MODERN MARKETING

PRINCIPLES AND PRACTICES

FOURTH EDITION

R.S.N. PILLAI
M.A., M.Com., LL.B.
Professor and Head
Department of Commerce
Arignar Anna College, Aramboly
Kanyakumari, Tamil Nadu

BAGAVATHI
M.A., M.Com.
240, Chidambaranagar
Nagercoil
Kanyakumari, Tamil Nadu

S. CHAND
PUBLISHING

S. Chand And Company Limited

(ISO 9001 Certified Company)

S.CHAND
PUBLISHING

S Chand And Company Limited

(ISO 9001 Certified Company)

Head Office: D-92, Sector–2, Noida – 201301, U.P. (India), Ph. 91-120-4682700

Registered Office: A-27, 2nd Floor, Mohan Co-operative Industrial Estate, New Delhi – 110 044, Phone: 011-49731800

www.**schandpublishing.com**; e-mail: **info@schandpublishing.com**

Marketing Offices:

Chennai	:	Ph: 23632120; chennai@schandpublishing.com
Guwahati	:	Ph: 2738811, 2735640; guwahati@schandpublishing.com
Hyderabad	:	Ph: 40186018; hyderabad@schandpublishing.com
Jalandhar	:	Ph: 4645630; jalandhar@schandpublishing.com
Kolkata	:	Ph: 23357458, 23353914; kolkata@schandpublishing.com
Lucknow	:	Ph: 4003633; lucknow@schandpublishing.com
Mumbai	:	Ph: 25000297; mumbai@schandpublishing.com
Patna	:	Ph: 4011400; patna@schandpublishing.com

First Edition 1987

Subsequent Editions and Reprints 1990, 92, 94, 95, 96, 97, 98, 99, 2000, 2001, 2002, 2003, 2004, 2005, 2006, 2007 (Twice), 2008, Fourth Edition 2009, Reprints 2010, 2011 (Twice), 2012, 2014, 2015, 2016 (Twice), 2017, 2018, 2020 (Twice), 2021 (Twice), 2022, 2024

Reprint 2026

ISBN: 978-81-219-1697-4 **Product Code:** H8MKT48MKTG10ENAD09O

PRINTED IN INDIA

By Shri Shyamlal Printing Press Private Limited, Plot 20/4, Site-IV, Industrial Area Sahibabad, Ghaziabad – 201 010 and Published by S Chand And Company Limited, A-27, 2nd Floor, Mohan Co-operative Industrial Estate, New Delhi – 110 044

PREFACE TO THE FOURTH REVISED EDITION

We are encouraged by the widespread response from students teachers and colleagues t the previous edition of the book—**MODERN MARKETING**. In this revised and updated edition the text has undergone an exhaustive revision and a substantial value addition. Through 49 well—structured chapters, the book covers the subject comprehensively. We have not only revised and updated all the earlier 40 chapters to reflect the latest developments but have also added 9 more chapters. Thus, the latest book—**MODERN MARKETING** consists of 49 chapters.

While doing the revision work, it is kept in mind that the students—community needs a handy book, a simple book, that covers all the topics and the full syllabi prescribed by the Universities. The syllabi of all Universities, in India, have been consulted and accordingly the book, MODERN MARKETING, in its present capsule form, we believe, will be more helpful and useful to the students of the subject—marketing .

The book has been written in simple language with clarity of thought with examples. The important concepts have been high—lighted either in bold letters or in boxes so as to enable the readers to understand the themes at one glance, without loss of time. In the new edition, we have added a good number of case studies from discussion.

The purpose of the book is to offer adequate and uptodate information on the current marketing problems and we hope that the book will meet the growing needs of the student—community.

The book could not be authored without the support and professional contribution from colleagues and teacher—friends. The feed back from friends has enabled us to remove all types of omission. We express our deep gratitude to the students and teachers for their continuous response to the book—Modern Marketing, since 1987.

Suggestions and constructive criticisms from students and teachers aimed at improving the book are highly appreciated.

The authors are grateful to Mrs. Nirmala Gupta Chairperson and Managing Director, Mr Navin Joshi, Vice President, (Publishing) Mr. R. S. Saxena, Advisor and the entire staff of S. Chand & Company, Chennai for their sincere help and suggestions.

Nagercoil. July 2009 **Authors**

PREFACE TO THE FOURTH REVISED EDITION

We are encouraged by the wide [illegible] response from students, teachers and [illegible] to the [illegible] edition of the book—MODERN MARKETING [illegible] revised and updated edition. [illegible] [illegible] [illegible] [illegible] [illegible] [illegible] [illegible] MODERN MARKETING [illegible].

While [illegible] [illegible] [illegible] [illegible] [illegible] [illegible] [illegible] full [illegible] prescribed by the Universities [illegible] [illegible] [illegible] [illegible] [illegible] [illegible] [illegible] [illegible] [illegible] [illegible] students and [illegible].

The [illegible] [illegible] [illegible] examples [illegible] [illegible] [illegible] [illegible] [illegible] [illegible] [illegible] [illegible] [illegible] [illegible] [illegible] [illegible] [illegible] without loss of [illegible] [illegible] [illegible] [illegible] [illegible] [illegible] [illegible].

The [illegible] [illegible] adequate and up-to-date information on the [illegible] [illegible] [illegible] [illegible] [illegible] the growing needs of the students [illegible].

The book could not [illegible] [illegible] without the support and [illegible] [illegible] [illegible] [illegible] [illegible] [illegible] [illegible] [illegible] [illegible] [illegible] [illegible] [illegible] [illegible] [illegible] [illegible] [illegible] [illegible] [illegible] the book—Modern Marketing [illegible].

Suggestions [illegible] [illegible] [illegible] [illegible] [illegible] [illegible] [illegible] [illegible] [illegible].

The authors are grateful to [illegible] [illegible] [illegible] [illegible] [illegible] [illegible] [illegible] Mr. R. [illegible] [illegible] and the [illegible] [illegible] [illegible] Company [illegible] [illegible] [illegible] [illegible] [illegible].

[illegible] Authors

PREFACE TO THE FIRST EDITION

This book is meant for students of " MARKETING", a subject being taught in various colleges in India. Marketing is an important functional aspect of business. The success of any firm or industry is largely determined by its ability in marketing the products. In recent past years there were vast changes in the production and distribution of goods, throughout the world, especially in the developing and developed countries. The reasons for the changes are : advancement in technology, improvements in transport and communication, Changes in fashion, increasing standard of living, rapid economic growth, increased knowledge of the consumers etc. Mass production and mass distribution are the order of the day, followed by stiff competition from similar firms. So, firms use different and various techniques to promote the sales through advertisements, personal selling etc. Hence, those who want to attain success in business or marketing of the products must possess thorough knowledge of the subject marketing. This is essential, to be a made (trained) salesman rather than a born salesman. In India, many colleges offer the subject marketing because of its importance.

We are happy to bring out this book MARKETING.. We hope it will very soon be in the hands of friends and students. Sincere efforts have been taken in explaining the theories. The book comprises 34 chapters and is presented in a systematic manner. Almost all the books on this subject have been consulted. Maximum care has been taken to present the themes in a lucid, easy and understandable language specially to the student community. Yet, if any error be noticed by fellow teacher's and readers, it may kindly be intimated to us for rectification in subsequent editions. Suggestions, advice comments, criticism, from the readers are welcome and will be incorporated in the next edition .

We are grateful to our publishers, M/s S. Chand and Company (Pvt) Ltd ., New Delhi, specially Padmashri S.L. Gupta, Managing Director for taking personal interest in bringing out this book in an elegant form and at low price, apart from its speedy release.

Nagercoil
(Kanyakumari) **R. S.N. PILLAI**
July 1987 **BAGAVATHI**

PREFACE TO THE FIRST EDITION

[illegible]

CONTENTS

1. MARKET AND MARKETING **1–19**

● Introduction ● Evolution of Marketing ● Meaning of Market ● Definition of Market ● Classification of Marketing ● Marketing ● Micro and Macro Marketing ● What is Marketed ● Modern Approach ● Objectives of Marketing ● Importance of Marketing ● Merchandising ● Selling ● Selling and Marketing ● Marketing and Distribution ● Marketing and Business ● Kinds of Goods is Marketing a Science or Art ? Approach to the Study of Marketing ● Modern Marketing ● Marketing in Economic Development ● Marketing as a Subject to Study ● Relationship Marketing ● Questions

2. MODERN MARKETING CONCEPT **20–27**

● Evolution ● Factors ● Implementation ● Benefits ● Social Marketing ● Case Study-1 ● Questions

3. MARKETING SYSTEM, MARKETING MIX, MARKETING FUNCTION **28–41**

● Marketing Mix ● Meaning ● Definition ● Elements ● Problems; Marketing System ● Meaning, Marketing Process ● Concentration ● Dispersion ● Equalisation; Marketing Functions ● Classification ● Functions of Exchange ● Functions of Physical Supply ● Facilitating function ● Case Study-1 ● Case Study -2 ● Questions

4. BUYING, ASSEMBLING AND SELLING **42 –56**

● Buying ● Classes of Buyers ● Problem of Buying ● Elements of Buying ● Purchasing Methods Assembling ● Meaning ● Advantages ● Problems, Selling ● Elements ● Kinds of Sales ● Questions

5. TRANSPORTATION **57–71**

● History and Development ● Functions ● Classification ● Road Transport ● Railway Transport ● Water Transport ● Airway Transport ● Choice of Transport ● Questions

6. STORAGE AND WAREHOUSES **72–79**

● Storage Situations ● Advantages ● Essentials of Good Storage ● Storage Vs. Warehouses ● Functions ● Classifications ● Warehouse Receipt and Warrant ● Advantages ● Importance ● Warehouses in India ● Causes of Slow Growth ● Suggestions ● Questions

7. STANDARDISTATION AND GRADING **80–85**

● Meaning ● Standardisation ● Standard ● Elements ● Grading ● Inspection ● Labelling ● Grading Vs. Standardisation ● Methods of Grading ● Types of Grading ● Significance of Standardisation ● Benefits of Standardisation ● Contral of Standard ● Agricultural Produce ● Extractive Industries and Manufactured Products ● Controls ● ISI ● AGMARK ● Questions

8. MARKETING FINANCE **86–92**

● Introduction ● Finance ● Business Finance ● Fixed and Working Capital ● Factors which Determine Working Capital ● Types and Sources of Working Capital ● Trade Credit ● Consumer Credit ● Open Account ● Charge Account Banking ● Instalment ● Hire Purchase ● Agricultural Marketing Finance ● Questions

9. MARKETING RISK 93–97

• Marketing Risk • Causes • Handling the Risks • Prevention • Reduction • Shifting • Questions.

10. MARKETING INFORMATION AND RESEARCH 98–123

• Information • Marketing Information • What is Market Information • Importance of Market Information • Development of Marketing Information System • Market Information System • Requisites of Good MIS • Benefits of MIS • Characteristic of Good MIS • Marketing Research • What is Market Research? • Market Research Vs. Marketing Research • Marketing Research Vs. MIS • Scope of Marketing Research • Types of Marketing Research • Objectives of Marketing Research • Advantages of Marketing Research • Marketing Research Process • Types of Marketing Research • Users of Marketing Research • Method of Data Collection • Gathering Primary Data • Framing a Questionnaire • Sampling • Methods of Sampling • A Good Sample • Sources of Secondary Data • Precautions of Secondary Data • Primary Data Vs. Secondary Data • Organisation of Marketing Research • Limitation of Marketing Research • Status of Marketing Research • Contribution of Marketing Research • Marketing Research in India • Case Study-1 • Case Study-2 • Case Study-3 • Questions

11. MARKETING MANAGEMENT 124–137

• Meaning • Functions • Characteristics • Negative Demand • No Demand • Latent Demand • Falling Demand • Irregular • Demand • Full Demand • Overall Demand • Unwholesome Demand • Marketing Organisation • Principles of Organisation • Marketing and Sales Management • Functions of Marketing Executive • Responsibility • Types of Organisations • Military Type • Functional Type • Line and Staff System • Committee • Geographical Type • Product Type • Market Type • Questions.

12. MARKETING STRATEGY AND PLANNING 138–155

• Introduction • What is Planning? • Features of Planning • Marketing Planning • Importance of Marketing Planning • Benefits of Marketing Planning • Characteristics of Marketing Planning • Corporate Planning Process • Marketing Planning Activities • Marketing Audit • Barriers • Case Study-1 • Case Study-2 • Case Study-3 • Case Study-4 • Case Study-5 • Case Study-6 • Questions

13. MARKETING ENVIRONMENT 156–173

• Introduction • Scanning the Environment • Importance of Environment Analysis • Need for Analysis • Concept of Micro and Macro Environment • Company • Company's Supplier • Intermediaries • Customers • Competitors • Public • Deomographic environment • Economic Environment • Physical Environment • Technological Enviroment • Political Environment • Legal Environment • Social and Cultural Environment • Case Study-1 • Case Study-2 • Case Study-3 • Case Study-4 • Case Study-5 • Case Study-6 • Case Study-7 • Questions

14. MARKET SEGMENTATION 174–189

• Introduction • Definition • Criteria • Bases • Geographic • Demographic • Psychographic • Socio–economic • Benefit • User Status • Usuage Rate • Loyal Status • Attitude • Benefits of Segmentation • Philosophics of Market Segmentation Mass Marketing • Product Variety Marketing • Target Marketing • Micro Marketing • Customised Marketing • Personalised Marketing • Market Targeting Strategy • Case Study-1 • Case Study-2 • Case Study-3 • Case Study-4 • Case Study-5 • Questions

15 **MARKET TARGETING AND POSITIONING** 190–198

● Introduction ● Selection of Target Market ● Evaluating Market Segments ● Selecting Market Segments ● Product Positioning ● What is positioning ? ● Product Position Vs. Brand Position ● Product Oifferentiation ● Differentiating Market Offering ● Qualities of Successful Position ● Positioning Approaches ● Product Repositioning ● Case Study-1 ● Questions

16. **PRODUCT PLANNING** 199–213

● Introduction ● What is a Product ? ● Important Features of Product ● Classification of products ● Product Attributes ● Product Planning and Development ● Product Levels ● Product Line ● Product Line Decision ● Product Mix ● Product Line and Product Mix ● Goals of Product Mix ● factors Influencing Product Mix ● Major Product Mix Strategies ● Expansion of Product Mix ● Contra ● Ction of Product Mix ● Alteration of Product ● Positioning the Product ● Trading Up ● Trading Down ● Differentiations and Segmentation ● Determining Factors for Differentiation ● Benefits of Segmentation ● What is a Right Product ? Product Innovation ● Reasons for Innovation ● Case Study-1 ● Case Study-2 ● Questions.

17. **MANAGING THE PRODUCT DEVELOPMENT** 214–227

● Product Life Cycle ● Different Stages ● Advantages of PLC ● Development of New Product ● Managing product Development ● Planning Process ● Launching a New Product ● Product Diversification ● Product Elemination ● Product Modification ● Product Failure ● Questions

18. **PRICING STRATEGY** 228–241

● Introduction ● What is Price Strategy Imporantance of Price ● Pricing Objectives ● Factors Affecting Pricing Decision ● Procedure for Price Determination ● Kinds of Pricing ● Price Leader ● Factors Affecting Changes in Price ● Price as an Indicator of Quality ● One Price Vs. Variable Price ● Resale Price Maintenance ● Case Study-1 ● Questions

19. **PRODUCT RELATED STRATEGY** 242–261

● Understanding a Brand ● What is a Brand ? ● Branding ● Essentials ● Benefits ● Types of Brands ● Reasons for Branding ● Reasons for Branding individual Products ● Conditions Favourable to Branding ● Brand Mark ● Functions of Brand ● Kinds of Brand Name ● Elements of Branding ● Brand Identity ● Brand Image ● Brand Position ● Brand Equity ● Value of Brand Equity ● Brand Name Decision ● Branding Strategy ● Brand Loyalty ● Brand Association ● Brand Extention ● Brand Rejuvenation ● Brand Relaunch ● Brand Proliferation ● Brand Audit ● Advantages of Branding ● Desirable Conditions ● Undesirable Characteristics of Brand ● Trade Mark ● Labelling ● Types of Labels ● Funcitons of Label Advantages of Label ● Disadvantages of Label ● Package ● Packing ● Growth ● Functions of Package ● Kinds of Materials used ● General Functions ● Kinds of Packages ● Requisites of Good Package ● Case Study-1 ● Case Study-2 ● Case Study-3 Case Study-4 ● Questions.

20. **CONSUMER BEHAVIOUR** 262–278

● Birth of Buying Idea ● Two categories of Buyers ● What is Buyer Behaviour? ● Definitions ● Importance of Studying Consumer Behaviour ● Types of Buyers ● What are buying Motives? Determinant of Buying Behaviour ● Consumer Buying Decision ● Characteristics of Buyer Behaviour ● Buying Motives ● Six O's Approach ● Importance of studying Buyer Motives ● 7 O's Framowerk ● Buyer Behaviour Model ● Buying Decision Process ● Motives of Industrial Consumers ● Buying Process ● Case Study-1 ● Questions.

21. **THE INDIAN CONSUMERS** 279–285

● Indian Culture ● Profile of Indian Consumers ● Classification of Indian Consumers ● Questions

22. **CONSUMERISM** 287–297

• Introduction • Evolution of Consumecrism • How did Consumerism originate ? • Unique Problems of Indian Consumers • Consumer Orientation • Consumer Exploitation in India • Major Problems of Consumers Exploitotion • Enactments • Carlill Vs. Carbolic Company • Consumer Protection Act 1986 • Rights of Consumers • Questions

23. **LAW RELATING TO SALE OF GOODS** 298–302

• Contract of Sale • Sale vs. Agreement to Sell • Essentials of a Contract Sale • Goods • Conditionsand Warranties • CaveatEmptor • DeliveryofGoods • RulesRegarding Delivery • Rights of Unpaid Seller • Questions

24. **THE PROMOTIONAL PROGRAMME** 303–316

• Introduction • PromotionalActivities • Selling • PromotionandSalesPromotion • TheNeed for Promotional Activities • Importance of Promotion • Objectives of Promotional Activities • Communication and Promotion • Elements of Communication • Promotional Campaign and Promotional Decision • Promotional Mix • Promotional Mixes and Strategies • Forms of Promotion • Relative Costs • Case Study-1 • Case Study-2 • Case Study-3 • Case study-4 • Questions

25. **SALES PROMOTION** 317–327

• Introduction • Definition of Sales Promotion • Purpose of Sales Promotion • Importance • Objectives • Reasons for Growth • Advantages • Effectiveness of Sales Promotion • Limitations • Kinds • Consumer Sales Promotion • Dealer Sales Promotion • Sales Force Sales Promotion • Promotion Planning • Case Study-1 • Questions

26. **ADVERTISING** 328–372

• Introduction • Evolution • Definitions • BasicFeatures • Whatisadvertising? • Advertising and Advertisement • Advertising and publicity • Advertising and Salesmanship • Advertising and Sales Promotion • Advertising Objectives • Additional Benefits • Advertising Goals and Models • Functions of Advertising • Central Theme • Importance of Advertising • PLC and Advertising • Advantages of Advertising to Manufacturers, Salesman. Wholesalers. Retailers, Customers and Community • Objections against Advertising • Classification of Advertising Copy • Types of Advertising • Headlines • Qualities of a Good Copy • Elements of an Advertising Copy • Scientific Advertising • Why and When to Advertise ? • Causes of Failure of Advertising • Determinants of Advertisability • Kinds of Advertising • Selction of Advertising Media • Kinds of Media • IS Advertising a Waste ? Follow up System • Keying the Advertisement • Advertising Agency • Advertising Budget • Evaluation of Advertising • Slogans • Questions

27. **PERSONAL SELLING** 373–394

• Introduction • ObjectivesofPersonalSelling • Salesmanship • Definition • ModernConcept • Science or Art • Is Salesmanship a Profession • Objectives • Importance • Duties of Salesman • Qualities of Successful Salesman • Sales Personality • Knowledge of Products • Knowledge of Customers • Classification of Customers • Types of Salesman • Theories of Personal Selling • AIDAS Theory • "Right of Set of Circumstances" • "Buying Formula" • "Behavioural Equationnn • Features of Personal selling • Process of Personal Selling • Why Salesman Fail ? • Questions

28. **SALES ORGANISATION** 395–401

• Introduction • Need for a sales Organisation • Importance Function • Structure • Sales Management • Function of Sales • Sales Management • Field of Sales Management • Sales

Manager • Qualities of Sales Manager • His Knowledge and Attitude • Duties and Responsibilities • Types of Sales Manager • Questions

29. **SALES FORCE MANAGEMEFNT** 402–413

• Introduction • Importance of Selection • Sales Force Decision • Sales Force Size • Recruitment and Selection • Selection Process • Training • Significance • Objectives • Advantages • Training Programmes • Training Methods • Evaluation • Questions

30. **CONTROL OF SALES FORCE** 414–424

• What is Control ? • Control Necessary ? Pre • requisites of Control • Elements Involved in Control • Method of Control • Bases of Control • Reports and Records • Sales Territories and Sales Quotes • Saleman's Authority • Field Supervision • Remuneration Plan • Motivation of Salesman • What is Motivation? • Need • Types • Techniques • Methods • Questions

31. **SALES FORECAST** 425–431

• Meaning • Factors Influencing a Sales Forecasting • Importance • Methods • Types • Questions

32. **REMUNERATION TO SALESMEN** 432–436

• Introduction • A Good Remunerative Plan • Objectives • Essentials • Developing a Remunerative Plan • Methods • Incentives • Frings Benefits • Questions

33. **CHANNELS OF DISTRIBUTION—I** 437–455

• Introduction • Definition • Function • Importance • Types Differnt Channels • Market Considerations • Intensity of Distribution • Channel Conflict • Causes of Conflict • Meaning of Conflict • Logistic Management • JIT Techniques • Benefits of JIT Techniques • Questions.

34. **CHANNELS OF DISTRIBUTION—II** 456–479

• Middlemen in Distribution • Agent Middlemen • Functions • Kinds • Merchant Middlemen • Functions • Wholesalers • Basic Characteristics • Services to Manufactures • Services to Retailer Retailer • Importance • Functions • Services • Essential Requisites of Retailers • Types • Itinerant • Fixed Shops • Small Scale • Large Scale • Wheel of Retailing • Elimination of Middlemen • Arguments in Favour of and Against • Questions

35. **MARKETING OF CONSUMER GOODS** 480–485

• Consumer Goods • Industrial Goods • Characteristics of Consumer Goods • Classification of Consumer Goods • Consumer Goods Marketing • Shopping Goods • Marketing Speciality Goods • Marketing • Comparative Study • Channels of Distribution • Questions

36. **MARKETING OF INDUSTRIAL GOODS** 486–492

• Buying Motives • Characteristic of Industrial Goods • Classification • Marketing Consideration • Questions

37. **MARKETING OF SECURITIES** 493–499

• Functions • Benefits • Organisation • Management • Membership Rules • Procedure for Dealings • Kinds of Dealers • Kinds of Speculators • Listing Advantages • Disadvantages • Reasons for Price Fluctuations • Questions

38. **MARKETING OF AGRICULTURAL GOODS** 500–507

• Classification of Agricultural Goods • Characteristic • Problems in the Marketing • Kinds of Markets • Defects of Marketing • Remedies • Questions

39. THE MARKETING OF SERVICES 508–520

• Introduction • Definition • ReasonsforGrowth • CharacteristicsofServices • Intangibility • Inseparability • Heterogeneity • Perishability • Ownership • Goods and Services Compared • Marketing Mix in Service Marketing • Product • Price • Promotion • Place • People • Physical Evidence • Process • Services Quality • Questions

40. REGULATED MARKETS 521–525

• Introduction Growth Development • Organisation • Constitution • Finance • Functions • Advantages

41. ORGANISED MARKETS 526–536

• Demerits of Unorganised Market • Organised Market • Meaning • Characterstics • CommodityExchange • CommodityExchange Vs StockExchange • Importance • Functions • Services • Organisation • Membership • Management • FutureContract • Types • Kinds • Advantages • Hedging • Hedging Vs Speculation • Questions

42. CO-OPERATIVE MARKETING 537–544

• Co-operative Marketing • Objectives • Need • Features • Structure • Functions • Advantages • Working Methods • Questions

43. MARKETING CONTROL 545–556

• Introduction • MeaningofControl • ConceptofControl • NatureofControl • Relationship between Planning and Control • Purpose of Control • Significance of Control • Limitation of Control • Control Process • Requisites of Control System • Marketing Control • Tools and Techniques of Marketing Control • Questions

44. INTERNATIONAL MARKETING 557–560

• Introduction • Deciding Whether to go Abroad • Main Activities • Importance of International Marketing

45. RURAL MARKETING 561–567

• Introduction • UrbanMarkets • SignificanceofRuralMarkets • KeyDecisionAreas • Media Mix • Questions.

46. MARKETING AND SOCIETY 568–571

• Introduction • Social Responsibility • How Marketing Influence Society • Economic Aspects • The Enviroment • How Society Influence Marketing • Social Criticism of Marketing • Consumer Movement • Questions

47. E-BUSINESS 572–576

• Introduction • Telemarketing • Automatic Vending • E-Business • E-Commerce • ElectronicDataInterchange • E-Mail • Internet • E-Auctioning • E-Marketing • E-Banking • E-Trading • Questions

48. TOTALQUALITYMANAGEMENT 577–583

• Introduction • Quality • Customer Satisfaction • Customer Expectations • Total Quality Management • Quality Assurance • Quality Circles • Guidelines • Measuring Quality • Benefits of TQM • Investors in People • Questions

49. RECENTTRENDINMARKETING 584–592

• Relationship Marketing • Word-of-mouth Marketing • Test Marketing • Case Study-1 • Case Study-2 • Case Study-3 • Case Study-4 • Case Study-5 • Case Study-6

APPENDIX 593–594

CHAPTER 1

Market and Marketing

- Introduction
- Evolution of Marketing
- Meaning of Market
- Definition of Market
- Classification of Market
- Marketing
- Micro and Macro Marketing
- What is marketed? Modern Approach
- Objectives of Marketing
- Importance of Marketing Merchandising
- Selling
- Selling and Marketing
- Marketing and Distribution
- Marketing and Business
- Kinds of Goods. Is marketing a Science or Art? Approaches to the study of Marketing
- Modern Marketing
- Marketing in Economic Development
- Marketing as a subject to study
- Relationship Marketing
- Questions

INTRODUCTION

The development of marketing is evolutionary rather than revolutionary. There is no single answer to the question of what is marketing ? To understand, it may be explained in brief, as ''Marketing is what a marketer does.'' But this meaning lacks clarity in understanding the subject. The evolution of marketing is as old as the Himalayas. It is one of the oldest professions of the world.

Marketing is indeed an ancient art; it has been practised in one form or the other since the days of Adam and Eve. The word, marketing has been defined differently by authorities in different ways. The traditional objective of marketing had been to make the goods available at places where they are needed. This idea was later on changed by shifting the emphasis from ''exchange'' to ''satisfaction of human wants.'' Different authors tried to give suitable definition from their viewpoint. Some are very broad, others are rather too narrow. Some emphasise on the traditional view of producing goods and finding out customers, others emphasise on the modern view that marketing must first find out what customers want and then plan a product to satisfy that want. As any other subject, it has its own origin, growth and development. Let us briefly trace the evolution of marketing.

EVOLUTION OF MARKETING

The barter system existed in the initial stage of marketing. The caveman, with his surplus products, approached and tried to exchange his products by accepting the products he needed–exchange of products for products. At that time, human beings were in nomadic hunter stage. In this primitive period, the human beings were nothing more than hunters or food gatherers. Then New Stone Age followed. In the stage of backward economy human beings were self-sufficient. In such backward economy or agrarian period, family units were self-sufficient–making needed food, clothes, shelter, tools etc. As time passed, the division of labour began to play its role and man started producing more than he needed. The surplus was exchanged in terms of commodities needed. They, in possession of surplus goods, searched for those who had a surplus to be exchanged. Searching for others who needed the surplus product became a tedious job as time and energy had to be wasted. Therefore, the people assembled in places called local markets where goods were disposed of. And later, it developed into shops, bazaars etc. The people, according to their interest specialised in productions. Specialists like carpenters, weavers etc., developed at this stage. The appearance of specialisation developed the idea of marketing.

In the pre-industrial period, the difficulties of barter system were removed by adopting common mediums of exchange like cows, pigs, slaves, shells, sheep etc. Then these were replaced by metals like copper, iron etc.; and later this medium of exchange was changed to silver, gold etc. At this stage, producers began to produce the products in larger quantities, employed the services of labourers in their factories; and middlemen, through whom sales were conducted, appeared. In the words of Kotler, "As the size of wealthy class increased, some goods and shops emerged that cater to the rich, and here some of the characteristics of consumer-oriented retailing first appeared. But on the whole, early capitalism operated essentially in an economy of scarcity, and this meant there was little reason to study the needs or wants of consumers or to go out of the way to cater them." Further, "the appearance of specialisation in selling expanded the concept of marketing. Marketing was the process of exchange of economic goods and the set of specialised institutions that facilitated exchange."

In the industrial period, handicraft operations appeared in factories; similarly many factories came up and rural areas developed into urban areas, where people were attracted. People started life, spending their time in factories and facilitated mass production, *i.e.*, home production was replaced by factory system and hand operations were replaced by machines. Because of the introduction of new inventions along with new machines, the production was on large scale. With the advent of industrial revolution, there arose mass productions. Mass productions were followed by large-scale consumption. In order that the products may reach the hands of the ultimate user, new methods of marketing appeared. This industrial revolution is the cause for the creation of the modern marketing system.

In short, traditional marketing developed from time immemorial. The wants were few or limited. The surplus produce if any, after their consumption, was exchanged in a local market. In course of time, farmers began to concentrate on selling, storing, transporting, providing credit-facilities etc., and this created an opportunity to middlemen to play their vital role. Around World War Second, India was importing capital goods as well as consumer goods; and in such a stage, the marketing functions were more or less inactive. But, when India was freed, the importing of consumer goods was also controlled. Import-substitution came up. New products came into existence. Many varieties of consumer goods which were imported formerly, began to be manufactured in India. Many manufacturers came up with new products, and similar goods were manufactured by producers, followed by mass productions and competitions. This is the stage where marketing functions started expanding.

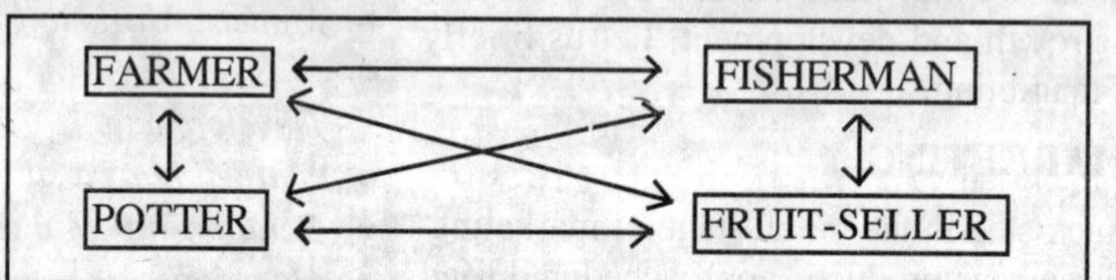

Decentralised Exchange

The farmer approaches all the other three persons to sell and buy goods; the potter approaches all the other three persons to sell and buy goods and so on.

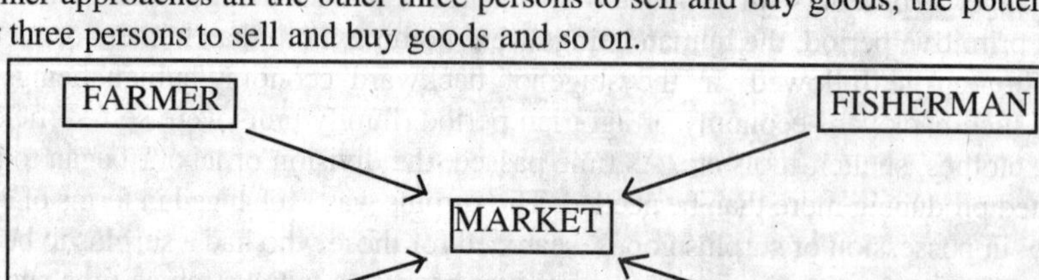

Centralised Exchange

The development of centralised exchange came up. Merchants appeared, located an area, called market. Thus we got all commodities from market or seller.

EVOLUTION OF MARKETING

1. **BARTER SYSTEM:** The goods are exchanged against goods, without any other medium of exchange, like money.

2. **PRODUCTION ORIENTATION:** This was a stage where producers, instead of being concerned with the consumer preferences, concentrated on the mass production of goods for the purpose of profit. They cared very little about the customers.

3. **SALES ORIENTATION:** The stage witnessed major changes in all the spheres of economic life. The selling activity becomes the dominant factor, without any efforts for the satisfaction of the consumer needs.

4. **MARKETING ORIENTATION:** Customers' importance was realised but only as a means of disposing of goods produced. Competition became more stiff. Aggressive advertising, personal selling, large scale sales promotion etc. are used as tools to boost sales.

5. **CONSUMER ORIENTATION:** Under this stage only such products are brought forward to the market which are capable of satisfying the tastes, preferences and expectations of the consumers–consumer satisfaction.

6. **MANAGEMENT ORIENTATION:** The marketing function assumes a managerial role to co-ordinate all interacting business activities with the objective of planning, promoting and distributing want-satisfying products and services to the present and potential customers.

MEANING OF MARKET*

The word 'Market' is derived from the Latin word 'Marcatus' meaning merchandise, wares, traffic, trade or a place where business is conducted. The common usage of market means a place where goods are bought or sold. In its strict meaning market need not necessarily mean a place of exchange. Let us define the market, as given by different authorities:

1. ''Market includes both place and region in which buyers and sellers are in free competition with one another.''– Pyle
2. ''The term market refers not to a place, but to a commodity or commodities and buyers and sellers who are in direct competition with one another.''– Chapman
3. ''Market is meant not any particular place in which things are bought and sold, but the whole of any region in which the buyers and sellers are in such free intercourse with one another, that the price of the same goods tends to equality easily and quickly.''– Cornot
4. ''Market, for most commodities, may be thought of not as a geographical meeting place but as getting together of buyers and sellers in person, by mail, telephone, telegraph or any other means of communications.''– Mitchell
5. ''A market is a centre about which or an area in which the forces leading to exchange of title to a particular product operate and towards which the actual goods tend to travel.''– Clark and Clark

The word market is commonly used and may mean or aim in any of the following manner, on the basis of the definitions by different authorities, given above.

---

*Need for markets:

1. for exchange (barter) of goods and services,
2. for adjustment of demand and supply by price mechanism,
3. for improvement of the quality of life of the society,
4. for the introduction of new modes of life.
5. for higher production (development of markets encourage production)

1. Market may mean a place, where buying and selling take place.
2. Buyers and sellers come together for transactions.
3. An organisation through which exchange of goods takes place.
4. The act of buying and selling of goods (to satisfy human wants).
5. An area of operation of commercial demand for commodities.

CLASSIFICATION OF MARKETS

Markets have been classified, on the basis of different approaches, in various ways. They are given below.

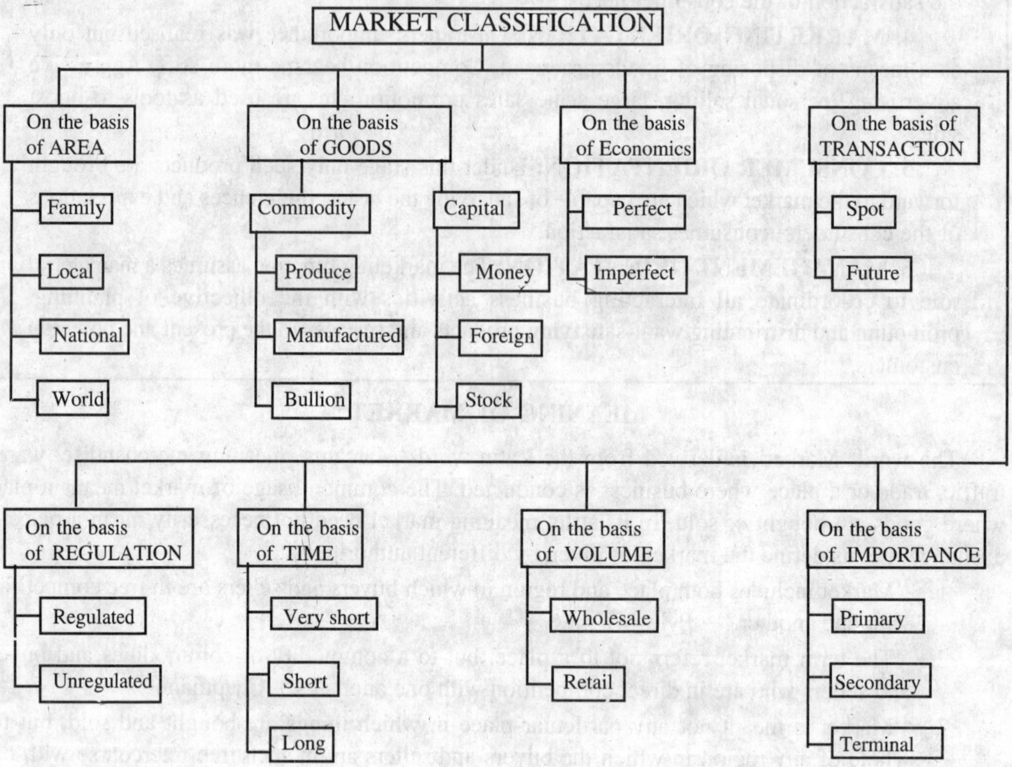

A. **On the Basis of Geographical Area**

1. **Family Market:** When exchanges are confined within a family or close members of the family, such a market can be called as family market.

2. **Local Market:** When people–buyers and sellers, belong to a local area or areas, say a town or village, participate in market, it is called local market. The demands are limited. For example, perishable goods like fruits, fish, vegetables etc. But strictly speaking such markets are disappearing because of the efficient system of transportations and communications. Even, then, in many villages such markets exist even today.

3. **National Market:** For a certain type of commodities, a country may be regarded as a market, through the fast development of industrialisation; it is called a national market. At the present stage, in India, the goods of one corner can reach another corner, because of the efficient systems of communications and transportation facilities. In the present decade almost all the products have national markets as the markets have widened to a great extent.

4. **World Market:** World or international market comes up when buyers and sellers of goods evolve on world level *i.e.*, involvement of buyers and sellers beyond the boundaries of a nation.

B. On the Basis of Commodities/Goods

Commodity Market : Produced goods or consumption goods are bought and sold. Commodity markets are sub-divided into:

1. **Produce Exchange Market :** This type of market is found only in developed industrial centres or cities. One market deals in one commodity only. Generally sellers and buyers of a particular commodity, set up such markets and run them regulated and controlled by certain rules. e.g., Wheat Exchange Market of Hapur, the Cotton Exchange Market of Bombay etc.

2. **Manufactured Goods Market :** Such type of markets deals with manufactured goods. e.g., Leather goods, machinery etc. The Leather Exchange Market at Kanpur, Piece Goods Exchange of Bombay are examples of such markets.

3. **Bullion Market :** This type of market deals with the purchase or sale of gold, silver etc. Bullion markets of Bombay, Calcutta, Kanpur etc., are examples of such markets.

Capital Markets

New or going concerns need finance at every stage. As such financial needs of concerns are met by capital markets. They are of three types:

1. **Money Market :** It is a type of market where money is borrowed or lent. This type of market helps or guides the public to invest their surplus fund in industrial concerns; and helps people to take loans through banks. London is the world's biggest money market.

2. **Foreign Exchange Market :** It is an international market. This type of markets helps exporters and importers, in converting their currencies into foreign currencies and vice versa.

3. **The Stock Exchange Market :** This is a market where shares, debentures, bonds etc., of companies are dealt with–purchased or sold. It is also known as Security Market. Stock Exchanges of Mumbai, Kolkatta, Chennai etc., are examples for this type of market

C. On the Basis of Economics

1. **Perfect Market :** A market is said to be a perfect market, if it satisfies the following conditions:

(i) Large number of buyers and sellers are there.
(ii) Prices should be uniform throughout the market.
(iii) Buyers and sellers have a perfect knowledge of market.
(iv) Goods can be moved from one place to another without restrictions.

It should be remembered that such types of markets are rarely found.

2. **Imperfect Market :** A market is said to be imperfect when

(i) Products are similar but not identical.
(ii) Prices are not uniform.
(iii) There is lack of communications.
(iv) There are restrictions on the movement of goods.

D. On the Basis of Transaction

1. **Spot Market :** In such a market goods are exchanged and the physical delivery of goods takes place immediately.

2. **Future Market :** In such a market contracts are made over the price for future delivery. The dealing and settlement take place on different dates.

E. On the Basis of Regulation

1. **Regulated Market :** These are types of markets which are organised, controlled and regulated by statutory measures.

Example : Stock Exchanges of Mumbai, Chennai, Kolkata etc.

2. **Unregulated Market :** This is a free market. There is no control with regard to price, quality, commission etc. Demand and supply determine the price of goods.

F. On the Basis of Time

1. **Very Short Period Market :** Markets which deal in perishable goods like, fruits, milk, vegetables etc., are for a very short period. There is no change in the supply of goods. Price is determined on the basis of demand.

2. **Short Period Market :** In certain goods, supply is adjusted to meet the demand. The demand is greater than supply. Such markets are known as Short Period Market.

3. **Long Period Market :** This type of market deals in durable goods.

G. On the Basis of Volume of Business

1. **Wholesale Market :** In wholesale market goods are supplied in bulk quantity to dealers.

2. **Retail Market :** In retail market goods are sold in small quantities directly to the users or consumers–consumer market. The consumer gets the goods for consumption and not for profit-making.

H. On the Basis of Importance

1. **Primary Market :** The Primary producers of farm produce sell their output or products through this type of markets to wholesalers or consumers. Such markets can be found in villages and mostly the products arrive from villages.

2. **Secondary Market :** The commodities arrive from other markets. The dealings are commonly between wholesalers or between wholesalers and retailers.

3. **Terminal Market :** The ultimate consumer gets the goods from such markets. Here the final disposal of goods takes place.

MARKETING

The essence of marketing is an exchange or a transaction, intended to satisfy human needs or wants. That is, marketing is a human activity directed at satisfying needs and wants, through an exchange process. A demand is a want for which the consumer is prepared to pay a price. A want is anything or a service the consumer desires or seeks. Wants become demands when backed by purchasing power. A need is anything the consumer feels to keep himself alive and healthy. A transaction consists of a value between two parties. A transaction differs from a transfer. A transferer may receive nothing in return. The aim of marketing is to make sales in order to earn reasonable profit for the producer.

Marketing, in its earlier definition and in **legal aspect** is said to be the effort by which the transfer of ownership in goods between the seller and buyer is effected–emphasises ownership transfer. It limits the scope of marketing to mere transfer of ownership. ''Marketing includes all activities which are concerned with effecting changes in the ownership and possession of goods and services.'' But marketing is concerned with several other economic aspects.

Marketing, in **economic point** of view, is defined as the exchange function by maintaining supply and demand in equilibrium. It aims at the creation of welfare and standard of living to the society as the object of marketing. It is also defined as ''That part of economics which deals with the creation of time, place and the possession utilities.'' ''That phase of business activity through which human wants are satisfied by the exchange of goods and services for some valuable consideration.'' It covers only few aspects of marketing.

Marketing, in its **descriptive definition,** explains the functions involved in the activities of goods from the producer to the consumer. ''That performance of business activities that direct the flow of goods and services from the producer to the consumer or user.'' This definition is a traditional one because the earlier view aims movement of goods and services from the producer to the consumer. In short, it makes marketing production-oriented rather than consumer-oriented.

MICRO MARKETING AND MACRO MARKETING

The term 'marketing' can be defined from two view points–micro and macro : that is, firm's point of view and national point of view.

(a) **Micro-marketing**

Under micro-marketing, if a firm formulates and implements such strategies (viz: product-development, pricing, promoting and distribution), that ensures flow of need satisfying goods and services at profit. According to Philip Kotler ''Marketing is a social and managerial process, by which individuals and groups obtain what they need and want through creating, offering and exchanging products of value with others. In the words of Stanton, ''marketing is a total system of interacting business activities designed to plan, price , promote and distribute want satisfying products and services to present and potential customers''. The ultimate aim of micro-marketing is satisfaction of human needs and wants, that is, it is consumer-oriented. Again, in the narrower sense, or what is known as 'micro-marketing, marketing is the process of managing an individual business firm in such a way as to satisfy its particular customers. Marketing also involves the management of every aspect of a business with the ultimate consumer in mind. It can be likened to close-up perspective of a scientist who inspects a small object through a microscope.

The concept of micro-marketing reveals two aspects. First, marketing must ensure need satisfying goods and services. That is, marketing begins with the customer and not with the production process. Secondly marketing rather than production should determine what products are to be made. The two aspects suggest that consumer is at the center of all marketing activities : producer does not determine the product.

(b) **Macro-marketing**

From the broader point of view or macro-marketing is the complex system of organisations and processes by which a nation's resources are distributed among the people, to satisfy their needs and wants. Thus, here the focus is on the total system, rather than the activities of a firm. So, it benefits the society as a whole. This concept keeps the producer informed of the changing needs of the ''consumers'' and equalises by ''distribution'', the ''demand'' and ''supply'' of commodities, thereby ensuring price-stability, in the long-run to the benefit of the society in general and buyers and sellers, in particular.

WHAT IS MARKETED?

Marketing is typically seen as the task of creating, promoting and delivering goods and services to consumers and businesses. In fact, marketing involves **ten types of entities:** goods, services, experiences, events, persons, places, properties, organisations, information and ideas.

1. GOODS : Physical goods constitute the bulk of most countries, production and marketing effort. Examples are : refrigerators, television sets, food products, machines etc.

2. SERVICES: As economics advance, a growing proportion of their activities is focussed on the production of services. Examples are : Services include the work of airlines, hotels, car rental firms, barbers, beauticians etc., and professionals such as, Accountants, bankers, lawyers, engineers, doctors etc.

3. EXPERIENCES: By orchestrating serveral services and goods, a firm can create, stage and market experiences. For examples : travels, climbing Mount Everest etc.

4. EVENTS: Marketers promote time-based events, such as tradeshows, artistic performances, Asian Games, Sport-events etc.

5. PERSONS: Celebrity marketing is a major business. Today, every major film star has an agent, a personal manager, and ties to a public relations agency. For Examples, artists, musicians, physicians etc.

6. PLACES: Cities, states, regions and whole nations compete actively to attract tourists, factories, company headquarters and new residents. Further examples, commercial banks, local business associations, real estate agents, Economic development specialists etc.

7. PROPERTIES: Properties are intangible rights of ownership of either real property (real estate) or financial property (stocks, bonds etc.) Properties are bought and sold, and this requires marketing.

8. ORGANISATIONS: Organisations actively work to build a strong, favourable and unique image in the minds of their target publics. Universities, museums, performing arts organisations and non-profits all use marketing to boost their public images and to compete for audiences and funds.

9. INFORMATION: Information can be produced and marketed as a product. This is essentially what schools and universities produce and distribute at a price to parents, students and communities. For examples, encyclopedias, magazines, news-papers etc., supply information.

10. IDEAS: Every market offering includes a basic idea. ''In the factory, we make cosmetics; in the store we sell hope''. Social marketers are busy in promoting such ideas.

Modern Approach is the Consumer Approach

We cannot find a single answer to the question of what is marketing. Marketing is a comprehensive term. Marketing is defined in different ways. A few definitions of notable authorities are given below:

''Marketing includes all activities involved in the creation of place, time and possession utilities. Place utility is created when goods and services are available at the places they are needed; time utility, when they are needed; and possession utility, when they are transferred to those who need them.''– Converse, Hugey and Mitchell.

''Marketing is the process of discovering and translating consumer needs and wants into product and service specifications, creating demand for these products and services and then in turn expanding this demand.''– Hansen

''Marketing is concerned with the people and the activities involved in the flow of goods and services from the producer to the consumer.''– American Marketing Association

''Marketing includes those business activities which are involved in the flow of goods and services from production to consumption.''– Converse

''Marketing is the economic process by which goods and services are exchanged and their values determined in terms of money prices.''– Duddy and Reizan

''Marketing consists of the performance of business activities that direct the flow of goods and services from the producer or supplier to the consumers or end-users.''

''Marketing is the business process by which products are matched with market and through which transfers of ownership are effected.''– Cundiff

''Marketing is a total system of business activities designed to plan, price, promote and distribute want-satisfying goods and services to present and potential customers.''–W. J. Stanton.

''Marketing is the creative management function which promotes trade and employment by assessing consumer needs and initiating research and development to meet them. It co-ordinates the resources of production and distribution of goods and services, and determines and directs the nature and scale of the total efforts required to sale maximum production to the ultimate user.''— UK Institute of Marketing.

The above definitions refer to the modern concepts of marketing as against the traditional definition by Clark who defines the term as ''marketing consists of those efforts which effect transfers in ownership of goods and care for their physical distribution.''

Previously market was considered to be a place where buyers and sellers would meet. But market does not necessarily mean a place. According to Barwell, marketing consists of identifying, anticipating and satisfying customer needs and desires. According to Stanton, ''marketing is the creation and delivery of a standard of living; it is finding out what customers want, then planning and developing a product of service that will satisfy those wants; and then determining the best way to price, promote and distribute that product or service.'' Peter Drucker observes that the purpose of business is to create a customer by which he lays stress on two aspects: (a) identification of consumer needs and (b) organising the business to meet these needs. The modern concept focuses on the consumers and their satisfaction. The approach of modern marketing is consumer-oriented instead of solely product-oriented.

''Marketing is not a high pressure selling, nor is it fancy advertising. The philosophy of marketing is the philosophy of consumer service. It is the chain of process backed by creative thinking that spreads from the concept of the product through strengthening the ''want'' for the product when it is consumed or used. ''Latif''. He also observed that ''marketing is an attitude of mind that should condition a whole enterprise in all economies. Rather it is the creative adaptation by a company of its practices to its changing environment. It concludes in its scope problems of location of the company, market segmentation, product differentiation, choosing the most appropriate distribution channels, doing profitable advertising, practising good public relations – all aimed at better selling.''

Marketing is not selling, nor is it a sophisticated word for selling but more comprehensive and could be termed as the ''cocktail science'', since it draws its materials, doctrines and principles from various other science, viz, Economics, Laws, Sociology, Psychology and anthropology.'' It is the base, the bedrock and the backbone of company's survival.

Objectives of Marketing

Barker and Anshen say, ''The end of all the marketing activities is the satisfaction of human wants.'' Through the satisfaction of human wants, profits are rewarded to the business and the reward is inducement for marketing. Now the time has changed and object of marketing is more than securing profits. The following are the aims of marketing:

1. Intelligent and capable application of modern marketing policies.
2. To develop the marketing field.
3. To develop guiding policies and their implementation for a good result.
4. To suggest solutions by studying the problems relating to marketing.
5. To find sources for further information concerning the market problems.
6. To revive existing marketing function, if shortcomings are found.
7. To take appropriate actions in the course of actions.

Importance of Marketing to the Society

1. Marketing is a connecting link between the consumer and the producer. Marketing process brings new and new items to retail shops, from where the consumers can have them.
2. Marketing helps in increasing the living standard of people. Because of mass production, costs of manufacturing and marketing have come down. This facilitates the fixing of cheaper rates and are a boon to the society. Thus, reduction in price will result in a higher standard of living.
3. Marketing helps to increase the nation's income. Efficient system of marketing reduces the cost to the minimum; this in turn lowers the prices and the consumer's purchasing power increases. This will increase the national income.
4. Marketing process increases employment opportunities. For continuous production, continuous marketing is needed. Continuous marketing invites numerous activities and thus job opportunities are provided to many people. In a country like India, it is really true, because these are sources of livelihood to many people.

5. Marketing creates modern cultivators. The poor farmer gets the new and developed methods of cultivation–useful implements, tools, fertilizers etc.–at his door and thus embraces the advantages of developed cultivation method.
6. Marketing removes the imbalances of supply by transferring the surplus to deficit areas, through better transport facilities.
7. Marketing helps to maintain economic stability and rapid development in underdeveloped or developing countries. If production is more than demand, the excess goods cannot be sold at acceptable price. Thus, there would be glut in the market, resulting in fall in price, and depression creeps in. Similarly, if production is less than demand, prices shoot up, resulting in inflation. In such situations, marketing maintains the economic stability by balancing the two aspects–production and consumption.
8. Marketing includes all activities in the creation of utilities–form, place, time and possession.
9. A reduction in the cost of marketing is a direct benefit to society. The man who makes such a contribution renders a service as important as that of the inventor of a labour-saving device.
10. Marketing adds value of goods by changing their ownership and by changing their time and place of consumption.
11. Scientific marketing has a stabilizing effect on the price level. Producers produce what consumers want and consumers have a wide choice of products, there are no frequent ups and downs in prices, Scientific marketing is the very antithesis of hoarding, profiteering and black-marketing.
12. Marketing helps to create awareness for non-business items for society's benefit like, family-planning, population-control, child-labour, child-abuse, anti-smoking compaign, polio immunization programmes and AIDS awareness campaigns, etc.

Importance to the Individual Firms

1. Marketing generates revenue to firms. A firm fulfils its motive only through marketing. Development of market is possible–local to world market. When markets are widened, sales increase, and thus profit to the firm increases.

2. Marketing section of a firm is the source of information to the top management for taking overall decisions on production. The information is the basis on which decisions will be taken by the management.

3. Marketing and innovations are the two basic functions of all businesses. The world is dynamic. Change is permanent. Change is the essence of life. Changing a business, on the basis of requirements of customers–new products, new methods etc.–is more important than running a business more efficiently. The behaviour and demand of customers keep on changing. In order to run a business successfully one should adopt the changing preferences, changing styles, changing fashions etc. The marketer informs retailers; retailers inform wholesalers, and they in turn inform manufacturers.

4. Marketing facilitates the development of business and creates employment opportunities for people.

Merchandising

Merchandising is only product planning. It aims at the internal planning relating to products or services for marketing at the right time, right price and in proper colour, qualities and sizes. Thus it is only a part of marketing study.

Selling

This is the last process of marketing. It is the needs of the sellers. It is an internal aim of a business.

Marketing is much wider than selling and much more dynamic. Selling revolves around the needs and interests of the seller; marketing revolves around the needs and interests of the buyer. Selling seeks profits by 'pushing' the products on the buyers. Marketing too seeks profits-but not through aggressive pushing of the products but by meeting the needs of the customers and by creating value satisfactions for them. To quote Levitt, "the difference between selling and marketing is more than semantic. A truly marketing-minded firm tries to create value-satisfying goods and services which the consumers want to buy. What it offers for sale is determined not by the seller but by the buyer. Selling is certainly a part of marketing. That is the last function in the process of marketing.

Selling Vs. Marketing

Selling	Marketing
1. Emphasises on the product.	Emphasises on customer's wants.
2. Sales are the primary motive.	Satisfaction of the customer is primary.
3. First production, then selling takes place at a profit without knowing customer's needs.	First customer's need is known and then production takes place; then the product is sold at a profit.
4. Internal, company orientation.	External, market orientation.
5. Company's need is the motive.	Buyer's need is the motive.
6. Cost determines price.	Consumer determines price; price determines cost.
7. 'Selling' views the customers as the last link in the business.	'Marketing' views the customer as the very purpose of the business.
8. It is an activity that converts the goods into cash.	It is a function that converts the consumer needs into products.
9. Core of business activity is the seller.	Buyer is the core of all activity.
10. Business is a goods-producing process.	Business is a customer–satisfying process.
11. Different departments of the business act independently.	All departments work in an integrated way to satisfy customers.
12. The seller determines what 'product' is to be offered.	What should be offered as a 'product' is determined by the buyer.

Distribution

It means the physical transfer of goods. It is one of the processes of marketing. It covers the methods to get the products to the market. It is concerned with physical movement of goods–from producer to the wholesaler, from wholesaler to the retailer, from retailer to the consumers.

Business

The term 'business' originates from the word 'busy' which denotes a state of engagement in some work. In the world of commerce, business refers to the economic or money-earning activities only. Business means either producing or purchasing of goods and services and selling those goods and services for the purpose of earning a profit. The Business people create markets. The development of skill, appearance of division of labour, endless human wants etc., are the causes for developing the business. Society produces surplus and it has to be disposed of through markets–business, and of course at a profit. Profit is an inseparable element in business or business aims at profit. The function of marketing is a boon to business. Business creates customers.

Kinds of Goods

Goods may also be called as product. They are tangible. They are :

A. Consumer's Goods

This type of goods are purchased by ultimate users or consumers for their personal use. For example, food, biscuits, toys, clothes etc. are purchased by consumers to satisfy their non-business wants. These goods may be further classified as:

(i) **Convenience Goods :** Consumers or purchasers get commodities such as bread, drug, perfumery, soap, sugar, tooth paste, newspapers, petrol, cold drinks, stationery items etc., at minimum effort and at low cost. They are often required by the consumers. These types of goods are available at places, where consumers need. The purchase of such goods cannot be postponed because they are daily necessities of life.

(ii) **Shopping Goods :** Before making final selection, the consumers make an enquiry as to the products' comparative prices, durability, style etc., from different shops. Goods like jewellery, furniture, ready-made garments etc., are more costly than convenience goods. Their need is also less when compared to the convenience goods. Shopping goods are generally available from particular shops where similar but same type of goods are sold.

(iii) **Speciality Goods :** Certain products possess special attraction to the consumers. As such the consumer may wait or suffer inconveniences to get the desired goods. This type of goods are of high value and manufactured by reputed firms. For example, cars, refrigerators, fancy goods, televisions, fans, scooters, photographic equipment, high grade shoes, stereo equipment, electrical appliances etc.

B. Industrial Goods

Goods which are used for production or used in producing other products are industrial goods. This type of goods are generally sold to manufacturers who in turn use them to make other own products. The difference between the consumer products and industrial goods is based on their ultimate use. If a product is brought by ultimate consumer, it is consumer goods. If a product is bought and used for making other products, it is an industrial product. The industrial goods can be further classified as:

(i) **Raw Materials :** Raw materials are the basic materials entering physically into the final products. For example, building stones, raw cotton, raw jute etc.

(ii) **Fabricated Materials :** Materials of this category will enter physically into the final products, but some type of processing is already undergone. For example, bricks, copper sheets, leather, yarn etc. As the processing is incomplete, further processing is required.

(iii) **Component Parts :** Such type of parts are already undergone some processing and more or less the parts can be called as final products. That is, the assembly of several component parts, makes the final products. The components are visible in the final products, such as batteries, tyres, speedometer, spark plugs, spare parts etc.

(iv) **Installation :** Machines, buildings, equipments etc., do not enter into final products and are durable for a long period. They are essential for production. For example, gas, power installation etc. They need heavy expenses for installation and sometimes decide the nature, scope and efficiency of an organisation.

(v) **Accessories :** They are light machines or tools which are used for the operation of a business. This is not used for manufacturing a product. For example, hand-tools, cash-register in retail shop, type-writers, calculators, accounting machines etc.

Services

Services are intangible activities which are offered for sale as such or in connection with sale of goods. For example, consultation, banking etc.

Services may be of two types—(i) Personal: It comprises of education, communication, medical, legal services etc. (ii) Business services: It comprises of advertising, mercantile credits, collection agencies etc.

Is Marketing a Science or Art ?

This is a matter of debate. Science is a classified and systematised body of knowledge. Art means the application of principles laid down, to the practical life. The word art means, it is the application of a set of rules to practice. The application needs skill. Skill must be developed by applying the rules. In short, it can be said that art involves the exercise of systematic knowledge to reap a good result.

It is an art because :

(1) The practice or method of marketing is applied by a marketing manager in his own way. He must have good knowledge of the situations, which are always, dissimilar from situation to situation. That means, he has his own method to get success in his field.

(2) The aim is to get satisfaction from the consumers. The marketer adjusts or tackles the situation, aiming to get success in his field.

(3) The success of a marketer depends upon his ability and skill. His brain is applied and follows in his own ways. The prosperity of marketing depends upon the ability of the marketer or salesman and not on marketing rules.

(4) As an art, it creates profits to firm, creates interest in the mind of users and develops the standard of living as one likes.

(5) As other social sciences, it deals with human beings. The behaviour of human beings cannot be measured accurately as those of sciences.

The field of marketing has been slow in developing a unique body of theory, because it is not a science. It is rather an art or practice much more closely resembling architecture. For example, the medical professionals, called practitioners are not scientists. As a practitioner, he applies the findings of many sciences to the solution of problems. Engineers, architects etc., called practitioners, make use of sciences–chemistry, physics, psychology etc. Thus, it is a characteristic of practice that brings about the solutions to each problem. One problem is different and distinct from others. Since marketing possesses all the important characteristics of an art, it may be concluded that it is an art.

Men of science have to develop a systematic approach to their problems which is known as the scientific method. Hypothesis are developed and facts are collected and tested to know the soundness of the hypothesis. That is, scientific approach is made, but not as a scientist. For instance, a doctor studies the symptoms of a patient before prescribing the medicine as a practitioner and not as a scientist.

In marketing research, scientific method of study is adopted. Like science, theoretical knowledge is derived, tested and generalised into theories, law etc. Science has systematic knowledge. Marketing managers by experience derive scientific approach and apply to the problems. Modern market is a science in the field of prediction of marketing result. One may conclude that marketing is a science.

Marketing, we can conclude, is both a science and art base.

Approach to the Study of Marketing

The study of marketing has been approached in more than one way. To some it has meant to sell something at a shop or market place; to some it has meant the study of individual product and its movement in the market; to some it has meant the study of persons–wholesalers, retailers, agents etc., who move the products and to some it has meant the study of behaviour of commodity movement and the way the persons involved to move them.

The approach to the study of marketing has passed through several stages before reaching the present stage. There is a process of evolution in the development of these approaches. To facilitate the study, these different approaches may be broadly classified as follows:

1. **Product or Commodity Approach:** Under the commodity approach the focus is placed on the product or it is an approach on the marketing on commoditywise basis. In other words, the study relates to the flow of a certain commodity and its movement from the original producer right up to the ultimate customer. The subject-matter, under this study, is commodity. When one studies the marketing on this basis–commodity approach, one must begin to study and analyse the problems relating to a commodity *i.e.*, sources and conditions of supply, nature and extent of demand, mode of transporting, storage, standardisation, packing etc. Again, take an example of a commodity, say rice. One has to study the sources of rice, location, people involved in buying and selling, means of transport, problems of selling the product, financing, storage, packing etc. Thus, we get a full picture of the marketing from the original producer to the ultimate consumer. The method of study is repeated for each item.

The system claims that it is simple and gives good result over the marketing of each product; description study is possible. But at the same time this approach is time-consuming and repetitive process which is a drawback.

2. **Institutional Approach :** In the institutional approach, the focus is on the study of institutions–middlemen, wholesalers, retailers, importers, exporters, agencies, warehousing etc.,–engaged in the marketing during the movement of goods. The approach is also known as middlemen approach. Here, emphasis is given to understand and analyse the functions of institutions, who are discharging their marketing functions. The activities of each institution form a part of marketing and collectively complete the marketing functions. In the process of moving the goods from the producer to the final consumers, a large number of persons are engaged. This system pays attention to the problems and functions of marketing institutions–transporting, banks and other financial institutions, warehousing, advertising, insurance etc.

This method does not give adequate knowledge of the entire marketing functions and also fails to explain the interrelations of different institutions.

3. **Functional Approach :** The functional approach gives importance on the various functions of marketing. In other words, one concentrates attention on the specialised services or functions performed by marketers. In this approach, marketing splits into many functions–buying, selling, pricing, standardisation, storage, transportation, advertising, packing etc. This may be studied one after another. Here each function is studied in detail in order to understand it and analyse the nature, need and importance of each function.

In this approach, marketing is regarded as "business of buying and selling and as including those business activities involved in the flow of goods and services between producers and customers."

This system gives too much importance to various marketing functions and fails to explain how such functions are applied to the specific business operations.

4. **Management Approach :** This approach is the latest and scientific. It concentrates upon the activities or marketing functions and focuses on the role of decision-making at the level of firm. This approach is mainly concerned with how managers handle specific problems and situations. It aims through evaluation of current market practices to achieve specific marketing objectives. Generally there are two factors–controllable and uncontrollable, which are more concerned with the decision-making. Controllables include price adjustment, advertisement etc. Uncontrollables–economical, sociological, psychological, political etc. are the basic causes for market changes. And these changes cannot be controlled by any firm. But controllables can be controlled by the firm. The uncontrollables limit the marketing opportunities. As such, managerial

approach is concerned with the study of uncontrollables and then taking decisions for controllables within the scope set by uncontrollables.

Managerial or decision-making approach emphasises on the practical aspects of marketing, but ignores the theoretical aspects of marketing. At the same time, this approach, provides an overall information of the entire business.

5. **System Approach :** The system approach can be defined as "a set of objects together with the relationsnips among them and their attributes." Systems focus on interrelations and interconnections among the functions of marketing. The system examines marketing connections (linkage) inside as well as outside the firm. Inside the firm there is a co-ordination of business activities–engineering, production, marketing, price etc. On the basis of feedback information proper control is exercised to modify or alter in the producing process, so that the desired output can be produced. Here, the aim is to secure profit through customer-satisfaction. Markets can be understood only through the study of marketing information. For instance, business is composed of many functions, which are composed of subfunctions. Each function or sub-function is independent, but interrelated and enables the other to achieve marketing objectives.

6. **Societal Approach :** This approach has been originated recently. The marketing process is regarded as a means by which society meets its own consumption needs. This system gives no importance as to how the business meets the consumer's needs. Therefore, attention is paid to ecological factors (sociological, cultural, legal etc.) and marketing decisions and their impact on the society's well-being.

7. **Legal Approach :** This approach emphasises only one aspect *i.e.*, transfer of ownership to buyer. It explains the regulatory aspect of marketing. In India, the marketing activities are largely controlled by Sales of Goods Act, Carrier Act etc. The study is concentrated only on legal aspects, leaving other important aspects. This does not give an idea of marketing.

8. **Economic Approach :** This approach deals with only the problems of supply, demand and price. These are important from the economic point of view, but fail to give a clear idea of marketing.

Modern Marketing

Marketing occupied an important place in all stages of economic life, even from barter system. But today, marketing is a complicated stage. Modern marketing possesses special characteristics. Modern marketing covers all business activities in order to ascertain the demand, product planning, distribution and facilitating the entire marketing process. The modern marketing emphasises the need for integrated and well-coordinated marketing programme. It aims to attract the customers. The features of modern marketing are discussed next :

1. **Consumer Orientation :** Modern marketing recognises consumer's supremacy in marketing. The managerial attention was focussed on the market and the consumer. The management becomes consumer or marketing-oriented. Consumer-orientation or market-orientation may be defined as the "managerial state of mind concerned with consumer satisfaction and profit, and not sales volume alone." Consumer becomes the pivot of all business decisions.

In production-orientation, large-scale production becomes the rule of the day. By ignoring the marketing side, the managements focus their attention only on production. Under sales orientation stage, attention is focussed on attaining maximum sales. But the production-orientation stage continues, though with declined sales. In consumer-orientation, the consumer becomes the pivot around whom all business is developed. Creation of satisfied customers is the main goal of modern marketing. Profit can be earned only by serving the consumer's need.

2. **Modern Marketing Begins with the Customers :** The producers of the last century had little care for the consumers. Now, the production is carried on in large quantity. The manufacturer produces more than what the society needs. The marketer aims to develop the market; the market

becomes seller's market. Similar marketers appear in the market and there arises competition. The consumer, who comes in the last stage, accepts the goods; there is no alternative. But the situation has changed. Market has developed from national to international. Competition is the order of the day. Businessmen have started realising it. Earning profit is possible only through the consumer's satisfaction. To satisfy a customer, his needs are to be known. Under consumer-oriented marketing, it becomes essential to know what the consumer needs. This is possible only when information is collected from the consumers. Modern marketing begins with the consumers and ends with the consumers. Marketing research starts at this stage. Through market research, information of current consumer needs can be known. Therefore we can say that the task of marketing starts with the consumer and ends with the consumer. Levitt says, "Instead of trying to market what is easiest for us to make, we must find out much more about what the consumer is willing to buy. In other words, we must apply our creativeness more intelligently to people, and their wants and needs, rather than to products."

3. **Modern Marketing Begins Before Production :** In early periods, there were less competitions and as such sales were easily made. But now this stage has changed. The consumer looks for the usefulness and acceptability of a product. As such it has become essential to find out the needs and desires of consumers, through marketing research. The information from the market or the consumer will decide the future of the product. Thus, product planning and development is undertaken before the actual production takes place. The pricing, distribution etc. are secondary. These enable a marketer to face the customer, who is the king.

4. **Modern Marketing is a Guiding Element :** At present competition is more acute, because many entrepreneurs produce similar commodities **en masse.** Marketing has also become a still competition. The ability of the marketer depends on the ability of finding a consumer and to satisfy him. Businessman has to understand the economic development of a country and must aim to raise the standard of living. People may choose one among the products. They decide what product to purchase and what product not to purchase. Reasons may be the advantages, a purchaser looks for or may not be found in the product.

Role of Marketing in Economic Development

The term 'Marketing' has widespread wings encompassing a wide range of activities. Marketing plays a pivotal role in the growth and development of a country. The development of marketing has always kept pace with the economic growth of the country. Both have experienced evolutionary rather than revolutionary change. Rather, we say that marketing is the bye-product of economic development.

A country is poor because it is underdeveloped or a country is underdeveloped because it is poor. It remains poor because it does not have the necessary resources for development. When people invest in productive industries, enterprises come up and thus the entrepreneurs get profits, in turn, ploughing back of profits is encouraged. These actions invite a chain of reactions–more investment, more employment, more output, more income, more savings etc. These economic forces ensure economic growth. The components of economic growth are savings, investments, production and consumption. All the components are equally important for economic growth. Marketing as a business function and an economic activity influences economic development of a country. Marketing plays a dominant role in every economy.

For several reasons, marketing has been neglected in India. It is so, because : (1) Our national economy is characterised by our overdependence, on agriculture. (2) There is always excess demand for many products–supply is less and demand is more. (3) Manufacturers concentrate their attention on production rather than marketing. (4) Markets are mostly sellers' markets. (5) The management is not a professionalised body and so gives no importance to functions of marketing.

In underdeveloped countries, the marketing functions are neglected or are in the infant stage. In the initial stage, farmers and industrialists are interested in production and not in marketing. Industries are quick in adopting new techniques in production, but not so much in marketing. Even today some industries follow production-oriented stage. The manufacturer produces products for which a ready market exists, but neglects the development of marketing. This wrong notion causes the problem of recession and stagnation in many countries.

At the present stage, marketing has gained a wide recognition because of the increasing pace of production. To a great extent, economic growth of a country depends on the performance of marketing activities which stimulates the demand for goods and services, and leads to higher production. Marketing is further widened. Thus, production and marketing along with other activities become vital for economical development. Production may be the door to economic growth of an underdeveloped and developing country, but Marketing is the key to economic deadlock. The modern marketing helps to explore the means of expanding and supplementing them, but not to accept the limitation of resources. Marketing, to a great extent, helps in the development of the standard of products and services and increases the standard of all fields. Marketing, itself being a complex mechanism, involves a number of functions and sub-functions, which call for different specialised persons for employment. The field of marketing engages about 35% of total labour force, directly or indirectly.

Marketing plays a significant role in under-developed countries as it is a multiplier. The increased capital formation is considered a key to economic development. Nurkse says, ''Society does not apply the whole of its current activity to the needs and desires of immediate consumption, but directs a part of it to the making of capital goods, tools and instrument, machines and transport facilities, plant and equipment.'' Thus marketing provides a systematic discipline to economic activity. It promotes the growth of exchange economy. Further, ''Without marketing there can be no democratic economic development. Without marketing as the hinge on which to turn, economic development will have to take the totalitarian form.''

In the present highly competitive economy which can be called a buyers' market, it is the customers who wields full power. Customers can make or wreck a company. The customer who was considered the ''king'' is now treated almost like ''God'', emulating the highly successful marketing people of Japan. Marketing, in modern times, means learning from customers, listening to customers and transforming the organisation around customers. Marketing, in practice, does not refer to any single activity such as selling, advertising or distribution. It involves the interaction of several business activities whose ultimate objective is the gratification of customer needs and desires. By satisfying the existing needs of the consumers and creating new needs and wants for better and improved products, marketing sets the pattern of consumption and improves the living standards of the people.

MARKETING AS A SUBJECT TO STUDY

Marketing is one of the oldest professions. Marketing is relatively new although it is an old subject and has emerged from the older concept of exchange. The complex marketing system of to-day has evolved through different stages of economic development. To-day, marketing is a complex activity because a marketer has to coordinate and manage several things before reaching the target market. A lot of changes occur in consumer habits, tastes and aspirations and these changes are visible everywhere. Consumers in developing countries like India tend to emulate high material standards of living from advanced western societies. Automobiles, consumer electronics, household appliances, computers, cell phones etc., have become common, consumer products of daily use. Under this changed environment, a marketer is expected to cater to the needs of consumers and act as an effective link between the firm and customers. What Adam Smith stated more than two hundred years ago sounds applicable even today and is actually what modern marketing is all about. Marketing has higher significance in an emerging economic development. The success of business is known by its achievement in the marketing front, measured in terms of profits, market share and cash flows. Marketing is also important for a consumer as it provides more alternatives to choose from, controls the price machanism, allows the consumer to bring a balance between his income and level of consumption. It is important to the economic progress of the country as it opens up new vistas of reasearch by supporting product innovation and enhancing the quality of life for the ultimate consumer. Marketing managers use different strategic and management tools like environmental scanning, marketing opportunity analysis, forecasting technique, tools for evaluation and tracking of consumer choices. Marketing, as a serious subject of study and as a major managment function, emerged in the last six decades. As a subject of study, it has borrowed concepts, theories and empirical models from other disciplines, particularly from 'economics' the mother of modern marketing. However, other disciplines such as psychology, sociology, statistics etc., have contributed a lot to the marketing discipline. Hence, marketing is a new subject of study concerned with disseminating knowledge, skills and strategies through the development of concepts, theories and models in order to enable marketing practitioners to approach the markets scientifically both for consumer satisfaction and for corporate profit.

RELATIONSHIP MARKETING

As marketing has been different eras of development, the outlook of companies toward customers has also totally changed in these eras. In the sales era, companies concentrated only on pushing products to customers and services were virtually nonexistent. Then the marketing era began. Companies started focusing on customer needs and wants. They realized that they needed to focus on the long-term profitability of customers. This is possible only when marketers develop a long-term relationship with the customers. Relationship marketing refers to understanding and responding to customer needs and perferences to build more meaningful and long-term connections with customers.

The goal of relationship marketing is to satisfy the customer in such a manner that he becomes loyal to the company and is unlikely to switch to the competitors. Companies try to convert the customer into clients by giving them special treatment and then try to convert these clients into members who join the company's club to avail of special benefits. The members turn into advocates who recommend the company's products to other potential customers and ultimately, the company aims at converting the advocates into partners who work actively with the company in producing quality products. It creates a mutually beneficial relationship between the company and the customers.

As the market-place becomes more and more competitive and the environment more and more volatile, organisations are fighting hard to attract and retain customers. Organizations need to retain their existing customers because the cost of retaining a customer is much lower than the cost of acquiring a new customer. The cost of losing a costomer is not just the loss of a one-time sale but also the lifetime value of that particular customer. So, marketers are engaging themselves in building lasting relationship with customers to achieve profitability. To retain customers, it is essential that organizations focus on customers' needs and wants and increase their service standard levels.

QUESTIONS

1. What is the essence of marketing ? (*B.Com., Bharatiar University*)
2. Bring out the importance of marketing. (*B.Com., Madurai*)
3. What are the objectives of marketing ? (*B.Com., Chennai*)
4. Define marketing and state its importance. (*B.Com.*)
5. Define market and state the various classifications of markets. (*B.Com., Andhra*)
6. Discuss the importance of marketing to a firm and to a society. (*B.Com.*)

7. Is marketing an art or a science? Discuss. (*B.Com., Chennai*)
8. What are the three approaches to the study of marketing ? (*B.Com., Andhra*)
9. What is commodity approach to the study of marketing ? (*B.Com., Madurai*)
10. What is the modern marketing system? (*B.Com., Madurai*)
11. What is meant by consumer-orientation? (*B.Com., M.Com., Madurai*)
12. ''Marketing begins before production and ends after production.'' Discuss. (*B.Com., Madurai*)
13. Define and explain the significance of marketing. How does it differ from market ? (*M.Com., Mysore*)
14. What is marketing? Discuss clearly the modern concept of marketing. (*B.Com., Allahabad*)
15. Trace the evolution and development of marketing. (*B.Com., Madurai*)
16. ''Marketing is the creation and delivery of standard of living.'' Do you agree with the definition? (*B.Com., Mumbai*)
17. Distinguish between marketing and selling. (*B.Com., Delhi, Punjab, Madurai*)
18. Distinguish between marketing and merchandising. (*B.Com., Madurai*)
19. Write a short note on classification of consumer goods. (*B.Com., Madurai*)
20. What do you understand by industrial goods? Explain the classification of industrial goods. (*B.Com., Madurai*)
21. Bring out the role of marketing in the economic development of a country. (*B.Com., Madurai*)
22. Distinguish among local markets, primary markets and regulated markets. (*B.Com., Chennai*)
23. What do you understand by 'Relationship Marketing'? (*B.Com., MS*)
24. Comment on the widened marketing concept. Can it be practised in India ? (*B.Com., Chennai*)
25. What is micro-marketing ? How does it differ from macro-marketing? (*B.Com., Kerala*)

CHAPTER 2

Modern Marketing Concept

- *Evolution*
- *Factors*
- *Implementation*
- *Benefits*
- *Social Marketing*
- *Case Study-1*
- *Questions*

HALLOW, BUSINESSMAN LISTEN !
In business you aim at PROFIT.
To make profits, SALES have to be made.
To make sales, CUSTOMERS are to be created.
To serve them better, they are to be SATISFIED.
To satisfy them better, what to do ?
Their NEEDS are to be translated into
WANT SATISFYING PRODUCTS REPEAT sales.
When sales are repeated, business PROSPERS.
When business prospers, PROFIT too INCREASES.
To enjoy GROWING PROFITS for a long time, what to do ?
You must SENSE their NEEDS, DESIRES and WANTS.
Then satisfy CONSUMERS NEEDS.

The old view of marketing concentrated totally on the functions of distribution of goods and commodities. The flow of goods from producer to the consumer is sales-oriented, aiming to maximise the profits through maximising the sales. In the past, various innovations, growth of mass communication, competition in the market, rapid growth in the field of science and technology etc., enlarged the scope of marketing. The producers face the changing conditions created by human behaviour. Thus a change in the marketing functions is necessitated. Realising the importance of marketing to the success of a firm, the business administrators began to think of a new idea. The aim, objectives, follow ups etc. are designed to suit the current needs, desires and changing behaviour of customers. The consumers are not to be told what to purchase but asked what to be provided for customer—creating value satisfaction. This modern marketing concept is developed through gradual change in the minds of business people.

Evolution

Marketing in the present stage is not merely aimed at profit through sales. In the self-sufficient stage, the concept of marketing was absent. In the exchange-oriented stage, where the evolution of marketing started initially, man invented money to solve the problems of barter. In the production-oriented stage, economy was in scarcity. Firms were trying to solve the problems of increasing the output. There was no market research. People were around the product. The firms aimed to increase the production and to reduce the cost. The consumer's needs and satisfaction were not considered, because they felt that the demand for their product will be continued. In the consumer-orientation stage, consumers get enough products they need. The consumers have additional funds to purchase products according to their tastes and preferences. Here the firms face uncertainty about the level of demand, expected from consumers. Hence the firms started, the sales orientation are stimulation devices–branding, packing, advertising, promotion, product style etc. That is, the sales concept is a product-orientation backed by selling and promoting aimed at generating high sales as the key to achieve high profits. Firms were practising the sales-orientation concept. Without market research and without understanding the market needs and desire, it became difficult to sell the products. The buyers' view was that they had been used by firms, rather than serving them. At this stage marketers began to feel the limitation of the sales-orientation stage. Thus, marketing-orientation stage developed and marketers began to find out the needs of consumers and tried to satisfy them. It became easy for the firm to sell what the consumers need rather than to sell the product, produced by the firm. The firms changed their attention and invested in consumer research to measure the needs and satisfaction of consumers.

"The marketing concept is a consumer's needs orientation backed by integrated marketing aimed at generating consumer satisfaction as the key to satisfying organisational goals."

The marketing concept holds that the key to achieving organisational goals consists in determining the needs and wants of target markets and delivering the desired satisfactions more effectively and efficiently than competitors. Perspectives on what constitutes marketing and on what place marketing holds in the firm, have undergone substantial changes in recent years. In earlier years, marketing was viewed as not much different from selling. But marketing concept can be expressed such as "FIND WANTS AND FILL THEM". "MAKE WHAT YOU CAN SELL, INSTEAD OF TRYING TO SELL WHAT YOU CAN MAKE". "LOVE THE CUSTOMERS AND NOT THE PRODUCT." Essentially, the marketing concept focuses on all the activities of the organisation for satisfying customer needs by integrating these activities with marketing to accomplish the organisation's long range objectives.

The ideas of the marketing concept are :

(a) **Consumer's Need Orientation :** "Selling focuses on the need of the buyer. Selling is preoccupied with the seller's need to convert his product into cash; marketing, with the idea of satisfying the needs of the customer by means of the product and the whole cluster of things associated with creating, delivering and finally consuming it." It is expressed in the following ways also :

* Consumer is the king. He gets what he needs.
* Consumer has voice and tops in the organisation chart.
* Consumer's need and desires are considered in production planning.
* Consumer's need and desires are shaped through products.
* Firms produce acceptable products and not the product easy to manufacture.

(b) **Integrated Marketing :** All the departments in an organisation recognise the importance of buyers. For instance, a firm may have many departments headed by department heads. When the buyer has any dealing with the departments, a good feeling or a goodwill must be created through the dealings. Another example, a buyer who is financially sound obtains credit purchases. Then the collection department should not treat him as a mere debtor. A customer should have a feeling that all the departments are doing something for him.

(c) **Consumer Satisfaction :** Firms aim to give satisfaction to consumers through marketing concept. The firms try to help the buyers in solving the problems, better than competitors. In the concept of consumer satisfaction, there are short-run consumer satisfaction and long-run consumer welfare. The short-run consumer satisfaction is achieved by supplying items like liquor, cigarettes, tasty but non-nutritious food etc., without making any social judgements about the consumer's wants. This reformulates the marketing concept into societal marketing concept.

"The societal marketing concept is a consumers' needs orientation backed by integrated marketing aimed at generating consumer satisfaction and long-run consumer welfare as the key to satisfying organisation goals."

The long-run consumer welfare further broadens the concept of marketing, *i.e.*, servicing one's market and society.

The marketer must see that consumers with purchasing power constitute a potential market. No sales can be made unless there are buyers. It is essential for the marketer to carry out the business in such a way that they give satisfaction to consumers' needs at a profit. In many cases consumers are ignorant about their needs. The marketer adopts the consumer's point of view and tries to make what they can sell, but not to sell what they can make. They become consumer-oriented. A manufacturer should study the consumers in relation to their needs, desire and satisfaction and then design and make products to match the taste of the consumers. Thus **consumers have been given supreme place** in the field of marketing through surveys to find out the real needs of different groups of buyers. Secondly, **buyers do not buy products** and services themselves but for the **promise of what these purchases will do for them**. For instance, buyers do not buy toothpaste, but they buy the promise of healthy teeth and an attractive smile. **Thus consumers buy satisfaction**. Thirdly, **consumers buy price**. That is, price is the basic consideration. Consumers have unlimited desire but with limited purchasing power. While buying, a consumer chooses the best product at a reasonable price, which is based upon the objectives of pricing policies. Thus price is a consideration in practically all consumer's decisions to buy or not to buy. Fourthly, **consumers buy images**. While buying, a consumer is greatly influenced by his images of the brands of various competing sellers. The brand images are products' personalities. For instance, design, colour, package, price etc. can be a strong influence in determining a brand's image–Bajaj Scooter, HMT Watches, Bata Shoes, Amul Butter, Nescafe Coffee, Pears Soap, Ponds Talcum Powder, Camel's Ink, Asian Paints, Sony T.V., Darjeeling Tea, Parley Biscuits, Godrej Furniture etc. have a strong and individual attraction for the buyers.

The marketing concept holds that achieving organisational goals depends on determining the needs and wants of target markets and delivering the desired satisfaction more effectively and efficiently than do competitors. Penny's motto also summarises the marketing concept: "To do all in our power to pack the customer's rupee full of value, quality and satisfaction."

The main premises on which the marketing concept based are :

1. The customer's needs and wants are varied and many and these must be understood and suitable products and services be offered to match the requirements.

2. The market consists of different segments and these segments can be grouped according to the customers' characteristics.

3. The consumers in any market look for products and services which carry attributes of features and these are perceived closest to solving their needs and wants and consumers' preference will be for such products and services.

4. The consumers in any market may not buy a product if they feel that it will not serve the purpose of solving their needs and wants.

5. The success of marketing concept lies in proper analysis of market research, segmenting the market and offering products specific to the segments, alongwith proper marketing programmes.

Factors Influencing Marketing Concept

There are several factors responsible for the thought of "the modern concept of marketing." A firm operating under the concept, receives direction from the market, *i.e.*, information regarding the customer's wants, needs and desires through market.

The factors, in brief, are :

1. **Population Growth :** The increase in population, naturally increases the demand too. Markets are made up of people. Increase in population causes increasing the markets, increasing the consumers, who have increased demand for goods, in kinds, varieties, preferences etc. Thus the producers have to meet the changing demands of people.

2. **Increasing Households :** The growth of demand for household products is more than it is to the total population at any time. Joint family system has become unpopular because of many

reasons. Most of the families are sub-divided and this increases the number of families and their demands. **Example :** Automobiles, refrigerators, electrical appliances, television sets etc.

3. **Disposal of Income :** Automation in industries, births of many new firms etc. open the door of employment. Thus people have increased their income and in turn aim for more satisfaction and more comforts. When the income continues to increase, the purchasing power also increases.

4. **Surplus Income (discretionary income):** The people have surplus income left after meeting the expenses on essential items. This surplus amount will be spent on non-necessary products or luxury goods. Such items are selected by people, if they can give satisfaction to their needs and desires.

5. **Technological Development :** Science and technology improves day by day. New inventions of products take place often. None will have the guarantee that his products will always possess good demand in the market. Some technological advancement may outmode the existing products, in turn the whole industry may come to a standstill. People always prefer to have the latest model. A number of new products, in the place of old ones, are being introduced into the market often. Consumers are at liberty to choose from the new products. Therefore, consumer-oriented marketing system is essential.

6. **Mass Communication Media :** The growth of mass communication media–Newspapers, magazines, radio, television etc. facilitates the buyers to learn about the new products available for sale. The buyer gets information about the new products, faster and more effectively before the products come to the market.

7. **Credit Purchases :** Credit purchases through hire-purchase schemes and instalment schemes are common today. Credit purchase pushes sales. The customers can enjoy the facilities and this widens the market.

8. **Changing Social Behaviour :** The social pattern is changing. It is essential for any product or service to keep pace with the change in order to survive in the market. The western style has tremendously affected developing countries, including India. The demand for electronic entertainment items and consumer products have changed tremendously in the last 20 years.

9. **Transport Facilities :** The fast and easier transport facilities have resulted in urban-rural interaction regularly and also global tours are becoming very common. These have helped to change consumer's attitude towards marketing activities. The demand for frost free refrigerators, high quality soaps, moisturising creams, fuel-efficient cars, battery operated machines, remote controlled electronic machines are increasingly in demand everywhere. Buyers and consumers are searching for better products.

10. **Increased Competition :** With rapid industrilization, the manufacturing base gone up and a large number of organisations are manufacturing consumer products and giving rise to competition. Consumer have now the option to select a suitable product or brand which could meet their requirements. Thus, the marketing activity of all competing products has become an important day-to-day matter and the same cannot be ignored.

All the factors mentioned above have changed the traditional thinking of business managers and have dragged the producers to change their idea of marketing to the modern concept of marketing.

Implement the Marketing Concept

Implementation of the marketing concept called for some definite steps, some of which are briefly described as :

1. Company policies and operations should be customer-oriented. Firms should attempt first to ascertain consumer's needs and desires before production starts. Customer's preferences shape the business decisions. Customer is the king.

2. Profitable sales volume should be the goal of the firm, and not just volume for the sake of volume alone.

3. Under sale-orientation, marketing task starts only after production. But under modern marketing concept, marketing is broadened and includes first market research, then product planning, selling, pricing, distribution etc.

4. All marketing functions are to be brought together and integrated under a new department–marketing department.

5. Market research should provide the base for all marketing decisions. ''Research is any relatively systematic, formal, conscious procedure for evolving and testing hypothesis for making decisions. The words 'systematic' 'formal' and 'conscious' differentiate 'research' from 'intuition'.''

6. Marketing concept insists upon constant innovation. Constant innovation is essential to implement marketing concept, because creation of a customer is essential.

MARKETING CONCEPT

What I can sell ?

MAKE WHAT YOU CAN SELL, BUT DO NOT TRY TO SELL WHAT YOU CAN MAKE.

Shall I first create products ?

NO, FIRST CREATE A CUSTOMER, THEN CREATE PRODUCTS.

Shall I love my products ?

NO, LOVE YOUR CUSTOMERS AND NOT THE PRODUCTS.

Who is supreme in markets ?

CUSTOMER IS SUPREME OR KING.

Who will shape my decisions ?

CUSTOMER'S PREFERENCES SHAPE YOUR DECISIONS.

Benefits

The following are the advantages of marketing concept :

1. It is possible to enjoy long-term success when the enterprise recognises the likes and needs of the buyers.
2. It enables the firm to capitalise on market opportunities.
3. Marketing risks can be avoided on knowing the market needs.
4. 'Consumers are the king.' This prestige gives prominent importance to the consumers.
5. Product-planning becomes more effective.
6. The demand for goods equalises the supply position on the basis of research and innovation.
7. Marketing concept assures the integration of the different departments of a firm.
8. Profit through service is emphasised.
9. Marketing research is a management tool for making fruitful decisions and future plans.
10. Examples are not few, when ample opportunity for improving after sales services is adopted by enterprises.

SOCIAL MARKETING

''Social marketing is the design, implementation and control of programmes seeking to increase the acceptability of a social idea or practice in a target group. It utilises concepts of market segmentation, consumer research idea configuration, communication, facilitation, incentives and exchange theory to maximise target group response.''–Philip Kotler.

Not only the product, but ideas can also be marketed. Social orientation or social marketing concept is of recent origin. It broadens marketing concept. In social marketing, it is aimed that the social marketer is primarily acting in the interest of the target society. There is a difference between propagandist and a social marketer. A propagandist has no influence on product design, pricing or distribution; but the firm's given objectives are promoted through communication media. But the social marketer participates actively in the organisation's planning. Social marketer advises the type of products acceptable to the consumer, distribution system to be adopted etc. Social marketers may pursue different objectives. A few examples are :

Doctors want people to stop smoking in order to safeguard them against cancer.

Government has introduced family planning programmes in order to control the alarming population growth.

The Tamil Nadu Government has made it compulsory that all children above 5 should be schooled to increase literacy.

The Tamil Nadu Government supplies tooth powders, free of cost to school children to keep their teeth clean against decay. Government compels scooter user to wear helmets to avoid fatal head injuries.

Social planning aims to produce an optimal plan for bringing about a desired social change. A desired goal cannot be achieved without social marketing. The social marketer has to design a social change. For instance, the objective is to reduce the percentage of people who have drinking (alcohol) habits. First analyse the attitude of the people. People may be educated about the bad effect of drinking. To enforce the objectives, the four Ps suggest several possible ways of solution to bring about a social change. For instance, take the case of cigarette smoking and see how the four Ps can be applied :

Product :

* Manufacturers may be asked to make cigarettes with filter-fitters.
* Cigarette may be made with less harmful ingredients.
* The attention of smoker may be diverted to substitutes.

Promotion

* Create a fear of death or disease in the smoker's mind.
* Advise them to cut down the number of cigarettes.
* Instil into them the fatal consequences of smoking.

Place

* Availability of cigarettes may be reduced.
* Let smokers understand the advantages of not smoking.
* Reduce the number of shops selling cigarettes.
* Shift the cigarette shops to remote places.

Price

* Increase the price of the cigarettes.
* Increase the premium (LIC) of smokers.
* Policies may be adopted to stop smoking habits–praising, non-monetary rewards etc.

The four Ps can be used in order to have a good effect to achieve the goal. New smokers may be protected which is easier than correcting smokers.

Marketing can be used not only to channelise the products in the hands of the consumer, but also to bring the social objective to the market or the consumers. The application of marketing theories to social welfare (social objectives) is known as social marketing.

Elements

1. The social marketing technique is used to achieve the society's satisfaction as a whole, as against consumer self-interest.
2. The social marketing is an instrument to achieve the aim of the society. For example, population control, introduction of computer as a subject in schools etc.
3. Creating a healthy and favourable attitude among people.

"The social marketing concept is a management-orientation aimed at generating customer satisfaction and long-run consumer and public welfare as the key to satisfying organisational goals and responsibilities."

QUESTIONS

1. Explain the concept of marketing. (*B.Com., Madurai*)
2. Distinguish between marketing and marketing concept. (*B.Com., Madurai*)
3. Explain the term 'Social Marketing'. (*B.Com., Madurai*)

CASE STUDY–1

MARKETING CONCEPTS

Company

MAR Ltd. founded in 1993 was a high technology products company. The company specialized in making electronic measuring device for process control, communications and instrumentation industries. It was largely an owner managed company. The president of the company, who himself was an inventor, had raised enough capital to finance expanding operations. A major oil company had recently supplied capital in exchange for a minority share in the company. The growth in business was enormous in the last four years. The shipments grew from $ 15 million in 1997 to over $ 50 million in 2000. The company's R&D had made several innovative changes to give MAR an excellent reputation in the industry.

The business growth, however, was good because of MAR's new technical advance. The company essentially responded to the customer demand. In 1998, several other companies entered the field with similar products. One of them, 100 per cent owned subsidiary owned by a major multi-national oil company, was especially aggressive in marketing the devices. It had spent capital in automating production line and essentially met or beat the prices of MAR in the market place acquiring a considerable market share within two years.

In 2001, it was estimated that MAR and its major competitor each held 30 per cent market, while 10 smaller companies had the rest of the market. Recently, it was rumoured that Japanese had come up with a major technological breakthrough that would lower the prices of the electronic measuring devices in half.

Marketing Concept

The executive vice-president of the company was alarmed by the recent trends in the marketplace. In spite of the number of competitors, he was confident that the technological capabilities of MAR would enable it to maintain the necessary edge to continue the growth at 30 per cent a year. The market for the devices itself was growing between 30 and 40 per cent each year. He was also convinced that his current sales department was incapable of "marketing" the products as aggressively as the competitors. There was virtually no market analysis, product planning was uncoordinated and market intelligence was poor.

He made several recommendations to the President of the company.

1. The director of sales be given early retirement or should be reassigned to a staff function.

2. The sales department should be replaced by full-fledged marketing department, composed of four divisions : sales, technical services, marketing planning, and product management.

3. Marketing planning should survey the market constantly, recommend innovations and coordinate long-range planning.

4. Technical services should assist Engineering Department in new product development and render technical support to sales.

5. Product Managers should monitor their products and competitor introductions, look for increased penetration of old products, foster market growth with new products.

6. Sales department should concentrate on enlarging sales in present markets in coordination with other divisions.

To implement the recommendations, MAR hired a new director of marketing. The new director interviewed all the personnel in the sales department and found that Sales Managers more or less ran independent operation making their own pricing decisions in many cases. They constantly came up to the executive vice-president for reducing price levels complaining that competitor prices were low. The exceptional low price approval became more of a norm. The advertising budget was $ 500,000, one per cent of sales. Most of the budget was spent on advertising aimed at enhancing corporate image in various trade magazines. The company offered numerous products with almost no standardization. Every order required special design and production considerations. Sales managers insisted on broad product line to keep customers satisfied. The competitors, on the other hand, had rationalized their production line and offered only a few standard products.

QUESTIONS

1. What actions should the Director of Marketing take to implement the marketing concept? How long would it take to implement these actions ?
2. Evaluate each one of the six recommendations made by the executive vice-president.
3. What are MAR' s most pressing problems ? Assign priorities for resolution.

Comments

The case reveals lack of marketing research, marketing intelligence as well as absence of coordination between different departments, particularly between production and sales. Under systems approach to marketing, and the new marketing concept, these handicaps can be easily removed. The customer will be the centre of the marketing universe and all departments/divisions will offer coordinated efforts to achieve overall mission of the firm. Product line shall be rationalised to smoothen the production of efforts as well as marketing activities. Standardisation without sacrificing customer interest is always desirable.

Marketing (management) concept demands integrated managerial approach to marketing and it rotates around customer needs (discovered by marketing research), customer-oriented marketing planning, evolution of right marketing-mix, co-ordination of all departments, and above all around adequate serving of market demand. Then only profitability and progress can be assured.

CHAPTER 3

Marketing System, Marketing Mix, Marketing Function

- *Marketing Mix*
- *Meaning*
- *Definition*
- *Problems*
- *Marketing System*
- *Marketing Process*
- *Concentration, Dispersion, Equalisation*
- *Marketing Functions*
- *Classification, Functions of Exchange, Functions of Physical Supply, Facilitating Function*
- *Case Study-1*
- *Case Study-2*
- *Questions*

Marketing Mix

Marketing mix is the policy adopted by the manufacturers to get success in the field of marketing. Those days, when goods were matched with the market, have gone. The modern market concept emphasises the importance of the consumer's preference. Manufacturers take various policies to get success in the market and the marketing mix is one of the important policies. In marketing planning, we make use of marketing information to assess the situations. Therefore, a manufacturer first analyses the nature of the consumer's needs and then plans his product to give satisfaction to the consumers. All the marketing effort focuses attention around the consumer's need. The management, therefore is concerned with the markets and market behaviours to identify the target groups of consumers through market information. Then the management plans to meet the consumer's needs and to face the competitors. All these programmes involve a number of functions, which are to be planned carefully; and plannings need analysis of the market to take a decision—prediction and forecasting, to the future needs of the public. Marketing departments perform the operations and the market offering mix is the result. Thus, the identification of demand and supply involves various functions of marketing to attain success in the market and the combination of these functions is known as marketing mix.

Definition

According to Borden, "The marketing mix refers to the appointment of efforts, the combination, the designing and the integration of the elements of marketing into a programme or mix which, on the basis of an appraisal of the market forces will best achieve an enterprise at a given time". According to Stanton, "Marketing mix is the term used to describe the combination of the four inputs which constitute the core of a company's marketing system–the product, the price structure, the promotional activities and the distribution system."

Thus marketing mix is the combination of the product, the distribution system, the price structure and the promotional activities. The term marketing mix is used to describe a combination of four elements–the product, price, physical distribution and promotion. These are popularly known as "Four Ps." These four elements or sub-mixes should be taken as instruments, by the management, when formulating marketing plans. As such, marketing manager should have a thorough knowledge about the four Ps. The marketing mix will have to be changed at the change of marketing conditions like economical, political, social etc. Marketing mix is developed to satisfy the anticipated needs of the identified markets. A brief description of the four elements of marketing mix (Four Ps) is:

1. **Product :** The product itself is the first element. Products must satisfy consumer needs. The management must, first decide the products to be produced, by knowing the needs of the consumers. The product mix combines the physical product, product services, brand and packages. The marketing authority has to decide the quality, type of goods or services which are offered for sale. A firm may offer a single product (manufacturer) or several products (seller). Not only the production of right goods but also their shape, design, style, brand, package etc., are of importance. The marketing authority has to take a number of decisions as to product additions, product deletions, product modifications, on the basis of marketing information.

2. **Price :** The second element to effect the volume of sales is the price. The marked or announced amount of money asked from a buyer is known as basic price-value placed on a product. Basic price alterations may be made by the manufacturer in order to attract the buyers. This may be in the form of discount, allowances etc Apart from this, the terms of credit, liberal dealings will also boost sales.

3. **Promotion :** The product may be made known to the consumers. Firms must undertake promotion work–advertising, publicity, personal selling etc., which are the major activities. And thus the public may be informed of the products and be persuaded by the customers. Promotion is the persuasive communication about the products, by the manufacturer to the public.

4. **Distribution (Place) :** Physical distribution is the delivery of products at the right time and at the right place. The distribution mix is the combination of decisions relating to marketing channels, storage facility, inventory control, location, transportation warehousing etc.

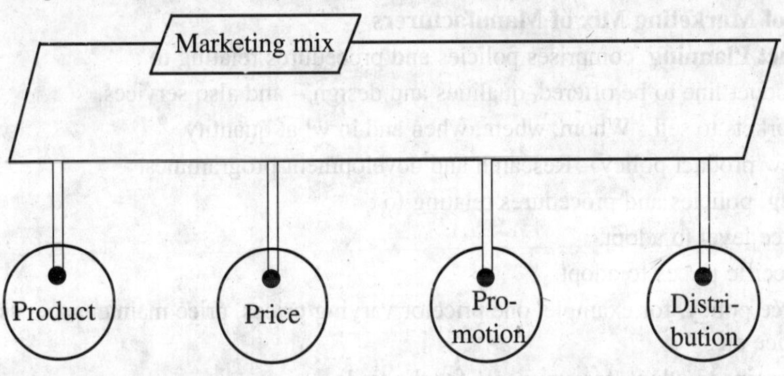

The Sub-components of the Four Ps.

PRODUCT	PRICE	PLACE	PROMOTION
Features	Credit Terms	Channels	Advertising
Design	Payment Period	Location	Sales Promotion
Brand	Discount	Stock	Publicity
Package	Commission	Delivery	Selling
Service	Price	Transport	Communication
Warranty	Differentials	Wholeselling	
Quality		Retailing	
Style			

Companies should view the four Ps in terms of the customer's four Cs.

Four Ps	*Four Cs*
Product	Customer needs
Price	Cost to the customer
Place	Convenience
Promotion	Communication

A firm's marketing efforts should start and end with the customers. The marketing mix–Four Ps, are the important tools or instruments used by the marketing manager in formulating marketing planning to suit the customer's needs. A share in the market and the goodwill depends upon the marketing plans. Change is constant. The customer's need and desire may change oftenly, because of the changes that take place in the market. The decisions on each element of four Ps are aimed to give greater consumer satisfaction. The elements of Four Ps are interrelated, complementary and mutually supporting ingredients. Thus marketing mix is used as a tool towards the customers in order to ascertain their needs, tastes, preferences etc. Marketing mix must face competition. It must satisfy the demands of the society. Then firms can attain the objectives–profit, market share, return on investment, sale-volume etc.

Concept of Marketing Mix

The concept of marketing mix, according to Borden consists of (I) a list of the important elements or ingredients that make up the marketing programmes, and (II) a list of the forces that bear on the marketing opearation of a firm and to which the marketing manager must adjust in his search for a mix or programme that can be successful. In brief, the four ''ingredients'' in the mix are interrelated. These are also known as **marketing decision variables.**

Elements of Marketing Mix of Manufacturers

1. **Product Planning**, comprises policies and procedures relating to :
   (a) Product line to be offered–qualities and design – and also services.
   (b) Markets to sell : Whom, where, when and in what quantity.
   (c) New product policy – Research and development programmes.
2. **Pricing,** policies and procedures relating to :
   (a) Price level to adopt.
   (b) Specific prices to adopt.
   (c) Price policy, for example, one price or varying prices, price maintenance, use of list price etc.
   (d) Margins to adopt, for company, for the trade.
3. **Branding,** policies and procedures relating to :
   (a) Selection of trade marks.
   (b) Brand policy – individualized or family brand.
   (c) Sale under private label or unbranded.
4. **Channels of distribution,** policies and procedures relating to :
   (a) Channels to use between plant and consumer.
   (b) Degree of selectivity among wholesalers and retailers.
   (c) Efforts to gain cooperation of the trade.
5. **Personal selling,** policies and procedures relating to :
   (a) Manufacturer's organisation.
   (b) Wholesale segment of the trade.
   (c) Retail segment of the trade.

6. **Advertising,** policies and procedures relating to :
   (a) The amount to spend.
   (b) Copy platform to adopt : (1) product image desired and (2) corporate image desired.
   (c) Mix of advertising : to the trade, through the trade, to customers.
7. **Promotions,** policies and procedures relating to :
   (a) Special selling plans or devices directed at or through the trade.
   (b) Form of these devices for consumer promotions, for trade promotions.
8. **Packing,** policies and procedures relating to formulation packages and labels.
9. **Display,** policies and procedures relating to :
   (a) Amount to be spent on display to help effect sale.
   (b) Methods to adopt to secure display.
10. **Servicing,** policies and procedures relating to services needed.
11. **Physical handling,** policies and procedures relating to :
    (a) Warehousing
    (b) Transportation
    (c) Inventories
12. **Fact finding and analysis,** policies and procedures relating to :
    Securing, analysis and use of facts in marketing operations.

Problems

Each element of marketing mix is under the control of a separate personnel. Therefore, it is necessary to the marketing manager to co-ordinate all the elements in marketing mix in order to achieve the aim. There arise problems in the process of co-ordination.

Controllable Factors

There are certain factors which can be controlled by the marketing management. Some of them are as follows:

1. **Product Planning :** A wise product policy is essential to meet the market demand. Marketing is a managed process through which products are matched with markets. A good poiicy is a guide for decision making. Consumers must be satisfied in a better way, through design; quality, size, market segmentation etc. The plan includes introduction of products and modification of products to suit the demand and elimination of unprofitable lines.

2. **Price :** It deals with price competitions. It also deals with policies of prices, discounts, allowances, terms of credit etc. A reasonable profit is aimed at by the offerer, and the price of the product is fixed to suit the market.

3. **Branding :** It must create a particular image in the minds of the consumers. Decision of the trade mark is important in developing the products. In a similar manner, packaging is also decided by considering its objectives and economies, in attractive style.

4. **Personal Selling :** Personal selling is good to increase the sale and at the same time to know the consumer's needs and desire.

5. **Sales Promotion :** The marketing manager makes out programmes, to increase the sales through exhibitions, displays, advertising etc. The process must inform and persuade the customers of company's product.

6. **Physical Distribution :** It includes the channels of distribution, transportation, warehousing, inventory control etc. Distribution is the delivery of products at the right time and at the right place.

7. **Market Research :** Market research is a system by which one can analyse the market conditions. It helps a marketer in formulating the policies by which the product reaches in an efficient way in the hands of the consumers.

8. **Internal Competition :** A firm may have many departments headed by specialists. There must be co-ordination among the departmental heads to achieve a good result.

Uncontrollable Factors

Uncontrollable factors are also known as external factors. Borden classifies these forces under four heads–behaviour of consumers, trade competitors and the Government. Apart from this, a firm may have no control over forces of economic, social, political etc. In brief:

1. **Consumer's Buying Behaviour :** Consumer's buying behaviour is affected by buying habits, buying power, motivation in buying, living standard, social environment, technological changes etc.

2. **Trader's Behaviour :** The behaviour of intermediaries–wholesalers or retailers, and their motivations, practices, attitudes etc. affect the marketing of the products and volume.

3. **Competitors' Behaviour :** New business firms come up. This attitude invites competition among the industrialists. The competition may be of supply and demand of the product, choice offered by the consumers, technological changes, new invention etc. The marketing manager must be vigilant about the market trend.

4. **Governmental Behaviour :** The marketing manager should consider the rules and regulations of the Government in respect of products, pricing, competitive practices, advertising etc. Firms have no control over the laws.

MARKETING SYSTEM

According to Stanton, ''marketing system is an interacting set of institutions, activities and flows designed to facilitate exchange transactions between an organisation (business or non-business) and its market.'' Philip Kotler says, ''The exchanges that take place in a society along with the facilitating institutions, make up its marketing system.'' In short, we mean, the marketing system is an exchange between two parties *i.e.*, business activity. As an example for the marketing system, we take a remote Indian village, which consists of a small market, few traders and bullock-carts for transportation. This is a marketing system which existed earlier in villages. But gradually changes took place and the marketing task became more complex. The manufacturers and the end users have no direct contact. The new concept of marketing–consumer-oriented marketing took shape. All these cause the appearance of middlemen–a large number of intermediaries and by the different channels of distribution, communication, etc.–in the field of marketing. Thus the modern marketing system is capped by mass production, stiff competition, complex channels of distribution, communication etc. Hence the meaning of marketing system involves (1) business institutions engaged in marketing functions; (2) the marketing environment; (3) customers served by business firms; and (4) the marketing tasks performed by the system. In brief:

Marketing institutions such as producers, manufacturers etc., perform one or more of the marketing functions. They are primarily engaged in production. They produce raw materials, semi-finished goods or services (bank), and are the first marketing institutions. Intermediaries like agents, retailers, competitors, facilitating institutions (transport) etc. add time, place, form and possession utility to market. All these institutions facilitate the flow of goods from the firm to the markets. The ultimate or household consumers are those who consume the products or services to enjoy the satisfaction contained in the products.

Institutional users or industrial users are those, who use the goods or services in the course of business so as to produce goods for ultimate consumers–consumer goods or industrial goods. Marketing mix is another plan through grouping of buyers or segmenting the markets, by customer characteristics–in terms of age, sex, income, education etc. Then marketing function performs the task, by which the producer and consumer are linked together. The marketing system must aim at necessary physical distribution, passing information of the product to the market through advertising, personal selling, display etc. A firm that changes its views on the changing situations, will prosper. Kotler says, ''The passive firm is doomed; the adaptive firm may survive; and innovative firm should succeed.''

MARKETING PROCESS*

Marketing is a process by means of which goods and services are exchanged. The goal of marketing is to move the products from the producer to the consumer. The flow of goods from the place of origin to the place of destination, involves a number of activities which is not a simple task. These activities of transfer, are functions which are known as marketing process. The marketing process involves three major activities viz.,

(1) Concentration; (2) Dispersion; and (3) Equalisation.

(1) Concentration

The first process of marketing is concentration. Concentration aims at the collection of products at a central place. It is because of:

(a) **Small Lot Output:** Agricultural produce, eggs, fruits, vegetables, dairy products, such as milk, butter, ghee etc., are collected at a central place from innumerable farmers, scattered here and there. These are marketed in natural form. To make other marketing services such as grading and standardisation, for the benefit of consumers, all produces–rice, wheat, cotton, tea, etc., are brought to a central place.

(b) **Assembly of Parts:** Some types of manufactured products need assembly work; for example, spare parts of products. These parts are manufactured at different firms and at different places. To make the final products, assembly or concentration is essential.

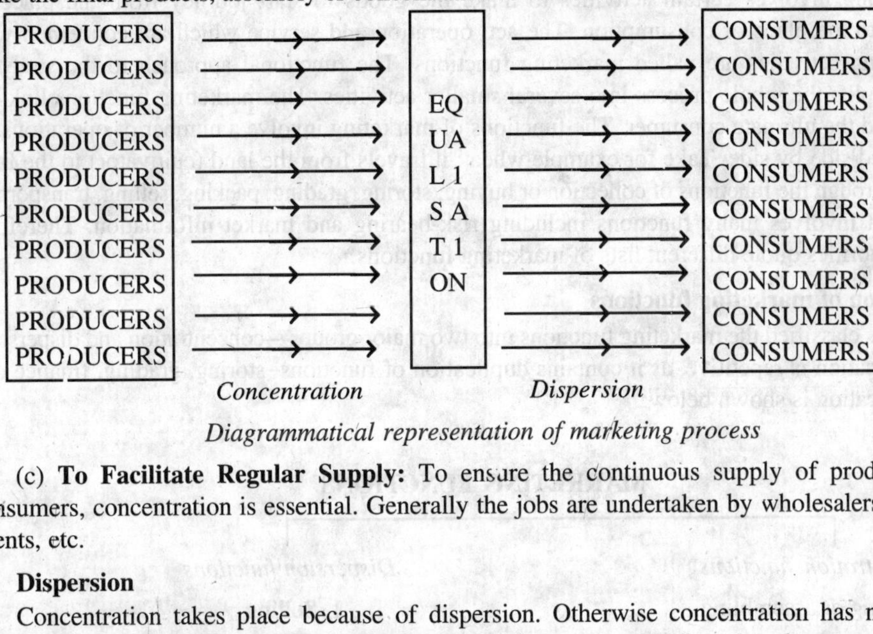

Diagrammatical representation of marketing process

(c) **To Facilitate Regular Supply:** To ensure the continuous supply of products to the consumers, concentration is essential. Generally the jobs are undertaken by wholesalers, exporters, agents, etc.

(2) Dispersion

Concentration takes place because of dispersion. Otherwise concentration has no meaning. The goods or products, assembled at a central place, have to be distributed to the consumers. Some of the products are dispersed to manufacturers or processors and the remaining goods are dispersed to the final consumers through a chain of wholesalers, retailers, agents, middlemen etc. The products meant for ultimate users are subdivided into small lots required to meet the final consumption.

Dispersion is essential, because the buyers are scattered or located not near the firm or in a concentrated place. In the absence of consumption, production has no meaning. The purpose of production and its concentration aims at finding consumers at profitable and accepted price.

A MARKETING SYSTEM is the set of significant institutions and flows that connect an organisation to its market.

A MARKETING FUNCTION is an act, operation or service by which the original producer and the final consumer are linked together. They represent the flow of the product and title to the product from the seller to the buyer.

(3) Equalisation

Between the two activities *i.e.*, concentration and dispersion, there is the equalisation process. It implies the reconciliation between demand and supply through storage and transportation, in needed quantity and quality at the required time and place. Adjustments of supply to demand are effected.

Equalisation aims at regular supply of goods which are produced in particular season, but consumed throughout the year, e.g., paddy, wheat, jawar, fruits, vegetables etc. Similarly some types of goods have only seasonable demand: but production takes place continuously. For example, rain coats, umbrellas, sweaters, woollen socks, mufflers etc. This equalisation facilitates regular supply. Then transport bring equalisation of supply, place-wise; and warehousing enables equalisation of supplies, time-wise.

Concentration, dispersion and equalisation constitute the soul of marketing. All the functions are performed by middlemen. Each process is not independent, but mutually interdependent and equally important. Middlemen assist in the transfer of ownership to consumers, but do not take title. Such middlemen are called functional middlemen. The middlemen who buy goods under an outright sale, are called merchant middlemen, who sell to consumers.

MARKETING FUNCTIONS

Marketing involves certain activities to make the goods to start journey from the place of production to the place of consumption. The act, operation and service which are concerned with the marketing activities are called marketing functions. The functional approach to the study of marketing splits the whole process into several smaller activities. The marketing functions link the producer and the ultimate consumer. The functions of marketing involve a number of operations, to be performed side by side. Take for example wheat; it travels from the land (cultivator) to the final consumer through the functions of collection or buying, storing, grading, packing, selling, transporting etc. Thus, it involves many functions including risk-bearing and market information. Therefore, various authorities quote different lists of marketing functions.

Classification of marketing functions

Pyle has classified the marketing functions into two major groups—concentration and dispersion. The classification is repetitive, as it contains duplication of functions–storing, grading, finance etc. The classification is shown below:

MARKETING FUNCTIONS

Concentration functions	*Dispersion functions*
1. Buying or assembling	1. Selling
2. Transporting	2. Transporting
3. Storing	3. Storing
4. Grading	4. Grading
5. Financing	5. Financing
6. Risk-bearing	6. Risk-bearing
	7. Dividing

* MARKETING MIX is the term used to describe the combination of four inputs which constitute the core of a company's marketing system - the product, the price structure, the promotional activities and the distribution system.

Conversely, Huegy and Mitchell classified the functions from the economic point of view. According to them, marketing functions are those which are capable of creating time, place, possession and form utilities. It is elaborate and includes functions like accounting, supervision etc., which are non-essential. The classification is reproduced next :

MARKETING FUNCTIONS

Physical Movement (Creating time & place utility)	*Movement of Ownership* (Possession utility)	*Market Management*
1. Transportation	1. Determining needs (gathering information)	1. Formulating Policies
2. Storing	2. Creating demand	2. Financing
3. Packing	3. Finding buyers & sellers	3. Providing organisational equipment
4. Dividing	4. Negotiating (prices & terms)	4. Supervising
5. Grading (inspecting, testing, sorting)	5. Giving advice (adjusting goods & services to the needs of buyers)	5. Accounting
6. Order assembly	6. Transporting title	6. Securing information especially by research
		7. Risking

Clark and Clark divided the marketing functions under three major groups–functions of exchange, functions of physical supply and facilitating functions. All the essential functions are included. It is an accepted classification. The classification is shown below:

MARKETING FUNCTIONS

Functions of exchange	*Functions of Physical supply*	*Facilitating functions*
1. Selling	1. Transportation	1. Financing
2. Assembling, (buying)	2. Storage	2. Risk-Bearing
		3. Standardisation
		4. Market formation
		5. Promotion

Thus the marketing functions are classified as under for the present purpose:

1. **Exchange functions**
   (a) Buying and Assembling
   (b) Selling
2. **Physical functions**
   (a) Storage
   (b) Transport
3. **Facilitating functions**
   (a) Financing
   (b) Risk-bearing
   (c) Standardisation
   (d) Market information
   (e) Promotion

A brief explanation of the above-mentioned classification is given below. (Again a detailed study of each function is done in subsequent chapters).

Functions of Exchange

Exchange brings about changes in the ownership of products. In the process of changes *i.e.*, transfer in the ownership, the two important functions are buying and selling. Thus, it is a two-way process involving two separate, but supporting activities. Both, buying and selling are complementary to each other but not contradictory with a different view-point. For better understanding of the activities, this function is sub-divided into buying and assembling and selling.

(a) **Buying :** It is needless to say that buying is the first step of marketing functions. It is carried out by all marketers–the manufacturers, the wholesalers, the retailers etc. Buying and selling are inseparable. Both happen at the same time. For example, if I buy a thing, then there should be someone to sell the thing. That is without selling, there is no buying. Seller is the person who sells the product. When the buying function is over, the buyer gets the title to the product. Buying may be done either directly or through middlemen. Buying implies business.

(b) **Assembling :** Assembling is concerned with the collection and concentration of goods of the same type from different sources at a place for further movement. Generally goods are bought from many sellers. When they are purchased from different small producers, scattered over a wide area, they are to be assembled together at a central place. For example, retailers buy different commodities of different sizes in different quantity, in different quality for their further movement. The main aim of assembling is to bring the products at a central place in order to disperse them either for production or consumption purposes. The job of assembling is carried out by middlemen, manufacturers etc.

(c) **Selling :** Selling and buying are complement to each other. Marketing efforts evolve around the buying and selling functions. In business, the selling function is very important. The primary objective of marketing is to sell the products at a profit. By selling, the ownership is transferred to the buyer. Sales are concerned with the activities, which convert the desire into demand. Creation of demand, its maintenance, expansion etc., are the soul of sales efforts. In this modern period, with mass productions, stiff competitions in market etc., the process of selling is a complicated function.

Functions of Physical Supply

The second group of marketing process is the physical supply. These are the functions that are related with creation of place and time utilities. Physical transfer of goods from the manufacturer to consumer takes place by means of (a) transportation and (b) storage.

(a) **Transportation :** As transportation, marketing function assumes unique importance because of mass production, mass distribution and ever widening markets. Since markets are geographically separated from the production place, transportation is essential. The function of exchange *i.e.*, buying and selling provide the transfer of ownership from seller to buyer. When ownership changes, possession is also changed. And through transport the possession is enjoyed by the buyer. When the distance between the production place and the consumption place increases, the importance of transport expands. The goods from a place where they are not needed, are transferred to place where they are needed. The function of transport can be as that of a nerve system, through which the blood circulates and keeps the body working at ease. Goods are sent to the markets through land, sea and air. The cost of transport is justified by the creation of place utility.

(b) **Storage :** Storage creates time utility. Products are preserved from the time of production to the time of consumption. Production may be during a particular season, but demand is regular. In the same way, production may be regular, but demand may be only in seasonal time. In both the cases, products have to be stored. Storage function is necessary in concentration as well as in dispersion. The function is done by the manufacturers, wholesalers, and professional warehouse keepers. Marketers can easily adjust the supply with demand through warehousing and transportation. Storage function is performed through warehouses. Storage is the base for consumers to get the goods.

Facilitating Function

In addition to functions of exchange and physical supply, there is facilitating function. Facilitating functions are (a) Financing, (b) Risk-bearing, (c) Standardisation, (d) Market information, and (e) promotion. All these are supporting activities. But these activities contribute in carrying out other functions. In brief, they are:

(a) **Financing:** Finance is the most fundamental aspect for any merchandise transactions. Funds are required to hold the stocks and to meet the cost of marketing. Finance is needed for production as well as for marketing–a self-blood of industry. Generally, there is a gap of period between the purchase of raw materials and the production of finished goods. It means that the manufacturer who invests in raw materials has to wait till the consumers pay for the finished goods. This waiting period is undertaken by financial institutions by granting loans. At every stage of buying or selling, the question of payment of price arises. The bankers, who are dealers in money, provide money on credit to the business. Merchandising machines are lubricated constantly by such financial institutions. There are various kinds of finance needed–short term, medium term, long term etc., and the source are commercial banks, co-operative credit societies, other agencies etc.

(b) **Risk-bearing:** In marketing, there arise numerous risks–damages to goods, physical loss, changes in economic values of goods, mismanagement, credit losses etc. These are more or less inherent in the marketing process. These are losses–on account of fire, flood, deterioration, bad debts etc. On all these occasions, an intelligent businessman reduces the possibility of risks. Thus, the risks are to be shouldered, shifted or reduced. Some of the risks are insurable, while others are not. For example, loss on account of fire, accident, etc. can be insured with insurance companies. But the loss on account of fall in demand, prices, competition etc., cannot be insured

(c) **Standardisation :** Standardisation is related with the division of commodities into distinct groups. Standard is used in providing certain basic qualities to the goods for their use. Standard is a specification. It is a 'norm', 'grade' or 'category'. Standards are fixed on physical characteristics of products. The standardised products possess uniform characteristics. For example, shape, weight, size etc.

Grading applies certain qualitative specifications. For example grading of fruits, agricultural produces etc. according to their size, colour, juice content, taste etc. Grading starts where standardisation ends. That is standardisation precedes grading. Both are closely related activities. Standardisation and grading are important and they widen the markets. Buying and selling becomes easier. It also facilitates purchase or sales by description.

(d) **Market Information :** The desired success of marketing depends on correct and timely decisions. These decisions are based on market information or market intelligence. Modern marketing must have information of size, location, characteristics of markets etc. The customer's wants, habits, purchasing power etc., are to be considered; the strength or weakness of competitors, trend in market, supply and demand etc. are also to be taken into account. Marketing conditions are dynamic and affect the industry to any extent. Market information includes all facts, estimates, opinions and other information used in making decisions, which affect the marketing of products or services. Most of the major decisions of business firms are based on the interpretation of the available data. Plans and programmes of marketing are not based on the information through market research and marketing intelligence services.

(e) **Promotion :** Promotion is a wide term including advertising, personal selling, sales promotions etc. Marketing communications are essential for both sellers and buyers. Sales promotions are marketing device to stimulate or restimulate demand for products. The behaviour of buyers can favourably be influenced only through promotion. Promotional programmes are needed for both consumer goods and industrial goods. Persuasive communication or effective promotion will facilitate the marketers to increase and maintain their market share.

A marketing function is an act, operation or service by which the original producer and the final consumer are linked together. This functional approach to the study of marketing has made it possible to split economic structure of exchange into smaller parts so that equal weight may be given to its each operation and by studying each function separately the best and most economical method of performing them, may be discovered. Marketing embraces every step which affects transfers in the ownership of goods and care for their physical distribution. Goods must be moved from producers to the customers and that too through a marketing machinery *i.e.*, buying and selling, until their ownership is transferred to the user.

Edmund D McGarry has stated that the term 'function' should be so defined as to meet the purpose for which it is used. To illustrate, he said, ''the function of the heart is not simply to beat, which is its activity, but rather to supply the body with continuous flow of blood. In like manner functions of marketing should be used only in connection with activities that must be performed in order to accomplish the general purpose. He classifies marketing functions into six categories:

1. Contractual - Buyers and sellers are brought together for marketing transactions.
2. Merchandising - Making products acceptable to market.
3. Pricing - Fixing a price to motivate buyers to accept the goods
4. Propaganda - Creation of customers or consumers.
5. Physical Distribution - Transportation and storage services.
6. Termination - End of the marketing activity.

The functions classified above provide a bird's eye-view of the area of marketing. They provide a basic knowledge, before proceeding further for a deeper study. The selection of classification really depends on the necessity, circumstances and the purpose of study. The importance of each function depends on the peculiar circumstances of each case. For efficiency in marketing it is not necessary to perform all the functions but only a balanced combination of these activities which are essential for success.

QUESTIONS

1. Explain the concept of marketing mix and describe various factors that determine it. (*M.Com., Karnataka*)
2. What are marketing functions? (*B.Com., Madurai*)
3. Explain briefly the various functions of marketing. (*B.Com., Madurai*)
4. ''Concentration, equalisation and dispersion are the soul of marketing.'' Discuss. (*B.Com., Madurai*)
5. What do you understand by the meaning and task of the marketing system?
6. Define marketing process. What are the major processes of marketing? Explain the functions involved in concentration and dispersion. (*B.Com., Madurai*)
7. ''Marketing functions represent the functional approach of marketing.'' Explain. (*B.Com., Madurai*)

Case Study-1

Marketing Strategy

In the white toothpaste market colgate is the undisputed market leader with virtually no threat from any other brands. There are many brands in the marketplace that have been trying to nibble at the market share of Colgate but with little or nil success. Some of the brands such as Macleans & Forhans's which tried to dislodge Colgate in the past are not in the reckoning today. Balsara's Promise toothpaste, which was introduced as the only toothpaste with ''time tested clove oil'', was hugely successful in a two-digit market share but could not hold on to it. Only Balsara's product management team knows why have they frittered away such a unique competitive advantage!

For the past two years two brands ''Pepsodent'' for the white toothpaste market and 'Close-up'' for the gel formulation have been trying to snatch market share from Colgate. Pepsodent advertisements deliver the message that it can check the growth of germs in the mouth and that too for long hours at a stretch. Close-up is fighting on competitive advertisements and sales promotions.

Colgate does not wish to be dragged into retaliatory advertisement. They feel that the message ''Meri big Shakti, meri big Suraksha'' (safety) has started sinking with distant second in the market. New product lauch is ruled out for the present. Colgate does not believe in the price war.

In view of the above situations help Colgate to formulate marketing strategies to effectively counter competition.

QUESTIONS

1. What positioning stand has Pepsodent taken ?
2. What is competitive advantage ? How does it help ?
3. Why reducing price is not advisable for a leading brand ?
4. Formulate marketing strategies for Colgate and justify your answer. (*AIMA*)

Case Study-2

Marketing Mix of Dabur Hommade

When talked to the sales person at Renume Enterprises and asked him about the number of sales call per day. He said that on an average we make 25–30 calls per day and there are 70% productive calls.

PRODUCT

Hommade: we can read it as "home made" obviously this brand can be nothing but ethnic. "Hommade is ethnic because ethnic is what we understand best. What the consumer repeats us for– an Indian company catering to Indian tastes", Says Amit Burman, D.G.M of Dabur Foods.

Dabur Hommade launches attempts at impacting the Foods market in urban India. Riding on nature's goodness and convenience, the brand has big plans to grab kitchen space. The brand name was chosen only after extensive research. Dabur should take in foods, after which a food line was decided upon. The research revealed that people believed Dabur's strength lay in product derived from nature, traditional enough to retain the product's natural goodness. The Dabur research revealed the following points:

1. Nuclear families were on the increase in urban India, replacing the support system that the joint family stood for.

2. Domestic help was getting to be a problem: while ten years ago, 53 per cent of all urban households had help in the kitchen, this figure has come down to 18 per cent by 1996.

3. Women were becoming more social and more caught to TV and didn't want to spend unnecessary time in kitchen, "Pressure of entertainment" is how Kartik Raina, CEO of Foods Division, puts it.

4. At the same time, what was not changing was the pride the urban housewife took in her cooking.

The range of products under Hommade includes ginger, garlic, ginger-garlic, red chilly, ginger-green chilly and tamarind paste.

The packing was in bottles and pouches. In packing, consumer research again showed that though the glass bottles were working out more expensive than pouches, housewives did not mind paying the Rs. 2 for extra convenience it gave them. Today 70 per cent of the sales are from glass bottles.

At a turnover of Rs. 3.5 crores now, Hommade appears to have successfully made it into urban homes.

PROMOTION

The company took a conscious decision to promote the category rather than the brand name since it was pioneering branded cooking paste. A series of 15 seconds ads—showing the hassles of grinding, cutting and pasting—was compared to the advantages of using Hommade.

The efforts seem to have worked. In May 1997, says Raina, Delhi used to average 8,000-10,000 unit sales of Hommade a month; by December, it increased to 65,000 units. National volume of sales for December was an impressive 3,70,000 units.

To increase acceptance, Dabur has decided to educate the consumer by launching door-to-door campaign, targeting 50,000 households, each in Delhi and Mumbai. The response, says Raina, has been very encouraging. Acceptance from door to door for a new product is usually 5-10 per cent . Hommade, he claims, notched a 28 per cent level of acceptance.

Dabur has pinned high hopes in Hommade and Burmans have a big plan "to be a really big, in the entire chain: right from growing the raw materials to processing and packing. Today 45 per cent of the produce goes waste due to obsolete techniques. We want to change that by setting up infrastructure, right from the farmer's level." Apart from all these, offers are also given to increase the knowledge of customers.

PLACE

Hommade is very well placed in the market because there are ten distributors in Delhi and all the distributors have adequate number of sales person and transportation facility is also very nice. All the distributors are well located. When talked to Mr. Kapil of Renuka Enterprises, the response was very good and he enlightended my knowledge by lot many information. He said that he is incharge of North Delhi and also includes the Sadar Bazar area. The distributors are same as of Real.

THE DISTRIBUTION CHANNEL OF HOMMADE PASTE

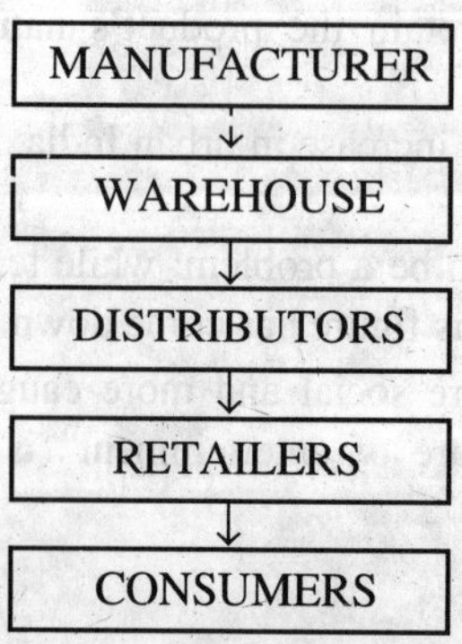

The coverage of the products is also the same as of Real fruit juice. The warehouse is at Vikas Marg, in New Delhi.

PRICE

A very critical marketing-mix tool is price, the amount of money that customers pay for the product. A dipstick research was done to fix the price of Hommade. Previously the 200 gm pack costed Rs. 22 but now it costs Rs. 20 expect for the tamarind, which comes for Rs. 12.50.

COMPETITORS

Dabur's Hommade has a small time competition with HLL's Kissan cooking paste. They have 3 flavours—ginger, garlic, ginger-garlic—and they have also launched tomato-ginger-garlic.

Another minor competitor is Kafros, which is manufactured by Kamakhya Fresh Foods Limited. The 200 gm paste costs Rs. 19.

TARGET MARKET

Another reason for the success of Hommade was that the company never lost sight of the fact that it was an urban phenomenon restricted to the upper classes of the society. This helped in controlling distribution and promotion cost. "Out launch was restricted to the 45 towns with access to cable TV," says Kartik Raina, CEO, Dabur Foods.

Source : A student project submitted in March 2002.

QUESTIONS

1. Discuss the issues involved in marketing strategies.
2. Suggest a marketing plan for Dabur Hommade under the present conditions.
3. What are the alternative strategies that could be considered by Dabur Hommade ?

CHAPTER 4

Buying, Assembling and Selling

- *Buying*
- *Classes of Buyers*
- *Problems of Buying*
- *Elements of Buying*
- *Purchasing Methods.*
- *Assembling*
- *Meaning*
- *Advantages*
- *Problems*
- *Selling*
- *Elements*
- *Kinds of Sales*
- *Questions*

Clark and Clark defined the marketing functions into three groups *i.e.*, Functions of exchange, Functions of physical supply and Facilitating functions. The first group of marketing functions is functions of exchange. And this group consists of buying, assembling and selling. An intelligent buying is followed by a successful selling. Both the functions *i.e.*, buying and selling are vital to the success of a business.

Buying or Purchasing*

Marketing is concerned with buying and selling. Buying and selling are very close to each other. They are inseparable. If one person wants to buy a product, then another person who is having that product, must be willing to sell it. Only if he sells the product, the buyer can buy that product. Hence both buying and selling happen at the same time. Buying and selling are complementary, as the title to goods is transferred from the seller to the buyer. Without purchasing, there is no selling. The primary object of the marketing process is the transfer of ownership from the seller to the buyer.

The person who buys the product is called the buyer. Pyle defines, ''Buying comprises all those activities involved in finding a suitable source of supply, selecting the desired quantity, quality, grade, style and size and coming to an agreement with reference to the price, delivery data and other conditions.''

Buying is an important function. Business concerns and consumers spend more time in buying goods. Buying includes the determination of one's need, finding out the source of supply, the making of business connections, the negotiating of prices and other terms and conditions and the transfer of title from the seller to the purchaser.

Product selling begins with product buying. The success of selling depends upon buying. It is generally experienced that the costs of the raw materials, supplies etc., are about half of the sales amount of manufactured products. Therefore, almost all the producers or manufacturers are basically interested in buying the best quality as purchasers only try to minimise the cost of buying. This is the case with middlemen, agents etc. Because the businessmen are interested in selling, successful selling, is guaranteed by wise-buying. Selling is at a profit. Thus we can remark that, ''Goods well-bought are half sold.'' For good buying, correct buying decision is essential. Perfect knowledge of consumers' demand and consumers' want must be studied by the marketing manager.

* The basic objective of the BUYING FUNCTION is to procure materials of the right quality, in the right quantity, at right time, at the right price and from the right sources with delivery at the right place.

Kinds or Classes of Buyers

Buyers can be classified into the following groups, depending upon the purpose of the purchase.

1. Manufacturers and Businessmen
2. Middlemen
3. Consumers

1. **Manufacturers :** Manufacturers purchase goods for production. According to the size of production the manufacturers buy large quantities. Manufacturers buy raw materials, equipments, machinery, spare parts etc. They use them in their operations. The manufacturers must be intelligent buyers. They must collect the market information of the purchasing goods. They must have the technical people to get the best equipment and machinery. Manufacturers aim at producing the best quality products, at a cheaper rate.

2. **Middlemen :** There are two types of middlemen. They are wholesalers and retailers. They buy goods for sale. Wholesalers buy large quantities. They sell the product to the manufacturers or retailers. The retailers buy small quantities and sell them to the ultimate consumers. Middlemen study the wants, needs and preferences of the consumers. According to the tastes of the consumers the goods are bought. When the middlemen purchase goods for sale, they must consider the following points:

1. They must estimate the demand.
2. They must know the sources of supply.
3. They must know the market news.
4. They must know the seasonal variation in demand, which depends on the distribution of income, custom, festival, behaviour of the people, consumer's preferences, fashion etc.

3. **Consumers :** The consumers are the persons who buy things for their own satisfaction. Consumers buy small quantities of goods for their needs. Buying of consumers depends upon their income. The buying behaviour of consumers is influenced by cultural, social, personal and psychological factors.

Problems of Buying

There are many problems in buying products. The main buying problems are :

1. What to buy ?
2. How much to buy ?
3. When to buy ?
4. Where and how to buy ?
5. How to negotiate prices and terms ?

1. **What to buy ?** It is difficult to determine the quality, size, type and style of goods which will be liked by the consumers. It is very difficult to take a decision regarding these factors. It is not possible to buy goods to satisfy consumers' wants, without finding the tastes of the consumers. So a decision must be taken in a proper way. Make a list of the things that are to be bought considering what are preferred by consumers.

2. **How much to buy ?** The quantity of goods needed must be known. Proper quantities of goods must be purchased for regular supply. As such, maintenance of balanced inventory method must be adopted to supply goods regularly to the consumers.

3. **When to buy ?** The time to purchase the goods must be decided. The time factor plays a vital role in this problem. Buying in correct time will give good profit. Correct purchasing will lead to correct supply to consumers.

4. **Where and how to buy ?** The sources from where purchase could be made is another problem. The availability of necessary products must be searched. There may be different places where the required products are available. There arises the selection problem from where we have to buy. We must select the place where we can get good quality with minimum cost.

5. **Negotiation of prices and terms :** This includes the terms and conditions on which the goods can be purchased. If the purchase price is less, the negotiation of prices and terms and conditions are favourable. As a result, the selling price will decrease, and competition with another trader is possible. On the other hand, if the negotiation of prices and terms are not favourable, the selling price will increase and hence competition fails.

Thus there are many problems before getting the proper quality and quantity of goods ; and that too in time and at the proper place. Again there is the problem of getting the goods at the lowest cost. If there is any problem of buying, we must consider the SIX R's. The SIX R's are : right quantity, right quality, right price, right delivery, right suppliers and right place.

Elements of Buying or Sub-functions of Buying

According to Thousley, Clark and Clark, the buying functions are :

1. Planning of Purchases (determination of demand)
2. Contactual (locating and maintaining the sources of supply)
3. Assembling
4. Negotiation
5. Contractual (entering into contract to buy)

1. **Planning of Purchases**

In planning of purchases there are three points. They are :

(a) Preparation of Budget

(b) Fixing the Rate of Turnover.

(c) Accounting for Changes in Fashion and Prices.

(a) **Preparation of budget :** The manufacturer should forecast with reasonable amount of accuracy the probable sale in a given period of time in the future. It is the management that estimates the probable sale during a given period of time. The management decides the required rate of production to meet the estimated sales. The management has to prepare the purchasing budget by estimating the expected demand, expected sales and probable production. Thus purchasing budget gives an estimate of the quantity of goods bought with reference to quality requirements. Budget is a strong plan of operation for efficient purchasing.

Budget is prepared for normally one year and forecast on the basis of the past purchase and sales records. It is a money budget. There is close relation between purchase budget and sales budget.

The marketing manager of manufacturing company prepares a list of materials for the production according to the production schedule. Then he gives orders. Before that he must know the benefits of large-scale buying. He can order for large quantities if there are storage facilities.

The budget must be suitable under inflationary condition and so it must provide for contingencies, anticipated rising prices, rising costs etc. While preparing the purchase budget the management must remember the following points :

1. Balance stock against sales.
2. Minimise investment on inventory.
3. Help finance department to plan and buy materials.
4. Help buyers in purchasing.
5. Increase enterprise's profit

Middlemen prepare a basic stock list. This contains the items of stock and also shows the minimum quantity of stock to be kept. Depending upon the past sales record, the stock list is prepared. If there is any change in the rate of item, the stock list is revised. The revised lists are useful whenever items are added or dropped from the stock.

(b) **Fixing the rate of turnover :** Profit is the measuring rod of the success or failure of an enterprise. Sale determines the profit. Hence profit depends on sales, profit is also determined by the rate of turnover. According to Clark and Clark, stock turnover is "the number of times the average inventory of stock is sold (and replaced) during a certain period, as usually one year." Quicker the sale of products, greater is the scope for profit in a firm. The rate of turnover refers to the numbers of times the average inventory of stock is sold *i.e.*; the speed in which the stocks are sold. The rate of stock turnover, is also known as the barometer of merchandising efficiency. The purpose is to find out whether the product is slow or fast moving, and on this basic decisions will be taken.

$$\text{Rate of stock turnover} = \frac{\text{Cost of goods sold}}{\text{Average stock}}$$

$$\text{Average stock} = \frac{\text{Opening stock + closing stock}}{2}$$

Illustration

The value of opening stock Rs. 4,000

Purchase during the year Rs. 52,000

Closing stock Rs. 6,000

The rate of stock turnover is calculated as follows :

Value of opening stock	Rs. 4,000
Add : Purchases	52,000
	56,000
Less : Closing stock	6,000
Cost of goods sold :	50,000

$$\text{Average stock} = \frac{4{,}000 + 6{,}000}{2} = 5{,}000$$

$$\text{Rate of Stock turnover} = \frac{\text{Cost of goods sold}}{\text{Average stock}}$$

$$= \frac{50{,}000}{5{,}000} = 10 \text{ times}$$

Higher the rate of stock turnover, the better it is. Faster rate is advantageous because :

1. Less capital is locked up in stocks,
2. Less risks due to deterioration are involved.
3. Price changes are avoided.
4. Savings are possible in the cost of rent, insurance, preservation expenses, salaries etc. Arrival of fresh stock is invited.

The rates can be improved by maximising sales. A good or desirable stock turn over rate is based on efficient buying and good sales policies.

(c) **Accounting for changes in fashion and prices:** A well-defined purchase plan gives importance to fashion changes and price changes. In brief :

(i) **Changes in Fashion :** Fashions are changing day by day. It is the most uncertain. The standard of living of the people in all the countries is increasing. Hence people require changes in each and every thing. That is the reason why fashions and tastes change.

Clark and Clark defined fashion as a style movement When a style is widely accepted it remains as a fashion. If somebody makes a change, then others also follow that style. Thus one fashion is replaced by another. As such it is a very difficult task for the marketer to calculate the fashions trend. Every marketer must carefully observe the style movement to be on the safe side, he has to keep in touch with the latest fashion. Hence he has to keep a close watch over the items, colours and designs which are selling well. The marketer, *i.e.*, the producer or the middleman keeps a minimum stock of fashion goods, otherwise he will incur losses if the fashion changes.

(ii) **Changes in Price :** The price-line trend can be classified into three. They are falling price, stable price and rising price. Generally producers and middlemen wish rising trend in prices, so that they can make good profit. On the other hand consumers want falling trend. Rising price trend leads to fall in demand.

2. Contactual

It is a sub-function of buying. It is concerned with the location and determination of sources of supply. The buyers maintain contact with the suppliers. Hence it is called the'contactual function'. When selecting the supplier, the buyer may consider the efficiency, financial resources and reputation of the supplier. The buyer must gave first preference to the local supplier, if he gives fair and competitive terms. Suppliers must be honest and fair in their dealings. The best supplier charges reasonable prices and offers best services to his customers. If more than one supplier are there, we are sure about a purchase.

Nowadays locating the sources of supply of product is not difficult due to improvements in communications and trade magazines. National as well as international sources are located very easily. Manufacturers are having salesmen and agents. Hence the establishment of contact is easy. There are numerous wholesalers and retailers. It is easy for the consumers to find the source of supply. Advertisements in newspapers, radio and T.V., also give information about the source of supply. Every purchaser should make contact with the supplier who is having the latest products.

3. Assembling

Assembling is the most important sub-function of buying. Assembling or concentration is the collection of goods from different sources of supply and making them available at the time they are needed and at the place they are wanted. (Full explanation is given in this chapter separately).

4. **Negotiation**

The buyer has to buy the product after deciding the factors which we have explained. Buyer invests money on the product which he buys. Hence he must get maximum benefit from his investment. Before buying a product, he must know the concessions like trade discount, cost of transport, time of delivery etc. Buyer gives the order in writing. All the details are written in that order. The price of the product is agreed. Briefly, the buyers and suppliers get together with a view to discuss the contents of contract as to price, payment, quality, quantity etc. This can be said as negotiation. After a detailed discussion, the parties settle the terms and conditions.

5. Contractual (contract of purchase)

When the terms and conditions are finalised between the buyer and the seller, they enter into a contract or the buyer gives the order to be executed by the seller. The provisions of the Sale of Goods Act will be applied in the interest of both the parties.

Purchasing Methods

The following purchasing methods are followed by the manufacturers or purchasing manager.

1. Concentrated buying
2. Diversified buying
3. Reciprocal buying
4. Hand to mouth buying
5. Forward buying
6. Contract buying
7. Buying by inspection
8. Buying by samples

9. Buying by description
10. Period buying
11. Buying by requirements
12. Open market buying.

1. Concentrated Buying

The buyer purchases all his needs from a single seller, selected from a few sellers. This depends upon the nature of goods. If the purchase are made from a single or from a very few suppliers, it is referred as concentrated buying.

Merits

1. There is less cost of contactual function. It is possible to make contact with the best suppliers.
2. Large orders lead to lower price and quantity discount.
3. Cost of handling and transporting will be less.
4. Reasonable price, best service and prompt delivery of goods are possible

It has got its limitation too. If the supplier fails to maintain regular supplies and if the buyer is a manufacturer, they may find much trouble in maintaining the production and business.

2. Diversified Buying

If the purchases are made from a large number of sources, then it is called diversified purchasing. It is also known as scattered buying.

Mertis

1. There is a flexible buying plan.
2. The buyer enjoys competitive price.
3. There is a wider choice to the buyer.
4. The danger of ''putting all eggs in one basket'' is removed.

3. Reciprocal Buying

The buyer and the seller enter into a contract to buy and sell their products mutually. It is a good policy. ''If you buy from me, I buy from you.'' For example, a sugar factory may buy sugarcane from the members of a society and sells its product *i.e.,* sugar to the members of the same society.

Merits

1. Better quality of goods at a reasonable price is made.
2. Purchasing and selling will increase.
3. It builds better connection and good will.

Demerits

1. It reduces the choice of suppliers.
2. Under unfavourable conditions prices may be higher.
3. The choice of buyer is limited.

4. Hand to Mouth Buying (conservation buying)

This is a kind of buying in small lots or quantities. It meets the current needs of the business. So it is called as 'current need' buying. It is conservative buying. There is no risk of loss. There is no speculation. If the middlemen expect a downward price, they adopt this policy.

Merits

1. Minimum capital is invested in stocks.
2. There is no problem of storage,
3. There is minimum risk of price fluctuation.

4. There is quick stock turnover.
5. There are flexibilities–buying and selling programme.

Demerits

1. There is no price concession or discount.
2. Buying is costlier.
3. There is high cost of transport, storage, etc.
4. There is the danger of out of stock, which leads to loss of orders.

5. Forward Buying (speculative buying)

It is a big lot purchase. By expecting a higher price in the future, buyers make a lot of purchase. They speculate a rising price and want to sell the stock at a higher price, to get a handsome profit. This type of speculation is prevailing in commodity exchanges.

Merits

1. Correct speculation leads to high profit.
2. Price concession and discount is possible.
3. It costs less in transport.
4. In a boom period it is the best policy.
5. It is suitable in sellers' market.

Demerits

1. There is heavy investment in stock.
2. There is the danger of overstocking.
3. There is inelasticity in buying and selling plan.
4. There is the risk of fall in price.
5. It is not suitable in buyer's market.

6. Contract Purchasing

In this method of purchasing, goods are purchased under a contract for a long period with fixed suppliers. The supplier supplies goods to the buyer at a fixed price. Investment of capital on purchasing is less. As there is contract, there is record-keeping and store-keeping.

This method is good when the prices are stable. When the prices decrease, the buyer cannot get the fruit of price-falling.

7. Buying by Inspection

It is the simplest and oldest type of purchasing. Now also it is prevailing in wholesale market. The buyer buys the goods by examining the goods directly. It is possible when the goods are purchased locally. This method is not suitable when the buying place is far away from the buyer's place.

8. Buying by Samples

This method is also very simple and old. The seller sends the sample and the buyer orders for the goods by seeing the sample. It is easy to purchase goods after examining the sample. Sometimes there are different qualities. Then they are graded. Those goods also can be purchased by seeing the samples. This method is prevailing in the agricultural goods like rice, cotton, tea etc.

It is easy to buy goods, which are in distant places, by inspecting the samples. Best selection of sample is necessary for the purchase of goods.

9 Buying by Description

When samples cannot be shown, the buyer makes the purchase on the basis of description given by the seller. It is because such goods cannot be carried to all places. A huge machine is an example. It cannot be taken with the seller. So he explains the size, performance and uses of the machine. The description is given by booklet or catalogue. Sometimes, buying is done by considering the name of the brand. Advertisement and standardisation help very much for popularising the brand names. For examples, Prestige Cooker, Sumit Mixy etc. They are purchased by their brand name.

10. Period Buying

Buying the goods regularly, *i.e.*, weekly or monthly or yearly etc., and usually monthly buying is prevailing among salary group people. Retailers also buy things monthly. It is easy to buy goods monthly. Transporting cost and other costs are incurred once in a month.

11. Buying by Requirements

Purchasing is done according to the demand. During the time of festivals like Onam, Deepawali, Christmas, Ramzan, etc, people purchase new clothes and other goods. As such the producers must purchase raw materials for meeting the increased demand. So they purchase things according to the requirements of their production. This purchasing happens only in time of festivals or occasionally.

12. Open Market Buying

When the price is reduced, the goods are purchased in the open market. Buyers are attracted by the reduction in price. Buyers buy goods and stock them. Non-perishable commodities are purchased and stocked.

Group Purchases : Sometimes manufacturers, institutions etc. go for joint purchase at a reasonable price. When the buyers are in group, and buy a large quantity, they enjoy favourable price, better selection, more concessions and discounts etc.

Buying Job-Lots : Some firms may sell their old stock or inferior stock or seconds at low prices or attractive prices. Insolvents also dispose of their goods at a very low price. In all these cases, the suitability or durability of the goods may be studied by looking at the whole lot.

ASSEMBLING

According to Holtzcla, assembling means, "the seeking out of sources of supply, buying wisely as to quantity, quality and variety and making commodities available when and where they are wanted." Goods are collected from big and small towns and villages at a central place for their further movement to the factory, mill or consumer etc. Assembling is helpful to the producers and the consumers. The meaning of assembling is finding the source of supply, buying the commodities and making them available at the time when they are needed and at the place where they are wanted. In agricultural products, assembling plays a vital role. As soon as the farm products leave the farm, assembling begins. Assembling of products in one market and distribution of the products to another market is possible, because of the improvement in communication and transportation.

Wholesalers assemble the product in one place while retailers buy small quantities and sell them to the consumers. Here both wholesalers and retailers are dispersing the product. Concentration of goods is to gather the goods in one point. In that place the producer's purposes can be solved. This object is fulfilled by the efforts of businessmen, manufacturers or consumers. For the middleman it is easy to get profit, by fulfilling the needs of his customer without searching for the source of supply. The manufacturer, without spending a lot of money can buy the required things at a single point. Consumers can satisfy their desire when and where they want.

Assembling is different from buying. In assembling goods of the same type, scattered in small lots, are brought together. Buying is the purchase of a variety of goods to sell to the needed persons. The following types of goods need assembling :

1. A number of small producers or manufacturers produce goods which are scattered over a vast area. Such types of goods need assembling.
2. Non-standardised goods and goods which are of different qualities.
3. Seasonal availability of goods

Assembling function is widely done in agricultural produce and is necessary since :

1. Small agricultural areas produce small quantity of agricultural products. So it is costly for the producer to carry them to the market.
2. The quality of agricultural products differs from place to place, farm to farm and season to season.
3. There is fluctuation of supply due to different crops which are produced in different seasons.
4. There is economy in large-scale handling, if large quantities are to be marketed.
5. Consumer's demand varies from place to place and consumer to consumer and produce to produce.

There are a number of agencies who are involved in assembling the agricultural produce.

1. Village businessmen collect the produce from the small farmers in villages and bring them to the wholesale market.
2. Cultivators collect the produce of other farmers and bring them to the market.
3. Growers bring their own produce to the market for sale.
4. Landlords collect produces from tenants and send them to the market.
5. Itinerant man who wander from village to village collect the agricultural produces and bring them to the market.
6. Commission agents also perform the assembling function.
7. Kuchcha arhatias assemble the produce from village merchants and pucca arhatias distribute the produce.

Assembling is not only important for agricultural products, but also for non-agricultural products and manufactured goods. Non-agricultural products like milk, minerals etc. need assembling. Milk is collected from individuals by Milk Co-operative Societies and it is distributed to consumers.

Manufacturers have their agencies for assembling. A car manufacturer manufactures some parts of a car. He then collects other parts from other manufacturers and then assembles the car for sale. Manufacturers are experienced people, and so they know the problems. Manufacturers have their assembling departments. The Chamber of Commerce has improved the position of the manufacturers in the market. In the assembling function of manufacturers, Trade journals and Directories give the best service.

Advantages of Assembling

It is important for the modern method of production and distribution. Following are the important advantages of assembling.

1. **Economy in the Cost of Transportation :** Goods are assembled in one place by gathering them from different places. When large quantities of goods are transported from different places to one place, it is natural that the transportation cost will be less. Bulk transport will be cheaper and so there is economy in the cost of transportation. This provides the economies of large-scale handling.

2. **Helps Standardisation and Grading :** The real aim of grading and standardisation is to give higher prices to the produces and provide standard quality to the consumers. When the total production is brought together, grading can be done. Standardisation is a marketing skill. And it leads to better price to the producers.

3. **Helps Bulk Sale :** Large orders can also be easily delivered to the consumers as goods are assembled in bulk. Manufacturers can order for a bulk quantity for their production. This can be possible only when the products are assembled in one central place.

4. **Wider Markets :** Wider markets for the commodities are possible only in the assembling centres. Wholesalers and retailers can have their large and small requirements at the assembling places. Wider markets of products are available and thus it provides time and place utility to manufacturers, middlemen and consumers.

5. **Cheaper Warehousing :** Storing and warehousing becomes easy as the products are assembled in one centre. The cost of ware housing is also less.

6. **Economic Processing :** If there is a large quantity, economic processing is possible. Economic processing leads to lower price. It is desired by all levels of people at any time.

7. **A Stable and Regular Supply can be Ensured :** Stable and regular supply can be ensured by assembling. Some products are seasonal in supply. Such a type of products is stored in one centre in large quantities at the season. The products can be supplied regularly throughout the year and even during shortage period. Thus assembling regulates the market condition. It assures stable supply of the products and this widens the market for commodities. It fulfills the consumer's satisfaction in terms of quality, price, choice etc.

8. **Variety of Products :** In the assembling centre there is the availability of a variety of goods at reasonable price.

Essentials of assembling are:

1. To know the source of supply
2. To know the quality of goods
3. To select the suitable centre for assembling
4. To have specialised market middlemen
5. To have market intelligence service

Problems in Assembling : Even though assembling is important, it has its own problems and they are:

1. **Need of Special Skill :** There are a number of producers. There are a number of small units of supply which are scattered over a wide area. The products are seasonal and irregular in character. There is difficulty in holding stock. To remove all these problems special skill is required.

2. **Lack of Transportation :** Assembling needs a developed means of transportation. But there is lack of proper transportation. Agricultural products which are mostly seen in the villages are to be transported. There are no proper roads connecting the villages and the market. The existing roads are also not in good condition.

3. **Absence of Properly Regulated Markets :** In India the properly regulated markets are less and they are also not functioning well. This leads the producers to sell their produce in the private market, at a low price.

4. **Lack of Standardisation and Grading :** This leads to the danger of adulteration, which leads to many problems.

SELLING

Selling is the other side of exchange function. Selling is the heart of the marketing task. Selling in business means the transfer of ownership of goods or services to a buyer in exchange for money. According to Cundiff and Still, "Selling, in its broad sense, aims not just at making sales but also finding buyers, stimulating demand and the providing of advice and service to buyers." According to Pyle, "Selling comprises of all those personal and impersonal activities involved in finding, securing and developing a demand for a given product or service, and in consummating the sale of it.'' Further American Marketing Association defines, ''Selling is the personal or impersonal process of assisting and/or persuading a prospective customer to buy a commodity or service and to act favourably upon an idea that has commercial significance to the seller.'' Demand is created for a product by selling. Only through selling, demand can be developed. The Six R's have to be considered and made possible by performing the sales function. Hence selling function plays an important role in the process of marketing.

Selling function is also called a creative function. It creates demand. Without selling there is no buying. The main object of selling is to sell or to dispose of goods at a satisfactory price. The title of goods is transferred to the buyer. Selling is an important factor in business. Production will be increased, if selling function is performed simultaneously. To increase sales, demand must be created. Skilled salesmen are required. They must find out buyers and give information about the availability of goods, their usefulness, price etc. The old proverb is, ''Goods well-bought are half sold.'' Sales are the life-blood of business. Successful selling depends on intelligent buying and efficient merchandising.

Elements of Selling

Following are the five elements of selling function:

I. Product planning and Development

II. The contactual

III. Demand creation

IV. Negotiation

V. The contractual function

I. Product Planning

The product planning function is also called merchandising function. It is very important in marketing. The starting point of marketing is with a satisfactory product through which consumer's satisfaction is aimed. It also aims at disposing of the products at a satisfactory price. Profit is earned by the producers. Satisfactory product with satisfactory price helps the consumers also. Selling function is a consumer-oriented function. The production of commodities must suit the needs of the consumers. Hence the production of commodities must be carefully analysed according to the needs, requirements and desire of the consumers. According to Stanton, ''A product is a complex of tangible and intangible attributes, including packing, colour, price, manufacturer's prestige, retailer's prestige, their services which the buyer may accept as offering satisfaction of wants or needs.'' Product is the combination of some attributes as to colour, size, design, dimension, appearance, utility, value etc. From these factors we can see the image of the producers. All the producers must aim to make the product a 'quick mover.' Hence every aspect of the product must be analysed and decided. According to Lemon, ''Product planning is an input-output device which translates a 'customer proposition' in terms of value and vice versa''.

Product planning is a process which covers the technical knowledge of the product as to its cost and profit consideration available from sale. It is a continuous process, from the starting of the new idea of one product up to the day it has gone out of the market. The nature of the product is decided by product planning. It must investigate the problems of production from the point of view of the consumer.

Product development acts according to plan *i.e.*, it makes the goods available as per the plan in connection with the quality, quantity, price, place and time of a customer. Hence it is right to say that product planning 'plans the work', product development 'works the plan'. Product planning and development make decision regarding the following:

(a) **Decision Regarding Variety :** The producer must be wise to decide the variety of products to be produced. Decision, regarding variety must decide the extent of choice and satisfaction of the consumers. He must decide about the limited or larger varieties to keep, based on size, colour, shape etc.

(b) **Decision Regarding Quality :** The producer must decide whether he has to produce a single quality or more. Price will be fixed according to the quality of the product. Higher quality goods fetch higher price. The policies of trading up and trading down must be known.

A firm trades up when it adds higher priced and better items to gain sales of a present lower priced article. For example, a firm producing at present Janata model sofa set (Rs. 800), introduces a new delux model sofa set (Rs. 1,200) along with Janata models. A firm trades down, when it adds or introduces low priced articles along with the existing high priced products.

(c) **Decision Regarding Diversification or Simplification of Product Lines :** Diversification of product line refers to finding of new products falling in the same line of product. For example, if a radio dealer adds to his product the television set, he is said to have diversified his product line.

Diversification takes place :

1. To take advantage of existing reputation
2. To increase the sales
3. To meet the customers' demand
4. To increase the profitability of the firm
5. To avoid the inevitable obsolescence of the present product
6. To minimise the risks of fashion changes
7. To utilise the existing capacity of plant and manpower.

Simplification refers to the practice of limiting the product line. It is the opposite of diversification. It reduces the number of products a seller deals in. It claims : (1) to reduce capital locked up in the products. (2) to minimise the confusion among consumers regarding products. (3) to specialise which is possible.

(d) **Decision Regarding Branding :** Branding the products is one of the devices of product differentiation. Product differentiation is the feature of manufactured goods. A brand is a name, a mark, a colour or a symbol. Brand is the value and quality of a product. It acts as a means of communication. It aims to give personality to the product. For the benefit of the consumers, the brand is given to the product. Consumers give preference to the branded product.

It aims at controlling the price of the commodities. The purpose is to provide product identification for assistance in buying and selling. The producer must select the name, mark or symbol that is easy to remember. It must be short, sweet and attractive and appealing to the eyes, ears and brain.

(e) **Packing of Products :** The fundamental function of packing is to preserve the products till they are sold to the consumers. It also helps in product differentiation and sales promotion. Hence it plays a very important role in marketing.

The producer must select the best material for packing. It must attract the attention of the consumers. It must be durable. It must have a good colour and an appealing nature. Some time consumers buy things, because they love not the contents but the containers. Nowadays plastic packages are widely used to attract customers. Thus product planning and development play a vital role in selling the products.

II. The Contactual

If the customers are prepared to buy the products, the aim of selling will be fulfilled. Only if there is contact between buyers and sellers, selling function will be in good swing. For the establishment of contact with the world, the following steps must be taken into account:

1. Choosing between limited or wider markets.
2. Choosing of buyers whether small or large.
3. Finding out or locating the customers.
4. Establishing contact with those buyers to create and maintain business relations.

1. **Limited or Wider Markets :** The nature of markets must be decided first. Markets are local market, state level market, national market and international market. It depends on the nature of the product *i.e.*, durable or perishable, quality, price of the product and financial position of the producer. The marketer must make the choice to maximise his sales.

2. **Large Versus Small Buyers :** It is another important decision of the marketer. There are a large number of small buyers and small number of large buyers. If the seller has a large number of lines of product, he must prefer large number of small buyers and vice versa.

3. **Finding out the Customers :** After deciding the nature of market and the number of buyers, the seller must find out the customers for his product. The seller must know the answer for the following questions.

Where they are located ? What they want ? At what price they want ? and when they want ?

4. **Establishing Contacts :** This is the function of establishing business relationship with the consumers. Establishment of contact must be widened and the buyers must act as the chain of communication. The relation must be expanded. This can be done through the best channel of distribution. (This will be explained in this book later).

III. Demand Creation

The demand creation may be defined as all special efforts to stimulate a desire for goods with the ultimate objective of sale at a profit. Clark and Clark are of the opinion that demand creation refers to "all special efforts to stimulate a desire for goods with the ultimate objective of sale at profit." Conversion of a desire into a demand is demand creation. It is the process that is designed to stimulate the existing desire to take the shape of demand.

There are variety of promotion tools to capture and maintain demand against competition. Those important are (i) Personal selling (ii) Advertising and (iii) Sales promotion.

(i) **Personal Selling :** Salesmanship is of paramount importance. It means the "ability to persuade people to buy goods or services at a profit to the seller and with benefit to the buyer." The salesman, in order to effect a sale, must persuade the customers to buy his products by applying A I D A S formula (Attention, Interest, Desire, Action and Satisfaction). By applying this formula, a prospective buyer can be converted into a customer.

(ii) **Advertising :** It is an impersonal approach. By advertising we mean "all the activities involved in presenting to a group of persons a non-personal, oral or visual, openly sponsored message regarding a product." The message is called an advertisement. It is relatively less costly method of demand creation, because it conveys the messages to a large number of customers at a time.

(iii) **Sales Promotion :** Sales Promotions are those activities which supplement and co-ordinate the personal sales and advertisements. Sales promotions are a group of activities. For example, displays, demonstrations, samples, exhibitions, show-rooms etc.

IV. Negotiation

It is the discussion between the buyer and the seller to determine the terms and conditions of sale. They exchange their ideas of the product in relation to price, quality, quantity, delivery date, terms of payment, discount if any, mode of transport etc. The period of settlement depends upon the nature of transaction.

V. The Contractual Function :

Functions of selling come to an end at this stage. The terms and conditions are agreed upon by the buyer and the seller and bind on both the parties. If there is any dispute, the parties can proceed to the court of law to get redress.

Kinds of Sales

1. **Sale by Inspection :** Under this, the buyer inspects the goods before he makes the purchase. This is a very old method. The rule 'caveat emptor' (Let the buyer beware) is implied on the purchaser.

2. **Sale by Sample :** A sample is a specimen or representation of the goods stocked. When goods are supplied by sample, it is guaranteed by the seller that the supplied goods will correspond with the sample. When goods are bulky and are in different qualities, sale by sample is better. It is unnecessary to carry the whole goods before the sales take place. The buyer has the right to reject the goods, if the supplied goods do not correspond to the sample shown.

3. **Sale by Description :** Under this, the seller gives a description of the goods through a catalogue, brochure etc. Where standardisation is possible, this type of sales is easy. Huge type of plants, machines etc., cannot be shown as samples or sent for inspection. In such cases only sale by description is possible.

In agricultural marketing, usually sales are effected in the following manner:

1. **Under Cover :** In this method, the buyer intimates the price by clasping the hand of the seller, under a cover. Sometimes, the buyer or his representative indicates the price by pressing or manipulating the fingers of the seller under cover. In the end, the highest bidder is announced. This method is practised in U.P., M.P., Maharashtra, Punjab etc.

2. **By Open Auction :** All those who take part in the auction sales, can inspect the goods. Open prices are offered during the scheduled time *i.e.*, the times fixed for transactions. The sale will be made to the highest bidder. This system is followed in Punjab, M.P. Rajasthan, Andhra, Karnataka etc.

3. **By Private Agreement :** Under this system the buyers at their convenience announce their prices, individually. The prices may or may not be accepted by the seller. At the closing of the transaction time, the decision about the price will be disclosed by the seller.

4. **Closed Tender System :** Under this system, the buyers have to write the price, place it in a cover and deposit in a box. At the fixed time, the tenders are opened. Then, whoever quotes the highest price, will become the buyer *i.e.*, sales are made to the highest bidder.

5. **Maghum Sale :** This type of sales takes place without mentioning the sales rate. Generally cultivators borrow finance from traders or if the marketplace is far away from the place of the seller, the product is given to the trader. The trader pays the amount to the cultivator on the basis of the price, at which it has been sold in the market.

6. **Dara Sales :** Large heaps of produces of different quantities are sold at a flat rate under this system. Thus large number of sales can be made within a short span of time.

QUESTIONS

1. What are the problems faced by a buyer ? How can he solve these problems ? (*B.Com., Madurai*)
2. What are various methods of buying ? Which method is the most suitable ? (*B.Com., Madurai*)
3. Would you prefer concentrated or diversified buying ? Under what circumstances can a dealer rely on limited number of sources.

4. What is stock turnover ? (*B.Com., Bangalore*)
5. Define buying. What are the sub-functions of buying ? Explain.
6. "Goods well bought are half sold." Explain the statement bringing out the problems of buying. (*B.Com., Madurai*)
7. What is reciprocal buying ? (*B.Com., Bangalore*)
8. What is the significance of assembling ? (*B.Com., Bangalore*)
9. "Selling is the most important activity." Do you agree ? Justify your position. (*B.Com., Madurai*)
10. Define selling. What are the sub-functions of buying ? Explain any two.
11. What is AIDAS theory of selling ? (*B.Com., Madurai*)
12. Explain the product planning and development as a sub-function of selling.
13. Discuss the need for demand creation.
14. Explain sales by description and sales by samples. (*B.Com., Madurai*)

CHAPTER 5

Transportation

- *History and Development*
- *Functions*
- *Classification*
- *Road Transport*
- *Railway Transport*
- *Water Transport*
- *Airway Transport*
- *Choice of Transport*
- *Questions*

Physical supply or the physical distribution of goods is one of the functions of marketing. What is transportation? Transportation means the physical movement of persons and goods from one place to another. For the large-scale development of trade and commerce, cheap and rapid transport is essential. Transport is the blood stream of a nation's economy.

Transportation is described as 'physical marketing', because without the physical supply of goods there will not be any transaction *i.e.*, buying and selling. Transportation is the 'key link' between the production and other marketing functions.

Transportation plays a very important role in the economic development of a nation. It is correct to say, "If agriculture and industry are the flesh and bones of the country, transport is the nervous system of the same."

According to Lionel Robbins, "Transport industries which undertake nothing more than the mere movement of persons and things from one place to another, have constituted one of the most important activities of men in every stage of advanced civilization."

Goods produced in factories or produces grown in the fields are not consumed at the place of their origin. Transport moves the goods from those places where they are abundant, to those places where they are scarce. Transportation is a necessary function of marketing, because markets are located far from the areas of production. They require some kind of transportation to create place-utility.

All the goods are not consumed where they are produced and all the goods are not consumed in the same period of their production. The purpose of the production will be achieved only if it reaches the hands of the consumers. As such transportation of goods from the place of production to the place of consumption is also a stage of production. Thus transportation creates place and time utility.

Transportation helps the growth and distribution of wealth. It develops trade and commerce. It encourages specialisation, division of labour, large-scale production and the extent of market. Better use of labour and capital is possible. An adequate and efficient transportation system is a corner-stone of modern marketing. It reduces regional imbalances. It promotes social integration of people of different nations in a country. It helps in the economic development of a country.

History and Development

The most primitive means of transport are the human beings. Due to the increase in the activities of man, he took a forward step. Domestic animals such as, ass, camel, elephant, horse, bullock etc., were used for transporting goods. Then were introduced wheeled carts. It was an important development in the history of transport. But the progress in transportation was very slow before the industrial revolution.

After the Industrial Revolution in the 18th century, there occurred a revolutionary change in each and every sphere of the economy. Due to that, there is increase in the production. Increase in trade leads to increase in the transportation system.

In England in the 18th century, an important development took place. That was the construction of canals. This happened in other countries also. It helped to carry raw materials at a low cost. Then steam engines were introduced. In the 19th century, Metcalf and Telfort, the great road builders brought much progress in roads. From 1825 to 1840 railways were introduced and improved in many countries of the world. Ocean transport also increased due to the mechanical invention of diesel engine. In the early stages ships were built with wood and iron. But after 1970 steel has been used. Then motor vehicles have been used. In this modern time air transport has increased very much.

Functions of Transport

Man produced everything he needed before man understood the merits of division of labour. Man was self-sufficient and not required any help of transport. As time passed, specialisation separated the producer and the consumer. Modern trade and industry depend largely on transport and transport brings together the producer and the consumer.

Transport helps the movement of persons and things from one place to another. It reduces the distance between the consumer and the producer. It helps in specialisation and large-scale production. The important functions are :

1. **It Encourages Large-Scale Production :** Conversion of raw materials into finished products is known as the production of goods. For large or small-scale production of goods movement of raw material is essential. Then finished products must be transported. Transportation of goods takes place from the abundant area to the scarce area. Transport is necessary at every stage of production of goods.

Transportation extends the existing market and creates new market. It increases the demand for goods. It leads to increase in the production level. Thus large-scale production is possible. Movement of products from one place to another place creates place utility. Transport moves the products in the required form to the required place. It equalises the supply.

2. **It Increases the Mobility of Factors of Production :** Growth of industries depends on the transport system. The four factors of production (raw materials, labour, capital and entrepreneur) are essential for the development of industries. It is only through transportation, the mobilisation of factors is made possible from one place to other places and from one country to other countries. It encourages migration of people and movement of labour and capital. Quick and reliable means of transport are essential for the industries which produce perishable commodities like, products, fruits, meat, fish, poultry etc. Thus it creates time utility.

3. **It Encourages Specialisation and Division of Labour :** Transport facilitates regional and geographical concentration. It helps the region or the country which may concentrate on the production of that commodity for which it is most suited. It will rely on other countries for those goods which it cannot produce. Thus it helps in territorial division of labour. Exploitation of local resources is also possible. Location of industries also is decided by the transport. Thus transportation helps everyone in the world to reap the benefits of specialisation.

4. **It Helps in Stabilising Price :** Transport brings about regional price equalisation. It helps in the movement of goods from surplus areas to deficit areas. This leads to the equalisation of demand and supply conditions. Prices are elastic or static according to the demand and supply conditions. This reduces the price of goods to the consumers. Thus transportation is good for both the consumers and the producers. It intensifies competition among dealers and thus reduces price.

5. **It Provides Employment Opportunities :** Transportation provides employment opportunities to skilled and unskilled workers. Millions of people are needed to perform the function of transport throughout the world. There are three modes of transport–land, water and air. Thus transport lends a helping hand to employment.

6. **It Strengthens the Defence of a Nation :** Transport is the most important element for strengthening the defence of a nation. Men and materials to fight wars are moved by the transport system. The National Defence Force consists of Air Force, Navy and Army and these three categories, transport are essential.

7. **It Reduces the Danger of Shortage :** In this world everything is in short supply relating to its demand. The danger of shortage can be eradicated with the help of transport. Transport creates place utility. American wheat, Russian kerosene, Burmese rice etc., are bought by us. We are in shortage of these commodities. Due to shortage of one commodity in one place the price will be high. But that commodity may be in abundant supply in other places at low price. Transport helps the shortage area by bringing the goods from the abundant area.

8. **It Helps in the Transformation of the Economy :** Transformation of agriculture from subsistence farming to commercial farming is possible through the development of transport. Development of industries is possible only by the movement of raw material, labour, capital etc. This movement is possible only through transport. Thus transport leads to transformation in agriculture and industrial economy of a country.

9. **It Transforms Social and Cultural Structures :** Social and cultural contacts between one country and another country are increased through transport. Social homogeneity and unity are created. Religious ideals are known. Standard of living, education and day to day life are known and exchanged. It broadens the knowledge of the society. In contrast, absence of transport makes a society stagnant; it can never enjoy the benefits of a modern and progressive society. National unity and integrity are promoted by transport. Transport increases the knowledge of the people. It spreads the culture and civilisation all over the world. Now all the nations have closer social and cultural contacts.

10. **It Increases Demand for Goods :** Today markets have become national or international only because of transport. It widens the market. Both consumers and producers are benefited by the extention of the market. New-comers in newer places can easily be contacted and thus demand is created. It helps the product to be distributed in the minimum possible time.

Classification of Transport

The means of transport can be classified into three main divisions and they are called the medium of movement or transport — 1. Land transport, 2. Water transport and 3. Air transport.

Due to the inventions of modern scientists, we have another means of transport *i.e.*, space transport which is used for going to the moon and other planets.

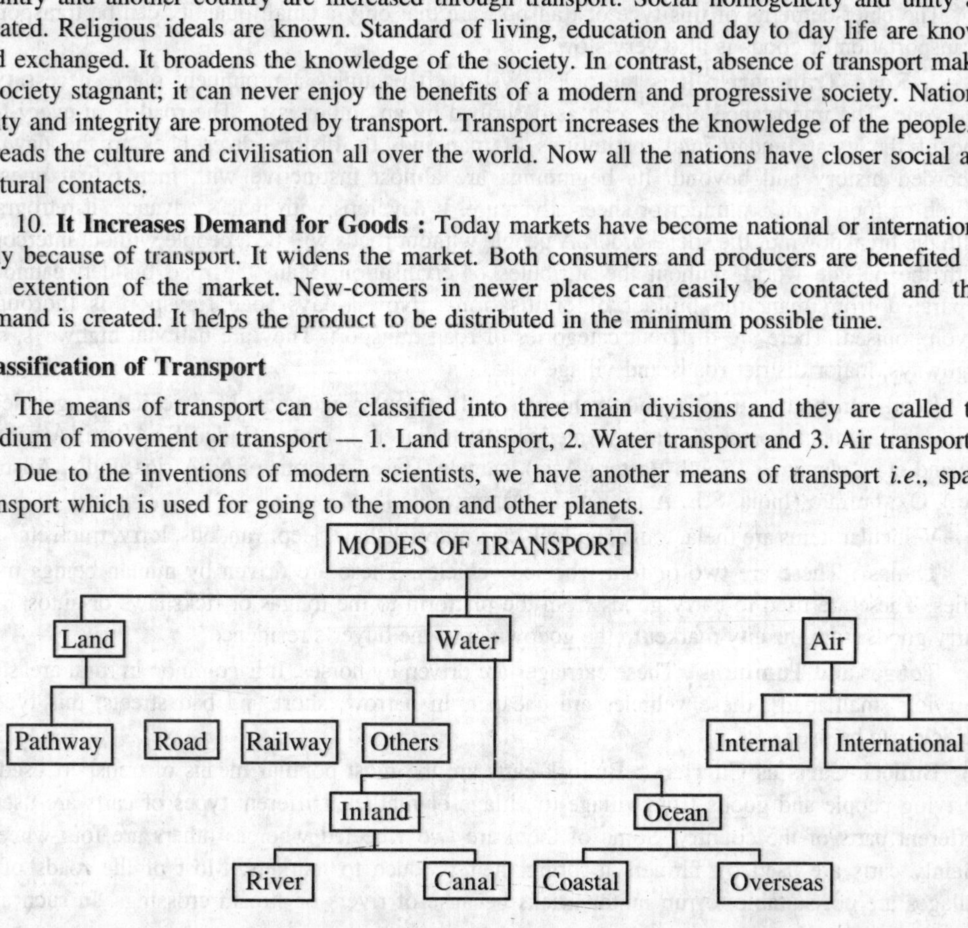

Land Transport

Land transport is the oldest one and is very important to each and every person. Without land transport nothing can be done. Land transport can be divided into four: they are pathways, roadways, railways and other ways consist of tramways and pipe lines.

Pathways can be studied under the following headings :

1. **Pathways :** It is used in small villages, hills, forest areas, deserts etc. In these places roads cannot be constructed. The two means of pathway transport can be studied under head load and pack animals.

(a) **Head Load :** This form of transport is used in hilly areas and forests. Roads cannot be constructed in these areas. The distance is also very short. Commodities like vegetables, fruits, fodder, firewood etc., are brought from small villages to neighbouring cities on head load. The cost is also very low.

(b) **Pack Animals :** In villages and deserts, animals like horse, donkey, buffalo, bullock, elephant, camel etc. are used to transport goods from one place to another.

The animals serve good purpose for transport of small quantities of grains, firewood etc., when roads are damaged. Carrying capacity of pack-animal varies; 75 kg. (average) in case of asses to 4 tonnes, in case of camels. Carrying of load also depends on the season, the strength of animal and condition of the road. The main advantage is that animals can pass through small tracts, muddy roads etc. where vehicles cannot be used. Though it is out of date it is used, because no other modes of transport can be used in those areas.

The chief demerits of this type of transport are that only a small quantity can be transported. Transportation of goods is also very slow.

2. **Road Transport :** It is the oldest system. It occupies a prominent place, necessary to everyone. The importance of the road as described by an author is : "The road is in every truth one of the great fundamental institutions of mankind. Its history dates back to the dawn of recorded history and beyond. Its beginnings are almost instinctive with man's first quest in search of food, water, plunder or sheer adventure. It develops with man's advance; it retrogrades with the breakdown of the social order. A people without roads will be a people without intercourse with the outside world–without the attributes of civilisation. Man, the road builder, cannot be separated from man, the builder of civilisation." Now-a-days road transport is thoroughly revolutionised. There are different categories of road transport. They are national highways, state highways, major district roads and village roads.

Road transport is used by non-vehicular and vehicular agencies. Non-vehicular agencies of roads are animals–horses (Eurasia, America, Australia etc.), mules (India, S. Africa, Argentina, Ireland etc.), elephants (South Eastern Asia), camels (Desert regions of N. Africa, India, Australia etc.), Ox, buffalo (India, S.E. Asia, Russia, America etc.).

Vehicular items are thela, tonga, bullock cart, autorickshaw, jeep, van, bus, lorry, truck etc.

Thelas : These are two or four-wheeled vehicles. These are driven by human beings in the cities. These are used to carry goods from the platform to the tongas or rickshaws or autos. They carry goods from the city market to the godown or to the buyer's residence.

Tongas and Tumtums . These carriages are driven by horses. It is common in rural areas. For carrying small loads, these vehicles are cheaper. In narrow, short and bad streets, this type of vehicle can be used.

Bullock-Carts as Carriers : Bullock-carts are the most popular means of transport used for carrying people and goods from village to village or market. Different types of carts are used in different parts of the country. Some of them are two wheeled whereas others are four-wheeled. Mainly carts are used by farmers to bring their produce to markets. Most of the roads of the villages are not suitable to run motor trucks because of rivers or stream crossings. In such areas pack-animals or bullock carts are suitable. They are locally made and available in most villages, apart from easy repairs. There is economy as the bullocks are also used for other farm-operations. However, the bullock-cart transport is declining due to its slow-driven, low carrying capacity etc.

Motor-truck Transport : After the industrial revolution this means of transport increased in the world. In modern days, motor transport has become a very popular means of transport. Usually metal roads are used by motor vehicles. Under motor-truck transport come the automobiles, motor-cars, trucks, buses, lorries, vans etc.

There are a number of reasons for popularity of motor-truck transport. First, motor-truck transport is cheaper for short distance when compared to railway transport. When the destination is not on a rail line, it is faster. During post-harvest period, there arises a sudden rush for transport facilities; it is the only alternative for movement of foodgrains. It carries perishable goods to their destination speedily and safely. However, there arises a great variation in the charges made by motor-truck owners.

Importance of Road Transport

Roads are the ''conveyor belts of a nation.'' Road transport is of vital importance for trade. All the movements of goods and passengers begin and end by taking roads. For the transportation of any goods and for any scheme of transportation roads are indispensable. Different kinds of roads are used by different kinds of vehicles. It is used for multipurpose. It provides maximum social advantages. Without spending money the poor as well as the rich can use it. Road is very necessary for the community development. Roads are the best means of transport to create demand for the industrial goods. A network of roads is essential for the transportation of raw materials and finished products. It is important for the economic development of the under-developed countries. Road transport is a major branch. It acts as a feeder for railways, airways and shipping, where people and goods are to be moved over a distance. Thus it is a link between other means of transport. It plays a significant role in bringing about social, political and economic development of a country.

Merits of Road Transport

1. **Quicker:** Quick delivery of goods is possible. It is of great advantage to the producers and consumers. This type of advantage is not offered by any other means of transport. It is worthy to be noted that the goods consigned will reach at the door of the consignee.

2. **Flexible:** It is more flexible than any other means of transport. Road transport is not fixed. Passengers and goods can be picked up at any place at any time. It has no particular time or specific route. Anyone can hire a vehicle at any time. If there is inefficient traffic in one route, it can be diverted to any other route. Motor vehicle can directly come to the warehouses to take the goods and deliver them at the appropriate place. Door to door delivery of goods is possible.

3. **Less Costly:** The cost of road construction and maintenance is lower than that of the railway construction. Hence road transport involves less capital. In terms of time and money, it is less costly and cheaper for consumers.

4. **Safety:** Motor transport has minimum handling in loading and unloading operations. It has the advantages of safety and reliability. Thus it eliminates breakages, losses and thefts. It is easy to carry perishable commodities like vegetables, milk, fruits, flowers etc. For short distance, it is less expensive.

5. **Wider Coverage:** Motor trucks cover wider areas, but railway covers only selected towns. Motor trucks cover the areas which cannot be covered by railways. For hilly regions, only road transport can be used.

6. **Provides Wider Market:** Businessmen can reach the market on distant places by motor truck and buy or sell things which could not be transported by railways. Merchants can buy things and sell them in the required place.

7. **Encourage Farm Products' Movement:** It is very advantageous to the farmers. They can send the perishable and non-perishable goods from the village itself. The green revolution is achieved by the improvement of road transport to a great extent.

8. **Delivery of Goods in Better Condition :** It takes less time and leads to the delivery of goods in a better condition. Trucks are equipped with specific accessories to handle specific goods.

9. **It is Part of Defence :** The extensive use of roadways is necessary for modern defence. For the movement of army and equipments, roadways are necessary. To maintain law and order within the country, movement of reserve police is necessary and this is possible only through roadways.

10. **Serve the Rural Areas :** A network of road transport helps the people in rural areas and brings them to the door of development.

11. **Easy to Carry Livestock :** It is easy to carry livestock from one place to another by the motor truck. Short delivery to the needed place, limits the expense of feeding, loading or unloading of livestock. Thus it saves time and money.

12. **A Source of Employment :** Employment opportunity is available both to skilled and unskilled workers. Millions of engineers, technicians, office workers, manual workers are engaged. Thus it is a source of employment.

13. **Helping Under-developed and Developed and Developing Countries :** Development of road brings integration of rural and urban economics. It broadens the market growth in an economical way.

14. **Minimum Middlemen Charges :** Truck owners buy goods from the farmers directly and sell them in the market. Hence there are no middlemen charges.

15. **Less Packing Expense :** When goods are transported through trucks, there is no need for packages as in the railways.

16. **Less Overhead Expenses :** Comparing to the railways, overhead expenses such as signals, station upkeep etc., are not needed for roadways.

Demerits of Road Transport

1. **Unsuitable for Long Distance :** Long distance cannot be covered by road transportation. Transporting of goods to foreign countries is not possible.

2. **Unsuitable for Bulky Goods :** It cannot carry bulky goods. Limited load carrying is the drawback of the system.

3. **Less Speed :** It moves at a less speed than the railways and airways. ''Early birds will fetch the fruit.'' Speed is very necessary for marketing goods. For this modern world of competition, speed is essential.

4. **No Protection of Goods :** Goods sent by trucks and other vehicles are not fully protected against wind, heat, rain, cold etc. As Johnson says, ''Goods in transit cannot be protected against wind and rain in road transport.''

5. **Chances for Accident :** Accident is more common in road transport. Often accidents occur in highways and in the hilly areas.

6. **Irregular Running** : There is frequent irregularity due to breakdown or accident or non-punctuality of workers.

7. **More Expense :** For long distance it is expensive. There is increase in the cost of petrol and other charges. Wear and tear have to be taken into account.

8. **Less Reliable :** During the rainy season roads are unfit and unsafe for travel. Hence it is not reliable. The transport is not free from hindrances.

9. **Not an Integrated System :** It is not an integrated system of transport. Public and private agencies operate this. There will be difference of opinion among them which creates clash. That will affect the interest of the public.

Even though the road transport has many drawbacks, it is popular and is used in almost all the parts of the world.

RAILWAY

In land transport, railway had the monopoly before the coming of the motor transport. It is the principal means of transport of the world. Railway development took place in India in the 19th century. There were a few railroads during those days. Its development was very slow due to the ignorance of its advantages. Now-a-days the importance is known by all and the development of railways has increased. Railways were built for military purposes before independence. Now it is used for transportation of goods and passengers.

Railway has been the pioneer of the modern mechanical transport. It is the means to move the goods and passengers by mechanical devices. Indian railway system is the largest in Asia. India stands fourth in the world in having maximum railway mileage next to the U.S.A., the U.S.S.R. and Canada. The nature of this system is that it requires the right of ownership of the land which the government can get without difficulty. It needs a heavy capital expenditure to start and recurring expenses to run the operation. It has now become a public utility in India. It renders high services to the community. To avoid public inconvenience and to enforce safety regulations, railways are given the status of social monopolies in almost all the countries.

Importance

Railways are the cheapest and quickest means of transport. It covers long distances and carries heavier types of goods. It is the central ''nerve system'' in the economy of a nation. It helps in the starting and running of industries throughout the world. It helps greatly trade. Through railways movement of food for workers, movement of raw materials to feed the machines and the movement of finished products to the markets are possible. It is of great help to agriculturists that the utilities of perishable goods are increased and urban and rural areas are brought close in contact. It strengthens the defence of a nation.

Merits of Railways

1. **Cheaper :** It is cheaper to transport heavy and bulky goods over a long distance and is very economical. Railways work on diminishing cost structure; transportation of heavy quantities leads to cheap rates. Railways are the common man's transport, because the rate is cheaper.

2. **High Speed :** Its speed is higher than the motor transport. Hence time is saved. There is no check-post as in road transport. Hence time is saved. The delay in shunting operation, loading and unloading of goods at different points is made up by extra speed. Due to the use of diesel oil and electricity, the speed of railways has further increased.

3. **Safer :** There are less railway accidents. It protects goods from exposure. Goods are not exposed to sun, rain or snow as in road transport. There is less fear of theft. There are specially designed bodies to safeguard and protect the goods.

4. **Suitable for Bulky Goods :** It is more suitable for transporting bulky goods. Materials made of wood, iron and steel and machine can be transported by railway. Industrial goods and engineering goods and raw materials can be transported at a cheaper rate.

5. **Long Distance Travel :** Long distance travel is safe and convenient in railway transport. There is unbroken journey from one part of the country to another part. This is beneficial to the trade.

6. **Dependable :** Railway renders regular service. It is not affected by weather conditions like rain, flood, fog, heat etc. Railways operate throughout the day. The regularity is due to control and efficient management of the government.

7. **Employment Opportunity :** Employment opportunity is greater for both skilled and unskilled workers. More than 15 lakhs of people are depending on railways to earn their livelihood.

8. **Helps Government :** It helps government in many ways. It is a source of income to the government as it is the monopoly of the government. It provides for the improvement of rural areas by connecting urban areas. It regularises labour supply and equalises prices.

Demerits of Railways

1. **Inflexible :** Railways have fixed routes which are suitable only for railways. Railways do not make door to door delivery. Their services are available only between certain definite points. Hence goods have to be carried to the railway station. For that it depends on road transport. It cannot compete with roadways in respect of door delivery. Deviation of rail route is not possible if any accident or natural calamity occurs in the route.

2. **Costlier :** It is costly for short distance. For light traffic also it is costlier than the road transport. This works on increasing returns principle; short distance leads to increase in cost. This system is not suitable for a lot of business requiring shorter haulage. Railway trains run regularly; sometimes they are not punctual.

3. **Inconvenient for Rural and Hill Areas :** It cannot serve rural areas. Villages and hill areas are beyond the reach of railways. Railways need heavy initial investment. Hence they can serve places where the volume of traffic is equal to operation cost. But villages cannot justify this and hence railways are not extended to hill areas and rural areas.

4. **Require More Capital :** Heavy investment is required for railways. Administration and operation expenses are fixed in nature. The cost of maintenance is also very high when compared to the rates of other means of transport. There must be guaranteed work load to meet these expenses. If it fails, there will be a heavy financial loss. Withdrawals of routes due to lack of traffic leads to heavy loss of capital.

5. **Effect of Centralised Administration :** Railways are the monopoly of the government. Hence there is centralised management and administration. Sometimes they work against the interest of the community. Personal considerations are not given importance.

Other Ways

Tramways : It is mainly used for transporting people in highly populated cities. It is suitable for carrying traffic in large cities during peak hours. It is run by diesel or electricity. Its large carrying capacity leads it to a better position to cope up with the heavy rush of traffic during certain hours.

Merits of Tramways are

(1) Less Capital is needed.
(2) Life of tramways is longer than that of the motor car.
(3) There is less chance of accidents.
(4) It is quick and simple to load and unload things.
(5) It is cheap and it attracts customers.
(6) Rains and other seasonal calamities do not affect this.

The Limitations of Tramways are :

(1) It is inflexible.
(2) The speed of tramways is very slow.
(3) More initial capital is needed to begin its operation.

Pipe Lines : It is the latest improved method of transport. It is a land transport. Grains, gas and liquid commodities like, crude oil, petroleum and other petroleum products etc., are transported. Usually pipe lines connect oil fields and refineries. This system avoids handling of products as well as other problems of transportation. It is cheaper than other means of transport. It is used in developed countries. India is also now using this system. With the help of pipe lines, loading and unloading of grains to and from a ship is conveniently done. This system saves time and cost.

WATER TRANSPORT

Water transport is cheaper when compared to other modes of transport. It is cheap because there is no need for highways or railway lines. It is the oldest means of transport. It was used for bulky goods and low grade goods in the olden days. But now it is used for traffic and for transportation of all kinds of goods. It also carries bulky goods over long distances, much longer than railways. It is the water transport which led to the discovery of several continents. It leads to the development of world trade.

Merits of Water Transport

1. **Cheaper :** It is cheaper as the cost of construction is less than that of the railways. Transportation of heavy and bulky goods is the cheapest.

2. **Bulk Carriage :** Items like sand, coal, bricks, sugarcane, iron, steel etc., can be transported by this at a cheaper rate. Water transport carries the heaviest of bulky goods. A boat can carry six times its weight. A ship can carry more goods.

3. **Safer :** It is safer to transport glasswares, scientific instruments, chemicals etc. These items must be handled with care. In water transport there is no shaking, vibration or jerking. Therefore, the above said goods are not damaged by water transport.

4. **Feeder :** Inland water transportation system of a nation is the connecting link between land transport and ocean transport.

5. **International Trade Creator :** International trade development is possible through this water transport. Oceans are in between nations. Trade of bulky and heavy goods is possible only through water transport. For international trade, it is the cheapest and most economic when compared to the other modes of transport.

6. **No Congestion :** Its capacity for traffic is greater than the railways. Hence there is no delay due to congestion.

7. **Suitable for Certain Areas :** Roadways and railways cannot be constructed in forest areas. If there is water transport in that area, it is the best suitable means of transport. Hence for transportation of forest products this is the only medium of transport.

Demerits of Water Transport

1. **Low Speed :** Water transport can create place utilities. But it cannot create time utilities. Water transport is very slow. The speed is very slow due to many reasons. The maximum speed of a ship is less than that of a train or a motor truck. It must adjust to the flow of water. Goods, requiring quick delivery, cannot be sent through it.

2. **Limited Areas Are Served :** Water transport is inflexible. The areas, which are touched are very few. If there is a canal route, then those places along its banks are benefited. People must bring things to the jetty for transportation, which leads to additional expenditure. As it is a natural way, the construction of new route is impossible.

3. **Not Dependable :** It is not at all weather-friend. Water transports depend on seasons. The winter season makes the rivers frozen. In the summer season the depth is lessened. There are falls and shallowness which are not suitable for navigation. In ocean transport also there are many difficulties. Wind and storm affect it. Ports and harbours cannot be constructed in all the coastal areas.

4. **Political and International Problems :** Ocean is the gift of nature. It must be free from political problems. Since it is a natural gift, everyone can use it. Often conflicts arise. Beyond seven miles from the shore, a country possesses no right of claim.

5. **Longer Journey Required :** A ship must sail a longer journey if one route is closed. The course of rivers is often zigzag. These cause delay. When the Suez Canal was closed, the ships took forty days to reach the U.K., and other European countries as against nine days through the Suez Canal.

The main branches of waterways are :

1. Inland waterways
2. Ocean waterways. The chart will give a clear idea :

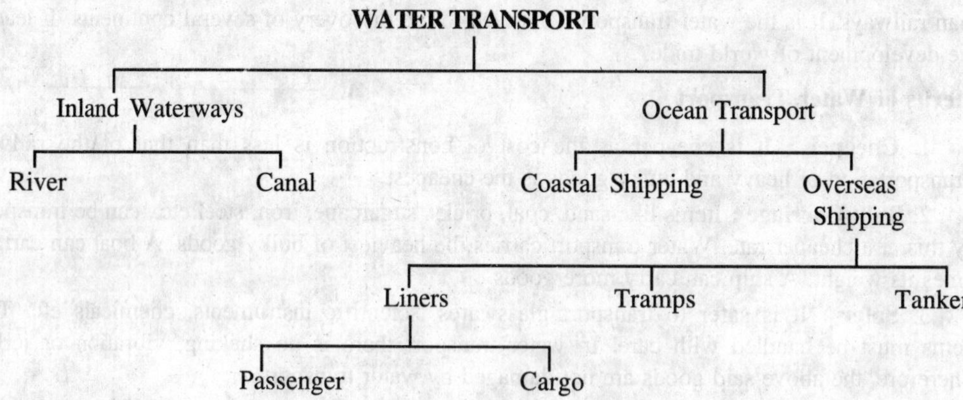

Ocean Transport

It is the big mode of transport between one country and another. It is the unifier of the world, as it brings different parts of the world closer and makes one market. Ocean transport of shipping may be divided into two. The chart gives a picture of ocean transport.

1. **Coastal Shipping :** It is an important means of transport to those countries that have sea-coasts which are well placed to move the goods and the people. It is an extended form of inland water transport. It is cheap and is a speedy form of transport. It renders services within the nation. At the time of civil emergencies and war, it is very important. It is flexible and is an economical means of transport. It is useful for the transportation of coal and other bulky and heavy cargoes. It makes easy the internal transport. It develops the trade between ports and continental ports.

Most of the coastal trade of a country is in the hands of the national shipping authority, for example, the U.S.A., Australia, Japan etc. Up to 1951, foreign shipping companies were involved in about 90% of the coastal trade. But after 1951, the coastal trades have been exclusively for Indian national shipping, except for petroleum products.

Overseas Shipping

It encourages international trade. It is a means of transport to move goods and passengers from one country to another. 96% of the total international trade is carried on by ships. The two divisions of overseas shipping are :

1. **The Liners :** Liners are the ships that move people and cargo on definite routes touching fixed ports as per scheduled time, which is declared in advance. There are passenger liners and cargo liners. They must make their journey at the scheduled time, whether the ship is full of cargo or not. They call at ports in a fixed route at regular intervals.

(a) **Passenger Liner :** The passenger liner carries passengers and mail and a small amount of cargo. It has luxurious facilities for customers. It is speedy. Some liners are very large in size, moving at a great speed and provided with the finest service.

(b) **Cargo Liner :** It carries large quantities of cargo. It is a large ocean-going ship. It does not have luxurious facilities as in the passenger liners. It has also a fixed time-table. Only a limited number of passengers can travel in this. It is suitable for traders. It makes delivery of goods within a particular period.

Tramps

These are ocean-going ships which have no fixed routes, fixed time-table or fixed freight rates. They go anywhere at any time. The load and route are decided by the tramp owner. Its main purpose is to transport cargo, grain and other seasonal products in bulk. The tramp may be ready to go to any place at any time as per the instruction of the hirer. The ship does not sail unless it is fully loaded or it is paid for the unfilled space. It can easily be compared to a taxi waiting for hire. Seasonal and unusual traffic are attended to by tramps, whereas normal trade demand throughout the year is met by cargo liners.

Difference Between Liners and Tramps

Liners	Tramps
1. Set routes and time-tables are followed.	1. They sail when they get cargo in full. They go wherever they like, as there is no route and time-table.
2. They are meant for passengers and cargoes.	2. They are meant for cargoes.
3. They sail on scheduled time and do not wait to get full load.	3. They wait for full load.
4. They have fixed rates.	4. They have fluctuating rates.
5. Their speed is quite fast.	5. Their speed is less than that of liners.
6. Liners are members of a fleet.	6. Tramps are individual ships.
7. They touch only scheduled ports.	7. They have no such scheduled ports.

Oil-tankers

Besides liners and tramps, there are oil-tankers. Tankers are huge ships. They are specially designed for carrying crude oil, petrol and other petroleum products. The tankers are known as 'Super Tankers' which are built for carrying great capacity of liquid items. Large tankers are built for this purpose and have a capacity of over 20 lakh tonnes of oil.

AIR TRANSPORT

Distances are shrunk due to the invention of air transport and credit goes to Wright Brothers. It is a gift to the community in the 20th century. Air transport is the most advanced mode of transport. After the two World Wars, it has developed vastly. Air transport has developed so much that it is able to compete with the railways. It is increasingly adopted in the U.S.A., Germany, United Kingdom etc.

In India, in 1911 and in 1921 the Civil Aviation Department was established. In Delhi, Bombay and Calcutta flying clubs were opened and they are functioning well, as there are favourable conditions for their development. In a vast country like India, such clubs are a necessity. They are running on profitable lines. There are Air India International and Indian Airlines Corporation in India. The former handles international and the latter, internal aviation.

The airway transports passengers, mail and also goods. It is helpful in times of emergency like flood, earthquakes and war. Air travel has gained speed and it is quite safe. Hence it is suitable for passenger and mail. The invention of Jumbo Jets (a palace in the Sky) has revolutionized the air travel all over the world. It is a practicable and economical method for transporting industrial and commercial goods. It is helpful to political, military and cultural aspects. It creates time utility in internal and international markets.

Merits of Air Transport

1. **Speed :** It is fastest and quickest means of transport. We can have a continuous journey over thousands of kilometres of distance. Perishable commodities can be transported very easily. No other means of transport can compete with air transport.

2. **Regular and Comfortable :** Planes are regular and punctual. They fly according to the time schedule. Air travel is comfortable. All the comforts are provided for the passengers. There is no jolting or jerk, which is common feature of land transport.

3. **Absence of Obstacle :** Mountains and oceans do not affect the air transport. It is beyond these barriers.

4. **Safer :** It is more safe for goods to be transported by the airways.

5. **Suitable for Perishable Goods :** Perishable goods can be transported. Today Indian rose flowers are transported to foreign countries to adorn the flower vases. Indian flowers and fruits are available in the international markets. Jasmine is exported to Singapore from Madurai.

6. **Suitable for Valuable Goods :** It is suitable for carrying high value goods, such as diamond, bullion etc.

7. **Spray of Insecticides :** Aerial spray of insecticides is possible and it is very useful to the agriculturists to eradicate insects.

8. **Emergency Remedier :** It is reliable for emergency remedy. At the time of flood after storm or war, helicopters and aeroplanes save the lives of stranded people by distributing food, clothes and other necessary items.

9. **Reduce Capital Investment :** Due to its regular, fast, efficient and quick service, it reduces the capital investment in stocking goods.

There are many developments taking place in airways. A Jumbo Jet (a Palace in the Sky) can carry 362 passengers at a speed of 1,000 kilometers per hour.

Supersonic Anglo-French Concord has been introduced recently. It travels at a speed of 2,000 kilometers per hour. Giant Air Buses carry hundreds of passengers at a time. All are becoming air-minded.

Demerits of Air Transport

1. **Costly :** The cost of air transport is very high and the freight charges are also high. The cost of construction and maintenance of aeroplanes and aerodromes etc., are also very high. But its carrying capacity is not very large when compared to its cost. It is beyond the reach of a moderate man. Air transportation costs are five times greater than road transport.

2. **Not safer :** In air transport also accidents occur. Accidents happen due to climatic condition and mechanical defects. These restrict the use of airways.

3. **Suitable to Only Costly Goods :** It is suitable only to high grade costly goods. Low grade and heavy and bulky goods cannot be transported. It gives more attention to passenger transportation than to goods. Cargo capacity is less than that in railways.

4. **Not Flexible :** It cannot serve all the areas. Only big cities have airports.

5. **Fair Weather Friend :** If there is unfavourable weather like stormy condition the scheduled flight has to be cancelled. Hence air transport is controlled by climatic conditions. Heavy rains, snow, storm, etc. dislocate flying operation. It will lead to uncertainty in its time-table.

6. **Limited Capacity :** Compared to other means of transport, the carrying capacity of airways is limited.

7. **Needs a High Degree of Training :** For operating air services, a high degree of training is essential. As such intelligent, careful and efficient hands are needed to operate.

8. **Law and Restriction :** There are international laws and restrictions over its service. Air agreement and permission of a country are necessary for aeroplanes to fly over the territory of any other country. This restricts the growth of airways all over the world.

Choice of Mode of Transportation

There are many means of transport. There are several national and international means of transport. It is the marketer who has to select the best mode of transport. There are merits and demerits for each means of transport. The marketer must prefer the transport system which is economical and convenient for him. Transportation cost is the highest *i.e.*, about 45% of the total distribution cost. Transportation medium is the main problem in deciding the marketing system. The marketing manager must select the appropriate means of transport. He must decide by considering the following factors :

1. Usefulness or combination of modes.
2. Specific carriers.
3. Own or lease transportation.

The management or the marketer must consider the following points :

1. **Suitability :** The mode of transport must meet our needs. For bulky commodities sea transport is suitable. For the transportation of petroleum, fuel, oil, building items, minerals, foodgrains, waterways are suitable.

2. **Speed :** For perishable goods quick delivery is necessary. Airways are the quickest and fastest means of transport. Hence perishable goods like fruits, flowers, fish, vegetables, eggs. etc., can be sent through airways.

3. **Cost :** People want the cheapest means of transport. Transport cost is the highest cost. Air transport cost is very high and it cannot be used for transporting heavy goods. Production and marketing cost can be reduced by going in for cheaper and economical transport system. If the transport cost is less, consumer can buy goods at a cheaper rate. It leads to the expansion of markets resulting in increasing sales and profits. Thus transport costs are important in trade and commerce.

4. **Safety :** Safety of goods is necessary during transportation. But commodities are damaged due to uncertainties and risks. As a result loss arises when they are transported. Safety and security of goods are very essential. Damages and losses are less in truck transport. Higher degree of safety and security is ensured in the motor transport.

5. **Flexibility :** When compared to other means of transport, road transport is more flexible. The most direct and economical routes are necessary for the success of a marketer. Regular supply is necessary for the marketer. For that roadways are suitable. Railway transport is not so flexible as road transport.

6. **Regularity and Punctuality :** The marketer should consider the regularities and punctualities of the transport system. He needs regular supply of goods. Railways are more regular and punctual than airways, which are affected by bad weather. Water transport is also affected by bad weather.

7. **Availability :** There are irregularities in all the modes of transport. Hence the marketer must depend on the means of transport which is available in that place.

Container Service

This system is the latest one and is designed for low cost, easy loading and unloading of goods. Standard containers are used to carry the goods. The containers are built boxes, which are filled with goods. With a powerful crane, the containers are placed in a ship or taken out. That is, the commodity-filled boxes are taken out with the help of a crane and so the ship need wait for long at the port to take out the goods. When the container is taken out, the ship is free to move. Then, the goods are to be taken out from the containers. Now the containerisation system is followed in roadways and railways because it saves cost and time.

Fishy Back Service

Loaded trailers are drawn by ship, trucks and railways. A trailer, filled with goods is attached to the vehicle-ship or truck. At the destination, it is detached and at the starting, it is attached to the vehicle. This eliminates time taken for loading and unloading.

RELATIVE RANKING OF VARIOUS TRANSPORT MODES

	Rank	*Cost*	*Speed*	*Damage in Transit*	*Dependa-bility*	*Reliable Delivery*	*Points Served*
High	1	Air	Air	Road	Pipe Line	Pipe Line	Road
↑	2	Road	Rail	Rail	Road	Water	Rail
	3	Rail	Road	Air	Rail	Road	Air
↓	4	Pipe Line	Pipe Line	Water	Water	Air	Water
Low	5	Water	Water	Pipe Line	Air	Rail	Pipe Line

SUITABILITY OF MODES OF TRANSPORT FOR DIFFERENT ITEMS

Mode of Transport	Items suitable
1. Airways	Perishable items like flowers, eggs, vegetables, fruits, fish, costly instruments etc.
2. Vehicle (Road)	All consumer goods, books, clothes, fruits, paper goods, industrial goods etc.
3. Pipe Lines	Petroleum, gasoline, gas, lubricants, crude oil, etc.
4. Waterways	Fuel oil, petroleum, sand, stones, heavy goods, food-grains, etc.
5. Railways	Iron and steel, timber, minerals, automobiles, canned food, agricultural crops etc.

ECONOMIC SIGNIFICANCE OF TRANSPORT

1. **Transport and Production :** Transport has considerably facilitated production and particularly large-scale production which is impossible without it. Large scale production requires huge quantity of raw materials, large number of workers, wider markets etc. Transport ensures regular supply of raw materials and workers to keep the factory running and distributes finished products over markets.

2. **Transport and Consumption :** Consumers use articles produced in different parts of the world. We can get watches of Switzerland, handicrafts of Japan, industrial goods of USA, milk products of Denmark etc. This is because of modern transportation.

3. **Transport and Exchange :** As different industries grow in the different parts of the world, it facilitates exchange and promotes competition. The world market economy is not merely a territorial expansion of commodity exchange relations, but a whole transformation brought about in these exchange relations by the modern means of transport.

4. **Transport and Distribution :** Transport has a great bearing on distribution. The international flow of labour and capital is due to transport. Entrepreneurs can also find new opportunities to start various trade and industries where profit opportunities are greater.

5. **Transport and Utility :** Transportation enhances transformation, place and time utilities of the commodities. Transport helps in the process of transformation *i.e.* transformation of raw material by capital, labour and organisation into goods which have the ability to satisfy human wants.

6. **Transport and Industries :** Industrial development would not have taken place if there were no transport. Both go hand in hand. Industries depend upon transport and transport creates new industries. They are the cause and effect of development for each other.

7. **Transport and Employment :** Transport provides employment to millions of people. Millions of people all over the world are directly or indirectly employed in this sphere of transportation.

8. **Transport and Agriculture :** The role of transport in the sphere of agriculture cannot be over-emphasised. Before and after sowing and after the stage of harvesting, transport plays a very significant role. The increased application of manures and fertilizers has, undoubtedly, increased farm production all over the world.

9. **Transport and Planned Economy :** Location of industries, development of backward areas, better distribution of products, better maintenance of administration etc. necessitate a proper system of transport in a planned economy. Transport being of prime importance to economic development becomes the integral part of planning.

10. **Transport and Price Stabilisation :** Consumers get commodities throughout the year at fixed and reasonable rates. If adequate transport facilities exist, the surplus would necessarily be transported to deficit areas. When large quantity of industrial goods have been produced or bumper crop is harvested, the surplus cannot be sent to other consuming centres in the absence of transport facilities.

QUESTIONS

1. Write a short note on Air transport. *(B.Com., Karnataka)*
2. How is transport important in marketing ? *(B.Com., Karnataka)*
3. Which mode of transport is useful for vegetables ? State your reasons. *(B.Com., Madurai)*
4. What are the various transportation agencies? What are the merits and demerits of motor transportation in marketing of goods ? *(B.Com., Chennai)*
5. Explain the modern development in the field of transportation. *(B.Com., Chennai)*
6. "For transporting perishable products to distant places air transport is most suitable and cheaper." Explain. *(B.Com., Chennai)*
7. Point out different modes of transport. Explain the advantages and disadvantages of railway transport. *(B.Com., Chennai)*
8. Explain the function of transport in marketing goods. Give out the comparative advantages of road and railway transport in marketing of goods. *(B.Com., Mysore)*
9. What are the factors that influence the selection of a particular mode of transport. Briefly explain modern developments in the transportation of goods. *(B.Com., Madurai)*
10. Explain the importance of transportation in marketing. What considerations weigh in the selection of a particular mode of transport? *(B.Com., Madurai)*
11. Discuss the merits of water transport. *(B.Com., Chennai)*
12. Explain the choice of mode of transport. *(B.Com., Mumbai)*

CHAPTER 6

Storage and Warehouses

- *Storage Situations*
- *Advantages*
- *Essentials of Good Storage*
- *Storage vs. Warehouses*
- *Functions*
- *Classifications*
- *Warehouse Receipt and Warrant*
- *Advantages*
- *Importance*
- *Warehouses in India*
- *Causes of Slow Growth*
- *Suggestions*
- *Questions*

Storage, like production, is a very important function of physical distribution. Even in the primitive days, human beings learnt to preserve food and essential items for the future or for the dull days. Storage is the process of holding and preserving the goods. It is an important function of marketing process. Through storage the excess products are preserved during the time of production until they are required for use or consumption. Increased demand or consumption is followed by increased production. Carry over of the products from one production period to another production period is important to assure the continuity of supply of products. Storage is the function of safeguarding the excess products for future consumption in seasons of scarcity. Storage creates time utility. Storage of goods is essential in the marketing process. It equalises the price in marketing. Under the modern era, storage is a major function of marketing.

What is Storage?

Storage can be defined as one of the marketing functions, involving preservation of goods between the time of production and the time of consumption. It is a process of holding and preservation of goods from their production time to the consumption time. There must be a gap between the time of production and the demand for it, as long as the production continues. Storage is essential to protect the goods carried over from deterioration in order to use them in the period of scarcity. The development of science and technology has improved the methods, ways and means of storage. As such, storage adds to the depth of market. Storing of goods is essential for transportation and transportation follows storing; this is physical distribution.

Situations Require Storage

The need for storage arises fundamentally out of lack of adjustment between the time of production and the time of consumption of goods. Thus storage brings an adjustment. The storage of products becomes necessary in the following cases:

1. **Seasonal Production, but Uniform Consumption :** Many goods, specially agricultural goods, are produced in different seasons. At the same time, such produces are consumed regularly or throughout the year and the demand is quite constant. As such, to bring an adjustment in demand and supply, storage plays its role by giving weight to the time factor. That is, matching the supply with demand. For example, fruits, vegetables, dairy products, fish etc.

2. **Uniform Production, but Seasonal Consumption :** Certain types of goods are demanded only in particular seasons. For example, refrigerators, electric fans, coolers etc., are demanded in the summer season; woollen blankets, room heaters, sweaters etc., are in demand in the winter season.

But, irrespective of the demand, they are produced throughout the year. As such, the produced commodities have to be stored in order to protect them from possible deterioration.

3. **Protection of Goods :** The excess goods have to be stored for future demand and safeguarded till they are wanted by consumers.

4. **To Maintain Balance Between Demand and Supply :** Surplus goods must be stored until the arrival of transportation facility. Such goods may be transported to the place where there is a demand. Goods may also be stored, until enough has been collected to make up a truck-load or wagon-load.

5. In our complex economic system products are generally produced in anticipation of market demand. Similarly many farm produces are harvested in only one season but are bought and consumed throughout the year. Thus storage is necessary and important.

Advantages of Storage

The storage facility is essential and the following are important benefits that can be had from the storage function:

1. Almost all the farm products produced seasonally are in demand throughout the year and as such producers have to store them.
2. Some types of goods are demanded seasonally and their production is uniform. The goods must be stored in order to effect timely supply to meet heavy demands.
3. Certain types of goods are to be preserved in the store, as the inherent quality increases. For example, rice, tobacco, liquor, wine, honey, gur, pickles, cheese etc.
4. When goods are manufactured, they must be transported. For this, they must be stored near the market to avoid delay in transportation.
5. Storage is always essential for easy transportation arrangement. Goods are stored at a particular place and from there, they are transported easily.
6. Production is always in anticipation of demand. So, the produced goods must be preserved in safety and free from deterioration.
7. Whenever the customers want the products, they can be made available. To satisfy the needs of the customers, an inventory has to be maintained.
8. Present era is a period of mass production. For mass production, storage is necessary to store raw materials. Large-scale production is regularised only when abundant supply of raw materials is there.
9. Cold storage facilitates longer life to perishable items, such as fruits, vegetables, fish, dairy products etc.
10. Products may be stored at seasonal times and in non-seasonal times; the products fetch good prices.
11. Continuous sales can be effected because of the storage facility.
12. It is regarded as an important aid in equalising prices by matching the demand and supply position.
13. Creation of employment opportinities to millions of people is made available.
14. Financial aid can be made available against the goods stored as a collateral security.
15. Storage is necessary to carry out other marketing functions, such as, grading, cleaning, mixing, packing etc.

Essentials of a Good Storage

1. The storage must aim at reducing spoilage, damage, breakage etc.
2. Storage must facilitate to know the volume and conditions of products, without much labour.
3. There must be material handling equipments.
4. The storage place should be free from rapid changes of temperature.

5. It must be located in a suitable place or as near to the factory and market as possible to avoid transportation cost.
6. It must enable goods to be moved in and out easily and speedily.
7. Goods must be so stored as to be picked up easily and quickly.
8. Inventory level of goods must be optimum to meet two points:–
   (i) regular demand and (ii) avoidance of tied up capital.
9. Facility in store must be suitable to the goods.

WAREHOUSES

The place, where the goods are stored is known as warehouse. Warehouse implies a house for wares. Wares means products. A warehouse or a godown is a room or a building for the accumulation of goods, possessing facilities to perform other marketing functions. A warehouse must provide a better view and a clear differentiation chart regarding the articles stored.

Difference between Storage and Warehouse:

Storage	Warehouse
1. It is generally located near the factory.	1. It is always located near the market.
2. Its aim is for personal use.	2. Its aim is for commercial purpose.
3. Additional marketing functions cannot be performed.	3. Allied marketing functions, such as grading, standardisation, blending, mixing, packing ing etc., are performed.
4. It gives facility for stocking raw materials and finished products.	4. It is meant for final products.
5. It is only a holding place.	5. It holds the goods as a distribution centre.

IMPORTANCE OF STORAGE

1. Stabilisation of pricing;
2. Price reduction by eliminating waste;
3. Easy availability of goods;
4. Bulk buying and selling is possible;
5. Cutting of transport cost;
6. Reduction of risk by storing goods;
7. Promotion of orderly marketing;
8. Availability of funds against stored goods;
9. Equalisation of demand and supply;
10. Avoidance of deterioration of goods.

Functions

Warehouses perform the following functions which are essential in the process of marketing:

1. Warehouse is a convenient resting place of surplus goods which are produced in seasonal periods and made available to the market when needed.
2. Warehouse assumes the responsibility to care for the goods of intrinsic quality free from deterioration due to climatic change. It gives diversified arrangements to safeguard the products in original condition.
3. Warehouse-keeper accepts the responsibility based on Bailment Act. Thus if the warehoused goods are lost or damaged or destroyed, the warehouse-keeper has to reimburse the loss. Therefore, the risk is transferred by the producer.

4. Warehouse receipts help the bailers (owners of the goods) get finance from the bankers by pledging them. Thus, without selling the goods at a low price, business people enjoy financial help in the dull days, when money is needed.
5. Warehouse-keeper takes the responsibility of mixing, grading, packing etc., at the direction of the producers.

Classification of Warehouses

Warehouses are classified, on the basis of ownership, into:

(1) **Public Warehouse**

It is used by the public. The operation system and rates of rent are regulated by the Government. It functions on commercial line. It gives facilities of scientific storage. Private warehouses are rarely constructed, because of heavy expenditure on construction. The warehouses are equipped with modern machineries. Risk of loss on account of life, accident, spoilage can be reduced.

Advantages of Public Warehouses

1. Public warehouses are built in modern methods which reduce all types of losses and safeguard the goods.
2. Facilities are open to all. Rental and other charges are generally low.
3. They have their own loading and unloading systems, such as cranes, rail-road etc. These heavy investments cannot be afforded by private warehouses.
4. They employ skilled persons, who give the best suggestions and better services to the users.
5. The users have to pay only for the space used and for the period of use.
6. The receipt issued by them will serve as a collateral security, which facilitates further finance.

(2) **Private Warehouse**

It is owned by private and large business-houses, such as manufacturers, wholesalers, retailers etc. They own and operate for their own use. This type of warehouse is rarely found because of the high cost on construction. It may be within the factory building or a separate building or near the market place. At the present stage, the importance of such warehouses is decreasing because of many reasons.

The following are the important types of warehouses:

1. **Bonded Warehouse**

This type of warehouse plays a significant role in international trade. It is situated at the port-towns and is generally owned by Dock Authorities. If owned privately, then licence is essential. Generally importers have to remit the duties in one lumpsum. But here, the imported goods, on which import duty has not been paid, are accepted for storage till the payment. The bonded warehouse offers valuable service to the importers. The importer has to enter into a bond along with sureties, assuring the payment of duty before removing the goods from bonded warehouses. The goods on which duty is not paid while they are in the bonded warehouses, are known as goods-in-bond.

Advantages of Bonded Warehouses

1. The importer can remit the duty in instalments. Delivery of a part of goods can be effected by remitting the proportionate duty.
2. The importers are allowed to do further processing on goods-in-bond, such as blending, mixing, racking, bottling etc.
3. The importer can take buyers to the bonded warehouse and the buyer can inspect the goods; this facilitates selling of imported goods which are in the warehouse.

4. It further facilitates the importer to re-export the imported goods without paying any duties. Thus the duplication of the work–first payment of duty and secondly claim for refund–is avoided.

2. **Duty-paid Warehouse :** This is situated at port-towns and is usually owned by Dock Authorities or public authorities. An importer remits the duty of imported goods and then stores them in the duty-paid houses.

3. **Special Commodity Warehouse :** Goods, produced to be stored, may require varying types of storage facility. This type of warehouse gives storage facilities only for a particular commodity. That is, the warehouse, where fishes, perishable produces are stocked, is not suitable for wool, cotton etc. The purpose of this type of warehouse is to keep the goods of intrinsic value in original form. Different types of warehouses are constructed according to the nature of the goods to be stocked.

4. **Refrigerated Warehouse (cold storage) :** Cold storage is of recent development in the field of warehouses. Perishable goods such as eggs, fruits, meat, milk, apple, etc., require cold storage facilities during the peak season for a longer period and they are released to the market, where there is a demand. Generally, such a type of cold storage is located at the consuming centre. The benefit of storage, in brief, are as follows:

1. Goods are available, throughout the year.
2. It widens the market.
3. It maintains reasonable price in the market.
4. It prevents temporary glut in the market.
5. It facilitates longer life to perishable goods.
6. It helps the producers by maintaining the price.
7. It lowers the marketing cost.
8. It maintains the intrinsic value of goods.
9. It promotes the health of users.
10. It releases goods on the basis of demand.

5. **General Merchandise Warehouse :** This is the most common type. It provides facility to all kinds of goods. No special facilities are required as all commodities are stored. It is a place of store for manufactured, semi-manufactured and raw materials until they are required by the manufacturers, distributors, retailers, consumers etc. This is located in the distribution centres.

MISCELLANEOUS

Tank Storage Warehouses

These facilitate by providing tanks which store liquids like, oil, gas, petrol etc., in bulk quantity.

Field (Custodian) Warehouses

Industrialists, wholesalers, retailers etc., use this type of warehouses or godowns. A portion of the building or a separate building is used for this type of warehouses, where goods are stocked. A public warehouse-keeper will be the custodian of the warehouse, without legally transferring the ownership of the goods housed in the godown. The main idea behind this is that the owner of the goods can get financial assistance from a bank on the strength of the warehouse receipt.

Household Warehouse

This warehouse is purely temporary in nature and is meant for safety of household articles, furniture etc., when one has to move away for a short period.

Yard or Ground Storage

There are places in the open space to keep goods, which do not deteriorate with the changes of climate. The ground is enclosed with protected walls. Goods like wood, iron etc., are stored there.

Differences between Warehouse Receipt and Warehouse Warrant

Warehouse Receipt	Warehouse Warrant
1. It is only an acknowledgement receipt of goods.	1. It is an acknowledgement receipt of goods and authority to obtain the goods by himself or his order.
2. It is not a collateral security.	2. Is is a collateral security.
3. It cannot be negotiated.	3. It can be negotiated.
4. Surrendering of the receipt along with a letter of authority effects the delivery of goods.	4. Delivery of goods is effected by surrendering of warrant with endorsement.

Advantages of Warehouse

1. Goods can be safeguarded and protected from loss, damages, fire, theft, deterioration etc., till demands arise.
2. It offers storage facility to merchants or manufacturers who own no warehouse or limited storage capacity.
3. The users of warehouses are relieved from the burden of expenses in construction of warehouses, and the available funds may be diverted into business.
4. Customers are being served more economically and quickly.
5. It gives facility for other marketing functions–grading, standardisation, packing etc.
6. Easy movement of goods is facilitated as warehouses are located in important routes, with provision for their own loading and unloading. This increases sales turnover.
7. The user of warehouses can dispose of the goods to a buyer; the buyer can also sell it to a third party; third party to fourth and so on, without moving the goods from the warehouse.
8. Bonded warehouses and their facilities are great advantages to users. (See the advantages of bonded warehouse).
9. Warehouse receipts/warrants are the basis on which financial assistance can be had from the Bankers.
10. It facilitates the user to sell the goods at the best possible price and thus derive better profit.

Importance

The study of marketing is not complete when one neglects to understand the importance of storage and warehousing. Warehousing services are demanded by ever widening markets because of mass production. The produced commodities are to be stocked at convenient places to facilitate easy distribution. The surplus products have to be stored in warehouses and the flow of goods to the consumers is to be regulated.

The life of perishable goods has been prolonged through the use of cold storage facilities and this covers a wider market. To have a wider market, we need storage or warehouse facility at each marketing point. Warehouse smoothens the operations of buying and selling. Stability in price in market is brought by warehousing. Productions, in anticipation of demand, need a good system of mass distribution.

It is roughly estimated on average basis, in India, that nearly 5 to 10% of foodgrains are lost a year, in the absence of storage facility. There is a substantial loss in storage in India, because the susceptibility to insect attack is high in the case of foodgrains. This loss can be controlled only by scientific method of storage.

Warehouses in India

The majority of the Indian farmers are usually in the habit of selling the produces, even when they are in the field *i.e.*, before bringing them to their house. This happens because of the hard need for cash and lack of facility to stock them. Indian cultivators accept loans even in pre-harvesting time against the crops. There is a forced sale to the moneylenders. Then the farmers have to make money for the next agricultural operations and other needs. The farmers have no storage facility to safeguard the balance produce in their own village against rodents, pilferage, insects, dampness, germination, birds etc. Preservation methods adopted by the villagers are traditional and crude and even these are not available to them.

The Royal Commission of India in 1928 pointed out the significance of storage and warehousing. But even today, the facilities are not enough and not scientific. On the recommendations of the Rural Banking Enquiry Committee of 1950 and the Committee of Directors of the All India Rural Credit Survey of 1954, the Central Government set up Central Warehousing Corporation in 1957, passed the Agricultural Produce (Development and Warehousing) Act of 1956. Organised development of storage and warehousing took place under our economic plans only after 1956, by recognising warehousing as extension of transportation. Thus more capital was invested for the accelerated growth of transport and warehousing–twin wings of physical distribution. For this purpose, Central and State warehousing Corporations were established.

Central Warehousing Corporation

It came into existence in 1957. Its functions are:

1. To provide godowns and warehouses in Centres at suitable places in India.
2. To run warehouses for storage of agricultural produce, seeds, fertilizers and agricultural implements offered by individuals, co-operative societies and other institutions.
3. To arrange facilities for the transportation of agricultural produce to and from warehouses.
4. To subscribe to the share capital of State Warehousing Corporations.
5. To act as an agent of the Board or of the Government for the purpose of purchase, sale, storage and distribution of agricultural produce, seeds, manures, fertilizers and agricultural implements.

State Warehousing Corporation

Each State Government is empowered to establish its own Warehousing Corporation, by getting the approval of the Central Warehousing Corporation. 50% of the capital is contributed by CWC and 50% by the State Government. Its functions are:

1. To provide godowns at places other than those earmarked or reserved for central warehouses.
2. To run licensed warehouses.
3. To manage regulated markets at those centres where its activities are extended.
4. To act as an agent of the Central or State Government or Central Warehousing Corporation.
5. To subscribe to the share capital of co-operative societies, which are specialised in warehousing.

Causes of Slow Growth

1. The surplus of products with the farmers is small, and it is not economical to keep them in warehouses.
2. Often failure of crops is experienced because of the mercy of monsoons–causing drought areas or flooded areas. The available produce is damaged, which is too little to be sent to godowns.

3. Cold storages are not available at the consuming centres.
4. The poor farmers are not able to meet the cost of warehousing. The cost of storage is often more than the price rise expected.
5. Warehousing receipts are papers of intrinsic value having unrestricted negotiability.
6. Grading is a must for the successful working of warehouses; but agricultural produces are heterogeneous.
7. There are irregularities in the transportation system.
8. Warehouses and godowns are situated in cities.

Suggestions for Improvement

The following measures are to be adopted to achieve the purpose of warehousing.

1. The godowns or warehouses must be located at the consuming centres, looking to the transport facility.
2. Storage facilities may be made available at the place of production.
3. The beneficial advantages of scientific storage should be taught to the producers and traders. Experimental trials of grading and storage facilities are to be arranged by the werehouses.
4. Warehouses should be equipped with modern machineries and well-trained persons.
5. Warehouses must secure fair prices to the producers.
6. The present warehouse charge, which are high, must be reduced by allowing some type of discounts to producers.
7. Banking facility in rural areas should be promoted. Conditions of loan system must be relaxed against warehouse receipt.

QUESTIONS

1. What are the functions of warehousing ? *(B.Com., Bangalore)*
2. Describe the services rendered by the public and bonded warehouses. *(B.Com., Bangalore)*
3. Assess the warehousing facilities in India. *(B.Com., Madurai)*
4. Write a detailed note on refrigerated warehouses. *(B.Com., Chennai)*
5. What are the characteristics of a good storage facility ? *(B.Com., Chennai)*
6. What is a bonded warehouse? How does it differ from other warehouses ? *(B.Com., Madurai, Chennai)*
7. Bring out the significance of storage and warehousing in modern marketing. *(B.Com., Madurai)*
8. Bring out the significance of storing and warehousing in marketing, and state the advantages of public warehouse. *(B.Com., Madras)*
9. Briefly write a note on public warehouse. *(B.Com., Madurai)*
10. Explain the role played by warehouses in marketing. *(B.Com., Madurai)*
11. Explain the need for providing cold storage. *(B.Com., Madurai)*
12. "Warehousing is not a marketing function." Explain. *(B.Com. Bhopal)*
13. Explain the various types of warehouses and their functions. *(B.Com., Madurai)*
14. What is the relation of storage to the behaviour of prices for a given commodity ? *(B.Com., Mumbai)*
15. Discuss the uses of warehouse receipt. *(B.Com., Chennai)*
16. Explain the functions of bonded warehouse. *(B.Com., Chennai)*

CHAPTER 7

Standardisation and Grading

- *Meaning*
- *Standardisation*
- *Standard*
- *Elements*
- *Grading*
- *Inspection*
- *Labelling*
- *Grading Vs. Standardisation*
- *Methods of Grading*
- *Types of Grading*
- *Significance of Standardisation*
- *Benefits of Standardisation*
- *Control of Standard*
- *Agricultural Produce*
- *Extractive Industries and Manufactured Product*
- *Control*
- *ISI*
- *AGMARK*
- *Questions*

When one has learnt the functions of exchange (buying and selling) and the functions of physical supply (transportation and storage), we take up the facilitating functions *i.e.*, standardisation, grading, financing, risk-bearing, market research, information etc. We take up standardisation and grading in this chapter.

Standardisation and grading are important for an efficient marketing. Of several functions of marketing, standardisation and grading solve some of the major problems. Standardisation facilitates effective performance of marketing functions, mainly buying and selling. Standardisation means the establishment of certain standards on the qualities or the intrinsic physical properties of a commodity. It signifies that the products produced are of a certain quality. The quality, we aim, is determined on the basis which depends upon size, colour, flavour, appearance, strength etc. To standardise is to determine or fix basis, limited to classes of products. It involves setting up of standards and maintaining those standards during the period. A standard carries the idea of uniformity. It means and implies that a standardised product bought from different sellers is the same. For example, lux soap, bought at Madras or Delhi, is similar. It ensures uniformity. When we speak of quality, it does not mean that the standard product should be of the best quality. Standardisation signifies that goods are of certain specified quality.

What is Standardisation ?

Duddy and Revzan define, ''Standardisation is the process of determining of classes or grades of a product or service that have fixed limits.''

International Organisation defines, ''Standardisation is the process of formulating and applying rates for an orderly approach to a specific activity for the benefit and with the co-operation of all concerned and in particular for the promotion of optimum overall economy, taking due account of functional conditions and safety requirements.'' Standardisation is mainly concerned with the division of products into distinct groups or classes on the basis of some common characteristics. Like other marketing functions, standardisation involves sub-divisions–(1) Determination of Standard, (2) Grading (3) Inspection, and (4) Labelling.

1. **What is Standard ?** A standard is a measure that is generally accepted as having a fixed value. It is a model. It is an example. It is a grade or a class. Anything serving as a basis of comparison is called a standard. It consists of basic limits or specifications to the qualities, that products must have to be of a designed grade. Again by standard is meant the established measures or specifications, covering the extent, quantity and quality of a product. For example, Horlicks bought at Bombay and

Calcutta is similar. It guarantees uniformity. The standard may be based on a number of factors, *i.e.*, pre-determined characteristics, such as colour, quality, weight, shape, sweetness, strength etc. These convey the idea of uniform quality. It means that goods of a particular standard will be of the same quality, irrespective of the seller from whom it is bought. That is, a standard often means that the commodities are of certain quality, regardless of the producer. Trade is based on standards.

Standardising means the determining of basic measures or limits to different groups of products. The process of fixing the grades is known as standardising. It is the use of standards. Standardising plays an important role in the marketing of agricultural goods and minerals. Manufactured goods are standardised in the process of production. To be effective, the standards described must be relatively permanent and used by a large number of buyers and sellers of the commodity concerned.

Types of Standards

Standards are determined on the basis of certain fundamental characteristics of the product concerned–basis for standards. There are three types of standard:

(1) **Quantity Standard :** Weights and measures are the standards usually used for the determination of quantity. Standardisation of weights and measures and enforcement of them are under the responsibility of Central and State Governments and local bodies. The standard weights and measures are kilogram, metre, litre.

(2) **Standards of Size and Measurement :** This is important as far as the manufactured goods are concerned. The standards are determined on the basis of the size of the products. For example, Ready-made garments, shoes, thread, nut, bolt, pipe etc. Such products are purchased or sold on the basis of size and measurements.

(3) **Quality Standard :** This is a standard, which is difficult to be established. This standard depends on the prescription of consumers and users. However, branding, product differentiations, positive quality etc., are the basis for standardising.

Standards may be positive or negative. **Positive standard** refers to the presence of the expressed qualities or specifications in the product. **Negative standard** refers to the absence of the expressed qualities in the product. Standards are also classified as general standard and private standard. **General standard** refers to the standard found in the product, no matter who produces them. **Private standards** are the standards prescribed by the individual firm.

2. **Grading :** Grading means the division of products into classes made up of units possessing similar characteristics of size and quality. It is the task of separating the products on the basis of predetermined norms or standards. Determination of standards to be established is known as the process of standardisation. It is the classifying process of the commodity as per the needs of the standards. It is important in standardisation and refers to the service of sorting out products into groups of uniform kind, quality, and size. Thus standard determines the quality and grading. The process of dividing a quantity of the same kind of goods into uniform groups according to certain standards of size, shape, colour, texture, degree of cleanliness, acidity or other significant characteristics.

Need of Grading

Generally farm products are of different qualities. For example, raw cotton and jute, coal, iron, ore, milk, ghee etc. Producers want to manufacture products of uniform quality; and for this, they want the raw materials in uniform quality. It is made possible only through storing out the raw materials on the basis of the standard or quality or size fixed.

Types of Grading

There are two types of grading (1) Fixed grading and (2) Variable grading. **Fixed grading** refers to sorting out of goods on the basis of standards (size, quality etc.) already set, to be followed from year to year. **Variable grading** refers to varying standards for goods from year to year.

Differences between Standardisation and Grading

Standardisation	Grading
1. It is fixed before grading.	1. It follows standardisation.
2. It is a process of fixing standards.	2. It is a process of separating the goods on the basis of quality.
3. It is a mental process.	3. It is a physical process.
4. It is applied in agricultural as well as manufactured goods.	4. It is applied in agricultural products.
5. It is meaningless without grading.	5. It is not possible without standardisation.
6. ISI stands for standardisation.	6. AGMARK stands for grade.

3. **Inspection :** To know the effectiveness of grading, it is necessary to have a check. Inspection or check aims to test the goods ''in order to determine the characteristics.'' For example, oranges or apples are sorted according to standards fixed. In the case of wheat, rice, butter etc., a sample which is representative of the group, is drawn and examined to determine the standard. In the case of manufactured goods, a sample of the finished product is inspected.

4. **Labelling :** Some type of identification of grades is necessary for the buyer to know the characteristic of the product. It is confirming the work of grading. A label may be a piece of paper containing printed statement or a metal imprinted; it may be a part of package or attached to it, indicating the price, contents, name, place, quality, ownership etc., of a product. The process of attaching the labels is called labelling.

Object of Labelling

1. Information pertaining to the product or the characteristics of the product can be made known to the buyer through labelling. It describes the specialities of the product. And this will make an item move quickly. As far as the customers or buyers are concerned, it will fetch much importance.

2. Label will avoid confusion when a number of products are displayed in a shop. Label helps a buyer to get what he needs. It indicates the grade and standard of the products.

3. Labelling makes a product to be judged by the consumers; and at the same it gives a guarantee of the products' standard.

Types of Label

There are 4 types of labels. 1. Brand label, 2. Grade label, 3. Descriptive label, and 4. Informative label.

1. **Brand Label :** It is the brand name applied to the product to the package. It carries information relating to the brand. Through a brand label, a firm can be remembered. The purpose of brand label is to popularise the brand loyalty. For example, Sanforised (a mark for shrinklessness), Agmark (standard goods).

2. **Grade Label :** Grade Label gives more important information to the quality of a product. By a letter, number or word, the product identification is done. For example grapes may be labelled as A, B, C,; species may be labelled as No. 1, 2, 3, ; and other products may be labelled as better, best etc.

3. **Descriptive Label :** A detailed description of the product such as chemical analysis, size, colour etc. storing methods, directions for the use of the products, are given in the descriptive label. This type of label is sometimes used for ungraded products, such as clothing, mechanical goods etc. The label explains the use, for example, food products.

4. **Informative Label :** This type of label carries more information and is distinguished from descriptive labelling. Such a label may contain fuller details of the guidance to use and care to be taken of the products.

Significance of Standardisation

1. Standardised products can be sold by description, whereas ungraded products can be sold only on the basis of inspection. Thus the exchange function becomes more efficient and simple.

2. In the age of mass production, standardisation is a prerequisite.

3. Consumers' favourable attitude can be earned by selling graded products.

Benefits of Standardisation and Grading

1. **Simplified Sales:** Sales by grade need no sample or description. But to sell ungraded products, inspection of the product is essential. Thus the sale of standard products becomes easy and simple. Standard products can be sold or bought by letters or telegrams.

2. **Reduced Marketing Cost:** The expenses to be involved in sales by inspection or sample can be avoided. Sales returns on standard products do not occur.

3. **Future Sales Facilitated:** When the goods are under graded system, future sales can easily be effected because of the dealings in standard goods.

4. **Simplifies Financing:** The prices of graded goods can be fixed easily. Easy finance lending can be availed of on the strength of the graded items.

5. **Satisfaction of the Consumers:** Grading guarantees goods of standard quality to consumers.

6. **Wider Market :** Sales by grade name can widen the markets for standard products and standardisation facilitates mass turnover.

7. **Low Transport Cost:** When grading is adopted, inferior goods can be discarded at the producing place, and thereby transportation cost decreases.

8. **Buyer's Satisfaction:** When standard goods are available, it gives no place for adulterated goods. Consumers can blindly purchase graded goods.

9. **Consumers Pay Right Price:** There is a disparity between the price charged by the manufacturer and price paid by the consumer in the case of ungraded goods. This will give chances to earn extra profits by the middlemen at the cost of the manufacturer or buyer. Standardisation eliminates such margins.

10. **Easy Realisation of Claims:** In the case of accident in store or in transit, claims can be finalised without much displeasure. At the same time, the loss of ungraded goods can only be settled with great difficulty. Simply the receipts of graded goods are enough to calculate the loss.

11. **Long Period Contracts:** When buyers and sellers are assured, about the standards, they can easily enter into contracts for long period.

Demerits

The following objections are raised against standardisation:

1. It destroys manufacturing secrets.
2. It prevents adoption of new ideas.
3. It destroys personal skill and ability.
4. It treats the workers as machines.
5. It cannot\easily apply to farm products.

Control of Standarus

Standards must be subjected, of course, to some form of effective control, to have the full advantages of standardisation. Not only the establishment of standard is enough, but also the standard must be properly controlled. Control may be observed by the following agencies :

1. **Control of Standard and the Farmer :** Producers of agricultural commodities may try to improve their control over products by adopting standard methods of cultivation. The middlemen or assembling units determine the standard of products.

2. **Control of Standard and the Producer:** Products of extractive industry–minerals, ore etc., are in natural form. Personal inspection does not judge the exact standard. The quality has to be decided only through a laboratory test, which reveals the intrinsic value of the products.

3. **Control of Standard and Manufacturer:** The producers of manufactured goods possess a good control over the standards of the products, through quality control. They are graded materials and in turn standard products are produced. Thus they can easily maintain standards.

4. **Control of Standard and the Consumer:** Consumers do not control the standards of the products. When the ultimate consumers are not satisfied with the standard of the product, they refuse to accept it, and this may force the manufacturer to improve his product. The buying agencies, before purchase, make sure of the standards as to its size, quality, performance etc.

5. **Control of Standard and the Government:** Agencies of the central, state and local governments exercise control over the standard through legislative measures. State and local governments exercise their power in the maintenance of standards for weights and measures. Local self-government takes measures for purity in food articles. Ignorance on the part of consumers is an obstacle. To make the standardisation an effective one, such standard is legalised. In India, the standardisation movement is of recent years. Government has the responsibility to keep up the standards. The Central Agricultural Marketing Department, the Directorate of Marketing and Inspection, the Central and State Warehousing Corporations undertake grading of agricultural produce. Indian Standard Institution undertakes standardisation of manufactured goods.

The Agricultural Produce (Grading and Marketing) Act, 1937

As per the recommendations of the directorate of Marketing and Inspection and Indian Trade Commissioners, for defining standards and qualities of agricultural products in India, the Agricultural Product (Grading and Marketing) Act was passed in 1937. Under this Act, Government has set up grading stations for commodities. The Act authorises the Agricultural Marketing Adviser to grant certificates of authorisation to persons or corporate bodies, who may agree to grade and mark agricultural produce on the basis of the standards laid down under this Act. The graded goods are stamped with the official seal of the Agricultural Marketing Department–AGMARK grade specification–AG for Agricultural and MARK for grading. The Act has authorised the Central Government to frame rules relating to grades and standards for commodities included in the schedule. The Act was first passed in 1937 and was amended in 1943 to widen its scope and to include additional products. The Act now includes fruits, vegetables, hides, skins, dairy products, tobacco, coffee, oilseeds, rice, wheat etc. To ensure the purity and quality of products, many laboratories have been set up. Agmarking for exportable commodities was first started in 1942, followed by many items. Quality control laboratories were established to fix the standard and to give training to the personnel. To check the adulteration of food articles, the Prevention of Food Adulteration Act was passed in 1954 and rules were framed in 1955. The inspecting staff of the Central Agricultural Marketing Department inspects the grading stations and collects samples of graded products from markets. The samples are examined to see if they conform to the standards of quality laid down by the Central Quality Control Laboratory at Nagpur.

The Indian Standard Institution (ISI)

It was set up in 1947 by the Central Government to promote and adopt Indian standards in all branches of industry and commerce. The aims and object are:

1. To approve and promote the general adoption of standards, prepared by it on National and International levels.
2. To prepare the standards for products, commodities, materials and processes.
3. Certification of industrial goods.
4. Circulation of information relating to standards and standardisation.

For the preparation of Indian standards, ISI has set up about 2,000 technical committees, consisting of more than 26,000 experts, working in honorary capacity, in different fields. Apart from these, paid experts are also appointed in various fields. ISI lays down standards for 100 items every year.

ISI Certification Marks Act, 1952

Any product manufactured as per the standard laid down by ISI may be certified under the ISI Certification Act. Under this Act, ISI has been authorised by the Central Government to issue licences for the use of ISI marks to firms producing goods, which conform to the ISI specifications. ISI marks indicate:

1. That the goods are subjected to quality control.
2. That the goods are well safeguarded against sub-standard goods.
3. That they have more than a claim by the manufacturers.
4. That they earn the buyer's confidence.
5. That they will act as a third party guarantee.

The manufacturers are bound by the contract of procedures to be followed. ISI inspectors pay surprise visits, draw random samples, seal and send them for testing. Samples may even be drawn from the open market. If the samples fail to satisfy the prescribed standard, suitable action will be taken against the manufacturer.

The benefits are:

1. Consumer gets standard products.
2. Goods come to the consumer at lower rate, safer condition, better quality, cheaper repair services etc.
3. The manufacturer strives to reduce wastage, cost and rejects; and these will improve the chances of making more profits.

QUESTIONS

1. Distinguish between standardisation and grading. (*B.Com., Madurai*)
2. Discuss the reasons why standardising and grading are important. (*B.Com., Madurai*)
3. Discuss : "Established standards for farm goods are known as grades". (*B.Com., Madurai*)
4. Explain the significance of standardisation of products from the viewpoint of buyer. (*B.Com., Madurai*)
5. What is standardisation ? (*B.Com., Madurai*)
6. Write a short note on standardisation and grading. (*B.Com., Madurai*)
7. What is AGMARK ? Give two examples each for ISI and AGMARK products. (*B.Com., Madurai*)
8. What is ISI ? (*B.Com., Madurai*)

CHAPTER 8

Marketing Finance

- *Introduction*
- *Finance*
- *Business Finance*
- *Fixed and Working Capital*
- *Factors Which Determine Working Capital*
- *Types and Sources of Working Capital*
- *Trade Credit*
- *Consumer Credit*
- *Open Account*
- *Charge Account Banking*
- *Instalment*
- *Hire Purchase*
- *Agricultural Marketing Finance*
- *Questions*

Supporting activities, like finance, contribute considerably to get success in the field of marketing. Financing refers to money and credit. The present age is of mass production and this needs mass distribution. Hence sufficient amount is needed by a business firm. Finance is the most fundamental aspect for any merchandise transaction. Business firms cannot stand through ownership capital. Majority of transactions between firms are carried on through credit. A business firm, from its inception, requires fund. A firm may manufacture its own products for sale or may purchase for resale. Goods are not sold immediately after they are manufactured or bought for sale. Generally, it takes some time for the goods to reach the hands of consumers. That is, there is a gap between the time of purchase of goods or production and the time when it reaches the final consumers. Sometimes, payment may be delayed. Then firms have to hold inventories to meet demands. All the business activities are continuous in day to day actions. A firm or a business needs finance for various purposes, from its inception to its fall. If agriculture and industry are the **flesh and bones** of economy, then **finance is the blood circulating system.** Credit transactions are common in business and this stops the inflow of cash. But the firm has to keep stock of further sales. Thus, the firm needs further amount of cash for the smooth running of business.

What is Finance?

Finance may be defined as the provision of money. Finance is the study of methods to obtain money and credit. Financing is the act of providing money and credit. Ownership capital is limited. On the strength of owned capital, business firms try to secure borrowed resources. ''Finance is the life blood of the economic, commercial and industrial undertakings.''

In business, it is profitable to invite borrowed resources. Thus ''Credit is the life blood of business.'' The finance needed to run a business as a whole is known as **business finance** and the finance needed to market the products is known as **marketing finance.** The marketing finance, which we are concerned, is one of the facilitating functions of marketing.

Kinds of Business Finance

Business firm requires two kinds of capital viz., Fixed Capital (Permanent capital) and Current Capital (Working capital).

Fixed Capital

It is the money which is invested in fixed assets, to be used over a long period of time. Fixed assets include land, building, fixtures and fittings, furniture, machinery, equipment etc. It is a long-term investment and having permanent existence. It is sunk permanently in the business. It is not returnable to the investors on demand. It is the core of the business.

The requirement for fixed capital is less than marketing finance–warehouses, service centres, showrooms etc. The sources for fixed capital are: issue of shares and debentures, long-term loans, ploughing back of profits etc.

Working Capital

Working capital is also known as current capital or liquid capital or circulating capital. Working capital is required to purchase raw materials, inventories, spare parts, marketable securities etc; and to meet day to day expenses. It is required for running the business. It is raised out of one's own funds and short-term loans. The primary need of the business firm for the fund arises when one has to invest in stock of goods. In case of quick turnover, the amount of working capital required is less. When the unit cost is higher, greater amount is needed; but when the unit cost of production is less, small amount of working capital is needed. If it is a manufacturing concern, the raw materials can be acquired on credit basis.

Our need is concerned with the working capital *i.e.*, the fund involved in production, purchase and sale of goods. The need for working capital is to finance day to day manufacturing expenses and sales expenses. It indicates the cash flow cycles. It is revolving fund. This cycle starts by purchasing raw materials with cash (credit), engaging labour, meeting operating expenses and marketing expenses and finally recovering through sales of finished goods.

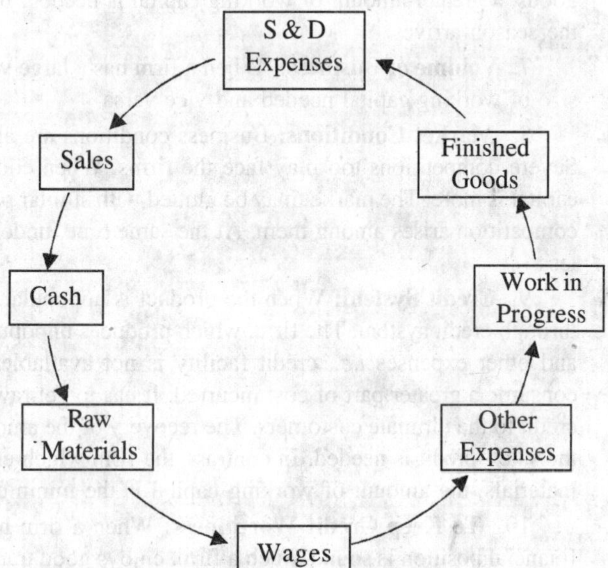

Thus, there is continuous flow of fund–mainly cash to inventory and inventory to cash. Again the working capital may be in the form of stocks, B/R, sundry debtors etc. Net working capital is the excess of total current assets over total current liabilities. There must be considerable margin of current assets over current liabilities. The working capital denotes the capital temporarily needed. Cash comes in and goes out of business. As such, the fund on working capital is more or less permanent in nature. The asset, under working capital, may change its form from one asset to another. For example, debtors to cash, stock to cash or debtors etc. Therefore, the fund is known as circulating capital.

Factors Which Determine the Working Capital

The following are the factors which decide the amount of working capital

1. **Cost of Production:** Industries, which use costly raw materials and expensive process of production, need larger amount of working capital. For example, the manufacturers of automobiles or durable consumer goods, need larger amount of working capital, because manufacturers of such goods invest in costly raw materials, production process, transportation expenses, other marketing costs etc.; and all these invested amounts are cashable when the goods reach in the hands of the ultimate consumer.

2. **Time Gap:** Normal working capital needs depend upon the time gap between input and output. That is the time taken to convert the raw materials into finished products, time lost in storage, time spent in transportation, time taken for the products to reach the hands of the consumer etc. are considered. Longer the time gap, larger is the amount of working capital needed. There is a time gap

between investment and turnover. Therefore, there is the need for more working capital for the smooth running of production. On the contrary, firms engaged in business of vegetables, fish, eggs, bakery products, flowers etc., need less amount of working capital, because cash is recovered quickly.

3. **Nature of Industry:** A greater amount of working capital is needed, if the industry is labour-intensive, and smaller amount of working capital is needed, if the industry is capital-intensive.

4. **Stock Turnover Rate:** A firm with higher rate of stock turnover *i.e.*, fast moving products, needs less amount to be invested in inventories. The lower the rate of stock turnover, the more the amount to be invested in inventories. If the demand is irregular, the rate of stock turnover will be less and therefore the need for the amount of working capital is more. Thus stock turnover rate is a basis to decide the amount of working capital.

5. **Size of the Unit:** Smaller the size of the firm, lesser is the amount required. A small-scale retailer needs limited working capital and a large-scale retailer needs a good amount of working capital.

6. **Nature of Products:** When the manufacturing concern is engaged in producing seasonable goods, a greater amount of working capital is needed. It is because products have to be stocked till the season arrives.

7. **Volume of Business:** When a firm has a large volume of business transactions, larger is the size of working capital needed and vice versa.

8. **Market Conditions:** Business conditions are always changing. The price may fall or rise. Severe competitions too may face the firms. When competition increases, the amount of working capital is more. The market may be glutted with similar products produced by different firms and thus competition arises among them. At the same time, under monopoly, the need for working capital is less.

9. **Credit System:** When the product is unpopular, there arises a situation to sell the products through credit system. The firm, which produces unpopular goods, has to pay cash for raw materials and other expenses *i.e.*, credit facility is not available for the purchase of raw materials, which consume a greater part of cost incurred. It has to get raw materials on cash and sell the products on credit to the ultimate customers. The recovery of the amount takes some time. Moreover, to boost up the sales, credit is needed. In contrast, the firm which enjoys credit facility for the purchase of raw materials, the amount of working capital is the minimum.

10. **To Keep Credit Worthiness:** When a firm has adequate working and fixed capital, the financial position is sound. Such a firm, enjoys good trade relations and thereby enjoys liberal credit facility. Bankers are interested in sound firms. A firm without adequate capital is like a landlord without land or a bank without cash.

Types of Working Capital

Current finance, also called working capital, is for financing current needs. They are of :

1. **Regular Working Capital:** Regular working capital is more or less similar to fixed capital. Therefore this type of capital is raised through share capital or long-term loans. A firm needs a certain excess of current assets over current liabilities so as to maintain the circulating capital. Working capital may be in the form of cash in hand and bank, raw materials, finished stocks, account receivable etc. The total amount of working capital under these heads does not change, but the form of current assets may change–stocks can be sold for cash, cash can be received from account receivable etc. Thus certain minimum amount of capital is required to maintain the regular working capital. For example, a minimum amount of goods must always be held in the stock. Thus the investment in it represents the permanent working capital.

2. **Seasonal Working Capital:** Certain supply is seasonal but demand is regular or supply is regular but demand is seasonal. The agricultural products are abundant in season time at low price and in off seasons, the price goes up. But demand may be regular. Businessmen, in order to take the

full advantage of low price, require capital to hold up the stock for off season. For example, production of wheat, jute cotton etc., is seasonal, but demand is regular. Woollen clothes, waterproof items, etc., are produced regularly, but demand is only seasonal. Finance for such seasonal working capital can be got from short-term loan.

3. **Emergency Working Capital :** There may be unexpected financial needs to meet certain situations arising from fire, flood, drought etc. This leads to a thrust on working capital all of a sudden. Special occasions, such as, extensive marketing campaign, emergency contracts for production, severe competitions, changes because of trade cycle, special jobs undertaken, introduction of new products into the markets etc., call for special working capital.

Financial institutions, public moneylenders etc., are there to mobilise the financial needs of firms. A corporation may issue shares and debentures. Banks grant long-term loans to improve the earning capacity of firms. Certain financial institutions provide long-term loans, while some provide short-term loans. All these types are external sources of finance which provide external working capital.

The following are the sources by which current financial needs can be met:

1. **Own Investment and Long-Term Borrowing :** A part of the long-term borrowing is utilised for current financial needs. Regular working capital needs certain amount of money to be kept in the floating fund. Own investment has limitations as to its availability. Therefore, the business has to depend upon the long-term borrowing to meet the current financial needs.

2. **Bank Loans :** Short-term financial needs are often met by bankers, through the sanction of loans. Such short-term loans are, generally, granted for short periods of a temporary nature, repayable within 6 months. Such loans may be secured or unsecured. Unsecured loans are given against the character, ability and credit standing of the businessman. Such loans are repaid by the businessman when sale of goods takes place, within a reasonable period. The bank may also provide cash, credit or the facility of overdraft to the businessman.

3. **Account Receivable Financing:** It is not possible to sell goods always on cash. Mercantile credit plays an important role in boosting the business transactions. Businessmen sell goods and the buyer's account is debited with the amount. Of course, this account receivable, known as sundry debtors in financial book, appears in balance sheet. On the basis of this account receivable, businessmen get loans or advances from factors. When funds are received from factors against account receivable, they are known as account receivables financing. They are of either of the two forms:

(A) Ordinary Account Receivable Financing

This is a system by which a business firm enters into an agreement with the financing institution, which agrees to purchase account receivable of the firm or gives advance against such account receivables. When sales take place, a statement of account is sent to the financing institution, which advances immediately about 70-90% of the face-value. Buyers make the payment to the selling firms, which settle with the financial institutions. For this, the financial institution charges about 2% of the invoice price. The loss on account of defaulted buyers is borne by the selling firms. It is called non-notification or ordinary account receivable financing and the buyer is not intimated with the arrangement, as he has nothing to do with it.

(B) Factoring

This is a system by which factor buys such account receivable (sundry debtors) of the seller, and assumes all the risk of non-payment. There is an agreement between the seller and factor or financing institution. The seller is paid off against such debt. The factor possesses the right to grant credit to the buyer or the seller. The invoice is forwarded by the factor, who receives the debt. Factor charges commission, say 1 to 3% of the invoice price.

Features of Factoring

1. Factor takes the responsibility of collection.
2. The firm increases operating efficiency.
3. The seller need not go for longterm loans
4. Marketing opportunity increases.
5. Bad debts do not affect the seller.

Differences between Factoring and Ordinary Account Receivable

Factoring	Ordinary Account Receivable Financing
1. Factor assumes liability of bad debts.	1. Seller is responsible for bad debts.
2. Factor is responsible for collection of debts.	2. Seller is responsible for collection of debts.
3. Factor forwards the invoice to the buyer.	3. Seller sends the invoice to the buyer.
4. Buyer must be informed.	4. No intimation to the buyer is needed.
5. It is notification of Account receivable financing	5. It is non-notification of Account receivable financing.

Trade Credit (Mercantile Credit)

Mercantile credit plays a significant role in financing marketing activities. By trade credit, it means the credit extended by one merchant to another, for the purchase of goods for sale, but not for personal use. This form of credit enables the firm to buy goods and services of a firm and settle at the specified date in future. This type of credit is not in the form of cash, but in the form of products or goods. Period of the credit depends upon the nature of the goods and the relation between the seller and the buyer. It is mainly based on the past records of the buyer. The seller measures the risk by considering the three C's basis–Character, Capacity and Capital. Character is the moral basis of credit; capital and capacity are the material bases which determine the limit of credit risk. More than 75% of sales of wholesale merchants and over 90% of manufacturer's sales are generally made on credit. Generally the credit period varies between 30 to 90 days. To such a credit, no collateral is offered.

Mercantile credit is of two types: (1) A regular buyer purchases goods; the seller prepares the bills and sends them to the buyer, who settles them in an orderly basis–date-wise. Practically, this type of transaction is done between merchants. As and when goods are sold, the bills will also be sent to the buyer, who usually settles them everyday or every week. Since the payments are made on rotation basis *i.e.*, date-wise basis, this system is known as Cycle Billing. (2) There is another practice, known as Revolving Credit Plan. Under this plan, the seller fixes a maximum limit for the amount of credit, Beyond this limit, no credit sales are made. The period may be fixed by the seller. The amount may be settled by remitting cash to the seller. For example, we are permitted by the seller to enjoy credit upto Rs. 1,000. Then, we can make credit purchases up to Rs. 1,000. After making credit purchases of Rs. 1,000, if we remit a part payment, say Rs. 100, then we are eligible again to get credit to the extent of Rs. 100 and so on.

The following advantages are claimed:

1. The trader gets the goods at credit, resells it at a profit. Thus a trader makes a profit without investment.
2. It reduces the needs for current working finance.
3. It creates a good relationship between the seller and buyer.
4. Sales increase as buyers are tempted to make purchases.
5. Under bulk purchase the buyer gets more discount, and the transportation cost will be less.

Disadvantages of the System

1. Trade credit creates bad debts.
2. It increases office cost for the collection of debts.
3. There is no possibility of cash discount.

Consumer Credit

1. **Open Account Credit:** Retail credit, also known as personal credit or customer's credit means the credit granted by a retailer to his customers. Customers are the last link. The credit is based on the capacity of the customer, who is able to pay within a specified time. This is a simple system whereby a seller opens an account in his books in the name of the consumer. As and when sales take place, the amount of the sales is debited in the customer's account, in the seller's book. A monthly statement is sent to the customer. Customer pays the outstanding amount once in a month or so. This type of credit is enjoyed by salaried people.

2. **Charge Account Banking (Credit Cards):** As in foreign countries, credit card system has come to India. If a person wants to avail of this facility, he must apply to the bank, in the prescribed form and he must have assumed income. The limit of the income is fixed by the bank. If the bank is satisfied with the credit worthiness of the party, the banker issues the credit cards and thereby informs the person of the credit limit. The credit card holder can make credit purchase from retail shops, repair shops etc., with the help of this credit card. As soon as a credit sale is made, the seller informs the bank or a copy of the invoice is sent to the bank. The banker makes the payment to the seller by debiting the card holder's account. In some cases, instead of paying cash, the sellers account is credited by debiting the card holder's account. At the end of the month, a statement of purchases made by the card holder is sent to the card holders. The card holder settles the statement with the bank depositing the amount. For payment, generally bank does not charge, but delayed payment carry interest. The system is a new trend. Sellers are relieved from the risk of non-payment. The displeasure of collection process on the part of the buyers is avoided.

3. **Instalment Credit:** In case of consumer durables–television, furniture, cycle, radio etc., instalment credit is generally allowed. Under this system, the buyer is allowed to own the article by paying a fixed amount, which is a part of the total price and this payment is also known as down payment on purchase. The price, which includes interest, is divided into instalments, which will be paid, generally monthly or at a fixed period as agreed upon between the buyer and the seller. In case of default, the buyer can be sued in a court of law for the recovery of the balance amount. By this system, the sales can be increased.

4. **Hire Purchase Agreement:** There is an agreement between the seller and the buyer, whereby the seller agrees to transfer the possession of the article to the buyer; but the ownership right of the article will be transferred to the buyer only on payment of the last instalment. As in instalment credit system, the seller hands over the article to the buyer. In case of default in payment of instalments, the seller possesses the right of possession of the articles and the amount paid will be treated as hire charges.

The significance of consumer credit is mainly aimed for boosting the sales. It is the system by which sellers can sell goods easily and quickly. The consumers, when they go for credit purchases, can increase their standard of living. Because of the consumer credit, the following merits are claimed:

1. Credit is the life blood of commerce.
2. Consumer credit has tonic effect.
3. Sales can be increased.
4. Consumer can increase standard of life.
5. Seller can increase his profits.
6. Mass production, in turn, decreases cost.
7. Consumers are tempted to save.
8. Employment opportunity increases.
9. Average men enjoy luxurious life.
10. Credit system increases the number of customers.

Drawbacks of Consumer Credit

1. Consumer credit creates inflation and boom condition.
2. It leads to over-buying.
3. It mortgages future income of buyers.
4. It is costly to buyers.
5. It tempts to buy unwanted goods.

Financing of Agricultural Marketing in India

The farmers in India cannot do cultivation without financial help. Finance is required for personal needs and productive needs. The financing of agricultural marketing means the fund required to move the crops from farmers to consumers.

Features of Agricultural Finance

1. The financial needs of farmers are recurring in nature.
2. The risk in agricultural loss cannot be shifted.
3. Climate conditions, often, go unfavourable.
4. Product is seasonal, but finance required for cultivation is round the year.
5. In the absence of standardisation and grade control, cultivators do not take advantage of the services of organised markets; but they sell forced sales to private village money-lenders which is a drawback.
6. Holding of the land is limited.
7. Produces are perishable.
8. Agricultural goods are bulky.

The financial loan that the farmers need is of three kinds: (1) Short-term loans or finance; for example, working capital needs. (2) Medium-term finance; for example, purchase of cattle, land improvement etc. (3) Long-term finance; for example, digging well, purchasing of machinery and land, farm construction etc.

The expenditure is of three types : (1) Directly productive; for example, purchase of cattle, fodder, holding stocks for more price etc., (2) Indirectly productive; for example, clearing old debts, education etc., (3) unproductive; for example, social and religious functions. According to the Rural Credit Survey Committee, these expenses are 28, 50 and 32 per cent respectively.

Village moneylenders play a greater part in financing the agricultural field. Various kinds of societies are there for financing the agriculturists. For example, Credit Institutions, the Government, Commercial Banks etc., play a limited role in financing the rural needs of the farmers. RBI provides credit through State Co-operative Banks. Agricultural Refinance Corporation which acts as a supplement to the existing institutions, offers long-term finance. Land Development Banks give long-term finance. Co-operative Credit Societies play an important role by giving short and long-term loans.

QUESTIONS

1. What is working capital ? Explain how a marketing firm estimates its working capital requirements. *(B.Com., Madurai)*
2. What are the various sources of meeting the current financial needs of a marketing concern ? *(B.Com., Madurai)*
3. What are various methods and sources of financing current financial needs ? Explain the types of credit extended by retailers to the consumers. *(B.Com., Mysore)*
4. Distinguish between hire purchase and instalment. *(B. Com., Mysore)*
5. Critically examine the factors responsible for estimating the working capital requirements of a marketing firm. *(B.Com., Madurai)*
6. Explain the important sources of marketing finance. *(B.Com., Chennai)*
7. Discuss the need for trade credit. *(B.Com., Madurai)*

CHAPTER 9

Marketing Risk

- *Marketing Risk*
- *Causes*
- *Handling the Risks*
- *Preventions, Reduction and Shifting*
- *Questions*

The entire marketing process has to face numerous risks and uncertainties. The aim of marketing is to get something in return for the services offered by the producers; the returns encourage them to increase output and services in the market. At the same time the entire marketing process involves risks. Risk arises due to uncertainties in regard to cost, loss or damage. Such risks are inherent in all forms of business activity. In a dynamic, free and competitive economy, marketing risks are inevitable. Marketing risks include changing demand and fashions, price falls, changes in desire and taste of consumers, changes in the market conditions and competitions, new and developed inventions, loss from bad debtors, fire, flood, accidents etc. Unforeseen conditions and uncertainties give rise to risks. Marketing risks are the elements of danger; loss from unforeseen circumstances in the future is always uncertain and gloomy. There are risks from the time of production to the time of sale.

What is Marketing Risk ?

Marketing risk may be defined as the danger of loss from unforeseen circumstances in future. It implies an element of uncertainty or possibility of loss. The uncertainty or risk is assumed by participants who are in marketing and more particularly by those who take title of goods. There arises a possibility of loss due to unpredictable or unfavourable happenings in the future. Market operations are based more on future conditions than on the present conditions. Exposition of business to the danger of financial losses, which are caused by multiplicity of reasons, in a nutshell, can be termed as marketing risks.

Causes of Marketing Risks

The risk is the result or effect of any unforeseen event on its happening. The business world is dynamic and full of risks of uncertainties. The future is unpredictable and full of uncertainties. Planning alone cannot solve or protect against uncertainties. In modern business, which has become the stage of severe competition, the element of risk is inherent in the marketing transactions. Modern business is usually carried on in large-scale basis and is based on anticipation of demand. Thereby risks are involved till the moment the product reaches the consumers. The producers and customers are separated by distance. The risks may be classified or grouped into :

1. Risks resulting from changes in market conditions.
2. Risks arising mainly or wholly out of natural causes.
3. Risks resulting from human behaviour.

1. **Risks Resulting From Changes in Market Conditions**

Important causes of marketing risks are greatly due to price fluctuations by market conditions. The price changes are chiefly responsible for the loss of expected profits. For example, there is a fall in the demand for electrical fans in the cold season; and fans remain unsold or to be sold at marked down price. This situation affects the producer and middlemen who stock them for the ensuing seasons; they face the loss of profits. At the same time if the season is favourably hot, the situations tend to more and more sales at marked up price. Almost all the producers and merchants have to face such risks caused by market conditions. This type of risks is generally of three kinds : (1) Time risks; (2) Place risks; and (3) Competition risks.

MARKETING RISKS

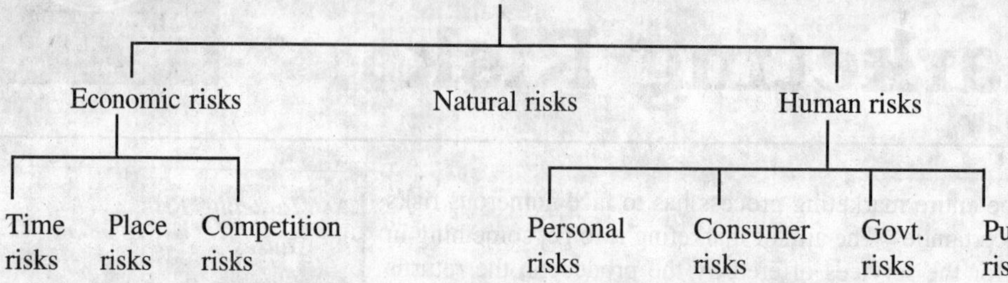

(i) **Time Risk:** The present stage is of mass production, which is in anticipation of demand. Products have been bought in the hope of selling them at a good price, which will realise a profit; but sometimes, the anticipated price is not realised. The wholesalers and retailers face such risks. Generally the wholesalers purchase goods from producers for selling them to the retailers, who sell them at a profit to the consumers. But sometimes, there arises an adverse change in the demand from customers, and customer have less demand for the product. Thereby the retailers have to face difficulty in disposing of the stocked products; and this trend insists upon them not to restock the products at such an expected quantity. Further, the wholesalers, who stocked them, in anticipation of demand from retailers, have to suffer loss. In turn, no fresh order is sent by the wholesalers to the producers, who have already invested a great amount in the production process in anticipation. As such the product which was got ready by investing a huge amount of money has not the expected demand nor any demand.

Time factor assumes prime importance on the market risk. Change in price is seen with the passage of time. This is caused by the improved products being offered for sale by the competitors or change in the weather conditions or new inventions as a result of scientific research or changes in the size of population or changes in fashion etc. Almost all the changes are unexpected and unforeseen. No one can say how long a particular product will be popular and when it will go out of demand.

(ii) **Place Risk :** The changes in price are caused by the passage of time which involves time risks. But place risk is different. The prices of a product are different in different markets at the same time. The demand and supply pattern differs from one market to another. This is because of price, which is based on demand and supply of the product. When businessmen purchase products from a market they aim to sell it at a higher price. But it so happens that sales have to be executed at a lower price than expected, because of low price at the selling market. Such losses are due to lack of knowledge of market conditions. The rapid means of communication minimise such risks. However, possibility of such risks exists in the market, which is unorganised and permits different prices.

(iii) **Competition Risk :** Competition is normally witnessed in the market. Mass production is followed by mass selling, which is again followed by keen competition among marketers. A producer or a marketer must always be alert to the attitude of competition. The absence of competitive attitude will cause closure of the firm. A competitor may change the method of production in order to improve the quality and durability of goods or lower the prices or adopt the best methods of selling, or offer special guarantee etc., to maintain the position of the market. All these cause the price reduction or divert the demand in the market. Thus every businessman must be alert in the actions of his competitors, who try to capture the market. At the present stage of severe competition, when one wants to be in the market one must be alert of the changes introduced in the market.

2. **Natural Risks**

Natural risks such as, earthquakes, fire, storm, rain, heat, cold etc., are uncontrollable by human beings. Pests, rats etc., cause physical damage to grains. Extreme cold or heat may deteriorate the quality of products. A farmer may not be able to raise his crops because of drought, flood, plant disease etc. Normal precautions only limit the losses but total avoidance is not possible.

3. **Risks from Human Behaviour**

Some uncertainties arise out of human elements, perhaps the major source of risks. In brief, they are :

(1) Dishonesty, carelessness, incompetence etc., of the employees cause risks in the business. Death of responsible officers is disastrous to the firm as a whole.

(2) Strikes, war, riots, theft, burglary etc., adversely affect the business.

(3) Loss from bad debts because of dishonesty of the customers is detrimental to business.

(4) A retailer/manufacturer may lose customers due to arrival of new products at lower prices, better service facilities, attractive terms etc.

(5) Legal liability under Workmen's Compensation Act.

(6) Changes in taxation policy of the Government or freight.

(7) Careless handling of materials will incur heavy loss.

Other Business Risks

(1) Price risks are difficult to avoid. In free and competitive market, prices always fluctuate.

(2) Credit sales will increase the sales; so also bad debts. To a certain extent bad debts can be avoided with the help of factors, del credere agents etc.

(3) Supply of raw materials must be regular to the producer. The irregularities in supply of materials will affect the production. This can be overcome by vertical combination.

(4) Consumer's preference always changes and is dynamic. Consumer's preference must be aimed at; otherwise produced goods cannot be sold. To overcome this, marketing research is a good guide.

(5) Commodities exposed to the open air may deteriorate and this will affect the quality of products. Air-tight packing and cold storage will preserve the loss of quality.

(6) Substitutes can divert the sales, thus leading to low sales. Device of branding and packages will solve this to some extent.

(7) The actions of the Government in the country and foreign countries affect the profitableness of a business. Price hikes of oil, petrol etc., levy of new taxes, imposition of tariffs etc., are examples.

(8) Physical losses that may happen due to fire, flood, storm, earthquake, burglary etc. can be avoided through insurance.

(9) Fluctuations in the rate of exchange may constitute losses in foreign trade. This risk can be avoided with the Forward exchange market.

(10) Market conditions greatly affect the sales. Over-stocking is profitable in rising market; but is fatal in falling market. One must possess the latest market news.

Methods of Handling the Risks

Marketing risks are common in day to day business; all precautions are to be adopted in protecting them against unforeseen risks. The businessmen find out means to eliminate the risks or at least minimise the effect of such risks. The risks occur by multiplicity of causes. There are business people, who undertake risks because of the belief ''larger the risk, greater the profit.'' A sensible businessman tries to minimise the risk, if losses are unavoidable.

The following methods are usually adopted :

(1) Prevention of risks

(2) Reduction of risks

(3) Shifting of risks

1. **Prevention of Risks :** "Prevention is better than cure." Preventive measures are designed to eliminate the risks or the causes of risks. It is not possible to find out a formula to avoid the risks completely, but to a great extent the risks can be reduced. The following steps are generally used in preventing the risks :

(a) Losses from theft, shop-lifting etc., can be minimised by giving effective training to the employees of the firm. Apart from this, Burglar alarms, watchmen, safety vaults etc., help to a great extent in preventing or avoiding the risks.

(b) Losses from bad debts can be prevented if creditableness of the party is known before granting credit. We can also get the help of factors and del credere agents.

(c) Loss from fire, weather change etc., can be completely avoided by constructing fire-proof building for stocking products.

(d) To avoid the non-availability of raw materials, it is advisable to adopt vertical integration, in which full control from the supply of raw materials to the distribution of final goods can be exercised.

(e) Loss from overstocking or understocking should be avoided by producing the products to meet the orders. Overstocking will block the capital and understocking will result in the loss of profits. This can be avoided in production to the orders.

(f) Reduced demand for the products can be regulated by effective sales-efforts through trade marks and brands. This will overcome the loss through bogus sales.

(g) To reduce the market risk, the pulse of the changes in the market has to be known at the proper time. The prices of the raw materials may be low or high in the future, and this information must be obtained from the market.

(h) The marketing risk is mainly due to price fluctuations, and the changes in demand and supply. These risks must be overcome by obtaining proper and accurate knowledge of the market by the management.

2. **Reduction of Risks :** Many risks are neither transferable nor avoidable. But market risks are reduced by the concentrated efforts of the marketers. In this modern period, it is difficult to predict the market conditions.

Suggestions to Overcome Loss

(a) Loss on sale on account of fashion change, improved products can be overcome by stock clearance sales at discount.

(b) Loss on account of market change may be minimised by market research.

(c) Innovations invite risks and at the same time changes may lead to progress. Business cannot progress without innovations. At the same time we are unable to forecast changes in the future which are beyond our control.

(d) Re-organisation of firms–amalgamation, conversion to company, etc.–greatly helps in improving the managerial ability, financial strength etc.

3. **Shifting of Risks :** Some types of risks involving loss can be shifted to other's shoulders. There are professional agencies which accept the risks as their responsibility.

(a) In the business world, there are many risks, uncertainties or losses. Generally business people are unwilling to bear such risks which create losses to the firm and so want to transfer them. Many natural risks or losses can be avoided through insurance. The importance of insurance of marketing lies in the fact that it helps in eliminating uncertainty. Insurance companies cover many risks for the payment of a sum, known as premium, for instance, Marine Insurance, Fire Insurance, Credit Insurance, Burglary Insurance etc. A businessman can easily transfer the risk to the insurer. Insurance is contract by which the assurer (insurance company) in consideration of the payment of a sum (premium), agrees to pay a specified sum of the insured on the happening of a certain event. The insurer undertakes to indemnify the assured for the loss on the happening of the event.

(b) The loss on account of price changes can be shifted through hedging by means of future contracts. The marketing risks, generally found in agricultural marketing, due to price changes are shifted effectively by entering into simultaneous contracts of sales and purchase at a future date. (A detailed study is made under chapter ''Organised Markets'').

(c) Government also plays its role. Government places tariff on imports of products and thereby, a demand for home products arises. Restriction on imports of goods is favourable to internal traders.

QUESTIONS

1. What are the causes of market risks ? Explain how they can be minimised.(*B.Com., Madurai*)
2. Explain the process of hedging. (*B.Com., Madurai*)
3. What are the economic risks associated with marketing ? (*B.Com., Madurai*)
4. Examine the nature of risks in marketing. (*B.Com., Madurai*)
5. Differentiate between time risk and place risk. (*B.Com., Mumbai*)
6. What are the methods through which risks may be avoided or minimised ?(*B.Com., Mumbai*)
7. What is marketing risk? What are the different types of marketing risks ? Explain their causes. (*B.Com., Madurai*)

CHAPTER 10

Marketing Information and Research

- *Information*
- *Marketing Information*
- *What is market Information*
- *Importance of Market Information*
- *Development of Marketing Information System*
- *Market Information System*
- *Requisites of Good MIS*
- *Benefits of MIS*
- *Characteristics of Good MIS*
- *Marketing Research*
- *What is Market Research?*
- *Market Research Vs. Marketing Research*
- *Marketing Research Vs. MIS*
- *Scope of Marketing Research*
- *Types of Marketing Research*
- *Objectives of Marketing Research*
- *Advantages of Marketing Research*
- *Marketing Research Process*
- *Types of Marketing Research*
- *Users of Marketing Research*
- *Method of Data Collection*
- *Gathering Primary Data*
- *Framing a Questionnaire*
- *Sampling*
- *Methods of Sampling*
- *A Good Sample*
- *Sources of Secondary Data*
- *Precautions of Secondary Data*
- *Primary Data Vs. Secondary Data*
- *Organistion of Marketing Research*
- *Limitation of Marketing Research*
- *Status of Marketing Research*
- *Contribution of Marketing Research*
- *Marketing Research in India*
- *Case Study-1*
- *Case Study-2*
- *Case Study-3*
- *Questions*

INFORMATION – (The basis of effective marketing)

Marketing managers spend much of their time in making decisions. An integral aspect of decision making is the analysis and evaluation of information. Timely information improves decision making. To be effective, the marketer needs to gather enough information to understand past events, to identify that is occurring now, and to predict what might occur in the future. Good marketing information is an extremely valuable management tool because it reduces uncertainty and the risks associated with decision making. Marketing information can lead the marketing manager to new products, to improvement of existing products, and to changes in price, promotion or distribution strategies and tactics. Information can also help to define problems or identify opportunities. Once a marketing problem or opportunity is identified, systematically gathering further pertinent information helps the marketing manager to deal objectively with the situation.

Marketing information is generated in many ways. Besides surveys and laboratory research, marketers can use internal records, government and trade association figures, and trials run in test markets, as well as other valuable information sources. Whatever the source, systematically gathered information reduces uncertainty and improves the quality of the decision-making process. Too often intuitive decisions based on personal experience and made with the benefit of research-based information lead to costly mistakes.

MARKETING INFORMATION

Marketing, an economic activity, which is as old as civilisation, is vital for the economic well-being of modern society. Although mass marketing was accepted by the Industrial Revolution, research in general and marketing research, as we know it today, were not considered important elements of the marketing mix until firms accepted the fact that marketing begins and ends with consumers. Consumer satisfaction is the key element for the success or failure of a firm. Business and product failure are the most common problems that face entrepreneurs. Now-a-days, the marketing manager is charged with the responsibility of decision making in various fields connected with the marketing of goods and services. Market research is conducted by manufacturers, middlemen and consumers, who are largely affected by marketing problems. Some firms use the term 'market research' instead of 'marketing research.' 'Market' means effective demand or potential buyers. The term "market research" is loosely used as synonymous with "marketing research". Market research is an intelligent investigation or study of the potential buyers. It deals with research on customer demand–behaviour and attitude of buyers and dealers, share of a product in the market etc. Marketing research has a wider meaning and scope. Marketing research involved a study of all those factors which have a direct impact upon the marketing of products and services. To understand the scope of marketing research, basic knowledge is needed about the activities included in the modern marketing concept. First, define what is marketing? Marketing is defined as including all the activities which involve providing potential consumers with goods and services to satisfy their demand. Research is the process of gathering, recording and analysing of critical and relevant facts about any problem in any branch of human activity. It is a method of clarifying and rationalising decisions, by replacing guesswork with facts and additional knowledge.

In earlier days, producers or salesmen went out, met the people and tried to sell the products. But now the times have changed. Mass production is followed by mass distribution campaign through a study and awareness of market conditions, competitions, consumer's taste and desire etc. Production-oriented stage had been replaced by consumer-oriented stage, in which consumers have been given importance as to their taste, likings, demand etc. The expansion of market and severe competition have necessitated the study of the consumers and their behaviour. The goods, produced or purchased for the customers, are in anticipation of demand. Thus, it has become essential for the marketer to depend upon the knowledge of the customers' demand for his products. A modern producer or manufacturer must study the market by collecting information or do research in order to decide as to what the customers need. The consumer is the pivot around which the marketing operations revolve, and to satisfy the customers' desire is important. To get success in the market, the marketer has to supply the right type of goods, at the right time, at the right place. He must take proper decisions through facts and figures. Thus, a marketer, to avoid sales risk, must possess correct information on:

1. What type of goods are needed by the customers ?
2. Where are the customers located ?
3. What is the customers' expectation of product feature ?
4. In what quantity the products are needed ?
5. Are there any special considerations on the product by the customers ?
6. The degree of competition existing in the market.
7. Why do they want the product ?
8. What is the size of the market (big, small etc.) ?
9. How can the products be made available to the customers ?
10. What are the purchasing powers of the customers ?

To get success in the field of marketing, a marketer must have knowledge pertainting to the above questions. Lack of knowledge will be a hurdle in the field of marketing.

What is Market Information ?

To perform the complex task of marketing, the marketer needs many pieces of information as a basis, for drawing marketing decisions. Market information, as a basis, is of great importance to the management of firms. Market information includes all facts, estimates, opinions, etc., considered in making decisions which affect the marketing of goods. Market information is an important feature of marketing. In drawing and formulating policies and directing the marketing activities, a marketing executive must have adequate information about the firm and the market regarding the products of the firm. The ability of the marketing executive is vital for success in marketing operations. He must be able to evaluate the uptodate information pertainting to:

1. The customers' expectation regarding the product.
2. The degree of competition to be faced.
3. Government policies.
4. Channel of distribution.
5. Defects of rival products.
6. Buying motives of the customers.
7. Supply, demand and price of similar products.
8. Size of the market to be covered.
9. Customers' opinion about the product–size, shape, type etc.
10. Satisfactory inflow of information.

The market information really helps a producer to retain, create and expand the market for his products. Information is needed relating to current and future market for the products. A business-man has to take decisions often. He can take wise decisions to tackle the situations effectively, only when he possesses the relevant information. For a company to operate successfully, the management must develop an orderly method for gathering and analysing the mass of information which is available and relevant to the firm. As mentioned earlier, market information includes all facts, estimates, opinions etc., taken into account in making decisions that affect the marketing of the goods and services.

When any problem has been known or understood, the foremost function is the collection of information relevant to the problem. After the collection of information, it must be communicated to those who need it. Then the available data must be wisely interpreted in terms of the problem to be solved. This is the objective and motive of collection of information.

Importance of Market Information

1. Successful marketing of the products greatly depends upon "sound knowledge of the market." This facilitates a marketer to create an expansion of market for the products. Marketing information is the life blood of marketing, along with other resources–capital, land, machinery, man-power etc., on equal footing.

2. Risk bearing can be minimised by collecting timely information. When the collection and interpretation of information collected are perfect, an accurate forecast can be made easily.

3. Mass productions followed by mass distributions are based on consumer-demand in anticipation. Up to date information is needed under consumer-oriented marketing approach. Changes are constant as far as the consumers are concerned; changes are often witnessed according to the consumer's taste, behaviour , fashion, likings etc. A marketer must have details of facts and figures relating to customers to get a desired result in the stage of competition.

4. Technical progress and innovations appear quite often. A marketer, who knows the development of the market, can attain success in the field of marketing. All types of progress, new products, new development etc., are based on information of facts and figures.

5. The marketing information is a major tool, to be used by the management in solving problems relating to marketing and taking decisions.

Development of MIS

All aspects of information including its collection, storage, processing, retrieval and use must be managed. The marketing oriented firm needs a system developed to the management of the entire information needs of the organisation. Such a system is called MIS of which research is a component part. The marketing environment is changing at an accelerating rate. Given the following changes, the need for marketing information is greater than any time.

1. **From buyer needs to buyer wants:** As income improves, buyers become more sensitive in their choice of goods. To predict buyers' response to different features, styles, and other attributes, the sellers must turn to marketing research.

2. **From local to global market:** As company expands their geographical market coverage, their managers needs more information more quickly to facilitate decision-making.

3. **From price to non-price competition:** As sellers increase branding, product differentiation, advertising and sales promotion, information on these marketing tools and techniques.

Therefore, the companies now extensively use MIS. Philip Kotler defines MIS as "consists of people, equipment and procedures to gather, sort, analyse, evaluate, and distribute needed, timely, and accurate information to marketing decision makers."

Marketing Information System (MIS)

Collection of information is a basis to make decisions. Information collected unsystematically and unscientifically is irrelevant in making decisions. The marketing managers need many pieces of information to carry out the marketing responsibilities. There are occasions when the information is not available or available lately or untrusted or found even improper. Therefore many firms adopt method to improve the situations. Marketing information system is one, but means as a set of procedures and methods for the regular, planned collection, analysis and presentation of information for the use in marketing decisions. Philip Kotler says, "A marketing information system is a continuing and interacting structure of people, equipments, and procedures to gather, sort, analyse, evaluate, and distribute pertinent, timely and accurate information for use by marketing decision makers to improve their marketing planning, execution, and control."

Essential Requisites of a Good MIS

The main purpose of marketing information system is to gather co-ordinated, systematic and continuous flow of relevant information. Marketing information system (MIS) is an organised set of procedures and routine. In brief, the requirements for a MIS are:

1. MIS makes available only the required information and is less time-consuming in making decisions.
2. It is a system which excludes unwanted marketing information, thus saving the time of decision-makers.
3. The operation and design of the system is handled by specialists, who gather information and deal with it to meet the desired objectives.
4. To the top executives, MIS provides fast and accurate marketing information.
5. It facilitates in taking suitable and quick decisions promptly.
6. It is a unified system.
7. It adopts the principle of selectivity in information.
8. It is economical.
9. It is conceived and used as a marketing decision support system.
10. It is an ongoing process. It operates continuously.

Benefits of MIS

The various benefits that flow from market information are listed below:

1. It helps marketing planning by making available correct information on the external environment and the internal company realities.
2. The information if free from any bias towards the pre-conceived conclusion will have more value than otherwise.
3. The information if free from any error will have more value than otherwise.
4. The quality of marketing decisions are decided to a great extend by the quality of marketing information available to the decision maker.
5. It facilitates the development of action programmes for achieving set goals.
6. It helps the controlling of marketing activities.
7. It helps effective tapping of marketing opportunities and effective defence against marketing threats.
8. It helps the firm to adjust its product and services to the needs and tests of customers.
9. It provides market intelligence to the firm.
10 It helps rapid spotting of trends and facilitates the formulation of basic assumptions on economic and business conditions.

Characteristics of Good MIS

1. Relevance (to decision making)
2. Accuracy
3. Completeness
4. Precision
5. Cost reasonableness.
6. Timeliness
7. Confidentiality
8. Clarity
9. Unbiasedness
10. Authenticity
11. Reliability
12. Strategic value

Marketing Research

Marketing research is defined as, "The systematic, objective and exhaustive search for the study of the facts relevant to any problem in the field of marketing." Marketing research may be described as a method of getting facts to be used by the executive in formulating policies and plans. It can also be defined as the systematic gathering, recording and analysing of data about problems relating to marketing of goods and services. It is a systematic search for information. It involves data collection, analysis and interpretation. Research cannot draw decisions, but it helps the marketers in the task of decision making. A successful executive will never depend upon guess work. He looks for more accurate information through research. The main idea of marketing research is to know more about the consumers, dealers, and the products. As the business grows, the distance between the manufacturer and consumers also widens. The management depends upon the marketing research as a tool in solving the marketing problems. It helps in taking a fruitful and efficient decision as to the flow of goods and services in the hands of the customers.

What is Market Research ?

The market research is an important element of the process of marketing research. Marketing research includes the complete analysis of the market. Information regarding the nature, size, organisation profitability of different markets, changes in markets and various factors – economic, social and political – effecting those changes are studied vigorously. The main purpose of market research is to know about the consumers and the markets of its products or services. It is a technique to know:

* Who are customers of our products or services ?
* Where do they live ?
* When and how do they buy the product and services ?
* Are customers of our products satisfied with the products ?
* Who are our main competitors in the market ?
* Are the company's products inferior or superior to competitors' products ?
* What policies and strategies are they following ?

In order to know the answer to such questions, market research is conducted so that the marketer may come to know the shortcomings in his product or policies and strategies and can make the improvement to make them effective in the best interest of the consumers and thus to increase the profitability of the concern.

Market research is a branch of marketing research and covers only a few aspects of marketing. It is only a sub-function of marketing research. It is concerned with the investigation and measurement of market demand.

Market Research and Marketing Research

Market research is about determining the characteristics of a market, for example in terms of its size, requirements, growth rate, market segments, and competitor positioning.

Marketing research is broader and is about researching the whole of a company's marketing activities. In most organisations, such research would probably include monitoring the effectiveness of its advertising, intermediaries and pricing position.

Research gets the facts needed to solve a problem. "*Research looks forward to see what industry may do when it can no longer do what it is doing*." Research is the process of gathering, recording and analysing of critical and relevant facts with regard to any problem in any branch of human activity. We have seen that marketing basically consists of spotting the needs of customers and meeting them in the best possible manner. Marketing research plays a key role in this process. Starting with market measurement, marketing research helps the firm in every component of the total marketing task. It helps the firm acquire a better understanding of the consumer, the competition and the marketing environment. It also aids the formulation of the marketing mix. Decisions on each element of the marketing mix, need marketing research support. A few definitions are given below:

Marketing research "is a systematic objective and exhaustive search for and study of the facts relevant to any problem in the field of marketing."

Marketing research is "that part of business research that studies the transfer and sale of goods and services. It may includes study of their physical distribution, wholesale and retail merchandising and financial problems. The real function of marketing research is to help the manufacturer or the producer to increase his sale." — Mitchell

"Marketing research" may be defined as, "the systematic gathering, recording and analysing of data about problems relating to the marketing of goods and services under essentially non-recurring conditions." — Ronald

''Marketing research is a part of the marketing information system, and a key to the implementation of the marketing concept. It is usually designed to aid planning and often involves evaluation of previous marketing efforts.'' — Frederick

''Marketing research is concerned with getting the best possible answer to certain major questions of business, namely, what to produce or handle, when and how much to produce, where to place the product over the market, where to direct sales effort, and what price to charge.''

According to the Report of the Committee on Definitions (USA), ''Marketing Research is the inclusive term which embraces all research activities carried on in connection with management of marketing work. Among other things, marketing research involves the study of the relationship and adjustments between production and consumption, preparation of commodities for sale, their physical distribution, wholesale and retail merchandising, and financial problems concerned. Such research may be undertaken by impartial agencies or by specific concerns to their agents for the solution of their marketing problems. It includes various subsidiary types of research such as Market Analysis, Sales Research, Consumer Research, Advertising Research."

According to Giles, ''Market research applied to a study of the market, while investigations into sales methods and terms of trade, advertising reaction, design, packaging acceptability and the effectiveness of sales promotions are perhaps more accurately describes as "Marketing Research".

Marketing research is defined as the systematic gathering, recording and analysing of data about marketing problems towards the end of providing information useful in marketing decision-making. It helps in solving problems. It is used in wider scope and greater importance and includes market research, as it is only a part of marketing research. In other words, market research is only a sub-function of marketing research. Market research is solely concerned with the collection of information about the market. In modern method of marketing, it is necessary for a producer or manufacturer to possess exact and accurate information relating to :

1. The type of goods needed by customers.
2. The time when they want the products.
3. The means of transport.
4. The rival products available in market.
5. Competitions if any.
6. The quantity wanted.
7. The actual buyers.
8. The reason for requiring a particular product.
9. The size of the market.
10. The price acceptable by the buyers.

Differences between Marketing Research and Marketing Information System

MR	MIS
1. It is concerned with solving problems only.	1. It is concerned with preventing complaints and solving problems.
2. It operates on specific problems.	2. It is a continuous process.
3. Its emphasis is on handling external information.	3. It handles both internal and external information.
4. Focus is on past information.	4. It tends to be future-oriented.
5. It is pertaining to a particular field of activity.	5. It suggests solution to problems for the whole organisation.

Scope of Marketing Research

Clark and clark define marketing research as "The careful and objective study of product design, markets and such transfer activities as physical distribution, warehousing, advertising and sales management. Thus the scope of marketing research lies in its variety of applications.

1. Diagnosing the current situation or problem based on detailed information.
2. Clearly identifying competitive strengths and weaknesses.
3. Constantly analysing what is happening in the market-place.
4. Planning to watch company's strengths with market opportunities by outlining objectives for product and market development and devising strategies and tactics to achieve them.
5. Watching out continuously for threats to the achievement of those plans.
6. Monitoring the progress of strategy implementation.
7. Research creativity, at its best, marketing research develops innovative ways to solve problems.

The main objective of marketing research is to enable manufacturers to make goods acceptable and saleable and to see that they reach the market more easily, quickly, cheaply and profitably without sacrificing consumer interest.

What Marketing Research can do for business ?

There are six faithful service-men at the disposal of Market Researchers.

1.	What ?	What is the product ?	Product Research.
2.	Who ?	Who are the buyers ?	Consumer Research.
3.	Why ?	Why do they buy?	Motivation Research.
4.	How ?	How do they buy ?	Research in buying
5.	When ?	When do they buy ?	habits and channels
6.	Where ?	Where do they buy ?	of distribution.

Scope of Market Research

Market research covers the following items of study :

1. Size of the present and potential market.
2. Consumer needs, wants, habits and behaviour.
3. Dealer wants and preferences.
4. Analysis of the market size according to age, sex, income, profession, standard of living etc.
5. Geographic location of customers.
6. Analysis of market demand.
7. Knowledge of competitors and their products.
8. Knowing the profitability of different markets.
9. Study the market changes and market conditions.
10. Analysis of various channels of distributions.

Objectives of Marketing Research

1. To understand the economic factors affecting the sales volume and their opportunities.
2. To understand the competitive position of rival products.
3. To evaluate the reactions of consumers and customers.
4. To study the price trends.
5. To evaluate the system of distribution.
6. To understand the advantages and limitations of the products.

7. To find new methods of packaging, by comparing other similar packages.
8. To analyse the market size.
9. To know the estimation of demand.
10. To evaluate the profitability of different markets.
11. To study the customer's acceptance of products.
12. To assess the volume of future sales.
13. To study the nature of the market, its location and its potentialities.
14. To find solutions to problems relating to marketing of goods and services.
15. To evaluate policies and plans in the right course of action.
16. To know the development of science and technology.
17. To know the complexity of marketing.
18. To measure the effectiveness of advertising.
19. To estimate the potential market for a new product.
20. To assess the strength and weakness of the competitors.

Advantages of Marketing Research

Marketing research has several advantages. They are :

1. Marketing research is used to measure market potential, characteristics and share of markets for a company.
2. Companies can use marketing research to evaluate new product opportunities and product acceptance and to test existing products relative to the competitor's products.
3. It helps to make better advertising decisions.
4. It helps to evaluate the effectiveness of marketing activities and draws attention to a potential problem.
5. It helps the manufacturer to adjust his productions according to the conditions of demand.
6. It helps marketing of goods in efficient and economical way by eliminating all types of wastage.
7. It helps a dealer to find out the best way of approaching potential buyers.
8. It helps to find out defects in the products and take corrective steps to improve the product.
9. It guides a dealer in planning advertising and promotion effort.
10. It helps to assess the effectiveness of advertising programmes.
11. It helps in evaluating the relative efficiency of different advertising media.
12. It facilitates to evaluate the selling methods.
13. It helps to minimise the risks of uncertainities.
14. It helps in exploring new markets for its products.
15. It guides a firm in making sales forecasts for products.
16. It helps to explore new uses of existing products.
17. It is quite helpful for a firm to launch a new product.
18. It helps the firm in knowing general conditions prevailing in the market.
19. It helps in determining pricing policies and pricing strategy of competitors.
20. It reveals the causes of consumer resistance etc.

Major areas for marketing research identified by the management are:-

1. Research on Markets

This includes market trends, market share and market potential. It is a study of the size, location, nature and characteristics of markets; and market is segmented on the basis of many variables–age, sex, income, education, occupation, religion etc. In short, it can be restricted to the study of ''who, what, where, when, why and how'' of actual and potential buyers.

2. Research on Sales

It covers sales forecasting, quota selling, sales territory design and other sales related activities. It analyses sales volume, salesman performance data, new product performance in test markets, opinion on customer-related product data etc.

3. Research on Product

It involves new product development, brand image, concept tests, product tests, test marketing of new product etc. It analyses the strength and weakness of present products in relation to diversification, simplification etc.

4. Advertising and Promotion Research

It includes media research, copy research, merchandising, packaging and measuring and effectiveness of various methods of advertising and promotion.

5. Corporate Growth Research

It emphasizes the studies on economic and technological forecasting, measuring company image, profitability measurement, merger, acquisitions, location etc.

6. Business Economic Research

It is concerned with economic forecasting and business trend analysis. Planning and product mix, price and profit analysis etc. are included.

Types of Marketing Research

There are different types of marketing research depending on the objectives that the research is designed to achieve and the sources of data which are to be used. Marketing research may also be either qualitative or quantitative depending on the form of data generated and the degree of mathematical accuracy level to which it is subjected. The most widely used category of marketing research is based on the functional objective of investigation. Marketing research can be defined as :

1. Exploratory
2. Descriptive
3. Casual, and
4. Predictive.

(1) **Exploratory Research**

Exploratory research gives valuable insight, generates ideas and hypotheses rather than measuring or testing them. ''Exploratory research is concerned with identifying the real nature of research problems and perhaps of formulating relevant hypotheses for various tests''. Crimp stated that the researcher undertakes exploratory research in order to generate an adequate basis for designing research and it includes searching for data that are already available both within the company and from external sources, consulting experts, conducting observational studies, getting feedback from market place and surveys.

A marketing researcher uses this type of research when very little is known about the problem being examined. The major benefit is that it is less expensive and less time consuming. For example, if a researcher is interested in finding out ''Which features or factors are vital in a purchase decision ? and ''What will be the best mode of communication to reach the consumers ? For all these purposes, exploratory research gives an insight into the problem.

(2) **Descriptive Research**

Descriptive research is concerned with measuring and estimating the frequencies with which things occur or the degree of correlation or association between various variables. It has been seen that market research reports are often descriptive and they measure market size, market structure, and the behaviour and attitudes of consumers in the market place. In general as the data obtained by descriptive research is put to various statistical analysis, it is very necessary to make a list of the variables to be investigated and how these variables will be measured.

(3) **Casual Research**

Casual research is basically concerned with establishing cause and effect relationship and an attempt to explain why things happen. For example, to what extent the price elasticity of demand or the degree to which advertising campaigns have affected the sales may be explained by casual research. However, there are two important aspects of casual research : (i) necessary condition and (ii) sufficient condition which should be kept in mind.

An event may be considered as the cause of another event, if its occurrence is the necessary and sufficient condition for the latter event to take place. A necessary condition means that the caused events cannot occur in the absence of the causative event. A sufficient condition means that the causative event is all that is needed to bring about the caused event.

(4) **Predictive Research**

The main purpose of predictive research is to arrive at a forecast or prediction or some measurement of interest to the researcher. The ultimate target may be the future sales level of the firm. Other goals of predictive research may involve industry sales level, projection or growth or defining of firm's product line and the use of a test market to predict the likely success of a new product.

Users of Marketing Reserach

Marketing research highlights issues and problems relating to marketing and consequently helps to solve many problems of marketing. It is an effective aid in implementing marketing concepts by obtaining information that identifies the consumers' problems and needs. The major users are :

(1) **Consumers :**

It goes without saying that, in any competitive environment, consumer is the King. In the final analysis, all sales proceeds flow from consumers. Therefore, knowledge of consumer behaviour of a target market is a must for every business concern. Marketing research locates the consumer requirements of goods and services and the factors upon which they depend.

(2) **Market Intermediaries :**

Market intermediaries are an integral link between the producers and the final buyers. Selling a product requires a channel for bringing it to the market and distributing it to the final buyers. Marketing research helps a manufacturer to select a right kind of channel.

(3) **Business Firms :**

Every business concern is interested in improving its position in the market by (i) increasing its market share, and (ii) increasing its profitability. In these cases, marketing research is essential and highly useful tool that is used while taking a decision.

(4) **Marketing research agencies :**

There are numerous specialised agencies engaged in conducting marketing research covering different segments of markets, both actual and potential. They have experts for conducting specialised research. These research agencies can be assigned the relevant projects, by the parties concerned. On the basis of their findings, they prepare research reports of their clients.

(5) **Government :**

Research in various areas is also done by Government. For example; Price indices, per capita income etc.

(6) **Producers :**

A competitive market is flooded with new products, new brands and new substitutes almost everyday. The thread of cut-throat competition is always there. He finds that the strategies that worked in the past but are not longer workable. Here, MR helps in the analysis of the situations.

Procedure of Marketing Research

Marketing manager has to do many jobs, but he is not expected to be a qualified researcher. He is the user of the findings of the marketing research, but he is not a researcher. At the same time, he should know the marketing research procedure. To understand the marketing problem in a better way, one must aim at marketing research through which solutions against problems can be had. The design and implementation of the marketing research project greatly depend upon the skill of the researcher. The exact procedure cannot be laid down for marketing research, as the procedure may change from firm to firm and from situation to situation. The following is the procedure generally followed in handling marketing problems through marketing research :

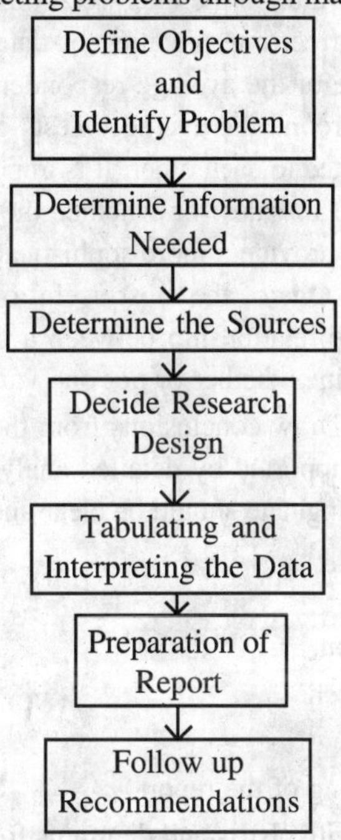

The Marketing Research Process

1. **Defining the Problem:** In order to carry out the research programme, the researcher should know the basic problem. He must be clear in mind as to what is exactly needed. The basic problem, *i.e.*, marketing problem is given importance and not the marketing research problem. A competent researcher will not accept a research project, until he understands the problem clearly. Thus crystallising the marketing problem is fundamental.

After identifying the problem, the researcher formulates a plan when the problem is defined. The purpose of the project determines the nature of the problem and the ways to solve it. When the researcher gets a clear idea of the problem, he analyses the situation and understands more about the problem. He analyses the company, its markets, its competition etc. The informal investigation or preliminary exploration consists of getting background information relating to the problem.

2. **Determining the Information Needed:** The researcher must consider the information and decide which is relevant and which is irrelevant to the study. In determining the kind of information needed, the objectives of the research must be borne in mind. The information should be necessary and relevant. If the available data are insufficient, fresh data have to be collected.

3. **Determining the Source of Information:** The Source of information may be classified into primary source and secondary source. When the information is obtained directly, specially for the problem, it is known as primary data. When the information is already collected by someone for some other purpose, and at the same time is helpful to the problem on hand, it is known as secondary data (see collection of data).

4. **Deciding Research Methods:** When secondary data are insufficient, the researcher has to be satisfied with the primary sources of data. The sources may be by experimental method, observation method or survey method (dealt separately in this chapter).

5. **Tabulation, Analysis and Interpretation of the Data:** After the collection of data, they are to be classified and tabulated into statistical summarisation. They may be in percentage, average, ratios etc., so as to give the greatest value in the interpretation work. Interpretation is the important stage in the process of research. Correct interpretation of data makes a research meaningful. The mean or median classifies the nature of the average respondent, and the standard deviation shows how far respondents are dispersed around the average. Tests of significance are useful in measuring whether two occurrences are related to each other. It is important, for example, to know whether a price decrease caused an increase in sales, or whether the two events just happened simultaneously. Correlation and association provide a more sophisticated method of making the same kind of analysis done in cross tabulation. One of the most useful of these is regression analysis, which allows the researcher to estimate the relationship between a dependent variable and one or more independent variables and to determine whether or not one variable causes another.

6. **Preparation of the Report:** Draw conclusions from the tabulated summaries. Conclusions, recommendations and suggestions supported by detailed analysis of findings, must be in a written form–report of the researcher. The language should be clear and properly paragraphed. Generally, a report may be in the following form :

1. Title of research.
2. The name of the organisation.
3. The objectives of the research.
4. The methodology used.
5. Organisation and the planning of the report.
6. A table of contents, along with charts and diagrams followed in the report.
7. The main report.
8. Conclusions drawn and recommendations suggested.
9. Appendices.

7. **Follow up study :** Follow up will ensure the implementation of recommendations made by the marketing researchers. Otherwise, the report may be left unopened.

Methods of Data Collection

There are two sources of data for investigation :

(1) Internal sources, and (2) External sources.

The internal sources mean and include a company's profit and loss account, balance sheet, sales figures, sales reports, inventory records, registers, documents etc. A proper analysis of these records, will reveal the degree of efficiency of the business. The collection of information from internal sources, is inexpensive. When information cannot be collected from the internal sources, or when available information is irrelevant and insufficient, then one will have to depend upon the external resources–facts collected from outside the company.

Other sources of information are : (1) Primary data, and (2) Secondary data.

Primary Data : Primary data are those which are collected for the first time and they are original in character. These are collected by the researcher himself to study a particular problem.

Secondary Data : The secondary data are those which are already collected by someone for some purpose and are available for the present study. For instance, the data collected during census operations are primary data to the department of census and the same data, if used by a research worker for some study, are secondary data.

Methods of Gathering Primary Data

The following are the methods adopted to obtain primary data:

(1) Experimental method

(2) Observation method

(3) Survey method

1. **Experimental Method**

"This method of gathering primary data involves the establishment of a scale model or a controlled experiment which stimulates the real market situation as much as possible. The theory is that the small-scale experiment will furnish valuable information in designing a large-scale marketing programme." Under this experimental approach, the producer carries out a small-scale experiment, tries to get valuable information, which can be of great help in designing large-scale marketing programme. This is a method intended to evaluate the effect of a proposed course of action. It seeks to find the buyer-reaction and can successfully apply it in several cases. For instance, a soap manufacturer gives different colours to the soaps–white in Kerala, green in Tamil Nadu and pink in Karnataka; except for the colour all the other factors are the same. Now the marketing manager records the sales over a period of time and decides the colour of the soap, in terms of highest percentage of sales. This method includes test marketing, *i.e.*, testing sales, promotion campaigns, fixing right price, products, packages, design etc.

Merits

1. This method is more realistic and gives best results.
2. This approach is more effective and profitable.
3. Relative efficiency can be measured.
4. It gives room to improve future research techniques.

Demerits

1. This method is expensive.
2. It takes a long time to get the results.
3. Careful planning is needed.
4. The test markets selected for the experiments must possess the same characteristics, which is difficult.

2. **Observation Method**

In Observation method, the data are collected by observing some action of the respondent. No questions are asked in data collection. No interview is made. The actions or behaviour of the customers are watched personally or mechanically. Buyers may be observed personally by the observer while making purchases. The observer or researcher poses as a customer, and observes the marketing situations. A buyer is unaware that he is being observed and acts in his usual way. The observer, posing as a customer, knows the ability of salesmen and the brand that is being pushed through and also the motivating factors of the purchasers.

Merits

1. It is more accurate.
2. Interviewer's bias is reduced.
3. Inaccuracies in answering questions are eliminated.
4. Actual market behaviour is recorded.
5. It is possible to get additional data.

Demerits

1. The method is expensive.
2. The field observer's bias may creep in.
3. It consumes more time.
4. It tells "what happened," but fails to tell "why it happened."
5. This method is less flexible.

3. **Survey Method**

A survey consists of gathering data by interviewing a limited number of people (a sample) selected from a larger group. A survey has the advantage of getting to the original source of information. In this method, the researcher obtains information from the respondents by interviewing them. This is the most common method of getting primary data. This method is more effective than the experimental and observation approach.

In the factual survey, respondents are asked to report actual facts, as exemplified by questions such as: What brand of cigar do you smoke? How many persons live in your house? Opinion survey, is designed to gather expressions of personal opinions, to record evaluations of different things or to report thinking on particular matters. For instance : How do you feel about this new cordless electric shaver? In the interpretative survey the respondent acts as an interpreter as well as a reporter. Interpretative data are gathered by using such questions as: Why do you use brand 'A' of the product in your house? What feature of the new pack of this product appeals to you most?

The survey can also be conducted in two ways: sampling survey and census survey. Under census survey, the marketer conducts surveys covering the entire market. The data are collected from each and every person in the market. But under sampling survey, only a part of the whole group will be studied. We may study a sample drawn from the large group and if the sample is adequately representative of the group, we should be able to arrive at valid conclusions. As such, sampling survey is widely accepted. Data collection under the survey method is of three types (A) Personal interview, (B) Main questionnaire, and (C) Telephone interview.

(A) **Personal Interview Method**

Under this method, the enumerator makes personal contacts with the informant and obtains more information than under any other method. The researcher can clarify the questions, if they are not understood by the informant. This is of two types:

(a) **Direct Personal Observation :** Under this method, the data are collected by the investigator personally. The investigator must be a keen observer, tactful and courteous in behaviour. He asks or cross-examines the informant and collects necessary information, which is original in character.

This method is adopted in the following cases:

(1) Where greater accuracy is needed.
(2) Where the field of enquiry is not large.
(3) Where confidential data are to be collected.
(4) Where the field is a complex one.
(5) Where intensive study is needed.
(6) Where sufficient time is available.

Merits

1. Original (first hand information) data are collected.
2. True and reliable data can be had.
3. Response will be more encouraging, because of personal approach.
4. A high degree of accuracy can be aimed.
5. The investigator can extract current information.
6. Misinterpretations, if any, on the part of the informant can be avoided.
7. Uniformity and homogeneity can be maintained.

Demerits

1. It is unsuitable where the area is large.
2. It is expensive and time-consuming.
3. The chances of bias are more.
4. An untrained investigator will not bring good result.
5. One has to collect information according to the convenience of the informant.

(b) **Indirect Oral Interview :** When the informant is reluctant to supply information, the method of indirect oral investigation can be followed. Under this method the investigator approaches witnesses or third parties, who are in touch with the informant. The enumerator interviews the people, who are directly or indirectly connected with the problem under study. For instance, we are asked to collect information relating to the gambling or drinking habits of people. In such cases, the informants will be reluctant to supply information relating to their own socially evil habits. On such occasions, we may approach the dealer of liquor shops, friends, neighbours etc., to get the needed information. Generally this method is employed by different enquiry committees and commissions. The police department generally adopts this method to get clues of thefts, riots, murders etc. The police interrogate third parties who possess knowledge about the happenings under study.

Suitability

This system is more suitable, where the area to be studied is large. It is adopted when direct information cannot be obtained. This system is generally adopted by governments.

Merits

1. It is simple and convenient.
2. It saves time, money and labour.
3. It can be followed in the investigation of a large area.
4. The information is unbiased.
5. Adequate information can be had.
6. As the information is collected from different parties, a true account can be expected and all aspects of the problem can be ascertained.

Demerits

1. Absence of direct contact is there; the information cannot be fully relied upon.
2. Interview with an improper man will spoil the results.
3. In order to get the real position, a sufficient number of persons are to be interviewed.
4. The careless attitude of the informant will affect the degree of accuracy.
5. Informants may colour the information according to their interests.

The researcher prepares a list of questions in the form of a questionnaire and either hands over the questionnaire to the informant, who fills the questionnaire or asks questions from the questionnaire and notes down the replies himself.

(B) The Mail Questionnaire Method

In this method, a questionnaire consisting of a list of questions pertainting to the survey is prepared. There are blank spaces for answers. This questionnaire is sent to the respondents, who are expected to write the answers in the blank spaces. A covering letter is also sent along with the questionnaire, requesting the respondents to extend their full co-operation by giving the correct replies and returning the questionnaire duly filled in time. To get quick and better response, the return postage expense is borne by the investigator, by sending a self-addressed and stamped envelope. This method is adopted by research workers, private individuals, non-official agencies and State and Central Governments.

Merits

1. Of all the methods, the mailed questionnaire method is the most economical.
2. It can be widely used, when the area of investigation is large.
3. It saves money, labour and time.
4. Error in the investigation is small because information is obtained directly from respondents.
5. It eliminates the danger of the bias by the interviewer.

Demerits

1. In this method, there is no direct contact between the investigator and the respondent. Therefore we cannot be sure about the accuracy and reliability of the data.
2. This method is suitable only for literate people. In many countries, there are illiterates who cannot understand and reply the questionnaire.
3. Generally there is long delay in receiving questionnaires duly filled in.
4. People may not give the correct answer and this leads to false conclusion.
5. The questionnaire is inelastic. Asking supplementary question is not possible.
6. Sometimes the informant may not be willing to give written answers, apart from causing delay.

Framing a Questionnaire

The questionnaire is the medium of communication between the investigator and the respondents. The success of an investigation depends on the framing of the questionnaire. As such, utmost care and caution are essential for designing or drafting the questionnaire. In addition, it requires skill, wisdom, efficiency and experience. There are no hard and fast rules to be followed, but the following general points may be borne in mind:

1. The Questionnaire should be brief.
2. The questions should be simple to understand.
3. The questions should be arranged logically.
4. There must be choice (simple alternative, multiple choice etc.)
5. Ask only what we want to know.
6. All questions should be numbered serially.
7. Proper words should be used in the questionnaire.
8. Necessary instructions should be given to the informant.
9. The questions should be capable of an objective answer.
10. A questionnaire should look attractive.
11. Avoid ambiguous questions.
12. The accuracy of the questionnaire must be judged.

(C) Telephone Survey

This type of survey is conducted over the telephone and resembles personal interview. Where the respondents are scattered in distant areas and where the telephone communication is advanced, the researcher can contact the informant to obtain information.

Merits

1. The cost is less.
2. It is quick in getting data.
3. This is most simple in collecting data.
4. It is flexible.
5. It gives accurate answer.
6. It saves time and travel of the researcher.

Demerits

1. Persons who have no phone connection are omitted.
2. Personal bias may creep in.
3. Lower income group respondents are not covered.
4. The interview will be of short duration.

Sampling

Only a part of the whole group population will be studied in the case of sample enquiry. According to Croxton and Cowdon, "It may be too expensive or too time-consuming to attempt either a complete or a nearly complete coverage in a statistical study. Further to arrive at valid conclusions, it may not be necessary to enumerate all or nearly all of a population. We may study a sample drawn from the large population and, if that sample is adequately representative of the population, we should be able to arrive at valid conclusions." The results obtained from sample study can be applied to the whole universe or population. We can study the characteristics of the population or universe from the sampling. A study of a sample will give a correct idea of the universe or population.

A truck load of product is accepted or rejected on the evidence gained from testing only a few items. A physician makes inferences about a patient's blood through the examination of a single drop. Samples are devices for learning about large masses by observing a few individuals.

Merits

1. It saves time because fewer items are studied.
2. It reduces cost also.
3. Where the population is infinite, only sampling method is possible.
4. Degree of accuracy is higher than that in census method.
5. It is more scientific.

Methods of Sampling

There are many methods of sampling. The choice of method will be determined on the purpose of sampling. The various methods can be grouped under two heads :

1. Random Sampling method (Probability samples).
    - (a) Simple or unrestricted random sampling.
    - (b) Restricted random sampling
        - (i) Stratified sampling
        - (ii) Systematic sampling
        - (iii) Cluster sampling

2. Non-random sampling method (Non-probability samples).
   (a) Judgement or purposive sampling
   (b) Quota sampling
   (c) Convenience sampling

Probability samples result from a process of random selection, whereby each member of a universe has a known chance of being selected for the sample. Non-probability samples result from a process in which judgement of bias enters into the selection of members of a universe included in the sample.

Random Sampling Method (Probability Samples)

A random sample is one where each item in the universe has an equal chance of known opportunity of being selected. ''Every member of the parent population has equal chances of being included.''

(a) **Simple Random Sampling :** This is a technique in which sample is so drawn that each and every unit in the population has an equal and independent chance of being included in the sample. Several methods have been adopted for random selection of the sample.

(i) **Lottery Method :** This is the most popular and simplest method. In this method, all the items of the universe are numbered on separate slips of paper of the same size, shape and colour. They are folded and mixed up in a drum or container. A blindfold selection is made. The required number of slips are selected for the desired sample size. The selection of items thus depends on chance.

(ii) **Table or Random Number :** As the lottery method cannot be used, when the population is infinite, the alternative is that of using the table of random numbers.

Merits

1. It is a scientific method.
2. Personal bias is absent.
3. Samples are more representative.
4. Sampling error can be measured.
5. This method is economical.

Demerits

1. This method requires a complete list of the population.
2. If the size of the sample is small, then it will not be a representative of the population.

(b) **Restricted Random Sampling**

(i) **Stratified Sampling :** When the population is heterogeneous or of different segments or strata with respect to the variable or characteristic under study, then it is stratified. First the population is divided into a number of sub-groups or strata. Each stratum is homogeneous. A sample is drawn from each stratum at random. There are two types of stratified random sampling. They are proportional and non-proportional. In the proportional sampling, equal and proportionate representation is given to sub-groups or strata. If the number of items is large in the population, the same will have a higher size and vice versa.

In disproportionate or non-proportionate sample, equal representation is given to all sub-strata, regardless of their existence in the population.

Merits

1. It is more representative.
2. It ensures greater accuracy.
3. It is easy to administer as the universe is sub-divided.
4. Greater geographical concentration reduces the time and cost.
5. When the original population is badly skewed, this method is an appropriate one.
6. For non-homogeneous population, it may yield more reliable results.

Demerits

1. To divide the population into homogeneous strata, it requires more money, time and statistical experience which is a difficult one.
2. If proper stratification is not done, the sample will have an effect of bias. If different strata of population overlap, such sample will not be representative one.

(ii) **Systematic Sampling :** It is also known as quasi-random sampling. A systematic sample is selected at random sampling. When a complete list of the population is available, this method is used. We arrange the items in numerical, alphabetical, geographical or any other order. If we want to select a sample of 15 students from 150 students, under this method K th item is picked up from the sample frame and k is the sample interval.

$$k = \frac{N}{n}$$

k = Sampling interval

N = Size of universe

n = Sample size

In the above example $k = \frac{150}{15} = 10$. 10 is the sampling interval. Every 10th student will be taken as sample, *i.e.*, 10th, 20th, 30th and so on (OR) 1st, 11th, 21st and so on. (OR) 6th, 16th, 26th and so on.

Merits

1. This is simple and convenient.
2. The time and work are much reduced.
3. If we take care, the result will be satisfactory one.
4. It can also be used in infinite population.

Demerits

1. It may not represent the whole population.
2. There is the element of personal bias of the investigators.

(iii) **Cluster Sampling (multistage sampling):** It is also called as sampling stages. It refers to a sampling procedure, which is carried out in several stages. The whole population is divided into sampling units, and these units are again divided into sub-units. This process will continue till we reach the last number.

For instance, we want to take 5,000 students from Madhya Pradesh. We must take universities at the first stage, then the number of colleges at the second stage, selection of students from the colleges at the third stage etc.

Merits

1. It introduces flexibility in the sampling method.
2. It is helpful in large-scale survey where the preparation of list is difficult, time-consuming or expensive.
3. It is valuable in under-developed countries, where no detailed and accurate framework is available.

Demerit

It is less accurate than other methods.

2. **Non-random Sampling Method (Non-Probability Samples)**

(a) **Judgement Sampling** (purposive or deliberate sampling): The investigator has the power to select or reject any item in an investigation. The choice of sample items depends on the judgement of the investigator. He has the vital role to play in collecting the information. For example, if a sample of 5 students is to be selected from a B.Com. Class of 50 students for analysing the habit of picture seeing, the investigator would select 5 students, who according to his opinion are the representative of the class.

Merits

1. It is a simple method.
2. It is used to obtain a more representative sample.
3. It is very helpful to make public policies, decisions etc. The executives and public officials use this method for their urgent problem.

Demerits

1. Due to individual bias the sample may not be representative one.
2. It is difficult to get correct sampling decisions.
3. The estimates are not accurate.
4. Its results cannot be compared with other sampling studies.

(b) **Quota Sampling :** This sampling is similar to stratified sampling. It is used in the U.S.A. for investigating public opinion and consumer research. To collect data, the universe is divided into quota according to some characteristics. Each enumerator is then told to interview a certain number of persons who are his quota. The selection of sample items depends on personal judgement.

It is stratified-cum-purposive sampling and thus has the advantages of both the methods. There is saving of time and money. If there are trained investigators, the sampling will give quite reliable results.

Personal prejudice and individual bias are there. It is not based on random sampling, and so sampling error cannot be estimated.

(c) **Convenience or Chunk Sampling :** Chunk is a convenient slice of a population which is commonly referred to as a sample. It is obtained by selecting convenient population units.

Merits and Demerits

1. It is suitable when the universe is not clearly defined.
2. Sample unit is not clear.
3. Complete source list is not available.

A sample obtained from automobile registration, telephone directories etc., is a convenience sample. The results of this sampling cannot be representative. They are unsatisfactory. They are biased. But they are used for pilot studies.

Qualities of a Good Sample

A sample selected should have the following essentials:

1. It must be true representative.
2. It must have homogeneity.
3. It must be random.
4. It must be adequate.
5. It must be proportional.
6. Items of the sample must be selected independently.
7. Selection of sample must be based on "the law of statistical regularity" and "the law of inertia of large numbers."

Sources of Secondary Data

1. Internal accounts, records and reports of the company.
2. Libraries.
3. National and international publications.
4. Publications of research institutions.
5. Publications of commercial and financial institutions.
6. Reports of various committees and commissions.
7. Journals, newspapers etc.

Precautions in the Use of Secondary Data

We must take extra care when using secondary data. The degree of reliability of secondary source is to be assessed from the source, the compiler and his capacity to produce correct statistics. The users for the most part, tend to accept a series, particularly one issued by a government agency as its face value without enquiring its reliability. Prof. Bowley says, "Secondary data should not be accepted at their face value." Therefore, before using the secondary data, the investigators should consider the following factors:

(a) Suitability of data
(b) Adequacy of data
(c) Reliability of data

The investigators should be careful in using secondary data and should consider the following points:

1. Were the data collected for a similar object?
2. Are they free from errors?
3. Were they collected by efficient and experienced agency?
4. What was the type of enquiry adopted?
5. What was the definition of the units?
6. What was the degree of accuracy aimed?
7. Was there any bias in the collection of data?
8. Were the data collected through a good method?
9. Were they collected in boom or depression or normal period?
10. Were the data properly edited and analysed?

Without knowing the meaning and limitations, we cannot accept the secondary data. Bowley points out, "It is never safe to take published statistics at their face value without knowing their meaning and limitations, and it is always necessary to criticise arguments that can be based on them".

Differences between Primary Data and Secondary Data

Primary Data	Secondary Data
1. Information is obtained from the original source.	1. Information is collected from those data which have been obtained by some other researcher.
2. They are originally collected for the project at hand.	2. They were collected for some other project, but are relevant to the research.
3. Information has to be created.	3. Information is already existing.
4. They give latest information.	4. Since they are already existing, they lack latest information.
5. They are collected at high cost and are time-consuming.	5. To the present project, they save time and money.
6. They are unpublished information.	6. They may be published or semi-published.

Organisation of Marketing Research

Generally producers want to market all the products produced. They would not like to hold the stock idly, which means blocked or dead capital amount. Whenever a fall in the sales is smelt, the businessman tries to find out the reasons through marketing research. There are two ways in getting the job done (a) by the company's own personnel and (b) by an outside agency. It is always better to have a separate marketing research department, within the organisation and at the same time it is advantageous that the researchers are well-versed in company procedures and know the information available. There are many institutions, having highly qualified specialists in the marketing research field–outside agency. They offer their expert services for hire.

There are no clear cut solutions to the problem of budget to be fixed. It is difficult to assess the expenditure of the research and the value of the result of a research project. Costs will be more as the precision increases. Nature of the research work and the size of the firm will decide the amount to be spent for the marketing research.

Limitations of Marketing Research

1. Marketing research needs the services of qualified and trained persons. Such persons are rarely found.
2. It is highly expensive and time-consuming.
3. If the researcher is biased to the problem, the results will be unsatisfactory and misleading.
4. Marketing research studies the behaviour of customers; so it is quite impossible to achieve mathematical accuracy.
5. It is not an end itself. It presents the correct information for decision making. Unless the information is used by a qualified manager, the study will be of no use.
6. By the time the results are ready, the circumstances might have changed; then the whole study will be valueless.
7. It deals with human behaviour and as much cannot be examined in a controlled environment. There are various and uncontrolled factors which influence marketing forces. This gives for wrong conclusions. Hence this leads to marketing research as not being an exact science.
8. The complicated problems may not be comprehensively studied and their impact is properly analysed by the researcher on account of insufficient fund, time and technique. This leads to erroneous findings, which disappoint the management.
9. The validity of marketing research is also limited by the limitation of tools and techniques involved.
10. It's use and effectiveness largely depends upon the ability of executives to get the most value of it.

Status of Marketing Research

In earlier stages, the market was a smaller one. But now the gap between the consumers and the producers is wider. Competition may enter at any time in the market. Changes are always there. The taste of the buyers changes at any time. For example, the higher demand, in the past, for radio is replaced by television; the higher demand for terylyn is replaced by polyester. Thus day-to-day changes take place in the market. Changes may occur in the market because of technological progress, expansion of markets, complexity growth of market, changes in the consumption pattern etc. The changes that take place in the markets must be understood by the management. For this, the management must depend upon the marketing research as a guide. It is an aid to the management. It places all necessary facts before the management, who can shape the solution to the problems. Marketing research plays an important role in decision-making.

Contribution of Marketing Research

1. Marketing research, as a guide will shape the products suitable to the demand.
2. Prices can be adjusted in accordance with the demand.
3. It helps to stimulate the sales through sales promotions.
4. It will not only increase sales, but also cut down the unnecessary expenses.
5. It will guide to achieve consumer satisfaction and sales profitability.

Marketing Research in India

The marketing research is unpopular with Indian manufacturers because of the following reasons:

1. Demand exceeds supply; in such a condition the sales are guaranteed and the market is favourable.
2. Firms earn profits without a marketing research.
3. The management thinks that the amount to be spent on marketing research can be used profitably for expansion and improvements of the products.
4. Available sources of information are adequate.
5. The management concentrate their interest on production and raw materials.

But marketing research in India will certainly in the long run, increase the profits, eliminate the wastes, fetch consumer satisfaction, guide progress etc.

Case Study-1

Research and Competition

INDIAN ALUMINIUM

Indian Aluminium, a reputed aluminium company, currently having a turnover of about Rs. 900 crore, was set up in 1971 at Kolkata. The company had set up the foil division in 1986 at Lonawala near Mumbai. The foil division commenced manufacturing of superwrap in 1987. The demand for aluminium foil by the pharmaceutical, cigarette and other industries was what the company initially had in mind when the foil division was set up.

The decision to manufacture household foil for wrapping foodstuff was basically an offshoot of its British partner. Since the British company was already marketing the product abroad, it was decided to do the same in India. The product was packaged in white paper and no advertising was done from 1987 to 1992 during which time it sold just 2,500 rolls per month. The company had always been catering to the needs of institutional buyers. The distributor for the aluminium foils was given the rolls superwrap which he would hand over to retailers or sub-distributors to sell as part and parcel of a whole consignment, besides what the distributor's salespersons could sell. The company was the first to launch the product in India and the target audience at that time was housewives of an income group of Rs. 3,000 per month and above. The product was launched in Mumbai alone and its availability extended beyond Mumbai later.

In 1989, the foils division had requested for money to be allocated for market research but was turned down because the management didn't think it worthwhile. It was only in 1995 (after three proposals were turned down) that the division at last got the go ahead. However, in 1990, another company started manufacturing household foils and the Indian Aluminium started facing problems as the new company did systematic market research and advertising.

QUESTIONS

1. What is the problem in this case ?
2. What strategy would you like to suggest to push up the sale of the product in view of the growing competition ? *(Pune, MBA)*

Case Study-2

Marketing Research
ALFA POWER LTD

Every year, with the onset of summer, demand for the petrol/kerosene operated domestic generators and battery-operated invertors increases. The total market for portable generators and invertors is estimated to be around Rs. 150 crores for North India which is badly affected because of the massive power cuts. There are two leading manufacturers of petrol/kerosene-operated portable generators. Both, along with a few other manufacturers have 80 per cent of the market share. The rest of the.market is captured by a large number or small-scale invertor: manufacturers. The invertor uses one or two batteries and has a back-up time of 3-6 hours whereas the generator sets can operate uninterrupted for a longer period. The voltage obtained from the portable generator set is consistent whereas in the case of invertors, the voltage reduces drastically after the back-up time.

The batteries which are used in the invertors are automatically charged but have a life of 2 to 3 years. Not much maintenance is required for the invertors, but in the case of portable generators, proper service is recommended after every 6 months. Some drawbacks which people have been observing in the use of portable generators are that they make lot of noise, vibrations and emit lot of smoke also while ın operatıon. Besides, the users will have to stock kerosene/petrol/diesel in the house for the operation of the set which has become a problem especially in small flats having working parents and small children. Recently in an incident it is alleged that because of the smoke emitted by the portable generator set, two kids of a family died.

Alfa Power is a professionally managed concern. The chief executive of the concern, Sh. Ish Kapoor, after completing electronic engineering, opted for self-employment instead of wage employment. He set up a unit for manufacturing electronic power generators in 1995 and within a period of one year other products such as CVT and Online UPS systems were added. All the products with state-of-the-art technology proved highly reliable and user-friendly. The foremost aim of Alfa Power is to produce high quality products for total customer satisfaction.

The products of the concern are being, used as OEM's for various concerns. Looking at the vast opportunities available for the invertor market, Sh. Kapoor decided to engage a marketing research agency to carry out a market survey for its product which may be used for homes/shops/establishments as a substitute for the portable generator sets. The cost in the case of portable generator sets ranges from Rs. 15,000 to 30,000 (fuel extra). In case of invertors; the range is Rs. 7,000 to 19,000 (the cost of battery varies from Rs. 3,000 to 5,000 depending upon the size and the brand).

QUESTIONS

1. What should be the objectives of marketing survey in this case ?
2. What changes, do you feel, Sh. Ish Kapoor should bring about in the company's marketing department? *(Pune, MBA, 2001)*

Case Study-3

Marketing Research
TARGETING TEENAGERS MARKET

Marketers of pimple creams, cosmetics, record albums, movies and other products already widely used by teens do focus a lot of advertising and promotion targeted at age group between 12 and 19. But most other companies ignore it. Many of the large food concerns do not make any effort to appeal to that group because of the belief that most food products are bought by home-makers—women who are married. Another reinforcing fact is that the post-war baby boom generation is now mostly in its thirties.

However, companies with such attitudes may be overlooking a key market. A recent survey of 1,002 teenagers found that 64% do some of their family's food shopping. Of that group, more than one-third shop at least once a week. The average teenagers' grocery bill is $24. It was also evident that teenagers in the household influence the choice of brand purchased. Six out of every 10 teenager supermarket shoppers have a hand in making the family groccery list, four out of 10 select brands to be bought.

Although the number of teens is expected to drop to 23 million in 1990 from 28.6 million in 1980, the youths have impressive spending power. This is because three out of five of them hold either full or part-time job. Based on a survey of 2,000 consumers between the ages of 12 and 19 years, the estimated weekly earnings of U.S., teenagers amount to about $600 million. In addition, four of every 10 of them receive allowances from parents of $80 million a week. Thus the clout (garment) of teenage market is about $35 billion a year. Nearly all of the teenager income is disposable. They don't pay rent or electric bill. It all goes to spending on consumer goods.

QUESTIONS

1. What is your opinion of the teenager market ? Do you feel this marketing research data is enough to convince management to target or concentrate on the teenager market ?
2. If you were a marketer of food products, how would you structure your marketing efforts to attract the teenager spending ?
3. Some marketers believe that teenagers do not form a distinct segment and, hence, need not be approached as a special group. In fact modern teenagers are matured and intelligent people who are capable to respond to the same type of advertising as other people do. Do you agree ? Please comment.
4. Modern marketers also cater to the youth market at a distict segments. Outline a research design for ascertaining the typical demand for *jeans* by the youth market in India.

QUESTIONS

1. What are primary data? Briefly analyse a few methods of collecting primary data. *(B.Com., Bombay)*
2. How is a good questionnaire prepared?
3. What are the various stages through which marketing research is organised? Briefly describe them. *(B.Com.)*
4. Differentiate between Market Research and Marketing Research. *(M.Com., Allahabad)*
5. What do you mean by marketing research? Describe its scope and importance. *(B.Com. Bharati Dasan)*
6. What are Secondary data? Mention a few sources from where secondary data are collected.
7. Discuss the advantages and disadvantages of observational method of collection of data. *(B.Com., Delhi)*
8. What type of sample would you select for each of the given projects?—a study of purchasing habits of buyers of carpets AND a study of brand loyalty in the cosmetic market.
9. "The use of postal questionnaire rather than personal interviews, normally has the advantage of cheapness." Discuss the advantages and disadvantages of postal survey. *(B.Com., Madurai)*
10. Explain the methods adopted for gathering primary data in marketing research. *(M.Com., Madurai)*
11. Explain the general nature of marketing research procedures. *(B.A., Poona)*
12. "Marketing information system has been called the life-blood of Marketing." Comment on this statement. *(B.Com., Delhi)*
13. What is the importance of marketing information systems? Discuss. *(M.Com., Chennai, Kolkatta)*

CHAPTER 11

Marketing Management

- *Introduction*
- *Meaning*
- *Characteristics*
- *Functions*
- *Negative Demand*
- *No Demand*
- *Latent Demand*
- *Falling Demand*
- *Irregular Demand*
- *Full Demand*
- *Overall Demand*
- *Unwholesome Demand*
- *Marketing Organisation*
- *Principles of Organisation*
- *Marketing and Sales Management*
- *Functions of Marketing Executive*
- *Responsibility*
- *Types of Organisation*
- *Military Type*
- *Functional Type*
- *Line and Staff System*
- *Committee*
- *Geographical Type*
- *Product Type*
- *Market Type*

Introduction

In the earlier chapters we discussed the importance of marketing. Marketing has been developed since the Industrial Revolution. In the olden stage, or we may say, production-oriented stage, the job of marketing was simple. Manufacturers produced goods or services and disposed them off. The consumers' desires were not taken into account. The sales managers were not included in the top management force. In the next stage, *i.e.*, sales-oriented stage, there were mass production and competition. This was the stage where the appearance of personal selling and advertising was a tool to stimulate the sales. Thus, the sales managers and advertising managers were included in the top management force. Then, in the next stage, *i.e.*, marketing oriented stage, the function of marketing became important. A number of marketing activities were performed by the marketing unit. The importance of the marketing manager also broadened. The marketing manager participated in top level decision-making functions. In the marketing-oriented stage, the businessmen paid more attention to satisfy the wants of the buyers. Then, under the total marketing concept the business is managed so as to give satisfaction of the customers through production, which is based on the desire of the buyers. Thus the entire firm has become a marketing organisation. For instance, the production department produces goods by meeting the customers' preference and the finance department helps the customers by granting credit. In short, different functions, which were under different managers have been brought under the marketing manager, who is to take even the policy decisions. The function of business is to create, retain and to satisfy a profitable buyer.

Meaning of Marketing Management

The importance of marketing has been widened through many evolutionary processes and shaped as consumer-orientation stage, in which the existence of a firm is measured of its ability to satisfy the consumers. A producer or firm can serve its share-holders, management and workers, when the firm is successful in its marketing.

The achievements of marketing objectives are two-fold–customer satisfaction and profitable sale. Customer satisfaction is gained, and it greatly depends upon the manner in which the marketing functions are organised. The marketing has special significance in an organisational structure of a firm. Markets are not created by God, nature or economic forces, but by businessmen.

Marketing management is the creative management function which promotes trade and employment by assessing consumer needs and initiates research development to meet them. It co-ordinates the resources of production and distribution of goods and services, determines and directs the nature of efforts required to sell profitably by maximum production to the ultimate user." Therefore marketing management is the functional area of business management which deals with the problems of consumers' satisfaction. Marketing management represents marketing concept in action. The process of management is the set of managerial functions, *i.e.*, planning, implementation and control of programmes to achieve pre-determined objectives. Marketing management, in fact, represents an important functional area of business management efforts under which goods and services flow from the producers to consumers.

Characteristics of Marketing Management

The important characteristics of marketing management may be obtained as under :

1. Marketing is a specialised business function. In the early days, the selling function did not call for any specialised skills as the sales could have been effected on production-basis. But at present, the business environment has undergone tremendous changes in social, economic, political and cultural aspects. The management of a firm, therefore, has to develop a particular organisation with a view to absorbing new ideas, new approaches and new market demands.

2. Marketing is a social function. It requires constant interaction with the various strata of society. It is instrumental in manipulating the factors of production, distribution, promotion and price, and also in influencing the patterns of consumption and consumer attitudes.

3. Marketing is an integrative function. It integrates and combines the other business functions like production, finance, personnel etc. with a view to accomplishing the organisational objectives.

4. Marketing reflects the business mission of a firm before the public and society.

5. It is said that change is the only basic law of economics. Marketing, which is the art of distributing the products and services among the various claimants, has also only one basic law, change.

6. Marketing is an universal function. It has a universality in the sense that it can be applied to both profit-motive and non-profit motive organisations. A profit-seeking business unit is dependant on marketing. The institutions like hospital, school, political association also practise marketing in popularising the services offered by them.

7. Marketing is a management function like the management of other functions such as production, finance, personnel etc. The business policies, strategies and programmes related to marketing are mostly of managerial functions. These are needed to be planned, organised, directed, coordinated and controlled so as to achieve the marketing objectives.

The study of marketing management is nothing but the critical evaluation of various marketing functions. The functions necessary to determine consumer wants and needs and to supply necessary goods and services to meet those demands can be broadly classified as follows :

(1) **Marketing Research :** Marketing research is the careful and objective study of product design, markets and other activities such as physical distribution, warehousing, advertising and sales management. Its main aim is to provide management with factual information as a basis for marketing decisions and actions. The major areas in which marketing research helps management to formulate its policies are : products, markets, marketing policies and sales methods.

(2) **Product Planning Development :** Product planning is the act of making out and supervising the search, screening development and commercialisation of new products, the modification of existing lines and discontinuance of managerial or unprofitable products. Business concerns must satisfy consumer's wants and needs for their continued existence. This existence is

assured by offering products and services that meet consumer requirements. Hence, product planning is a very important function.

(3) **Standardisation and Grading :** Standardisation is the process of setting up standards, and manufacturing products in conformity with those standards and includes the process by which this conformity is assured. Thus, it ensures the uniformity of size, shape, design, colour and physical properties of the product. Grading is a part of the process of standardisation. It is the process of storing out goods into a number of grades or classes according to some characteristics such as quality and size. It helps not only the producer but the sellers and consumers also.

(4) **Product Pricing :** Pricing is a very important and crucial decision as it affects all the parties involved in the production, distribution and consumption of goods. Price of the product affects volume of production and the amount of profit. It is the source of income to the distributors of the product. Hence, the marketing manager has to take pricing decisions very carefully.

(5) **Packaging :** Packaging is also an important marketing function. A package is used to contain, protect and identify a product. Besides, it is an important sales tool which makes a product attractive and attention-captivating. Good and attractive packing is a plus-point in facilitating the sale of a product. Hence, the marketing manager has to take decision regarding the type and material of packing, its shape, size, design and colour etc.

(6) **Advertising and Sales Promotion :** Advertising is a method of business communication to the prospective customers. Such communication includes information about business institution, its products, product qualities, the time and place of availability etc. The main object of advertising is to promote the sale of products. The marketing manager has to take a number of decisions relating to advertising such as selection of a suitable and economical medium, planning advertising programme, preparing the advertising budget etc.

(7) **Distribution Management :** Distribution of products is also an important function of marketing management. It involves the decision to channels of distribution and their management. A long series of middlemen-sole selling agent, wholesalers and retailers etc. work between the producer and consumer. The marketing manager has to manage all these distribution channels.

(8) **Management of Sales Forces :** Personnel is very important component of marketing activity. The success of a business concern depends considerably upon the performance of its salesmen. Salesmen play a crucial role in communicating company and product information to customers. Hence, the company should have a trained sales force. Marketing manager will be intimately concerned with the task of selection, orientation, training, supervision, motivation, compensation and evaluation of the sales force of the company.

In the words of Pride and Farrel, ''Marketing management is a process of planning, organising, implementing and controlling marketing activities in order to effectively and efficiently facilitate and expedite exchanges. The effectiveness and efficiency dimensions are two important components.''

Functions of Marketing Management (in brief)

1. Determination of marketing goals to be achieved.
2. Market analysis to improve sales.
3. Formulation of marketing plans, procedures, policies etc.
4. Evaluation of unsatisfied and potential customers' needs and desire.
5. Organising the marketing functions and marketing mix.
6. Develon detailed sales plans and budgets.
7. Sponsors a continuing programme of market research.
8. Determination of most desirable channels of distribution.
9. Encouraging good employee relation within the organisation.

10. Exercises effective marketing communication.
11. Participation in the product planning to match with demand.
12. Periodical review of over-all marketing programmes to increase the sales volume and net profits.
13. Proper control and co-ordination of all marketing functions.
14. Evaluation of actual performance with the standard performance.
15. A plan ''to do right things and not to do things rightly'' that is importance is given to demand side.

Philip Kotler has defined marketing management as ''marketing management is the analysis, planning, implementation, and control of programmes designed to bring about desired exchanges with target audiences for the purpose of mutual or personal gain. It relies heavily on the adaptation and co-ordination of product, price, promotion and place of achieving effective response.''

Marketing management looks after the marketing system of the enterprise. It is that part of the business management which is concerned with marketing, *i.e.* leading and co-ordinating the various activities of the business firm in getting its goods and services to its customers. Marketing management plays an important role in any business concern. It looks after marketing system of the business concern. It performs all managerial functions in the field of marketing. It evaluates the effectiveness of each part of the marketing mix continuously and makes necessary modifications to eliminate discrepancies, if any, discovered in the execution of marketing plan, policies and programmes. For satisfying the needs and wants of customers, organisations have to sense such needs and wants and create products and services which are capable of satisfying them.

''Marketing management is the creative management function which promotes trade and employment by assessing consumer needs and initiative research development to meet them. It co-ordinates the resources of production and distribution of goods and services, determines and directs the nature of efforts required to sell profitably by maximum production to the ultimate user.'' The task before the marketing management is the responsibility of finding a market for the products. Thus, the tasks relate to ''regulating the level, timing and character of demand in a way that will help the organisation to achieve its objectives. Marketing management may, therefore, be rightly described as demand management.''

The broad objectives of Marketing Management

1. To satisfy customers.
2. To increase profits for the growth of the business.
3. To generate more and more customer base for the business.
4. To increase the quality of life of the people.
5. To determine marketing-mix that will satisfy the needs of customers.
6. To create good image of the organisation.

The organisation forms an idea of a **desired level** of transactions with a market. At any point in time, the actual demand level may be below, equal to, or above the desired demand level. That is there may be no demand or there may be weak demand, adequate demand, excessive demand and so on. Thus the different levels of demand–low, equal to or above the required demand, lead to the right market tasks or the demand situations. They are :

1. Negative demand
2. No demand
3. Latent demand
4. Falling demand
5. Irregular demand
6. Full demand
7. Overall demand
8. Unwholesome demand

1. **Negative Demand :** Major part of the market dislikes the product. This stage is also referred as **conversional marketing**. This is an unfavourable condition. Sometimes, a consumer even pays a price in order to avoid it. People have a negative desire to travel in bus or airways. This situation is challenged in the marketing management who have to analyse the dislikes and prepare a plan to convert the negative demand into a positive one *i.e.*, create a favourable demand. They have to develop a plan redesign, lower the price and include other promotional activities to create an interest in the consumers.

2. **No Demand :** As far as certain products or services are concerned, people are indifferent towards them. Thus there is a stage of no demand; *i.e.*, people have no interest in getting the products. This may also be happened because they are not found in the market or people are unaware of the product because of lack of publicity by the firm. For instance, the book bank of a college may possess good books written by foreigners in foreign language or English and the students may not be interested in going through the books. Thus, there is no demand. Therefore, marketing management has to stimulate the situation, which is a difficult task, by trying to convert demand from **'no demand'** to **positive demand**. This task is referred to as **stimulational marketing**.

3. **Latent Demand :** Many consumers may share a strong desire for something that cannot be satisfied by the existing products or services. The latent or hidden desire for the products is an opportunity to the management in developing or improving the existing products; or services. **Development marketing** is, thus, a process by which the latent demand is converted into actual demand. For instance, bike-riders have a latent desire to have self-starter in the bike, instead of kick starter. A marketing management, by new innovation or changes in the production, produces bikes with self-starter. A good marketer, who has experience and farsightedness will produce effective goods or services that will satisfy the demand.

4. **Falling Demand :** Certain firms may find a falling tendency of demand for the products or services. **Faltering demand** for the products refers to a situation in which the demand is less than the target. For instance, private colleges may face decline in the number of incoming students. There, the marketer analyses the situation or finds out the causes of faltering demand, and involves remarketing through the creation of new satisfaction.

5. **Irregular Demand :** In certain organisations, seasonal demand causes the problems of idle capacity or overworked capacity. For instance, water pumps are in great demand in summer and no demand in rainy season, fans have good demand in summer, but no demand in winter etc. This type of irregular demand may be converted into regular demand and this process, taken by the management, is known as synchromarketing.

6. **Full Demand :** Organisations face full demand for their products. But at the same time, there is a task before the marketer that he should maintain the market demand. This is because consumer preference may be changed or competition may appear. Thus cost of products, sales force, consumer satisfaction etc., may be watched continuously. It is known as **maintenance marketing**.

7. **Overall Demand :** Some organisations may have more demands for their products. The firm may not be able to meet all the demands. This may be due to excessive popularity or due to shortage of supply of raw materials. Thus, the management faces the marketing task and tries to find ways to reduce the demand. This is known as **demarketing**. This happens when prices are raised, quality is reduced, ignoring promotional measures etc. Demarketing is opposed to marketing concept.

8. **Unwholesome Demand :** Smoking, use of alcohol, spurious drugs etc., are unwholesome. Certain goods or services have good demand. Certain items of products may be grouped as ''injurious products''. In such a situation, the sales of such unwholesome items are discouraged. This situation is known as **counter-marketing** or unselling. All types of socially undesirable products or services are counter-marketed in order to destroy the market altogether. For instance, cigarettes, alcohol, hard drugs etc.

Marketing Organisation

Sheldon says, ''An organisation is the process of so combining the work which individuals or groups have to perform with the facilities necessary for its execution, that the duties so performed provide the best channels for the efficient, systematic, positive and co-ordinated application of the available effort.'' All organisations have some aims and objects before them. An organisation consists of people, who run and manage them. The progress or the development of the organisation is facilitated by regulations, policies and procedures and defining the duties and responsibilities of its members. Thus, all organisations are made of objectives, people and procedures. They aim at dividing the work according to importance and regrouping them into one. The predetermined objectives are accomplished by the groups consisting of individuals.

Marketing organisation is a separate organisation for the purpose of marketing alone. It is defined as, ''A group of people brought together to participate in a common effort to accomplish certain goals.'' Organisation is the backbone of the management with proper care at all levels, it is possible for the management to attain the aimed goal.

An organisation structure and its design have to be planned by the management, as an architect designs a building. The architect has to look at the size and type of land, environment, materials and many other factors in designing the building for an aimed or specific object. In the same way, when the management of a firm designs the organisation structure, it is a job more than that of an architect. They have to look into many matters. Another example will be a game, in which an unlimited number of players assemble without specific role assigned to each. So, everyone has got his own rules and this will bring no result to the game. Therefore, when designing an organisation structure, the following principles may be followed to achieve the set aim.

Principles of Organisation

1. **Clear-cut Objective :** An organisation is created to fulfil certain goals or aims. In order to achieve the aim and objectives it has to identify the activities of goals in clear, precise and complete terms free from ambiguity.

2. **Specialisation and Definiteness :** The principle of specialisation is the division of work aiming at maximum results. The activities of a firm are divided into many units, sub-units and suitable groupings in relation to departmental activities, sectional activities etc. Fixed responsibilities aid in speeding up the work. Every employee must definitely know his position in the firm and purpose thereof, so that he realises his responsibility and works accordingly.

3. **Delegation of Authority :** A clerk gets his authority from his section-head, to whom the worker is responsible for the proper performance of the job assigned. Therefore authority always flows downward, while responsibility always moves upward. A clear definition of authority and responsibility is essential. In the lack of clear definition, the management cannot have a smooth function of work. A busy management allocates task among the subordinates. A successful office manager never performs the task himself, but gets the work done by others.

4. **Span of Control :** No executive must have too many subordinates reporting to him. If an office manager has many subordinates under him, then control becomes defective.

5. **Co-ordination :** Co-ordination is essential to bring unity of action in the organisation. Work of all departments should be balanced in order to avoid conflict or overlapping of functions, with the object of ensuring smooth and efficient working functions.

6. **Flexibility :** Organisation must be flexible, so that it can be adjusted to changing conditions. It must permit expansion, replacement, merger etc. It should not be rigid.

7. **Responsibility :** Without authority there cannot be any responsibility. Assignment of responsibility should be coupled with authority sufficient to carry them out. There must be parity between authority and responsibility. Each worker must have sufficient authority to discharge the responsibility assigned to him.

8. **Efficiency :** Available human resources should be utilised to the best and fullest capacity in order to achieve the highest efficiency through operations.

9. **Unity of Command :** Subordinates receive instruction from one authority. Too many high officials create confusion in the mind of the worker.

10. **Personal Ability :** As people constitute an organisation, proper selection, placement and training are necessary. Organisation structure must ensure optimum use of human resources.

Marketing and Sales Management

By marketing, we mean, ''Performance of business activities that direct the flow of goods and services from producer to consumer or user.'' By sales management, we mean, the planning, direction and control of personal selling including recruiting, selecting, training, equipping, assigning, routing, supervising, paying and motivating, as the tasks applied to the personal sales force. Thus, we see that marketing is a wider term and includes sales management.

Distinction Between

Marketing Management	Sales Management
1. It is a modern concept.	1. It is an old concept.
2. Its object is to satisfy consumer wants/ needs and then maximise profitability.	2. Its object is to maximise sales
3. It deals with the problems of buyers.	3. It deals with the problems of sellers.
4. Its scope is wider : –discovering needs –obtaining demand –customer satisfaction –aims repetition of orders	4. Its scope is narrow: –selling –sales promotion
5. It includes sales management.	5. It is a part of marketing management.

Functions of Marketing Executive (Manager)

Marketing executive is a very responsible person, who is entrusted with the task of looking after the entire marketing activities. The process of marketing must be achieved through the effective fulfilment of objectives. In a sellers' market the marketing function is mainly concerned with the distribution function, and the job of marketing executive is easy. But, at the same time, in buyer's market which has competitive market situation, the marketing operations have more emphasis. Under this situation, the executive is given more powers and authority as well as good status in the organisation. He may take decisions even without consulting the Board of Directors, to prevent any delay in arriving at a decision. He may as well be designated as Marketing Director.

Marketing Manager's Responsibility

The increasing marketing responsibilities and growing complexity of the marketing functions have increased the status of the marketing executive or director. Thus his position is gaining importance. The basic functions are :

1. To find out marketing opportunities.
2. To improve marketing plans, procedures etc.
3. To develop new innovations–product, market discovery etc.
4. To develop the sales force.
5. To have constant touch with the market–business research.
6. To avail of resources to be utilised effectively.
7. To interpret the market situations.

8. To adopt the most profitable and desirable channels of distribution.
9. To supervise and control the various departments under him.
10. To develop the existing market.
11. To review marketing programmes for improvement, if needed.
12. To control the marketing costs.
13. To exercise effective account to advertising.
14. To forecast effectively and profitably.
15. To adopt sound price policy for competing market, in consultation with other top members.
16. To keep sufficient inventory to meet demand.
17. To maintain good relation with customers, consumers etc.
18. To create good inter-relationship within the firm.
19. To facilitate growth and diversification of products.
20. To evaluate the effectiveness of management performance.

TYPES OF ORGANISATION STRUCTURE

Organisation is the vehicle for accomplishing the goals and objectives of the business. Organisation is essential, when human beings have to collaborate and work for a common purpose. In fact, an organisation is often defined as ''a group of persons working together towards the attainment of certain common objectives.''

When the enterprise expands, some pattern of organisation should be adopted. Generally, the following are the types of organisation.

1. Military Type of Organisation

This is the simplest and oldest form of organisation. It is also referred as **line organisation, scalar** or **hierarchical organisation**. Under this type of organisation, a superior delegates authority to a subordinate, who in turn delegates authority to another subordinate and so on. Authority descends from the top to the bottom level, through downward delegation of authority. Subordinates become responsible to their immediate superiors. The topmost management has full control over the entire field.

MANAGING DIRECTOR
↓
MARKETING MANAGER
↓
AREA SALES MANAGER
↓
SALESMEN

(OR)

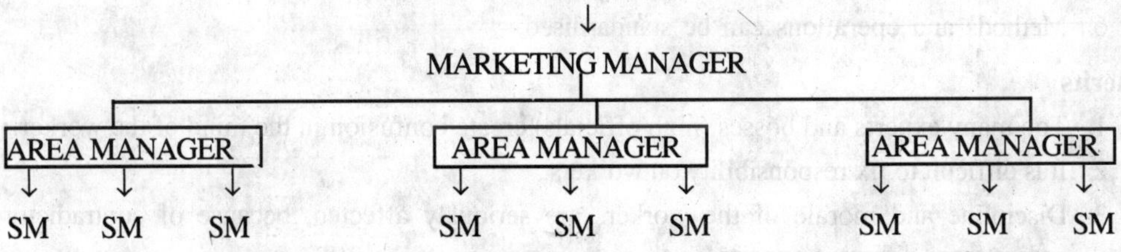

SM=SALESMAN

Suitability

This form is suitable :

1. if the business is comparatively small.
2. if the labour management problems are easy to solve.
3. if the processes are easily directed.
4. if the work is of a routine nature.

Merits

1. It is simple to work.
2. It is economical and effective.
3. It is easy to fix responsibility.
4. It facilitates quick decisions and prompt actions.
5. Quick communication is easy.
6. Discipline can easily be maintained.

Demerits

1. The organisation is rigid and inflexible.
2. It works on a dictatorial basis.
3. Departmental heads act on their own whims and desire, as it is difficult to secure co-ordination of the activities of workers and departments.
4. In big business it does not operate satisfactorily.

2. **Functional Type Organisation**

The limitations of line organisation have been removed under this system. All types of work of the organisation are grouped and managed by the top executive. There are separate functional departments for major functions of the enterprise; example personnel department, purchase department etc. Each department does its function for the entire organisation. Sales department does the function for the whole enterprise. The functional organisation works through the line organisation. Functional organisation is based on expert knowledge and makes the greatest use of division of labour resulting in high efficiency and specialisation.

Merits :

1. Greatest use of division of labour is possible.
2. The system is based on expert knowledge.
3. Functional efficiency of the worker can be maintained.
4. Mass production is made by standardisation and specialisation.
5. Separation of mental and manual functions is possible.
6. Methods and operations can be standardised.

Demerits

1. Too many experts and bosses (high officials) create confusion in the mind of the worker.
2. It is difficult to fix responsibility on workers.
3. Discipline and morale of the workers are seriously affected, because of contradictory orders from different experts.
4. There is heavy overhead expense.

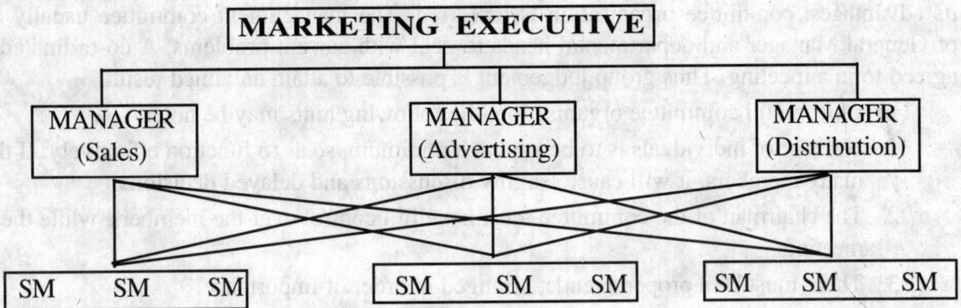

FUNCTIONAL TYPE

3. **Line and Staff System**

In this type, the organisation is based on the line organisation and the functional experts advise the line officers as to the functions of the enterprise. The line officers are the executives and the staff officers are their advisers. Though the staff officers do not have the power to command the line officers, their advice is generally adhered to. The combination of organisation with this expert staff forms the type of organisation–line and staff. The 'line' keeps the discipline and the staff provides expert information. The line gets out the production and the staff carries on research, planning, fixing standard etc. This type of organisation is suitable for large concerns. The line officers give orders, decisions etc., to subordinates in consultation or guidance with the staff officers. The underlying idea of this method is that specialised work is to be left to experts who will give advice on specialised groups–investigation, research etc. The staff officers who have no executive positions in the concern, but are only the thinkers, while the line officers are the doers.

Merits

1. This type is based on specialisation.
2. It brings expert knowledge of the whole concern.
3. Increased efficiency of operations may be possible.
4. Mass production is possible.

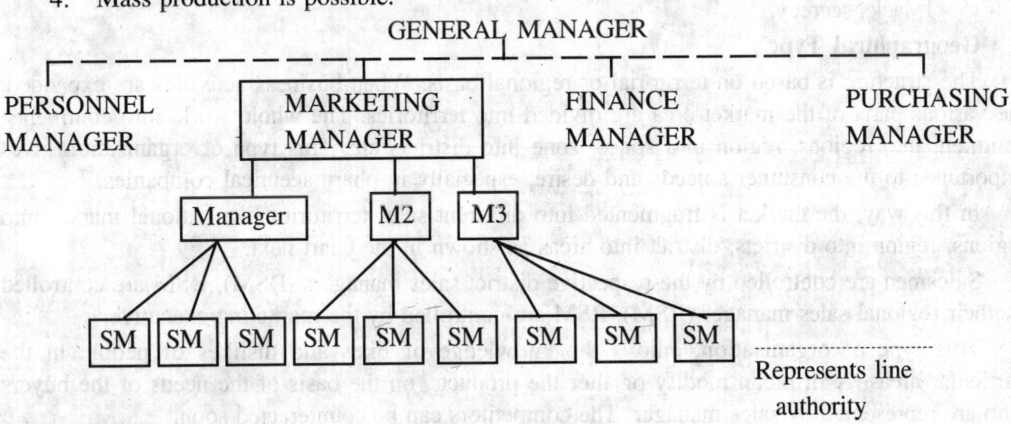

Demerits

1. There arises confusion unless the duties and responsibilities are clearly indicated by charts and office manuals.
2. Advice and expert information are given to the workers through the line officers. It is possible that the workers may misunderstand or misinterpret.

4. **Committee Organisation**

Committee organisation is widely used for the purpose of discharging advisory functions of the management. Committees are formed in different levels of organisation. A committee is a group of people who meet by plan to discuss or make a decision on a particular subject. Because of its advantages, committee organisation is preferred. The management committee usually consists of General Manager and departmental heads to deal with current problems. A co-ordinated plan is agreed to in a meeting. Thus group judgement is possible to attain an aimed result.

For a successful committee organisation, the following hints may be noted :

1. Number of individuals is to be kept at a minimum, so as to function effectively. If there are many members, it will cause lengthy discussions and delayed decisions.
2. The chairman of the committee must have full control over the members, while they are in meeting.
3. There must be a proper agenda, arranged in order of importance.
4. All the members are to be informed before the meeting about the points to be discussed, so that they may prepare for the meeting.
5. The meeting must be started on time and must end on time.

Merits

1. It stimulates co-operative action.
2. It can promote better understanding.
3. A problem is discussed in detail and decision taken.
4. It facilitates co-ordination of activities of various departments.
5. Group discussion and decision will bring better results.
6. It gives demographic management.

Demerits

1. Committees are expensive.
2. Committee weakens individual responsibility.
3. Committee may sometimes become time-consuming rather than time-saving.
4. Responsibility cannot be fixed on any person.
5. It lacks secrecy.

5. **Geographical Type**

The structure is based on territorial or regional basis. When business activities are expanded, the various parts of the market area are divided into territories. The whole world into continents, continent into regions, region into zones, zone into districts etc. This type of organisation gives importance to the consumer's needs and desire, especially in pharmaceutical companies.

In this way, the market is fragmented into different sales territories like national market into regions, region into districts, district into areas as shown in the chart next.

Salesmen are controlled by the respective district sales managers (DSM), DSM are controlled by their regional sales manager (RSM), RSM are controlled by the marketing executive.

This type of organisation, enjoys the knowledge of likes and dislikes of people in the particular areas. A firm can modify or alter the products, on the basis of the needs of the buyers who are represented by sales manager. The competitors can be counteracted soon.

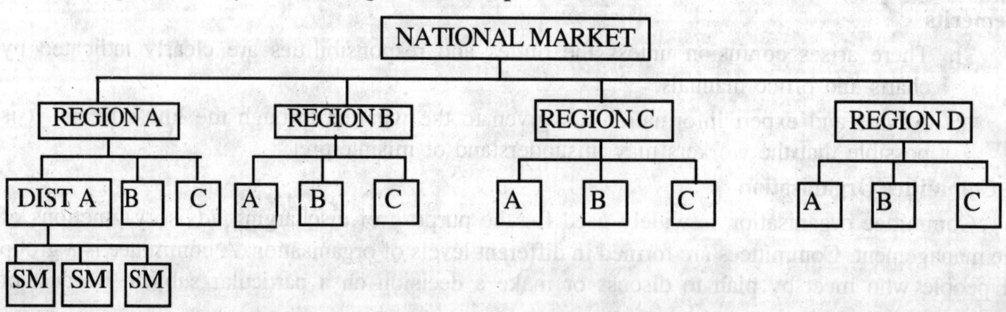

Merits: (Geographical Type)

1. Geographical type of divisions allow a manager to pay special attention to the needs and problems of the local markets.
2. Geographical type of organisation provide opportunities for local talent to be utilised.
3. Geographical division helps managers to gain extensive knowledge of diverse activities.
4. This type of organisation improve an organisation's relationship with customers.

Demerits: (Geographical Type)

1. This type of organisation require more people to work.
2. There arise communication problems.
3. Cost of operations are high.
4. Top managers at HO find it difficult to control and supervise the activities in different locations.

6. Product Type

Certain companies produce different varieties of products and it is advantageous to boost the sales on the basis of product or product groups. A separate product manager is appointed for each product. He attends to the production and marketing of his products. When the market is competitive, the product type organisation with the product manager can concentrate its attention on the performance of a particular product or brand. Sales promotion, advertising, marketing research etc., remain as the centralised activity for the product group.

7. Market Type (Consumer)

This type of organisation is based on the different types of customers. The enterprises have adopted customer-oriented marketing and thus there arise two sets of organisations through which the needs of customers or market are met; *i.e.*, sub-division of markets on the basis of government and non-government customers, industrial individual customers, rich and poor customers and on the basis of sex, income, taste, age etc. A firm may have different groups of customers, who have different needs and problems. Thus, each section can look into the needs of each group of consumers and facilitate their buying–wholesale section, retail section etc.

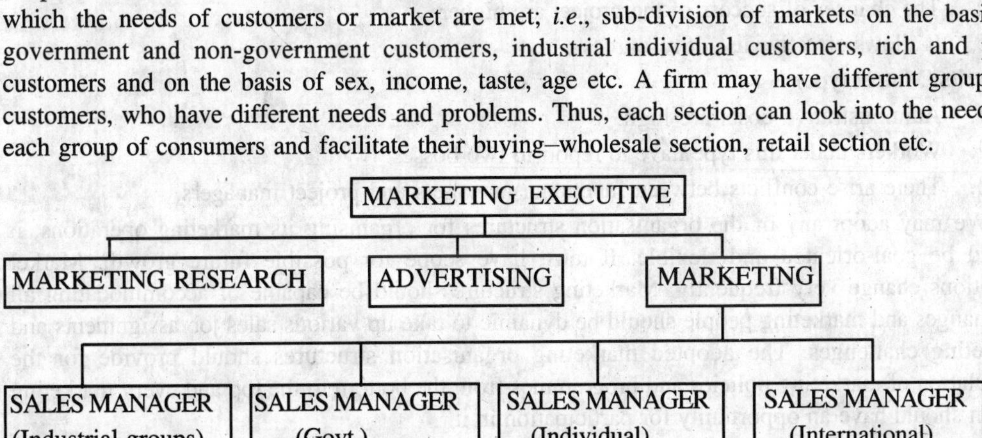

Merits: (Consumer Type)

1. This type of organisation can encourage consumers with clearly defined services.
2. The specialists can understand the needs of a particular segment of customers.
3. This type of organisation is useful to serve different type of customers.

Demerits: (Consumer Type)

1. Coordination between sales and other functions of marketing is difficult.
2. More man-power is required: thus expenditure is high.

8. **Matrix Type**

Matrix organisation is also known as grid or project organisation. Matrix organisation is created by merging the two complementary organisations, the project and functional. A team may be set up within the existing organisation, to conduct a study of a particular product or design or to complete a specific assignment in time. A project manager has a project team consisting of people from several functional sections. For instance, a project team is formed to market the television, and for this people will be drawn from different functional departments, say, production, research, marketing, engineering etc. These specialists are drawn from respective departments, borrowed to perform their part in the project work. When the project work is complete, they go back to their respective departments. This type of organisation is needed when a special type or urgent assignment of jobs or complicated job or a new product etc., is introduced. Generally, such organisation may be temporary.

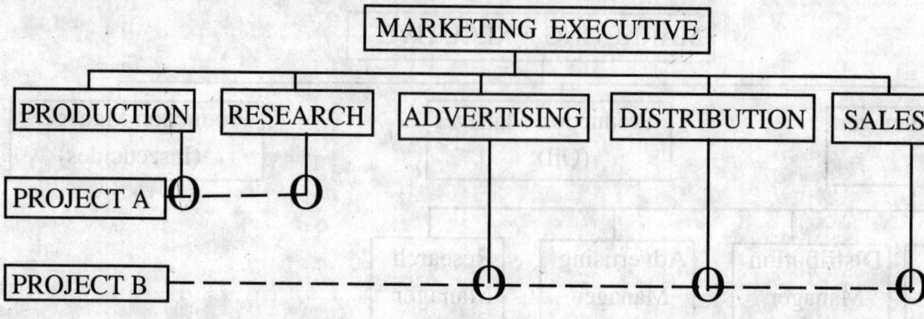

Merits

1. Specialised product knowledge is acquired.
2. It is economical to draw experts from various sections.
3. Expansion, improvements, diversification etc., are the result.
4. The chances of success of the project are higher.
5. It allows effective use of resources.

Demerits (Matrix type)

1. Adiministrative costs are high.
2. Workers under this type have to report to two bosses.
3. There arise conflicts between functional managers and project managers.

We may adopt any of the organisation structures for organising its marketing operations; it should be goal-oriented and flexible. It must have scope for possible future growth. Market conditions change very frequently. Marketing structure should be capable of accommodating all the changes and marketing people should be dynamic to take up various sales job assignments and marketing challenges. The adopted marketing organisation structures should provide for the formulation of marketing policies and programmes from the bottom to the top and every marketing person should have an opportunity for participation in it.

QUESTIONS

1. Analyse the impact of the marketing concept on the marketing organisation and the company organisation. (*B.Com., Mumbai*)
2. Explain how you will determine the structure of marketing organisation. (*M.Com., Delhi*)
3. Define 'marketing management' and explain its functions. (*B.Com., Madurai*)
4. Discuss the scope and importance of sales organisation. Examine briefly the structure of a sales organisation. (*B.Com., Madurai*)
5. Briefly examine the role of marketing management. (*B.Com., Madurai*)
6. Describe the various types of marketing organisation structures. (*M.Com., Delhi*)
7. Explain the following :
   (a) Line type organisation.
   (b) Functional type organisation.
   (c) Line and staff system organisation.
8. Write short notes on :
   (a) Geographical type organisation.
   (b) Product type organisation.
   (c) Consumer type organisation.
9. Is there any difference between Sales Management and Marketing Management? If so, explain how these two functions differ in scope and activities. (*B.Com. Meerut*)
10. Explain the functions of Marketing Manager. (*B.Com. Mumbai*)

CHAPTER 12

Marketing Strategy and Planning

- *Introduction*
- *What is Planning*
- *Features of Planning*
- *Marketing Planning*
- *Importance of Marketing Planning*
- *Benefits of Marketing Planning*
- *Characteristics of Marketing Planning*
- *Corporate Planning Process*
- *Marketing Planning Process*
- *Marketing Planning Activities*
- *Marketing Audit*
- *Barriers*
- *Case Study*-1
- *Case Study*-2
- *Case Study*-3
- *Case Study*-4
- *Case Study*-5
- *Case Study*-6
- *Questions*

INTRODUCTION

Strategic market planning (also mentioned as Strategic Planning or Strategic Market-oriented Planning, or Strategic Marketing Planning) essentially refers to planning that is conceptually and functionally long-term, typically covering a period of five years or more for the entire corporation. **Strategic market planning is a process yielding a marketing stratetgic that is framework for marketing plan.** The aim of strategic market planning is to adapt, adjust or reshape on an ongoing basis the corporation's different businesses to accomplish the target growth and profit objectives. The whole process involves keeping in focus the changing market opportunities and developing a viable fit between the corporation's objectives, resources and competencies.

The importance of planning can be best understood from the following poem:

For want of a nail, the shoe was lost
For want of a shoe, the horse was lost;
For want of a horse, the rider was lost;
For want of a rider, the battle was lost;
For want of a battle, the kingdom was lost;
AND all for want of a horse-shoe nail.

The importance of planning lies in the fact that it is like a navigator operating under varied business circumstances. A marketer has to work in an environment which is uncertain and ever-changing. It is a proper planning only that enables a manager to carve out the future course of action. Drucker has rightly defined business planning, "as a continuous process of making present entrepreneurial decisions systematically and with best possible knowledge of their futurity, organising systematically the effort needed to carry out these decisions against expectations through organised feedback."

What is Planning ?

Planning refers to the determination of a course of action to achieve a desired result. Planning is the process of thinking before doing. It is an intellectual process. All types of organisations prepare plans. Even individuals formulate plans. In its simplest form, planning is the process of establishing individual or organisational goals and the ways to achieve the goals. A plan is a predetermined course of action to be taken in future. Planning is a deliberate and conscious process. In the words of Fayol, "the plan of action is at one and at the same time the result envisaged, the line of action to be followed, the stages to go through and the methods to use.'' Planning begins with an analysis of external environment and internal resources and ends with the formulation of goals and detailed plans of achieving these goals. According to Koontz and Donnell, ''planning is deciding in advance what to do, how to do it, when to do it and who is to do it.''

Features of Planning

The following are the features of planning, in brief :

1. **Purposeful :** Planning is goal-oriented in the sense that plans are prepared and implemented to achieve certain objectives.

2. **Primary :** Planning is the most basic function of management. Without plans, there is nothing to organise and no need for control.

3. **Pervasive :** Planning is the function of each and every manager irrespective of his rank and area of work.

4. **Forward Looking :** Planning involves looking ahead and preparing for the future.

5. **Intellectual Process :** Planning is a rational and mental exercise.

6. **Continuity :** Planning is an ongoing process. Old plans have to be revised and new ones have to be prepared when the environment undergoes a change.

7. **Integrated Process :** Every lower level plan serves as a means towards the achievement of higher plans.

8. **Choice :** There is no need for planning if there is only one way of doing it. Planning problem arises only when an alternative course of action is discovered.

Marketing Planning ?

A business firm has to make various marketing decisions. These decisions actually emerge from the complex interaction of a large number of persons carrying out diverse responsibilities in the marketing organisation. Being part and parcel of the over-all management, the marketing executives are deeply involved in the process of planning. Marketing planning defines the role and responsibilities of marketing executives in such a way as to achieve the goals of the firm. It lays emphasis on the allocation of marketing resources in the best and most economical way. It gives an intelligent direction of marketing operations. Marketing planning involves the preparation of policies, programmes, budgets etc. in advance for carrying out the various activities and functions of marketing to attain the marketing goals. According to American Marketing Association, ''marketing planning is the work of setting up objectives for marketing activity and of determining and scheduling the steps necessary to achieve such objectives.'' Planning is the first management function to be performed in the process of management. It governs survival, growth and prosperity of any enterprise in a competitive and ever-changing environment.

The connecting link of markets to marketing is the process and the function of marketing management. Marketing management is the blending factor of markets and marketing. Today the consumer is a complicated, emotional and confused individual. His buying is based on subjectivity and not often backed by objectivity. The introduction of innumerable brands of toilet soaps, talcum powders are examples. Planning precedes activity in any purposeful endeavour. Business firms naturally undertake a good deal of planning. Business firms have to master the environment and score over their competitors. Thus in the case of a business firm, planning is always strategic in character. A firm cannot afford to travel in a haphazard manner, it has to travel with the support of a route map.

Every company must look ahead and determine where it wants to go and how to get there. Its future should not be left to chance. To meet this need, companies use two systems–a strategic planning system and marketing planning system. Strategic planning provides the route-map for the firm. Strategic planning serves as the hedge against risk and uncertainty. Strategic planning is a stream of decisions and actions which lead to effective strategies and which in turn help the firm to achieve its objectives. Strategy is not something that can be taken out of one's pocket and pushed into the market all of a sudden. ''No magic formula exists to prepare for the future. The requirements are excellent insight to understand changing consumer needs, clear planning to focus our efforts on meeting those needs, and flexibility, because change is the only constant. Most important, we must always offer consumers–products of quality and value, for this is the one need that will not change.''

Marketing has been described as the railway engine which pulls all the other departmental carriages along. Marketing planning is the interface between the enterprise and its market. We had explained that marketing places the consumer at both the beginning and the end of the business process. Any firm practising marketing in the proper sense has to identify correctly the needs of the consumer, translate the needs into suitable products and services, deliver those products and services to the total satisfaction of the consumer and through the process generate profits for the firm.

Importance of Marketing Planning :

Marketing planning is a systematic and disciplined exercise to formulate marketing strategies. Marketing planning can be related to the organisation as a whole or to strategic business units (SBU). Marketing planning is a forward looking exercises, which determines the future stategies of an organisation with special reference to its product development, market development, channel design, sales promotion and profitability. We may now summarise the importance of marketing planning in the following points:

1. It helps in avoiding future uncertainties.
2. It helps in management by objectives.
3. It helps in achieving objectives.
4. It helps in coordination and communication among the departments.
5. It helps in control.
6. It helps the customers in getting full satisfaction.

Benefits of Marketing Planning :

1. Marketing planning promotes successful marketing operations.
2. Planning helps to co-ordinate activities which can facilitate the attainment of objectives over time.
3. It forces management to reflect upon the future in a systematic way.
4. Resources can be better balanced in relation to identified market opportunities.

Marketing Strategy = The marketing logic by which the business unit hopes to achieve its marketing objectives.

5. A plan provides a frame work for a continuing review of operations. It will make the firm to give more attention to market enlargement rather than market maintenance.
6. Marketing planning helps to appraise performance, capitalise on strength, minimise weaknesses and threats and finally open up new opportunities.

7. Planning can be advocated to minimise the risk of failure.
8. Marketing planning reduces the adverse consequences of unfavourable circumstances beyond the influence of management.
9. A marketing plan promotes a comprehensive view of the business firm and acts as a process of communication and co-ordination between marketing department and other departments.
10. A greater preparedness to accommodate change can be stimulated.

Characteristics of Marketing Planning :

Marketing planning has the following characteristic features :

1. The success depends to a large extent upon human behaviour and response.
2. They are complicated in nature.
3. Marketing decisions have long term effects on efficiency, profitability and market standing of the firm.
4. Marketing planning is a formal and systematic approach towards planning of all marketing activities–product positioning, price setting, distribution channels etc.
5. Marketing planning, as a rational activity, requires thinking, imagination and foresight. Market analysis, market projection, consumer behaviour analysis and marketing-guided conclusions are based on data and measurements drawn from internal and external environments.
6. Marketing planning is a forward-looking and dynamic process designed to promote market-oriented or consumer-oriented business actions.
7. Planning is concerned with two things : (i) avoiding incorrect actions and (ii) reducing frequency of failure to exploit opportunities. Thus, marketing planning has both an optimistic and a pessimistic component.
8. Marketing planning is done by the marketing department. Various sub-divisions and sections under the department give their proposals based on which the overall company marketing plans are developed and designed.
9. Planning is a process of deciding in advance what to do and how to do it. If the marketing planner desires to achieve a target market at some future date and if he needs some time to decide what to do and how to do it, he must make the necessary marketing decisions before taking action.
10. Planning is basically a decision-making process. Marketing planning is a programme of marketing-based actions regarding the future with the object of minimising risk and uncertainty and producing a set of interrelated decisions.

Corporate Planning Process

Steps in Corporate Planning Process:

1. Establishing corporate mission, objectives and goals.
2. Establishing Strategic Business Units.
3. Assigning resources to each Stategic Business Unit.
4. Planning for Business Growth.

Establishing Corporate Mission, Objectives and Goals

Top management prepares statements of mission, objectives and goals that play the role of a framework within which divisions and business units prepare their plan. They are guiding force for the organisation and express the reasons of being in business and what specific goals the firm is pursuing at a given point of time. A mission statement addresses the organisation's fundamental reason for existing and specifies the functional role that the organisation is going to adopt in its market place. When the top management is convinced about the irrelevance of mission, the famous management thinker Peter F Drucker recommends in answering some fundamental questions;

1. What is our business?
2. Who is the customer?
3. What is the value to the customer?
4. What will our business be?
5. What should our business be?

Apparently these questions do not seem to be complicated at all. A casual approach to answering these questions is difinitely going to be counter-productive. In fact, these are among the toughest yet most important questions that any corporation can answer. Creating or revising a mission statement is quite difficult because of the many complex variables that must be examined.

The enterprise mission that provides a sense of direction with repect to where it wants to go and what it aspires to achieve in overall business, often also reflects much idealism. The next step is to establish a specific set of objectives. (here objectives and goals are synonymous).

Objectives provide direction to stay focused on common purpose. Every activity is directed towards the objectives and every individual contributes to accomplish the objectives.

Objectives coordinate the activities and keep them on the right track. They make behaviours in an organisation more rational and coordinated and thus more effective.

Objectives serve as performance standards to compare actual results.

Objectives provide a basis for motivation of employees to be result oriented because they know towards what ends they are working.

Establishing Strategic Business Units

Once the organisation mission, objectives and goals are set, they will provide a framework for determining what kind of organisational structure and business models are a 'best fit' for the organisation's marketing efforts. The organisation structure for a single product will be simple as it can be designed by management function or geographic territory. But in case of multi-product organisations, the structure can be very complex. So Companies prefer establishing strategic business units (SBUs). A SBU is a distinct business unit of the business organisation in the form of a subsidiary company, department, division or product line with a specific product-market focus and independent authority and responsibility of the manager to take business decisions. A strategice business unit operates like a company within a company which is organised around a business model and cluster of offerings that share some commonalty in the form of similar production process, similar targets markets or similar investment requirements. A SBU has control over its own business model and marketing strategy. A strategic business unit has the following characteristics:

(a) Separate responsibility for strategic planning and profit performance and profit influencing factors.

(b) A separate set of competitors.

(c) Single business or a collection of related businesses, which offer scope for independent strategic planning from remaining organisation.

The understanding of an SBU is, therefore, a convenient starting point for planning since the company's strategic business units have been identified. In practice, big companies in India work on the basis that strategic planning at SBU level has to be agreed to by the corporate management.

Planning for Business Growth

Intensive growth strategies are appropriate when current products and current markets show the potential for sales increase. There are three main strategic options that seem to be appropriate to accomplish intensive growth.

1. Market Penetration
2. Market Development
3. Product Development

1. **Market Penetration :** It is a strategy of increasing sales of existing products in current markets. For example, Procter and Gamble reduced the price of its detergent ariel in the Indian market to increase its sale among existing and new consumers in the current market. Depending on the product category, other approaches can be to increase advertising, sales promotion, personal selling and increase distribution network in the current markets.

2. **Market Development :** It refers to increasing sales by introducing current products into new markets. This strategy often involves expanding business in new geographic areas. For example, with globalisation and opening up of Indian borders for businesses, many organisations have introduced their products in the Indian market. These companies were marketing these products in their domestic and other markets for quite sometime.

PRODUCT

MARKET	Current	New
Current	Market penetration	Product development
New	Market development	Diversification

3. **Product Development :** It means increasing sales by improving current products in some way or developing entirely new products for current markets. For example, Gillette has modified its razor and named it Vector for Indian consumers. In auto industry, manufacturers regularly introduce redesigned or new products.

Marketing Planning Process

The steps involved in the marketing planning process are :

1. Scanning the marketing environment.
2. Internal scanning.

3. Setting the marketing objectives.
4. Formulating the marketing strategy.
5. Developing the functional plans.

We shall briefly discuss these steps :

1. **Scanning the Marketing Environment :** First, a firm scans its marketing environment. The purpose is to find out (i) the favourable and unfavourable factors prevailing in the environment and (ii) the specific business opportunities available to the business unit and their relative attractiveness. Study of marketing environment analysis helps to locate marketing opportunities and discover unsatisfied consumer demand. It also undertakes customer sensing, reactions of the customer to its products and tries to locate the causes of the customers patronage of a particular brand and who remain closest to the customer, and why.

2. **Internal scanning :** Internal scanning is the process of assessing the firm's strength and weaknesses and identifying its core competencies and competitive advantages. While environmental scanning may help to identify the various possible opportunities in areas of interest to the firm, the firm obviously cannot tap all the identified opportunities. It has to be selective and decide on the opportunities it has to tap and the business it has to pursue. It also has to build defences against impending problems.

3. **Setting Marketing Objectives :** The very purpose of setting objectives is to provide clear cut direction to the business regarding its future course of action. Objectives are set in all the key areas of marketing such as sales volume, market share, market standing, innovation, productivity, profit etc. The business unit has to develop its marketing objectives after weighing the opportunities available in the environment, the threats, the forces of competitions, the resources and capabilities of the unit and its marketing organisation.

For example, marketing objectives may be set as follows :

* The distribution costs per unit of the product will be reduced by 10% in the current financial year.
* Market share of the product will be increased by 10% during the next financial year.
* The sales volume of the product will be increased by 15% during the coming financial year.

4. **Formulating Marketing Strategy :** Marketing strategy formulation is the core of marketing planning. Marketing strategy is a set of objectives, policies and rules that guide over time marketing efforts of the concern. Stated in simple terms, marketing strategy is the complete and unbeatable plan designed specifically for attaining the marketing objectives of the firm, the marketing objectives indicate what the firm wants to achieve, the marketing strategy provides the design for achieving them.

5. **Developing Functional Plans :** Once the marketing strategy is formulated, the next step is elaborating the marketing strategy into detailed plans and programmes. The detailed functional plans will emanate from and be in tune with the marketing objectives and marketing strategy of the firm. Even the best marketing strategy may turn out to be a failure in the marketplace, if the detailed functional plans are drawn up in a haphazard manner. A plan may have to be developed for each marketing function.

A mechanism for monitoring at regular intervals, the attainment of key results areas is an essential part of the whole process. This mechanism, with its supportive procedures, should seek to provide the appropriate feedback upon which corrective measures can be taken.

The Marketing Planning Appraisal Process

1. External Appraisal
2. Internal Appraisal
3. SWOT Analysis
4. Gap Analysis
5. Forecasting

NB: These have been explained later in this book

Marketing Planning Activities

Marketing Planning is concerned with the determination of marketing objectives. These objectives may be long-term and short-term nature – long range and short range.

(a) **Long-term Marketing Planning (LTMP)**

Long range planning involves tentative determination of the enterprise's broad goals to be achieved and the strategies to be adopted for the purpose over a long period of time. LTMP covers a time which is long enough to provide the marketing management with an opportunity to anticipate future problems and thus to have a greater freedom of action to resolve them in an orderly manner.

According to Peter F. Drucker, ''long range planning is not master-minding the future. It does not deal with future decisions. It deals with the futurity of present decisions. It is not an attempt to eliminate risk. Rather it seeks to raise the capacity to take risks.'' These have great relevance to a long term planning for marketing also. The goals generally relate to sales, market share, the range of new products, markets to be pursued, the lines of business which the enterprise should go in etc.

For LTMP, Philip Kotler suggests consideration of the following situations :

(1) **Diagnosis :** It refers to the company's standing with respect to sales, market share, recent trend etc.

(2) **Prognosis :** It refers to the estimation where the company is likely to go if present market condition continues; how much will be its sales and profit in the long run.

(3) **Objectives :** On the basis of prognostic studies, the company may assess bright future or doubtful future and accordingly decide new objectives.

(4) **Strategy :** It stresses on the company's competitive advantages and consists of plans for high-quality products, premium price, vigorous advertisements, and highest order of salesmanship, after a careful evaluation of alternatives under the circumstances.

(5) **Tactics :** It suggests how to make use of the company's strategies to achieve its objectives. That is, the tactics indicate the particular method that are to be used to achieve the goals of the enterprise.

(6) **Control :** It requires two things to be incorporated : (i) monitoring device to check the planning effectiveness, and (ii) contingency plans to meet new situations.

(b) Short-term Marketing Planning (STMP)

Short term planning for marketing is generally made for one year or less. STMP has two objectives (a) implementation of LTMP through programmes and budgets and (b) improvement of operating performance. The plans are normally sub-divided into monthly or weekly plans for control purpose. Mostly short term plans are in the form of budgets. Periodically, the budgeted figure is compared with the actual performance, variations are considered for corrective steps.

Tools and Techniques of Marketing Control

1. Marketing Audit
2. Market Share Analysis
3. Marketing Cost Analysis
4. Credit Control
5. Budgetary Control
6. Ratio Analysis
7. Contribution Margin Analysis
8. Marketing Information
9. Variance Analysis
10. SWOT Analysis

The Marketing Audit

Marketing audit is the final method of marketing evaluation and refers to a thorough, systematic, objective examination of its objectives, strategies, organisation and performance. The primary purpose of audit is to identify weak areas in executing marketing activities and recommends actions to improve performance in these areas. It also highlights activities where the company does well. Companies regularly conduct accounting or financial audit. Likewise, the marketing audit should also be conducted on a regular basis and not just when performance evaluation points to problems with the system, or when there is a crisis.

Marketing audit may focus on all of the firm's marketing, or it could include some specific marketing activity or activities. For example, the audit could be only for customer service, focusing solely on customer service objectives standards, and comparing them with achieved standards. Similarly, the audit might be conducted for sales, advertising, sales promotion, or any other activity. The extent of marketing audit depends on involved costs, number of target markets served, marketing mix composition, and environmental conditions. The audit findings can be useful to take corrective actions where required to be necessary such as target markets, opportunities, marketing strategies, marketing mix etc. Marketing audit helps evaluation by understanding the following:

- Describing the present activities and realised results in the areas of sales, costs, prices, profits and feedback with respect to other areas of performance.
- Analysing information about factors that may have an impact on marketing strategy such as environmental conditions, target customers and competition.
- An analysis of opportunities, threats and deciding suitable alternatives for marketing strategy.
- Develop a comprehensive database to be used in the evaluation of objective and achievements.

A company may use external consultants or company personnel. Hired auditors are more expensive though experienced in this specialised work, and not being from within the company, adopt an objective approach while devoting full time to this work.

The process of conducting marketing audit has no specific method or is bound by any set of rules or procedures. There are only some guidelines to develop a step-by-step plan to make marketing audit methodical and objective to accomplish the purpose. Professionals in this field often use a series of carefully designed relevant audit questionnaires to focus on the appropriate issues and interview diverse group of personnel from different departments of the company. These interviews starts at the top management level and subsequently move down through other hierarchical levels. After the audit is complete, a comprehensive written report of findings is prepared and handed over to the top management. Many firms conduct marketing audits informally by attempting to verify operating results against set performance standards.

In addition to sales, the management wants to assess the costs to determine the relative profitability of its territories, product lines, or other marketing units. A marketing cost analysis is a detailed study of the operating expenses from a company's profit and loss statement. On the basis of this analysis, the management should examine any variations between budgeted costs and actual expenses. One challenge in marketing cost analysis costs–especially indirect costs – to the marketing units. The findings from these analyses can help to take decisions regarding a company's marketing programme.

Barriers or Obstacles

No manager can predict completely and accurately the events of the future. There are various barriers in the path leading to successful planning. The height of each barrier may differ from company-to-company.

Obstacles to Effective Planning

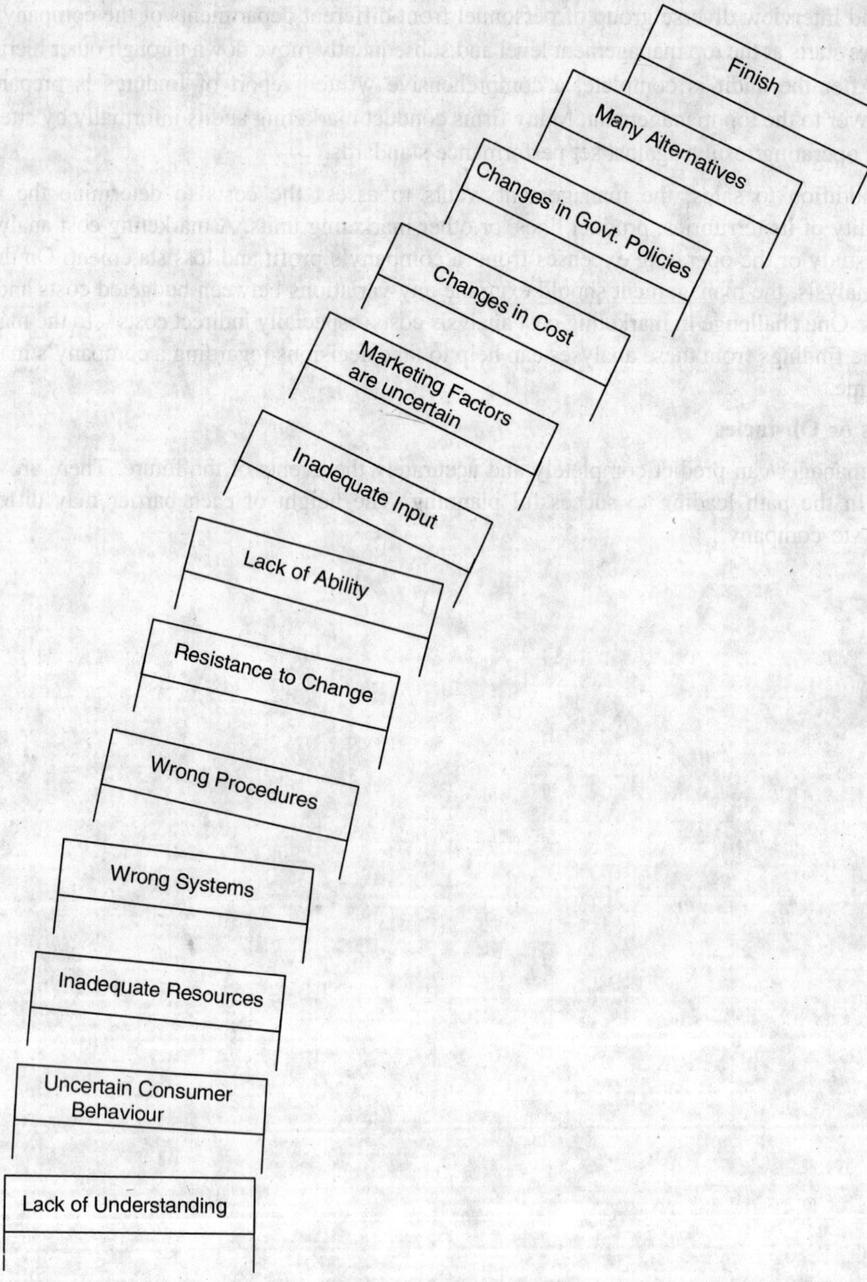

The following measures are helpful in overcoming obstacles to planning :

1. Set clear-cut objectives.
2. Develop a sound management information system.
3. Keep plans flexible.
4. Undertake a cost-benefit analysis of all plans.
5. Provide required resources.
6. Develop a dynamic outlook among managers.

Case Study-1

NEED FOR STRATEGIC PLANNING FOR SURVIVAL AND GROWTH

Company

Alpha, S.A., is a Mexican Corporation in the industrial city of Monterrey. The original company began in 1890 when six local businessmen founded a brewery. This company expanded, putting many operations into a holding company. However, in 1974, the management fued and split the company into two concerns—Valores Industrials and Alpha.

Alpha was quite aggressive and management believed in expansion through diversification. Starting with little more than steel mills and paper factories, Alpha diversified into tourism, hotelling, food processing, capital goods and petrochemicals. Between 1976 and 1980, Alpha's subsidiaries grew to 157 from 37, while the number of employees tripled to 48,000. Assets increased 450 p.c. to $2 billion. Revenues rose 460 p.c. to $1 billion; and profits increased 440 p.c. to $80 million.

The expansion plans were executed primarily through foreign bank loans. After Mexico discovered huge oil reserves in 1976 bankers wanted a piece of action. Since Alpha was aggressively expanding and was the biggest private enterprise, bank lent money to Alpha. The result was $2.5 billion debt mainly from 130 foreign banks.

Corporate Expansion

Alpha's expansion, however, did not follow any planned strategy. For many of its subsidiaries, Alpha did not have management expertise to run companies. It did not have management development plans to ensure management stability and growth. Integrated business planning was conspicuous by its absence.

In 1980, Alpha bought a food processing company, which was a thriving undertaking. But the new management (of Alpha) did not know the intricacies of commodity business. As a result, the Food Division lost $2 million in 1981; major problem of Alpha's executives was their complacency. The feeling was that their executives was special and could do no wrong. Employees of acquired companies resisted some of the decisions but new management belived in over optimistic forecasts. There was also tremendous waste of corporate resources in hiring executives with degrees. Alpha hired inexperienced graduates with Harvard MBA than experienced executives with appropriate experience.

Several people tried to warn the company that it didn't have money or the manpower to handle its growth and over-spending. In 1979 and 1980, as acquisition and investment projects accelerated, Alpha needed money quickly and piled up short-term debt. Management consultants told Alpha that eventually bankers would balk (shirk) at lending more money and the company wouldn't have the cash to pay its debts. The manager of strategic planning for the capital-goods group also brought to management's attention the cash flow problems which began to appear in fourth quarter of 1980. The manager recommended liquidating as many acquisitions as possible. But expansion proceeded unchecked.

External Environment

Under normal business conditions, Alpha could have managed to survive, but the bubble burst in the late 1981. The U.S. recession decreased the demand for goods and the world-wide oil glut caused Mexico's economy to deteriorate rapidly. Reduced oil production caused Mexico's revenues to drop and which in turn made the peso overvalued. The overvalued peso hurt exports even more. Furthermore the high interest rates hurt the cash-flow of the debt ridden company. The 40% devaluation of peso increased the debt-burden by $140 million. The company stopped paying principal in December, 1981, on its short-term loans and in April, 1982, on its long-term debt. It posted a loss of $124 million in 1981. The loss in 1982 is projected to be $308 million. Alpha laid off 4,000 employees last year.

Commentary

Alpha's size made it a special company in Mexico. Its 1980 sales represented some 2% of Mexico's gross domestic product. Since the company created jobs and brought in industrialization, the Mexican Government also encouraged Alpha to grow.

For some of their lendings, the bankers also were to blame. Many bankers conceded that they didn't always do their homework. Since so many banks were involved and due to Alpha's complicated financial statements, the bankers assumed that any further loans would be good. However, the major banking institutions should have seen the coming crisis. To weather this crisis, Alpha must sell at least 20% of its assets, but most potential buyers are short of cash due to bad economic environment. Mexican Government cannot help because it needs cash itself. Alpha due to its size and place in Mexican industry, cannot be allowed to fail as these difficulties may foreshadow a wave of other corporate failures.

QUESTIONS

1. What are lessons learned from Alpha's predicament ?
2. What specific steps in strategic planning should have been taken in 1976 prior to adopting expansion strategy?
3. What should Alpha have done in 1979 when first signs of trouble began to appear?
4. How important is it to have realistic forecasts of external uncontrollable parameters to take a rapid corrective action?

Case Study-2

LONG-RANGE PLANNING FOR SUN OIL COMPANY

Sun Oil Company

Sun Oil Company during 1970's was mostly a refiner and marketer of petroleum products. It was content with buying oil domestically and from Iran and Venezuela and distributing the products through its own network or retailers. Its own exploration and production of oil amounted to less than one third of the refining capacity. Like other oil giants it went on a diversification fling (rush) into other businesses outside oil. Real estate, industrial distribution, trucking interest were acquired. It had an oil-services subsidiary, Sperry-Sun. It had a 66 year old Sun Ship Company and in 1978, it acquired a 34% stake for $293 million in Becton, Dickinson & Co., a medical supplies concern. Investment analysts charged that Sun Oil lacked continuity in strategic planning.

Long Range Strategy

Several external events prodded (aroused) Sun's management into taking a hard look at the far-flung corporate interests. In 1979, oil prices rocked again while Sun's U.S., production of oil declined at an alarming rate. The overall drop-off exceeded the industry average. The same year, Sun lost its Iranian supply due to the U.S. Hostage crisis. Its Venezuelan supply had been lost due to nationalization four years back.

Furthermore, the company went too far a field into businesses from health care field to aquaculture. Becton Dickinson acquisition created some violation of security laws in addition to being an unrelated field. Its brief venture into aquaculture, breeding shrimp-like prawns native to Malaysia, demonstrated obstacles to company's diversification strategy : finding businesses large enough to amount to something for an integrated oil company.

The lesson learned was there is no better business to be in than oil and no other large enough to put the cash flow to generate sound future growth. Sun Oil Company began to put strategic planning at work. It divested Becton, Dickinson & Co. shares through an issue of exchangeable debentures. It sold Sperry-Sun Inc. oil services subsidiary, and the Sun Ship Company. It also reduced its holdings in a Canadian Oil Company, Suncor, from 75% to less than 50% to take advantage of the tax incentives available to Canadian-controlled oil companies.

Sun Oil Company needed oil reserves to increase its exploration and production capabilities. In 1980, it acquired Texas Pacific Company for $2.39 billion from Seagram Company. Taxas Pacific acquisition gave Sun Oil four million acres of potential oil producing properties. To concentrate more on exploration it sold off two of its refineries. The sale of refineries and divestiture of other unrelated ventures generated cash to partially offset the acquisition of Taxes Pacific. The strategy was to become a top energy producer with all the inherent risks in development and exploration of oil wells.

QUESTIONS

1. Do you agree with Sun Oil Company's strategy of capturing energy reserves rather than other diversified corporate acquisitions ?
2. The risks in oil exploration are high. It requires enormous outlays for exploration and production. Are the risks worth in the current corporate strategy ?
3. With a worldwide glut in the demand for energy, what opportunities do you see for integrated energy companies ?

Case Study-3

GENERAL ELECTRIC—CHANGING WITH TIMES

General Electric Company

General Electric Company is a large conglomerate multinational holding company, with presence all over the world and products ranging from light bulbs to jet engines to sophisticated computers. Reginald Jones was the chairman of GE until he retired in 1980. Mr. Jones was known for his financial wizardry. He steered GE into high technology businesses and de-emphasized its dependence of electrical equipment. Mr. Jones built the company to be profitable year after year with keen attention to the bottom line. Today, the comany is enormously successful with its profits rising comfortably than those of many other American industrial companies.

Strategy to Meet Foreign Competition

Mr. Welsh, a 22-year GE Veteran, became Chief Executive of the $27 billion giant succeeding Mr. Jones and is bringing new strategy for the period ahead. What must GE do to keep it profitable in the "long run" ? Mr. Welsh insists that GE either must keep gaining the market share or risk being overrun by foreign competitors that can produce higher-quality goods faster and cheaper. Many of GE's old-line manufacturing businesses such as consumer appliances, electronics and industrial equipment have been buffeted by foreign competition and recession. The company had strong performance in its high technology products and services and by its General Electric Credit Corporation.

The strategy to long-term profitability is to put a greater emphasis on market share and to implement the change with urgency but not responding to a financial emergency. Mr. Welsh wants to transform the company's bottom-line wizards into "World-class Competitors". He wants GE's product lines, within three to eight years to be No. 1 or No. 2 in market share in all 250 GE businesses. Many are already there, but others will have to fight to get there.

GE unloaded several businesses that were marginal or did not fit into GE's strategic thrusts. GE also made about $700 million worth of acquisitions. Mr. Welsh eliminated layers of mandatory review for capital expenditures, acquisitions and divestitures. He gave broader decision-making authority to GE's six "sector-executives", who run divisions into which all GE's businesses are grouped. The new management style encourages entrepreneurs.

GE has a commitment to make those businesses leaders that are not currently No. I or No. 2 in the marketplace. The managers of these units feel threatened. But Mr. Welsh demands a plan to turn things around with plenty of incentives for executives, to stay and develop alternatives.

QUESTIONS

1. Is GE's philosophy of market share as a primary objective to bottom-line profits appropriate?
2. What does GE need to do to gain market share ? What are the strategies for gaining market share ?
3. Is three to eight year time frame enough to achieve the industry leadership position ?

QUESTIONS

1. Define the term Marketing Planning.
2. Discuss the scope of Marketing Planning Activities.
3. Explain the Marketing Planning Process.
4. Discuss the importance of Marketing Planning.
5. What are the difficulties in Marketing Planning ?
6. What are the objectives of Marketing Planning ?
7. What are the advantages of Marketing Planning ?
8. What are the major problems in Marketing Planning ?
9. What are the components of the marketing Planning ?
10. Discuss the elements of strategic marketing Planning.

Case Study-4

HELIX LATEX INDUSTRIES

Helix Latex Industries, a partnership concern which was in the business of surgical and medical equipments, manufacturing between 25 to 30 items like feeding nipples, B.L.B. mask equipment, saline and blood transfusion tubing, soil testing sheets, etc., entered into the business of manufacturing surgical and post-mortem hand gloves in December 1968. It invested Rs. 5 lakhs in plant and equipment to manufacture this item and started manufacturing 2,000 pairs per day. There were about 30 other manufacturers in this field, nearly all of them coming under the classification of small-scale industries. Helix Latex faced competition mainly from Dial Rubber Works of Mumbai, Phoenix of Bhavnagar, and Swastik Rubber of Pune.

The first two companies were selling about 60,000 pairs of hand gloves everyday. Swastik Rubber, which was the biggest company of the lot, was marketing about 30,000 pairs per day. These concerns were selling gloves on an approximate rate of Re. 1 per pair.

When Helix first started manufacturing gloves it tried to sell its product at the rate of Rs. 1.25 per pair. In terms of quality its product was superior to two of its competitors but occupied a second place when compared to Dial Rubber Works of Mumbai. Being a surgical item the product, however, had to satisfy the minimum specifications in respect of T.S. (Tensile Strength) and E.B. (Elongation at Break) laid down by the Government which required testing of the product in the Government laboratories before permission to market them was granted.

The market for gloves consisted of hospitals, surgical trade, D.G.S.&D. and State tenders, individual doctors and packets of medicines. Helix sold their brand of gloves, which they called super-tax, through wholesalers and dealers and were able to keep to delivery schedules. They had an open channel policy. Helix appointed one dealer each in Chennai, Calcutta and three in Delhi. No dealer was appointed in Mumbai where the competition was very tough.

In promoting the sale of gloves Helix put up sign boards in important surgical and medical equipments markets. To push the sale of its gloves it also advertised its products in medical journals and put up stalls in medical and surgical conferences.

The above marketing mix did not, however, help Helix in selling its daily production of 2,000 gloves in the market. One of its partners, who had his training in the area of marketing in one of the best business schools of U.S.A., finding that its product was not moving notwithstanding the fact that Helix's marketing mix compared favourably with its competitors, decided to experiment and identify the effect of price reduction on the sale of this product. As a result of this decision the price of its brand of product super-tax was reduced from Rs. 1.25, initially fixed price, to Re. 1. The reduced price also did not make any difference in the sale of super-tax. It again reduced the price to 87 paise per pair. On finding that the reduced price of 87 paise, which was lower than its three main competitiors' prices in the neighbourhood of Re. 1 per pair, again failed to tick, a decision was taken to further reduce the price to 75 paise per pair. No tangible difference was, however, made to sales of super-tax by this downward exercise in price reduction.

On reviewing other elements of the marketing mix, it was found that the Mumbai concern was selling for cash and was not giving any credit facilities while its two other competitors were allowing 30 days credit. Helix in order to improve upon its competitors' strategy decided to grant 3 months' credit facilities. Unfortunately all these changes did not help Helix in marketing all the 2,000 pairs it could produce every day. The firm was really at a loss to understand what mix and strategy it could adopt to achieve success in its sales efforts?

QUESTIONS

1. What are the basic problems being faced by the company in marketing its products ?
2. What are the strengths and weaknesses of the company ?
3. What marketing mix and strategy would you recommend to the company ?

Case Study-5

Marketing Plan

CUSTOMER COMFORTS LTD.

'A glorious morning!' muttered Ms. Shakti Rohilla to herself as she arranged her agenda for the day. Ms. Rohilla was the newly appointed marketing manager of Customer Comforts Limited (CCL)—a Rs. 20 crore company in Bombay. First on her engagements for the day, she had a meeting with her Director (Marketing) early in the morning. This meeting was to evaluate the initial thoughts of Ms. Rohilla on how to plan marketing efforts for 'water-beds'—a major product developed recently by CCL.

Customer Comforts Limited (CCL) was set up about a quarter of century ago in New Delhi by Harjinder Singh to create and market a variety of inflatable products. The organisation manufactured rafts, boats, life-jackets and collapsible containers for bulk storage purpose. It had acquired both quality image and customer satisfaction. Over the years, the only change that Mr. Singh had allowed in company philosophy, was to innovate and add more vigorously to the consumer products in the inflatable category to meet new customer desires.

Water-bed was a major offer in the series by CCL in the middle of 1991 to the Indian markets. The product had already been accepted, to a large extent, abroad and it was hoped that Indian consumers too will accept it. It may be noted that water-beds are made of PVC with mattresses full of water. This water needs to be changed once in six months. In winter, if customers desired, the water could be heated to a required temperature.

Among the major benefits of water-beds over the conventional beds and mattresses whether made of jutes, cotton, or foam, was that a water-bed applied equal pressure on every point in the body. This ensured its users a healthy and comfortable night's sleep. Ms. Rohilla believed that this benefit will be its chief attraction and needed to be communicated.

Further, the PVC used in making water-beds was of high quality. They are sturdy enough as the in-house research and limited field experiments proved to withstand children romping on them. One could even stub a cigarette without springing a leak. Ms. Rohilla knew that this would be a major hurdle to cross as it would take some communication to convince customers. However, she felt confident that the benefit would reach customers.

Ms. Rohilla was to design a comprehensive market plan for the water-bed. Before it, however, she consulted her Director (marketing) with her initial thoughts. The Director seemed to agree but asked her to marshall them in writing and discuss the same again that afternoon.

As she began, as if on cue, her study room clock chimed. "Oh, nine-thirty! time to get ready for the office," said Ms. Rohilla and spurted out of her study.

QUESTIONS

1. Critically examine the opportunity as seen by the CCL ?
2. Suggest a suitable plan for marketing water-beds. (*AIMA*, *June, 1997*)

Case Study-6

SOYABEAN MILK—AS AN ALTERNATIVE

Market Strategy

Dr. S. Chakraborty was domiciled in Los Angeles, U.S.A. for the last eight years. After getting his Masters in Food Technology from the University of California, he obtained a Ph. D. specialising in 'high protein products.' After completing his education, he joined a company, HyPro Inc., as a Director of R & D. The company developed different types of high protein products which were marketed through a large number of departmental stores throughout U.S.A. The company enjoyed a good reputation.

Dr. Chakraborty was seriously thinking of returning to India and settling down in his hometown of Bangalore. He was also toying with the idea for the last two or three years to set up a plant to produce high protein products in India. During his earlier visits, after talking to different people, he had noticed the availability of Soyabeans in abundance. He had carried out several experiments in his laboratory and had developed what he called **"Soyabean Milk."** He felt that for a country like India with the majority of the children being undernourished, this would be an ideal product.

Soyabean Milk would have some percentage of normal milk, water and other raw materials added to give it a high protein value. It will be pasteurised, so refrigeration would not be essential and will have almost the same or even better life than average milk. Soyabean Milk would cost about 15 per cent more than the regular milk, which, he felt, was justified due to its high protein values. To obtain same proteins, the other substitutes or medicines, he felt, would be ten times costlier.

As he was about 25,000 kms away from his potential market, he first wanted to ascertain the feasibility of his project. He had several questions to which he wanted the answers. Some of these were :

(i) Whether the tradition-bound Indian population would accept a new concept like Soyabean Milk ?

(ii) In which town should he set up his first plant ? And of what capacity ?

(iii) In what form should he introduce the Soyabean Milk ? As a substitute to normal milk or by adding different flavours, as a competitive product to the already existing soft drinks market ?

(iv) What sort of distribution arrangement should he have ?

Technically he was confident about the production of the Soyabean Milk. Marketing-wise and commercially, whether such a project will be viable, was his main doubt. His friends had informed him that recently two companies have already introduced Soyabean Milk in India which was, however, very costly in the market. This did not worry him much as he felt that his product would be superior and that with such a large population in India, even a dozen competitors should do reasonably good business. Thus, he felt encouraged by the news of two companies introducing the soyabean milk.

QUESTIONS

1. What type of information should Dr. Chakraborty collect and consider before setting up his project ?
2. What marketing strategy would you recommend for marketing of Soyabean Milk in India.

(AIMA)

CHAPTER 13

Marketing Environment

- *Introduction*
- *Scanning the Environment*
- *Inportance of Environment Analysis*
- *Need for Analysis*
- *Concept of Micro and Macro Environment*
- *Company*
- *Company's Supplier*
- *Intermediaries*
- *Customers*
- *Competitors*
- *Public*
- *Demographic Environment*
- *Economic Environment*
- *Physical Environment*
- *Technological Environment*
- *Political Environment*
- *Legal Environment*
- *Social and Cultural Environment*
- *Case Study-1*
- *Case Study-2*
- *Cast Study-3*
- *Case Study-4*
- *Case Study-5*
- *Case Study-6*
- *Case Study-7*
- *Questions*

INTRODUCTION

Marketing activities are influenced by several factors inside and outside a business firm. These factors or forces influencing marketing decision-making are collectively called marketing environment. It comprises all those forces which have an impact on market and marketing efforts of the enterprise. According to Philip Kotler, marketing environment refers to ''external factors and forces that affect the company's ability to develop and maintain successful transactions and relationships with its target customers".

The marketing programme of a firm is influenced and shaped by a firm's inwardly need to begin its business planning by looking outwardly at what its customers require, rather than inwardly at what it would prefer to produce. The firm must be aware of what is going on in its marketing environment and appreciate how change in its environment can lead to changing patterns of demand for its products. It also needs to assess marketing opportunities and threats present in the surroundings. An environment can be defined as everything which surrounds and impinges on a system. Systems of many kinds have environments with which they interact. Marketing can be seen as a system which must respond to environmental change. Just as the human body may have problems, it fails to adjust to environmental change. Similarly, businesses may fail if they do not adapt to external changes such as new sources of competition or changes in consumers' preferences.

Scanning the Environment

Marketing activities do not take place in a vacuum, isolated from all external forces. In fact all marketing operations are conducted in a highly complex, dynamic and changing environment. According to Philip Kotler, "A company's marketing environment consists of the factors and forces outside marketing that affect management's ability to build and maintain successful relationships with target customers".

The marketing environment offers both **opportunities** and **threats**. Successful companies know the vital importance of constantly watching and adapting to the changing environment. A company's marketers take the major responsibility for identifying significant changes in the environment. More than any other groups in the company, marketers must be the trend trackers and opportunity seekers. Although every manager in an organisation needs to observe the outside environment, marketers have two special aptitudes. They have disciplined methods - marketing intelligence and marketing research – for collection of information about the marketing environment. They also spend time in the customer and competitor environment. By conducting systematic environmental scanning, marketers are able to revise and adapt marketing strategies to meet new challenges and opportunities in the market place.

Marketing as a function is basically all about matching the offerings of the organisation to the outside world, in particular, the market-place. Not surprisingly, many functions within marketing, such as selling, product development and market research, concern themselves with issues, problems and opportunities outside the organisation, and focus on responding to outside events and circumstances. Kotler identifies in this external role the need for markters to develop an 'outside-in' perspective, an ability to work on external cues and stimuli to the profit of the whole organisation.

Environment scanning is a constant, important activity of successful companies. This process includes gathering, filtering and analyzing information related to the marketing environment. It also includes monitoring the changes taking place in the environment and forecasting future status of each factor. Such analysis helps to spot opportunities and threats in the environment, and pinpoints the ones that are specifically relevant to the company. The company's marketing people have the responsibility for scanning and identifying significant changes or trends in the marketing environment. As already mentioned that marketing research and marketing intelligence system are the methods used by companies for environment scanning and gathering vital information about changes. Customers' behaviour and competitors' activities are also important factors to be watched in the environment. Successful companies know the vital importance of constantly scanning and adapting to the changing environment. The environment continues to change at a rapid pace.

Importance of Environment Analysis

The following are the benefits of environment analysis:-

1. It helps in marketing analysis.
2. It can assess the impact of opportunities and threats on the business.
3. It facilitates the company to increase general awareness of environmental.changes.
4. It is possible to develop effective marketing strategies on the basis of analysis.
5. It helps to capitalise the opportunities rather than losing out to competitors.
6. It facilitates to understand the elements of the environment.
7. It helps to develop best strategies, in the light of analysing "what is going around the company.

Need for Environment Analysis

Environmental analysis attempts to give an extensive insight as to the current market conditions as well as of impact of external factors that are uncontrollable by the marketers. These variables play an important role in convincing potential customers regarding changes in market trends, market conditions etc. Facilitating the corporation's strategic response to the changes taking place in environmental factors is the ultimate purpose of environment analysis. The firm has to come up with alternative programmes and strategies in line with environmental realities. This is possible only with proper environment analysis. It helps strategic response by highlighting opportunities, the pursuit of which will help the firm to attain its objectives. It helps to assess the attractiveness and probability position of these opportunities, and helps to prepare a shortlist of those which are relevant to the firm and which can be pursued by it.

Spotting the opportunities and threats is the central purpose here. It is in the environment that the firm finds its opportunities, it is in the environment that it finds the treats it has to encounter, and, it is by tapping the opportunities present and countering the threats embedded therein that the firm achieves its growth objective. The starting point is thus to spot the opportunities and threats.

Concept of Micro and Macro Environment

A marketing oriented company looks outside its premises to take advantage of the emerging opportunities, and to monitor and minimize the potential threats face by it in its businesses. The environment consists of various forces that affect the company's ability to deliver products and services to its cuotomers. The marketing environment is made up of:

1. Micro-environment and
2. Macro-environment.

We discuss them in detail.

1. Micro Environment

The micro-environment of the company consists of various forces in its immediate environment that affect its ability to operate effectively in its chosen markets. This includes the following:

(a) The Company (b) Company's Suppliers (c) Marketing Intermediaries
(d) Customers (e) Competitors (f) Public

A brief explanations are given below:

(a) **The Company**

In designing marketing plans, marketing management takes other company groups into account – Finance, Research and Development, Purchasing, Manufacturing, Accounting, Top Management etc. Marketing manager must also work closely with other company departments. Finance is concerned with funds and using funds to carry out the marketing plans. The R & D Department focuses on designing safe and attractive products. Purchasing Department is concerned with supplies of materials where as manufacturing is responsible for producing the desired quality and quantity of products. Accounts department has to measure revenues and costs to help marketing know-how. Together, all of these departments have impact on the marketing plans and action.

INTERNAL ENVIRONMENT (Within the Co.)

The marketing management, in formulating plans, takes the other groups into account:

* Top Management
* Finance
* R and D
* Manufacturing
* Purchasing
* Sales Promotion
* Advertisement etc.

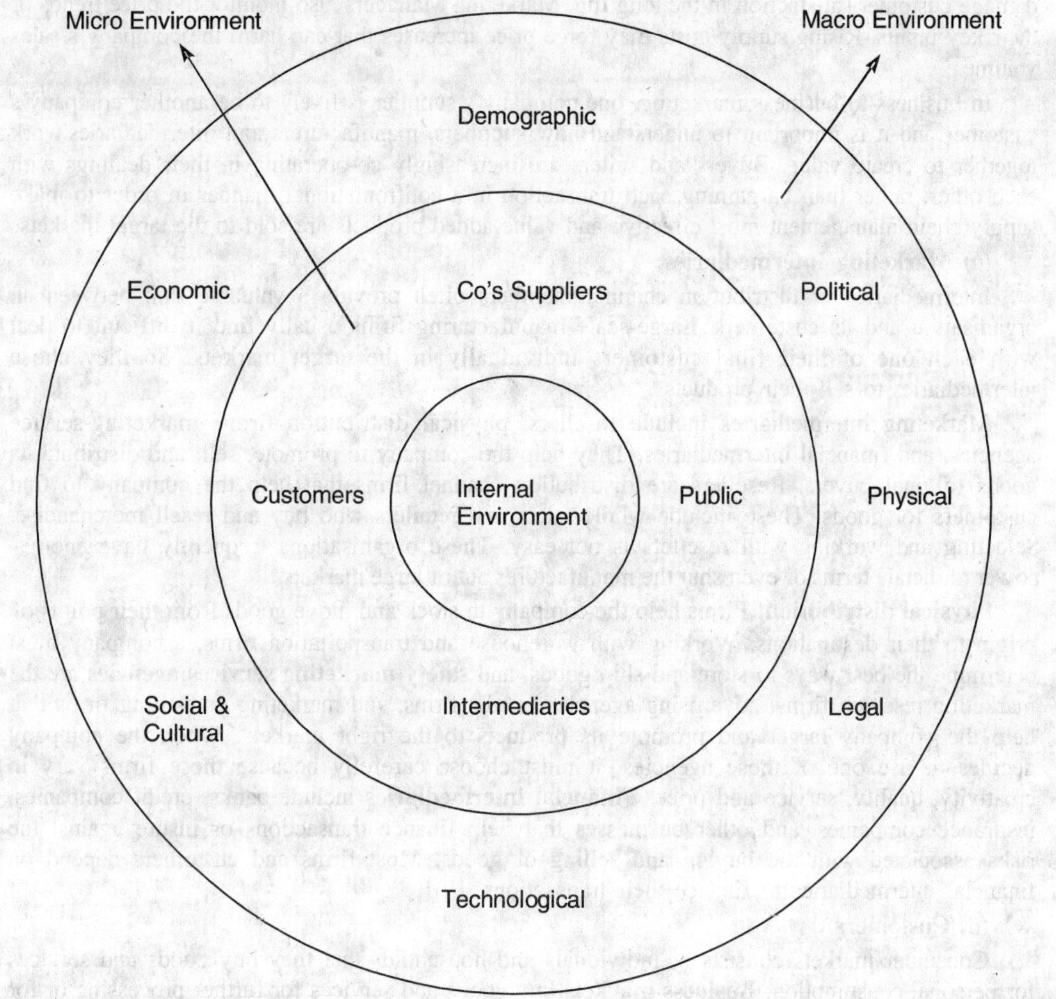

The Organisation's Marketing Environment

Environmental forces are dynamic and any change in them brings uncertainties, threats and opportunities for the marketers. Changes in the environmental forces can be monitored through environmental scanning, that is, observation of secondary sources such as business, trade and Government, and environmental analysis, that is, interpretation of the information gathered through environmental scanning. Marketers try to predict what may happen in the future with the help of tools like marketing research and marketing information or marketing intelligence system, and continue to modify their marketing efforts and build future marketing strategies.

The company should think about the consumer and work in harmony to provide customer value and satisfaction.

(b) **Company's Suppliers:**

Suppliers provide the resources needed by the company to product its goods and services. They are important links in the company's overall customer "value delivery system". Supplier developments can seriously affect marketing. Marketing managers must watch supply availability–supply shortages or delays, labour strikes and other events can cost sales in the short run and damage customer satisfaction in the long run. Marketing Managers also monitor the price trends of their key inputs. Rising supply costs may force price increases that can harm the company's sales volume.

In business-to-business marketing, one company's supplier is likely to be another company's customer and it is important to understand how suppliers, manufacturers and intermediaries work together to create value. Buyers and sailers are increasingly co-operating in their dealings with each other, rather than bargaining each transaction in a confrontational manner in order to make supply chain management most effective and value-added products are sold to the target markets.

(c) **Marketing Intermediaries:**

Intermediaries or distribution channel members often provide a valuable link between an organisation and its customers. Large-scale manufacturing firms usually find it difficult to deal with each one of their final customers individually in the target markets. So they chose intermediaries to sell their products.

Marketing intermediaries include resellers, physical distribution firms, marketing-service agencies, and financial intermediaries. They help the company to promote, sell, and distribute its goods to final buyers. Resellers are distribution channel firms that help the company to find customers for goods. These include whole-salers and retailers who buy and resell merchandise. Selecting and working with resellers is not easy. These organisations frequently have enough power to dictate terms or even shut the manufacturer out of large markets.

Physical distribution: Firms help the company to stock and move goods from their points of origin to their destinations. Working with warehouse and transportation firms, a company must determine the best ways to store and ship goods, and **safety marketing services agencies are the** marketing research firms, advertising agencies, media firms, and marketing consulting firms **that** help the company target and promote its products to the right markets. When the company decides to use one of these agencies, it must choose carefully because these firms vary in creativity, quality, service and price. **Financial intermediaries** include banks, credit companies, insurance companies, and other businesses that help finance transactions or insure against the risks associated with the buying and selling of goods. Most firms and customers depend on financial intermediaries to finance their transactions.

(d) **Customers:**

Consumer markets consists of individuals and households that they buy goods and services for personal consumption. **Business markets** buy goods and services for further processing or for use in their production process, whereas **reseller markets** buy goods and services to resell at a profit. **Government markets** are made up of government agencies that buy goods and services to produce public services or transfer the goods and services to others who need them. Finally, **international markets** consists of the buyers in other countries, including consumers, producers, resellers and governments. Each market type has special characteristics that call for careful study by the seller.

(e) **Competitors:**

No single competitive marketing strategy is best for all companies. The company's marketing system is surrounded and affected by a host of competitors. Each firm should consider its own size and industry position compared to those of its competitors. These competitors have to be identified, monitored and outmaneuvered to gain and maintain customer loyalty. Industry and competition constitute a major component of the micro-environment. Development of marketing plans and strategy is based on knowledge about competitors' activities. Competitive advantage also depends on understanding the status, strength and weakness of competitors in the market. Large firms with dominant positions in an industry can use certain strategies that smaller firms cannot afford. But being large is not enough. There are winning strategies for large firms, but there are also losing ones. And small firms can develop strategies that give them better rates of return than large firms enjoy.

(f) **Public:**

General public do take interest in the business undertaking. The company has a duty to satisfy the people at large alongwith competitors and the consumers. A public is defined as "any group that has an actual or potential interest in or impact on a company's ability to achieve its objectives". Public relations is certainly a broad marketing operation which must be fully taken care of. Goodwill, favourable reactions, donations and hidden potential future buyers are a few of the responses which a company expects from the public. Kotler in this regard has viewed that "companies must put their primary energy into effectively managing their relationships with their customers, distributors, and the suppliers, their overall success will be affected by how other publics in the society view their activity. Companies would be wise to spend time monitoring all their publics understanding their needs and opinions and dealing with them constructively" Every company is surrounded by seven types of public, as shown below:

1. Financial – banks, stock-brokers, financial institutions.
2. Media – Newspaper, magazines, TV.
3. Government – Government departments
4. Citizen – Consumer Organisations, environment groups.
5. Local – Neighbourhood residents, community groups.
6. General – General Public, public opinions
7. Internal – Workers, officers, Board of Directors.

2. MACRO-ENVIRONMENT

The macro-environment consists of broader forces that not only affect the company and the industry, but also other factors in the micro-environment. The components of a macro-environment are:

(a) Demographic Environment (b) Economic Environment (c) Physical Environment
(d) Technological environment (e) Political Environment (f) Legal Environment
(g) Social and Cultural environment

Brief explanations are given below:

(a) **Demographic Environment:**

Demography is the study of population characteristics that are used to describe consumers. Demographics tell marketers who are the current and potential customers, where are they, how many are likely to buy and what the market is selling. Demography is the study of human populations in terms of size, density, location, age, sex, race, occupation and other statistics.

Marketers are keenly interested in studying the demography ethnic mix, educational level and standard of living of different cities, regions and nations because changes in demographic characteristics have a bearing on the way people live, spend their money and consume. For example, one of the demographic characteristics is the size of family. With the number of small families increasing in India, the demand for smaller houses and household items has increased significantly. Similarly, the number of children in a family has reduced significantly over the years. So, per child spending in a family has increased significantly.

According to the 'World Health Organisation, young people in the age group of 10–24 years comprise 33% of the population and 42% of our population consists of age group, 0-24 years. Teen-agers in the age group below 19 years comprise 23%. The senior citizen age group (above 65 years comprise only 8% of total population. About 58% of the working population is engaged in agricultural activities, with highest, that is, 78% in Bihar and Chattisgarh and lowest 22% in Kerala.

Since human population consists of different kinds of people with different tastes and preferences, they cannot be satisfied with any one of the products. Moreover, they need to be divided in homogeneous groups with similar wants and demands. For this we need to understand the demographic variables which are traditionally used by marketers, to segment the markets.

Incomes: Income determines purchasing power and status. Higher the income, higher is the purchasing power. Though education and occupation shapes one's tastes and preferences, income provides the means to acquire that.

Life-style: It is the pattern of living expressed through their activities, interests and opinion. Life-style is affected by other factors of demography as well. Life-style affects a lot on the purchase decision and brand preferences.

Sex: Gender has always remained a very important factor for distinction. There are many companies which produce products and services separately for male and female.

Education: Education implies the status. Education also determines the income and occupation. With increase in education, the information is wider with the customers and hence their purchas decision process is also different. So the marketers group people on the basis of education.

Social Class: It is defined as the hierarchical division of the society into relatively distinct and homogeneous groups whose members have similar attitudes, values and lifestyle.

Occupation: This is very strongly associated with income and education. The type of work one does and the tastes of individuals influence one's values, life-style etc. Media preferences, hobbies and shopping patterns are also influenced by occupational class.

Age: Demographic variables help in distinguishing buyers, that is, people having homogenous needs according to their specific wants, preferences and usages. For instance, teenagers usually have similar needs. Therefore, marketers develop products to target specific age groups. The youth are being targeted through advertisements and promotional campaigns, stores are being designed with 'youthful' features, youth events are being sponsored, and even new technology is developed with their tastes in mind. The age groups that attract the attention of marketers can be classified as:

(i) **Infants:** The population of India is growing at an alarming rate. The rate of infant deaths has declined considerably due to the advancement in medicine. Although infants are consumers of products, their parents are the decision makers. The size of a family is decreasing and the average income of family is increasing.

(ii) **School going teens:** In this segment, there is a great demand for school uniforms, bags, shoes, books, stationary, confectionaries, food, albums, bicycles and other similar products.

(iii) **Young Adults:** Marketers target the young adults in the age group 18-30 years with products like motorbikes, music systems, clothes, sports cars etc. Two-wheeler manufacturers in India target this segment of people. In the last five years, various companies like, Bajaj, Hero-Honda, Kinetic, TVS etc. have introduced a large number of models to attract young adults.

(iv) **Adults:** (35-45): Consumers, in this age group, are more health conscious and look for stability and financial independence. The industries that are benefited by them are: Pharmaceuticals, personal products, fitness products, gym equipments, cars, home appliances, consumer durables, banks, insurance companies etc. Marketers push products specifically designed for this age group.

(v) **Senior Citizens:** This consumer group boosts the demand for health care services, select skin care products, financial planning etc.

(vi) **Women:** Women constitute nearly 50% of India's population. They are actively taking up professions. This shift in their role has generated a greater demand for childcare and convenience products that save time in cooking, cleaning and shopping.

Marketers are trying to come up with products that are easier to handle, less heavy, convenient to use etc. The change in the role of women is paving the way for a change in the role of men. Advertisement portray men cleaning, cooking and caring for their children, which was unthinkable in the past.

(b) **Economic Environment:**

Economic environment is the most significant component of the marketing environment. It affects the success of a business organisation as well as its survival. The economic policy of the Government, needless to say, has a very great impact on business. Some categories of business are favourably affected by the Government policy, some adversely affected while some others remain unaffected. The economic system is a very important determinant of the scope of private business and is therefore a very important external constraint on business. The economical environmental forces can be studied under the following categories:

(i) **General Economic Conditions:** General economic conditions in a country are influenced by various factors. They are:

Agricultural Trends
Industrial output trends
Per capita income trends
Pattern of income distribution
Pattern of savings and expenditures
Price levels
Employment trends
Impact of Government policy
Economic systems.

(ii) **Industrial Conditions:** Economic environment of a country is influenced by the prevalent industrial conditions as well as industrial policies of a country. A marketer needs to pay attention to the following aspects:

Market growth
Demand patterns of the industry
Its stage in product life cycle.

(iii) **Supply sources for production:** Supply sources required for production determines inputs which are available for production. They are:

* Land
* Labour
* Capital
* Machinery and equipment etc.

Economic environment describes the overall economic situation in a country and helps in analysing GNP per capita rate of economic growth, inflation rate, unemployment problems etc.

(c) **Physical Environment**

The physical environment or natural environment involves the natural resources that are needed as inputs by marketers or those that are affected by marketing activities. Environmental concerns have grown steadily in recent years. Marketers should be aware of trends like shortages of raw materials, increased pollution, and increased governmental intervention in natural resources management. Companies will have to understand their environmental responsiblity and commit themselves to the 'green movement'.

Potential shortages of certain raw materials, for examples, oil, coal, minerals, unstable cost of energy, increased levels of pollution; changing role of Government in environment protection are a few of the dangers the world is facing on physical environment forces. Other aspects of the natural environment which may increasingly affect marketing include the availability and cost of raw materials, energy and other resources, particularly if those resources and energy come from non-renewable sources.

(d) **Technological environment:**

The technological environment is the most dramatic force now facing our destiny. Technological discoveries and developments create opportunities and threats in the market. The marketer should watch the trends in technology. The biggest impact that the society has been undergoing in 'the last few years is the technological advancement, product changes and its effects on consumers. Technology has brought innumerable changes in human lives, be it in the field of science, medicine, entertainment, communication, travel or office equipment. Name any field, and one can see changes in product or efficiency and faster services.

One of the most dramatic forces shaping people's lives is technology. Technology has released such wonders as penicillin, open-heart surgery and birth control pill. It has released such horrors as the hydrogen bomb, nerve gas, and the sub-machine gun, Every new technology is a force for "creative destruction". Transistors hurt the vacuum tube industry, xerography hurt the carbon paper business, autos hurt the railroads, television hurt the newspapers. Instead of moving into the new technologies, many old industries fought or ignored them and their business declined. Yet it is the essence of market capitalism to be dynamic and tolerate the creative destructiveness of technology as the price of progress.

Technology essentially refers to our level of knowledge about 'how things are done'. That is understanding this aspect of the marketing environment is much more than simply being familiar with the latest hi-tech innovations. Technology affects not only the type of products available but also the ways in which people organise their lives and the ways in which goods and services can be marketed.

Computer-aided design (CAD) and computer-aided manufacturer (CAM) have shortened the time required for new products to reach the market and increased the variety of products that can be produced cost effectively. The benefits of CAD/CAM are clearly evident in the car .industry. Mass production is in standardised models. Computer systems have also contributed substantially to the growth of various forms of direct marketing such as direct mail, direct response marketing etc.

(e) **Political Environment:**

The political environment consists of factors related to the management of public affairs and their impact on the business of an organisation. Political environment has a close relationship with the economic system and the economic policy. Some Governments specify certain standards for the products including packaging. Some other Governments prohibit the marketing of certain products. In most nations, promotional activities are subject to various types of controls. India is a democratic country having a stable political system where the Government plays an active role as a planner, promoter and regulator of economic activity. Businessmen, therefore, are conscious of the political environment that their organisation face. Most Governmental decisions related to business are based on political considerations in line with the political philosophy following by the ruling party at the Centre and the State level. Substantial number of laws have been enacted to regulate business and marketing to protect companies from each other, to protect consumer from unfair trade practices, to protect the larger interests of society against unbridled business behaviour. Changing Government agency enforcement and growth of public interest groups also bring in threats and challenges.

(f) **Legal Environment:**

Marketing decisions are strongly affected by laws pertaining to competition, price-setting, distribution arrangements, advertising etc. It is necessary for a marketer to understand the legal environment of the country and the jurisdiction of its courts. The following laws affected business in India :–

1. Indian Contract Act 1872
2. Factories Act 1948
3. Minimum Wages Act 1948
4. Essential Commodities Act 1955
5. Securities Contracts Regulation Act 1956 (SEBI Act)
6. The Companies Act 1956
7. Trade and Merchandise Act 1958
8. Monopolies and Restrictive Trade Practice Act 1969
9. The water (Prevention and Control of Pollution) Act 1974
10. The Air (Prevention and Control of Pollution) Act 1981
11. Sick Industrial Companies (Special Provisions) Act 1985
12. Environment Protection Act 1986
13. Consumer Protection Act 1986
14. Securities and Exchange Board of India Act 1992
15. Different Taxation Laws.

(g) **Social and Cultural environment:**

Socio-cultural forces refer to the attitudes, beliefs, norms, values, lifestyles of individuals in a society. These forces can change the market dynamics and marketers can face both opportunities and threats from them. Some of the important factors and influences operating in the social environment are the buying and consumption habits of people, their languages, beliefs and values, customs and traditions, tastes and preferences, education and all factors that affect the business.

Understanding consumer needs is central to any marketing activity and those needs will often be heavily influenced by social and cultural factors. These cover a range of values, beliefs, attitudes and customs which characterise societies or social groups. Changes in lifestyle of people affect the marketing environment. As health problems in people have increased because of significant changes in their lifestyle' they have become concerned about their food. They prefer to eat low fat, low or no cholesterol food. This is specially true for people above 40 years. To a great extent, social forces determine what customers buy, how they buy, where they buy, when they buy, and how they use the products.

In India, social environment is continuously changing. One of the most profound social changes in recent years is the large number of women entering the job market. They have also created or greatly expended the demand for a wide range of products and services necessitated by their absence from the home. There is a lot of change in quality-of-lifestyles and people are willing to have many durable consumer goods like TV, fridge, washing machines etc. even when they cannot afford them because of their availability on hire-purchase or instalment basis.

Culture influences every aspect of marketing. Marketing decisions are based on recognition of needs and wants of the customer, a function of customer perceptions. These help in understanding of lifestyles and behaviour patterns as they have grown in the society's culture in which the individual has been groomed. Thus a person's perspective is generated, groomed and conditioned by culture.

Marketing environment can also be classified as: (i) Controllable Forces and (ii) Uncontrollable Forces.

Controllable forces consist of marketing policies and marketing strategies. Marketing policies are framed by the firm depending on its marketing philosophy. The top management is responsible for framing broad policies. Marketing strategies are developed by middle level management. Internal forces are inherent to the firm and can be controlled by the management. Marketing mix elements are the tools often used to harmonise the internal variables with that of external variables. The controllable factors are well within the grip of the firm and comparably easy to adjust them to suit the changes. These factors are combined into what we have referred to earlier as Marketing Mix. For instance, if the price appears to be on the higher side a decision to reduce it for a short term or even a long term is possible and could be implemented as quickly as possible. Off-season prices or discounts are examples in this connection.

Uncontrollable forces: Various elements called uncontrollable variables affect an organisation and its marketing efforts. It is now recognised by all that even a well conceived marketing plan may fail if adversely influenced by uncontrollable factors. The offering of the firm and the impact of the uncontrollable environment interact to determine the firm's level of success or failure in reaching its objectives. The external forces are divided into micro-environment and macro-environment. The micro-environment consists of the suppliers, marketing intermediaries, customers etc. while the macro-environment consists of the demography, socio-cultural, political, economical, tachnical, legal environments etc.

Examples of Threats are :

1. Electronic type-writer with memory replaces manual type-writer.
2. Twin blade shaving system replaces razor shaving system.
3. Fuel efficient small cars against old model cars.
4. Entry of MNCs into Indian Market increased competition.

Examples of opportunities are :

1. Marketing opportunities to produce cheap small cars.
2. Marketing opportunities to introduce fully auto-matic washing machines in the areas where husbands and wives are working.
3. Marketing opportunities to start business in low cholesterol food items.
4. Dismantling of price controls and introduction of market-drive price policy.

Case Study-1

MANVILLE FIGHTS A WAVE OF PROBLEMS

Company

Johns Manville is a big construction and forest-products concern. The company's business grew with the boom in housing industry and other commercial and industrial construction. After 1974 oil embargo, the housing industry suddenly became aware of the increasing importance of solid construction with super insulation to reduce the energy bills. In response to the market demand, Manville began a $ 200 million expansion to double the glass fibre capacity. It also expanded roofing products facilities and was ready to increase production. In 1979, Manville bought Olinkraft Inc., a Lousiana based forest-products company, to increase geographical coverage. The price for Olinkcraft came to $ 600 million after a bidding war raised the price of shares purchased to $ 65. The purchase was for cash, long-term debt and preferred shares.

Economy

The company began to slow down in 1979 due to affected construction industry. First the rapidly rising interest rates and inflation began to put a damper in buying power of consumers. The inflationary boom was then followed by a recession accompanied by high persistent interest rates and unemployment which almost caused depression in housing industry. The effect of the slower economy on the earnings of the Manville Corporation is shown in the enclosed figure.

Manville earned in 1981 $ 60.3 million on sales of $ 2.2 billion. This was down from $ 120 million in 1978. It sank into the red by $ 5.5 million in 1982 first quarter, registering its first, loss in 50 years. The company was troubled on three fronts. First the acquisition of Olinkraft proved burdensome. Second, the market began shrinking due to recession and finally, it was hit with a wave of suits charging health damage from exposure to asbestos produced by Manville.

The balance sheet of Manville did not recover from the big outlay required for the acquisition. Compounding this difficulty, Olinkraft had problems ranging from cash flow to mechanical to management. This took significant Manville management resources to straighten out Olinkraft.

In order to cope with shrinking markets, Manville took, several drastic actions to cut costs. Manville cut operations and trimmed its workforce. Two senior vice-presidents were given early retirement and were not replaced. It closed executive dining room, leased the corporate jet, resorted to energy conservation through dimmed lights to save on the utilities bill. If the economy improves the company could quickly snap back into profitability.

However, the biggest cloud that is left untouched is the asbestos law suits pending against the company. Manville is the free World's largest producer of asbestos. Recently, as the health damage due to breathing of asbestos fibres became apparent, thousands of people exposed to the product claimed huge damages. Manville became one of history's most sued companies.

Two years ago, shareholders were told at the annual meeting that these suits would not amount to more than a ripple. But the suits turned into a tidal wave. The outcome of the whole affairs now cannot be reasonably determined. Manville faces suits by 15,000 plaintiffs in 10,400 cases, and new suits are coming at the rate of 400 per month this year. What is more threatening than these numbers is that several juries have awarded not only compensatory but punitive damages based on findings that company covered up the health hazards of asbestos. Some awards have exceeded $ 2 million, although those still are awaiting final ruling.

Compensatory damages are covered within limits by insurance. The company has $ 600 million coverage. However, insurance carriers are claiming that the company defrauded them by not telling them about hazards. The legal bills to fight these claims are running close to $ 2 million per month.

Future

General consensus is that Manville will weather the storm, but only after a tough selling. The company has in-place capacity to meet the demand when the economy expands. The company may breakeven in 1982 under a most optimistic scenario, otherwise it could be in the red substantially.

QUESTIONS

1. Could Manville have done better in responding to the external uncontrollable factors ?
2. What is Manville's social responsibility in asbestos law suits ?
3. Should Manville have foreseen potential problems of slower economy and the Olinkraft acquisition?

Comments

A business enterprise is an open social institution. It must adapt itself with the changing and uncontrollable external environment. The environment must accept its outputs and receive reasonable satisfaction. Then only it will tolerate and support the firm. Hence, the survival, growth and prosperity of anybusiness ultimately depends upon harmonious and enduring relationship between the firm and its environment—economic, technological, social and political forces of the dynamic environment.

Case Study-2

ISSUES MANAGEMENT

Many corporations feel that their strategic and marketing planning groups focus too narrowly on forecasting of products and services provided by the company and thus fail to spot important trends in the business conditions. If such trends are detected early enough the corporate management can be alerted as to the consequences of the trend and can select an appropriate strategy to mitigate its impact on the corporation revenues. For example, the business and economic planners failed to predict the Arab oil embargo or the environmental revolution.

To supplement the business and marketing planning activities, top management executives set up trend-spotting departments. The mission of these departments is to deal with the upcoming issues. The issues manager considers the immediate future and the next one to five years, and is charged not only with identifying issues but also setting forth specific ways the company might deal with them. Essentially, the issues managers were assigned tasks previously done somewhat haphazardly by top executives. By tracking trends and issues early in their cycle, the top management could eliminate unpleasant surprises.

Today, about 70 corporations have issues managers. These include large oil companies, banking and insurance concerns and retailers. There are several examples that demonstrate the usefulness of this new kind of executive. When President Reagan cut the federal budgets, the issues managers at Atlantic Richfield Oil Company saw trouble ahead. They predicted that these budget cuts would prompt one state after another to try to compensate for lost federal money by taxing business. Atlantic Richfield with operations in 28 states felt that it may become a prime target. To deal with this situation, Atlantic Richfield mobilized corporate resources to defeat many bills aimed specifically at oil companies.

Atlantic Richfield has five clusters of issues: resources, environment, corporate and planning, manufacturing processes, and trade association participation. The group monitors hundreds of publications, opinion polls, and think-tank research reports. The information on any topic is available to top executives on one day's notice.

At Monsanto Company, an issues manager organizes a task force of middle managers and other employees to do the work and the results are sent to top executives.

Most issues tend to follow an eight-year cycle. For the first five years or so, nascent issues are emerging in local newspapers, are being enunciated by public-interest organizations and can be detected through public-opinion polling. It is easier to deal with issues at this stage as they are low-keyed and flexible. If it affects the corporate interests, companies can intervene and prevent the issue from reaching the legislative or active stage. In the fifth or sixth year, the national media get interested in an issue ; then governmental action typically results in seventh or eighth year.

There are several examples where corporations anticipated issues and recommended actions that saved companies millions of dollars. With the advice of issues managers, S.C. Johnson & Sons, a privately held maker of floor waxes and other chemicals, removed fluorocarbons from its aerosol sprays three years before federal legislation forced others in industry to do so. Sears Roebuck & Co. spotted flammable nightware controversy early and got non-flammable goods into its stores well before governmental action required this.

QUESTIONS

1. Do you feel that issues managers are needed to spot trends and suggest early strategies to prevent later, adverse impacts ?
2. Is there a possibility that an early intervention to mitigate the impact of an issue would encourage corporations from discharging their social responsibility ?
3. How should the issues management department be organized to supplement corporate and market planning groups ?

Comments

Marketers must anticipate well in advance the impending problems or issues due to every-changing environmental forces, particularly economic, social, political and legal forces, and on the basis of such contingent changes, formulate most desirable plans and strategies so that changes when they occur can be met successfully and possible losses can be reduced. Issues managers are experts in forecasting issues and offering best solutions to them.

Case Study-3

REVAMPING OF AN OLD-LINE INVESTMENT BANKER

Dillon Read & Co.

Dillon Read & Co. has been one of the nation's pre-eminent investment banking houses, built by Clarence Dillon, a Wall Street leader for decades. Dillon Read for years relied heavily on its enviable list of blue-chip clients such as Union Oil of California, Grumman, R.J. Raynolds Industries. They did little to generate new business areas. The company imposed a stringent code of honour that went beyond federal regulations. Each business was scrutinized and anything below standard was rejected.

Changing World & Competition

Dillon Read relied on the traditional approach which involved offering financial advice to big corporations and managing securities underwritings. On the other side, there was a new brand of money makers, aggressive risk-takers who were aiming for profits through plunges into the frantic corporate-takeover game. They created merger ideas and sold them to companies and by betting their own money on stocks of takeover candidates. They also invested in new ventures.

Rival firms changed rapidly. Morgan Stanley & Co pushed through a typical diversification drive and grew to 2,200 employees from mere 264 in 1970. Soloman Brothers, which boasts unmatched abilities in institutional trading established itself as a top under-writer. So did Merrill Lynch & Co. which commands the largest retail distribution system for securities in the country. Giant outsiders such as Prudential Insurance, American Express, and Sears Roebuck bought securities firms.

At the same time, big companies were turning less loyal to their traditional investment bankers. Dillon Read, as a result, lost some prominent clients, including Superior Oil, CPC International and the New York Power Authority.

During 1980's, the outlook was for even more turbulent and drastic changes. With markets more volatile, investment banks have become bigger and diversified. In addition, increasingly aggressive foreign institutions and the huge commercial banks were eager to enter the investment banking field.

Dillon Read's Response

Dillon Read faced an uphill battle to play the catch-up with competition. It was already hurt by exodus of employees who were disappointed at the corporate strategy. Dillon Read brought in John Birkelund to become the chief operating officer and to *spur diversification.* He began to build retail brokerage business which would give Dillon Read a capability to distribute new securities. Mr. Birkelund began pursuing profits in venture capital, arbitrage and money management in addition to traditional corporate finance. Mr. Birkelund proposed developing actively a secondary market (over-the-counter market) for debentures—the fast-growing popular investment.

QUESTIONS

1. Did Dillon Read wait too long to change in response to the changing environment ?
2. What other actions should Dillon Read take to stop its slide and regain a position of preeminence?
3. Should Dillon Read go against the trend of "bigness" and find a market niche in venture capital and arbitrage business ?

Comments

Usually we have very keen competition among the marketers. Under competition, 'innovate or perish' is the rule. Hence, marketers must develop innovations and introduce them successfully. Innovation alone can assure favourable conditions to meet the changing environment. Marketer can fight competition and maintain or develop market share only through innovative management.

Case Study-4

USING THE INTERNET AS A VIRTUAL PRIVATE NETWORK

Sandal, shoe, and bootmaker Deckers Outdoor Corporation recently switched to an Internet Networking technology called *virtual private network* to interconnect their global company.

Virtual private networks (VPNs) use the power of the Internet instead of using private telecommunications lines or other network links. A virtual private network is a secure and encrypted connection between two points across the Internet. It transfers information by encrypting and encapsulating telecommunications traffic into packets and sending the packets over the Internet. Most VPNs are built and run by Internet service providers. Companies that go with a VPN from an Internet service provider essentially outsource their networks to a save money on having to acquire and manage their own wide area network equipment and bandwidth requirements.

Deckers is a $ 100 million company whose 20-person office in Hoek Van Holland, the Netherlands, collaborates on product development with its staff in Goleta, California. The VPN costs roughly $ 31,000 to implement and saves Deckers $ 10,000 per month compared with leasing their previous high-speed network connections.

"We needed a network that would serve as the foundation for our international expansion, "says Steve Miley, MIS director at Deckers". It will be critical ...because our offices will use it to make sure projects are done on time."

Employees at the two sites use the VPN to update the status of product development projects through Lotus Notes groupware databases. The VPN supports Note's ability to replicate databases of project information at each work site, which is crucial to groupware support of project team collaboration.

VPN performance "is slow but workable for interactive Notes database access," Miley says. And as the quality of Internet service improves, VPN performance can only improve, he adds.

Security, a reported shortcoming of virtual networks, is improved with Net Fortress software from Fortress Technologies. It automatically changes encryption keys every 24 hours. "We feel very secure with their products on our network," he says.

Offices for production management in Hong Kong, Mexico, and Macao will be added to the VPN this year. Miley says. Those sites currently use expensive International telephone calls to access servers in Goleta. Desktop video conferencing over the VPN, to cut international travel costs, is also planned.

Deckers doesn't mind being among the first to implement a virtual private network. "VPNs are here to stay". Miley says, "And we are on the leading edge, not the bleeding edge.

QUESTIONS

1. What are the business benefits of Decker's switch to a virtual private network?
2. What can be done to overcome several limitations of virtual private networks ?
3. Does it make business sense for any company to use the internet as their private telecommunication network? Why or why not?

Case Study-5

USING THE WEB FOR ELECTRONIC COMMERCE

After deciding that its extranet and private World Wide Web site for large corporate customers was a success, $ 6.7 billion Office Depot, Inc., launched a public version that targets small and at-home businesses.

The new Web site ties a Web browser application with the Company's inventory and ordering systems and conducts realtime warehouse checks to ensure stock is available nearby. The site, at *www.officedepot.com*, also verifies addresses and credit cards on the fly.

"What they've created seems to be a highly integrated Web site, leveraging their sales delivery systems," said Gregory Wester, research director at The Yankee Group, in Boston.

Office Depot, in Delray Beach, Florida, won't disclose how much it is spending on its new Internet storefront. But savings could be substantial if customers move online: Processing an electronic order costs about 10 per cent of the cost of a telephone order, said Paul Gaffney, senior vice-president of systems development.

The new Website is taking advantage of tens of millions of dollars the company have invested in its computing and telecommunications systems, he said. "It's an incremental investment", Gaffney said. Issues of how to integrate a Web interface with back-end systems were hashed out a year and a half ago when the private Website was launched.

The site is using Microsoft Internet Information Server and Commerce Server software on a 12-processor IBM AS/400 messaging and ordering system and an IBM mainframe center for delivery data. The company uses its own trucks and drivers for nationwide shipping.

Office Depot outsourced the design of the site to Studio Verso, in San Francisco, after determining it didn't have the expertise to do the work in-house. Studio Verso developed the look, selected art elements and fonts, and determined Web-specific issues such as how much information to put on one page and how to make it easy for customers to find what they want.

The Website allows users to find specific products by keyword or numbers as well as by browsing the catalogue. It uses characters from the popular *Dilbert* comic strip to keep surfers interested. Office Depot tested initial concepts with focus groups, said Beth Van Story, vice-president of Office Depot Online, in San Francisco.

Although it may seem late to establish a consumer Website for business machines and office supplies, Wester said he believes Office Depot's marketing muscle carries enough weight to make up for the timing. Office Depot said it is first in the fragmented office supply market, with about a 4 per cent share. "There's no such thing as bcing late when you're carrying a big brand name," Wester said.

QUESTIONS

1. What business benefits does Office Depot hope to gain with their new Website?
2. Was their delayed entry into public electronic commerce a good business decision ? Why or why not ?
3. Visit the *officedepot*.com Website. Did Studio Verso and Office Depot do a good job of Website development? Why or Why not?

Case Study-6

A Unique Marketing Problem

RADIX PHARMACEUTICALS LTD.

"Radix Pharmaceuticals Ltd." is a small scale, sole proprietorship concern based in Ludhiana. It is engaged in the production and marketing of drug formulations. At the time of its inception, the firm introduced only liquid formulations. But later on, as the market for its product started growing, it also launched some, table formulations. At present, it offers a good range of more than ten different medicines, though the products are all of a general nature, *e.g.*, cough syrups, paediatric suspension etc. and can also be treated as OTC drugs.

At present, the firm's products enjoy a good reputation in Chandigarh, Haryana, Punjab and Uttar Pradesh. They are selling both on doctor's prescription and otherwise. As a part of the strategy to expand the market, the Chief Executive of the firm, Mr. Sunil Kumar sent one of his representatives to explore the possibility of selling his products in Gujarat. The representative visited a few stockists and wholesalers of drugs in Ahmedabad and Baroda with an intention to appoint a propoganda stockist who will not only keep the stocks and distribute them but will also try to get the drugs prescribed by the doctors in his region. For this he offered :

(*i*) a commission of 25-40% (negotiable) of the written price, and (ii) a credit facility of 45 days.

Inspite of all his efforts, the representative failed to find any stockist who could be interested in selling his products. He described the situation like this: "There are many small manufacturers of medicines in and around Ahmedabad. Many of these restrict their markets to nearby areas and hence particularly in Gujarat the competition is very tough. All the stockists I talked to have described the commission offered by Radix Pharmaceuticals as low. Some of the problems is something else. The moment I talk of a firm from Chandigarh, the stockists refuse to work without any further thought. They say that nobody, here, would buy a medicine made by a small concern in Punjab. People of Gujarat are so scared of the name, Punjab, that they do not have faith in medicines made there and they can't afford to do so because, after all, none of the products of Radix is a speciality item".

After a careful investigation of the situation, Mr. Sunil Kumar and his colleagues came to the conclusion that under the existing circumstances, they cannot penetrate the market in far off states. Also, it is well known that Ahmedabad has an established reputation for fine chemicals and drugs manufacture. Therefore, they devised one scheme. As per this, Radix Pharmaceuticals would open one small office in Ahmedabad and get registered there. This address of the firm's registered office will be printed on the labels of the medicines. Thus, in the market, the firm will be recognised as one from Ahmedabad while, for all practical purposes, it will operate from Chandigarh only.

QUESTIONS

1. How do you evaluate the pros and cons of Sunil Kumar's long term strategy ?
2. What alternative steps could he take under the situation described in the case?
3. If you were the marketing executive what steps you will take for creating a market base in Gujarat?

Case Study-7

Entrepreneurship or Exploitation

VENTURA PAINT LTD.

Mr. S. Ghosh, basically from traditional rural and agricultural background, managed to get the licence for setting up a factory through his political contacts. He started M/s Ventura Paint Ltd. (Public Limited Company) to manufacture certain sophisticated building products with foreign technical know-how. The project was estimated to cost about Rs. 200 lakhs which was raised through contributions by associates, public issue and term loans from state financial corporation. The required machinery was imported and installed and actual production was started. A turnover of Rs. 6 crores was projected in the first year of its operation but the sales hardly reached Rs. 15 lakhs. Due to various reasons, the financial position of the company became critical and it failed to meet even its daily expenses. The production stopped and Mr. Ghosh's request for sanction of an additional term loan of Rs. 20 lakhs from state financial corporation was also declined. He appointed

Mr. Ajay Sharma a passed out from IIM, Ahmedabad as Vice President, Marketing. Mr. Sharma had worked earlier with a number of leading MNCs in various capacities. Immediately after joining, he decided to start an aggressive promotion strategy for M/s Ventura Paints Ltd.

QUESTIONS

1. What are the main reasons for failure of M/s Ventura Paints Ltd.
2. Do you think that Mr. Sharma shall be able to save M/s Ventura Paints Ltd.? If yes, why? If no, why?
3. If you were the Vice President of Marketing, what marketing strategies would you recommend to the management?

QUESTIONS

1. Explain the concept of Marketing Environment? *(B.Com., Chennai)*
2. What forces determine external marketing environment? Discuss any three forces with examples. *(M.Com. Agra)*
3. What are uncontrollable forces of marketing environment? Discuss them. *(M.Com., Kerala)*
4. What is marketing environment ? Explain its main dimensions. *(B.Com., MS)*
5. Explain the impact of environmental forces on marketing. *(B.Com., Delhi)*
6. "Every change is Government regulatory environment creates adjustment problems for the marketer. Explain. *(B.Com., Banaras)*
7. Why is it necessary to scan marketing environment ? What are controllable and uncontrollable variables in the marketing environment. *(M.Com., Allahabad)*
8. What are the various types of factors which influence the marketing environment? *(M.Com. MS)*
9. What are the factors that influence the marketing environment of an organisation ? *(B.Com. Andhra)*
10. "Marketer has to be more aware of changes in the external environment than any other department in the organisation". Do you agree. *(M.Com.Bangalore)*
11. How do macro-environment forces provide opportunities and pose threats to a company. *(M.Com., Mumbai)*
12. What are the forces affecting marketing in the micro-environment. *(M.Com., Jammu)*

CHAPTER 14

Market Segmentation

- *Introduction*
- *Definition*
- *Criteria*
- *Bases*
- *Geographic*
- *Demographic*
- *Psychographic*
- *Socio-Economic*
- *Benefit*
- *User Status*
- *Usage Ratio*
- *Loyal Status*
- *Attitude*
- *Benefits of Segmentation*
- *Philosophies of Market Segmentation*
- *Mass Marketing*
- *Product Variety Marketing*
- *Target Marketing—Micro Marketing*
- *Customised Marketing*
- *Personalised Marketing*
- *Market Targeting Strategy*
- *Case Study-1*
- *Case Study-2*
- *Case Study-3*
- *Case Study-4*
- *Case Study-5*
- *Questions*

INTRODUCTION

Market segmentation is a recent development in marketing thinking and strategy. It is based on the natural variations found in a general or total market. Diversity is the basic characteristic of a market, be it a consumer market or industrial market. Marketers must understand natural diversity for effective marketing. In today's highly competitive environment, market segmentation, target market selection and effectively positioning the offerings are very essential requirements for gaining competitive advantages. For instance, a ready-to-wear garment seller must first identify his customer segment groups. He may subdivide his customers in terms of sex and age group-men's wear and ladies wear. Then he may go on selecting a particular segment or all the segments. Accordingly, he may cater to the needs of each segment efficiently. Likewise, a hotelier may subdivide his customers as vegetarians and non-vegetarians. A further sub-division can be average customers and affluent customers. For affluent customers he may provide air-conditioned and luxurious services. What we understand from the examples given above is that customers are not alike and they differ in many aspects including purchasing power and buying habits.

Business organisations operate in different markets consists of all types of existing and potential customers with their widely varying needs and wants. The markets exhibit widely heterogeneous characteristics with widely differing and scattered consumers. The buying practices are different it is indeed difficult for any organisation to operate and serve such markets effectively, both from organisation's point of view as well as consumers' interest. The business organisation, instead of competing everywhere to cope with the entire market, may decide to identify those markets or territories of markets which can be served most effectively by offering them correct products and matching their needs and long-term business and consumer interests are served in the most desired manner. Thus, the firm tries to break up the market into smaller units, club them so that each submarket has more or less homogeneous characteristics. Therefore, it is sub-dividing or breaking up the market into different cohesive and homogeneous market characteristics with a distinct marketing programme and effort. *The process of dividing a market into smaller homogeneous markets with similar characteristics is called market segmentation.* The firm will focus only on those submarkets which can be served most effectively on the basis of their evaluation of market requirements. *This is called target marketing.*

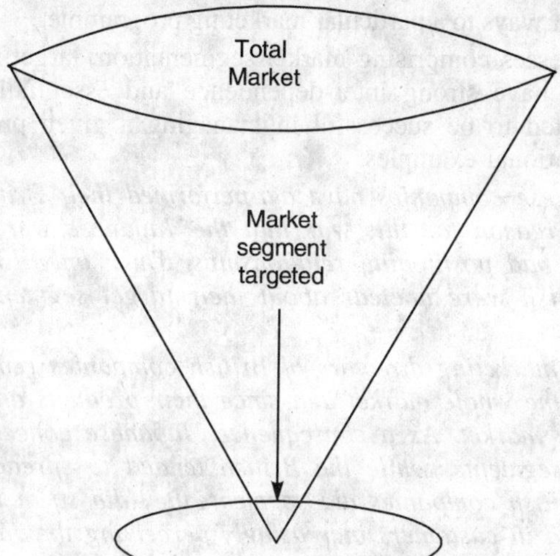

From mass market to market segmentation

Definition

According to Philip Kotler, "Market segmentation is the sub-dividing of market into homogeneous sub-sections of customers, where any sub-section may conceivably be selected as a market target to be reached with a distinct marketing mix."

According to Stanton, "Market segmentation consists of taking the total heterogeneous market for a product and dividing it into several sub-markets or segments, each of which tends to be homogeneous in all significant aspects."

Market segmentation is just the first step in a three-phase marketing strategy. After segmenting the market into homogeneous clusters, the marketer must select one or more segments to target. So the second step is target marketing, which is the process of evaluating each market segment's attractiveness and selecting one or more segments to enter. To accomplish this, the marketer must decide on a specific marketing mix-that is, a specific product, price, channel and promotional appeal for each distinct segment. The third step is market positioning, which involves arranging for a product to occupy a clear, distinctive and desirable place relative to competitive products, in the minds of target consumers.

The concept of market segmentation emerged as an extension of the marketing concept in the latter part of 1950's. It is based on the simple observation that all the existing and potential consumers are not alike: there are significant differences in their needs, wants, tastes, background, income, education and experience etc. and these characteristics change over time with lifestyle changes. Had they been alike, it would have eliminated the need to have different variations of the same basic product and one promotional campaign is all that would have been needed. For instance, there would have been only one type of soap, one detergent, one scooter, one computer, one car and so on.

A market is composed of individuals and they are rarely homogeneous in benefits wanted, purchase rates, price and promotion elasticitiy. Their response rates of products and services and promotion programmes differ. Since consumers have dissimilar needs and wants in a market, is is called a heterogeneous market and most markets are heterogeneous. Differences in product preference, size and growth in demand, media habits and competitive structure of the market also affect the differences and response rates.

A **market segment** is a portion of a larger market in which the individuals, groups or organisations share one or more characteristics that cause them to have relatively similar product needs; whereas **market segmentation** is the process of dividing the total market into relatively distinct homogeneous sub-groups of consumers with similar needs or characteristics that lead them to respond in similar ways to a particular marketing programme.

Three-decision processes comprising market segmentation, target marketing and positioning are closely related and have strong inter-dependence and essentially need to be examined carefully and implemented to be successful in managing a given product-market relationship. Peter Doyle cites international examples:

"In England, Japanese companies have out-performed their British rivals across a range of industries. A major reason for this was that the Japanese were better at managing the segmentation, targeting bad positioning relationships. Thus, only 13% of the Japanese firms versus 47% of the British were unclear about their target segment of customers and their special needs."

"All too often, the marketing directors of British companies remarked that they see their target market as being the whole market and since their products and wide appeal, there was no need to segment the market. As a consequence, Japanese concentrated their resources in specific high-potential segments, while the British tended to spread theirs thinly across the entire market. When British companies did segment, they did so at the lower, cheaper end of the market. This resulted in customers increasingly perceiving the Japanese, in contrast to the British, as offering quality and status."

Market segmentation and the identification of target markets are an important element of each marketing strategy. The importance of market segmentation results from the fact that the buyers of a product or service are no homogeneous group. Actually, every buyer has individual needs, preferences, resources and behaviours. Since it is virtually impossible to cater for every customer's individual characteristics, the marketing people group customers into various market segments by variables they have in common. These common characteristics allow developing a standardised marketing mix for all customers in this segment. They are the basis for determining any particular marketing mix.

The interlinking of segmentation, targeting and positioning

Corporate and Marketing Objective

↓

SEGMENTATION
- Consider varibles for segmenting market
- Look at profile of emerging segments
- Validate segments emerging

↓

TARGETING
- Decide on targeting strategy
- Decide which and how many segments to be targeted

↓

POSITIONING
- Understand customer perceptions
- Positioning products in the wind of the customer

↓

MARKETING MIX

Criteria for Market Segmentation

The market segmentation to be worthwhile six criteria, as shown below, must be satisfied:

1. **IDENTITY:** The markating manager must have some means of identifying members of the segment, that is, some basis for classifying an individual as being or not being a member of the segment. There must be clear differences between segments. Members of such segments can be readily indentified by common characteristics which display similar behaviour.

2. **ACCESSIBILITY:** It must be possible to reach the different segments in regard to both promotion and distribution. In other words, organisation must be able to focus its marketing efforts on the chosen segment. Segments must be accessible in two senses. First, firms must be able to make them aware of products or services. Secondly, they must get these products to them through the distribution system at a reasonable cost.

3. **RESPONSIVENESS:** A clearly defined segment must react to changes in any of the elements of the marketing mix. For instance, if a particular segment is defined as being cost conscious, it should react negatively to price rises. If it does not, this is an indication that the segment needs to be refined.

4. **SIZE:** The segment must be reasonably large enough to be a profitable target. It depends upon the number of people in it and their purchasing power. For example, makers of luxury goods may appeal to small but wealthy target markets whereas makers of cheap consumption goods may sell a large number of persons who are relatively poor. The idea is that enough potential buyers must exist to cover the costs of production and marketing required in that segment. This is often called as substantiality.

5. **NATURE OF DEMAND:** It refers to the different quantities demanded by various segments. Segmentation is required only if there are marked differentiation in terms of demand.

6. **MEASURABILITY:** The purpose of segmentation is to measure the changing behaviour pattern of consumers. For example, the segment of a market for a car are determined by a number of considerations, such as economy, status, quality, safety, comforts etc.

Bases for Consumer Market Segmentation

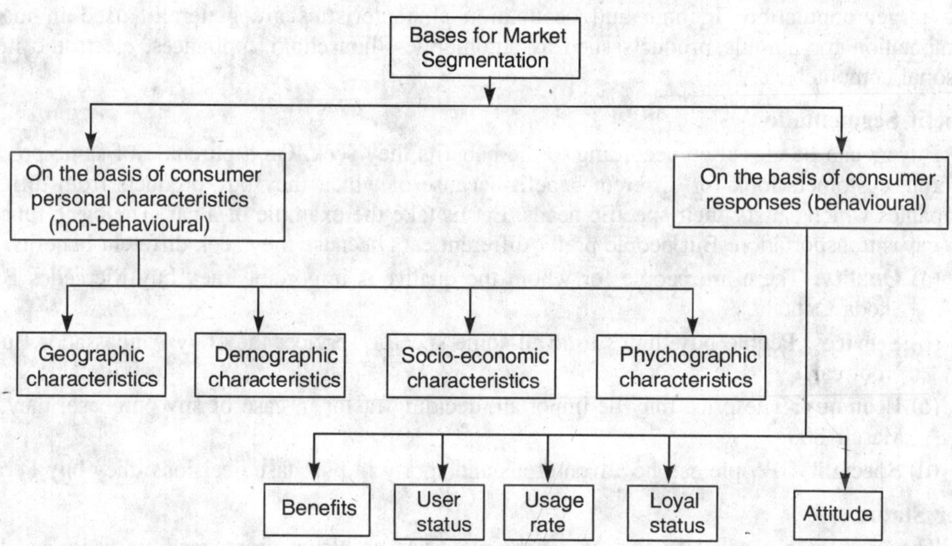

Geographic Segmentation

In geographic segmentation, the whole market is divided into different geographical units. Generally, the market is divided into regions – northern, southern, western eastern and so on.

Each region may consist of several states and districts. A national marketer may treat the whole nation as his market and divide it on the basis of region or zone for business operations. For example, in the detergent market, Hindustan Lever and Proctor and Gamble are all national markers in India. Moreover, a multinational company (MNC) may divide the global market on the basis of continental characteristics. For example, Coca-Cola may consider the entire Asia as its market but for further business operations, it may divide Asia into South Asia, Middle-east, Far-east Asia etc. Perhaps, each country may also be considered as a geographical segment.

Demographic Segmentation

In demographic segmentation, the market is subdivided into different parts on the basis of demographic variables – age, sex, family size, income, occupation, education, family life cycle, religion, nationality etc. Demographic variables have long been the most popular bases for distinguishing significant groupings in the market place. One reason is that consumer wants or usage rates are often highly associated with demographic variables; another is that demographic variables are easier to measure than most other types of variables.

Psychographic Segmentation

Consumers are subdivided into different groups on the basis of personality, life style and values. These characteristics lead to pschographic segmentation. People exhibit different life-style and they express them through the products they use. Some social segments are very orthodox and tradition bound at home. But the same people look very modern and conspicuous when in the outside world. Marketers of cosmetics, textiles, soft-drinks, fast-food providers etc. must understand the lifestyle of the target market. Personality is another psychographic characteristic which is used to segment the market. Particularly, automobile manufacturers – two wheelers and passenger cars – must consider different personality traits in dividing the market. Values are also used by marketers to segment a market. Value are beliefs which determine people's product choices and desires.

Socio Economic Characteristics

Income, occupation, education, religion and social classes are the important socio-economic data required for market segmentation. These are all components of socio-economic characteristics of a target population. Income and occupation characteristics are generally used in market segmentation for durable products such as automobiles, household appliances, electronic items, personal computer etc.

Benefit Segmentation

Buyers can be classified according to the benefits they seek. On a purchase of same product, different customers look for different benefit because of which they buy products from different companies which satisfy their specific needs. Let us take the example of a car. The basic function of a car is transportation. But people prefer different cars because they seek different benefits.

(a) **Quality:** There are people for whom the quality is important: they buy Mercedes Benz, Skoda Octavia.

(b) **Services:** People buy things to avail some specific service: they buy Ambassador Bullet-proof car.

(c) **Economy:** The price may be important deciding factor in case of any purchase: they buy Maruti 800.

(d) **Speciality:** People can be adventurous and sporty in purchase decisions: they buy Ferari.

User Status

The users of a product or service can be classified as heavy users, medium users and light users – heavy buyers, medium buyer and light buyers. Marketers of soft drinks, hot drinks etc. for example, many segment the market in terms of the above said criteria. A firm, generally, is interested in the heavy buyers or users. Sometimes, a firm may select light users as their target market with the intention of wooing and changing these customers into heavy users.

Usage Rate :

Markets can be segmented into various classes depending on usage rate. Considering the cosmetics usage, the different categories of usage rate are as follows:

(a) **Light:** These are the categories of the users who are very infrequent users. In case of cosmetics an average housewife who is not very fashion conscious is a light user of cosmetics.

(b) **Medium:** The fashion-conscious teenagers are the medium users of cosmetics, that is, they use it frequently.

(c) **Heavy:** There are people for whom the cosmetics are the most important purchase and they are heavy users of it. Celebrities in entertainment world, the models etc. need cosmetics on a regular basis, as it is the most important part of their profession.

Loyal Status

Consumers have varying degrees of loyalty to specific brands, stores and other entities. Buyers can be divided into four groups according to brand loyalty status.

(a) **Hard-core Loyals:** Consumers who buy one brand all the time. We find people who have been using colgate for years without caring which other brands are coming in and going out of the market.

(b) **Split or Safe Core Loyals:** Consumers who are loyals to two or three brands. Pepsodent after its launch found some customers of Colgate switching between the two brands.

(c) **Shifting Loyals:** Consumers who shift from one brand to another. Customors can be found to keep on switching off from Colgate to Close-up and then to Pepsodent without any consistency.

(d) **Switchers:** Consumers who show no loyalty to any brand. These are the people who will buy any brand that is available in the market.

Attitude

A market may be segmented by classifying people in it according to their enthusiasm for a product. Five attitude groups can be found in a market.

(a) **Enthusiastic:** These are people having tendency of impulsive purchase. They may not carry cash all the time but suddenly decide to buy something. They definitely need credit cards.

(b) **Positive:** They are serious but mobile people who need to buy suddenly at any time.

(c) **Indifferent:** There are some people who are technology averse with systematic purchasing pattern. They would prefer to purchase with cash after thinking over the need for purchase. They do not prove to be potential users of credit cards.

(d) **Negative:** People can be spend thrifts who fear of loosing money or misusing it. They would never go for a credit card.

(e) **Hostile:** People at times become very much irritated either by sales-people calling or meeting any time, giving false promise or by the service provided. For example, in case of credit cards, there are some hidden costs which are not clarified by the sales-person during selling.

Benefits

Benefits from segmentation are:

1. Sagmentation helps in focusing strategies more sharply on target groups.
2. It helps the company to know demand pattern of each segment thus increased the sale volume of the products.
3. It helps the marketer to understand the needs, behaviour, habits, tastes and expectation of consumers of different segments. Thus marketing opportunities increases.
4. It is possible to satisfy a variety of customers with a limited product range by using different promotional activities.
5. Marketing can be more specialised when there is segmentation as the element of marketing mix.
6. Segmentation helps in adopting different policies, programmes and strategies for different markets based on rival's policies, programmes and strategies.

7. New customers are attracted bacause of segmentation strategy and thus opportunities are created for growth.
8. Customers are benefitted as the products that serve customers interest and satisfy their needs and wants.
9. Segmentation supports the development of niche strategies.
10. It helps to achieve a better competitive position for existing brands.
11. Identify gaps in the market which represent new product opportunities.
12. It is possible to pay proper attention to a particular area.

The Philosophies of Market Segmentation

The marketers adopt several approaches to segmenting a market. The various approaches are given below: (Evolution)

1. Mass Marketing

Before the onset of the marketing age, there was widespread adoption of mass marketing, mass production, distribution and promotion. That is, offering the same product and applying the same marketing-mix to all customers assuming that there is no significant difference among consumers in terms of their needs and wants. The Coca-Cola Company follow this approach. The company feels that no segmentation is necessary. The company designs its marketing programmes to appeal to all buyers. This is undifferentiated marketing strategy. This type of marketing is well suited for fruits, vegetables, drugs, chocolates, bakery items, stationery items etc.

2. Product Variety Marketing

Once it is learnt that consumers would not accept standard products, the marketer might try to provide different sizes, colours, shapes, features, qualities etc. to attract them. For example, when Maruti 800 introduced into Indian roads it was a variety product because it used two versions – Standard and Deluxe with different colours.

3. Target Marketing

The modern marketing concept starts with the definition of target markets. The target marketing has its root in the marketing age. Target marketing requires marketers to take three steps:

(a) Market Segmentation
(b) Market Targeting
(c) Market Positioning

Two alternative approaches can be followed despite the fact that different customers have different needs:

(a) Shotgun Approach
(b) Rifle Approach

4. Micro Marketing

The target marketing is being changed to micro marketing. Micro marketing occurs when target market is further bifurcated and the needs of the small customer groups are addressed on a local basis. Thus, even though target customer has been identified in the target markeing, some specific modern styles of features products are made available at selected places on local basis. It has four levels:

(a) **Segment Marketing:** A market segment consists of a large identifiable group within a market with similar wants, purchasing power, geographical location, buying attitudes or buying habits.

(b) **Niche Marketing:** A niche is a more narrowly defined group whose needs are not well served. It has the following characteristics:

(i) The customers in the niche should distinct set of needs.
(ii) They will pay a premium to the firm that best satisfies their needs.
(iii) The niche in not likely to attract other competitors.
(iv) The niche gains certain economies through specialisation.
(v) The niche has size, profit and growth potential.

(c) **Local Marketing:** Target is leading to marketing programmes being tailored to the needs and wants of local customers. For example, different editions of newspapers for different areas cover local news are good examples.

(d) **Individual Marketing:** The ultimate level of segmentation leads to "one-to-marketing" or "customised marketing". Mass customisation is the ability to prepare on a mass basis individually designed products and communications to meet each customer's requirements. The concept of service has broadened to include both breadth of product offerings and the ability to customise to meet specific needs.

5. Customised Marketing

The focus of the target marketing is further shifting from local basis to individual customer basis. With the advancement in manufacturing because of breakthrough in information technology, for instance, use of computer-aided design and computer aided manufacturing: it has now become possible to manufacture a product as per the individual customer needs or of a buying organisation. Tailors and drapers (cloth merchant), boutiques (ladies and children), beauty parlours etc. are customise products.

6. Personalised Marketing

Although in case of customised marketing, the requirements for a customer are met by a custom-made product, but still the customer might not be willing to retain his loyalty with the company because of competition. For instance, one gets shirts made from a tailor as per personal fitting. Still, tailors find their customers shifting their loyalty to others. Heil, Parker and Stepens provide TEN RULES for building relationships with customers:

(1) The average customer does not exist.
(2) Make customer's experience special. Give customer something to talk about.
(3) If something goes wrong, fix it quickly.
(4) Guarantee customer satisfaction.
(5) Trust customer and customer will trust the company.

(6) Customer's time is as important as company's.

(7) Don't take customer for granted.

(8) The details are important to customer, as they should be to the company.

(9) Employ people who are ready and willing to serve customer.

(10) Customer cares to find out whether company is a responsible corporate citizen.

UNDIFFERENTIATED, DIFFERENTIATED AND CONCENTRATED MARKETING

Undifferentiated Marketing

Differentiated Marketing

Concentrated Marketing

Market Targeting Strategy

The concept of market segmentation identifies three strategic options of marketing, viz., Concentrated Marketing, Differentiated Marketing and Undifferentiated Marketing.

1. Concentrated Marketing

It is concerned with "focussing all available resources on one segment within the total market". It is an attempt to match what the firm can do the best with a market niche devoid of strong competitors, a strategy of differential advantage. It means one marketing mix, a rather narrow product and some unique competence, which is the basis for the firm's competitive advantage in a chosen segment.

Concentrated marketing takes a variety of forms, for examples, high fashion boutiques and design-oriented houseware shops. Such marketing has been followed by Ambassador cars, HMT Quartz, Rolex watches, Glass manufacturing units, Johnson and Johnson's strategy for infant market etc. is a good example of concentrated marketing.

2. Differentiated Marketing

It attempts to appeal to the entire market by designing different products and marketing programmes for different segments of the market. By so doing marketers hope to achieve additional sales and increased customer identification with brand or company name. This type of marketing is followed by most medium and large sized firms doing business in many markets with a broad product line. For examples, Golden Tobacco Company in India markets cigarettes under ten brand names: Panama, New Deal, Gold Flake, Taj, Sainik, Gaylord, Tajmahal, Square Target and Diamond. Hindustan Lever Ltd., manufactures and sells bathing soap under different names, such as Lux, Lux-supreme, Lifebuoy, Rexona, Saral, Pears, Lyril etc. Usha Fan Co. markets fans under three different names Usha Prima, Usha Delux and Usha Continental. Lipton and Brooke Bond reach all segment of the market through a large number of brands of tea priced at various ranges and promoted through a variety of appeals.

3. Undifferentiated Marketing

It treats the entire market as its target by competing successfully using the same marketing mix. Such marketing is resorted to when it is found that there are some products which have a broad-based appeal and hence there is no need for their segmentation.

Such marketing proves weak in every segments because there is specialised competition in each segment. For example: Coca-Cola, Pepsi-Cola, Thumps-up, Sprint, Canada Dry, Campa Cola etc.

Strategy

Strategy	Organisation Characteristics
Concentrated	The organisation targets a major offering to a specific market segment.
Differentiated	Each organisation targets several products, one product to each of several market segments.
Undifferentiated	All products from all organisations targeted to all or a majority of the market.

Examples of Market Segmentation:

1. **Cigarettes :** The market can be segmented on the basis of :
   (1) Type of cigarettes
      (a) Filter
      (b) Plain
   (2) Price :
      (a) High priced
      (b) Medium priced
      (c) Low priced
2. **Refrigerators :** The market can be segmented on the basis of :
   (1) Geograhical
      (a) North India
      (b) South India
      (c) East India
      (d) West India
   (2) Size of refrigerators:
      (a) 65 litres
      (b) 90 litres

(c) 165 litres

(d) 286 litres

(3) Nature of consumers:

(a) Households

(b) Industrial

3. **Washing Machines:** Segmented in the following ways :

(a) Density : Urban and suburban

(b) Economy : Middle and Upper income groups

(c) Benefits : Automatic, Semi-automatic, Fully-automatic

Case Study-1

MARKETING IN RETAIL SALES

Company

Morgan Department Store had been in business for 64 years in a small town in West Virginia. The department store sold all items such as shoes, gifts, small appliances, and apparel from children to adults. The store was hit by recession and was out of touch with its customers. It faced plunging sales and soaring debt. About 60% of its sales were on credit charge accounts and as the recession deepened, customers fell way behind on payments causing a cash squeeze for the store. To pay its bills, the store borrowed money at 21% interest while it could collect only 18% interest on credit card balances due to State laws. Morgans debt climbed and losses increased to $ 250,000 on sales of $ 1.6 million in 1981.

Survival Strategy

The banks shut off credit and manufacturers stopped shipping unless they were paid on delivery. Owners of Morgan decided to liquidate the business and called in Mr. Buxbaum.

Mr. Buxbaum upon his arrival noticed large manufacturing plants of Union Carbide, FMC and Volkswagen. He also found that the overall unemployment was much below national average and even lower among the store's middle income customers. For two days he surveyed the town's traffic pattern, competitor's merchandise and shopping habits at a new mall 30 miles away. He talked with local media about store's advertising strengths and weaknesses.

He recommended that the business could be salvaged if the store owners took certain actions. He said the store was trying to be everything to everybody. So he recommended that Morgan eliminate least profitable lines : shoes, gifts, small appliances and the children's department. Morgan reduced major appliance display area to make room for expanded ladies' and men's apparel.
The ladies' and, men's garments had high volume and higher profit margins. Mr. Buxbaum found people driving out of the town to buy sheets and towels at a distant store. Morgan, therefore, added a linen department.

To get shoppers, the store announced a three-month "Fight for Survival" sale offering discounts of as much as 50%. Previously Morgan had discounted only 20% or less. Mr. 'Baxbaum said that at least 40% of the merchandise must be sold off-price or you won't bring in customers.

Morgan also revamped its merchandise buying. With Mr. Baxbaum's help, they found suppliers who could offer better prices on furniture and apparel. Instead of buying from travelling salesmen, Morgan's buyers went to manufacturers' showrooms. These efforts provided 10 to 30% savings on most apparel and also allowed store to update its fashions more frequently.

These changes finally paid off. The store's sales went up for two months, in a row. Profits were slim but at least the cash started coming in. Morgan feels that its fight for survival is far from over. It needs more planning, more market research, and rapid changes to meet the customer demands. It must offer appropriate marketing-mix for each typical market segment. It must have enlightened promotion devices. It must have clear and precise marketing strategies.

QUESTIONS

1. Why was Morgan Store about to fail ?
2. The reason retailer fails is because he doesn't make changes. He doesn't ask himself basic questions : Who are we trying to reach ? What are our strengths ? Comment.
3. What other actions should Morgan take to continue on the road to profitability ?

Comments

Marketer must define mission or central purpose of firm's existence, basic objectives and goals. Then he should locate marketing opportunities as well as risks, evolve a happy balance between product offering and customer demand, and resort to market segmentation. For each segment most desirable marketing mix or offering must be made. This demands marketing planning and programming.

Case Study-2

CLASSIFYING MARKETS BY HOPES AND FEARS

The traditional method of analysing markets is to look at customer's age, sex, income, life style or patterns of using products. People with certain age, sex and income tend to have some common habits and marketers have concentrated on analysing these habits to develop their products. For banking and financial services companies, this classifications does not prove useful. Another way to classify consumers was developed which is based on people's hopes and fears.

A market research firm conducted extensive interviews with approximately 2,500 people with bank accounts. The purpose of this study was to help banking institutions to attract public's spare cash with competitive rates for services offered. The study would also tell banks which customers to pursue and which to avoid.

The largest group of financial services customers was classified as planners and dealers. These customers are optimistic, well-informed fairly affluent and confident about their ability to handle their finances. These people are more interested in profit than convenience. They tend to spread their surplus among several investments. They shop around for the best deal and interested in getting maximum return. The financial services companies like banks must offer competitive rates and service charges to lure these customers. Since they are sophisticated they can evaluate themselves the alternative options. The banks, in this case, must convince them why their services are best for the cost charged to them.

The second group, the conservators, are confident but are cautious. They have saved their money through steady savings habits and made themselves safe. Thirty per cent of customers in this category are 55 or older. These customers want service, privacy and convenience. They usually maintain high balances and do their cheque cashing at the bank. They are not interested in automatic banking machines, banking by mail or any other convenient services.

The first two groups account for 50 p.c. of the customers. The third group, service-seekers, 16 p.c. of the market, have less education, have lower incomes. The third group is also less sophisticated. Many of these (the third group) are widows. The top priority of service-seekers is not the biggest return on their money. They go to a bank because that is one of the few times in the day, somebody services them.

The customers in the fourth category, 19 p.c. of the market, spend imprudently, believe in luck, not planning. They are pessimistic about the future. They are suspicious about bank's motives and are not concerned about bank services, as it reminds them that they have very little savings. As many customers in these category have moderate incomes, they are not customers to be ignored.

The final category, about 12 p.c. of the market, are called hopefuls. These customers dream that financial institutions may help them to get a foothold on the slippery ladder of financial security. They consider bank credit as a stepping stone to enter into a suitable business or profession and secure firm settlement in their lives. Nearly half of them are between 18 and 35 years old. They are not aggressive. They have less education, and lower income than average. But they are eager to improve their financial status.

QUESTIONS

1. Evaluate the usefulness of this market (segmentation) research study.
2. Assume that you are a bank manager. How would you prepare bank-services package to attract business from these different segments of customers ?
3. Is there another way to segment customers of financial services ?

Comments

Market segmentation on the basis of psychological wants and personality traits as well as life styles of people is the modern approach for subdividing the market and formulating the package of most desirable product utilities/services expected by a typical group of customers.

Case Study-3

DIVERSIFICATION BEYOND DUSTPANS & DRAINERS

Company

Rubbermaid has been in the business of making rubber dustpans and drainers since 1970's. Its sales and earning's grew at a steady pace until 1979. The company's evolution began in 1934 when James Caldwell invented the rubber dustpans and convinced the company that the household gadgets had more profit potential than toy balloons that company was making. The company's name was changed to Rubbermaid from Wooster Rubber Company in 1957 to reflect its role as the housewife's helper. The company's main products were household products made from plastic. In 1970, the company made an ill-fated attempt to diversify into the booming recreational vehicle market. The main reason for the failure was that the company went too far a field in trying to sell motor boats and sleds.

However, this diversification failure did not cause problems, for the company. It relied on its solid business base of household products. Like other manufacturers, Rubbermaid had chosen to control the retail price of its products under so-called (resale price maintenance or RPM practices) fair-trade Laws. The demise of those laws, made Rubbermaid products attractive to discount and grocery stores instead of just to old line department stores, that wanted a guaranteed mark-up. With this change, Rubbermaid suddenly had a whole new market to serve, and sales quadrupled in 10 years. With this prosperity Rubbermaid did not seek innovations and new concepts. Meanwhile, competitors, especially foreign ones, were starting to make inroads with new household items like stackable storage bins. Rubbermaid's management chose to stay away from such new products calling them faddish.

The growing competition and slowing expansion of merchandisers began to signal stagnation for Rubbermaid. The board of directors suddenly realized that "more of the same and a little better" is not going to keep company healthy in the 1980's. Rubbermaid's retiring Chairman in his search for the top executive discovered Mr. Gault who was a marketing Vice-President at General Electric. Mr. Gault took over as the Chairman and Chief Executive Officer in the late 1981.

Corporate Reorganization

Mr. Gault's first move with Rubbermaid was to develop and market stackable storage bins. He sold three marginally profitable divisions-one made auto-floor mats and accessories, another sponsored in-home selling, parties, the third was a housewares subsidiary in Holland. He installed new general managers at the remaining three divisions. He also brought new management and replaced half of the sales force. He fired 60 middle management employees, or 11 per cent of white collar staff for the sake of cost cutting. He pushed Lester Gigax out of the presidency into early retirement.

These moves reinforced Mr. Gault's message that more of the same was not acceptable and new ideas were encouraged. With these changes new product introductions were stepped up to more than 40 a year from 20 in the past. These included flat sided beverage pitchers to fit into crowded refrigerators, a combination laundry basket and hamper, and cleaning pads with plastic handles.

Furthermore, Rubbermaid planned to get into other product areas. These included home-insulation products, such as weather-stripping, and outdoor beverage jugs. Although these products are not revolutionary, Mr. Gault, thinks he can outflank smaller regional competitors, using Rubbermaids brand name and extensive regional distribution.

In order to increase sales, Rubbermaid, for the first time ever offered promotions, rebates and coupons. The company, therefore, began to market a whole product line to fill consumer needs (systems approach to marketing) rather than its approach in the past which viewed each product *individually*.

The marketing research department started looking at the consumer needs more closely. With inflation and sky-roketing real estate prices, the space in new homes started shrinking. This trend was documented on a quarterly basis, which meant smaller refrigerators, shelves and closets. So Rubbermaid designed space organizers to battle the perils of cabinet clutter and crowded closets. Rubbermaid acquired a new company called Con-Tact which manufactured plastic coverings. Contacts products were designed for older generation. But Rubbermaid marketing executives thought, with the current do-it-yourself craze and the young generation's penchant for self-expression, Rubbermaid can sell Con-Tact products to younger customers, particularly two-income families.

These changes resulted in improved financial results. Rubbermaid's earnings rose 27% in 1981 to $25.6 million or 3.31 a rise in market share. Analysis expect annual 15% increase in 1982 and 1983. After languishing in the range of $ 20 to $ 30 per share, Rubbermaid stock jumped recently to above $ 42 a share on the New York Stock Exchange. Capital appreciation is the best indicator of customer-oriented integrated marketing plans.

QUESTIONS

1. What are the lessons learned from Rubbermaid's marketing experience ?
2. Did Mr. Gault go too fast and ruthlessly in making management changes at Rubbermaid ?
3. How much attention to the profit picture should the company devote in carrying on in a competitive business ?
4. How important is it to monitor changes in customer's environment to gauge the needs for new and innovative products ?
5. What are the main reasons Rubbermaid was losing to the competition ?

Case Study-4

SEGMENT TO SELL

India's diversity could provide plenty of opportunities should marketing strategies be designed and executed well. Unfortunately, several companies have failed to grasp the nuances of Indian consumer behaviour and hence, their products bombed in the marketplace.

Segmentation is a powerful tool through which markets can be handled and brands built. Two case studies illustrate how poor segmentation has led to miscalculation. Result: Companies entering India have either failed or taken a lot of time to succeed.

First, cars. Lack of proper segmentation of the automobile market resulted in most cars being launched in the mid-size segment. Soon, the mid-size segment was choked with cars like Daewoo's

Cielo, Opel's Astra and Ford's Escort among others. The mid-size segment is a niche market, but there were few takers here. Today, most of these companies are unable to achieve even 25 to 30 per cent of their target and have landed up with heavy inventory. Now they are forced to offer deep discount and resort to desperate sales.

Had proper segmentation been done, the focus would have been on small-size cars that are mostly affordable and comprise the largest and the fastest growing segment. This has been proved by the success of Maruti 800 and Zen. It took a lot of time for people to realise the segmentation folly. So car manufacturers are now making a beeline for the small car segment, which again is threatened by excess capacity and may ultimately lead to price wars.

Had proper segmentation been adopted, there would have been another brand to challenge the Maruti 800 and Zen monopoly long ago and that brand would have gained good sales and market share.

There are certain brands of cars which are doing well. Take the Zen, for example. Its better aesthetics, more leg space than the Maruti 800 and better technology inputs, make it popular. This car is ideal for a distinct segment.

The positioning of the Zen has been directed towards a segment defined by the parameter of usage. Segmentation for usage is a powerful weapon in the marketing armoury. Customers desirous of upgrading themselves from a Maruti 800 or those who desire a mix of aesthetics and manoeuvrability for regular usage, find the Zen an extremely lucrative option. Result: at a time when the car industry is facing rough weather, the Zen seems to have done better, primarily because it is segmented by usage-kids can be dropped at schools, it is decent enough to be driven to office or can even be used to comfortably drive down to an informal party.

Many a times, companies can track usage patterns and segment the market by usage and gain.

Let us take another case study of a recently-launched beverage which has also pegged usage as the criterion for segmenting its market and achieved considerable trials and healthy repeat purchases. Fosters beer has recently been launched in pint-sized bottled alongside the usual larger pack size. The shape and size of the bottle is targetted towards young, trendy, light-users who consider drinking beer as a part of their lifestyle. San Miguel and Ice have also been launched in the same size.

In my opinion this particular pack size, which is handy, shapely and international in its look, gained huge ground among light-users. In terms of segmentation, the usage pattern goes alongside a sport like bowling or as a quick accompaniment drink or even as a trendy teenage drink where holding the Fosters bottle transports young customers to a different world of lifestyle and minority. There is, of course, multiple usage which takes place and the fact that it is a low cash-ring product. The size also helps.

Since the segment defined by usage is the light, young, trendy user who apes the West, a certain chunk of the young women segment also fall in the consumption segment.

In both the cases of cars as well as the newly-launched beers, focussing and selecting specific usage criteria for segmenting the market helps increase trials and market share.

Segmentation by usage could be on the basis of light or heavy consumption, regular or occasional consumption, home-out-of-home consumption as well as the method and style of usage.

As the market becomes more competitive, whether in cars or in beer, a clear segmentation strategy would help launch, increase or even retain market shares and profitability. If a product is not segmented specifically and is aimed at everyone, then it is most probably aimed at no one. This could be the beginning of the end of any brand.

QUESTIONS

1. What criteria have been used in segmentation of the market ?
2. "Market segments are essential to reach target markets." Comment on this statement in context of above case.

Case Study-5

A CASE OF SEGMENTATION : LACOSTE

"Lacoste does not use price as an excluding factor". That is, the target wearer is described in psychographic, not demographic, terms. It is a brand for the arrived, for the early adopter "who runs a successful business, is respected in his field, has two children and no plans of having any more" according to SLA. The consumer "works harder and plays hard," and appreciates the value of finer, non-fashion-led leisure wear. Teeny-boppers are *persona non grata*. Puneet Malhotra, an employee of Junach Pvt. Ltd. (an SLA franchisee which runs seven outlets), says that most customers are "30 plus".

Lacoste's perceived value stays high because its wearers form a club of like-minded folk, snooty to the extent that all club members are. As the brand's wearers are walking-talking advertisements on the desired social circuitry, the prospective buyer charmed by the kind of people he see wearing the crocodile.

The quintessential Lacoste wearer is a mobile phone-equipped, leisure-loving, globetrotting yuppie in his 30s or 40s, bent on staying fit, and a keen golfer or weekend tennis buff, he's a great spender of self-earned money, casual at the right times, global in his thinking and with little time for woolly "intellectuals" who refuse to admit that clothes are a personality statement or think that getting mournful about Indian poverty is achieving more than what he does with his time (adding to GDP growth).

Of course, the audience is only a subset of India's wealthy. Casualness and leisure are not well-in-graned concepts here, shown by the weak response to Club Med's activity packed foreign holidays, "People come with an 'I am sorry' look when forwarding their leave application, "says Kochar, lamenting the stigma attached to splurging. Thanks to the Gandhi-Nehru legacy, "the belief is, if he's so rich he must have had a hand in some scam. We are not comfortable with wealth, with success."

Change has begun. Back in 1993, Lacoste came with the understanding that there were about half-a-million potential buyers. In four years, the tribe is said to have doubled. "Of these, about a lakh are buying Lacoste," believes Kochar. He predicts that the group should swell by half in the next five years. By then, much of the current segment of 20s, in fashionable professions, with good degrees from premier institutes, "in the words of Darlie O. Koshy, professor and chairman, apparel marketing and merchandising, National Institute of Fashion Technology (NIFT). "Their purchasing power is rising, aspirations are high and they can afford to buy on impulse as they pay by plastic."

QUESTION

1. Discuss Lactose approach for segmentation of their market.

QUESTIONS

1. Define market segmentation and discuss the significance in India.
2. "Marketing segmentation is very useful for effective marketing of any product." Elaborate. *(B.Com. MS)*
3. "Target market follows market segmentation" Discuss. *(M.Com. Kerala)*
4. What are the elements that influence in deciding the principles of segmentation ? *(B.Com. Andhra)*
5. What is meant by marketing segmentation ? What will be suitable base for marketing of televisions? *(B.Com. Mumbai)*
6. What are conditions precedent to successful market segmentation? *(B.Com. Bhopal)*
7. What are the objectives of market segmentation ? *(B.Com. Ujjain)*
8. What are the bases for market segmentation ? *(B.Com. Andhra)*
9. What are the various kinds of segmentation ? *(B.Com., Delhi)*
10. Discuss the benefits of market segmentation. *(B.Com., Jammu)*
11. Describe the criteria for segmenting the market. *(B.Com. Madurai)*
12. Why and how are market segmented ? Is segmentation always necessary ? *(B.Com., Allahabad)*

CHAPTER 15

Market Targeting and Positioning

- *Introduction*
- *Selection of Target Markets*
- *Evaluating Market Segments*
- *Selecting Market Segments*
- *Product positioning*
- *What is positioning?*
- *Product position Vs. Brand Position*
- *Product Differentiation*
- *Differentiating Market Offering*
- *Qualities of a Successful positioning*
- *Positioning Approaches*
- *Product Repositioning*
- *Case Study*-1
- *Questions*

INTRODUCTION

Once the process of segmentation of the market has been achieved, the next step follows, that is, selection of suitable segment or segments which the firm can serve most effectively. Thus, target marketing is the act of evaluating, selecting and focussing on these market segments that the company intends to offer its marketing programme and serve it most effectively. Market segmentation is the prelude to targeting. Through segmentation, a firm divides the market into many segments. But all these segments need not form its target market. Target market signifies only those segments, that it wants to adopt as its market. A selection is thus involved in it. In choosing the target market a firm basically carries out an evaluation of the various segments and selects those segments that are most appropriate to it. The evaluation of the different segments has to be actually based on those criteria and only on the basis of such an evaluation target segments be selected. The firm must assess the sales and profit potential of each segment to know whether the segment is relevant to the firm, whether it is sizeable, accessible, attractive and profitable. It must examine alternative possibilities, that is, whether the whole market has to be chosen for tapping, or only a few segments have to be chosen, and if so, which one. It may look for segments that are relatively less satisfied by the current offers in the market from competing brands. It must look at each segment as a distinct marketing opportunity. It must also evaluate its resources and choose the segments that match its resources.

Selection of Target Markets

The selection of target markets helps the market to correctly identify the markets and the group of target customers for whom the products or services are produced. In these days, market targeting is used for all types of markets including developing and emerging markets. It helps in sub-dividing the market into many segments, and then deciding to offer a suitable marketing offer to some selected segments. Market targeting is the act of evaluating and comparing the identified groups and then selecting one or more of them as the prospects with the highest potential. A marketing programme is developed which will provide the organisation with the best return on sales, by correspondingly deliver the maximum value to customers. After analysing different segments, the marketing manager must select one or many segments to serve. The marketing manager is required to evaluate the different segments in terms of market size, competition, growth rate, company's resources, profitability, scale of economies etc. It should also be absolutely certain that investing in a particular segment is sensible in terms of company's mission, objectives skills and resources.

Instead of aiming a single product and marketing programme at the mass market, most companies identify relatively homogeneous segments and accordingly develop suitable products and marketing programmes matching the wants and preferences of each segments. It should be realised that all segments do not represent equally attractive opportunities for a company. Companies need to categorise segments according to their present and future attractiveness and their company's strengths and capabilities relative to different segments' needs and competitive situation. The following points are worthy to be noted:

* Establish criteria to measure market attractiveness and business strength position.

* Evaluate market attractiveness and business strength factors to ascertain their relative importance.

* Assess the current position of each market potential segment on each factor.

* Project the future position of each market segment based on expected environmental, customer and competitive trends.

* Evaluate segment profitability.

* Evaluate implications of possible future changes with respect to strategies and requirement of resources.

Evaluating Market Segment

In evaluating different market segments, a firm must look at three factors - Segment's size and growth, segment's structural attractiveness and company objectives and resources. The company should enter only segments in which it can offer superior value and gain advantages over competitors. Several models for measuring segment attractiveness exist, although arguably the most useful is Michael Porter's five-force model, thus profitability is affected by the five factors:

1. Industry competiters and the threat of segment rivalry;
2. Potential entrants to the market, and the threat of mobility;
3. The threat of substitute products;
4. Buyers and their relative power;
5. Suppliers and their relative power.

Having segmented the market the strategist should then be in a position to identify those segments which, from the organisation's point of view, represent the most attractive targets. In deciding where to focus the marketing effort the strategist needs to give consideration to three elements:

1. The size and growth potential of each segment;
2. The structural attractiveness of different segments;
3. The organisation's objectives and resources. Once, a decision has been made on the breadth of market coverage the strategist needs them to consider how best to position the organisation, the product range and brand within each target segment. However, the following three most common positioning errors should be avoided:

1. Confused Positioning.
2. Over Positioning
3. Under Positioning.

Selecting the Market Segment

Once a marketer has evaluated the different segments for their size, growth and attractiveness, and found that they are compatible with the company's objectives and resources, the obvious step is to go for selecting the market segments. There are five patterns of target market selection, which was first putforward by D.F. Abell:

1. Single Segment Concentration
2. Selective Segment Specialisation
3. Product Specialisation
4. Market Specialisation
5. Full Market Coverage

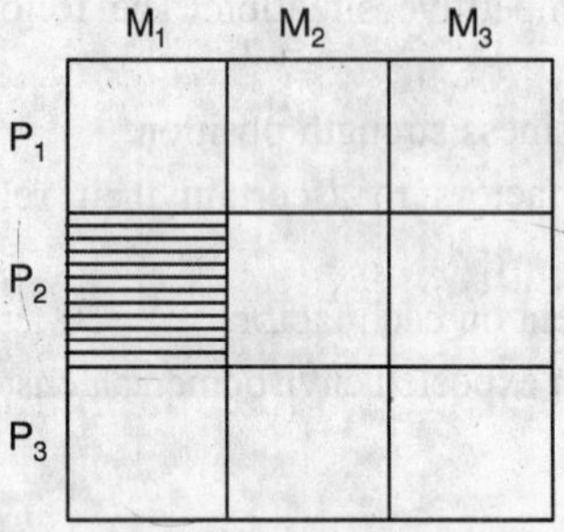

Single-segment concentration

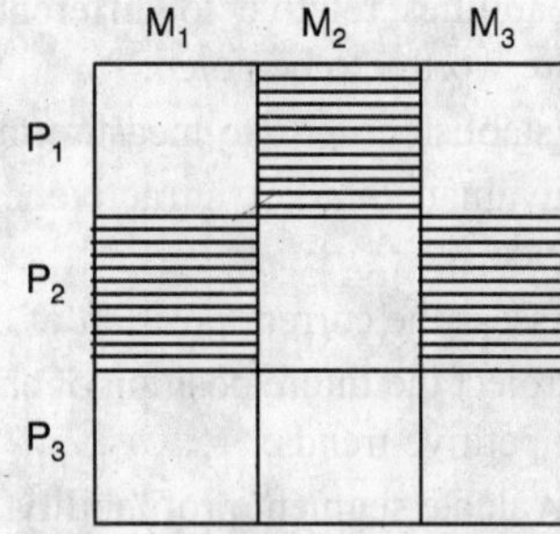

Selective specialisation

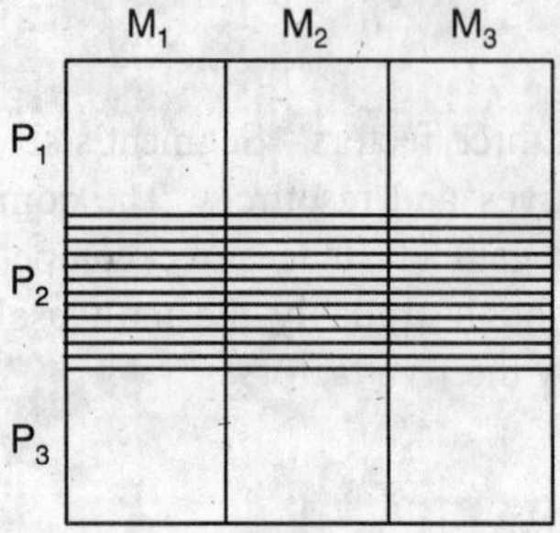

Product specialisation

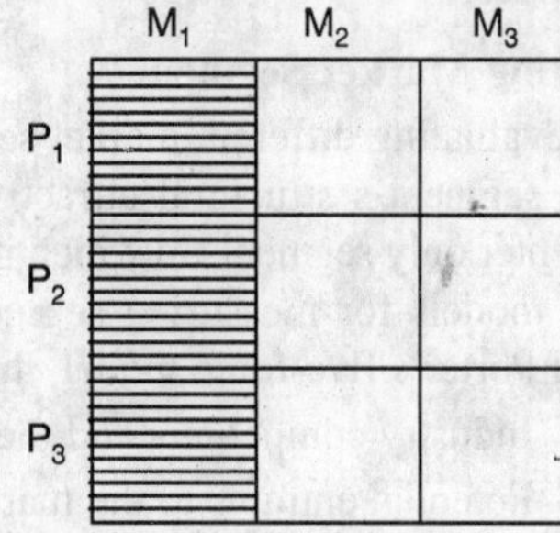

Market specialisation

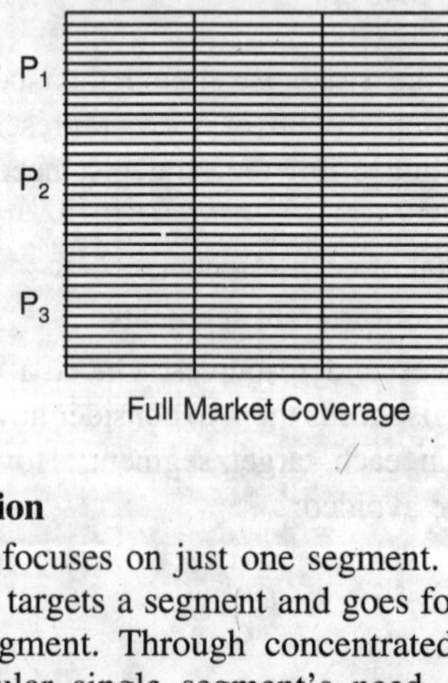

Full Market Coverage

1. Single Segment Concentration

In this case the organisation focuses on just one segment. That is, the marketer prefers to go for single segment. The company targets a segment and goes for a larger market share instead of a small share in larger market segment. Through concentrated marketing the company gains a strong knowledge of the particular single segment's need, thus it achieves a strong market position in the segment and enjoys operational economies, through specialising its production, distribution and promotion. For example the Allahabad Law Book Agency (specialised only in law books), BPB Publications (specialised only in computer books) etc. are good examples.

Concentrated marketing strategy may involve more than normal risks. At the same time, the strategy provides higher returns and therefore, it is possible that competitors might be attracted to find their place in the segment, which may deter the company to continue with this strategy.

2. Selective Segment Specialisation

In selective specialisation, the firm selects a number of segments, each objectively attractive and appropriate, as per the company's objectives and resources. There may be little or no synergy among these segments, but each segment promises to be a money-maker. This market coverage strategy has the advantage of diversifying the firm's risk. Even if one segment becomes unproductive, the firm can continue to earn money on other segments. For example, a company X produces television as well as walkman, the two different types of products obviously for two different types of markets, then it can be cited as example of selective specialisation.

3. Product Specialisation

Under product specialisation, the firm concentrates on making a certain product that it sells to several segments, for example, a microscope manufacturer sells microscopes to university-laboratories, Government laboratories and Commarcial laboratories. It makes different microscopes for these different consumer groups, but does not manufacture other instruments that these laboratories might use. Product specialisation promises strong recognition of customers within the product areas.

4. Market Specialisation

Here the organisation concentrates on satisfying the range of needs of a particulur target group. An example of this would be an agro-chemical manufacturer whole principal target market is farmers. For instance, X Company can implement market specialisation strategy by producing all sorts of home appliances - Television, Washing Machines, Refrigerators. Micro Ovens, Fans, Flasks etc. for middle class people. The firm gains a strong reputation to serve this consumer groups of middle class segment.

5. Full Market Coverage

When a firm attempts to serve all consumer-groups, with all the product that they might need, it is called the Full Market Concept. Only very large firms can adopt this strategy. Examples are IBM (Computer Market). General Motors (Vehicle Market) and Coca Cola (drink market). They cover the whole market, in two broad ways:

(a) Undifferentiated markets

(b) Differentiated Markets

(a) **Undifferentiated Markets:** Here the firm ignores market segment differences and goes after the whole market, with only one market offer. It primarily focuses on buyer's needs. It designs its product and its marketing programme that will appeal to the largest number of buyers, a sort of mass distribution, for example, Coca Cola company's early marketing of only one drink, in one bottle size, and of one taste, to suit everyone.

(b) **Differentiated Marketing:** Under this method, the firm designs different programmes for each segment. For example, IBM offers many hardware and software packages for different segments, in the computer-market. The other cases are those of American Drug and Edison Bros., which is a very large retail organisation, operating about 900 shoe-stores, in four categories, each appealing to a different market-segment. This type of marketing typically creates more total sales, than undifferentiated marketing. However, it also increases the costs of doing business, which includes:

(i) Product modification costs,

(ii) Manufacturing costs,

(iii) Administrative costs,

(iv) Inventory costs, and

(v) Promotion costs.

So, only big companies can afford to adopt this strategy.

Product Positioning

Why do buyers or consumers prefer one product to another ? In today's over-communicated society and highly competitive markets, consumers have numerous options in almost all product categories. For instance, buyers can buy a PC from IBM, Sony, Apple, Zenith and others including low-cost assemblers. Every day, an average consumer is exposed to numerous marketing related messages and the marketer must successfully create a distinct and persuasive product or service image in the mind of the buyer or consumer.

Once the organisation has decided which customer groups within which market segments to target, it has to determine how to present or position the product to this target audience. Segmentation, targeting and positioning (STP) constitute the fundamental pillar of any marketing function. Product positioning is the final stage in STP continuum. The marketing manager needs to decide which segment to enter and how to target that segment with a product offer through selection of market segment and target marketing strategy. The challenge is to decide what position the company wants its products to occupy in the selected segment or segments. A product's position is the definition that a consumer gives to the product on important attributes. It is the position in the perceptual space of the consumer's mind that the product takes in relation to competitor's products, which is often verbalized by customers on certain attributes. Positioning is an act of developing the company's offerings and image to occupy a distinct place in the minds of the target market. Positioning is a consumer driven strategy in which the objective is to occupy a unique place in the customer's mind and maximize its potential benefit for the firm.

What is Positioning?

Positioning is the act of designing the company's offering and image to occupy a distinctive place in the target market's mind. The end result of positioning is the successful creation of a market-focused value proposition, a cogent reason why the target market should buy the product. Each company must decide how many differences to promote to its target customer. The position of a product is the sum of those attributes normally ascribed to it by the consumers – its standing, its quality, the type of people who use it, its strengths, its weaknesses, any other unusal or memorable characteristics it may possess, its price and the value it represents. Many marketers advocate promoting only one central benefit what ROSSER REEVES has referred to as Unique Selling Proposition (USP) Numbar one positionings include "best quality", "Best service", "lowest price", "best value", "Safest", "more advanced technology" etc.

Positioning is a platform for the brand. It facilitates the brand to get through to the target consumer. Positioning is the act of fixing the locus of the product offer in the minds of the target consumers. In positioning, the firm decides how and around what parameters, the product offer has to be placed before the target consumers. The significance of product positioning can be easily understood from David Ogilvy's words: "The results of your campaign depends less on how we write your advertising than on how your product is positioned."

Positioning of a product or service is nothing but creating an image in the consumers' mind. Consumers genarally tend to use images while making a purchase; they buy brand images rather than actual products. There are many brands that have a powerful influence on the consumer's mind. Just think of Pepsi or Coca Cola in the soft drink market, Maruti or Santro in the passenger car market, BPL or Onida in the television market and so on. Brand names add to the offering and create a "meta product", an emotional loyalty with consumers. Consumers associate brand names with life-styles, social positions, professional roles and those associations combine to form an image or position. The terms "position" or "positioning" are frequently used to mean 'image'. To build up a brand image or corporate image, a marketer generally used advertising as a tool.

Product Position Vs Brand Position

Brand positioning is a major decision in marketing. It is believed to be the source from which all other decisions of marketing mix should flow. The entire combination of marketing mix elements attempts to communicate the brand's "position" to consumers.

Product position and brand position are different in scope. According to Smith and Lusch, product position refers to the objective attributes in relation to other products, and brand position refers to subjective attributes in relation to competing brands and this perceived image of the brand does not belong to the product but is the property of consumers' perceptions of a brand. However the terms "product positioning" and "brand positioning usually mean the same thing.

A product cannot exist unless it finds a place in the consumer's perception of the world of products around him. Any product or brand is noticed only when it occupies a particular point or space in the individual consumer's mind relative to other brands in the same product category. The perception of product is subjective and is governed by the individual's needs, values, beliefs, experience and environment. The position is the way the product or the brand is defined by consumers on important attributes. Positioning is the perception of a brand or product it brings about in the mind of a target consumer and reflects the essence of that brand or product in terms of its functional and non-functional benefits as judged by the consumer. Maggi Brand of noodles has been successfully positioned and the "two minute" noodle in the minds of target consumers and has created a distinctive brand image. HLL's Lux soap is hypothetically positioned as the "beauty soap" of female film stars and Dettol is the antiseptic for minor nicks and cuts, while possessing a plethora of uses, from preventing nappy rash to doubling as effective after shave lotion. BMW car is positioned as the "ultimate driving machine", and Volvo is positioned on safety and durability. As markets become more crowded and competitive with similar types of products, consumers rely more on the product's image than on its actual characteristics in making their buying decisions.

Product positioning brings us to the idea of functional value whereas brand positioning talks about something above and beyond functional value for which the customer is willing to pay more and when asked to recall, he may recall the brand more and given a chance to replay, he will associate the brand with so many elements which are beyond the functionality of the product. Therefore a product position refers to a brand's objective or functional attributes in relation to other brands in the category. It is a characteristic of the physical product and its functional attributes. Simply speaking, it stands for what it can do in the market.

Brand position on the other hand is an outcome of the perception of the target segment customers. It is brand's subjective or perceived attributes in relation to competing brands in the market. Let us take an example of Vicks Action 500. If you look at its product position, it's an anti-cold treatment, which has certain composition that reduces the congestion and helps during cold and cough.

Product Differentiation

Product differentiation and product positioning are central themes in the marketing strategy of a firm. The two ideas are also closely interlinked. When the firm is thorough with the differentiatio and positioning strategy for a given product, it completes one significant part of the marketing stratagy formulation for the product. A company's offer has to be distinct from those of its competitor and should fulfil the requirements of the customers of its target markets. Company's positioning is the result of whatever the company does. Marketing mix is the most tangible and the most flexible tool to create the dasired positioning. Companies use their marketing mix to create something specific and special for the customer.

Product differentiation results from added features which give customers benefits that rivals cannot match. Before adding features, a company should thoroughly research the need for the particular feature among customers in the intended target market. Companies keep on adding new features just because their competitors are offering them. Sometimes, deletion of features and benefits from a product may be a very effective differentiation because customers never really wanted these benefits.

Differentiating Market Offering

Differentiation is the act of designing a set of meaningful differences to distinguish the company's offering from that of competition. According to Theodore Levitt, all products can be differentiated to some extent. A differentiation strategy should meet the following criteria:

1. **Superior:** The chosen strategy should be superior than other ways in order to obtain the required benefits.
2. **Preemptive:** The difference should be crafted in such a way so that it is not easy to be copied by the competitors.
3. **Important:** The difference should deliver a highly valued benefit to the consumers.
4. **Distinctive:** The difference should be delivered in distinctive way.
5. **Affordable:** The difference should be available at affordable prices.
6. **Profitable:** The difference should make the company profitable through it.

Qualities of a Successful Position

Creation of a successful position comes from two sources, that is, physical product differences and brand communication, which helps in finding a memorable and meaningful way to describe the product. The objective of positioning a brand is to cause people to feel that there is absolutely no substitute for the brand. The following are qualities that help to make a successful position:

(1) **Relevance:** Often in search of a point of differentiation, brand managers identify and position the brand on an attribute, which is different but is of little concern for the customers. For example, the image of Ujala – whiteness – is an example of powerful position.

(2) **Distinctiveness:** Customers have few needs that are unfulfilled and the cosumers have many choices to fill the needs they have. If brand's position lacks distinctiveness, it will be forced to compete on the basis of price or promotion that are expensive propositions and may not build brand equity in the long run.

(3) **Coherance:** There is a need to integrate all forms of communication to bring coherence to the brand's position. for example, a brand being positioned as premium but being available in a discount store or with a price off very often dilutes the premium position of the brand. A11 the brand elements, in which the brand is positioned should have coherence in communication for building a strong position.

(4) **Commitment:** Brand managers have a tendency to get nervous when a strong position is threatened due to alienation. Once a position is adopted, it takes commitment to stay committed to the position in the face of competitor's threat to ensure the long-term position of the brand in the market.

(5) **Durability:** The brand's position is built over a period of time in customer's mind. Brands have taken long period of time to get a dominant market share. For example, Maggi noodles in Indian market took time to establish itself as a brand leader.

(6) **Clarity:** A brand'a position should have clarity so that it will be easy to communicate and quick to comprehend.

(7) **Courage:** Adopting a strong position requires clarity of vision and courage for the brand manager. A brand manager needs to have courage to believe that a strong position is a strategic intent for the brand.

Positioning Approaches

There are several approaches to positioning of product and service offerings:

1. **Positioning by product attributes or customer benefit:**

This approach to positioning is probably the most common and involves setting the brand apart from competitors based on specific brand attributes or the benefits offered. Many products, such as autos, cameras and other durable product brands offer excellent examples. A product that is well made usually offers more than one benefit. In case of toothpaste, brands are positioned on cosmatic, medicinal, taste or economy dimensions. Some brands are using one, two or even three of the above mentioned dimensions to create dual or triple positioning.

Examples: Promise is positioned on gum care.

Close-up is positioned on fresh breath and cosmetic benefit.

Colgate is positioned on fresh breath, decay prevention and taste.

2. **Positioning by price-quality:** This approach justifies various price-quaility categories of the products. Manufacturers deliberately attempt to offer more in terms of service, features or performance in case of certain products known as premium products and in return, they charge higher price, to cover higher costs and partly to communicate the fact that they are of higher quality.

3. **Positioning by product-user:** This deals with positioning a product keeping in mind a specific user or class of users. For example, cosmetic brands like Lakme position themselves targeting fashion-conscious women.

4. **Positioning by use or application:** The idea behind this approach for positioning is to find an occasion or time of use. For instance, Vicks Vaporub is to be used for a child's cold at night. Iodex is for sprain and muscle pains, Burnol ointment, is for burns and Dettol antiseptic is for nicks and cuts. These brands have used this positioning for decades now without any serious challenge from competitors.

5. **Positioning by corporate category:** This positioning is used so that the brand is perceived as belonging to another product category. This is often a strong positioning strategy when the existing product category is crowded. The consumers then perceive the brand in different context. For example, milk powder, with suitable additions and appropriate packaging, can be positioned as an 'energy drink' for sports people or a health-drink for players or a drink for 'growing school going children etc.

6. **Positioning by corporate identity:** Companies that become tried and trusted household names, use their names to imply the competitive superiority of their new brands such as Tata, Sony etc. Corporate credentials are added as a by-line. This offers a strong positioning and is used in line extensions or brand extensions.

7. **Positioning by competitor:** Positioning by competitor may be used because the competitor enjoys a well-established image in the market. The marketer wants the consumers to believe that the brand is superior, or at least as good as the brand offered by the competitor. It is like telling the people that you live next to some famous movie personality in Delhi rather than getting involved in explaining the locality and streets.

Product Repositioning

Products do undergo 'repositioning' as they go long their life cycle. In some cases, even products that are selling well are repositioned. This is done mainly to enlarge the reach of the product offer and to increase the sale of the product by appealing to a wider target market. The product is provided with some new features or it is associated with some new uses and is repositioned for existing as well as new target segments.

"Milkmaid" is a good examples of repositioning. When the product was introduced in the sixties, it was positioned as a convenient form of milk for use in tea and coffee. When the sales reached a plateau in the 1980's, the company studied the situation in detail and decided to reposition it as a produce for all uses involving milk. A well-planned advertising compaign was launched, repositioning 'Milkmaid' as an ideal ingredient for a variety of sweets and other preparations, in addition to daily use in tea and coffee.

Case Study-1

Wahaha—Taking the Fizz out of the Giant Cola Brands

Ehen Zong Qinghou, a Chinese farm worker, started a company of beverages and ice creams with two retired teachers in 1987, hardly anyone could have imagined that this company could give sleepless nights to global giants such as Coca-Cola and Pepsi Co. But the new company, Wahaha, the pride of many contemporary Chinese consumers, has managed to do just that.

Wahaha, one of the leading homegrown Chinese beverage brands, had revenues of US$1.37 billion (11.4 billion yuan) and profits of US$162.7 million (1.34 billion yuan) in 2004.

Wahaha, which is meant to mimic the sound of a baby laughing, demonstrates clearly what great brand stories are made of. The company started small, and in 1991, merged with the state-owned Hangzhou Canning Factory. The 1996 joint venture with the Danone Group gave the company foreign investmet to the extent of US$45 million. After dabbling in many product categories, it launched its trademark brand the 'Future Cola' in 1998 to compete against the global cola giants. Today, Wahaha's product portfolio includes milk and yogurt drink, purified and mineral water, carbonated soft drink, fruit and vegetable juice, sports drink, and iced tea including cognee (rice porridge), canned food and health products.

Wahaha has been careful in its strategy to compute against the global cola and food giants. As the fashion conscious Chinese consumers seem to prefer the global colas in the larger coastal Chinese cites, Wahaha has till now focused on rural and semi-urban Chinese areas. Further, the Wahaha brand has generously used home grown celebrities for all its products. This is in line with its overall strategy to position Wahaha as a patriotic company and to tap into the patriotic fervor of the Chinese consumers.

By projecting Wahaha's products as China's own, the Wahaha brand has carved out a clear positioning in the market against the global brands. But whether this strategy will work in the long run is a million dollar question and will require constant efforts to balance the brand promise and its careful delivery in a hostile and increasingly competitive Chinese market-place.

QUESTIONS

1. What aspects of consumer behaviour have been discussed in this case?
2. What is likely to be the adoption process of Wahaha products among consumers?
3. Discuss the positioning strategy of Wahaha.

QUESTIONS

1. What is market positioning?
2. What is product positioning?
3. What is meant by the term "market share"?
4. What do you understand by marketing strategy?
5. State the basic determinants of marketing strategy.
6. What do you mean by strategic marketing decisions?
7. What is perspective marketing strategy?
8. How is product positioning established?
9. How is companies evaluate and select target segment?
10. What do you understand by product differentiation?
11. What is meant by "product repositioning"?
12. Explain "product positioning" and "brand positioning"?

CHAPTER 16

Product Planning

- *Introduction*
- *What is a product ?*
- *Important Features of a Product*
- *Classification of Products*
- *Product Attributes*
- *Product Planning and Development*
- *Product Levels*
- *Product Line*
- *Product Line Decision*
- *Product Mix*
- *Product Line Vs. Product Mix*
- *Goals of Product Mix*
- *Fectors Influencing Product Mix*
- *Major Product Mix*
- *Strategy*
- *Expansion of Product Mix*
- *Contraction of Product Mix*
- *Alteration of Existing Products*
- *Positioning the Product*
- *Trading Up*
- *Trading Down*
- *Differentiation and Segmentation*
- *Determining Factors for Differentiation*
- *Benefit of Segmentation*
- *What is a Right Product ?*
- *Product Innovation*
- *Reasons for Innovation*
- *Case Study-1*
- *Case Study-2*
- *Questions*

INTRODUCTION

Good products are key to market success. The product represents a bundle of expectations of the consumers. The product satisfies the needs of society. A successful product ensures its own promotion if satisfies the needs of consumers, that is the product is right to the market. A good product should be able to generate extra amount to enthusiasm which is important to market organisations. It gives the marketer independence in decision making. For the marketer, the meaning of the product is determined by the needs and desires of the consumers. For instance, when one buys toothpaste, he buys in the hope of getting whiter teeth, avoiding bad odour etc. That is, a consumer buys the promise (product) of solving problems or avoiding one or enjoying one. For instance, one buys a car, expects troublefree journey, quick travel, comfortable seating etc.

Product and market are two essentials of successful marketing. If marketing can bring together products and markets in such a way that product and consumer demands are perfectly correlated, there is no reason why marketing cannot be successful. Both are equally important. If the product is sound and easily acceptable to the market, if it satisfies reseller's needs and customer preferences and is carefully filled to the needs and desires of the customers, sales success is assured. A right product is bound to reduce considerably the problems of pricing, promotion and distribution. Good products are key to market success.

A product or service is essentially offered to satisfy a need or want. Therefore, want-satisfying is the basic characteristic of a product. A firm's marketing plan must begin with the determination of its offerings – products or services – to the target market. For example, a woman does not buy a simple chemical compound for a lipstick. What she buys are aspirations and hopes in the form of a lipstick. The purpose of buying the lipstick is to beautify her lips. The producer must remember that lipstick is not merely a chemical compounds it is a beauty, in the form of chemicals.

Customers always expect a benefit while buying a product. It may be a bathing soap, toothpaste or motor cycle. For example, what one buys are his aspirations, hopes and expectations in the form of a motor cycle: the very purpose of which is to serve as a personal motorised form of transportation. But the customer expects a lot of benefits alongwith the basic benefit. What does he expect ? He may expect economy, fuel-efficiency, low maintenance cost, aesthetic appeals etc. In simple meaning, from the customer's point of view, the motor cycle is not only a personal motorised transportation but it is also expected to be fuel-efficient, have low maintenance cost, and serve as a life-style-symbol.

The ultimate aim of marketing is selling. Marketing is defined as the managerial process through which products are matched with markets. The success of business firms greatly depends upon how best they serve and satisfy their customers. A business can prosper only by satisfying the needs of customers. When a firm markets products or services, it should aim to enjoy **consumer satisfaction** and **profit maximisation**. Both these aims are attained through the product exchange. The product policy decisions based on the consumer's demand is an important factor in marketing the product successfully. A producer or a manufacturer takes into account many factors—customers' needs, desire, prestige, income, education etc., to make the product attractive and acceptable to its customers. A producer tries to create an image or a concept of the product in the customer's mind. For instance, a scooter manufacturer may give a guarantee as to the trouble-free performance for a run of 10,000 kilometers; a mixy manufacturer gives a guarantee for a period of 5 years within which all repairs and replacement of parts will be done free etc.

What is a Product ?

Anything that possesses utility is described as goods. A product is both what a seller has to sell and what a buyer has to buy. Thus, any enterprise that has something to sell, as tangible goods or not, is selling a product. People purchase products, because they are capable of realising some benefits to the purchaser. A product is one which satisfies the needs of customers. According to Philip Kotler, "A product is anything that can be offered to a market for attention, acquisition, use or consumption that might satisfy a want or need. It include physical objects, services, persons, places, organisation and ideas."

Alderson defines, "A product is a bundle of utilities consisting of various product features and accompanying services." Stanton defines, "A product is a set of tangible and intangible attributes, including packaging, colour, price, manufacturer's prestige, retailer's prestige, and manufacturer's and retailer's services, which the buyer may accept as offering satisfaction or wants or needs."

From these definitions, we realise the **important features of a product**, under modern marketing:

1. **Tangibility :** It should be perceptible by the touch. An item to be called a product, should have a tangibility character touch, seen or feeling. For instance, car, shirt, book etc.

2. **Intangible Attributes :** The product may be intangible, in the form of services, for instance, banking insurance services, repairing etc. It is an associated feature. For instance, scooter is a tangible product, and when free servicing is offered by the seller, then the product is not only a tangible item but also an intangible one.

3. **Associated Attributes :** Such attributes may be, brand, package, warranty etc. For instance, Hindustan Lever's vanaspati ghee has a brand name DALDA and with its package it can be identified by the consumers. It has developed an image that all kinds of vanaspati ghee sold are being referred to as DALDA ghee.

4. **Exchange Value :** Whether the product is tangible or intangible, it should have exchange value and must be capable of being exchanged between seller and buyer for mutually agreed price.

5. **Consumer Satisfaction :** Products should have the ability to offer value satisfaction to the consumer. The satisfaction may be both real or/and psychological. For instance, when we, buy SNOW we also buy beauty—a product with a bundle of utilities.

Generally when we think of products, we mean physical products, for instance, a car, radio, book etc. But products also include services (service products). For instance, when one employs a carpenter, he is not purchased, but his service is purchased—his time, his ability, his skill etc. Even an idea can be marketed, for instance, family planning or safe driving. Thus a product consists broadly of anything that can be marketed, including physical objects, services, persons, places, organisations and ideas.

> A Product is anything that can be offered to a market for attention, acquisition, use or consumption that might satisfy a want or need.

Classification of Products or Goods

In marketing the term **goods** is used in synonym for **products**. The products may be classified into the following categories (for details refer Chapter I) :

1. **Industrial Goods** are those which are used for further production of goods or services, and include capital goods, raw materials, component parts etc. These are used as input in producing other products. For instance, iron ore, machine tools etc.

2. **Consumer Goods** are meant for final consumption by consumers and not for sale. They are of three types :

(*a*) **Convenience Goods :** Items, the consumer buys frequently, immediately and with minimum shopping effort are convenience goods. For instance, food items, newspapers, drugs, soap, tooth paste, biscuit etc.

(*b*) **Shopping Goods :** There are goods purchased by the consumers, only after a careful comparison-suitability, quality, price, style etc. For example, clothes, furniture, household appliances, fans etc.

(*c*) **Speciality Goods :** These are goods with unique characteristics or brand identification and the purchasers make a special purchasing effort, for instance, fancy goods, special eating items etc.

According to durability or tangibility, products can be classified into three :

1. Non-durable goods, such as soap, salt etc.
2. Durable goods, such as clothing, tools, refrigerators etc.
3. Services, such as repair, haircut etc.

Product Attributes

As the product moves away from its core or generic form, a number of attributes will be added in order to differentiate that product from its competitors, These attributes will include a variety of additional features, quality levels, design, branding, packaging, customer service etc. In each case attributes should be developed to meet the needs of the target market and provide a competitive advantage for the product. Product attribute decisions involve deciding the **quality**, **features** and **design** of the product.

(*a*) **Product Quality:** It refers to the ability of the particular product item to perform its intended functions, and as such it summarises factors such as durability, reliability, precision, performance, and ease of operation. The selection of a quality level depends on the nature of the market or market segment being targeted and also on the position selected for the product.

(*b*) **Product Features:** Product features also qualify as an important source of product differentiation. In addition to the core product, the firm must offer a range of necessary features, that is, the features that a consumer would expect to see in the product. Features help in product differentiation with. respect to that of competitors.

(c) **Product Design:** A product design indicates its usefulness as well as makes it attractive. Decisions have to be taken in this regard too. Products can also be distinguished because of a unique style or design which helps to create a distinct "personality" for the product. A distinctive design is difficult to create, relatively rare and usually expensive. In consequence, most mass market goods are not characterized by distinctive designs and if anything, there is a tendency for businesses to use fairly standard styles for their products.

PRODUCT POLICIES

Product policies are the general rules set up by the management itself in making product decisions. Products of a firm are the backbone with which profit is earned, enabling the firm to exist. Therefore, the product is the fundamental feature which determines the firm's success or failure. Good product policies are the basis on which the right products are produced and marketed-successfully. The fundamental function of a product policy is that it guides the activities of a firm and is measured not only with the current profits, but also with the long life of the firm. The policies of the firm must be to manufacture right products for the consumers. **"Product policy is concerned with defining the type, volume and timing of the products, a company offers for sale."** The product policy is the objectives and guidelines, which determine the nature of the product or services, to be marketed. All types of commercial function must have a policy. And when a product is concerned, a policy is essential to make the product up to the standard expected by consumers. The product policy is a broad term and includes many activities.

A product policy, generally covers the following :

1. Product planning and development
2. Product line
3. Product mix
4. Product branding (Identification) (Chapter No. 19)
5. Product style
6. Product positioning
7. Product packaging (Chapter No. 19) etc.

We discuss topics 1,2,3,5 and 6 in this Chapter and the remaining topics will be dealt in subsequent chapters.

1. Product Planning and Development

In the modern competitive situation, producers try to bring out suitable products which are closer to and more attractive than, the substitutes. To make one's product, the producer must take utmost care in planning his product. The pressure of competition leads to drag out the existing products, and the management looks ahead for the development of new products, in the place of the existing product or through diversification or extension of product line. A product may be a physical product or a service as far as marketing is concerned. The product planning means an attempt to establish the product in line with market needs. It is defined "the act of making out and supervising the search, screening, development, and commercialisation of new products, the modification of existing lines and the discontinuance of marginal or unprofitable items." In this definition, there are three important considerations :

(1) Evolution and introduction of new products.

(2) Bringing alterations in the existing lines to suit the requirements of the market.

(3) The discontinuance of elimination or marginal or unprofitable products.

Product planning is the initial stage for the entire marketing programme of a concern. Product planning embraces all activities which enable producers and middlemen to determine what should constitute a company's line of products. Product development, a more limited term embraces the technical activities of product research, engineering and design. The effort of developing products or/and increasing the scope to satisfy the needs of the customers, who like a change, is called merchandising. Merchandising is often termed as product development. It is the function of the management through the co-ordinated efforts of specialists to design the products to satisfy the consumer's needs.

The product planning and product development include the decision-making of the following:

1. Which products should the firm make and which should it buy ?
2. Should the company expand or simplify its line?
3. What new uses are there for each item?
4. What brand, package and label should be used for each product?
5. How should the product be styled and designed; and in what sizes, colours and materials should they be produced?
6. In what quantities should each item be produced?
7. How should the product be priced?

A company cannot always be successful in selling poor products in the market over the long run. The survival and growth of the product depends upon many activities that make the product more acceptable to the intended customers.

Product Levels (The customer value hierarchy)

In planning its market offerings, the marketer needs to analyse the product at different levels. A product has different layers (levels), like an onion and each of the layers contributes to make the product. The identified levels are :

1. Core Benefit or Product
2. Basic or Generic Product
3. Expected Product
4. Augmented Product
5. Potential Product

1. **Core Benefit or Product**

This is the most fundamental level. The core product explains the reasons for which the customer is making the purchase. For instance, a hotel customer is actually buying the concept of "rest and sleep".

2. **Basic or Generic Product**

The marketer at this level has to turn the core benefit to a basic product. The basic product for hotel may include bed, toilet, towels etc.

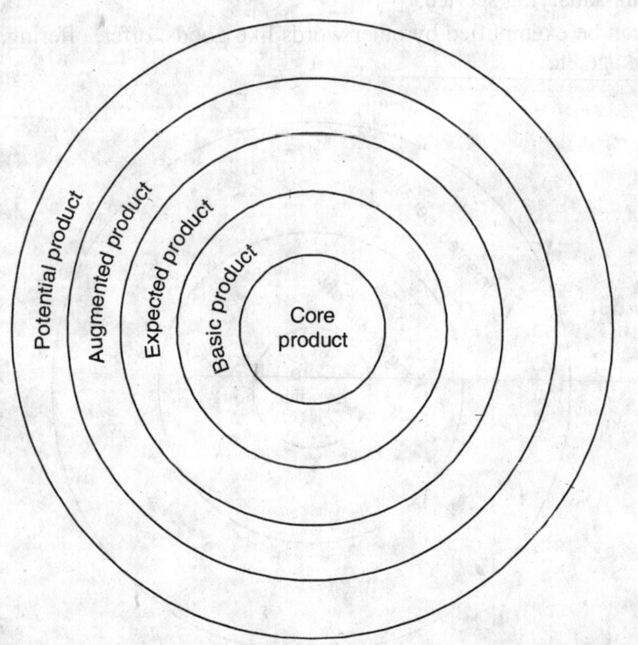

3. **Expected Product**

At this level, the marketer prepares an expected product by incorporating a set of attributes and conditions, which buyers normally expected when they purchase this product. For example, hotel customers expect clean bed, fresh towel, a degree of quietness etc.

4. **Augmented Product**

At the fourth level, the marketer prepares an augmented product that exceeds customer expectations. In developed countries, brand positioning and competition take place at this level. For example, today's hotel customers expect cable or satelite television with a remote control and high-speed internet access etc.

5. **Potential Product**

This levels takes into care of all the possible augmentations and transformations the product might undergo in the future. This level prompts the companies to search for new ways to satisfy the customers and distinguish their offer. Successful companies add benefits to thier offering that not only satisfy customers, but also surprise and delight them. Delighting is a matter of exceeding expectations. For example, ever-faster internet.

A customer will always evaluate the benefits that he will get from the ownership of the product, for the cost he has to bear for the ownership. The benefits associated with any product can be classified as:

1. Core Benefits
2. Tangible Benefits
3. Augmented Benefits

1. Core Benefits (Core Products/Services)

These benefits explain the core meaning of the product to the consumer. These are the intangible benefits at the core of the product that the consumer expects to obtain through ownership to consumers. For example, the core benefit of buying food is to overcome hunger; a car offers the generic benefits of convenience in travelling.

The product (service) has certain immediately identifiable characteristics and functions that distinguish it from other products or services. The most fundamental level is the Core Product, which answers the question, "What is the buyer really buying ?" Every product is really the packaging of a want-satisfying service.

The product can be exemplified by other words like goods, offer, offering, package, bundle of goods, benefit package etc.

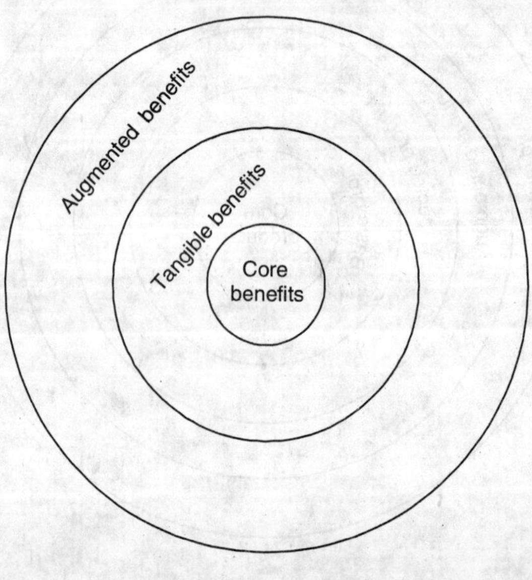

2. **Tangible Benefits**

These benefits are the tangible benefits that the consumer come across while making a choice. These are the physical attributes of the product that the consumer confront in the market place. These include features, colour, design, style, quality, size, weight, durability etc.

3. **Augmented Benefits**

Many basic products are a combination of core and tangible benefits. Companies augment the core and tangible benefits with warranty, guarantee and after sales service programmes so that the customer's experience with the brand increases. The other augmented benefits include facilities for credit, packaging, repair, after sales service facilities etc.

2. Product Line

"A product line is a group of products that are closely related, either because they function in a similar manner, or are sold to the same customer groups, or are marketed through the same types of outlets, or fall within given price ranges." According to Stanton, "A broad group of products, intended for essentially similar uses and possessing reasonably similar physical characteristics, constitute a product line." In other words, a broad group of products, which are meant for essentially similar uses and possess reasonably similar physical characteristics, constitute a product line. For instance, a range of toilet soaps is product line.

The product item is a specific version of a product that has a separate designation in the seller's list. That is, a product item is a specific product. For instance, Hindustan Motor's Ambassador Mark IV is a product item.

Product Line Decision Strategies

Taking of decisions or changing the composition of the product line, by either adding or subtracting products, depends upon a number of factors :

1. Consumer's preference
2. The tactics of competitors
3. The firm's cost structure
4. Changes in market demand
5. Buying habits
6. Marketing influences
7. Product influences
8. Company objectives
9. Product specialisation
10. Elimination of obsolete products

3. Product Mix

"A product mix (also called product assortment) is the set of all product lines and items that a particular seller offers for sale to buyers." An organisation with several product lines has a product mix. Product mix need not consist of related products. In other words, product mix is "the composite of products offered for sale by a firm." It is a collection of products manufactured or distributed by a firm. It is the full list of all products offered by a firm. For instance, a firm manufactures watches, machinery items, electric lamp etc. It has four main characteristics : (1) Length (2) Width (3) Depth (4) Consistency.

Length of product mix refers to the total number of items in its product mix. Width or breadth of the product mix refers to the number of different product lines offered by the company. Depth of the product mix refers to the average number of items offered by the company in each product line. Consistency of the product mix refers to how closely the various product lines are related in production requirements, distribution, channels etc. For instance, products manufactured by an electric company have an overall consistency, as most products involve electricity power.

Product Line and Product Mix

Most companies generally market several products rather than just one or two. It is necessary for them to understand the relationship among all their products to coordinate their marketing of total group of products. **Product item**, **Product line** and **Product mix** concepts help us to understand the relationship among a company's different products.

A **product item** refers to a particular version of a product that is distinct, such as Surf Excel is a (premium) product item offered by the Hindustan Lever Limited. A **product line** is a closely related group of products for essentially similar use, and technical and marketing considerations. Colgate product line includes Colgate Dental Cream, Colgate Gel, Colgate Total, Colgate Herbal. etc. **Product mix** is the total number of products that a company markets. **Product mix consistency** means how closely related different product lines are in end–use, production requirements, distribution etc. A company may have many product lines in its product mix. The **product mix width** refers to the number of product lines a company has. **Product line length** means the number of product variants available in a company's product line.

Goals of Product Mix

The efficient fulfilment of the marketer's goal to supply goods and services to consumer for satisfaction of their needs can be possible if due attention is given to three issues which govern the product mix – **sales growth**, **sales stability** and **profits**.

Sales growth can be achieved either by increasing its share in existing markets or by finding new markets. Four ways can be adopted by which product mix can be adjusted to achieve goals, that is, organisational goals.

(a) **Market Penetration:** under which market share is increased by expanding sales of present products in existing uses;

(b) **Market development**, under which markets are expanded by creating new uses of present products;

(c) **Product Development**, where market share is, increased by developing new products to satisfy existing needs.

(d) **Diversification**, where market is expanded by developing new products to satisfy new consumer needs.

Sales Stability: Stable sales allow for more efficient planning in all phases of production and distribution. It is also desirable to maintain a proper balance in total sales and product mix so that a market share losing product can be counteracted by another picking up market share. Sales stability is also possible by making an entry into a new market.

Profits are determined by the components of the product mix. Some items are usually more profitable than others. Low profit items may be performing a valuable part in helping to sell company's more profitable products; and they may also prove as insurance against an unforeseen failure in profitable products.

Factors Influencing Change in Product Mix

Generally it is very difficult for a concern to take a decision about the number of products it should produce at a given time because the number of products or product mix is affected by several factors. Changes in the product mix, that is, adding or eliminating products, may be due to the folowing factors :

(1) Change in demand of a product due to population changes,

(2) Changes in purchasing power or behaviour of the customers,

(3) Change in company desire,

(4) Development of by-products by using residuals, at low cost,

(5) The competitor's actions and reactions,

(6) To utilise the available marketing capacity fully,

(7) Financial influences of the firm,

(8) Advertising and distribution factors,

(9) Goodwill of the firm,

(10) Possibility of adding new product to its product line at less cost.

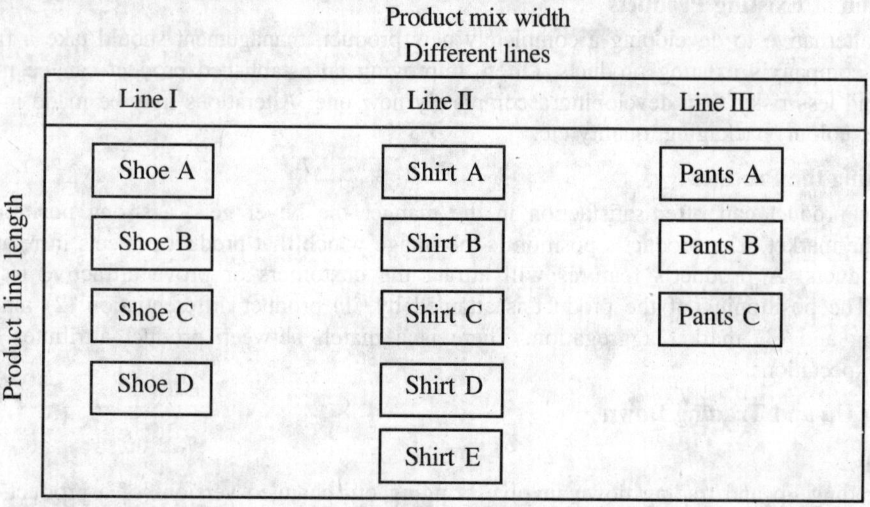

No. of items (length) = 12

No. of lines (width) = 3

Average depth $\frac{12}{3} = 4$

Major Product Mix Strategies

A company has several major strategies as its disposal, with respect to the width, depth and consistency of its product mix. One major management aspect involved in product policy is the decision concerning product mix. The product mix is one of the elements in the product policy. This is more important now-a-days since most of the manufacturers are diversifying their products.

The following strategies are generally employed by the producer or wholesaler of the product

(1) Expansion of Product Mix.
(2) Contraction of Product Mix.
(3) Alteration of Existing Products.
(4) Positioning the Product.
(5) Trading up and Trading down.
(6) Product differentiation and Market segmentation.

We discuss them briefly :

(1) Expansion of Product Mix

It is also referred to diversification. A firm may expand its present product mix by increasing the number of product lines or increasing the number of product items within the same line. New lines may be related or unrelated to the present products. For instance, a provision stores may add drugs, cosmetics, baby foods, dry fruits etc.

(2) **Contraction of Product Mix** (product line contraction)

In certain circumstances, the management has to drop the production of unprofitable products. A firm may either eliminate an entire line or simplify the assortment within a line, this is termed as contraction of product mix.

This is also termed as simplification. The process of avoiding or stopping the production of a particular product is called simplification. Simplification may be defined as deleting or eliminating those product items, which are unsatisfactory or unnecessary, from the product line. It is opposite to product diversification. It is also termed as pruning, deletion. elimination, contraction, dropping or abandonment.

(3) **Alteration of Existing Products**

As an alternative to developing a completely new product, management should take a fresh look at the company's existing products. Often, improving an established product can be more profitable and less risky than developing a completely new one. Alterations may be made in the designs size, colour, packaging, quality etc.

(4) **Positioning the Product**

When a product can offer satisfaction in the manner the buyer gets, a strong position is created in the market. The product's position is the image which that product projects in relation to rival products. A product's features will attract the customers or prove attractive to the customers. The positioning of the product is attained by (1) product differentiation (2) market segmentation and (3) market aggregation. There is a match between product attributes and consumer expectations.

(5) **Trading Up and Trading Down**

Trading Up

Both trading up and trading down involve bringing out changed versions of a product and altering the nature and direction of promotion. Normally, a firm will trade up or down, but not both. **Trading Up** refers to adding of higher priced and more prestigious products to their existing line, in the hope of increasing the sales of existing low priced products. In other words, when a marketer has already gained a good reputation through marketing his low priced products in the initial stage and later on introduces high priced products, it is termed as trading up. For instance, a factory marketing terrycotton is trading up by introducing polyester.

Trading Down is the opposite to trading up. A company is said to be trading down, when it adds a lower priced item to its line of prestige products in the hope that people who cannot effort the original products, will want to buy the new one, because it carries some of the status of the higher priced product. In other words, a manufacturer of high quality products, starts producing and selling a lower quality product. The manufacturer having already gained and established a good name in the markets wishes to widen the market for his products. In trading down new market is looked for, where the old product has not reached.

(6) **Product Differentiation and Market Segmentation**

When there is a fundamental difference between one product and another, there will be a product differentiation. The product differentiation involves developing and promoting an awareness of differences between the advertiser's products and the products of others. The purpose of this differentiation is to make one's product different from those of other competitors. Awareness of differentiation is developed and promoted on company's product from the product of others. This strategy is useful and facilitates a business to remove itself from price competition. This system is adopted by many firms that wish to engage a non-price competition in the market. Thus a firm establishes that its product is different from, and better than, other products. This differentiation sometimes, causes monopolistic competition. When a firm has exclusive features like trade-mark, trade-name patent-rights etc., the product is differentiated. Quality, design, colour, brand, packaging etc., also make a product differentiated. For instance, toilet-soap, tooth paste, paint etc., are differentiated by increasing the price, taking into account the cost of advertisement and promotion. The seller hopes that the demand can be directed to his differentiated market products which are reasonably standard.

Major Determining Factors for Product Differentiation :

1. The characteristics of the product that are considered important by the customers.

2. The extent of appreciation by the customers as to the differences or distinguishing features of the product.

3. The extent of money consideration that the customers are ready to pay for the extra quality of the product.

4. Generally speaking, the more a product or service can be differentiated from its competition, the more successfully price can be used to enhance this differentiation.

In the modern marketing concept, all marketing activities have to revolve around the customers. Effective marketing requires a clear picture of the consumers' characteristics that can be described as the "Customer Profile." Marketing effort should be towards the specific group of people or segment.

According to William J. Stanton, "Market segmentation consists of taking the total heterogeneous market for a product and dividing it into several sub-markets or segments, each of which tends to be homogeneous in all significant aspects."

A market consists of buyers and buyers who differ in one or more respects. They differ in their wants, resources, geographical locations, buying attitudes, buying practices etc. Again, buyers can be grouped in terms of sex, education, income level etc. This grouping of buyers (segmenting the market) is said to be **market segmentation**. That is grouping the buyers, based on income, age, education etc., is called market segmentation. As a market is segmented based on more characteristics, the seller achieves better precision. Different products are manufactured to meet the different requirements.

Market segmentation is used to sub-divide the market (or consumers) of the product in order to capture more and more sales effectively and efficiently. It is a technique of product differentiation which involves manipulation of either the product and promotion or pricing variables. Whenever there are two or more customers of a product they can be sub-divided into several positive buyers' group according to their common characteristics.

The different types of segments are :

1. Geographic Segmentation.
2. Demographic Segmentation.
3. Socio-Phycological Segmentation.
4. Product Segmentation.
5. Benefit Segmentation.
6. Volume Segmentation.
7. Marketing-factor Segmentation.
8. Life-style Segmentation.

Benefits of Market Segmentation :

1. If the market is properly segmented, if the buyers' respective preference systems are accurately defined, and if all segments are properly served, the sales volume should be larger than if the same product were offered to all buyers.

2. More specialised, hence, presumably more efficient media can be used and personal selling can be focused on segmented market.

3. The manufacturer can prepare and follow a sound marketing programme which leads to efficiency and more success in selling.

4. Manufacturer comes close to a particular group of customers. One can modify or develop a new product on the basis of market demand.

5. It leads the firm in the long-run towards better profitability.

6. It provides various types of information which are useful in marketing research, product development, evaluation of activities etc.

What Constitutes a Right Product ?

To make the product policies successful; one must raise the following 10 R's.

1. Is it a right product?	RIGHT PRODUCT
2. Has the product in right quality?	RIGHT QUALITY
3. Is the product packed in acceptable quantity?	RIGHT QUANTITY
4. Is it priced suitably and competitively?	RIGHT PRICE
5. Is the product acceptable to buyers?	RIGHT BUYERS
6. Is the product marketed at right time?	RIGHT TIME
7. Is it introduced in the right market?	RIGHT MARKET
8. Is the size of the product acceptable?	RIGHT SIZE
9. Is it in an attractive colour?	RIGHT COLOUR
10. Is it styled attractively?	RIGHT STYLE

PRODUCT INNOVATION

A product or a service, which is profitable today, may not be so tomorrow. It is either replaced by another one or it degenerates into profitless competition. The underlying reason is that markets are highly dynamic. The days have changed and science and technology have given rise to scientific marketing. Now the economy being more dynamic, we are compelled to produce what the market needs. This transformation of economy from static to dynamic calls for innovation. "Innovation is the design and development of something new, as yet unknown and not in existence, which will establish a new economic configuration out of the old, known existing elements. The success of a business largely depends upon how best it serves and satisfies its customers who may be ultimate consumers. The business tries to meet its social responsibility towards the society through the medium of its product-goods or service–For instance, when a buyer purchases a refrigerator, he not only purchases the conveniences-food preservation, cold drinks, cooling vegetables, but also satisfies his psychological needs social and economic status. Unless the consumer's needs are satisfied, the business cannot prosper.

The following factors are considered for product innovation :

(1) **Market Changes :** The market is dynamic, and therefore, existing products and product lines prove inadequate for meeting buyer's demand.

(2) **Change in Technology :** Changes in technology have not only widened the existing markets but also brought entirely new markets through the creation of entirely new products.

(3) **Profitless Price Competition :** Generally, the competitive forces in the modern system do not permit the continuance for a long time of a firm if it does not produce new products or make improvements in the existing products.

Thus, product line strategy involves a long term plan for changes and adjustments in the product line of the firm in order to realise the objectives of the firm efficiently and economically. A firm may adopt the following alternative product strategies :

(1) **Product Innovation**

The first strategy of product line may be adding more and more new products to the existing product line. It helps the management in diversifying the risk and attracting more and more sales. Continuous product and market research is necessary for it.

(2) **Product Improvement**

It is also necessary to modify or improve the existing products-size, form, design, new pack etc.

(3) **Product Dropping**

It is also essential to review the product line from time to time and drop those products from it which have lost their market and become uneconomic.

(4) **Policy of Planned Obsolescence**

Some manufacturers adopt the policy of planned obsolescence also. They bring, new models and drop the old ones to increase their sales and attract more customers.

(5) **Policy of Product Differentiation**

Some manufacturers adopt this policy just to attract the customers to their product through minor changes in their brand, packing, style etc.

What is a New Product ?

According to Stanton : Three recognizable categories of new products are :

1. Products that are really innovative-truly unique.
2. Replacements for existing products that are significantly different from the existing goods.
3. Imitative products that are new to a company but not new to the market.

Perhaps the key criterion as to whether a given product is new is how the intended market perceives it. If buyers perceive that a given item is significantly different (from competitive goods being replaced) in some characteristic (appearance, performance), then it is a new product.

Reasons for Product Innovation

1. To meet market changes.
2. To adopt technological changes.
3. To avoid profitless competitions.
4. To adjust diversification of risk.
5. To incorporate changes in fashion.
6. To effect development of new market
7. To meet consumer needs.
8. To cover inadequacy of present lines.
9. To serve buyers better.
10. To adopt product differentiation.
11. To overcome competitor's challenge.
12. To emphasise new uses of products.
13. To take advantage of existing reputation.
14. To improve product safety.
15. To produce goods more economically.

Case Study-1

Innovation for Leadership

ROTOMATIC ELECTRONICS LTD.

Rotomatic Electronics Ltd. was a small company offering accessories product for medium to large computers. The company specialised in the manufacture and sale of magnetic disc drives. The product, being: complex one, required extensive controls. As the product required high quality control, it had high unit cost and was manufactured to meet customer requirements.

Rotomatic's business in computer industry was highly competitive. Many larger companies manufactured their own magnetic disc drives and also there were quite a large number of small manufacturers who had entered in the field recently. Rotomatic's disc drives offered large capacity and high speed and could interface with any existing computer system. The company had capacity to expand its operations due to attractive features and flexibility.

However, as the company was not occupying leadership position in the market, the company had ,to constantly come up with innovations to increase sales. In order to attain more corporate ability, the management decided to diversify into new product areas. They asked the R&D department to design the single board efficient computer. As a result of six months' hard efforts, the R & D department gave the prototype.

QUESTIONS

1. Suggest the ways and means of positioning the new product in a highly competitive market.
2. Advise the alternatives to reach the customers with new and innovative computer product giving plausible reasons. (*Pune, MBA,*)

Case Study-2

Re-establishing Credibility with Changing Reality

LAXMI MILLS

Mr. Rajan Kohali, alongwith his brothers, started making and selling edible oils way back in 1910. In 1930, Rajan, alongwith his sons, started Laxmi Mills with factories operating in Bombay and Hyderabad. The change was not only in the name but also a major technological difference. The Laxmi Mills was subjected to a new process : refining. The mill had to get people to accept a "tasteless" cooking medium, because that's what the oil became after refining. By generating an export market, he covered the risk of being left with excess stocks while he experimented with the Indian market. At that time, there were a sufficient number of Europeans in India to form the base of his local market.

Rajan had chosen groundnut oil for the following reasons:

(i) It was very commonly used by Indian families with potential customer base.
(ii) Groundnut was grown widely in India.
(ii) The oil seeds yielded a good quantity of oil.

The oil was sold in 1.5 and 5.0 kg small barrels to cater to both the nuclear and joint family needs.

Rajan sold the concept of refined oil as one that is pure as it undergoes a thorough cleaning process retaining the flavour of the foodstuff itself. The concept being new, the buyers had to be convinced that it was not harmful.

The company enjoyed 80% of the market share till 1970. Other companies saw the growing potential in groundnut oil and entered the market. To remain in the market as a leader, the Laxmi Mills changed the pack size to one, two, five, ten, fifteen and twenty-five kg. However,a competition became fairly intense in 1980. A number of big players entered the market: In 1981, Bombay Oil Mills launched refined Kardai Oil which helped to lower cholesterol, levels; the primary cause of heart attacks. It explained this feature, and the doctors also started prescribing Kardai Oil. Any person-with a heart problem was immediately prescribed to change the cooking medium to Cardai oil.

Consumer queries started coming into Laxmi Mills. People wanted to know if it was safe to use refined groundnut oil. The market share dropped sharply to 65%.

QUESTIONS

1. What, according to you, should the Laxmi Mills have done immediately after sensing the change?
2. Advise the company to clear its reputation and re-establish its credibility.
3. Recently, it has been reported that Kardai oil is not helpful in preventing heart problems. What advice would you pass on to Bombay Oil Mills ?

[Pune, MBA]

QUESTIONS

1. What is the need for product policy ? Describe the qualities of a product policy. *(B.Com. Delhi)*
2. What is meant by a product ? *(B.Com. Mumbai)*
3. What do you understand by product differentiation ? *(B.Com. Mumbai)*
4. What do you understand by product planning ? *(B.Com. Delhi)*
5. Describe simplification and diversification as a part of product policy. *(B.Com. Madurai)*
6. What is meant by the expansion of product mix ? *(B.Com. Madurai)*
7. Define product. What are the essential characteristics of a product ? *(B.Com. Kerala)*
8. What are the goals of product mix ? *(B.Com. MS)*
9. What is meant by product line expansion ? *(B.Com. Poona)*
10. What is product planning and Development? *(B.Com. Andhra)*

CHAPTER 17

Managing the Product Development

- *Product Life Cycle*
- *Different Stages*
- *Advantages of PLC*
- *Development of New Product*
- *Managing New Product Development*
- *Planning Process*
- *Launching a New Product*
- *Product Diversification*
- *Product Elimination*
- *Product Modification*
- *Product Failure*
- *Questions*

PRODUCT LIFE CYCLE

As every being has life, a product has its life. Industrial goods may have a longer life than consumer goods. When a product idea is commercialised, the product enters into the market and competes with the rivals, for making sales and earning profits. Products, like human beings, have length of life. This has been described as life cycle in human beings and when applied to products, it is called as product life cycle. The product life cycle is generally termed as product market life cycle, because it is related to a particular market. For instance, an old product in the market of Mumbai, may have a new life in a remote village. The product life cycle may be short for some products and long for some other products. The period may differ form product to product. But the product passes througn the stages, collectively known as product life cycle. The chart below gives the life cycle of a product.

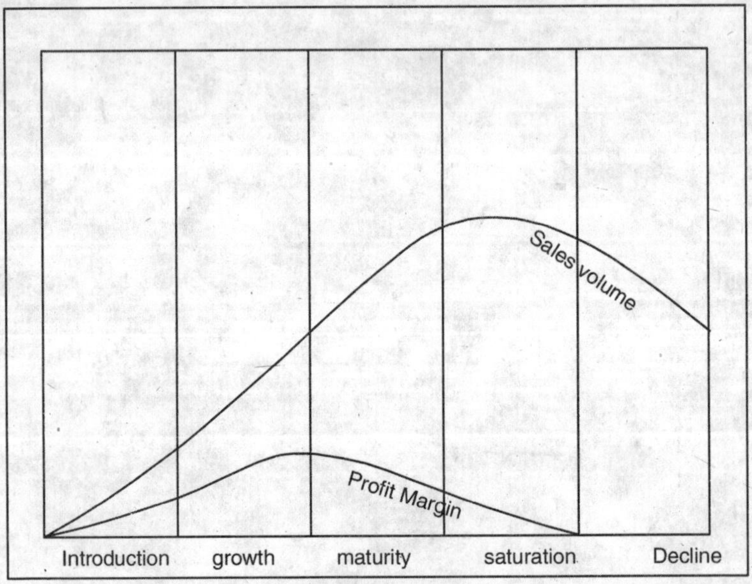

Product Life Cycle

Introduction : Product is new : awareness in market is low : cost of marketing is high : profits are low.

Growth : The product has given satisfaction to the first buyers. Others follow : Sales increase rapidly and product starts generate profits. Competitors notice the success and start planning competitive offering.

Maturity : The product reaching its maturity and sales are good. But battle for market share is about to begin.

Saturation : Total sales are not growing any more. The battle for market share is difficult. Try for strong brand loyalty and reduced price.

Decline : Sales and profits are starting to fall and future of the product does not look healthy. Remedial strategy–modifying, repositioning or even deleting the product, is needed.

Every product moves through a life cycle, having five phases and they are :

1. Introduction
2. Growth
3. Maturity
4. Saturation
5. Decline

1. **Introduction :** This is the first stage in the life of a product. This is an infant stage. The product is a new one. The new product means "a product that opens up an entirely new market, replaces an existing product, or significantly broadens the market for an existing product." The initial stage needs greater amount for investment. In this stage, the product is introduced into the market and made available to the customers with a slow rise in sales. The profit may be low, because of heavy advertising and sales promotion in order to stimulate the demand.

2. **Growth :** The product satisfies the market. In this stage, a product gains acceptance from the part of consumers and businessmen. Sales of the product increase. Profit also increases. This is the stage where competitors appear along with substitute products in large numbers. Previous buyers continue in their purchase and new buyers appear. Firms may find it difficult to meet the demand. The success of firms depends upon the efficient manufacturing and distributing systems of the product.

3. **Maturity :** At this stage, keen competition increases. Sales continue to increase for a while, but at a decreasing rate. Competitors go for mark-down price by increasing advertising deals. Market expenses increase, even after mark-down prices, which enable to face competition. Thus, profit is thinned. Additional expenses are involved in product modification and improvement in the marketing mix or/and product mix or style changes, to attract the customers and retain the market. Overall marketing effectiveness becomes the key factor in this stage.

4. **Saturation :** In the saturation stage, the sales are at the peak and further increase is not possible. The demand for the products is stable. The rise and fall of sale depend upon supply and demand. At this stage, a replacement of product is needed, because the sale of the existing product cannot be increased.

5. **Decline :** When sales start declining, buyers go for newer and better products. This is because of many reasons—technological advances, consumer shifts in taste, increased competition etc. At this stage, the product cannot stand in the market; many firms withdraw from the market, when sales and profits decrease. Price becomes the competitive weapon. Under such a situation, firms shift their attention to other products. The product becomes out of date and fashion. Then the firm will drop the product from the product line.

Management of PLC

The marketing manager should manage the life cycle of a product towards better progress and for a healthy growth of the firm. A marketing manager, while forecasting the PLC, must also anticipate the limitations and other drawbacks. Thus he may be able to chalk out programmes more successfully. We discuss how the PLC is managed under various stages.

I. Management of Introduction Stage

After successful test marketing of a new product, the company introduces the product in the market with full-scale marketing programme. The introductory stage is viewed as fairly risky and quite expensive because large amounts of money is spent on advertising and other tools of marketing communications to create consumer awareness in sufficiently large numbers and encourage trials. Profits are mostly negative in this stage or in some exceptional cases they may be very little.

Introducing a product category is relatively expensive, challenging, time consuming and quite risky. The aim of every company is to move quickly through the introduction stage and for this, research, engineering, production, are critically important to ensure the availability of quality products. The company must be able to provide promptly post-purchase service and availability of spares, if required. To encourage trial and repeat purchase, consumer goods companies use a combination of demonstrations on TV, samples, special introductory prices and coupons. The company also tries to gain distribution and shelf space with retailers.

Various factors affect pricing decisions of a new product, such as new product's perceived value to consumers, how fast competitors can copy it, the availability of close substitutes, the effect of price on sales volume and costs. Generally, for a pioneering product or a significantly improved new product, companies adopt high price and high promotion strategy. However, a company may use any one of the two important pricing strategies during introduction stage – skimming pricing strategy or penetration pricing strategy.

(a) **Skimming pricing:** This strategy can be appropriate when the market size is large and not much time is available before the competition appears. Similarly, this strategy can also work in niche markets where customers are relatively insensitive to price and owning the product is important, for example, Apple Computers keeps its price high when it introduces a new product. This helps company to recover its new product investment relatively fast.

(b) **Penetration Pricing:** This strategy allows the company to strive for fast market development and the focus is on long-term objectives of market share and profit maximisation. Price is kept low and promotion is high. The market is seen as large and characterised by intense competition and consumers who are aware or become aware are very willing to buy the product at an affordable price. This strategy can also work when the market is large and any serious threat from competition is not anticipated.

The importance of distribution set up is particularly significant for consumer product companies. The availability of consumer products at convenient locations where consumers generally shopping for such products is quite important, keeping in view the large amounts spent on promotion to make consumers in the target market aware and induce new product trial among customers. Most firms use their established distribution network for a new product.

There is a high percentage of product failures in the first stage. When a product is first introduced at the pioneering stage, since the product is new, profits are negative or low because of low sales and heavy distribution and promotion expenses. There is very little direct competition. The promotional programme is designed to stimulate demand. By looking ahead, one can know that competition will enter sooner or later and cause prices and its market share to fall. Once the product gains consumer acceptance the sales go up in growth stage. The PLC is the result, not the cause, of marketing strategies choosen by the firm. Since "the first impression is the best impression," the marketing manager should :

1. Make proper advertising before the products are released in the market.
2. Shorten the period of introduction, as far as possible.
3. Formulate new pricing and marketing strategies.
4. Undertake large scale promotional work.
5. Give proper attention to the distribution aspects.

II. Management of Growth Stage

This stage is marked by a rapid climb in sales. Potential buyers start buying the product. Buyers compare this product with the rival product, because new competitors enter the market with new product features and thus competition increases. The number of outlets are increased. Companies maintain their promotional expenditures at the same or at a slightly raised level to meet competition. Since this is a crucial stage, the marketing manager should:

1. Improve product quality.
2. Add new product features and improved styling.
3. Enter into new market segments.
4. Enter into new distribution channels.
5. Reduce the prices to attract buyers.
6. Increase promotional activities.

Characteristics of this stage :

1. New market segments are opened.
2. Sales increases rapidly.
3. Company earns higher profit.
4. Unit manufacturing cost falls faster.
5. Competition enters the market.
6. Competitors engage in frequent price cuts.
7. Competitors increase promotion activities.

III. Management of Maturity Stage

During this stage, a manufacturer gets maximum profit through maximum sales. Price competition becomes increasingly severe. A novel method of pushing sales as creative selling is called for. The sales and profits start scale down as the products gradually lose their significance in the presence of better goods substitutes. For an effective management, the marketing manager should :

1. Improve the quality of the product.
2. Give proper attention to increase the usage among the current customers.
3. Try to convert non-users into users of the product, that is, creating new buyers.
4. Give proper emphasis to advertisement and promotional programmes.
5. Try to discover new uses for the product.

At this stage, it is more likely that the competitors become more active. In case the product is novel one, by new competition would have come out with a similar product in the market to compete. Therefore, the sales are likely to be pushed downwards by the competitors while the promotional efforts would have to be increased to try and sustain the sales. This is called the maturity stage or saturation. At this point it is difficult to push sales up. With regard to the profits, the profits are likely to stabilise or start declining as more promotional effort has to be made now in order to meet competition.

In the maturity stage, the companies can take the following strategies to stimulate sales:

1. Market Modification
2. Product Modification
3. Marketing mix Modification
4. Systematic framework. (for the matured product)

1. **Market Modification:**

The company may try to expand the market in order to increase sales by adopting the following:

* Enter new market segments
* Attract new users
* Increase usage among the present customers
* Persuade customers to use the product
* Create new uses of the product

2. **Product Modification:**

The decline can be arrested by improvements in the product and promotion. We should however, at this time seriously think in terms of new product, new product-mix or redesign of the current product. The company can stimulate sales by modifying the product characteristics – improvements.

* Quality improvements (Durability, Reliability, speed etc.)
* Feature improvements (size, materials, weights etc.)
* Style improvements (new models, new styles etc.)

3. **Market Mix Modification:**

The companies can try to stimulate sales by modifying marketing mix elements:

* Price
* Distribution
* Advertisement
* Personal selling etc.

4. **Systematic Framework (for matured products)**

In order to handle matured products, the managers need a systematic framework for identifying new ideas to utilise any growth opportunities: a few examples are given below:

* Innovative product differentiations.
* Add new product lines.
* Stimulate non-users
* Create new product-line elements
* Expand distribution coverage
* Expand distribution intensity
* Penetrate substitute's exposure
* Stimulate light users.

IV. **Management of Saturation Stage**

This is a stage where a manufacturer finds it difficult to expand the sales volume beyond a particular point, that is, sales are at the peak and further increase is not possible. Since the sale of product cannot be increased, the marketing manager should :

1. Introduce new models.
2. Pursue new uses for the product.
3. Introduce new package and repricing.
4. Middlemen's margin is to be increased.
5. If the price is heavy, offer the product on instalment basis.

V. **Management of Decline Stage**

This is the last and most crucial stage. Sales may decline for a number of reasons–technical advances, arrival of new products at low cost, changes in fashion, consumer preference etc. Sales and profits continue to fall at this stage. If the substitutes are more attractive and in latest fashion, buyers may turn their eyes towards them. At this stage, cost control is increasingly important to generate profits by the following alternatives : (Suggested by Stanton) :

1. Improve the product in a functional sense, or revitalize it in some manner.
2. Make sure that the marketing and production programmes are as efficient as possible.
3. Streamline the product assortment by prunning out unprofitable sizes and models. Frequently, this tactic will decrease sales and increase profits.
4. "Run out" the product, that is, cut all costs to the bare minimum level that will optimize profitability over the limited remaining life of the product.
5. Abandon the product.

Advantages of PLC

1. When the product life pattern is known, the management must be cautious in taking advance steps, before the decline stage, by adopting product modification, pricing strategies, style, quality change etc.
2. The firm can prepare an effective product plan, by knowing the PLC of a product.
3. The PLC will greatly help the management in drawing future plans of the firm.

A management may be able to adopt some measures to **control** the PLC. They include :

1. Extension of the life at maturity and saturation stage by adopting new packaging, re-pricing or product modification etc.
2. Creation of new uses by expansion of the market.
3. Creation of more varieties of the product among current users. For instance, Amul Milk Powder, through advertisement emphasises many uses, in preparing milk, tea, curd etc. "It is like having a dairy in your home."
4. Adoption of the latest technological changes, fashion changes, market acceptance etc.

Product Identification (Branding)

Branding is the use of a distinctive name or/and mark on a product to differentiate it from similar competitive products. (For detailed explanation see Chapter 19)

DEVELOPMENT OF NEW PRODUCTS

The term 'new product' has many connotations. So, what should we call a 'new' product ? Most definitions of new-product have a common feature that new products offer innovative benefits. The development and introduction of new products have traditionally been seen to be a costly and risky activity. For an organisation intent on either maintaining or improving its position in the market-place, there are, however, few alternatives to new product activity of one sort or another. The issues faced by many marketing strategists thus revolve around the issue of the type of new product activity that is to be pursued and how best to manage and, hopefully, reduce risk levels.

A company can add new products through, **acquisition** or **development**. The acquisition route can take **three forms**.

(1) The company can buy other firms;

(2) The company can buy a licence or franchise; or

(3) The company can buy patents.

The development route can take **two forms**:

(1) The company can develop new products in its own laboratories. or

(2) It can contract with independent researchers or new-product development firms to develop specific new products.

We can identity six categories of new products.

1. **New–to–the–world–products:** New products that create an entirely new market.

2. **New product lines:** New products that allow a company to enter an established market for the first time.

3. **Additions to existing product lines:** New products that supplement established product lines (package sizes, flavours etc.)

4. **Improvements and revisions of existing product:** New products that provide improved performance or greater perceived value and replace existing products.

5. **Repositioning:** Existing products that are targeted to new markets or market segments.

6. **Cost reductions:** New products that provide similar performance at lower cost.

Managing New Product Development

The companies handle the organisational aspect of new product in following ways:

1. **Product Managers:** The manager in charge of a specific product division is bestowed the responsibility of new product development. The advantage of this method is that managers are quite knowledgeable about the consumers' changing needs and competitive activities.

2. **New Product Managers:** A new type of managers are appointed to take care of new product development professionally.

3. **New Product Committee:** This is a high-level body constituted of top level managers from all the functional departments.

4. **New Product Department:** A separate department for new product may be created to undertake new product development systematically on a continuous basis.

5. **New Product Venture Team:** Some companies assign new product development to venture teams. It is a unit within the company responsible for creating entirely new products aimed at new markets. Team members are generally drawn from different functional area of the company. They are removed from their normal duties, given a budget, a time frame, and provided informal workplaces that may even be garages to work as a team and develop new products.

In a growing economy like in India, to be successful in the field of marketing, new consumer needs must be discovered and satisfied. A new product must be suitable to meet the changing needs of the customers. The life of the firm is closely related to the development of new products through technological innovations. The technological innovations are important to the growth of established business as well as to the development of new business. Businessmen must make a detailed study of the market in relation to the products. New products mean new profits. For instance, a ready-made garment dealer has to plan the garments to be in line with the changing fashions. Product failure wastes the money, material and time, apart from defeating the objectives of the firm.

Product plan is the first step for an entire marketing programme. It is a wider term and includes product development also. Product plan has been defined as "the act of making out and supervising the research, screening, development and commercialisation of new products; the modification of existing lines and the discontinuance of marginal or unprofitable items." The top management, including specialists, takes decision on product planning.

New Product Planning Process

The new product planning is the function of the top management personnel and specialists drawn from sales and marketing, research and development, manufacturing and finance. This group considers and plans new and improved products in different phases, as given belows:

1. Idea generation (Idea Formulation)
2. Screening of ideas (Evaluation)
3. Concept Testing
4. Business analysis
5. Product development
6. Test marketing
7. Commercialisation (market introduction)

1. **Idea Generation:**

The focus in this first stage is on searching for new product ideas. Few ideas generated at this stage are good enough to be commercially successful. New product ideas come from a variety of sources. An important source of new product ideas is customers. Fundamentally, customer needs and wants seem to be the most fertile and logical place to start looking for new product ideas. This is equally important for both personal consumers and industrial customers.

Product planning starts with the creation of product ideas. The continuous search for new scientific knowledge provides the clues for meaningful idea formation. Drucker suggested that the sources can broadly be divided into: (a) Internal Source (within the company) and (b) External Sources (outside the company)

Sources of New Product Ideas (Internal)

1. Research and Development Department
2. Technical Service Staff
3. Company Salesman
4. Executive Personnel
5. Company Sales Records
6. Top Management
7. Company Patent Department
8. From Employees Suggestions
9. "Brainstorming" Sessions of Management

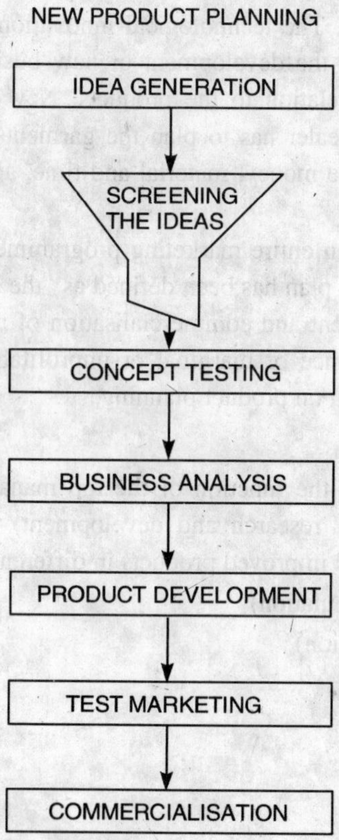

Sources of New Product Ideas (External)

1. Consumers
2. Competitors
3. Free-lance Inventors
4. Trade Literature
5. Consulting Organisations
6. Trade Fairs
7. Advertising Agencies
8. Government Agencies
9. Intermediaries (Distributors etc)
10. Wholesalers and Retailers.

2. **Screening the Ideas:** (Evaluation)

It means critical evaluation of product ideas generated. After collecting the product ideas, the next stage is screening of these ideas. The main object of screening is to abandon further consideration of those ideas which are inconsistent with the product policy of the firm. The product ideas are expected to be favourable and will give room for consumer satisfaction, profitability, a good market share, firm's image etc. All the ideas cannot be accepted, because certain product plans need huge amount of investments, for certain plans raw materials may not be available, certain plans may not be practicable etc. Many of the ideas are rejected on account of many reasons and thus eliminate unsuitable ideas. Only promising and profitable ideas are picked up for further investigation.

Answers are sought to questions like:

* Does the product meet a genuine need ?
* Is it an improvement over the existing product ?
* Is it close to our current lines of business ?
* Does it a totally new line of business ?
* Will it offer customers a superior value ?
* Will the new product bring in expected ROI ?
* Does the market accept the new product ? etc.

3. **Concept Testing**

After the new product idea passes the screening stage, it is subjected to 'concept testing'. Concept testing is different from test marketing, which takes place at a later stage. What is tested at this stage is the 'product concept' itself – whether the prospective consumers understand the product idea, whether they are receptive towards the idea, whether they actually need such a product and whether they will try out such a product if it is made available to them. In fact, in addition to the specific advantage of getting the consumers' response to the product idea, this exercise incidentally helps the company to bring the product concept into clearer focus. Concept testing helps the company to choose the best among the alternative product concepts. Consumers are called upon to offer their comments on the precise written description of the product concept, viz, the attributes and expected benefits.

4. **Business Analysis** (Market Analysis)

This stage is of special importance in the new product development process, because several vital decisions regarding the project are taken based on the analysis done at this stage. Estimates of sales, costs and profits are important components of business analysis and forecasts of market penetration and market potential are essential. More precise estimates of environmental and competitive changes that may influence the product's life cycle or its replacement or repeat sales are also needed to develop and launch a product. A complete cost appraisal is necessary besides judging the profitability of the project. Market analysis involves a projection of future demand, financial commitment and return thereon etc. Financial specialists analyse the situation by applying break-even analysis, risk analysis etc. Business analysis will prove the economic prospects of the new product.

5. **Product Development**

The idea on paper is converted into product. The product is shaped corresponding to the needs and desire of the buyers. Product development is the introduction of new products in the present markets. New or improved products are offered by the firm to the market so as to give better satisfaction to the present customers. Laboratory tests, technical evaluations etc. are made strictly.

6. **Test Marketing**

By test marketing, we mean, what is likely to happen, by trial and error method when a product is introduced commercially into the market. These tests are planned and conducted in selected geographical areas, by marketing the new products. The reactions of consumers are watched. It facilitates to uncover the product fault, if any, which might have escaped the attention in the development stage. By this, future difficulties and problems are removed. This type of pre-testing is essential for a product before it is mass produced and marketed. Sometimes, at this stage, management may take decision to accept or reject the idea of marketing products.

Designing the programme for test marketing involves making a number of decisions:

* Where and in how many markets should test be carried out ?
* What should be the duration of test marketing ?
* What to test ?
* What criteria should be used to determine success or otherwise ?

7. **Commercialisation** (Market introduction)

This is the final stage of product planning. At this stage, production starts, marketing programme begins to operate and products flow to the market for sale. It has to compete with the existing products to secure maximum share in the market-sales and profits. When a product is born, it enters into the markets; and like human beings, has a life span–product life cycle.

In launching a new product, the company must make four decisions:

(1) When should the product to be launched ?

– Right time.

(2) Where should it be launched ?

– a single locality,

– a region or

– national market etc.

(3) Which groups should be targeted ?

– Existing customers.

(4) How should it be launched ?

– Develop an action plan for introducing the new product into the rollout markets.

Consider the following before launching a new product.
1. Effective market research
2. Ensure product quality
3. Differentiation of product
4. Identification of consumer needs
5. Effective promotion
6. Proper distribution system
7. Correct pricing strategy
8. Knowledge of local needs
9. Choose correct time
10. Strength of sales force.

Factors that hinder the new product development
1. Shortage of ideas
2. Shorter PLC
3. Higher expenditure
4. Fragmented markets
5. Inappropriate incentives
6. High gestation period
7. Non-cooperation of staff

Product Diversification

Diversification occurs when a firm seeks to enter the market with a completely new product. "Diversification is a policy of an operating company, so that its business and profits come from a number of courses, usually from diverse products that differ in market or production characteristics." Generally it means adding a new product to the existing product line. It may be new products, new markets, new technologies etc. It is just the opposite of product line contraction and is also referred to product line expansion. For example, a firm making watches at present, has started making wall-clocks. This product is different from the existing product. The reasons for the diversification are :

1. To take advantage of the existing reputation;
2. To arrest the declining profit margins;
3. To meet new products of competitors;
4. To use more effectively the existing facilities;
5. To increase the sales of existing products;
6. To maintain market share;
7. To meet the customers' demand;
8. To utilise the existing spare capacity of factory;
9. To eliminate cyclical slumps;
10. To curtail market expenditure,
11. To compensate the loss of another product;
12. To use undistributed earnings.

The kinds of diversifications are:

1. **Products Sharing a Common Base :** It is an introduction of new products, which are akin to the present line. The new products, which are introduced into the market, will not affect the present product, in any way. For instance, a sugar industry can diversify to paper product.

2. **Products of Related Industries :** It is an introduction of a new product, a complementary item. For instance, a type-writer company may manufacture type-writer ribbon, which can be used as a complementary product to the typewriter. The new product may be used as an input for the old product.

3. **Products of Unrelated Industries :** The products of unrelated industries or lateral diversification as a move to expand product line, beyond the confines of the industry. That is, the company can produce any products. For instance HMT produces wrist watches, electric lamps etc.

Product elimination (Product Withdrawal)

It means that a product is removed from the product line. When there is no demand for a product or when the demand declines to obsolescence, marketing of such product is of no use. Moreover, certain products cannot be modified to suit the market. In such a case, it is better and profitable to withdraw the product. Such product brings decreased sales, and profit, and finally affects the reputation and financial strength of the firm. Such a process of withdrawal of products is known as product elimination. A sick product lost market appeal.

The indicator for elimination :

1. Downward profit trend
2. Decreasing price trend
3. Declining sales trend
4. Cheaper substitutes are appeared.
5. Greater utilisation of executive's time.
6. Contribution is not covering the fixed expenses.
7. Unfavourable customer reaction.
8. Emergence of superior substitute products.
9. Decreasing marketing share.
10. The product may be in the last stage of PLC.

Production Modification

The existing product has to be modified in order to suit the changing conditions, because of fashion change. When one makes improvements in the existing product, by changing its quality, size, form or design etc., the process is said to be product modification. When changes are made, the existing product may look almost new. The purpose of this change is to increase the sales or to attract the customers. Modification may facilitate : (1) Satisfying the additional needs of the buyers, (2) up grading or down grading the quality of a product to suit the market–rich or poor (3) Changing to attractive design, colour, shape etc. (4) Meeting the consumers' demand or for social responsibility.

Product Failure : Reasons

Generally it is witnessed that many products entering into the market, may not reach the target of sales and profits. Introduction of new substitutes, technological innovations, consumers, who are selective in their choice of products etc. reduce the span of life of products. The following are the general causes for the failure :

1. Conception of product idea or specification of the product may be faulty.
2. Design of product may not match with production facility.
3. The strength of competitions may not be accounted.
4. Marketing may be inefficient and insufficient.
5. Cost of production may be higher than the estimated cost.
6. The product performance may be unsatisfactory.
7. Operations may not be within control.
8. Market changes may not be understood properly.
9. Producers may be ignorant of consumers' preference.
10. Technical and production problems might have been underestimated.
11. Products may be introduced to the market untimely.
12. Introducing products for which there is no demand.
13. Stressing product attributes incorrectly.
14. Prices may be high.
15. Poor packaging, inappropriate size etc.
16. Weaknesses in distribution
17. Inadequate sales force
18. Poor timing
19. Lack of test marketing
20. Government policy

How to Avoid Product Failure ?

Many products are introduced in the market and many products go out of the market every year. Many of the problems can be solved by timely action taken by the management: Thus, the failure of some of the products can be avoided by the following steps :

1. The product must be suitable to the market.
2. There must be a good demand in the market.
3. The product must keep the company's image.
4. There should not be any legal restriction.
5. The product must be in tune to the consumer's need.
6. The product must fit into the existing product facility.
7. There must exist a good system of marketing.
8. The product must be compatible with the current environment and social standards.
9. There must exist a good demand creation method.
10. There must exist a good system of distribution.

QUESTIONS

1. Explain briefly the steps to be followed in new product introduction. *(B.Com., Madurai)*
2. What do you understand by "Evaluation of the Ideas"? *(B.Com.)*
3. What are normal functions involved in product planning ? *(B.Com., Madurai)*
4. Describe simplification and diversification as a part of a product policy. *(B.Com., Meerut)*
5. What is meant by product life cycle ? Explain its concepts with examples. *(B.Com., Allahabad)*
6. What is meant by product modification ? *(B.Com., Calicut)*
7. Why new products fail ? *(B.Com. Andhra)*
8. What do you meant by new product development ? *(B.Com., Kerala)*
9. What is a new product ? How is it developed ? *(M.Com., Madurai)*

CHAPTER 18

Pricing Strategy

- *Introduction*
- *What is price*
- *Importance of price*
- *Pricing Objectives*
- *Factors Affecting pricing Decision*
- *Procedure for Price Determination*
- *Kinds of Pricing*
- *Price Leader*
- *Factors Affecting changes in Price*
- *Price as an Indicator of Quality*
- *One Price Vs. Variable Price*
- *Resale Price Maintenance*
- *Case Study*-1
- *Questions*

INTRODUCTION

Pricing assumes a significant role in a competitive economy. Price is the main factor which affects the sales organisation. A good price policy is of great importance to the producers, wholesalers, retailers and the consumers. Marketers try to achieve their long-run pricing objectives through both price policies and price strategies. If the prices are high, few buyers purchase and if the prices are low, many buyers purchase. Thus market may be reduced or increased. That is, the price increases in relation to the sales revenue. Thus pricing is a critical situation. Therefore, a sound pricing policy must be adopted to have a maximum sales revenue.

In the early stages of men, prices were set by buyers and sellers negotiating with each other. The seller may demand a higher price than expected and the buyer may offer a price less than the expected one. Ultimately they arrive at an aggreeable price through bargaining. Now in the competitive economy, development of large business aims to have one price policy. In certain cases, the buyer looks at the price as an indicator of product quality. If the price is higher, the buyer believes the products to be of high quality. In case the quality is not up to the mark he expects, he feels that the price is high. Hence, one cannot say that the price is high or low, without considering the quality of the product to be purchased. The price is greatly affected or influenced for future production and marketing.

Prices play an important role in the economy. The time within which the product is sold varies. The goods, which are of a perishable nature and frequent changes of style, may not be stocked for long time. In the case of durable goods, they can be stocked for longer time, in the hope of getting favourable price rise. Holding the stock depends upon the financial resources of farmer, middleman, wholesaler etc., and the perishability of the goods.

What is Price?

Price may be defined as the exchange of goods or services in terms of money. Without price there is no marketing in the society. If money is not there, exchange of goods can be undertaken, but without price; *i.e.*, there is no exchange value of a product or service agreed upon in a market transaction, is the key factor which affects the sales operations.

What you pay is the price for what you get.

Price is the exchange value of goods or services in terms of money.

Price of a product or service is what the seller feels it worth, in terms of money, to the buyer.

You pay a PRICE →	When you pay tuition fees to a teacher. When you engage a labour on wages. When you pay rent on your house. When you pay commission to a broker. When you pay subscription. When you pay salary to salesmen. When you pay charges on your trip. When you pay premium. When you pay advertisement bill. When you pay interest on loans.

Importance of Price

The market price of a product influences wages, rent, interest and profits. In other words, the price of a product influences the price paid for the factors of production–labour, land, capital and entrepreneurship. The price is a matter of vital importance to the buyer and the seller. Exchange of the goods or services takes place only when the prices are agreed upon by the seller and the buyer. Price can decide the success or failure of a firm. Prices are important economic regulators. By transferring to money economy from barter economy, the importance of price has been increased. Price is a primary source of revenue which, all firms try to maximise by expanding markets. The marketing demand for a product or service to a large extent depends upon the price of the product. Price will affect the competitive position and share of the markets. Pricing policy, no doubt is a potential weapon, specially in a planned economy like ours where it can be used in such a way as to bring about a proper allocation of resources according to planned priorities.

When a firm sets a price for its goods, it has to consider many factors–demand, existing competition, legal restrictions etc. Only the cost of production is not enough to fix the price, but the objectives of the firm may also be considered. In consumer-oriented marketing, the product must have utility to the buyer, who must have satisfaction. If a consumer is not satisfied, he may refuse to buy the product. Then, in monopoly, a firm can fix the price of its product. The market is full of competitors and many substitutes also appear. When a new firm launches a promotion campaign, introduces a new product, or reduces its pricc to expand the market, the market goes to competitors. Under these circumstances, price reduction or changes in the price structure will help to overcome the situations.

Pricing Objectives

To perform the marketing job efficiently, the management has to set goals first. Pricing is no exception. Before determining the price itself, the management must decide the objectives of pricing. These objectives are logically related to the company's overall goal or objectives. The main goals in pricing may be classified as follows:

1. **Pricing for Target Return** (on investment) (ROI): Business needs capital, *i.e.*, investment in the shape of various types of assets and working capital. When a businessman invests capital in a business, he calculates the probable return on his investment. A certain rate of return on investment is aimed. Then, the price is fixed accordingly. The price includes the predetermined average return. This is seller-oriented policy. Many well-established firms adopt the objective of pricing in terms of "return on investment." Firms want to secure a certain percentage of return on their investment or on sales. The target of a firm is fixed in terms of investment. For instance, a company may set a target at 10 or 15% return on investment. Further, this target may be for a long term or short term. Wholesalers and retailers may follow the short term, usually a year. They charge certain percentage over and above the price, they purchased, which is enough to meet operational costs and a desired profit. This target chosen, can be revised from time to time. This objective of pricing is also known as pricing for profit. Certain firms adopt this method as a satisfactory objective, in the sense they are satisfied with a certain rate of return.

2. **Market Share :** The target share of the market and the expected volume of sales are the most important consideration in pricing the products. Some companies adopt the main pricing objective so as to maintain or to improve the market share towards the product. A good market share is a better indication of progress. For this, the firm may lower the price, in comparison to the rival products, with a view to capture the market. By reducing the price, customers are not exploited, rather benefited. The management can compare the present market share with the past market share and can know well whether the market share is increasing or decreasing. When the market share is decreasing, low pricing policy can be adopted by large-scale manufacturers, who produce goods needed daily by the consumers. So margin of profit comes down because of low price, but the competitors are discouraged from entering the market. By low pricing policy, no doubt, market share can be increased, besides attracting new users.

Objectives of a Firm in Pricing

1. To profit maximisation
2. To earn target return (ROI)
3. To face competition
4. To increase market share
5. To enter new market
6. To achieve a particular market share
7. To keep competition out
8. To keep parity with competition
9. To attain a target market
10. To bring price stability
11. To survive in competition field
12. To balance price over product line.

3. **To Meet or Prevent Competition :** The pricing objective may be to meet or prevent competition. While fixing the price, the price of similar products, produced by other firms, will have to be considered. Generally, producers are not in a haste to fix a price at which the goods can be sold out. One has to look to the prices of rival products and the existing competition and chalk out proper price policy so as to enable to face the market competition. At the time of introduction of new products to the market, a low price policy is likely to attract customers, and can establish a good market share. The low price policy discourages the competitors. This low price policy can be adopted before the obsolescent stage under PLC.

4. **Profit Maximisation :** Business of all kinds is run with an idea of earning profit at the maximum. Profit maximisation can be enjoyed where monopolistic situation exists. The goal should be to maximise profits on total output, rather than on every item. The scarcity conditions offer chances for profit maximisation by high pricing policy. The profit maximisation will develop an unhealthy image. When a short-run policy is adopted for maximising the profit, it will exploit the customers. The customers have a feeling of monopoly and high price. But a long-run policy to maximise the profit has no drawbacks. A short-run policy will attract competitors, who produce similar goods at low cost. As a result, price control and government regulations will be introduced.

5. **Stabilise Price :** It is a long-time objective and aims at preventing frequent and violent fluctuations in price. It also prevents price war amongst the competitors. When the price often changes, there arises no confidence on the product. The prices are designed in such a way that during the period of depression, the prices are not allowed to fall below a certain level and in the boom period, the prices are not allowed to rise beyond a certain level. The goal is to live and let live. Thus firms forego maximum profits during periods of short supply of products.

6. **Customers' Ability to Pay :** The prices that are charged differ from person to person, according to his capacity to pay. For instance, doctors charge fees for their services according to the capacity of the patient.

7. **Resource Mobilisation :** This is a pricing objective, the products are priced in such a way that sufficient resources are made available for the firms' expansion, developmental investment etc. Marketers are interested in getting back the amount invested as speedily as possible. A product may have a short PLC. The management may fix a higher price and this trend will invite competitors with low priced similar products.

Factors Affecting Pricing Decisions

The pricing decisions are influenced by many factors. The price policies should be consistent

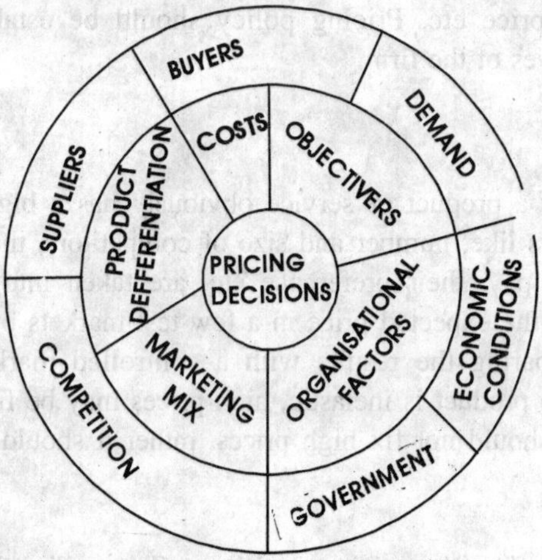

Factors Affecting Pricing Decisions

with pricing objectives. The influencing factors for a price decision can be divided into two groups: (1) Internal Factors and (2) External Factors.

(A) Internal Factors

(1) Organisational Factors

Pricing decisions occur on two levels in the organisation. Over-all price strategy is dealt with by top executives. They determine the basic ranges that the product falls into in terms of market segments. The actual mechanics of pricing are dealt with at lower levels in the firm and focus on individual product strategies. Usually, some combination of production and marketing specialists are involved in choosing the price.

(2) Marketing Mix

Marketing experts view price as only one of the many important elements of the marketing mix. A shift in any one of the elements has an immediate effect on the other three–Production, Promotion and Distribution. In some industries, a firm may use price reduction as a marketing technique. Other firms may raise prices as a deliberate strategy to build a high-prestige product line. In either case, the effort will not succeed unless the price change is combined with a total marketing strategy that supports it. A firm that raises its prices may add a more impressive-looking package and may begin a new advertising campaign.

(3) Product Differentiation

The price of the product also depends upon the characteristics of the product. In order to attract the customers, different characteristics are added to the product, such as quality, size, colour, attractive package, alternative uses etc. Generally, customers pay more price for the product which is of the new style, fashion, better package etc.

(4) Cost of the Product

Cost and price of a product are closely related. The most important factor is the cost of production. In deciding to market a product, a firm may try to decide what prices are realistic, considering current demand and competition in the market. The product ultimately goes to the public and their capacity to pay will fix the cost; otherwise product would be flapped in the market.

(5) Objectives of the Firm

A firm may have various objectives and pricing contributes its share in achieving such goals. Firms may pursue a variety of value-oriented objectives, such as maximising sales revenue, maximising market share, maximising customer volume, minimising customer volume, maintaining an image, maintaining stable price etc. Pricing policy should be established only after proper considerations of the objectives of the firm.

(B) External Factors

(1) Demand

The market demand for a product or service obviously has a big impact on pricing. Since demand is affected by factors like, number and size of competitors, the prospective buyers, their capacity and willingness to pay, their preference etc. are taken into account while fixing the price. A firm can determine the expected price in a few test-markets by trying different prices in different markets and comparing the results with a controlled market in which price is not altered. If the demand of the product is inelastic, high prices may be fixed. On the other hand, if demand is elastic, the firm should not fix high prices, rather it should fix lower prices than that of the competitors.

(2) Competition

Competitive conditions affect the pricing decisions. Competition is a crucial factor in price determination. A firm can fix the price equal to or lower than that of the competitors, provided the quality of product, in no case, be lower than that of the competitors.

(3) Suppliers

Suppliers of raw materials and other goods can have a significant effect on the price of a product. If the price of cotton goes up, the increase is passed on by suppliers to manufacturers. Manufacturers, in turn, pass it on to consumers. Sometimes, however, when a manufacturer appears to be making large profits on a particular product, suppliers will attempt to cash in on the profits by charging more for their supplies. In other words, the price of a finished product is intimately linked up with the price of the raw materials. Scarcity or abundance of the raw materials also determines pricing.

(4) Economic Conditions

The inflationary or deflationary tendency affects pricing. In recession period, the prices are reduced to a sizeable extent to maintain the level of turnover. On the other hand, the prices are increased in boom period to cover the increasing cost of production and distribution. To meet the changes in demand, price etc. several pricing decisions are available–(a) prices can be boosted to protect profits against rising cost, (b) price protection systems can be developed to link the price on delivery to current costs, (c) emphasis can be shifted from sales volume to profit margin and cost reduction etc.

(5) Buyers

The various consumers and businesses that buy a company's products or services may have an influence in the pricing decision. Their nature and behaviour for the purchase of a particular product, brand or service etc. affect pricing when their number is large.

(6) Government

Price discretion is also affected by the price-control by the government through enactment of legislation, when it is thought proper to arrest the inflationary trend in prices of certain products. The prices cannot be fixed higher, as government keeps a close watch on pricing in the private sector.

The marketers obviously can exercise substantial control over the internal factors, while they have little, if any, control over the external ones.

Procedure for Price Determination

There is no specific procedure applicable to all firms for price determination. However, the following steps may be followed to determine the price :

1. Determine demand for the product.
2. Anticipate and analyse the competitive reaction.
3. Establish expected share of the market.
4. Select pricing strategy.
5. Consider company's marketing policies.
6. Set the price.

1. Determining Demand for the Product

The marketer has to make out an estimation for his product. Each price that the company might charge will lead to a different level of demand. There is a relation between the price charged and the resulting demand. In the normal case, demand and price are inversely related, *i.e.*, higher the price, lower the demand. There are two practical steps in demand estimation. They are, first, to determine whether there is a price which the market expects and second, to estimate the sales volume at different prices. Comparison of the prices of rival products is a good guide in pricing products. In certain cases, the marketer conducts regular survey of potential buyers, retailers, wholesalers etc., to determine the expected price. When we know the expected price, we can compute sales volume at different price levels. If demand is elastic rather than in-elastic, sellers will consider lowering their price, to produce more total revenue. That is a product with elastic market demand. It is usually priced lower than the product with an inelastic demand.

2. Anticipate and Analyse the Competitive Reaction

The competitors can influence the price. Competition may arise from (1) similar products (2) close substitute and (3) unrelated products seeking the same consumer's disposable income. When the marketing field is easy to enter, then the number of competitors is greater, and there is a room for more revenue. To anticipate the reactions of the competitors, it is necessary to collect information about their product, cost structure, market share etc.

3. Establish Expected Share of Market

A marketer must decide the share of the market at the expected price. Low priced products may capture larger share of the market, and a high priced product may capture a small share of the market. Large share of the market can also be captured by advertisements and non-priced competition. Share of the market is also decided by the factors, such as present production capacity, cost of plant extention etc.

4. Select Pricing Strategy

A good and proper pricing policy may be employed to achieve a predetermined share of the market. There are two methods:

(a) **Skimming Pricing :** This price strategy is characterised by high initial price of the product, at the time of introduction of the product in the market. Manufacturers aim at profit maximisation at the shortest period, where market conditions are also favourable. The price is brought down when competitors enter into the market field. Under this, the price is fixed high, because the product is characteristic for its distinctiveness and exclusiveness etc. Skimming is suitable for new products, because (1) at the initial stage, competition is at minimum, and the distinctiveness of the product leads the market, (2) if the market is unfavourable the price can be brought down easily. And at the same time, if the price is too low, it is very difficult to raise the price, (3) High price creates a vision of superior product.

(b) **Penetrating Price :** Price skimming strategy adopts a high introductory price to skim the milk of the market, whereas penetration pricing strategy adopts a low introductory price to speed up or capture the widespread market acceptance. Penetrating pricing strategy is characterised by low initial price of the product, when introduced in the market. The aims is to catch the major portion of the market. The policy is satisfactory, when (1) the cost of production comes down because of large-scale operations, (2) there is fear of stiff competition, (3) the product's demand is highly price elastic, (4) the public accepts the new product as a part of its daily life.

5. **Consider Company's Marketing Policies**

The price of product is influenced by the nature of product's durability–perishability or non-perishability. Perishable products have to be disposed of within a limited time e.g., fruits, milk, vegetables etc. Durable products e.g., car, radio, cloth, scooter etc., are concerned prices which need not be reduced. But when the fashion changes, the marketer may compel the stockist to sell out the stocks before they become obsolescent.

Channels of distribution select the types of middlemen, and the gross marginal requirements of these middlemen will influence a manufacturer's price. Wholesalers as well as retailers may purchase from a producer, who often sets a different factory price for each of the above two. Larger the promotional methods used, larger will be the expenses and this will reflect in the manufacturer's price, as the set price has to cover the expenses.

6. **Setting the Price**

Study the business objectives, analyse each step (mentioned above) through its merits and demerits, then select a specific price for the products by the producer. There is no specific method for setting the price. Procedures used for setting a specific price vary under different competitive conditions. Complexity of the pricing policy has led to the development of numerous approaches to price setting. The following are the basic policies generally recognised for pricing:

1. Cost based
2. Demand based
3. Cost-demand based
4. Competition based

1. **Cost Based**

The price determination of a product, under cost-based method, is made on the basis of cost of production plus an additional margin of cost, that is, selling price is equal to cost of production plus anticipated profit. When the management adds to this cost some amount referred to mark up, this method is also called cost plus or target pricing method. Here, the cost of manufacturing serves, as a base, for price fixation. Cost-based price or floor price, sales below the floor price will be a loss to the firm. For instance, cost of a product is Rs. 100, the profit aimed (mark up) is Rs. 25 or the percentage mark up on cost is 25%, then the selling price will be hundred and twenty-five rupees. In India, a large number of companies follow this policy.

Its **advantages are**:

(1) Simple system
(2) Socially fair
(3) No price war among competitors
(4) Safe recovery of cost guaranteed
(5) Reasonable system in changing situation

Its **disadvantages** may be :

(1) Demand ignored

(2) Future cost not considered

(3) Unaccounted competition

(4) Inefficiency during manufacturing stage, not considered.

(5) Profitability of every product ceases initiation.

2. **Demand Based**

Weakness of the above cost based pricing is to determine the price on the basis of demand. On the basis of the demand for the product the price is fixed. One method is that the firm does not fix a price, but charges what a buyer can pay *i.e.*, charges what the traffic will bear. Price is fixed by simply adjusting it to the market condition. The price varies from consumer to consumer. A high demand is followed by a high price and a low demand is followed by a low price. Another method is that the management may enter into test marketing, through different prices and select the price which ensures the maximum revenue. In certain cases, the management may forecast prices on the basis of historical data available.

Merits of this policy are:

1. Consumer's price elasticity and preferences are considered.
2. Inefficiency is penalised.
3. New product pricing is facilitated.

Demerits, are:

1. It is socially unfair.
2. It does not ensure competitive harmony.
3. Consumers are at a disadvantage.

For a real price, both cost and demand are taken into account. Cost serves as a floor and demand serving as ceiling. The actual price lies in between these two.

3. **Cost-demand Based**

This method removes the deficiencies of the cost-based and demand based pricing. On the basis of cost data from accounting records, demand schedules are built so as to develop the break-even analysis. This is also known as break-even pricing. Because the interrelationship of costs and sales volume determines the amount of profit or loss, break-even analysis helps in estimating the effects of different prices on profits. The firm tries to determine the price that would produce the profit it is seeking. This is clear from the chart given below:

Illustration :

You are given the following data for the costing year of a factory:

Budget output	1,00,000 units
Fixed expenses	Rs. 5,00,000
Variable expenses	Rs. 10 per unit
Selling price	Rs. 20 per unit

Draw a break-even chart showing the break-even point. If the selling price is reduced to Rs. 18 per unit, what will be the new break-even point. (*B. Com., Jabalpur*)

Solution :

$$\text{B.E.P.} = \frac{\text{Fixed Cost}}{\text{Selling cost} - \text{Variable cost}}$$

$$= \frac{5,00,000}{20\text{–}10} = \frac{5,00,000}{10} = 50,000 \text{ units}$$

Break-even sales = 50,000 × Rs. 20 = Rs. 10,00,000

If the selling price is reduced to Rs. 18, then the contribution will be Rs. 8 *i.e.*, Rs. 18-10.

The new break-even point

$$= \frac{5,00,000}{8} = 62,500 \text{ units}$$

Break-even sales = 62,500 × Rs. 18 = Rs. 11,25,000

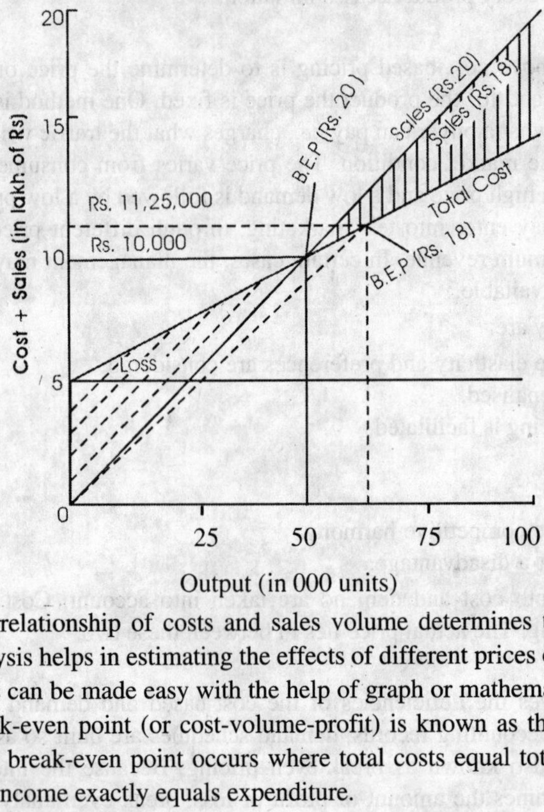

Because the interrelationship of costs and sales volume determines the amount of profit (or loss), break-even analysis helps in estimating the effects of different prices on profits. The technique of break-even analysis can be made easy with the help of graph or mathematical formula. Graphical representation of break-even point (or cost-volume-profit) is known as the break-even chart. It is important to note that break-even point occurs where total costs equal total sales revenue. At this point it indicates that income exactly equals expenditure.

Profit planning is a plan for future operation or planning budget to attain the given objective to attain the maximum profit. The volume of sales required to maintain a desired profit can be known from the formula :

$$\text{Desired sales} = \frac{\text{Fixed cost + Desired Profit}}{\text{P/V ratio}}$$

$$\text{(or)} = \frac{\text{Required contribution}}{\text{New contribution per unit}}$$

4. **Competition Based**

Before pricing a product, every firm takes into account the conditions of competition. Policies are to be determined to fix the selling price at above, below or in line with competition.

Thus :

(1) **Meeting the Competition :** Marketers competing on a non-price basis simply meet competitors' price. An important point of meeting the competition is that sellers have the means of non-price competition, for example, branding, packaging, sales promotion etc.

(2) **Pricing Above the Competition :** This policy is less common. Under this, the price is fixed above the market price, just to impress the buyers that the product is superior.

(3) **Pricing Under Competition :** Many firms set lower prices because of low production cost or low quality or to promote sales. There will be less profit.

Kinds of Pricing

By following the above principles, business firms may opt various kinds of pricing for their products. A few, important of them are explained below:

1. **Psychological Pricing :** Many consumers use the price as an indicator of quality. Costs and other factors are important in pricing. Yet, psychology of the prices is also considered. Certain people prefer high priced products, considered to be of high quality. Costly items like diamond, jewellery etc., reveal the status of the persons, who wear them. They demand highly priced items. For example, highly priced television sets carrying prestige prices are in demand. Then in the retail shops another pricing 'odd pricing' is used. The prices are set at odd amounts, such as Rs. 19.95 instead of Rs. 20; Rs. 299.90 instead of Rs. 300. Odd prices, by psychology, may bring more sales. An article priced at Rs. 9.90 will have more sales than when it is priced at Rs. 10.

2. **Customary Pricing :** Customers expect a particular price to be charged for certain products. The prices are fixed to suit local conditions. The customers are familiar with the rates and market condition. Manufacturers cannot control the price. Such products are typically a standardised one. Certain business people reduce the size of the product, if the cost of manufacturing increases. Sometimes, the firm changes the price by adopting new package, size etc. For example, confectionary items.

3. **Skimming Pricing :** It involves a high introductory price in the initial stage to skim the cream of demand. The products, when introduced in the market have a limited period free from other manufacturers. During this period, it aims at profit maximisation, according to the favourable market condition. Generally, the price moves downward when competitors enter into the market field.

4. **Penetration Pricing :** A low price is designed in the initial stage with a view to capture greater market share. That is if the pricing policy is to capture greater market share, then this is done only by adoption of low prices in the initial stage. Because of the low price, sales volume increases, competition falls down.

5. **Geographical Pricing :** The distance between the seller and the buyer is considered in geographic pricing. In India, the cost of transportation is an important pricing factor, because of the wide geographical distance between the production centre and consuming centre. The majority of the producing centres are located in Bombay, Delhi, Calcutta and Madras; and at the same time the consuming centres are dispersed throughout India. There are three ways of charging transit:

(a) **F.O.B. Pricing :** In FOB (original) pricing, the buyer will have to incur the cost of transit and in FOB (destination) the price influences the cost of transit charges.

(b) **Zone Pricing :** Under this, the company divides the market into zones and quotes uniform prices to all buyers who buy within a zone. The prices are not uniform all over India. The price in one zone varies from that of another one. The prices are uniform within a zone. The price quoted is by adding the average of the transport cost.

(c) **Base Point Pricing :** Base point policy is characterised by partial absorption of the transport cost by the company. One or more cities are selected as points from which all shipping charges are calculated.

6. **Administered Price :** Administered price is defined as the price resulting from managerial decision, and not on the basis of cost, competition, demand etc. But this price is set by the management after considering all relevant factors. There are many similar products manufactured by different firms and more or less the price tends to be uniform. Usually the administered price remains unaltered for a considerable period of time.

7. **Dual Pricing :** Under this dual pricing system, a producer is required compulsorily to sell a part of his production to the government or its authorised agency at a substantially low price. The rest of the product may be sold in the open market at a price fixed by the producer.

8. **Mark up Pricing :** This method is also known as cost plus pricing. This method is generally adopted by wholesalers and retailers. When they set up the price initially, a certain percentage is added to the cost before marking the price. For example, the cost of an item is Rs. 10 and is sold at Rs. 13. The Mark up is Rs. 3 or 30%.

9. **Price Lining :** This method of pricing is generally followed by the retailers than wholesalers. This system consists of selecting a limited number of prices at which the store will sell its merchandise. Pricing decisions are made initially and remain constant for a long period. The firm should decide the number of lines and the level of each price line. Many prices are not desired and the prices should not be too close to each other or too far from each other. For example, a shoe firm has several types of shoes, priced at Rs. 120, 140, 170 etc., a pair.

10. **Negotiated Pricing :** It is also known as variable pricing. The price is not fixed. The price to be paid on sale depends upon bargaining. In certain cases, the product may be prepared on the basis of specification or design by the buyer. In such cases, the price has to be negotiated and then fixed.

11. **Competitive Bidding :** Big firms or the government calls for competitive bids when they want to purchase certain products or specialised items. The probable expenditure is worked out. Then the offer is made quoting the price, which is also known as contract price. The lowest bidder gets the work.

12. **Monopoly Pricing :** Monopolistic conditions exist where a product is sold exclusively by one producer or a seller. When a new product moves to the market, its price is monopoly price. There is no competition or no substitute. Monopoly price will maximise the profits, as there is no pricing problem.

13. **Oligopolistic Pricing :** Oligopoly is a competitive market situation and the presence of a few large sellers, who compete for larger market share. None has control over the price it charges. Any firm may take initiative in fixing the price of a product and others will follow. For example, tyre, watch etc.

After the price is fixed, a businessman may face the problem of reduction in the quoted price. A difference between the price quoted and the net price charged, is known as price differential. This price reduction *i.e.*, price differential, is made in the form of incentives to buyers, to meet competitive pressure etc. It is considered before fixing the price. The price differentials are, in brief:

(a) **Trade Discounts:** Trade discount or functional discount is allowed in the form of deductions from the list price. Manufacturers give this type of discount to wholesalers and retailers as a consideration for the remaining marketing function to be performed by them.

(b) **Quantity Discounts :** Quantity discount is allowed to encourage a buyer to purchase in bulk. It is used as a sales device for slow moving items. For example, Rs. 3 for one pen, Rs. 25 for 10 pens, Rs. 45 for 20 pens etc. In certain cases, the quantity discount will be in the form of free units.

(c) **Cash Discount :** It is concession or deduction given to the consumer by the seller for remitting the bill within the specified period of time. It is a deduction from the invoice bill at the time of payment.

(d) **Seasonal Discount :** Seasonal discounts are allowed on purchases during slack season. For instance, air-coolers are generally sold during summer seasons, and to encourage sales during winter season (off season) where no sales may be possible, dealers will allow seasonal discount. This enables better utility of plant and reduce storage cost.

(e) **Allowances :** There may be special types of allowances offered to retailers, who are expected to perform promotional activities to push up the sales. For example, advertisement allowance, window display allowance, free samples, free display materials etc. Brokerage allowance is also offered to a trader or a firm, that links the buyers and sellers.

Price Leader

All the marketers should decide, whether as a matter of policy, they will initiate or follow price changes. The firm initiating price changes is called price leader and those following it, price followers.

Factors Affecting Price

Prices move up : reasons	**Prices move down :** reasons
1. There is more demand but less supply.	1. There is more supply but less demand.
2. Weak competitors exist.	2. Strong competitors exist.
3. Sellers hold up goods for higher price (bullish attitude).	3. Sellers push out goods. (bearish attitude)
4. There is increase in wage but not in productivity.	4. Wages are stable and productivity rises.
5. Factors of production are used inefficiently.	5. Factors of production are used efficiently.
6. Buyers are eager to possess ownership.	6. Buyers resist against purchase.
7. The supply of money increases.	7. The supply of money decreases.
8. Goods are non-perishable by nature.	8. Goods are perishable by nature.

Price as an Indicator of Quality

Price often seems to be perceived as an indicator of product quality by the consumer. This is based on the study of consumer behaviour. This is because:

(1) Customers trust price is more than their own evaluation of the product worth.

(2) "The more a consumer spends upon a product, the more he will like it."

(3) Price is taken as an important factor because of the snob appeal it offers.

(4) Price is an easy means of product measurement.

(5) Product satisfaction depends in part on the amount of effort the consumer has spent to obtain the product.

Once Price Versus Variable Price

Generally marketers prefer to sell at one price policy, that is, by offering all like buyers exactly the same price. The policy is papular in USA. There is no bargaining and no favouritism is shown to any buyer. It is a fair trade practice. It gains customer confidence. Through efficient management and best marketing mix, the manufacturers and dealers should bring down marketing costs and improve quality of services to the ultimate consumers. The consumers should be offered lower price and better quality under any normal pricing policy.

Under variable price, the seller sells similar quantities at different prices. The other name of **differential pricing** is **'price discrimination'**. Under this policy the price is usually set as a result of bargaining. Prices are subject to negotiation and higgling. Certain favoured customers are offered lower prices. Mainly in developing countries, sellers use variable pricing for most consumer goods and products. In retail business, the price discrimination is usual. The price discrimination takes in several forms – customer basis, time basis, location basis and product form basis.

Resale Price Maintenance

Retail price is a price at which a retailer sells the products to his buyers. Resale price maintenance is a policy where manufacturers want to control the prices at which retailers will resell the manufacturer's product. Manufacturers adopt this as marketing policy, identify their product by brand, patent, trade mark etc., and place restrictions and control on the price at which the products shall be sold by the retailers. The price will be fixed by the producer and at the same price the product will be sold. The price fixed by the producer should not be altered. The producer must see that the price is maintained till his products reach the ultimate consumer. This policy prevents unhealthy price competition, bargaining etc.

QUESTIONS

1. Describe the three bases on which firms usually set their pricing in practice. Illustrate them. (*MBA, Allahabad*)
2. What is meant by skimming the cream price policy ? What are the reasons for adopting this policy ? (*B.Com., Chennai*)
3. Explain the factors influencing price determination. (*B. Com., Mumbai*)
4. Explain the various objectives of pricing. (*B.Com., Delhi*)
5. Discuss the various methods of pricing. (*B.Com., Chennai*)
6. Briefly explain some of the bases of pricing policies. (*B.Com., Chennai*)
7. What are the alternative pricing strategies available to the marketer who wants to introduce a new product in a highly competitive market ? (*M.Com., Madurai*)
8. Explain the ROI pricing strategy. Under what circumstances can it be suggested ? (*M.Com., Madurai*)
9. What are the guiding principles for fixing product pricing ?
10. Write a short note on resale price maintenance.
11. Explain the factors affecting pricing decisions. (*B.Com., Madurai*)

Case Study-1

A Case of Price Revision and Marketing Strategy VIJAY LABORATORIES

Vijay Laboratories have been in the pharmaceutical industry for 4 decades. The company has a sound manufacturing infrastructure and good techniques and has been supplying bulk requirements to the government departments like ESI, Defence etc. The marketing department is headed by representatives in the Southern states and Orissa. Like all companies entering the market, Vijay Laboratories had to be contented with heavy odds in the initial stages.

The company's Chairman toured Germany, Canada, U.K. and struck a deal with a German company to manufacture and market a life-saving drug used extensively in surgery. Though the company had the German backup, it faced uncertain market. These are :

1. A similar product based on indigenous technology was already being marketed in India by a giant company, at least 10 times larger and more reputed than Vijay Laboratories.

2. The giant company had not been concentrating on this product with the result that the demand stimulation was very lukewarm and the market was very small and expanding slowly.

3. Though the product was-life-saving one, the Indian medical profession was not using it extensively as in Germany or US—because of its high price, the difficulty in assessing the need for the product and the fear about fatal reactions (though non-existent)

However, Vijay Laboratories had a certain edge over its giant competitor. Apart from the fact that it had the backing of a German collaboration, the giant company's product had a quality problem and was in and out of the market frequently. Thus, by projecting a foreign name and quality, Vijay. Laboratories was able to launch a product with success in the Southern states.

It so happened, the market for this life-saving product was several fold larger in Bombay than in any other city. Hence, the giant competitor diverted all its stock to Bombay, practically starving the other markets in the country of this drug.

Herculean Task

When Vijay Laboratories entered the Bombay market, it was faced with herculean task of marketing the drug because its competitors already enjoyed terrific patronage and brand reputation. However, the fortune smiled on Vijay Laboratories, when the giant competitor's product was out of stock for two months.

Being the only alternative brand available, the chemists were able 10 substitute all the giant's products with Vijay Laboratories's brand. Thus, the latter became popular. This spell, however; was brief and when the giant's product reappeared; Vijay Laboratories' sales slumped. Even though Vijay Laboratories has a German collaboration, it was marketing its product at Rs. 60 per unit while the giant was charging Rs. 164.

Then, the unexpected, happened. The giant suddenly revised its price from Rs. 164 to Rs. 208. This took Vijay Laboratories' marketing team by surprise. The Vijay Laboratories people attributed the increase in the price of their competitor to the following reasons :

1. The giant wanted to make as much profits as possible by putting up a stiff price, since in Bombay costly price means better quality. Moreover, the giant had its major sales from Bombay.

2. The revision in the retail price of the giant's products would enable the chemists to enjoy a better profit margin and lead them to substitute Vijay Laboratories' prescriptions with the giant's product since the latter enjoyed a better brand image and gave more retail margin.

Now, Vijay Laboratories' marketing, team was in a fix. It had to evolve a suitable counter strategy, and the options available to them were just two, namely:

1. Raise the price of Vijay Laboratories Labs' product and bring it at par with or somewhere near the giant's product Vijay Laboratories' product already enjoyed an excellent profit margin and any increase in price, while making the product less affordable, will add to the kitty of the company. At the same time, though the Bombay market may not be deterred by the higher price, it will surely dissuade the doctors from other parts of the country from using the product.

2. Launch a campaign highlighting the advantages of the economy in using Vijay Laboratories' brand over that of giant company.

Moreover, in a market which is slowly expanding, raising the prices may once again retard growth.

QUESTIONS

1. What are the key issues that emerge from the above case?
2. How far are Vijay Laboratories' presumptions about the reasons behind the price increase affected by its competitors valid?
3. What strategy should Vijay Laboratories' marketing team adopt in response to the price revision initiated by their competitor?

CHAPTER 19

Product Related Strategy

- *Understanding a Brand*
- *What is a Brand ?*
- *Branding*
- *Essentials*
- *Benefits*
- *Types of brands*
- *Reasons for Branding*
- *Reasons for branding individual products*
- *Conditions Favourable to Branding*
- *Brand Mark*
- *Functions of Brand*
- *Kinds of Brand Name*
- *Elements of Branding*
- *Brand Identity*
- *Brand Image*
- *Brand Position*
- *Brand Equity*
- *Value of Brand Equity*
- *Brand Name Decision*
- *Branding Strategy*
- *Brand Loyalty*
- *Brand Associations*
- *Brand Extension*
- *Brand Rejuvenation*
- *Brand Relaunch*
- *Branch Proliferation*
- *Brand Audit*
- *Advantages of Branding*
- *Desirable Conditions*
- *Undesirable Characteristics of Brand*
- *Trade Mark*
- *Labelling*
- *Types of Labels*

UNDERSTANDING A BRAND

Branding is the process by which companies distinguish their product offerings from competition. Marketers develop their products into brands which help to create a unique position in the minds of customers. A brand is created by developing a distinctive name, packaging and design, and arousing customer expectations about the offering. By developing an individual identity, branding permits customers to develop associations like prestige and economy with the brand.

In marketing, the brand name is a major selling tool and one of the most important components of the 'total product personality'. We are in fact, living in an age of brands. The intensive brand promotion undertaken by marketers of various products have made consumers extremely brand-conscious. These days no consumer asks for just bath soap. He specifically asks for Lux or Hamam, or some other brand. Similarly, no buyer asks for a toothpaste, he asks his brand. The brand image, developed through advertising and other promotional measures, creates strong brand awareness and loyalty among consumers. Corporations spend long years, lot of money and effort to build brands. A good brand is an invaluable asset for the owner.

Brands are all pervasive. The purpose of any business is to create customers at a profit and the most valuable asset for a company is its customers' loyalty. Brands explain the way people live in a society. The value of a brand comes from its ability to gain an exclusive, positive and prominent meaning in the minds of a large number of customers. Brands are valuable assets to organisations and also are important to customers. Brands can create wealth for the company depending upon how much value they add to the consumers' life. Brand is defined as a name, term, sign, symbol, design or some combination that identifies the products of the firm.

Products are the children of manufacturers. Unlike human children, product children are never brought into the world by accident. For the product, there must be a conscious decision to give birth. But the manufacturers are in a better position that they have an opportunity to assess the success of a product child beforehand, if necessary, they could make corrections. Once a manufacturer has decided to introduce a new product he will give his product an identity – a brand name. This is more difficult than naming a human child because of legal and marketing considerations peculiar to product. The name of the product creates the right image and is a basis for the whole marketing and public relations strategy.

Products are as dear as their own children to manufacturers and producers. When a manufacturer wants to introduce a new product to the market, he wants to identify the product rather with striking name—Brand name. The buyers identify the product and differentiate in from those of competitors.

In olden days, most of the products went unbranded. They sold the products without the supplier's identification. In the present age, almost all the products are branded and packaged successfully. At present, brand and package are the two attributes of a product. The study of marketing is incomplete, if we do not take into account the study of branding and packaging. Each firm wants to identify its products through brand names. Branding play a more important role than a mere name. The basic purpose of branding is to fix identity of the production of a given product. In India, branding process started with agricultural products meant for export as well as internal consumption (under Agmark scheme) and with manufactured products (under ISI mark).

- *Functions of Label*
- *Advantages of Label*
- *Disadvantages of Label*
- *Package*
- *Packing*
- *Growth*
- *Functions of Package*
- *Kinds of Materials used*
- *General Functions*
- *Kinds of packages Requisites of Good Package*
- *Case study - 1*
- *Case Study - 2*
- *Case Study - 3*
- *Case Study - 4*
- *Questions*

Whichever way you look at it, brands today are the most demonstrably powerful and sustainable wealth creator in the world. The term 'brand' and the practice of branding is applied across the full spectrum of businesses. Branding is also applied across any type of organization that seeks to create a relationship with its audience over and above day-to-day processes and costs. Brands and successful brands have a powerful value of endurance. The best of them stay etched in the mind space for generations, representing a set of values.

What is Brand ?

A brand is a "name, term, symbol or design to identify the goods or services and to differentiate them from those of the competitors." American Marketing Association defines a brand as, "the use of a name, term, symbol or design, or some combination of these, to identify the product of a certain seller from those of competitors." A brand identifics the product for a buyer. A seller can earn the goodwill and have the patronage repeated.

> **BRAND:** A name, term, sing, symbol or design or a combination of them which is intended to identify the goods or services of one seller or group of sellers and to differentiate them from those of competitors.
>
> **BRAND NAME:** That part of a brand which can be vocalised-utterable. For examples: Fiat Car, Sony T.V., Bata Shoe etc.
>
> **BRANDING:** It is a process by which a product is branded.
>
> **BRAND MARK:** That part of a brand which can be recognised but not utterable, such as a symbol, design or distinctive colouring or letrering.

Branding is the practice of giving a specified name to a product or group of products of one seller. Branding is the process of finding and fixing the means of identification. In other words, naming a product, like naming a baby, is known as branding. Parents have children and manufacturers too have children; *i.e.*, products. As parents, the manufacturers also eager to know the characte and capacity of their products on their birth, but not on their names. Thus branding is a management process by which a product is named *i.e.*, branded.

Brand Name is a brand or part of a brand consisting of a word, letter, group of words or letters comprising a name which is intended to identify the goods or services of a seller or a group of sellers and to differentiate them from those of competitors. It is nothing but a combination of letters, words or numbers. For instance, HMT, 501 soaps.

ESSENTIALS OF A GOOD BRAND

Robertson and others are of the view that brand names selected are simple and easy to pronounce, familiar and meaningful; and are different, distinctive and usual. There is no hard and fast rule to the selection of a brand name. However, through extensive research and past experiences, brand marketers have developed the following features or qualities while selecting a brand name:

1. Brand should suggest something about the product – purpose, quality, benefit, use, action etc. For example, Tiger Locks, Godrej Type-writer etc.
2. It should be simple, short and easy to pronounce and remember, for example, Lux, Hamam, Philips etc.
3. It must provide the benefit that customers' desire.
4. The brand is given proper support and the support is sustained over the long run.
5. Brand managers understand as to what the brand means to consumers. Managers of brands understand the totality of their brand's image.
6. It should be unique, attractive and distinctive: for examples, Quink, Maggy, Boost, Sunlight, etc.
7. It should not be used as a general or common name. For examples, Dalda, Kodak, Kerosene, band-aid, etc. Such identification is dull and flat because of their over-use. It causes confusion in the mind of consumers.
8. It should have a stable life and be unaffected by time. It should not depend upon fashions or styles, because they have a short life.
9. It should be capable of being registered and protected legally under the legislation.
10. The brand protfolio and hierarchy should make sense.
11. The brand is consistent.
12. The brand is properly positioned.
13. The pricing strategy is based on consumers' perception of value.
14. The brand name should be acceptable to the social settings.
15. It may be powerful.
16. It should be easy to advertise and promote.
17. Brand and trademarks must be suitable to markets, buyers and products.
18. It should be distinctive
19. It must have a pleasing sound to the ear, when pronounced.
20. It should be economical to reproduce.
21. It must be original
22. It should not be pronounced in several ways.
23. It should not be offensive.
24. It should create a good image.
25. It should not be out of date.

SUCCESS OF A STRONG BRAND

Buyers differentiate products based on specifications, delivery terms and quality. Brand success comes through differentiation. Brands provide a strong competitive advantage to the companies owning them and hence they are increasingly becoming important tradable assets.

The benefits of a strong brand are:

1. A strong brand name is company's most valuable asset. No one can take away the brand from the company.
2. A strong brand can command a premium price.
3. It helps the buyers in taking quick purchasing decision.
4. It creates trusts and emotional attachment to your product and the company.
5. A strong brand will help your customers to trust you and your product, without even knowing the product features.
6. Your customers will automatically think of you first when they think of your product category.
7. A brand builds a good name for your product and the company.
8. A brand impresses your firm's identity upon potential customers, not necessarily to capture an immediate sale but rather to build a lasting impression of you and your products.
9. A strong brand signals that you want to build customer loyalty, not just to sell product.
10. A strong brand will help your customers to trust you and create a set of expectations about the company.

Types of brands

1. **Individual Brand:** A firm may decide upon a policy of adopting distinctive brands for each of its products.
2. **Family Brand:** Family name is limited to one line of products. The term family brand refers to one brand name which a firm adopts for a variety of its products. For instance, Johnson and Johnson, Tata, Godrej, Amul (for milk products), Dippy (for fruit squashes).
3. **Company Brand:** We may have for all products the name of the company or the producer. When a firm manufactures many products, this type of brand is used, for instance Tata's textiles, engineering goods, chemicals etc.
4. **Combination Device:** Products have individual names and company brands to indicate the firm producing them. For instance, Tata's Taj Tea.
5. **Private or Middlemen's Brand:** Such brands are owned and controlled by middlemen rather than manufacturers. Manufacturer introduces his products under a distributor's brand name.

Reasons for Branding

1. It is an instrument for sales promotion in the market, where stiff competition exists.
2. It facilitates easy advertisement and publicity.
3. It creates special consumer preference over the product.
4. Sales can be increased through brands.
5. It arrests the immediate attention of buyers.
6. It differentiates the goods of a producer from the goods of competitors.
7. It ensures standard quality and satisfaction to buyers.

Reasons for Branding individual Products

According to Giles, amongst arguments in favour of branding are the following :

1. Memory recall is facilitated. This could lead to more rapid initial buying action or greater frequency of buying and, hence deeper loyalty.
2. Advertising can be directed more effectively and linked with other communication programmes.
3. Branding leads to a more ready acceptance of a product by wholesalers and retailers.

4. Self-selection is facilitated a very important consideration in self-service stores.
5. Display space is more easily obtained and special promotions are more practicable.
6. The importance of price differentials may be diminished.
7. Brand loyalty may give a manufacturer greater control over marketing strategy and channels of distribution.
8. Other products may be introduced more readily. (The failure of a brand may, of course, lead to undue resistance to other products).
9. The amount of personal persuasive selling effort may be reduced.
10. Branding makes market segmentation easier. Different brands of similar products may be developed to meet specific categories of users.

Conditions Favourable to Branding:

McCarthy suggests the following conditions which lead to successful branding :

1. The demand for the general product class should be large and strong enough to support a profitable marketing plan, involving additional promotion costs.
2.. The product should be easily identifiable by a brand and lend itself easily to conspicuous marking.
3. The brand must be economies of large scale production, whenever additional production is undertaken as a result of expanding sales volume.
4. The brand must carry through to the ultimate consumer.
5. The quality of the product should be best and it should be easily maintained.
6. There must be consistent and wide spread supply of the product.
7. The ideal brand is the one which becomes universally well known but at the same time retains a clear and independent identity.
8. The brand, once established, can command a premium price owing to the valuable psychological intangibles associated with its name.

Brand Mark is that part of the brand which appears in the form of a symbol, design, or distinctive colouring or lettering. It is recognised by sight, but not pronounceable. It is designed to easy identification of product. For instance, the symbol of Anacin's four fingers, Incremen Syrup's Giraffe, Murphy Radio's baby etc.

Functions

1. Brand facilitates distinctiveness from the rival products in the market.
2. Branded products possess individual identification.
3. Branded goods create a satisfactory or standard quality in the minds of the consumers.
4. Branding reduces the price comparison, because two similar items with two different brands may not be compared.
5. Brand differentiates the product, and facilitates advertisement to be more effective and successful.
6. Brands help or facilitate consumers' shopping.
7. Repeated sales are facilitated with minimum effort through brands.
8. A good brand signifies prestige, ensures legal right, forms the basis for successful demand, creational activity, sales-stability, and widening the market area etc.

Kinds of Brand Name

1. **Descriptive Name :** It includes all words that describe the products. For instance, Glucose biscuit, Colgate Tooth brush, Pond's face powder etc.
2. **Suggestive Name:** The name suggests something about the function of the product. For instance, Band-aid sticking-plaster, Quickfix etc.

3. **Arbitrary Name:** It is a name which neither relates to the product nor to the producer.
4. **Coined Name:** Importance is given to the producer's identity. For example, 'Vimal' alone is meaningless, unless attached to suitings.

ELEMENTS OF BRANDING

Brands are unique in many ways. Each brand has its position in the customer's mind and delivers a set of values perceived higher than these of other competing brands. Looking at the fundamental nature of the brand management, one may introduce four key concepts as elements of branding, viz., *brand identity, brand image, brand position* and *brand equity.*

BRAND IDENTITY

Different brands vary in the power and value they command in the market place. Many brands are largely unknown to consumers and for some others, there is very high level of awareness in terms of name recall and recognition. Aaker defines brand identity as, *"a unique set of brand associations that the brand strategist aspires to create or maintain. These associations represent what the brand stands for and imply a promise to customers from the organisation members". Brand identity* refers to an insider's concept reflecting brand manager's decisions of what the brand is all about. *Brand image* reflects the perceptions of outsiders, that is customers about the brand.

From customers' point of view, it is the image they have of a brand that matters. Brand image is the sum total of impressions created by the brand in the consumer's mind.

According to Kepferer, a brand is complex symbol and capable of conveying upto six meanings or dimensions.

(1) **Physique:** The term physique refers to a combination of independent characteristics, which may be either prominent *i.e.* springing readily to the mind when the brand is mentioned or dominant.

(2) **Personality:** If we identify the brand with a person, we form a picture of that person by the way in which he speaks and communicates. In this regard, the marketing communications and promotion of brand play a very important role.

(3) **Culture:** This implies a system of values, a source of inspiration and brand energy. The cultural facet relates to the basic principles governing the brand in its outward signs, that is, products and communication. It is a link between brand and the product.

(4) **Relationship:** A brand is a relationship. It often provides the opportunity for an intangible exchange between persons. It is something which permeates both products and the customer appeal, even though no personal presence may be evident.

(5) **Reflection:** A brand reflects a customer's image. It is the image of the brand offered to the brand's potential purchasers or users. It is a type of identification.

(6) Self-image: Its reflection is the target's outward mirror, self-image is the target's own internal mirror. Through our attitude towards certain brands, we develop a certain type of inner relationship with ourselves.

BRAND IMAGE

Brand image is the key concept intervening between the brand and its equity. It is the driver of brand equity. The image of a brand can adjust brand value upwards or downwards. When the coconut oil is "Parachute", its value moves upwards. This shift is the result of brand name. The name adds visual and verbal dimensions in consumer's mind and acts as intervening variable moving the value upwards. The name Rolex or Omega add radical value to the product. A customer who is not familiar with brands like Rolex or Omega will most probably assess the value of these brands as just another watch (a product) because these brands mean nothing to him. In such a case, these brands are unlikely to alter because there is not intervening variable between the brands and their valuation.

A brand exists as a complex network of associations in a consumer's mind. Alexander proposed that types of brand associations can be *hard* and *soft* and brand sub-images consists of three elements: *image of provider, image of product* and *image of user.*

BRAND POSITION

The brand manager needs to establish communication objectives and plan the creative execution strategy. The beginning of an execution strategy is the brand position statement. Brand position is that part of brand identity and value proposition that is to be actively communicated to the target audience which depicts advantages of the brand over competitors. Once the brand position decision is made, brand identity and value proposition can be translated into a suitable execution strategy in the form of an integrated advertising campaign. Creating a unique position in the marketplace involves the careful choice of target market and establishing a clear differential advantages in the minds of customers. This can be achieved through brand name and image, service, design, guarantees, packaging, delivery etc.

BRAND EQUITY

Brand equity is one of the popular and potentially important concepts in marketing that emerged in the 1980s. It has raised the importance of the brand in marketing strategy. Many scholars have expressed their views in defining brand equity. Aaker defines brand equity in the following words:

"Brands have equity because they have high awareness, many loyal consumers, a high reputation for perceived quality, proprietary assets such as access to distribution channels or to patents, or the kind of brand associations (such as personality associations."

Keller defines brand equity:

"Brand equity is defined in terms of marketing affects uniquely attributed to the brands, for example, when certain outcomes result from the marketing of a product or service because of its brand name that would not occur if the same product or service did not have the name."

VALUE OF BRAND EQUITY

Brand equity needs to be distinguished from brand valuations, which is the job of estimating the total financial value of the brand. Certain companies base their growth on acquiring and building rich brand portfolios. The following methods are useful for brand valuation:

1. Brand Contribution Method
2. Discounted Cash Flow Method
3. Market Value Method
4. Inter-brand Method
5. Price Premium Method
6. Brand Goodwill Method.

BRAND NAME DECISION

Giving a brand name is one of the crucial decisions in brand management. This is a crucial decision resting on two dimensions, viz., the name should be one, which satisfies several marketing criteria and secondly, the name should not be one, which is already being using by other firm. This necessitates extensive consumer research and mapping of consumer interest. A brand is defined as a composite set of beliefs and associations in the mind of consumers. So a brand name is believed to indicate the product's benefits, be memorable and help in reinforcing the belief and associations in the consumer's psyche. The name has to be unique so to rise above the clutter. However, when unique names become run of the mill, suddenly a simple name becomes a hit and people remember this name. Decision on branding a product should be done in such a way that it helps in 'decluttering' the brand. There is no hard and fast rule to the selection of a brand name. The essentials of a good brand, already mentioned in this chapter, may be followed.

BRANDING STRATEGY

This is a powerful strategy which is directly related to product strategy. A brand is used to identify an offering and set it apart from competing offerings. Brand plays an important role in marketing strategies. We can say that a product is something that is made in factory but a brand is something that is bought by a customer. A product can be copied, but a successful brand is unique and achieves its own brand personality. Brand personality creates goodwill for the product in the market as reflected in its wide acceptance and leads to customer satisfaction. It is the discriminator in the market place. For example, Surf, Colgate etc. are not just products of daily use; they have resplendent personalities in the consumers' mind.

BRAND LOYALTY

Brand loyalty is said to occur when a customer makes the choice of purchasing one brand from among a set of alternatives consistently over a period of time. In the traditional sense, brand loyalty was always considered to be related to repetitive purchase behaviour. For some products such as purchasing a house or a car, repetitive purchase behaviour may not occur. In these situations, attitudinal brand loyalty, that is, consumer feelings about the brand that was purchased, and their inclination to recommend the brand to others are measured. Brand loyalty is usually rated as the most important indicator of brand equity. The reason for this is that loyalty develops post purchase and indicates a consistent patronage of a customer over a long period of time whereas all other elements of brand equity may or may not translate into purchase.

BRAND ASSOCIATIONS

Anything that is connected to the consumer's memory about the brand is an association. Customers form associations on the basis of quality perceptions, their interactions with employees and the organisation, advertisements of the brand, price points at which the brand is sold, product categories that the brand is in product displays in retail stores, publicity in various media, offerings of competitors, celebrity associations and from what others tell them about the brand.

BRAND EXTENSION

Brand extension is an effective tool in brand management and it deals with the extending a brand name to more products. There are three types of brand extensions:

(1) Brand extension to other items in the same product line,

(2) Brand extension to items in a related product line, and

(3) Brand extension to terms in an unrelated product line.

BRAND REJUVENATION

It is the concept of adding new value, attributes to the existing product to enhance its overall appeal. This concept is intended to refocus the attention of consumers on an existing brand. This is commonly observed fact where in many of the brand names are added with the prefix like new, super, premium, extra strong etc.

Brand rejuvenation helps in revival of a brand, which may be showing signs of decline. Even in case of healthy and successful brands may also require brand rejuvenation, because of competition, some reformulation and refinement becomes necessary from time-to-time. It helps to keep the brand live and in focus.

BRAND RELAUNCH

Many a time in marketing, there comes a stage in the life of a brand when it needs to be re-worked and relaunched to take it to a different level. This happens not only for brands, which may not be doing well but also for brands that are doing well but would like to do better. Brands go through various stages of evolution in their life and often may need to be restructured and revitalised or rejuvenated to improve their sales and market share and profits. There are three ways in which brands can be relaunched: (1) Repositioning, (2) Change in channel and distribution strategy and (3) Revamption of whole marketing-mix.

BRAND PROLIFERATION

Brand proliferation is opposite of brand extension. In case of brand proliferation more items are brought in with new brand names. In other words, the firm has several brands in the same product or product category. It means that the list of independent brands increase.

BRAND AUDIT

A brand audit is a comprehensive examination of a brand that will assess the health of the brand while uncovering its courses of equity. During a brand audit company will construct a snapshot of where the brand stands today and you will also discover possible new sources of equity to build upon in the future. There are four steps in a brand audit: (1) The brand inventory, (2) The brand exploratory, (3) The brand Analysis and (4) The brand positioning.

Advantages to the Producer

1. Brand enables a firm to build reputation.
2. It is a device by which a good image and goodwill are established.
3. It facilitates introduction of new products, in a simplified process
4. It distinguishes products from rival firms and thus ensures constant returns
5. It is essential for sales promotion and building a demand.
6. It widens the markets, through demand creation.
7. It helps in reducing advertising cost.
8. It brings repeated sales.
9. It reduces the need for price comparison.
10. Individuality of a product is established.

Advantages to Wholesalers/Retailers

1. They require less time to get sold.
2. Branded products pose less risk.
3. There is a stabilised demand for the branded products.
4. Branding aids in advertising and display programmes.
5. Branding assists in increasing control over the market.
6. Branding reduces the price comparisons and helps to stabilise price.

Advantages to the Consumer

1. Brand distinguishes and differentiates the products of different producers.
2. An identification is possible through brands; consumers are at ease while shopping.
3. Consumer gets quality goods
4. Many people get satisfaction on certain brands, which are in great popularity.
5. It assures quality and standard of the product.

Desirable Conditions to Branding

1. There must be widespread supply of the products.
2. The quality and standard of the products must be maintained regularly.
3. Enforcement of product identification and differentiation by brands must be strictly adhered

to

4. There must be enough demand from the general public.
5. Brand must carry through the product to the ultimate consumer, to be more effective.
6. Product must have distinctive and special approach.

Undesirable Characteristics of Brand

1. Brand is not likely to deceive or cause confusion
2. It should not be contrary to any law.
3. It should not contain scandalous or obscene matter
4. It should not hurt religious sentiments.
5. It should not be similar to the existing one.

Trademark

Trademark has been defined as "Any sign, mark, symbol, word or words, which indicate the origin or ownership of a product as distinguished from its quality, and which others have not the equal right to employ for the same purpose." When a brand name or brand mark, is registered and legalised, it becomes a trade mark. So registered brand is a trademark. A trademark is registrable or non-registrable. Therefore, all trademarks are brands, but all brands are not trademarks.

LABELLING

"Label is a part of the product, which carries verbal information about the product or the seller. It may be a part of a package, or it may be a tag attached directly to the product." Label may be a small slip or a printed statement. It may be a part of a package or it may be attached to the product. It conveys verbal information about the product and seller. The producer gives necessary information to the consumers through the label. The act of attaching or tagging the labels is known as labelling. Labels are of three types.

(1) **A Brand Label** is simply popularising the brand name of the product. It gives only the brand names. For example, "sanforised" on clothes.

(2) **A Grade Label** identifies or emphasises the quality standards or grades as A, B, C or 1, 2, 3 etc. In other words, it identifies the quality.

(3) **A Descriptive Label** given written or illustrative objective information about the use, care, performance and other features of the product.

Functions of Labelling

1. It enables the producer to give clear instructions about the uses of the product.
2. Price variations caused by the middlemen are avoided because price is printed and maintained.
3. Manufacturer-buyer relation is established.
4. It encourages producers to make only standard products.
5. Buyers can easily identify the product.

A complete label gives the following information:

1. Brand name
2. Address of the producer
3. Gross and net quantity of the content
4. Ingredients in the product
5. Directions for the use
6. Precautionary measures
7. Nature of the product

8. Date of packing and expiry
9. Retail price

Advantages of Labelling

1. It grades the product
2. It facilitates buyers to pay the right price
3. It helps in avoiding confusion.
4. It brings home the characteristics of a product.
5. It helps advertising activity.
6. It gives all needed information to buyers.
7. It gives guarantee for the standard.
8. Label is the media to popularise the product.

Disadvantages

1. It is of no use to ignorant or illiterate population.
2. It increases the cost of the product.
3. Labelling must be preceded by grading and standardisation.
4. It aims at mainly popularising the product rather than giving information to the consumers.

PACKAGING

The packaging of a consumer product is an important part of the marketing plan. There are many factors to be considered while designing a package. A good number of companies adopt square packages in place of round packages which save space. Lip-sticks and eye brow cosmetics are designed as pencil to be carried in ladies' purses or hand bags.

Packing means wrapping of goods before they are transported or stored OR delivered to a consumer. On the other hand, **packaging** is the sub-division of the packing function of marketing "Packaging" has been defined as "an activity which is concerned with protection, economy, convenience and promotional considerations." Many marketers have called **packaging a fifth** P, along with four Ps *i.e.*, price, product, place and promotion. Thus packaging is one among the activities of designing and producing the container or wrapper for a product. The wrapper or the container is called package.

The Growth of Packaging

The following are the factors which influence the growth and recognition of packaging as a marketing tool.

(1) **Self-Service:** A number of products, are being sold year after year, through the super-markets, on a self-service basis. Thus, they are packed and kept ready for sale. Packages attract attention, telling product features, create overall impression and win consumers' confidence. So good package is a must

(2) **Consumer affluence:** Consumers are willing to pay a little more for conveniences, appearance, dependability and prestige of better packages.

(3) **Company and Brand Image:** To enjoy a distinctive attraction, there must be a good brand and packaging.

(4) **Innovational Opportunity:** Innovative packaging can bring large benefits to consumers and profit to producers.

Functions of Packaging

(1) **Product Protection:** Package protects the products and is fundamental in idea. Their journey from manufacturer to consumer is facilitated. Package prevents breakage, contamination, pilferage, chemical change, insect attack etc.

(2) **Product Containant:** Package means using just the space in which a product will be contained. Ordinary packing is in the form of throw-away containers.

(3) **Product Attractiveness:** The size and shape of the package, its colour, printed matter on it etc., must make the package attractive to look at. The psychological feeling is that a good package contains good quality product in it. Attractiveness is a major consideration in modern packaging. A pictorial label on the package plays a role of silent salesman.

(4) **Product Identification:** Packages differentiate similar products. Packaging and labelling are inseparable and are closely related to branding. Package has more significance, when the product cannot be seen by the buyer—packed milk, fruit juice etc. Buyers depend on the package label in understanding the product of the package. An attractive label is a means of success in marketing.

(5) **Product Convenience:** The purpose of packaging is not merely confined to consumer service. The design and size of the package must be in accordance with the contents *i.e.*, product, it must be convenient to the ultimate customers. Package which can be easily handled, opened, moved etc., is appreciably favoured by customers.

(6) **Effective Sales Tool:** A good package stimulates sales: A designed and attractive package invites customers. As is the product, so is the package. Many people think that a good package, taller in size, not shorter, contains bigger products. Women like round or curved shape of packages. Packaging, attractive and innovated, has value, as many people buy the products, for the sake of containers.

Kinds of Materials Used for Packaging

1. Earthen wares.
2. China Jars.
3. Wooden Boxes.
4. Card Board Container.
5. Straw Baskets.
6. Gunny Bags.
7. Glass Bottles.
8. Tin Containers.
9. Plastic Containers.
10. Clothes etc.

Some general functions of packaging are :

(1) It is an advertising medium
(2) It encourages re-purchases.
(3) It facilitates retailers' functions
(4) It creates product image and individuality.
(5) It enables easy display.
(6) It protects the contents
(7) It facilitates easy storing, transporting etc.
(8) It becomes easy to identify the products.
(9) It helps memory and recognition.
(10) It provides convenience, economy, adjustability etc.

Kinds of Packaging

A Consumer Package: Is a kind of package which holds the required volume of product for the household consumption. For example, tooth paste, shoe polish etc.

A Family Package: When products are related in use and are of similar quality, the firm makes the packages identical for all products by using common feature on all the packages. In this type of package system a producer uses similarity in packages, *i.e.*, material appearance, method etc.

Re-use Package: It is also known as dual package. A producer sells the contents in such a package, which can be re-used for other purposes after the product is consumed; the package has a secondary use, after the contents are consumed. For instance, the glass jar of Nescafe Instant Coffee, and many other products are packed in such a way that the package can be put into many uses.

Multiple Package: The practice of placing several units in one container is known as multiple packaging. For instance, Make-up set, Baby's care set etc.

Requisites of Good Package:

1. It must protect the contents.
2. It must look attractive.
3. It must establish identity.
4. It must provide convenience.
5. It must have less cost.
6. It must develop the interest to possess.
7. It must arouse the people to re-purchase.
8. It must enhance the image of the brand.
9. It must occupy less space.
10. It must give out a brief idea of the product.
11. It must build confidence.
12. It must have a clean look.
13. It must look like an asset.
14. It must possess a status to display.
15. It must minimise the seller's job.
16. It must resist soiling.
17. It must have trade characters.
18. It must have label-pasted.
19. It must have eye-catching look.
20. It must be simple in design.
21. It must be convenient to handle.
22. It must look like a fast-seller.

QUESTIONS

1. Distinguish the terms Brand, Brand Name and Trademark. (*B.Com., Bombay, Kolkata*)
2. Enumerate briefly the functions performed by packaging. (*B.Com., Indore, Mumbai*)
3. Mention the advantages of labelling (*B.Com., Madurai*)
4. Explain the advantages of brand name. (*B.Com., Madurai*)
5. What are the advantages of branding to a manufacturer?
   Explain the difference between brand and a trademark. (*Inst. of Mgt. and Research*)
6. What are the pros and cons of branding and packaging? (*M.Com. Chennai*)
7. What are the characteristics of a good brand ? (*B.Com., Chennai*)
8. Define packaging explain its role in marketing (*B.Com., Indore*)

Case Study-1

Creating Brand Image

TABEFFER INDIA

Soumitro Ghosh, the Managing Director of Tabeffer India, at the time of R & D review, felt that his company had developed a product with the potential to be a winner; a tablet based soft drink, branded '*Lorino*'. The results of the market research that he had commissioned indicated that consumers were not only interested in the concept, but also liked the flavours in which Lorino had been test-marketed. However, breaking into the soft drinks market would not be simple. While the concentrates segment was stagnant, the aerated drinks segment was dominated by global players with huge ad-spends. The product had two over-riding advantages. It didn't have the inconvenience of mixing, sugaring and stirring and disposing off the package unlike tetrapack. The company had worked out a third-party contract distribution arrangement with Gretas which is also distributing soaps, biscuits and hair-creams.

Tabeffer India hired the services of TNS-MODE, a leading market research firm. The initial research revealed the following facts:

(*a*) The consumption pattern in volumes was filter-coffee : 3.9% malted drinks : 2.2%; instant coffee : 1.8% and soft-drinks : 1.1%. The soft-drinks market, though a low-volume in comparison, was far more impressive in terms of value—Rs. 1,300 crore per annum.

(*b*) Aerated Soft Drinks (or ASDs) accounted for Rs. 1,100 crores; tetrapacks, Rs. 150 crores; concentrates, Rs. 60 crores; branded squashes, Rs. 25 crores.

(*c*) ASDs consisted of Colas (70%), Lemon drink (20%), Orange 910%).

(*d*) There are three brands in the Cola segment of ASD: Life, Prime and Vic. Life is a 100-year old global brand with a brand image built around fun, youth and group socialising. Prime is a close rival of Life in several markets around the world. Vic had a near-monopoly position, with a 60% share of Cola market, with its macho image it had tried to position directly against prime.

(e) In the lemon segment, Misty was the single largest selling brand in the 1970s and 1980s which initially used its hygienic and thirst quenching values.

Later, it projected the 'anytime-drink image' highlighting the occasion-brand association. Its cloudy appearance was well received. The following six broad conclusions were analysed by the company:

1. The brand image during the launch will be vital.
2. ASD brands have enormous ad-spends.
3. Global brands have been successful only in the Cola segments.
4. Tetrapacks have seen the largest number of failures, but also single largest success.
5. Brands targeting several demographic and psychographic segments have not been successful.
6. For five years, the concentrates market has defied all attempts at expansion.

QUESTIONS

1. Develop an image-plan for Lorino.
2. How will you develop product concept for Lorino before launching? (*MBA Pune*)

Case Study-2

Saree State of Affairs

It's a brand that put faces like Aishwarya Rai and Madhu Sapre on the beauty map. Way before that, back in the 1970s, textile brand Garden Vareli, owned by the Rs. 650-crore Mumbai-based Garden Silk Mills, set new standards for the fashion industry by launching chic sarees and dress material.

Two decades down the line, few women would want to be spotted buying–leave alone wearing – a Garden saree. In the past five years, sales of Garden sarees have dropped by 50 per cent. Until about five years ago, 25 shops in Mumbai alone – not counting the company's own showrooms – stocked the brand.

Today, the product is retailed only at company-owned showrooms. Garden operates through franchisee operations with outlets in about 104 locations across the country and six company owned showrooms (four in Mumbai and one each in Bangalore and Surat).

Why did Garden stop blooming? Ask company officials and their reply is stock: The brand is still flourishing and there's no downward trend.

But says Kamlesh Pandey, former creative head, Rediffusion DY & R (Garden's erstwhile agency), who was involved in the launch of the brand, "Garden started as an individualistic brand. It was known as an artist's brand. But somewhere along the way, it lost its way. It could not embrace the changes in the market-place as the company's passion got dissipated." In short, the brand failed to age gracefully.

The problem was one of complacency and lack of innovation. Says an industry observer, "Garden was an aspirational brand until about 15 years ago. Then, its image went for a toss because it was neither innovating in terms of new designs and prints nor re-inventing itself."

While lack of innovation was the root cause for the decline of the brand, there were many more creases that Garden should have ironed out. To begin with, the company could not take the brand beyond sarees and dress materials.

In 1997, Garden launched ready-made men's shirts and trousers under the Vareli brand name, while its sarees and dress materials were already selling under the Garden Vareli label. With such strongly feminine associations, the men's wear brand came apart at the seams.

Agrees Garden Silk Mills General Manager, marketing, Paresh V. Chothani, "People always confused the word 'Vareli' for an Italian company and thus it was always perceived as a dress material brand. We needed to separate the identities of the two brands".

To do just that, Vareli was removed from the brad name in 1998. The company has since been selling its sarees and dress materials under the "Garden" label alone and focusing on strengthening it.

Meanwhile, although Vareli still sells men's-wear, it remains a completely neglected brand, accounting for barely 5 per cent of the company's sale of fabric

Textile industry analysts aren't too convinced that the brand name was the only reason for the failure of Garden's foray into men's-wear.

They cite the example of Vimal, the competing brand from Reliance Industries, which in spite of its feminine association, was able to reach across all fabric categories, such as sarees and materials for dresses, suits and shirts.

The true culprit, therefore, was the image of the brand. In fact, one reason for the erosion of Garden's brand equity has been its increasing reliance on bargain or spot sales; the company holds 20-day discount sales twice a year at all it outlets.

Besides, Garden is no longer seen as a brand that is fashionable or stylish. "All loyal customers of Garden are grandmothers now," dismisses a Mumbai-based retailer.

Pandey points out that Garden's earlier target customers were working women who were urban, educated and fashion conscious, in the 18 to 25 age bracket.

As these customers grew older, unfortunately, the brand also aged, instead of teaching out to the newer generations of customers. In the meantime, the demand of the target audience changed.

Consider this Today, Garden retail outlets are visited only by women in the B and C socio-economic categories or those looking for low-priced outfits for daily wear: Garden sarees sell for between Rs. 200 and Rs. 2,000, while dress materials retail in the range of Rs. 250 to Rs. 850.

Says Chothani, "Till 2002, our saree business was growing at 18 to 20 per cent a year. But since the demand for sarees has been gradually fading, in the past two years, we have shifted focus to dress materials."

Until December 2001, 65 per cent of the company's sales came from sarees, with the balance made up by dress materials. By this year-end, the balance will even out more: The share of dress materials in total sales is likely to increase to 45 per cent.

Garden may consider that a step in the right direction, but it may be a case of too little, too late. For the problem extends beyond just Garden. Over the years, the demand for sarees per se has dropped.

Up to the late 1980s, sarees were the preferred wear for office-going women; today, the dress of choice is more likely to be salwar-kameez or western outfits.

With sarees being increasingly reserved as special occasion-wear, there's little room for the ordinary or garden variety of saree — customers demand more dressy and ornate varieties.

But Garden never invested in upgrading it sarees to that level; its stuck to its hopelessly outdated designs and image.

Also, while Garden has always manufatured polyester and silk fabric, consumers have moved on to more contemporary materials like linen, cotton and denim. And increasingly, the trend is for ready-made garments rather than tailored outfits.

As Pandey puts it, "Garden should have grown beyond the realm of sarees and dress materials. It had the potential to become a complete fashion house. But it never made any effort to stay on top while it could have easily encashed on the brand."

One way of ensuring that would have been increased brand visibility—but Garden's performance in that area has been dismal. Its last television advertising campaign was in 1995. With a minuscule advertising and marketing budget of about Rs. 3 crore, the brand now depends on print ads and hoardings for its recall.

Ironically, at the same time, smaller saree brands like Parag, Kunwar Ajay and Prafful sarees — which used to be in the unorganised sector — have grown exponentially in the past five years, riding on the cable and satellite wave.

Clearly, in today's time of cut-throat competition, visibility means electronic media. To quote Pandey, "If it's not on air, it's no there."

Chothani disagress. He says, "We don't really need to be present on television as our brand is a heritage one. So, we don't need to make its presence felt; people remember Garden from its early days. Besides, promoting a brand is an expensive exercise these days."

Garden's current advertising agency, Publicis Ambience, on the other hand, is busy attempting to modernise the brand and make it a desirable fashion garment.

Says Elsie Naji, vice chairman and chief creative officer, Publicis Ambience. "To keep the brand in sync with the times, through our latest print and outdoor ads, we are showcasing latest cuts, accessories and new ways of draping a saree."

Industry observers, however, think it will take more than that to revive the brand. "It will need an excellent communication strategy and a complete breakthrough, other than a huge investment," says a Mumbai-based analyst who tracks the textile sector.

Garden does seem to realise that — and perhaps does not feel equal to the task just yet. Tellingly, it has taken a step back from branding to manufacturing, yarn.

Garden ventured into manufacturing polyester filament yarn in 1997 and at present, 60 per cent of the company's revenues come from its yarn business and the rest from fabrics.

While the company currently produces 50,000 tonnes of yarn a year, there are plans to expand to 80,000 tonnes over the next year.

Of course, it's not quite ready to let go of the textile business. Plans are a foot to revive the Vareli men's-wear brand.

According to Chothani, the Vareli brand range will be retailed through exclusive "Vareli" showrooms instead of the existing Garden showrooms.

The company plans to set up about six franchised stores for selling just the Vareli range. But with Vareli accounting for just 5 per cent of the company's revenues, Garden is not aiming very high.

Points out Chothani, "It's a slow-growth area. Also, our current infrastructure is more suitable for production of women's wear."

QUESTIONS

1. What are the significant issues in this case? What went wrong with Garden Silk Sarees?
2. How can Garden make its brand contemporary? Suggest a plan to revive Garden's business.

Case Study-3

HAIER BRAND

Haier is the world's 4th largest white goods manufacturer and one of China's Top 100 electronics and IT companies. Haier has 250 subsidiary companies and 30 design centers, plants and trade companies and more than 50,000 employees throughout the world. Haier specializes in technology research, manufacture, trading and financial services. Haier's 2005 global revenue was RMB 103.9 billion (USD 12.8 billion).

Guided by business philosophy of CEO Zhang Ruimin, Haier has experienced success in the three historic periods - Brand Building, Diversification and Globalization. At the 21st anniversary of founding of the Haier Group December 26, 2005, Haier announced its 4th strategic development stage of Global Brand Building. In 1993, Haier brand was officially recognized as a famous brand and in 2005 valued at RMB 70.2 billion. Since 2002, Haier has consecutively been ranked first in the row of China's most valuable brands for manufacture of 15 products, including refrigerators, air-conditioners, washing machines, televisions, water heaters, personal computers, mobile phones and kitchen integrations. Haier was ranked first of China's Top 10 Global Brands by China State Bureau of Quality and Technical Supervision (CSBTS) for refrigerators and washing machines. On August 30, 2005, Haier was ranked Ist of China's Top 10 Global Brands by the financial Times.

Haier has been widely recognized as a leader of 9 products in terms of domestic market shares and the 3rd player of 3 products in the world market and world-class company in the fields of home integration, network appliances, digital and large-scale integrated circuits and new materials. Haier has long attached significance to innovation in satisfying the demands of worldwide consumers and realizing win-win performance between Haier and clients. Haier has currently obtained 6,189 patented technology certificates (819 for inventions) and 589 software intellectual property rights.

Haier has hosted and taken part in modification of about 100 China's technological standards. Haier invented technology, incorporated in the Safe Care water heaters and dual-drive washing machines, has been proposed to the IEC Criteria.

Haier's "OEC", "Market-chain" and "Individual-goal combination" management performances have been recognized worldwide. Haier's experiences have also been introduced into case studies of business mergers, and to financial management and corporate cultures of many foreign educational institutes, including Harvard University, University of Southern California, Lausanne Management College, the European Business College and Kobe University. Haier's "Market-chain" management practice has also been recommended to the EU for Case Studies, and its "Individual-goal combination" management concept has been recognized by worldwide management researchers as a feasible solution of commercial over stocks and accounts overdue.

Facing fierce global market competition, Haier has launched the global brand building strategy and updated the spirit, "Create resources, worldwide prestige" and work style "Individual-goal combination, swift action and success", with an aim to gain global recognition and sustainable development.

Haier is an example of how an Asian company can build a brand and take it beyond its national market. Haier brand which is built on quality and a commitment to offer innovative products at a competitive price, exports to over 150 countries around the world, has 13 factories spreading from Philippines to Iran to US and recently became the no.1 refrigerator maker in the world, overtaking Whirlpool.

Haier traces its history back to the Qingdao General Refrigerator factory, which founded in 1958 as a cooperative to repair and assemble electric appliances. Till Chinese entrepreneur Ruimin Zhang took charge of the factory in 1984, the company struggled with its quality and incurred huge losses. Haier attracted tremendous publicity when Zhang smashed faulty refrigerators with a sledgehammer, to send out a message about his commitment to quality. Today, Haier commands approximately over 30% share of the Chinese market in white goods and had revenues of US $9.7 billion as of 2003.

True to that event, Haier has built its brand on quality. Haier's strategy has been to establish a leadership position in the domestic market before venturing into global markets. Unlike most players who concentrate on the low end of the market by offering cheap products, Haier has focused on offering innovative products at a competitive price and the brand is starting to see results. A case in point is that Haier is the leading brand in the US in mini-refrigerator category.

Haier's commitment to quality and innovation is evident by the 18 international product design centers that it has established in Los Angeles and Tokyo which are in turn supported by production facilities in US, Japan and Italy.

Though it is common to see charismatic CEOs such as Sir Richard Branson, Steve Jobs and Bill Gates leading the brands in the western world, it is hardly the case in Asia. Many Asian executives shy away from publicity. Ruimin Zhang has set an example to many Asian companies about how the CEO can take charge of the brand and be the chief brand ambassador. Zhang's aggressiveness to build his brand, his commitment to quality and his business acumen has attracted much deserved global accolades.

Ruimin Zhang was placed nineteenth among the twenty-five most powerful people in business outside the US by Fortune magazine in 2003 and Haier was ranked the most admired Chinese brand in 2004 by a Financial Times/Price waterhouse Coopers survey.

QUESTIONS

1. Analyse the Haier case and identify significant issues.
2. Discuss Haier's branding strategy.

Case Study-4

LOOK MA, FAIR HANDS

The glow on Rakesh Kumar Sinha's face is hard to miss - and it's all due to FairGlow, the fairness soap from the Godrej stable. No, Sinha isn't a user, but as vice president for sales and marketing at Godrej Consumer Products, he has reason to be bright - again.

For the past three months, FairGlow has been growing at close to 40 per cent; Sinha claims that the advertising support for the brand has also doubled since last year. Agency Mudra, which handles the brand, says there will be "interesting activities" around the brand in the next few weeks.

The activity is urgently needed. FairGlow may be erupting like Etna at the moment, but until the last quarter of 2004, the brand bore of closer resemblance to Haleakala, the world's largest dormant volcano. Within two years of its launch in 1999, FairGlow had become a Rs 100-crore brand.

But now the entire fairness soaps category - Godrej FairGlow, Hindustan Lever's Fair & Lovely soap and Emami Naturally Fair herbal fairness soap - has shrunk to Rs 80 crore.

In comparison, fairness creams, which were around Rs 550 crore, crossed Rs 800 crore by end-2004. Even in the Rs 4,000 crore soaps market, the fairness segment has a minuscule 2 per cent value share (just 1 per cent in volume terms).

Although FairGlow still has the lion's share of the fairness segment, its 60 per cent share works out to just Rs 48 crore, which is less than half its earnings in year two.

In other words, even if FairGlow keeps up its scorching 40 per cent growth, it will take another two years or so for it to regain its 2001 position. So, is Sinha happy because FairGlow is getting a second opportunity to score?

When FairGlow soap was launched in December 1999, the dice were heavily loaded in its favour. The foremost reason is that most Indians associate beauty with fair skin.

Even the competition's research bears that out: According to a 1998 Hindustan Lever study, 78 per cent of women in India aspired to be two shades fairer because they believed it made them more attractive and confident.

"It is a colonial hangover," comments Ashish Mishra, head strategic planning, Mudra.

The decision to promote the fairness proposition as a soap also made strategic sense; in India, creams had a penetration of only 25 to 30 per cent.

On the other hand, soaps enter over 95 per cent of Indian households. And FairGlow was priced at Rs 11 for a 75-gram bar, compared to Rs 26 for a 25 gram tube of Fair & Lovely cream. "We offered fairness through a soap, which was more convenient to use at no extra cost," says Sinha.

With high expectations from the product, Godrej planned a high visibility launch. On the launch day, FairGlow created a "surrogate roadblock" on television channels (the 40-second television commercial ran simultaneously on all channels within a five- to 10-minute time frame to ensure that even viewers who surf channels during commercial breaks caught a glimpse of the brand).

Then, the product was advertised on all top rated programmes such as Kaun Banega Crorepati and Kynuki Saas Bhi Kabhi Bahu Thi. "The opportunity was big because it was a true innovation." says Mishra.

But there were huge credibility issues to be tackled: The stay-on proposition of creams - once applied, creams stay on all day- while soaps are washed off within seconds of application.

Sinha argues, "The same is true with hair conditioners or a face wash, which are also washed away. But consumers still believe that they work," True, but fairness soaps had to content with an established category (launched in 1975) like fairness creams. For hair conditions and face washes there was no close alternative product.

Godrej's solution was simple: It tailored its commercials to focus on customer testimonials. The result, within a year of launch, FairGlow was selling between 400 and 500 tonnes a month (a volume share of 1 per cent in the toilet soaps segment).

Hid did HLL, whose Fair & Lovely had more or less created the market for fairness products, react? Within a couple of month of FairGlow's launch, HLL retorted with a prolonged teaser campaign for Lux Sunscreen soap. The new variant was launched in March 2000 - and withdrawn barely a few months later.

In the second half of 2000, battle-lines had been drawn between the soap and the cream, FairGlow and Fair & Lovely aired similar television commercials on the marriage theme; only, Fair & Lovely launched two ads in response to FairGlow's single ad spot.

"We could not match their advertising muscle," admits Sinha. Instead, Godrej resorted to offers like buy-three-get-one-free in end-2000.

Even as Fair & Lovely and FairGLow fought it out on TV screens, the sun was eclipsing over the toilet soaps industry.

Consumers were downgrading to the sub-popular category: In 2000, while the popular category grew by just 1 percent, the sub-popular category was clipping along at a brisk 15 per cent. FairGlow being an offering in the popular segment of soaps, was naturally going to be hit.

Then, in December 2000, a year after the launch of FairGlow soap, it committed a vital strategic mistake. It extended FairGlow into creams with the proposition, Bedaag gorapan (spotless beauty).

But instead of being considered a natural brand extension, the move further fuelled a suspicion that consumers had harboured - fairness soaps may not be as effective as creams.

Importantly for Godrej, it lost the high ground of innovation that it had made its USP. Sinha admits that if he could change one thing about FairGlow's past, "We would never venture into creams".

Even as FairGlow's brand extension backfired, HLL engaged in battle on another flank - it launched Fair & Lovely soap. Naturally, the already thin dividing line between cream and soap further blurred.

Fiar & Lovely's soap was a high profile launch with its theme, Ek Tukda chand ka (A piece of the moon). While a barge backlit by the moon floated on the sea off Mumbai's Marine Drive, practically every hoarding in prominent places hollered the benefits of Fair and Lovely soap. But at Rs 15 per cake, (nearly 50 per cent more expensive than FairGlow), HLL's new battering ram did not find too many takers.

Analysts say that HLL used the soap as merely a flanking strategy to guard it cream user-base. "The idea was that even if consumers bought a fairness soap, it would be from the same brand basket," says one analyst. HLL executives did not meet. The Strategist for this Article.

Still, HLL did not rest after its soap launch. Over the next two years, the company launched several new Fair & Lovely cream variants.

FairGlow, on the other hand, was still fighting consumer perception that soaps may not work. It launched a "money-back challenge" to build up credibility in 2002. Fair & Lovely reacted by offering two soaps for the price of Rs 20 (coming down to the FairGlow price).

The sales graphs, though, remained dim. By mid-2004, FairGlow put the cap on its cream misadventure. It followed with an ad campaign in late 2004 that illustrates the efficacy of the soap. That's paid off dividends, and sales are currently up. Whether they'll be able to reach their previous highs, though, is anyone's guess.

QUESTIONS

1. What is the positioning of FairGLow soap? What is this positioning likely you appeal to Indian consumers?
2. SWhy was the extension of FairGlow to face cream a bad decision?

CHAPTER

20

Consumer Behaviour

- *Birth of Buying Idea*
- *To Categories of Buyers*
- *What is Buyer Behaviour*
- *Definitions*
- *Importance of Studying Consumer Behaviour*
- *Types of Buyers*
- *What are Buying motives ? Determinant of Consumer Buying Behaviour*
- *Consumer Buying Decision*
- *Characteristics of Buyer Behaviour*
- *Buying motives*
- *Six 0's Approach*
- *Importance bf Studying Buying Motives*
- *7 0's Framework*
- *Buyer Behaviour Model*
- *Buying Decision Process*
- *Motives of Industrial Consumers*
- *Buying Process*
- *Case Study-1*
- *Questions*

THE BIRTH OF BUYING IDEA

Mr. A owns a scooter. The scooter is causing dissatisfaction because of some defects or troubles in it. He decides to replace it with another scooter. He anticipates the idea of a trouble free and dependable scooter. He decides not to buy a scooter of the same made, because of dissatisfaction and lack of confidence. Thus a thought seed about a new scooter is born in him, the moments he thinks, "I must replace the scooter", the buying idea comes up. With the thought in his mind, he thinks of benefits. And this leads to further thinking; what sort of a scooter will give the benefits, he wants. The benefits made the desire. He may buy any one of many makes of scooter, which can give the desired benefits. He makes enquiries and observes through talking to his friends, he selects one or two possible scooters, which can satisfy his needs. He talks to the people, who own the particular make. By this, he wants to confirm his decision about the ,make he wishes to buy. He reads advertisements about the new scooters. He chooses one with all the possible advantages and which is wholly dependable. Mr A is a ***prospective customer*** to a dealer.

TWO CATEGORIES OF BUYERS

There are two categories of buyers – the ***individual buyer*** and the ***business buyer***. While the individual buyer buys things for his own personal and family consumption, the business buyer is a commercial buyer who buys things for manufacturing other products or for reselling or for use in running his enterprise. This distinctior is substantial and it separates the two categories into two different entities. In buying motivation attitude and purchase behaviour etc. of the two are different. These have been dealt with separatel under the chapters (a) Marketing of Consumer Goods and (b) Marketing of Industrial Goods.

WHAT IS BUYER BEHAVIOUR ?

The wealth of products and services produced in a country make our economy strong. Almost all the products, which are available to buyers, have a number of alternative supplies i.e. substitute products are available to consumers, who make a decision to buy products. Therefore, a seller, most of his time, seeks buyers and tries to please them. In order to be successful, a seller is concerned with:

- Who is the customer?
- What do consumers buy?
- When do consumers buy?
- How do consumers buy ?
- From where do consumers buy ?
- Why do consumers buy ?

A buyer makes a purchase of a particular product or a particular brand and this can be termed "product buying motives". And the reason behind the purchase from a particular seller is "patronage motives".

More or less, after the Second World War, the sellers markets have disappeared and buyers markets have come up. It means that the manufacturer's attention has switched over from the products to the consumers and specially concentrated on the consumer behaviour. The manufacturer possesses no control over the behaviour of consumers. A modern marketer first, tries to understand the consumers and their response, then he studies the basic characteristics of their behaviour. It can be said that consumers is the pivot, around which the whole marketing system revolves. The selection or choice of products or services by consumers greatly determines the fate of the producers. As such, the marketer must know the consumers, more and more, in order to manufacture the products, which give them satisfaction, in the way, the customers need. The marketing programmes and policies depend upon the consumer behaviours. If one makes out the marketing programme, neglecting the consumer behaviour, one will naturally invite failure. A careful study of consumer behaviour will facilitate the marketer in determining the size, form, style, colour, package, brand etc.

When a person gets his pay packet, and if he is educated, sits down along with his wife and prepares a family budget, by appropriating the amount to different needs. It may happen that after a trip to the market, they might have purchased some items, which are not in the budget, and thus there arises a deviation from the budgeted items and expenditure. The deviation is due to the new needs because of the arrival of new products, better display of products, credit-facilities, behaviour of salesmen, competitive price etc. The new needs may arise because the son has a friend's shoe in his mind, the daughter has a friend's dress in her mind, the wife has been thinking about a particular sari or he himself has been thinking about the design of the drawing hall at his friend's house etc. All the behaviour of human beings during the purchase may be termed as "buyer behaviour." The process whereby individuals decide whether, what, when, how and from whom to purchase goods and services can be termed as the customer's or the buyer's behaviour.

The buyer may take a decision whether to save or spend the money. When he decides to spend, then there are many problems as to what to purchase, because needs are numerous, which leads to ranking the needs in terms of priority. Then, the problems are purchasing problems – where to buy, how to buy, from whom to buy etc.

Marketing concept start with the consumer needs and behaviour in meeting the needs. Every action of a person is based on needs. The real problem is to learn what a customer takes intc consideration when he chooses a particular brand. Such a study is concerned with consumer behaviour. Consumer or buyer behaviour is that subset of human behaviour that is concerned with decisions and acts of individuals in purchasing and using products. Consumer behaviour, a subset of customer's behaviour, is concerned with decisions that upto the act of purchase.

DEFINITIONS

"Consumer behaviour can be defined as the activities and the actions of people and organisation that purchase and use economic goods and services, including the influence on these activities and actions." JF Engel

"Consumer buying behaviour refers to the buying behaviour of final consumers – individuals and households who buy goods and services for personal consumption". Kotler and Armstrong

"Consumer behaviour consists of the acts of individuals in obtaining, using and disposing of economic goods and services, including the decision processes that precede and determine these acts."

Kurtz

"Consumer behaviour may be defined as the behaviour that consumers display in searching for, purchasing, suing, evaluating and disposing of produces, services and ideas which they expect will satisfy their needs."

Schiffman and Kanuk

Thus, the study of consumer behaviour is the study of how individuals make decisions to spend their available resources – money, time and effort – on consumption – related items. However, it may be noted that consumer behaviour research today goes for beyond "what, why, how, when, where and how often" facets of consumer behaviour and also considers the uses which consumers make use of the goods they buy and evaluations of those goods after use. There may be many repercussions after the consumer makes a purchase. For example, a buyer may feel sorrow and guilt or dissatisfaction with his choice of particular scooter, because of continuing maintenance expenses over it. The buyer may decide not to buy the same make or model again and may also refer to his friends conveying the dismal performance of the scooter. Each of these possible consequences of consumer's post purchase dissatisfaction has significant implication for the marketer. For the marketer, the person is important, who makes the buying decision, not the one who actually makes the purchase or uses the product.

IMPORTANCE OF STUDYING CONSUMER BEHAVIOUR

The field of consumer behaviour studies deal with how individuals, groups and organisations select, buy, use and dispose off products and services to satisfy their needs and desires. Thus, according to Webster, "Buyer behaviour is all psychological, social and physical behaviour of potential customers as they become aware of, evaluate, purchase, consume and tell other people about products and services".

As a matter of fact, customer is the pivot around which the whole industrial of nowadays revolves. The economists call the 'customer' a "king". He is just like a voter in democracy. His selection of goods or services determine the fate of products/services. Therefore, in order to attract him more and more, the marketers should know their customers well so that they could treat them in the way they like to be treated, present them goods in the way, they will appreciate and close a sale in such a way that consumer satisfaction is created. The study of consumer behaviour is very useful in determining the form, style, packaging, brand, trademark etc. of the product. The whole aspect of buying behaviour determines the durability, price policy and utility aspect in goods. The consumer or buyer behaviour is extremely important for an effective marketing planning. The success or failure of marketing depends largely on target consumer's individual and group reaction that manifest in the buying patterns. The buyer behaviour is concerned with the study of factors that influence a person to buy or not to buy. Its concept lies in understanding the consumer and his motives and therefore, involves seeking as answers to pertinent questions like : Why a buyer buys or does not buy a particular brand or product ? Does a buyer devote much time and study to comprehend the benefits of a product and its services ? Does a buyer buy due emotion or impulse ? Does a buyer imitate others ? What factors does a buyer take into consideration in the buying decision ?

TYPES OF BUYERS :

The issue of the buyer's style and its implications for marketing strategy has been the subject of research in the United States by Dickinson, who identified seven types of buyers :

(1) **Loyal** buyers who remain loyal to be a source of considerable periods.

(2) **Opportunistic** buyers who choose between sellers on the basis of who will best further his long-term interests.

(3) **Best deal** buyers who concentrate on the best deal available at the time.

(4) **Creative** buyers who tell the seller precisely what they want in terms of the product, service and price.

(5) Advertising buyers who demand advertising support as part of the deal.

(6) Chisellers who constantly demand extra discounts.

(7) Nuts and bolts buyers who select products on the basis of the quality of their construction.

"Marketers should approach the study of a new market by asking the following questions, that may be called six 0's of any market :

1. What does the market buy ?	– Objects of Purchase.
2. Why does it buy ?	– Objectives of Purchase.
3. Who buys ?	– Organisation of Purchasing.
4 How does it buy ?	– Operations of Purchasing Organisation.
5. When does it buy ?	– Occasion of Purchase.
6. Where does it buy ?	– Outlets for Purchase."

WHAT ARE BUYING MOTIVES ?

You purchase a product, because of certain motives. Motives refer to thought, urge, strong feelings, emotion, drive etc. They make a buyer to react in the form of a decision. Motivation explains the behaviour of a buyer. Motives induce a consumer to purchase a particular product. The motives may be generally controlled by economic, social, psychological influences etc. When a consumer buys a product, his aims are desire of security, rest, comfort, curiosity, self preservation, fashion etc. People purchase products urged by mental and economic forces, which create a desire, and this desire is satisfied by the articles displayed for sale. Motive is an inner urge that prompts one to action, it is not a mere desire. The stimulated desire is called a motive.

Knowledge of the buying motives of consumers is essential for a marketer. The changes in the market are brought by the consumers. The needs and desire of the consumers and their buying behaviour greatly depend upon their income, social status, psychology etc. The consumer and the customer arc two different terms. Customer is not always the consumer and the consumer is not always the customer. Customers, like middlemen, agent etc., may or may not purchase products for their own use, whereas consumers get the products for their own consumption. Here we are concerned with consumer behaviour and the consumer is the important factor. "Buyer behaviour is all psychological, social and physical behaviour of potential customers, as they evaluate, purchase, consume, and tell others about the product and services".

DETERMINANTS OF CONSUMER BUYING BEHAVIOUR

A marketer is always interested to know how consumers respond to various marketing stimuli-product, price, place and promotion and other stimuli i.e., buyer's environment – economic, technological, political and cultural. The marketer studies the relationship between marketing stimuli and consumer response. These stimuli pass through buyer's box which produces the buyers' responses and is shown below :

Buyer Behaviour Model

Outside Stimuli	
Marketing	*Other*
Product	Economic
Price	Technological
Place	Political
Promotion	Cultural

Buyer's Black Box	
Buyer Characteristics	Buyer Decision

Buyer's Response	
Product	Choice
Brand	Choice
Dealer	Choice
Purchase	Timing
Purchase	Amount

The buyer is considered as a black box, because his mind cannot be imagined, as to his buying decision. The buying decision depends on his attitude, preferences, feelings etc.

Factors influencing the consumer behaviour are internal needs, motives, perception and attitude as well as external-family, social groups, culture, economics, business influences etc.

These influences are shown below:

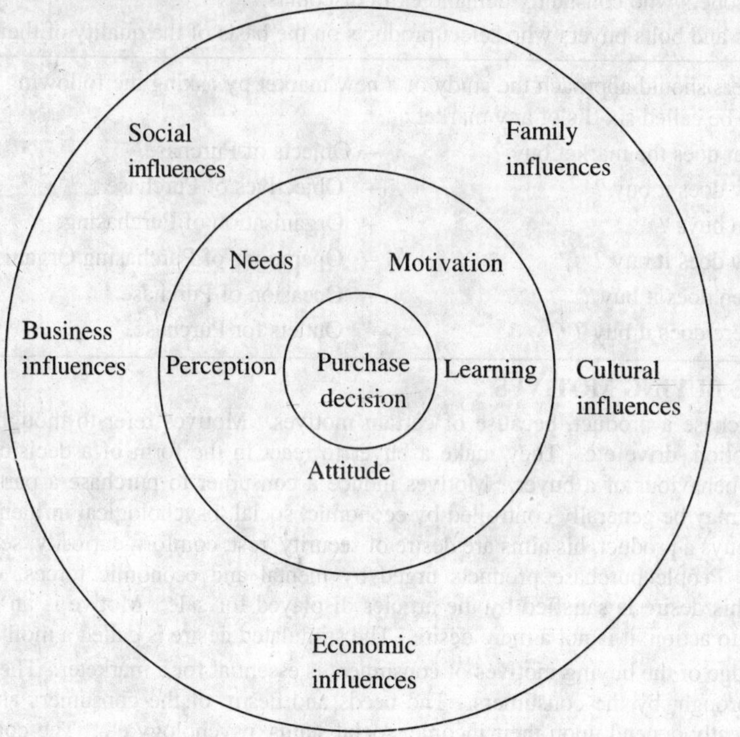

The study of the buyer behaviour is essential to understand what Marketing is. The success or failure in marketing depends upon the individual's reactions, expressed in the form of buying pattern. Mainly, the buyer behaviour has many approaches: the economic, the psychological, the socio-cultural etc. A buyer is subjected to many influences before the actual purchase. Aroused needs are forces which activate goal-oriented behaviour to bring want - satisfaction.

CONSUMER BUYING DECISION :

A very important area for marketing firms is to determine the decision maker or the real customer in the purchase decision of products and services. For purchasing a car, scooter etc. men take the decisions whereas for buying baby products, kitchen-wares, house-furnishing, etc. purchasing decisions are taken by woman. For buying a house or going for vacations, decisions are taken by majority members in the family. The firm must find out the characteristics of such persons who play a significant role in influencing the decision to make a purchase.

The following are the different participants in any consumer buying decisions;

1. **INITIATOR :** Initiator is the person who first suggests the needs of the idea or the need for a particular product which should be bought for satisfying certain requirement.
2. **INFLUENCER :** After the initiator has suggested the idea for a particular product, the influencer is the person who gives more information or gathers more information, which will influence the decision of the purchase.

3. **DECIDER :** The decider is the person who ultimately decides to buy a particular product depending upon the situation. He is generally the dominating member of the family or head of the family, who carries out the role.
4. **BUYER :** The decision has been made for certain goods, the buyer goes to purchase from the shop. The actual purchase made by the buyer, will depend on the convenience of the family members or of the group and it may depend on the earning members or head of the family.
5. **USER :** The user is generally one who actually consumes or uses of the product or service and he may or may not be the initiator, decider or buyer. For instance, parents purchase toys but the actual users are children.

It must be borne in mind that the consumers buy a product or services so that it is required to satisfy a variety of needs – social, psychological etc. Any product or service offered by the sellers should give maximum utility value to the consumers for which they have paid.

CHARACTERISTICS OF BUYER BEHAVIOUR :

1. Buyer behaviour is very complex
2. Buyer behaviour is the process by which individuals decide whether, what, when, from whom, where and how much to buy.
3. Buyer behaviour is very dynamic.
4. Consumer behaviour comprises both mental and physical activities of a consumer.
5. It is an integral part of human behaviour.
6. In many cases, it is the sum total of the behaviour of a number of persons.
7. It is influenced by a number of marketing stimuli offered by the marker.
8. Consumer behaviour is basically social in nature.
9. Consumers act differently at different times.
10. They learn and thereby change their attitudes and behaviour.

Why focus customer value ?

"A customer is the most important visitor on our premises.
He is not dependent on us, we are dependent on him.
He is not an interruption in our work. He is the purpose of it.
He is not the outsider in our business. He is a part of it.
We are not doing him a favour by serving him.
He is doing us a favour by giving us an opportunity to do so".

Mahatma Gandhi

BUYING MOTIVE

A motive is a drive or an urge for which an individual seeks satisfaction. A buying motive is the reason why a person buys a particular product. It is driving force behind buying behaviour and may be based on psychological or physiological wants. Thus a motive or purpose of the purchase is mental instinct. It is imposed or created. It comes from within the man.

"A motive may be defined as a drive or an urge for which an individual seeks satisfaction. It becomes a buying motive when the individual seeks satisfaction through the purchase of something". – *Stanton*

In a consumer-oriented marketing model, consumer is the king and a marketer should understand the needs, wants, buying motives and feelings of his potential customers, to be successful in his marketing efforts. Consumers have different kinds of needs and they do not pursue all their needs at all points of time. Whenever a need gets a direction or goal and all the energies of consumer are targeted towards achieving the goal, it takes the shape of a buying motive. Buying motives takes different forms. The important types of buying motives are as follows:

(1) Inherent and learned buying motives

(2) Emotional and rational buying motives

(3) Psychological and social buying motives

A brief discussions are given below:

(1) INHERENT AND LEARNT BUYING MOTIVES

Inherent buying motives are those which arise from the basic needs of the consumers such as hunger, sex, comfort, and safety. In order to satisfy these motives, a consumer has to make his best efforts. If these motives remain unsatisfied, he feels mental tension. Learned motives are those which a customer acquires or learns from the environment in which he lives or from education. These motives are social status, social acceptance, economic, social and political achievement, fear and security. These motives are much affected by education and social environment of the customers.

Both types of motives play a very important role in consumer decision process. These motives provide direction to a company's marketing activities. Out of these two motives, inherent motives are stronger, more useful and urgent. In satisfying the learned motives, customers do not care for the price of the product.

(2) EMOTIONAL AND RATIONAL BUYING MOTIVES

Emotional buying motives are those which are affected by the feeling of the heart. In such motives, heart dominates over head and mind. In satisfying these needs sometimes man is not rational. These motives are hunger, thirst, ego, prestige, comfort, pleasure, love and affection etc.

Rational buying motives are those motives where a consumer is rational in taking buying decision. Here head and mind dominate heart. Before making any purchase, he satisfies himself with the price, quality, durability, reliability and service and then decides to purchase the goods which are useful to him and are available at reasonable price. He takes more time in making rational purchases.

Both emotional and rational motives are important for a marketer. The marketer should decide which type of motive – emotional or rational – should be aroused in selling his product, keeping the merit of the product in mind. The advertisement programme for the brand should focus on the appropriate motive of the consumer.

Emotional and rational buying motives can be differentiated on the following grounds:

(*a*) **Time in Purchasing :** The purchaser needs little time in making emotional purchases because he decides immediately for the purchase. On the other hand, the purchaser has to consider many factors like price, quality, after sale service and other related matters and therefore, he takes time in taking decision for the rational motives.

(*b*) **Dominance :** Emotional buying motives are dominated the feelings of the heart whereas in rational buying motives head and mind dominate.

(*c*) **Nature of Product :** Emotional purchases are generally of the goods which are low-priced and non-durables. In rational purchasing the product is durable and comparatively of high price.

(3) PSYCHOLOGICAL AND SOCIAL BUYING MOTIVES

Psychological motives are those motives which are concerned with the social groups. It assumes that buying behaviour of an individual is influenced by his social environment and he is always anxious to conform to the standard of his environment.

Social motives are those motives which are affected by the society in which he lives. Man is a social being and he cannot remain unaffected by the society. He cannot purchase anything without the sanction and recognition of the society.

IMPORTANCE OF STUDY OF BUYING MOTIVES

If the marketer understood the intellectual or emotional process that leads potential customer to accept or reject particular product, he might conceive marketing strategies that would make one more of his instruments, more productive. If he has perceived the nature of the drive or appetite that results in a given pattern of a purchasing behaviour, and if this drive of appetite was sufficiently prevalent among potential buyers, the marketer might design his product mix, advertising any sales tactics more efficiently. In short, a knowledge of the 'why' or consumer behaviour offers an opportunity to influence that behaviour. Whether a marketing strategy is designed to conform to the buyer behaviour or to influence its determinants, the formulator of the strategy would benefit from knowledge of these determinants. This is especially true when the marketer is dissatisfied with established techniques and is seeking to innovations in his product or promotion instruments. Even if its current marketing practices are proving quite successful, the firm is confronted by the high probability that the future will be different. Changes in tastes, attitudes and behavioural patterns make particular marketing methods more or less efficient. By understanding the 'why' of consumer behaviour, the marketer can often detect trends that in effect allow him to peer into the future. This fore-knowledge will enable him to tailor future strategies and tomorrow's realities rather than today's.

THE 7 0'S FRAMEWORK

This framework is popularly known as 70's frame and is used for basic understanding of consumer behaviour.

Who is the consumer (occupants) : Answer to this question helps us to understand consumer's geographic, demographic, psychographic and media graphic profile. Obviously this question helps in explaining the state of being of the consumer. Demographic profile is the study of age, income, sex, occupation and education qualification etc. of the consumer. Psychographic profile is the study of the lifestyle of the consumer as expressed by activities, interests and opinions of the consumer. Geographic profile is the region to which the consumer belongs. Media graphics are the media habits of the consumer, for instance, fair and lovely cream sells more in the southern region than in the other regions.

A study of demographic profile of Frooti drinkers revealed only 5 – 12 years' age group drinks Frooti. Teenagers, the biggest market for soft drinks, did not drink Frooti because they found it too kiddish. Hence, the Digen Varma campaign was released for relaunching Frooti as "cool drink" for "cool dudes". The advertisements also show the typical psychographic profile of today's teenagers, using their language and talking about their interests like careers, computers etc.

What does the consumer buy (Object of Purchase) : Answer to this question explains what product proposition the consumer is buying. The answer is in terms of product (for examples, soft drinks, softdrink concentrates syrups etc.), product forms (in soft drinks – Cola Vs Lime Vs Orange) and brands (Coke Vs Pepsi). What the the features, sizes, colours, flavours etc that the consumer seeks ?

Why is the consumer buying (Objective) ? What benefit is he seeking ? What motives is he trying to satisfy ? For example, Fair and Lovely caters to a very strong motive of women, based on the desire to look fair, in a country obsessed with fair skin. Consumers today are also looking for sun protection in their cream.

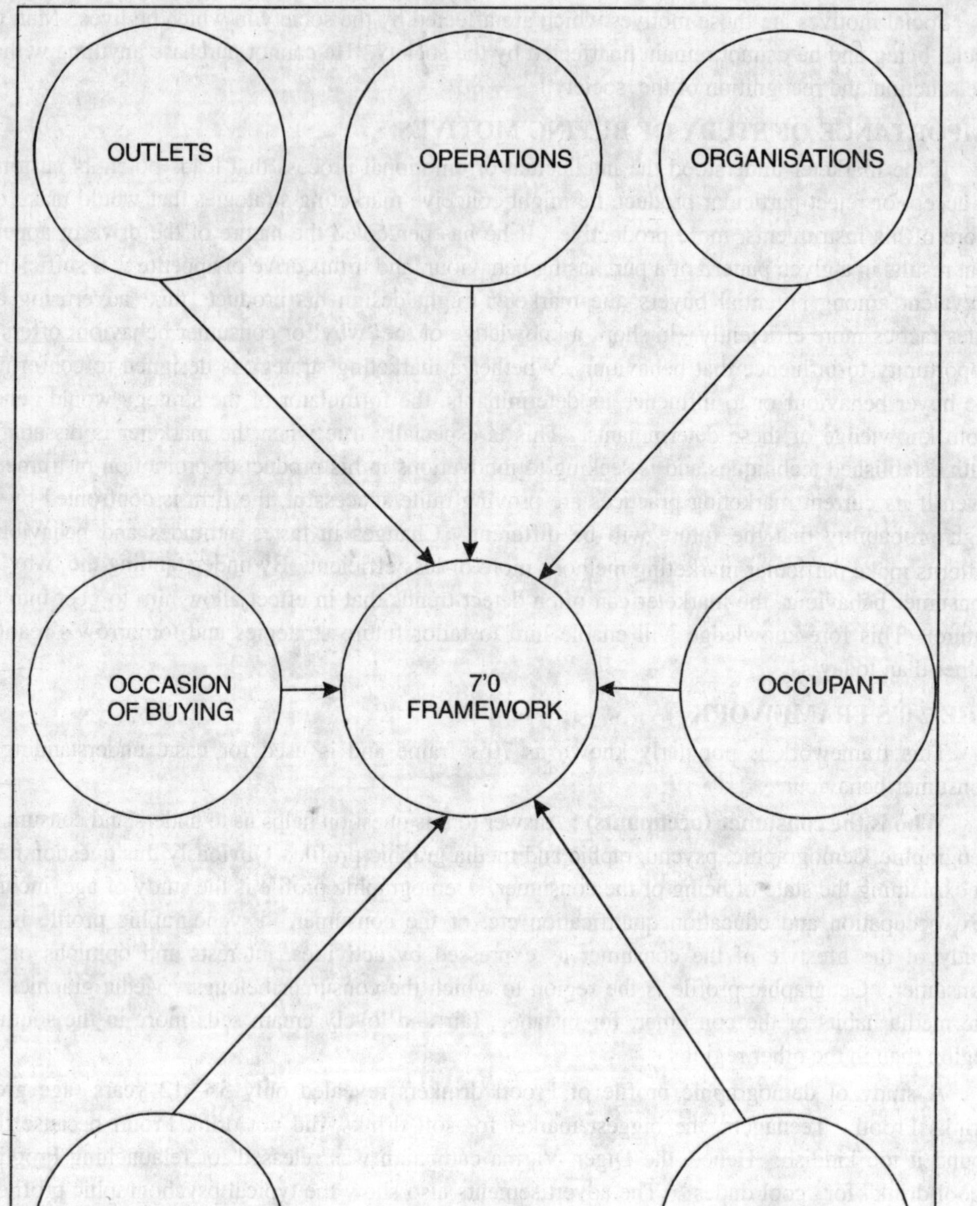

7 '0 Framework

When do they buy or How often do they Buy and use (Occasion)? This explains the buying rate or buying frequency of consumers and the occasion on which they would buy the product or services for desired benefits. For example, items like refrigerators, air conditioners etc. are bought during Diwali.

Where do they Buy (Outlets) : They explain the type and nature of outlets from where the customer makes a choice. The types of outlet may be a retail shop, grocery store and wholesaler's shop. The nature of outlets also include urban outlets, shopping malls or rural shops.

How do they Buy (Operations) : This explains what kind of background information do consumers collect before buying and from whom do they seek information ? For instance before buying a car the consumer collects a lot of background information from friends and does a lot of deliberation before buying. Also when he enters a dealer's showroom he asks the dealer or salesman many questions.

Who is involved (Organisation) ? This explains the organisation of information sources around the key players in the decision process. It describes the various roles played by people in the purchase process.

BUYER BEHAVIOUR MODELS

The influence of social sciences on buyer behaviour has prompted marketing experts to propound certain models for explaining buyer behaviour. Broadly, they include the Economic Model, the Learning Model, the Psychoanalytical Model, the Sociological Model etc. Let us discuss the models in brief :

(A) THE ECONOMICAL MODEL (MARSHALLIAN MODEL)

Economists were the first professional group to advance formal explanation of buyer behaviour. The theory holds that purchasing decisions are the result of largely "rational" and conscious economic calculations. An individual buyer seeks to spend his income on such goods which give the most satisfaction (utility) according to his tastes and at relative prices. Fundamentally, the income-its distribution and level-affects the purchasing power, which determine the behaviour of buyers. According to classical economists, consumers follow the principles of utility maximisation. The theory emphasizes on economic motivation. Alfred Marshall's work aimed at realism, but his method was to start with simplifying assumptions and to examine the effect of a change in a single variable, say price, when all other variables were held constant. He employed the "measuring rod of money" as an indicator of the intensity of human psychological desires. This method, over the year, and assumptions have been refined into what is now known as modern utility theory.

The following important economic factors affect the buyer's behaviour.

1. **Disposable Personal Income :** The economists made attempts to establish a relationship between income and spending. Disposable personal income represents potential purchasing power that a buyer has. The change in income has a direct relation on buying habits. Personal consumption spending tends both to rise and fall at a slower rate than what disposable personal income does.
2. **Size of family income :** The size of family and the size of family income affect the spending and saving patterns. Generally large families spend more and small families spend less, in comparison.
3. **Income Expectation :** The expected income to receive in future has a direct relation with the buying behaviour. The expectation of higher or lower income has a direct effect on spending plans.
4. **Propensity too consume and to save :** This goes to the habit of spending or saving with the disposable income of buyers. If the buyers give importance to present needs, then they dispose of their income. And buyers spend less if they give importance to the future needs.
5. **Liquidity of Fund :** The present buying plans are infuenced greatly by liquidity of assets i.e. cash and assets readily convertible into cash, for example, readily marketable shares and bonds, bank balances etc. However, these convertible assets influence and offer freedom to the buyer, who actually buys with current income.

6. **Consumer Credit :** Facility of consumer credit system-hire purchase, instalment purchase etc., play an important role in purchasing decision. A buyer can command more purchasing power. "Buy now and pay later" plays its role effectively in the rapid growth of markets for car, scooter, radio, fridge, furniture, television and the like.

Economic model suggests behavioural hypothesis,

(*a*) Lower the price of the product, higher the sales.

(*b*) Lower the price of substitute products, lower the sales of this product.

(*c*) Higher the real income, higher the sales of this product.

(*d*) Higher the promotional expenses, higher the sales.

However, "lower the price of a product, higher the sales" may not hold good, as buyers may feel that the product is a sub-standard one. Economic factors alone cannot explain all the variations in sales. The model ignores the fundamental question of how product and brand preferences are formed.

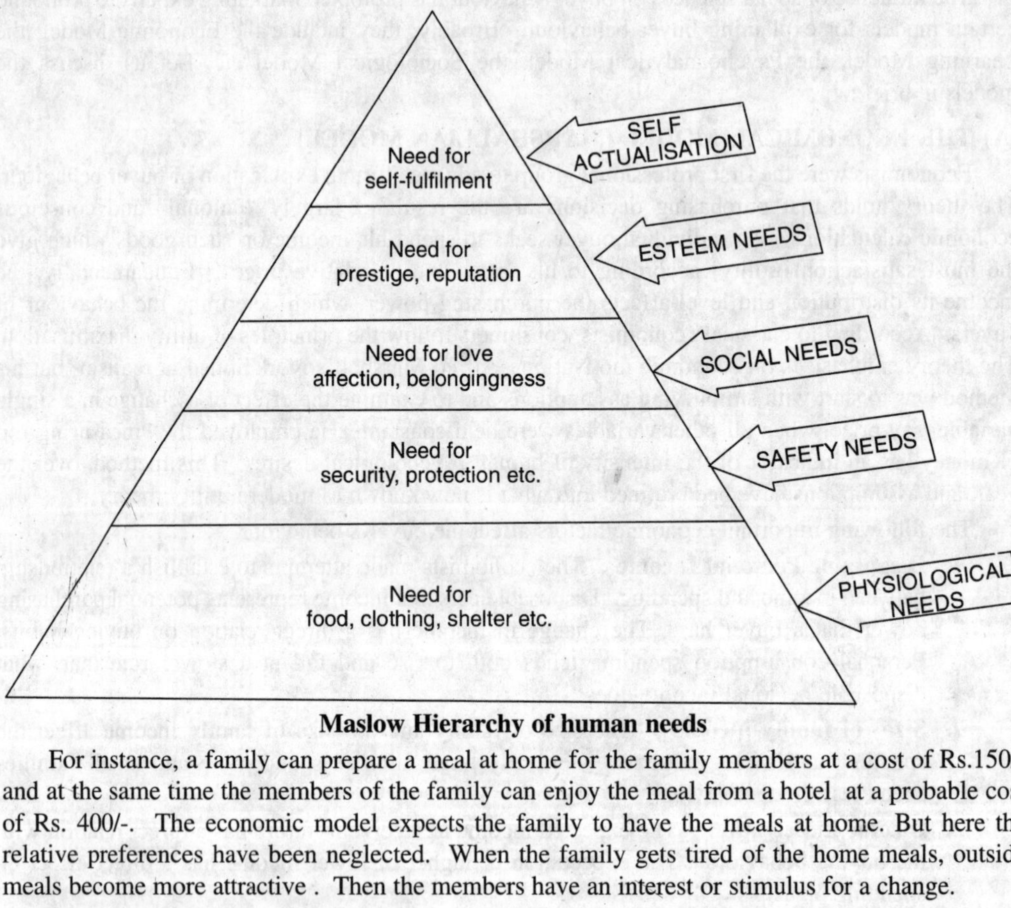

Maslow Hierarchy of human needs

For instance, a family can prepare a meal at home for the family members at a cost of Rs.150/- and at the same time the members of the family can enjoy the meal from a hotel at a probable cost of Rs. 400/-. The economic model expects the family to have the meals at home. But here the relative preferences have been neglected. When the family gets tired of the home meals, outside meals become more attractive . Then the members have an interest or stimulus for a change.

(B) PSYCHOLOGICAL THEORIES

Psychology has contributed much to the marketers to understand the buyers. Psychology explains how consumers learn about a product and how they can recall from the memory, the development of buying habits. This theory of learning is explained as a process of "repetition, motivation, conditioning and relationship. Repetition improves learning. For example, when advertisements are repeated, people may be able to understand further about the product. This approach-repetition-is aimed at repeated advertisements for drawing the attention and interest of the people. According to stimulus-response theory, learning is dependent on drive, cue, response and reinforcement. Drive is a strong stimulus. Drives may be primary-thirst, hunger etc. and secondary-desire for money, pride etc. Response is an answer given to drive or cue. For example, when you feel hungry, you try to get food at any cost. Reinforcement is a positive repetition of purchase of the same brand whenever same needs arise. The economic factors are related to the functional nature of products. Psychological motives of buying relate to personal feelings and emotions. The psychological factors play a more important role in motivating the consumer behaviour than economic factors.

Again psychology directs towards satisfying certain needs and they are (Maslow Hierarchy of human needs).

(C) PSYCHOANALYTIC THEORIES :

It is a theory developed by Sigmund Freud and is composed of three elements viz. the id (instinct), the super ego and the ego. The buyer behaviour depends upon the relative strength of the three elements in the personal ability. For example, you went to a shop to get a handkerchief. While leaving the shop, you noticed an automatic watch and you were impressed by its fine appearance. (Id is aroused). But you remembered about your younger brother's need for a dress (Super ego intervenes). The id and super ego are sometimes in conflict. The ego is the conscious and rational control which maintains the balance between the id and the super ego.

(D) SOCIAL CULTURAL THEORIES (GROUP THEORIES)

Veblen was an economist, but evolved into a social thinker greatly influenced by the new science and social anthropology. The individual decisions and behaviour are quite often influenced by the family and the society. He saw the man as a social animal. His wants and behaviour are largely influenced by the group in which he is a member. For instance, the decision my be made by one; actual buying may be done by another and the product is used by yet another member of the family. For example, a mother takes a decision to buy a tiny cycle for her little boy; the cycle is purchased by the father and the user is the little boy.

Most of the luxury goods bought by us are mainly because people of the same status have bought them. As such, culture, social attitude, family are the different factor groups that influence buyer behaviour.

An individual mixes with the people of strong influences. He speaks of their behaviours for gaining group acceptance. An individual is much more influenced by the people, with whom he has regular contacts. The activities of popular heroes are watched and friendly imitated. These groups are known as reference groups. The influence exerted by peers may not affect everyone. A new style may creep in and may be picked up by a few in the initial stage; later it may spread to others and is known as diffusion process. The marketers have to deal with the groups and individuals and thus the sociological approach is necessary.

The following are some of the important motives, influencing the ultimate buying behaviour of customers :

1. Fear	:	To overcome theft, you may purchase a burglar alarm (out of fear)
2. Desire for money	:	Purchasing when the price falls down
3. Vanity	:	Getting costly items, to be admired by others.
4. Pride	:	Possessing luxurious items for high position in the Society.
5. Love and affection	:	When you purchase toys, dresses for your sister, it is out of affection

6. Sex and romance	:	Spending much on dresses, ornaments etc.
7. Fashion	:	Imitation motives : Old people dress like young ones.
8. Possession	:	This refers to collection of stamps , coins etc.
9. Health and physical Well-being	:	Purchasing healthy foods, vitamins etc.
10. Comfort and Convenience	:	Purchasing equipments like refrigerator, pressure cooker, mixy etc.

Mortimer has given ten kinds of convenience to be reckoned with in marketing :

1. Form	:	A product may be available in different forms for Example ; Vitamins may be in the form of tablets, or Liquids, or syrup or powder.
2. Quantity	:	Products are offered in sizes : for example pastes are available in family size, medium and small size.
3. Time	:	The products are available at any time : for eg: tea, cigarette and the like are always available.
4. Packaging	:	Packages are easy to open, use and store.
5. Place	:	The product must be available all places : for eg: tea, coffee, newspapers etc.
6. Combination	:	Convenience is found in service industries.
7. Automatic	:	People prefer push button model. For example, bike with a self-starter model.
8. Credit	:	Credit facility is offered by the seller : hire purchase, instalment purchase etc.
9. Readiness	:	The product must be ready for use: for example, tinned meal.
10. Selection	:	Facility to select : There may be choice-to-choose items

Buying Decision Process

The process consists of :

1. Recognition of an unsatisfied need
2. Identification of alternatives
3. Evaluation of alternatives
4. Purchase decision
5. Post Purchase behaviour

1. **Recognition of An Unsatisfied Need :** When a person has an unsatisfied need, the buying process begins to satisfy the needs. Generally the unsatisfied need leads to tension. The nature of the want indicates the speed with which a person moves to fulfil the unsatisfied want, which is of high pressing need. On the basis of need and its urgency, forms the order of priority. Marketers should furnish the information of selling points.

2. **Identification of alternatives :** Different alternatives are available in the market. The consumer must know the brand of the product, which gives maximum satisfaction. And the person has to search out for relevant information of the product brand, location etc. There are many sources—friends, neighbours etc., and the marketers, salesman, advertising display, sales promotions, newspapers, television etc.

3. **Evaluation of alternatives** : This is a critical stage, especially with regard to the costly items. Consumers have different views on different alternatives. The attributes-taste, colour, price, durability etc., have different preferences. All the details of the attributes are provided by the marketers. On the basis of attribute preferences say price, colour etc.,

consumers reduce the number of alternatives. For instance, when we buy a table on the basis of price range, we may be able to eliminate the alternatives, then colour etc. This process must be understood by the marketers.

4. **Purchase decision :** By considering the likes and dislikes of alternatives, one is about to take a decision as to buy or not to buy. One will consider with reference to product, type, price, quality etc. A seller can facilitate such consumers to understand the product through advertisements.
5. **Post purchase behaviour :** Feedback information is important as far as a seller is concerned. A brand preference naturally repeats sales to a marketer. A satisfied buyer is a silent advertisement. If the purchased brand fails to give the expected satisfaction to the buyer, it affects the sales negatively. A satisfying experience of a buyer tends to strengthen the brand preference.

A list of motives that impel organisational customers to make a purchase, according to Nystrom, is given below :

Motive	Objective
Efficiency	In performance, practicability and increased capacity
Economy	In money, in use or in time
Good quality	In material and workmanship
Simplicity	In construction, operation and application
Saleability	In increasing saleability of user's product
Ease of operation	In easier handling, greater convenience, handiness or light touch
Space saving	In compactness, ease for storage and holding
Obsolescence	In which it needs improvement, replacement or additions
Safety	In providing safety to employees, clients and customers
Cleanliness	In plant, user's product, or for the workmen

THE BUYING PROCESS

Researchers have identified eight stages in buying process : They are :

(1) Problem recognition (Need Recognition)

The process of buying normally starts with the recognition of a need by the consumer. He recognises a problem and develops a perception of the problem. Then he seeks information for solving his problem.

(2) Awareness

The customer turns to his environment of information around him. It makes him aware of the existence of the product that would solve his problem.

(3) Comprehension (Evaluation)

Comprehension comes out of his ability to reason with the information. The awareness and comprehension stages represent the information processing stage. These two stages constitute the cognitive field of the purchase process. Cognition refers to acquisition of knowledge.

(4) Attitude :

It is the sum total of the individual's faith and feelings towards a product. As a result of his awareness and comprehension, the consumer develops an attitude – favourable or unfavourable – towards the product. The purchase process will continue only if he develops a favourable attitude or a liking for the product.

(5) Legitimisation

The buyer must be convinced that the purchase of the product is the legitimate course of action. This stage often stands as a barrier between a favourable attitude towards the product and actual purchase. Only if the buyer is convinced about the correctness of the purchase decision, he will proceed. At this stage, he may seek further information regarding the product or attempt to assess the information already available. Attitude and legitimisation constitute the attitude field of the purchase process.

(6) Trial

Conviction leads the consumer to try the product on a small scale; he may buy a sample. He tries to evaluate the product from his own experience.

(7) Adoption

A successful trial leads him to buy/adopt the product. Trial and adoption stages constitute the behavioural field in the buying process.

(8) Post Purchase Behaviour

The purchase leads to a specific post-purchase behaviour. Usually, it creates some restlessness in the minds of the individual. He is not sure about the product. He may feel that the other brand would have been better. He may even feel that the salesman has taken him for a ride. At this dissonance is uncomfortable, the individual, by himself, will seek all means to recover his conviction and poise. He will seek reassuring advertisements of the products or he may deliberately avoid positive stories about the competing brand.

QUESTIONS

1. What are the psychological factors that influence in consumer decision maker *(M Com. Madurai)*
2. Define the concept of Buying Behaviour. Why is it desirable to study it in marketing *(M Com. Andhra)*
3. What do you mean by buying motives ? Explain the importance of studying consumer behaviour in marketing
4. When an individual is member of several peer groups, are his consuming activities likely to be affected by all groups ? Explain.

Case Study-1

END OF ALL WORK AND NO PLAY CULTURE ?

Every year, about 100 million Japanese spend about $75 to see Mickey Mouse and wait two hours in line to rocket through Space Mountain at Tokyo Disneyland. They flock to hear Aron Narikiyo, "Elvis-san", a wildly popular Elvis impersonator. They ski, attend cultural events, go bowling, take juggling lessons, and play pachinko, a vertical version of pinball. What they also do in great numbers is shop. One hundred and twenty million Japanese consumers with rising disposable incomes translates into lots of buying power. Long considered a society of all work and no play, Japan finds both its culture and its consumers changing.

- In the conventional picture of modern Japan, men work most of the time, and women are relegated to background positions of stay-at-home wives and mothers. Indeed, many older Japanese accept without complaint endless, unquestioned hard work. But the old ways are changing. Japanese men are discovering that fun is sometimes more important than earnest dedication to the workplace. And Japanese women are assuming professional roles outside the home. Declaring that its citizens should start enjoying life, the government officially shortened the work week from forty-eight hours to forty and funded the Leisure Research and Development Centre to teach its citizens the value of leisure time. With more money to spend and more time in which to spend it, the Japanese are becoming active and experienced consumers, dedicated to make their country a seikatsu taikoku – a "lifestyle superpower".

- Two of the most powerful groups of Japanese consumers are the more than 8 million Dankai Juniors, children of Japan's post war baby boom, sand women, whose status and affluence continues to grow. Raised during a prosperous time in an affluent society, young Japanese spend a lot of money on sports, audiovisual equipment, entertainment, and fashion. Although looking for value more than they did in the 1980s, these young consumers still splurge on new products that improve the quality of their leisure time. One of their favourite places to go for fun is Namco's Wonder Eggs, and arcade specialising in virtual reality games. As for tastes in fashion, this group prefers American and European styles and colours. To attract these trendy customers, some small shops in areas frequented by young people carry only imported clothing.
- In today's Japan, women comprise about 40 per cent of the country's 64.5 million person work force, and more than 50 per cent of mothers work outside the home. Following the Equal Employment Law of 1986, women began to pursue more education, entered a variety of professions, began earning their own salaries, and became champion consumers. Besides attending concerts and plays, travelling, engaging in sports, and frequenting "relaxation parlours", where the sounds of birds singing or waves crashing on the shore relieve stress, Japanese women shop. Choosy about labels, many Japanese women favour distinctive brands, such as Armani suits, Yves St. Laurent towels, and $1,600 Gucci handbags.
- Benefiting from Japan's growing appetite for consumption, retailing – both upscale and value-oriented – is booming. To attract consumers by providing more spacious and attractive surroundings, venerable department stores and such as Mitsukoshi and Takashima are remodelling and modernising their interiors. New speciality shops are springing up, as are large shopping centres with avenues of stores and abundant parking space. Although many Japanese equate a good product with a high price tag, many others are becoming increasingly value-conscious, looking for high quality at low prices. Retailers are responding by opening giant discount stores. One of them, I world, is recording annual sales of over $180 million on discounted top-of-the-line brands such as Nordica and Sony. What the Japanese call "roadside chains", freestanding retail buildings, are springing up in suburbs. Two such competing chains, Aoyama and Aoki, sell name brand men's clothing at lower-than-department-store prices.
- When Japanese leaders commanded the country to relax, the leisure industry rushed to provide places to do it. Just as retailing is profiting from larger numbers of Japanese shoppers, the leisure industry is profiting from the greater amount of time that Japanese are spending on recreation. In one year alone, two hundred companies applied for permits to develop new theme parks. To enable ski enthusiasts to make one day trips from Tokyo, a bullet train station opened at popular ski resort, Gala Yuzawa. For those who prefer to schuss in climate controlled comfort, indoor ski slopes are available within city limits. Built on top of one of Tokyo's numerous skyscrapers, the International Aquarium gives city dwellers a chance to escape temporarily to an undersea world. Having discovered the pleasures of camping, Japanese are pursuing this pastime in record numbers. American commercial camp ground developer KOA recently opened its first Japanese compound in Okayama. Vacationers can swim, play tennis, visit the mini zoo, or join in recreational group singing at the Karoake Kabin.

- With all these choices and more, people don't have trouble deciding how to have fund on a day off or a week-long break, but the Japanese are still novices at "hanging out". A Leisure Development Centre survey revealed that 40 per cent of respondents wouldn't know what to do with a month off. To help them, the National Recreation Association offers a one year course on how to enjoy life. Many Japanese, however, are convinced that the art of having fun is "Made in the U.S.A".

QUESTIONS

1. What are the significant issues in this case ?
2. "The changing role of Japanese women has influenced their buying behaviour" Discuss this statement in the light of what you have learned in this case.
3. To market leisure facilities in Japan, what aspects of Japanese consumers' behaviour is of interest ?

CHAPTER 21

The Indian Consumers

- *Indian Culture*
- *Profile of Indian Consumers*
- *Classification of Indian Consumers*
- *Questions*

INDIAN CULTURES

India is said to be a country of multi-cultures. It is because of long history of many many years. At different times, different rulers ruled over the country. Further, at the same time there had been different rules in different parts of India. Then, there was invasion from outside specially from Arab countries; and then many years India was under the British rule. In certain part of the country for sometime there had been French and Portuguese rule. The different rulers had different systems of governance and social practices. All these factors left a deep imprint on culture. In olden days, the means of transport and communication were very poor; large numbers of languages, systems, habits etc. are followed. These facts of history made India a multi-culture nation.

LANGUAGE

India is a multi-language country. There are eighteen languages officially recognized in the constitution which are spoken or used in different parts of the country. Besides the recognized languages, English is the official language in most private offices and for interstate correspondence. Besides official language, there are many other languages which are quite populat in certain parts of the country, like Bhojpuri in certain part of UP and Bihar, Marwari in certain parts of Rajasthan, Dogri in J and K etc. The local language have great influence on consumers specially in rural areas. There are also wide variations of languages from place-to-place (in spoken languages) and if they are used by marketers in communication, they have greater impact on consumers.

RELIGION

Religion has great impact on culture and buying behaviour of consumers. In India, there are major religions-Hindus, Muslims, Sikhs, Christians, Jains etc. Every religion has its own values, faith, beliefs and greatly affect consumer behaviour. For instance, Hindus by and large are vegetarians. Cow is considered as Matha by Hindus and therefore, they do not eat cow-meat. Muslims do not eat pig meat. Sikhs do not consume tobacco in any form. The faith in vegerarianism is so strong in Hindus and in restaurants, only vegetarian food are supplied. The impact of religion on culture and consumer behaviour is so strong that it is not possible to describe fully.

India has large number of races. Anglo Indian communities are found largely in Kolkata and there are Chinese who settled down in shoe businesses. There are tribes and each tribe has its own customs and preferences. Customs of Sindhis are different from that of Parsis and others and each one of them has to be approached differently by a marketer.

EDUCATION

The level of education has great impact on knowledge. It also affects values, faiths and beliefs. The poor educated country has greater faith in superstitions and traditions, because one believes more on luck, fate, stunch believer in God. Since there is less education, tribes should be properly studied and researched to find out consumer behaviour and about preferences for their products and services.

According to 2001 sensus, India has a population of 102.7 crore, on March 2001, of which 65.38 percent were literate. The literacy is the highest in Kerala which has reduced its birth rate to the lowest and helped migration of persons to other states in India and abroad. All these factors influence behaviour of customers and should be properly taken into consideration by marketer

RESPECTS TO ELDERS:

In Indian culture all those, who are elders in age than oneself, are not only given respects but also often what they say is accepted and acted. A son does what his father says, a younger brother or sister give respect to their elder brothers and sisters, and often are willing to act on their advice. This respect is powerful in purchasing high value items like land, buildings etc. They are credible sources of information and in many matters, their advice is sought because it is felt that with the age, one gathers more experience and knowledge which must be utilized. Actually age is given big respect. But gradually, the respect for elders is declining, however, their influences on buying habits and behaviour is still very strong and should not be ignored by marketers.

CARE FOR TOMORROW:

Indians think more deeply for tomorrow, they save a good percentage of their income for future, (around 20-25% in 2000-01): for their children's education, marriage etc. Because of sense of insecurity, people do not enjoy life but care more for their children than for themselves.

Though certain cultural factors are common to all countries, there are other attributes which differ widely from country to country, like beliefs, languages, food habits, concept of beauty, attitudes etc. So, marketers take these facts into consideration, otherwise, he may loose the market rather than increase its share. The technological changes specially development in information technology, high speed aeroplanes, fast communications etc. made the world very close and small. One can send and receive messages in few seconds across the world: markets have become globalised through internet and e-commerce etc.

ACHIEVEMENTS:

Personal achievements and success whether as a scientist, sportsman, artist, educationalist or businessmen etc. is a matter of great pride and prestige. Therefore, they are always busy in making efforts for vision and mission. Persons of achievements are actually honoured and respected all over the world but Americans are more fusy and make greater efforts to achieve higher and higher goals because of this instinct more inventions and researches have been done in USA, but gradually many other countries like India and China are achieving more in scientific fields and in sports. The American achievements are often measured in terms of material achievements.

MORALITY AND SEX:

There are wide differences on morality and sex from country to country. The laws of America, Europe, Japan, Australia, India etc. provide equal opportunities to education and job to ladies and gents. However, there are certain restrictions on their education and job. Even today in India everyone wants at least one male child, and in rural India, girls are not given same opportunities for learning, but in the West, Japan, Australia etc. there are no such taboos and restrictions. Western world including American believe in polarized morality and sex except for top politicians. Here as per various studies there are pre-marriage sex increasing in number and there are also cases where couples stay together without marriage.

ATTITUDE:

Americans believe that every problem has a solution and therefore it must be identified when any problem is faced. In Hinduism, nature and people are one and human being has to act as God wants. But Americans have an attitude to conquer nature. Because of this, they have come out and succeeded and many researches have been carried out. The attitude to conquer nature is one of the belief that man is supreme, and different from other forms of life on the universe. Therefore, they feel that problems which are in existence in nature can be solved; for example problems like shortage or surplus of water, extreme heat or coolness etc. through researches to find out solutions.

In America, UK, Japan etc. people are punctual and activities are held as per schedules. But in India and many other countries, it is a fashion to be late in social functions, marriages etc.

PROFILE OF THE INDIAN CONSUMER:

India being very vast, consumers here are naturally scattered over a vast territory. As the country is also marked by great diversity in climate, religion, language, literacy level, customs, lifestyle, economic status etc. here the consumers present a complex group. The heterogeneity holds many implications for a marketer, especially to those going in for national marketing.

According to the Census 2001, the population of India stood 1,027 million, of which 742 million lived in rural areas and 285 million in urban areas. And according to the census 2001, the nation's average literacy rate is 65.4%.

On the one hand, India has the highest concentration of illiterates in the world and on the other hand, it has the second highest concentration of literates and the third largest pool of educated and technically trained manpower in the world. India has a strong pool of engineers, scientists, and technically educated persons. In modern fields like information technology, India has been displaying its strength very clearly in recent years.

DIVERSITY:

Indian consumers are marked by great diversity; diversity in religion, language, culture, tradition, dress, food-habit, custom etc. The people of India belong to different religious groups – Hindus, Muslims, Christians, Sikhs, Jains, Budhists and Parsee. Further there are sects, sub-sects, castes and sub-castes. Each caste has its own customs established over generations. In birth and death, in marriage and family life, the individual is entangled in the chores of his religion. What is welcome for one religion is taboo for the other and something totally banned in one religion is an accepted practice in another.

Apart from the recognized languages, specified in the Constitution of India, there are hundreds of dialects. And many amalgams of languages have been formed as a result of shifting of population. This linguistic diversity is a big challenge to a marketing man.

India holds out the picture of widely varying styles. Almost every religious community, has its own traditional styles of dress and the same is the case with ornaments and jewellery. Rice is staple food in South and wheat in the North. However, in several of the Southern States, people now consume wheat products and like-wise, certain Southern dishes have become popular in the North. But the basic difference in food habits remains. There are certain communities, which are strict vegetarians. Some use coconut oil as the cooking medium, some use ground-nut oil and some others, mustard or gingely oil.

India is a vast country with a land area of 3.29 million sq.km and population of 1027 million (1.5.2001). Within the urban segment, there is a great concentration of consumers in the metros. The six cities – Kolkata, Mumbai, Delhi, Chennai, Bangalore and Hyderabad, are large by global standards. The second tier of cities, Ahmedabad, Kanpur, Pune, Nagpur, Lucknow and Jaipur, also has high consumer concentration. Large cities are concentrated in the South and West zones. There are about 3,750 towns in India. 64% of urban population lives in 350 such towns. The rest scattered across the remaining 3,400 odd towns. The rural consumers are spread over the five lakhs villages.

CHANGES IN LIFESTYLES:

The Indian consumer is not a single homogenous entity and is not possible to draw a generalized characteristic of Indian consumers. Indian population has different religious groups. Each religion, subsect and caste has its own culture and customs and given rise to different behaviour towards their consumption, use and purchase of products and services. Culture and subculture vary from region-to-region. The North Indian culture is vastly different from South Indian. Social marketing also varies from region-to-region and place-to-place. Therefore, marketing companies cannot make a composite single marketing programme and strategy for the Indian consumers but will have to make changes in the marketing programme depending upon consumer characteristic based on geographical and religious consideration. This is quite evident from the food-habits, fashion, dress-materials, life-style etc. and above all attitude and behavioural differences towards purchase and use of products and services.

As Indians are used to a system of hierarchy in the work-place, senior colleagues are obeyed and respected. Supervisors are expected to monitor an individual's work. Educated Indians have learnt to adapt to Western methods of monitoring one's own work and completing it on schedule. In a groups discussion, only the senior most person might speak, but that does not mean that others agree with him. They maintain silence, without contradicting him out of respect for seniority. Westernized Indians, on the other hand, can be quite assertive and direct and should be treated in the same manner.

CLASSIFICATION OF INDIAN CONSUMERS

The classification of Indian consumers based on economic status is suitable for the present study. Accordingly, we may divide Indian consumers into four classes- Wealthy Class, Middle Class, Lower Middle Class and Poor Class. Let us take each class, one by one.

(1) Wealthy Class

The senior successful top business executives drawing salary of Rs. one lakh or more per month fall in this class. The persons in this group often believe in showing their new acquired richness. They buy high priced cars, house, get best education for their children and get treatment in the best hospitals etc. This class wants to have best enjoyment of life and looks for the future of their family.

The next group is of high level professionals. These persons do not have family status and have acquired wealth because of proficiency in their professions. Therefore, they are career oriented and their priority is to build career of their children too through best education in India or abroad. Young successful professionals, senior corporate executives and small scale and medium scale new businessmen fall in this group, who have come up through their education and hard work. They are all well educated and many of them have advanced Indian degrees in their professions. These persons are active in professional, social and community activities but most of them do not take much interest in religious functions. They believe in high standard of living and try to buy best things in life-house, furniture's, furnishings, automobiles, health-care, insurance, education of their children etc. so that they may also become good in professions. They prefer to live in posh colonies and buy goods in the best stores.

This group has a good deal of marketing significance. This is because firstly, it is useful segment for luxury products. Secondly, in respect of other products too, super premium brands depend on it. Stanley in one of his study reports said that the pattern of income distribution in India is such that the top 20% of the population- about 180 million people

– which roughly translates to the upper crest of the middle class. Data from the NCAER has estimated the affluent population in India with an income of over Rs.10 lakhs p.a to be in the range of one million households. It means that audience of 5.6 million individuals are available for Products priced at the top-most end of the scale.

(2) Middle Class

The next class according to economic status is middle class, whose mean income in India varies between Rs. 10,000 and Rs. 20,000 per month, though some have higher income. They are mostly junior executives. They are white collar or workers but also include blue collar persons and small traders. These people have great ambition to move up and is one of the biggest class in every society. Sometimes, they are celled cream of the society. They are generally well educated or technical hands and always try to improve their skills so that they can move up. They want respectability in the society and therefore on certain occasions they spend more than their capacity. Most of them spend some time for worshiping their faith and participate in religious and social functions. They take all possible care that their children do well in competitive admission tests of medical, engineering, management and other professional cources.

The middle class has emerged as the result of several socio-economic developments that took place over the years. The industrial units that came up created a sizable chunk of well-to-do industrial workers, engineers and managers. In the service sector, a sizable population of teachers, doctors, and other supporting staff emerged. The continuous expansion of the Government machinery at the Centre and the States swelled up the strength of Government servants of different categories. The trader class also expanded considerably; and so did service providers of different type. While these developments taking place largely in the urban areas, rural India was also undergoing a welcome change.

CONSUMPTION SCENARIO:

The middle class is now emerging as the 'Consumption Community' of the country. As the members of the class are better educated and better exposed to global life-styles, their aspirations have been constantly growing. Their spending is steadily on the increase. They often spend more than what they earn at any given point of time in order to cope with their new social image. Their expenditure on non-food items is continuously on the increase. Toiletries and cosmetics, including premium brands, have become common items of consumption for them. Instant coffee and soft drinks find a place on their daily menu. Costly fabrics, ready-mades, furniture, fans, stereo-music systems, TVs, refrigerators, electric mixers and grinders, appliances like washing machines, dish-washers, vacuum cleaners etc. are gaining a rapid entry into the homes of this class.

Besides the economic factors, socio-cultural and lifestyle factors have also contributed to the rapid shift in the consumption pattern of the middle class, The growth of urbanization is the first among these factors. The breaking down of the joint family system and the rise of small families is the next factor. More and more women taking to employment is the third factor. These and other similar factors acting in concert have brought about a new lifestyle among the middle class. Thus, the growth of lifestyle requires several time-saving conveniences or devices. The economic improvement and the lifestyle change have collectively brought about the shift in their consumption pattern. The income from the employed wife has made it possible for the family to buy a variety of house-hold appliances. In fact, the boom in house-hold appliances that we see today has been caused jointly by the change in lifestyle and the increased affordability of the middle class. It can be seen that these time-saving devices or appliances are mostly sold on planks such as '*save time*', '*make your job easy*', '*enjoy a new recipe*' etc. These planks go well with the lifestyle profile of the neo-middle class women, whether she is a working woman or a non-working woman. She needs the time saving devices; she is also willing to take the suggestions of the advertisers to fry, grill, or bake and bring the new, exotic to the dinning table.

The Indian middle class is considered the largest group which buys and consume products like, food, music system, kitchen and comfort appliances, scooter, motor-bikes, fashion and cosmetic products, health care products, jewellery, and many other lifestyle products. The Indian middle class is further pushed up by very high growth in IT and software industry and this sector is predominantly in the age group of 25 to 40 years.

CONSUMER CREDIT FACILITY

Compulsions on the social and economic fronts are driving him towards consumer credit. Basically, he lives on a fixed income and manages within a rigid budget. But he stays in fairly decent house, hired or owned. He has some furniture. His wife selects reasonably good furnishing and uses modern cooking gadgets. He has his personal transport. His children study in good schools. How does all these happen? He obviously manages such a lifestyle through credit facilities made available to him by different agencies. Today, practically anything - from sewing machine to personal computer – is available to him on instalment payments. The availability of credit facility acts as a temptation to buy. His desire to possess more and more material comforts is realized through credit. It is estimated that more than 50% of most durables are bought with credit facility. The middle class is *pledging future income for current consumption.*

Important segments within the middle class:

The important segment-wise classifications are

(*i*) The middle class male

(*ii*) The middle class female and

(*iii*) The middle class teenager.

(i) ***The middle class male :*** This class has been moving towards more materials comforts. It has already been led into new lifestyle – fusions between the traditional and the modern, between the east and the west. In contrasts to the 'spend - for - others, not for yourself' philosophy of the older generation of this class, the modern generation happily lavishes things on itself. Earlier, family need based purchases were the norm, but today one's own desire based purchase is catching up. These trends are more visible among the younger members of the group.

Ready-mades are preferred: The change in the dress habit of the average middle class male is one good example of the new trend. The market for ready-made garments is growing at the rate of 25%. Men are fast shifting from tailor-stitched garments to ready-mades, with emphasis on branded and designer ones. More than 100 well-known menswear brands are now competing in the market.

Holiday travel: Holidaying is now becoming very popular. Earlier, holidaying meant visiting one's parents and relatives and the traditional home or places of worship. Now, it is sight seeing, people travel to unknown parts of the country for enjoyment and relaxation from work.

Prestige Conscious: The middle class consumer acquires many of his possessions, because he is a 'status-conscious' or 'prestige-conscious' man. He is very particular to maintain a standard of living. His finances may be tight; still he plans for more possessions. They are his status symbols. Marketers can motivate him by appealing to his sense of prestige.

Family-ties: The middle class man is still basically a home-loving man with strong family ties. He assigns a lot of importance to the well being of his family. The 'family tie' binds him so strongly that anything that appeals to this 'human bond' will get a positive response from him. The needs of his family, particularly children, get priority in his budget. He adjusts to the changing fashions of his college going children, without much resistance, though these changes are expensive for him. He spends a good portion of his income on the education of his children. A son's education/career and daughter's marriage are life long dreams for him.

Decision maker: Another important dimension is that the middle class male is not the sole decision-maker in purchases for the family. He is influenced in his buying decisions by his family, especially his wife. Whether it is a car or TV or toothpaste, hair-oil, magazines etc., the wife plays a role in the purchasing decisions.

(*ii*) **The middle class female:**

The woman is a crucial part of the middle class home. At present, the profile and role of the middle class woman has been undergoing significant changes. Today, she is educated and in many cases employed. The percentage of working woman has actually been growing at a steady pace. Their purchasing power has increased: thus the demand for product categories like cosmetics, packaged foods, beverages, two-wheelers, holiday packages etc. are of great appeal to them, In urban parts, the middle class woman is an active partner in the family. She is no longer confined to the four walls of the kitchen. She has acquired a place in society by virtue of her education and employment. She is a major factor in all purchase decisions of the family. She is practically the sole decision-maker. Her role is main in purchasing-decisions. She is the cashier and budgeter. For several products, she is the 'gate-keeper'. New items cannot find an entry into the house without her consent and clearance. Purchases meant for children too are mostly decided by her. In buying household appliances, she is often the sole decision-maker.

Cautious buyer: The middle class woman is generally a cautious buyer. Her education and social background makes her a discriminating buyer. She is willing to try new things. She is not opposed to change. But she does not adopt any product instantly. She may do a sample purchase: she enquires with somebody who has known the product: she may listen to advertisements of the product: she decides to purchase only if she is fully satisfied.

The middle class women is quality conscious as well as cost conscious buyer. She often cross-checks the price details with other stores. She bargains, She compares one brand with another on price and quality. She has a tight family budget to follow and within this budget, she develops her own preferences-whether it is baby food, cooking medium, tea or coffee, cosmetics or ready-made garments etc. Sales promotional incentives like prize-coupons, rebates, bonuses, free-gifts etc. definitely attract her. She finds out what product or brand her neighbour or friend is using. She always get direct information from an existing 'user' about the product.

Time-saving devices:

The middle class woman also seeks leisure. Time saving appliances hold out great charm to her. She prefers for gadgets like electric grinders, Washing machine, Dish-washers, Pressure-cookers, Microwave ovens, Vacuum cleaners, etc. as they reduce her workload and save her time to a great extent.

The middle class woman possesses a good awareness of the changes taking place in her environment. Her education level and the growth in media has contributed to this development. TV and magazines, etc. carry a lot of information targeted at her. They carry information on social, personal and family issues and massages on a variety of products and services. Since manufacturers need her patronage, they communicate with her through every possible media.

Sense of beauty: To quote Ogilvy and Mather Advertising, "Global influences are affecting them more intensely, whether it's apparel, accessories, cosmetics or shoes, they opt for what is most modern. Dressing has become bolder, more Western and varied. The tremendous media exposure has taken her close to the fashion trends internationally. The time lag for trends to percolate to India from the major fashion centres like Paris and London has decreased tremendously". She is generally fashion loving, but seldom fashion-crazy. Soap or shampoo, face cream or moisturizer, perfumes or hair oil, in selecting her brand, she is greatly influenced by the messages that appeal to her sense of grooming, sense of beauty is a strong motive force behind several of her purchases.

(*iii*) **The middle class teenagers: (14 – 20)**

This is a sizable segment within the middle class. They are certainly more modern and adventurous than their elders. We can witness the blend of the Western and Indian lifestyle, in them. They care less for 'religion and tradition'. They are after a new look, 'variety' interests them, and most of them are quick in adopting fashions. Their tastes and preferences can be influenced relatively more easily. It is, of-course, not easy to dupe them, but it is easy to motivate them. The teenage market is of special importance to certain product categories, like garments, cosmetic, personal care products, fast food, soft drinks etc.

(3) **Lower Middle class**

Though their purchasing power is low, their size is very large. NCEAR has found that 75% of the purchases, like, cooking oil, tea, detergent cake, bath soap, tooth powder, footwear, transistors, mobile phones, etc. are made by this class. In recent years, this group is receiving the benefits of several social, educational and economic programmes. Over time, a good part of this group may advance economically and join the upper middle class. Already, a good part of this group is a part of the upper middle class.

(4) **The Poor class:**

The 'below the poverty line' (BPL) is large in size. They are consumers of unbrand products. However, this class is coming up and emerge as consumers of branded consumer products.

QUESTIONS

1. What do you understand by social class?
2. Describe lifestyle of different classes of consumers.
3. What do you understand by wealthy class and how they behave?
4. What are the characteristics of middle class female?
5. What are different economic classes in India? Describe major characteristics of each class.

CHAPTER 22

Consumerism

- *Introduction*
- *Evolution of Consumerism*
- *How did Consumerism Originate ?*
- *Unique Problems of Indian Consumers*
- *Consumer Orientation*
- *Consumer Exploitation in India*
- *Major Problems of Consumers Exploitation*
- *Enactments*
- *Carlill Vs.Carbolic Company*
- *Consumer Protection Act 1986*
- *Rights of Consumers*
- *Questions.*

Consumer movement is a universal phenomenon. The goods or services available may be in abundance or in short supply, but the position of the consumer is weak, in relation to the seller. Sellers want customers, as buyers and not as complainants. The frustration and bitterness on the part of consumers, who have been promised much is indeed great, but they realize less. It may be due to the existence of sellers' market, where consumers are voiceless. There are many practices whereby consumers are not only being denied their basic rights but are being deceived too. Who is a consumer? A consumer is an individual who consumes goods – manufactured by firms or created by nature (air, water etc.) and services offered by Government or firms – hospitals, educational institutions etc.

Consumerism is defined by Richard H.Buskirk and James as "Organised efforts of consumers seeking redress, restitution and remedy for dissatisfaction they have accumulated in the acquisition of their standard of living."

Philip Kotler says that "Consumerism is not limited to organized efforts only but, is a social movement seeking to augment the rights and powers of buyers in relation to sellers".

Harper W. Boyed and David analyse the consumerism as "the dedication of those activities of both public and private organizations which are designed to protect individuals from practices that impinge upon their rights as consumers".

Thus, consumerism, as social movement, may be defined as an organized effort of consumers seeking redress, restitution and remedy for dissatisfaction, that they have accumulated in the acquisition of their standard of living".

Consumerism is a public movement which protests against certain marketing practices. It is a social movement and not just protests by an individual consumer or a group of consumers. It is not even a criticism by the press or few public speeches against the firms or businessmen indulging in marketing malpractices that affect the consumers. Consumerism, to be precise, is an important social movement which aims at protecting the consumers against unethical or immoral marketing practices of private companies as well as public enterprises. It is neither opposed to profits or monopoly, not antagonistic to the large companies or big business houses. It has no concern with the monopoly legislation or foreign exchange control measures. There would be no consumerism if the business firms practice and follow the norms of good conduct and service in the areas of their selling and marketing activities.

EVOLUTION OF CONSUMERISM

The idea of 'consumerism' was first conceived in USA around the beginning of this century. Its evolution can be studied in three distinct phases as follows:

1. **AROUND 1900:** The business firms dealing in meat packing were least concerned with the consumers. Meat used to be sold in the most unhealthy manner. This affected the health of the consumers. Even many other firms used to produce dangerous, unwanted products and drugs and sell them to the consumers by adopting manipulative devices. Conscious and sensible become disgusted with this sort of affairs and started campaign to preserve the interests of the consuming public.
2. **AROUND 1930:** Consumerism assumed more importance because people in general become more enlightened and concerned with the standards of good quality products. This was possible on account of education, awareness and political consciousness. Although consumerism did not become a serious public movement during this time, the Government came up with a legislation called Miller-Tiching Act 1936 in order to regulate certain marketing mal-practices.
3. **1960's:** It is in the sixties of this century consumerism became a very forceful social movement. Late President Kennedy, in the year 1962, passed a legislation to protect the consumers' rights particularly with regard to false advertising and unhealthy packaging of food and other articles. The consumerism movement reached its height when a serious criticism was levelled against the 'unsafety' of automobile companies to adopt safety methods. The Government also passed many other legislations to control pollution. Business firms in the beginning criticized consumerism stating that they had been taking due care in regard to product quality etc. But later on they started setting up consumer affairs cell to deal with consumer disputes of allegations.

In India, consumerism has been active for some time past. A few years ago, adulteration of food articles was sought to be presented by the Food Adulteration Act in India. Inspectorate Departments were set up in all States of India to implement and supervise the way the Act was followed. To a certain extent, it has done good because false weights and measures have been checked and food adulteration has been controlled to a great extent.

The major causes of consumerism in India have been identified as rising prices, poor product performance and service quality, product shortages and deceptive advertising – shortages and inflation. Government has been very responsive to the consumer needs through legislative action. Economic discontent has been generated out of spiraling inflation. Thus it has become necessary for the consumers to stand up for their rights through an effective organization in order to redress the grievances.

HOW DID CONSUMERISM ORIGINATE?

The majority of the consumers in advanced countries are well educated, well-informed and are in a position to protect themselves. But our Indian situation is different from the Western, where adequate production and proper distribution of products exist. In India, industries have not achieved the level of affluence of technology and the existing markets of products run in shortages, adulteration and black market prices. Indian people have less money at their disposal. The profit-making attitude of the business failed to discharge social responsibilities for maintaining fair price, quality of goods and providing services etc. In short, consumerism is an outcome of sufferings and exploitation of consumers, and some businessmen, aim to make abnormal profit, which is at the cost of consumers' safety and health. However, it has been accepted and agreed that "A consumer is a king of the Market" but in fact he is not. The majority of the Indian problems relating to consumers are adulteration, artificial scarcity, unreasonable prices etc.

There are different religious customs, traditions and languages in India, and about three-fourth of the population live in rural areas, where cultivation is the source of livelihood, and there is wide disparity of income of people. Majority of the people, who are most illiterate, have low income. To save or protect themselves, against exploitative practices of trade, consumerism has emerged and has been accepted as a defensive force to safeguard the interest of the customers.

UNIQUE PROBLEMS OF INDIAN CONSUMERS:

Indian consumers face several unique problems requiring more involvement and support from the Government and the consumer organizations to protect their rights. Some are given below:

1. Consumerism is still in its infancy and not well organized. Majority of Indian consumers are not consciously aware of their rights.
2. Shortage of essential commodities occur very often in India. Such imbalances lead to hoarding and black-marketing, profiteering and corruptions.
3. Many consumers are ignorant and uneducated and in such situations, the marketer exploit the consumer. There are many such cases in India.
4. Producers advertise their products, not with a view to serve the public, but with a view to dispose of their dead products at a good profit.
5. Consumers become easy victims, in the absence of information, and buy sub-standard and defective products.
6. The court procedure in India is a time consuming and tiresome process. Thus, consumers avoid legal actions. People are unaware of the simple procedures under the Consumer Protection Act.
7. Supplier, and not the consumer, become the king in the market. etc.

CONSUMER ORIENTATION

We have seen in earlier chapters that the consumer orientation has been given maximum importance by the marketers. Satisfaction and well being of the consumer should be the objective of all business units. In real practice, he is not protected or safeguarded but, he is cheated and looted.

CONSUMER EXPLOITATION IN INDIA

Consumers at large become a prey to the exploiters. Examples are not few but countless:

1. Supplied materials are of sub-standard.
2. Goods, in many cases, fall short of their weight.
3. Goods and services are priced high.
4. Consumers are tortured with false advertisement.
5. Interested persons or profiteers create artificial scarcity to earn illegitimate profits.
6. At the time of price rising stages essential commodities are hoarded and black marketed at boosted price.
7. Rude behaviour of rationing shops – controlled by government.
8. Funs and contests advertisements have been a method of cheating innocent people.
9. People are made fools by advertising tall and false claims.
10. Mail order business is another form of crookedness.
11. Consumers have been harassed during the guarantee period, where free repair is warranted.
12. Adulteration is at the maximum. About 50% of the food items, we are consuming now, are adulterated.

Further Examples

1. Tooth paste tubes filled with air at the other end.
2. Buying a package of biscuits, one finds more package materials than the quantity of biscuits
3. 300 gms of vanaspati is found in a 500 gm tin of ghee, but labeled as 'PURE GHEE'
4. A 250 gm of pure tea consists of 150 gms of exhausted tea leaves, which is artificially coloured and prepared, but the script of the label reads as "A 1"
5. 500 gms of chilly powder packet consists of 150 gms of red brick powder or coloured saw dust, where label reads "PURE".
6. One litre milk packet contains 40% of water, where packet is sealed with label "PURE MILK".
7. One Kg of sugar packet weighs only 970 grams, where as labeled as NET WEIGHT ONE Kg.
8. When applying sandalwood (wet powder) on forehead, it leaves black scars on the skin.
9. When someone wants to commit suicide by taking poison, he will not die, as the poison is adulterated.
10. In a packet of one kilogram of black rum, one ean easily find 100 grams of black coloured pebbles.
11. A match box does not contain the labeled number of sticks.
12. Making the bottom of the bottle or tin bulged inwards, thereby eating into the quantity of the content.

Further, consumerism in India is to be seen differently from that of affluent societies of the Western countries. Some of the major problems of consumers' exploitation are given below:

1. **Pricing:** A rupee was a rupee in 1949. It rose to Rs 1.04 in 1955. But today, it is worth Re 0.10 (1949 as a base year). Pricing theory says that the price is related to quality and quantity, but in actual practice it is not so. Prices of daily convenience items such as soaps, tooth paste, washing powders etc. are fixed by the producers. Producers generally stamp the price, which is 10%–20% above the real price. This ensures a good margin to wholesalers, to whom the producers sell and create a demand from them. Shortages are created but at the same time such goods can be had from black marketers.
2. **Adulteration:** Adulterations make illegitimate profits. Businessmen aim at profit – more profit. Profit is inherent in the business. When one wishes to have undue profit, one tries to adulterate the products. For example, mixing of coconut oil with palmolein, or cheaper fats in ghee, presence of stones in grains etc. About 25–35% of the food we eat today is adulterated. Adulteration has become a commercial activity, causing so many harmful effects.
3. **Duplication:** Duplicates are available for all types of products – milk, automobile parts, blades, pens, watches, radios, medicines, clothes, and even currency notes. Duplicate medicines are prevalent in large measure from Cape to Kashmir. Persons, unfamiliar with the original products can easily be fooled by the traders. There are industries, within India, manufacturers of everything duly stamped "Made in Japan" or "Made in USA" etc.
4. **Artificial Demand:** There are situations where the shop-keepers hang the board "No Stock" in front of their shops, where stocks are in abundance. Consumers, who need such items, may pay higher price. Even in cinema houses, board may be hung in the main entrance "House Full". But black marketers offer tickets to needy cinema goers. People may not bring these to the government's notice.

5. **Sub-Standard:** There is a general tendency among the middlemen or manufacturers that reducing the quality and quantity of the products, is common after gaining good popularity for the product. Products are packed and sealed. Unless one makes an out-right purchase, goods cannot be inspected. If defective or damaged items are found in a pack, one cannot return it and the consumers have to blame themselves at their own cost. Generally, when one gets a product, no bill is made. Thus there is no proof. Even if a bill is made, print appears like "goods once sold will not be taken back". Thus the seller does not accept the defective or damaged goods. Concealed sub-standard, reduced quantity and defective items are sold in the market. The innocent people, who are unaware of these, are cheated and they suffer.
6. **Product Risk:** In the absence of adequate information to the consumers, dangers do appear. There are many harmful medicines, electrically operated kitchen appliances etc. sold to the consumers, without giving adequate information. Beauty aid cosmetics, most of them, have reactions in the long run. Mainly poorly designed kitchen ranges cause injuries- even fatal to many who handle them. Certain type of small tablet of one paise size is packed in big packet, where one hundred of such tablets can be easily packed in it.
7. **Advertising**: The main purpose of advertisement is to make product familiar among the public. But advertisement contains least information about the product. The role of advertising has been criticized in many ways – makes false claim, misrepresentation, fraud, cheating etc. The words- Super, A-1, Wonderful, magical action etc. may possess no meaning in relation to the product.
8. **Warranty and Services:** When guarantee is given against the good performance of the product, it is made ineffective through pretext. Even during the guarantee period, if the product goes inoperative, the poor consumers have been charged by making false charge on consumers' ignorance. There are many people who possess vehicles – cycles, scooter, bike, car and other products such as, radio, television, watches, tape recorders etc. and if they go under repair, the servicing mechanic or service station charges exorbitant charges, which is a punishment on the innocent consumers. There are many quacks (doctors) who make tall claims and, if approached, it is at the cost of our life. Businessmen have unlimited tactics to cheat the consumers, who are like a sheep before a lion.
9. **Fitness:** The product quality and durability along with suitability etc. may come under category of product fitness. What is claimed by the product advertiser must tally with the product. But in actual practice, it is not so. For instance, clothes having a seal of "sanforised" may shrink, battery having a label "leak proof" starts leaking, products, having a label of "unbreakable" break at use etc. For all these calamities, the possessor of the products becomes responsible instead of the producer.

Thus, consumerism is an outcome of sufferings and exploitation of consumers, who aim to secure protection from commercial terrorism, and exploitative practices, in order to safeguard the interest by establishing the rights and powers in relation to products and sellers. The former President of the USA, Mr Kennedy, defined the basic consumer rights – **"As the Right of Safety, The Right to be informed, the Right to choose and the Right to be heard".** Increased product information for the consumers has been widely prescribed as a remedy. The government of India has enacted certain laws to protect the well being of the consumers and to safeguard them. A few are described below:

CARLILL VS. CARBOLIC SMOKE BALL COMPANY

In the above case, the Carbolic Smoke Ball Company issued an advertisement in which the Company offered to pay £ 100 to any person who contracts influenza, after having used their smoke balls three times daily for two weeks, according to printed directions. It was also added that £ 1000 are deposited with the Alliance Bank showing the sincerity of the company. One Mrs. Carlill used the smoke balls according to the printed directions. But she subsequently suffered from influenza. She sued the company for the promised reward, and it was held that the company was liable to the reward.

From the above, it is to be learned that consumers themselves must be alert and active. One should not tolerate cheating and victimization. "Self help is the best help". Therefore, the consumers should take the cheaters to task.

THE PREVENTION OF FOOD ADULTERATION ACT, 1954

This is a consumer–oriented legislation designed to protect the health of the public by prohibiting adulteration of food. An adulterated food article is one which is injurious to public health. It is deemed injurious when:

The product quality is not as demanded or claimed;

It contains an injurious substance;

Any constituent of the article has been taken away;

It has been prepared, packed or kept under unsanitary conditions;

It is unfit for human consumption;

It is obtained from deceased animals;

It is poisonous or deleterious;

It contains a prohibited preservative;

Its quality or purity falls below the prescribed standards.

THE ESSENTIAL COMMODITIES ACT, 1955

It is one of the major consumer-oriented legislations of the country whose object is to control, in the interest of the general public, the production, supply and distribution of trade and commerce in certain commodities declared essential. A number of products are included under it. Whenever a company markets these products, the provisions of this act apply to it and influence its product, distribution and pricing decisions. In 1974, it was further amended with provisions against hoarders, black-marketeers and profiteers. It is made compulsory to display the prices of essential commodities.

WEIGHTS AND MEASURES ACT, 1958

This Act was enacted to safeguard the consumers against the exploitation of weighing measures of commodities by traders. Under this Act standard weights and measures are introduced and metric system of weights and measures has been introduced.

THE MONOPOLIES AND RESTRICTIVE TRADE PRACTICES ACT, 1969

This Act was enacted in order to regulate the monopolistic and restrictive trade practices followed by companies. It applies only to such undertakings, except government and public undertakings. Monopolies and Restrictive Trade Practices Commission (MRTP) has been set up to enquire into monopolistic and restrictive trade practices upon a complaint by any trade or consumer association. The main objectives, in short, are checking concentration of economic power which is detrimental to the society, checking such monopolistic and restrictive trade practices which are injurious to public well-being and welfare and vesting the powers with the Central Government to investigate and control mergers and expansions.

DRUGS AND COSMETICS ACT, 1940

Just as in food products, drugs of sub-standard quality are manufactured and marketed. The prices charged for medicines are not proportional to the cost of production. The high prices charged by the manufacturers are high enough to exploit the consumers. There is the problem of spurious drugs – manufactured by unscrupulous producers, and they are not only harmful but also dangerous to life.

PACKAGED COMMODITIES ACT, 1975

This is an important measure for consumer protection. This order provides that producers of several packaged commodities should print on the packages and contents, weights, price, month of manufacture, the date of expiry of the products, the name of manufacturer meant for retail trade so that consumer will come to know what they purchase. It has valuable provisions to consumers.

Further:

Drugs Control Act, 1950

Dangerous Drug Act, 1930

The Drugs and Magic Remedies (Objectionable Advertisement) Act 1954

Household Electrical Appliances (Quality Control) Order, 1976 and many other Acts in favour of consumers.

The Indian Contract Act, 1872

The Sale of Goods Act 1930

The Air (Prevention and Control of Pollution) Act 1981

The Bureau of Indian Standard Act 1981

The Hire Purchase Act 1972

The Specific Relief Act 1963

The Protection of Civil Rights Act 1955

The Drugs Act 1940

The Foreign Trade (Development and Regulation) Act 1992

The Indian Patents and Design Act, and so on.

The various laws provide no direct relief to the consumers as the focus is on punishment to persons violating the laws.

CONSUMER PROTECTION ACT 1986

The Government of India has passed the Consumer Protection Act in1986. This is a landmark in the history of consumer movement in India because it is applicable to the whole of India and to all goods. It is not applicable to public enterprises. It seeks to setup courts in each state with powers to punish the guilt by heavy fine and imprisonment. It seeks to set up elaborate inspectorates to implement this Act. For this purpose, active co-operation of all State Government is necessary. However, it is too early to comment whether it is successful or not. Much depends on the role of public and merchants, and on the honesty of Government officials.

One redeeming feature of the above Act is that there is a provision for penalty and imprisonment for managers of manufacturing companies. The Food Adulteration Act is applicable to merchants only. But the Consumer Protection Act applies to the manufacturing companies so that any defect or impurity of the product at the manufacturing stage can be detected and if proved, the concerned executives can be sent to jail. The middlemen like wholesalers and retailers can, thus, be excused if the product is defective or harmful at the production stage of the plant. It is important to mention that the Government of India deserves admiration and appreciation for this bold step.

Also about two years ago, the Government of India passed Environmental Act under which a separate Ministry was established to enforce regulation of pollution. It is applicable to whole of

India. In all big cities and towns, pollution has become not only a nuisance but also a dangerous thing. The public health is affected by contamination of drinking water and food and many have died. In spite of this, this problem continues to be serious even today. It is essential that the Government takes stringent measures to control pollution.

Consumerism in the wider sense includes environmentalism and also refers to the senseless waste of scarce natural resources by the private companies. The resources of the country must be conserved for long-term growth of the economy. In India, this is a very important public issue. The leading economist of USA, has strongly criticized the depletion of resources, pollution of environment etc. by irresponsible business policies and practices in USA. It is more true in India and stringent steps are extremely necessary to combat environmental pollution and degradation in all big cities and towns in India.

The consumers, particularly in India, are unorganized and relatively uninformed. On the other hand, the traders and businessmen are organized and well-informed,. Unscrupulous businessmen take this advantage and exploit the consumers in a variety of ways. Aggressive mass advertisements, deceptive sales promotion tactics, misleading publicity and campaign etc. create confusion in the minds of the consumers when they are confronted with making a choice of products.

To a certain extent, the Government is also responsible because the bureaucrats do not take adequate steps to solve the above problem. The public is unaware of their own interest and thinks that it is the job of the Government and Government thinks that it is the task of the businessmen and executives. Really speaking, it is the responsibility of both Government and businessmen. Self-regulation is better than Government regulation and this requires that businessmen practice marketing management very seriously. The professional management at the top of a business concern must have a high order of business leadership with democratic values. That means it should have the deep insight into social issues or social problems and take steps to solve them because it is the only way to avoid interference by the Government. Why the tax payers' money be wasted on regulations and the bureaucrats and thereby pave the way for 'Totalitarianism' . The top management must be seriously involved in and committed to business development within the broader perspectives of 'societal marketing concept'.

RIGHTS OF CONSUMERS

1. Right to choose:	A consumer has a right to choose the best quality products at fair price
2. Right against exploitation:	A consumer has a right against exploitation by unfair trade practices including fraudulent and misleading advertisements.
3. Right to protection	A consumer has a right to protect and enhance the quality of his life.
4. Right to Safety:	A consumer has a right to protect health and safety from the goods and services he buys.
5. Right to seek redress:	A consumer has a right for the redressal of his grievances, if any.
6. Right to be informed:	A consumer has a right to be informed of the quality, price, ingredients of the products, purity, quantity and other pertinent facts relating to the product, he purchase.
7. Right to be heard:	The right to be heard and assured that consumer interests will receive due consideration at appropriate forums.
8. Right to receive after-sale service:	A consumer has a right for services after sale and for warranties and guarantees.

The Consumer Protection Act provides for three-tier machinery for the redressal of consumer grievances at the District, State and National levels, as discussed below:

(A) DISTRICT FORUM:

The State Governments are required to establish District Forums in each District. The important features of District Forum are as under:

(*i*) Each District Forum consists of a chairman and two members appointed by the State Government. It has the powers of a Civil Court for enquiring into any complaint. i.e. summoning, and enforcing attendance of witness, examining them on oath, receiving documents, evidence etc.

(*ii*) A District Forum can receive consumer complaint where the value of goods or service and the compensation claimed is less than rupees five lakhs.

(*iii*) The complaint can be filled by a consumer to whom goods are sold or services rendered, or any recognized consumer association.

(*iv*) On receiving the complaint, the District Forum shall refer the complaint to the opposite party concerned and send the sample of goods for testing in a laboratory. The opposite party is the seller, manufacturer, or any organization against whom the complaint has been filed.

(*v*) The District Forum, after being satisfied that the goods are defective or there is some unfair trade practice, can issue an order to opposite party directing him to either remove the defect or replace the goods or return the price paid or pay compensation to the consumer for loss or injury etc.

An appeal against the order of the District Forum can be filed to the State Commission within 30 days.

(B) STATE COMMISSION:

The State Commission is set up by the State Government and its jurisdiction is restricted to the boundaries of the State concerned. The Consumer Protection Act lays down the working of the State Commission as under:

1. The State Commission shall consist of a President who either is or has been a Judge of a High Court and two other members. All the three shall be appointed by the State Government.
2. Only those complaints can be filed where the value of goods or services and compensation claimed is between rupee five lakhs and twenty lakhs. The appeals against the orders of any District Forum can also be filed before the State Commission.
3. The State Commission is required to refer the complaint to the opposite party concerned and send the sample of goods for re-testing in laboratory, if necessary.
4. The State Commission, after being satisfied that the goods were defective, can issue an order directing the opposite party to either remove the defect or replace the goods or return the price paid or pay compensation to the consumer for loss or injury etc.

Any person, who is aggrieved by the order of the State Commission, can appeal against such order to the National Commission within 30 days.

(C) NATIONAL COMMISSION:

The National Commission is set up by the Central Government. An appeal against the order of the National Commission can be filed to the Supreme Court within 30 days.

REDRESSAL OF CONSUMER GRIEVANCES

DO YOU FEEL

- As a result of an unfair trade practice adopted by any trade, you have suffered loss or damage.
- The goods purchased by you suffer from any defects.
- The services in respect of the goods purchased by you suffer from deficiency in any respect.
- A trader has charged for the goods a price in excess of the price fixed by or under any law for the time being in force or displayed on the goods or any package containing such goods.

DO YOU KNOW?

YOU HAVE A RIGHT OF REDRESSAL OF YOUR GRIEVANCES.

WHOM TO APPROACH:

- You may make complaint in writing to the following Forums set up by the State, Central Government for redressal of Consumer Grievances:

  District Forum: If the compensation claimed is less than Rs 5 lakhs.

  State Commission: If the compensation claimed is between Rs 5 lakhs and Rs 20 lakhs.

  National Commission: If the compensation claimed is more than Rs 20 lakhs.

APPEAL:

- You may prefer an appeal before the State Commission against the orders passed by the District Forum.
- You may prefer an appeal before the National Commission against the orders passed by the State Commission.

NO COURT FEE:

- You are not required to pay any court fees or engage a counsel to present your case before these forums. You may present your case YOURSELF.

Consumers may be facilitated with the following expectations:

1. Unadulterated goods
2. Correct weight and measures
3. Quality of Goods
4. Replacement provision
5. Uniform and reasonable price
6. Choice in selection
7. Service after sale, if necessary
8. Complete information of goods
9. Absence of fraud and misrepresentation
10. Availability of essential commodities

To make the movement of consumerism more effective the following steps are useful:

1. Attending the breach of guarantee or warranties by forming Legal Action Committees.
2. Conducting short-term courses for the members about their rights and also appreciation of the products.
3. Consumers must be conscious of establishing their rights.

4. More and more consumer organizations have to be opened.
5. Consumerism may be taught even from elementary school level.
6. United and organized actions by the consumers are essential.
7. Introduction of more legislation in favour of consumers' welfare.
8. Consumer service (guidance) centres should be opened.
9. Government must take initiative to safeguard the interest of the public.
10. Black marketers, hoarders, profiteers must be convicted and their names must be published in newspapers; and the government should try offenders summarily.

The consumer movement should be strengthened in our country so that the tendency to push up the prices could be curbed and the quality of services and products ensured. Among consumers under Indian condition, the literacy level is low and purchasing power is poor. But one must be aware of one's rights and should not hesitate to exercise them in right direction. To face the businessmen, who are well organized, the consumers should also create strength by organizing themselves into a strong body-cooperation. Consumer problems must be reduced by making them good buyers through education and implementing various Acts. The consumers themselves have to protect themselves through powerful consumer movement.

QUESTIONS

1. Trace the evolution of consumerism in the world.
2. Critically examine the Consumer Protection Act 1986.
3. Describe the need for consumer protection in India. *(B.Com., Uggain)*
4. Discuss the causes for growing consumerism. *(B.Com., MS)*
5. What is consumerism?
6. Comment on the need of consumer protection in a free market economy.
7. State the consumers' right against exploitation. *(B.Com., Kerala)*

CHAPTER 23

Law Relating to Sale of Goods

- *Contract of Sale*
- *Sale vs. Agreement to Sell*
- *Essentials of a Contract Sale*
- *Goods*
- *Conditions and Warranties*
- *Caveat Emptor*
- *Delivery of Goods*
- *Rules Regarding Delivery*
- *Rights of Unpaid Seller*
- *Questions*

In business or trade, exchange of goods takes place. Human beings do the business with buyers as a seller and with suppliers as a buyer. In all the dealings, a set of rules is to be observed by purchasers and sellers. Marketing involves purchases and sales of goods between sellers and buyers. In all transactions, both the parties are to be satisfied. But, in certain cases, either one or both may be disappointed over the terms of transaction. Naturally the aggrieved party seeks the assistance of the law in order to enforce the rights. The laws relating to these rights are defined and they are codified in an enactment known as the Sales of Goods Act, 1930, which came into force from 1st July, 1930. The following are the various terms given in the Act.

Contract of Sale

A contract of sale of goods is a contract whereby the seller transfers or agrees to transfer the property in goods to the buyer for a price (Sec. 4). It includes an actual sale as well as an agreement to sell. Here the agreement to sell is not a sale, but becomes a sale in future or subject to some conditions to be fulfilled at a later date.

The differences between the two are given below:

Sale	Agreement to sell
1. It is an executed contract, *i.e.*, the property in goods (ownership) passes to the buyer immediately.	1. It is an executory contract *i.e.*, the property in goods passes to the buyer at a future date.
2. If the goods are destroyed, the loss falls on the buyer, even if the goods are in the possession of the seller, because ownership has been passed on to the buyer.	2. If the goods are destroyed, the loss falls on the seller, even if the goods are in the possession of the buyer, because the ownership has not been passed on to the buyer.
3. If there is a breach of contract by the buyer, the seller can sue for the price, as the ownership lies with the buyer.	3. If there is a breach of contract, by the buyer, the seller can sue for damages and not for the price as ownership lies with the seller.
4. The seller cannot resell the goods, and even if the seller resells, the buyer does not acquire the title to goods.	4. In case of resale, the final buyer gets a proper title over the goods.
5. It gives right to the buyer to enjoy the goods–**jus in rem.**	5. It gives a right to the buyer against the seller to sue for damage–**jus in personam**

6. If the buyer becomes insolvent before he pays, the goods are to be transferred to the Official Receiver. The seller makes a rateable claim for the price, but the goods cannot be claimed (because ownership has been passed on to the buyer).	6. If the buyer becomes insolvent and if the seller has not been paid, the seller will refuse to deliver the goods unless paid for (because ownership lies with the seller.)
7. If the seller becomes insolvent, the buyer, being the owner, can recover the goods from the receiver.	7. If the seller becomes insolvent. the buyer's remedy is to claim only rateable dividend and not the goods–as property in goods has not been passed on to the buyer.

Distinction Between

Sale	Hire Purchase
1. Ownership is transferred from the seller to the buyer immediately.	1. Ownership is transferred only when a certain agreed number of instalments is paid.
2. Buyer becomes the owner.	2. The authority of the buyer becomes as that of a bailee.
3. The buyer cannot terminate the contract and is bound to pay the price.	3. Under hire purchase, the purchaser has the option to terminate the contract and he cannot be forced to pay further instalments.
4. If the buyer makes the payment in instalments, the amount is treated as payment against the principal amount.	4. The amount paid under each instalment is regarded as hire charges and not as payment against the principal amount.

The Sale of Goods Act and its knowledge is of utmost importance to the people, who deal in purchase and sale. The Act gives definitions of various terms which are commonly used in marketing. They are given below :

Essentials of a Contract Sale

1. There must be two parties–a buyer and a seller.
2. There must be some goods. Transfer of ownership of goods from seller to buyer is essential.
3. The price in money must be paid on transfer of property on sale.
4. The subject-matter of the contract of sale must be movable property and not immovable property.
5. All the essentials of a valid contract must be present in the contract of sale.

Goods

Sec. 2(7) : "Goods means every kind of movable property other than auctionable claims and money, and includes stocks and shares, growing crops, grass and things attached to or forming part of land which are agreed to be severed before sale or under the contract of sale." A debt due to a man, is an auctionable claim and cannot be sold or bought as goods. By money we mean current money and recognised currency in circulation in the country. For example, trademarks, copyrights, patent rights, goodwill, electricity, ship, water, gas etc.

1. **Existing Goods**

These are goods which are owned and possessed by the seller at the time of the contract. These goods may be:

(a) **Specific Goods :** These are the goods which are identified and agreed upon at the time of sale.

(b) **Ascertained Goods :** These, though sometimes used similar to specific goods, are the goods which become ascertained, subsequent to the determination of contract of sale.

(c) **Unascertained Goods :** These are goods which are not specifically identified, but are defined by description.

For example : A, who wants to purchase a radio, goes to the dealer, points at a particular set; He agrees to purchase. The set so agreed to be bought is a **specific set** (goods). On the other hand, if A makes a promise to buy one set, the agreement is for **unascertained goods.** The set becomes **ascertained goods** when A makes up his mind as to which one, among the sets, he intends to buy.

2. **Future Goods**

These are the goods which a seller does not possess at the time of the contract, but which will be manufactured or produced or acquired by him after making the contract of sale.

3. **Contingent Goods**

Though a type of future goods, these are the goods the acquisition of which by the seller depends upon a contingency which may or may not happen.

Conditions and Warranties

The buyer and the seller are at liberty to enter into contract on any terms they like. The agreement for sale of goods may contain many terms or stipulations relating to the quality and quantity of goods, time, place, mode of delivery, settlement of price etc. The stipulations, imposed on the seller and on the buyer, in a contract of sale made with reference to goods, which are the subject matter thereof, may be either a condition or a warranty. That is, the stipulations, on the basis of which the sales are agreed, may be described as conditions or warranties.

Condition : A condition is a stipulation which is essential to the main purpose of the contract. It goes to the root or backbone of the contract. If there is a breach of a condition, the aggrieved party can cancel the contract.

Warranty : A warranty is a stipulation which is collateral to the main purpose of the contract. It is not of such vital importance as a condition. A contract may contain various terms and promises, some of which may be important while others may not be. The distinctions between a condition and a warranty are as follows:

Condition	Warranty
1. It is a stipulation which is essential to the main purpose of the contract.	1. It is a stipulation which is collateral to the main purpose of the contract.
2. In breach of condition, the aggrieved party repudiates the contract.	2. In case of breach, the aggrieved party can claim damage only.
3. It goes to the root or backbone of the contract.	3. It does not go to the root of the contract.

Express and Implied Conditions and Warranties

Conditions and warranties may be express or implied. An express condition or warranty is one stated definitely in the contract. Implied conditions and warranties are those which are attached to the contract by operation of law. Further, the law incorporates them into the contract, unless the parties agree to the contrary. It is not necessary that all the conditions should be expressed in the contract.

For instance, in sale by description, the goods must correspond with the description; or in case of sale with sample, the bulk should correspond with the sample in quality, or the buyer should have the right to enjoy the possession of goods or the goods bought should be free from any encumbrances etc.

Caveat Emptor

Caveat emptor means ''let the buyer beware.'' The seller is supposed to reveal all necessary truths. When a man buys goods after thorough inspection and makes his own selection, and if the goods turn to be unsuitable, he cannot blame anybody except himself. But this doctrine does not apply where the consent of the buyer, in a contract of sale, is obtained by fraud or knowingly concealing the defects in the goods.

Delivery of Goods

A contract of sale always involves reciprocal promises. That is buyer has to accept the goods and pay for them. Delivery is not only the physical transfer of goods, but also the transfer of ownership by the seller. The delivery of goods may be:

1. **Actual Delivery :** Actual or physical delivery takes place where the goods are handed over by the seller to the buyer or his agent authorised to take possession of the goods.

2. **Symbolic Delivery :** Where the goods are ponderous or bulky and are incapable of actual delivery, they are accepted by means of obtaining possession; the delivery may be symbolic. For instance, handing over the key of a warehouse to the buyer is a symbolic delivery of goods.

3. **Constructive Delivery :** Constructive delivery or delivery by attornment takes place when the person in possession of the goods, acknowledges that he holds the goods on behalf of and at the disposal of the buyer. For instance, where the seller holds the goods as a bailee for the buyer, there is a constructive delivery.

Rules Regarding Delivery

1. Delivery of goods and payment of price must be strictly according to the terms of the contract. (Sec. 32).
2. Delivery should have the effect of putting the goods in the possession of the buyer or his duly authorised agent. Delivery of goods may be actual, symbolic or constructive. (Sec. 33).
3. A delivery of part of the goods in progress or the delivery of the whole, has the same effect, for the purpose of passing the property in such goods, as a delivery of the whole; but a delivery of the goods with an intention of severing it from the whole, does not operate as delivery of the remainder (Sec. 34).
4. Apart from any express contract, the seller of goods is not bound to deliver them until the buyer applies for delivery. (Sec. 35). If the goods are subsequently to be acquired by the seller, he should inform this to the buyer and the buyer should then apply.
5. The place of delivery may be stated in the contract, and where it is so stated, the goods must be delivered at the place during business hours on a working day. Where no place is mentioned, the goods are to be delivered at a place at which they happen to be at the time of the contract of sale, or if the contract is with respect to future goods at the place at which the goods are produced. [Sec. 36(1).]
6. Where the goods at the time of the sale are in the possession of a third person, there is no delivery by the seller to the buyer unless and until such a third person acknowledges to the buyer that he holds the goods on his behalf. [Sec. 36(3).]

7. The goods must be delivered as per terms of the contract. Where the contract uses words like ''directly,'' ''immediately,'' ''forth-with,'' ''without loss of time,'' it has been held that quick delivery is contemplated. Where no such time for sending the goods is fixed, the seller is bound to send them within reasonable time. [Sec. 36(2) and (4)].
8. The seller has to bear the cost of delivery unless the contract otherwise provides. All expenses of and incidental to making of delivery are borne by the seller; but all expenses of and incidental to obtaining of delivery are borne by the buyer. [Sec. 36(5)].
9. The delivery of quantity of goods contracted for should be strictly according to the terms of the contract. A buyer has the right to reject defective delivery. (Sec. 37).
10. Unless otherwise agreed, the seller is not entitled to deliver the goods by instalments. If he does so, the buyer has the right to reject the goods. (Sec. 38).

Rights of Unpaid Seller

The seller of goods has been deemed to be an unpaid seller when (1) the whole of the price has not been paid, or (2) bill of exchange or–other negotiable instrument has been received as conditional payment and has been dishonoured.

Rights of Unpaid Seller Against Goods

Where the property in the goods passed to the buyer, an unpaid seller has the following rights against the goods:

1. **Right of Lien :** Lien is a right of an unpaid seller to retain possession of the goods which are under his actual possession until he is paid or tendered the price of those goods. The unpaid seller can exercise the right of lien in the following cases:

(a) Where the goods have been sold without any stipulation as to credit;
(b) Where the goods have been sold on credit, but the term of credit has expired;
(c) Where the buyer becomes insolvent.

2. **Right to Stoppage In Transit :** While the goods are in transit, the right of stoppage can be exercised when :

(a) The seller is unpaid.
(b) The buyer becomes insolvent.
(c) The property in goods has been transferred.
(d) The goods have parted with the possession of seller.

3. **Right of Resale :** An unpaid seller has a right to resell the goods:

(a) Where goods are perishable.
(b) Where the right is expressly mentioned in the contract.
(c) Where a notice of his intention of resale is given to the buyer.

Right against the Buyer Personally

The unpaid seller of goods has the following rights against the buyer personally :

(a) Suit for price.
(b) Suit for damages for non-acceptance.
(c) Suit for interest.

QUESTIONS

1. Distinguish between sale and agreement to sell.
2. Who is an unpaid seller ?
3. Discuss the rights of an unpaid seller.
4. Define and distinguish between a condition and a warranty.

CHAPTER 24

The Promotional Programme

- *Introduction*
- *Promotional Activities*
- *Selling, Promotion and Sales Promotion*
- *The Need for Promotional Activities*
- *Importance of Promotion*
- *Objectives of Promotional Activities*
- *Communication and Promotion*
- *Elements of Communication*
- *Promotional Campaign and Promotional Decision*
- *Promotional Mix*
- *Promotional Mixes and Strategies*
- *Forms of Promotion*
- *Relative Costs*
- *Case Study-1*
- *Case Study-2*
- *Case Study-3*
- *Case Study-4*
- *Questions*

INTRODUCTION

Today's market is full of offers and discounts. Marketers use multiple promotion programmes to entice customers to buy products and services. While objectives of advertising are long terms and generally of brand building, sales promotion programmes often pursue a single goal, that is, to maximise sales in short run. The consumer promotion programmes are visible to the audience because they are often advertised in the mass media. Companies also undertake trade intermediary promotion and sales force promotion programme to increase sales. This is important because in both direct and indirect marketing programmes, sales and trade play an important role in the product and information flow process. Hence, without adequately promoting the product at trade and sale force and, many consumer promotion programmes will not achieve its desired objectives. Sales promotion programmes are short term programmes aimed at maximising sales in a period of time but what is most important to remember is that the sales promotion programme should be designed in such a way that it does not effect the overall brand image of the firm and its product. Many companies offer sales promotion programmes more frequently. Though they are able to optimize their sales in a short run period but frequent use of sales promotion leads to brand values erosion. Sales promotions are increasingly being used to accomplish an ever-expanding list of marketing objectives.

Companies pursue short terms and long-term marketing goals. In the long run, they wish to build brands, which deliver value over long period of time. In the short-term, they pursue sales market share goals. The demand for products and services is affected by various extraneous factors like seasonality of business, entry of new competitor into the business. In off seasons, sales are not healthy and there is a fall in market demand which creates excess inventory in the pipeline and companies use sales promotion schemes to promote sales during off-season period.

The definition of promotion is ''the co-ordination of all seller-initiated efforts to set up channels of information and persuasion to facilitate the sale of goods or service or the acceptance of an idea.'' The promotion refers to the activities to push forward or to advance an idea, in such a way as to gain its approval and acceptance. Promotion is telling and selling.

Brink and Kelly have defined promotion as, "the coordination of all seller initiated efforts to set up channel of information and persuation to facilitate the sale or a product service or the acceptance of an idea."

Product planning, pricing and distribution are marketing activities that are performed mainly within the company or between the company and its marketing 'partners'. Sales are the life-blood of the business. The ultimate aim of production is sale. Sales revenue is the important source of income. Sale is not self-generating activity. The stiff competition has increased the importance of sales promotion efforts on the part of the producers. Thus, sales promotion means all the steps that are taken for the purpose of obtaining or increasing sales. In the words of Hopkins ''Sales promotion is an organised effort applied to selling job to secure the greatest effectiveness for advertising and for dealers 'help.' Sales promotion, as a tool of marketing promotion, gives rise to increase in product usage as well as expansion of a product or introduction of a new product. Promotion means ''any marketing effort whose function is to inform or persuade actual or potential consumers about the merits of a given product or service for the purpose of introducing a consumer either to continue or to start purchasing the firm's product or service at same (given) price.''

Promotion is the fourth major component of company's total marketing mix (along with product planning, pricing and distribution). Its intent is to inform, persuade and influence people. Promotional activity in marketing is basically an exercise in communication. It is a basic ingredient in non-price competition and it is an essential element in modern marketing. It is an exercise in information, persuation and influence. Communication is necessary in exchange activities. For instance, we have the best products with good package, fair price etc. The products cannot be sold to consumers unless buyers know it. People must know that the right products are available at the right place and at the right price. This is the job of promotion in marketing. Promotion is a spark plug in marketing mix. It can be defined as ''the coordinated, self-initiated efforts to establish channels of information and persuation to facilitate or foster the sale of goods or services, or the acceptance of ideas or point of view.

Thus, promotion refers to activities and processes designed to change or reinforce behaviour and/or ideas of the consumers, through communication, so that they are persuaded to buy what they might not otherwise buy, and what they don't really want to buy. Promotion is "*telling*" and "*selling*". It is an exercise in information, persuation and influence. These three are inter-related in the sense that to "inform is to persuade;" and if "a person is persuaded he is informed".

Promotional Activities

In the present era, selling is a complicated task. There may be stiff competition. There may be many substitute products. Products have become more consumer-oriented. Consumers have become more sophisticated. For instance, they possess the best products at a fair price. The products are of a better quality than the substitute produce for sale. But sales are not automatic. The prior idea of the production is for the sales. How will the buyers get the products, when they have not heard of our products? Therefore, people must have knowledge of the existence of the product and its availability. This is possible only through a good propaganda. There arises a need for proper flow of information along with products from producer to consumer. Thus promotion is the process of marketing communication aimed to inform, persuade and influence people.

The statement ''Nothing happens until somebody sells something'' gives in a nutshell the place of promotional activities in today's business. The promotional activities must aim:

(a) To inform prospective buyers about the existence of a product and its want-satisfying capabilities.

(b) To remind the users of past and present to its various roles on consumption.

(c) To persuade the prospective buyers in a most effective manner.

Selling, Promotion and Sales Promotion

Selling and promotion are propagated synonymously. Selling is a narrow term and refers to the transfer of title from the seller to the buyer. It does not include advertising and other demand creating methods. But promotion is a broader term; it includes advertising, personal selling, sales promotion and other selling tools. Promotion and sales promotion are different terms. Sale promotions are only a part of promotion. Promotion covers all other marketing activities more efficiently and effectively. Sales promotion helps the selling activity only. To attract customers, awaken their demand and stimulate them to act in the desired manner are the main purposes of promotion. Sales promotion acts as a bridge between advertising and personal selling to co-ordinate efforts in these two areas. The main tasks of promotional activities are to establish and maintain communications with large market segments. Promotion is essential in modern marketing and is in the form of non-price competition.

Promotion is a very wide term including advertising, personal selling, sales promotion and other promotional tools that can be devised to reach the goals of the sales programme. On the other hand, *sales promotion* is only a part of it. "*Sales promotion*" has been defined as "activities, other than personal selling, advertising and publicity, that stimulate consumer purchasing and dealer effectiveness, such as displays, shows and expositions, demonstrations etc."

The Need for Promotional Activities

Promotion is the final element in the marketing mix. The manufacturer has to take effective steps in meeting the consumer in the market after taking the decision relating to the nature of products, its price and its distribution. The present age is of consumer-oriented markets and therefore, it is the responsibility of manufacturer to know what is required by the buyers. Even the most useful and want-satisfying product will be a marketing failure if no one knows it is available. Thus it becomes essential, rather a duty, of the manufacturers to make the customers know from where, how, when and at what price the product would be available. As the distance between producers and consumers increases and as the number of potential consumers grow, promotional activities are necessary. More and more promotional activities are required to induce the consumers to purchase more and more products and thus demand for the product is created. A basic purpose of promotion is to let potential customers know about the products.

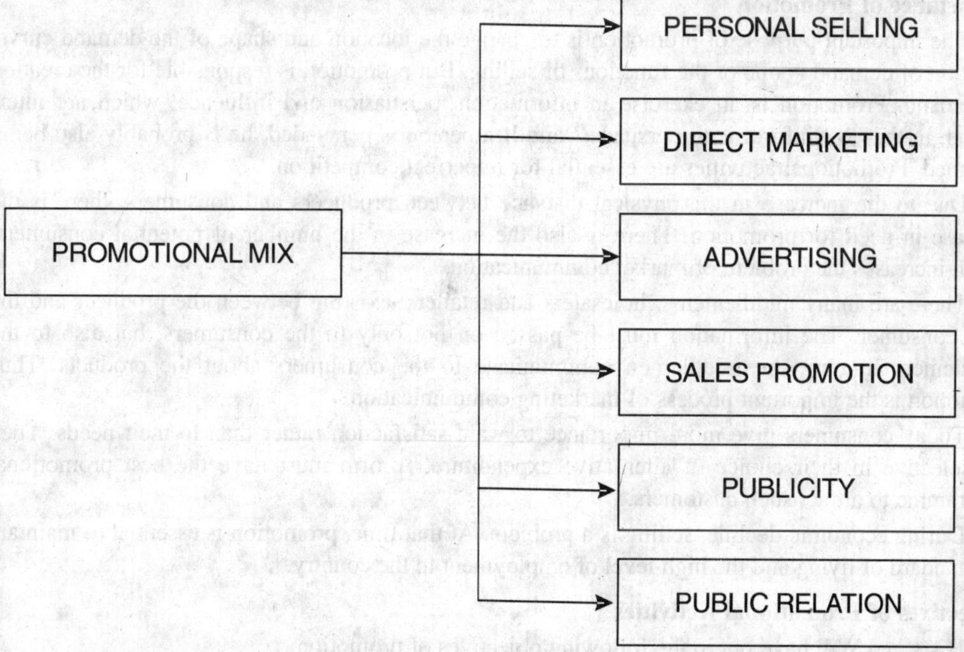

Secondly, there is stiff competition among the manufacturers. Therefore, promotional activities are necessitated. When a producer increases his promotional activities, others also follow the same and this leads to promotion war.

Thirdly, large scale production can be achieved only with methods of large scale selling, which is possible only through the promotional activities.

Fourthly, when there is an imperfect market condition, product cannot easily be sold on the basis of product-differentiation. In such a situation, only the promotion activities draw the attention of consumers. The customers are attracted to buy the products on the basis of promotional activities.

Main Purpose of Promotion

The overall purpose of promotion, as said in the above para, is (a) *to communicate*; (b) *to convince* and (c) *to compete*. Communication is the basis of marketing, it is not enough merely to communicate, but communication should be convincing enough to supplement and provide adequate advantages as compared to competitors' product. The favourable change in the pattern of consumer demand is secured through commercial information, persuation and influence with the help of personal selling, advertising, publicity and sales promotion devices.

Four Major Promotion Tools:

* *Advertising* : Any paid form of non-personal presentation and promotion of ideas, goods, or services by an identified sponsor.
* *Personal Selling* : Oral presentation in a conversation with one or more prospective purchasers for the purpose of making sales.
* *Sales Promotion* : Short-term incentives to encourage the purchase or sale of a product or service.
* *Public Relations* : Building good relations with the company's various clients by obtaining favourable response building up a ''corporate image'' and handling or heading off unfavourable rumours, stories and events.

Importance of Promotion

The important purpose of promotion is to change the location and shape of the demand curve. Creation of demand is one of the functions of selling. But promotion is responsible for the creation of demand. Promotion is an exercise in information, persuasion and influence, which are interrelated, in that to ''inform is to persuade'' and if a person is persuaded, he is probably also being informed. Promotional activities are essential for imperfect competition.

Due to the increase in the physical distance between producers and consumers, there is the increase in need for promotion. There is also the increase in the number of potential consumers, which increases the problem of market communication.

There are many middlemen–wholesalers and retailers–existing between the producer and the final consumer. The information must be passed on not only to the consumers, but also to the middlemen. In turn, the middlemen communicate to the consumers about the products. Thus promotion is the important process of marketing communication.

Today consumers give more importance to want-satisfaction rather than to their needs. They are selective in their choice of alternative expenditure. A firm must have the best promotional programme to attract such customers.

During economic decline, selling is a problem. At that time, promotion is essential to maintain the standard of living and the high level of employment in the country.

Objectives of Promotional Activities

Histy and Will have put in the following objectives of promotion:

Demand Objectives : The idea of promotion is to influence, stimulate, maintain and create demand for a product. Promotion is responsible for demand creation. To create demand for products, a number of promotional activities must be taken. These activities can be employed to maintain the demand and to capture demand from competitors. They are alternative instruments for meeting competition and for the creation and maintenance of consumer demand.

Communication Objective : It aims at creating awareness. It provides information to consumers and retailers about product features, where the products can be obtained and what the products are capable of doing or achieving brand preferences.

Specific Objectives : (Performance Objectives). It gives specific information about a product, and influences the consumer's decision of purchasing.

Communication and Promotion

In marketing system, promotional activities are exercised through communication. If the executives know the benefits of communication, they can manage the promotional programme in a better way.

The word "Communication" is derived from the Latin word "Communis" which means 'common'. When, we communicate, we are trying to establish a commonness with someone. The fundamental four elements of communication process are 1. a message 2. a source of this message 3. a communication channel and 4. a receiver. The sender sends the message and the receiver receives the message. True communication takes place only when the two parties mean the same thing or have in common the same message.

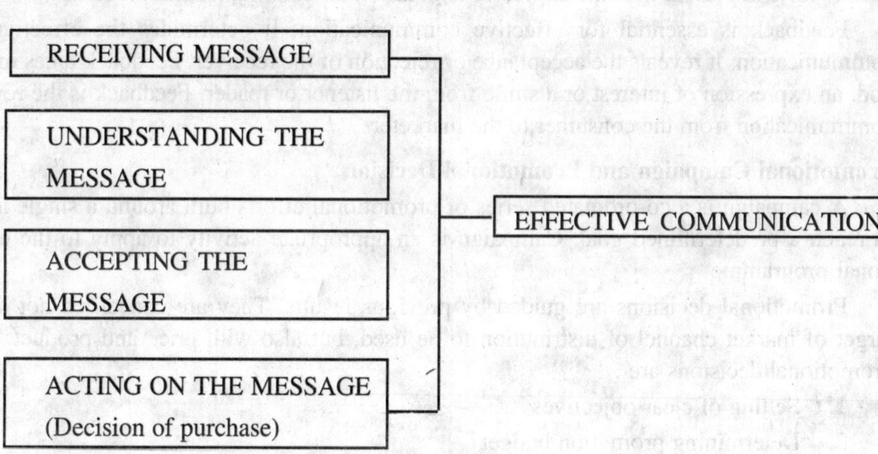

Elements of Communication

(The process of communication has two divisions, explicit and implicit. Explicit communication means the use of language that is verbal. Implicit communication is in the nature of non-verbal communication, *i.e.*, understanding a message through symbols).

Elements of Communication

The three elements or stages of a communication process are a message, a source and a receiver. But to be more elaborate, the communication process is of five stages.

At the first stage the source originates the communication. The person is a sender of the message. For example, the marketing executive communicates the ideas or information to his subordinates.

The second stage is encoding–the idea to be communicated is converted into a message form *i.e.*, the idea is translated in a language (explicit) or medium of expression (implicit) suitable for transmission.

In the third stage, the message carrying the idea flows or moves from the source towards the receiver by print media or sound wave.

In the fourth stage decoding takes place *i.e.*, the message is interpreted.

In the fifth stage the receiver receives the decoded messages and acts as per the message received. It is the largest of the communication. This is shown in the chart.

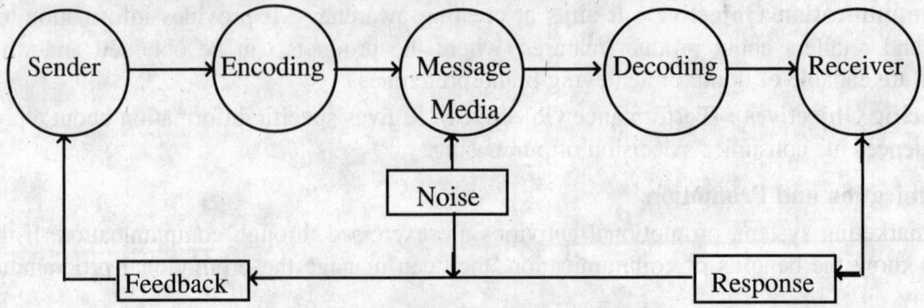

Elements in the Communication Process

The other elements affecting communication process are noise and feedback. Noise consists of extraneous interferences with communication. It creates many obstacles in reducing effectiveness of the communication process. It can be actual noise, such as thundering or other kinds of interferences. Any sort of disturbance affecting the receiver's attention while receiving the message is noise. Noise is present in some degree or another, in all communication processes.

Feedback is essential for effective communication. It determines the effectiveness of the communication. It reveals the acceptance or rejection of the receiver. Feedback takes many forms–a nod, an expression of interest or a smile from the listener or reader. Feedback is the reverse flow of communication from the consumer to the marketer.

Promotional Campaign and Promotional Decision

A campaign is a co-ordinated series of promotional efforts built around a single idea designed to reach a predetermined goal. Campaign is an appropriate activity to apply to the entire promotional programme.

Promotional decisions are guided by previous results. They are concerned not only with the target of market channel of distribution to be used, but also with price and product. The steps of promotional decisions are :

1. Setting of clear objectives
2. Determining promotion budget
3. Knowing about the market
4. Appealing to its nature and timing
5. Patterning the promotion mix

Promotion Mix

The purpose of promotion is to reach the desired consumers and persuade them to act. A company may have a well-designed product offering, with a price and distribution system appropriate to its target market. But if it is unable to reach that market, then all its efforts will have been in vain. Promotion is responsible for awakening and stimulating consumer demand for the product. Promotion, in its broadest marketing sense, encompasses all selling activities–advertising, personal selling, sales promotion and public relations. The particular way an individual marketer combines these activities is called promotion mix. To many customers, promotion and selling are synonymous with marketing. Promotion certainly represents a very large part of the marketing efforts of most firms, but it is, of course, only one part of marketing mix. Promotion is not limited to business activity, but is also used by a variety of non-profit organisations. Of the four elements of marketing mix, promotion is the one used to the greatest degree by non-profit organisations. For instance, colleges use promotion to get students join, political candidates holding meetings (promotion) aim at winning votes, the government uses promotional technique for popularising family planning programmes etc. Thus promotion is heavily relied upon by non-business organisations too.

Promotion activity ultimately comes under the direction of the marketing manager. In many large firms, however, each method of promotion mix operates independently. The marketing manager has the responsibility of coordinating and inter-relating all the methods to achieve the marketing objectives. Within the marketing frame-work, advertising, personal selling and sales promotion are termed as promotional mix. (For details refer chapter 25, 26 and 27).

There are two types of promotion blends : (1) Push Blend and (2) Pull Blend. They are closely related to the channel of distribution.

A push promotional blend emphasises personal selling. The producer pushes the product to intermediaries, who organise promotion to reach consumers and sell the product. Firms develop strong sales forces at both the distributor and dealer level. Products are pushed through the channel of distribution and dealer.

On the other hand, a pull promotional blend emphasises on impersonal selling. Here it is the producer who organises advertising and sales-promotion campaign. Pull strategies have proved to be very effective for difficult distribution cases. A firm adopting this strategy would spend more on advertising and sales promotion.

The distinction between the two is shown below:

PUSH versus PULL STRATEGY

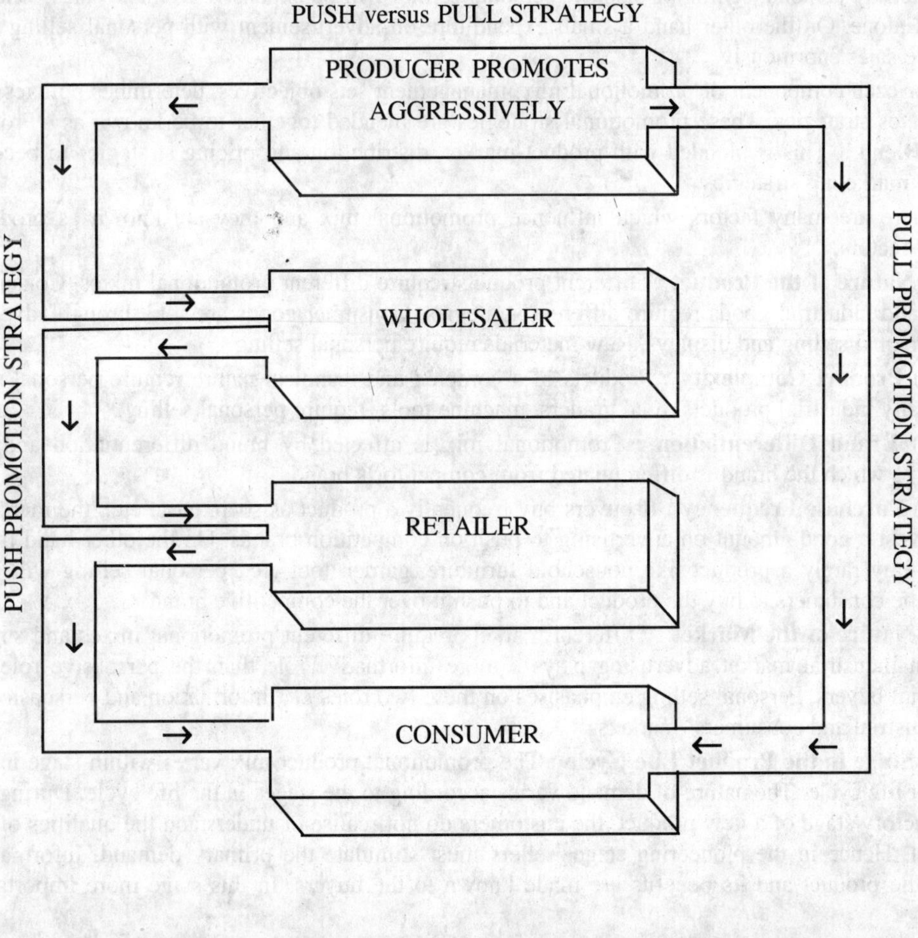

A PUSH STRATEGY calls for using the sales force and trade promotion to push the product through the channels. The producer aggressively promotes the product to wholesalers; wholesalers aggressively promote the product to retailers and the retailers aggressively promote the product to consumers.

A PULL STRATEGY calls for spending a lot of money on advertising and consumer-promotion to build up consumer-demand. If the strategy is effective; consumers will ask their retailers for the product, the retailers will ask their wholesalers for the product and the wholesalers will ask the producers for the product.

Promotion may be informative, persuasive or reminiscent (reminder). Informative promotion is needed when a firm has distinctly new products for sale. For instance, when a firm that manufactures radio sets decides to produce television sets also, this fact must be known to the buyers *i.e.,* informative promotion. Persuasive promotion is needed when a firm has a product, which is similar to other products. Consumers are persuaded to purchase a particular product, which is better than others *i.e.,* persuasive promotion. Reminiscent promotion is used after the products are well established in the market. Customers are frequently reminded of the product by the brand name, which is made a household name by repetitive advertisement.

Promotional Mixes and Strategies

Marketing professionals use the term promotional mix to refer to the combination of personal selling, advertising, sales promotion and other forms of promotion. It becomes the promotional strategy. A combination of at least of two methods is essential for the promotion. Advertising is supported by personal selling or display. Personal selling will be expensive to make sales, when it is used alone. On the other hand a small expenditure on advertisement with personal selling will increase sales enormously.

For each component of promotional mix, management sets objectives, determines policies and formulates strategies. These promotional strategies are blended together to be known as ''Promotional Blend.'' This is blended with product-market, distribution and pricing strategies to become overall marketing strategies.

There are many factors which influence promotional mix and they are known as product-market factors.

1. **Nature of the Product :** Different products require different promotional mixes. Consumer goods and industrial goods require different strategies. Consumer goods are sold through advertising, personal selling and displays. Raw materials require personal selling.

(a) **Product Complexity :** Products of a complex and technical nature require personal selling. Many industrial products–road graders, machine tools–require personal selling.

(b) **Brand Differentiation :** Promotional mix is affected by brand differentiation and the degree to which the brand is differentiated from competitor's brand.

(c) **Purchase Frequency :** If buyers buy frequently a product as soap, paste etc., the marketer will invest a good amount on advertising to push on competition brands. On the other hand if the buyers buy rarely a product like household furniture, garden tool etc., personal selling will persuade the consumers to buy the product and to push it over the competitive brand.

2. **Nature of the Market :** Different markets require different promotional mixes and strategies. In industrial market advertising plays a more informative role than the persuasive role for industrial buyers. Personal selling emphasises on these two roles *i.e.*, information and persuasion in the industrial and consumers' markets.

3. **Stage in the Product Life Cycle :** The promotional product mix varies within stage in the product life cycle. The nature of demand varies according to the stages in the life cycle. During the introductory stage of a new product, the customers do not realise or understand the qualities of the product. Hence in the pioneering stage, sellers must stimulate the primary demand. Information about the product and its benefits are made known to the buyers. In this stage more importance

must be given to personal selling and trade shows. In the growth stage, customers know the qualities of the product. Hence to stimulate selective demand, advertising must be increased. In the maturity stage advertising is used as a tool of persuasion. In the decline stage, sales and profits decline and hence all the promotional activities should be cut down.

4. **Market Penetration :** *i.e.*, the product is already well known to the buyers. In that situation a sustaining promotional strategy is suitable. The retailers and middlemen try to stock the products. They try to become 'best sellers.'

A brand has insignificant market penetration *i.e.*, it has a small market or struggling market. In that condition, a developmental promotional strategy is suitable. Personal selling or push strategy or advertising or a full strategy is required.

5. **Market Size and Location :** Product market size and location influence the promotional mix. In narrow markets where the number of potential buyers is small, direct mail is used. In a broad market, advertising is used.

The location of market is in the urban and rural areas. In urban markets where buyers are many, advertising can be used. In rural markets where buyers are few, personal selling can be used.

6. **Characteristics of Buyers :** The characteristics of prospective buyers strongly influence the promotional mix. Experienced professional buyers such as industrial purchasing agents need personal selling. Inexperienced buyers like housewife, need advertising. Some buyers give importance to time, some to the purchase of products; some buyers act according to the influence of friends, relatives etc. Promotional mix and strategy are affected by these.

7. **Distribution Strategy :** Companies fighting more through distribution for establishing their brand, invest more money on personal selling and advertising. Companies which have already established their brand in the market have to invest only a small amount in personal selling and advertising.

If the product is sold directly to the consumers, the method to be adopted is personal selling. If the product passes through a longer channel of distribution, the marketer gives more importance to advertising and less importance to personal selling. For consumer products, sold through channels, advertisement to final buyers is essential. Effective promotional packaging and display are also essential.

8. **Pricing strategy :** Pricing strategy influences the promotional mix strategy. If the brand is priced higher than the competition, more personal selling is needed to get a middleman to stock and push the brand. If the brand is priced lower, little promotion is needed. If the marketer allows middlemen mark ups on the brand to be lower than on competitive brands, heavy advertisement is needed 'to force' them to handle the company's brand. There is considerable need for personal selling to retain its present customers and secure new customers.

FORMS OF PROMOTION

Personal selling and advertising are the two best known forms of promotion. In terms of cost and market impact, it is the most important form. Personal selling is an important part of promotional programme. It is commonly supported by advertising. The other forms of promotion are sales promotion, publicity and public relation. These are explained in detail in the following chapters. It is important for the successful promotional programme. The other methods of promotion are point of purchase display, packaging and direct mail.

1. **Personal selling :** It is the most important, the most effective and the most costly form of promotion. It is the best means of oral or face-to-face or direct communication. Personal presentation has the prospect of effecting sales. Its effect is to push the product through the distribution channel.

2. **Advertising :** It is an impersonal method of communication as well as an impersonal salesmanship for mass selling and it is a means of mass communication. Advertising is also an important form of promotion and it costs less than personal selling.

3. **Sales Promotion :** The marketing activities other than advertising, publicity and personal selling are known as sales promotion. It serves as a bridge between personal selling and advertising. It is an aggressive method of a selling.

4. **Publicity :** It is a non-personal stimulation of demand as advertising. It stimulates demand for a product or service or a business unit by making publicity in radio, television or stage.

5. **Public Relation :** It is a form of promotion. It creates, develops and maintains a bright image of an organisation on the public. Thus the goodwill of the seller increases and leads to good selling and promotes the sale of goods. Under competition and consumer-oriented marketing it is very effective.

6. **Point of Purchase display :** It is the silent salesman that attracts the buyers' attention to the product and makes them decide to buy. Promotion at the point of purchase is more effective. Proper display of products is done by manufacturers or distributors. It varies widely. Automobile show-room with promotional literature and pricing information helps the buyers to test the products. Display serves to examine the product and make buying decision. With the combination of personal selling and advertising, display gives the maximum effectiveness.

7. **Packaging :** It differentiates and protects a product. It plays two critical promotional roles. First it calls the attention of the customer to the product in retail stores. Secondly it carries the selling messages and other information to make buying decision as is explained in an earlier chapter. Package provides product protection, ease of handling, selling ability, convenience and information. It attracts the customers. It serves the same purpose as printed advertising.

8. **Direct Mail :** Newspaper advertisement reaches lakhs of people, while direct mail is sent to the selective customers. It will attract the customers to buy the goods. It is more effective than advertisement, because it gives information directly. It is a supplement to other forms of promotion. It helps the product awareness or acceptance. It increases purchase probabilities, when buyers are contacted directly or when they see displays.

9. **Other Forms of Promotion :** Sampling is one form of special promotion. Sampling of new food products, and other consumer products, especially sample medicines to doctors are to introduce the new products to the consumers.

Couponing is yet another form of promotion. Coupon offers a price reduction to stimulate purchase of new products. It is inserted as "Tear outs" in magazines or newspapers.

Trading stamp is a powerful incentive to develop strong customer store or brand preferences.

Special premiums are also offered for the same reasons. Though these special forms of promotion are not so important, they play key role in the overall marketing strategies of companies.

Relative Costs of Different Forms of Promotion

The methods of promotion vary considerably according to the cost for messages delivered. If there is less availability of fund, low cost promotional input is used. More combination of promotion mix may prove more productivity. The decision is taken according to the availability of fund. Cost is given importance. A better approach will decide what promotional goals are to be achieved; and then the cost to be involved can be figured out.

QUESTIONS

1. Define promotion. What is meant by the concept of the promotion blend ?
2. Explain the process of communication in marketing.
3. What are the objectives of promotion ? What are the basic types of promotion strategy ?
4. What do you mean by demand creation ? To what extent can elements of promotion act as methods of demand creation ?
5. What is promotional mix ?
6. Name and describe three important objectives of promotion, with respect to demand stimulation.

7. What do you mean by informing, reminding and persuading ?
8. Examine the various discounts and allowances offered to traders or buyers to promote sales. (*B.Com., Madras*)
9. What are the factors governing basic promotional strategy ? (*M.Com., Madurai*)
10. Discuss various forms of promotional activities. (*B.Com., Madurai*)
11. Define the concept of promotion-mix. What are its elements ? What are the determinants of promotion-mix ? (*B.Com., Madurai*)

Case Study-1

Dealership Problems

SWITCHEX GEARS LTD.

SWITCHEX is an eight-year old organisation manufacturing entire range of switchgear products. It has a foreign collaborator. Its manufacturing unit is located near Delhi with sales spread over the entire country. The market of switchgears is dominated by two major companies having market shares of 40% and 37% respectively. SWITCHEX has established a market share of 14% and remaining 9% market share is divided among three other manufacturers. The competition between the first three organisations is quite fierce. During the initial years, SWITCHEX concentrated in the Northern region and established itself as a reputed manufacturer of switchgears. Since the last two years, the company is trying to establish its presence in the Western region.

The pricing strategy of the company is always to be lower than the major two competitors by about 8-10%. Its discounting policy is also flexible and sometimes it deals directly with the customers and offers them suitable discounts.

It has appointed dealers in all its markets, usually district-based. For servicing its dealers in the Western region. SWITCHEX has opened up a Regional Office at Mumbai and Branch Offices at Pune, Vadodra and Indore.

Its Pune office is headed by Mr. Patil, a competent Electronics Engineer with a Post-graduation in Management. Since the company wants to establish in the Western region. Mr. Patil is pressurised to (accept) higher quotas. In turn, he has no option but to increase the quotas of his dealers. These days, Mr. Patil is faced with a tough decision. His dealer at Kolhapur is the major cause for concern. The dealer is a partnership firm, M/s. Kadam Brothers. This dealer is with Mr. Patil for the past two years. Except for the last six months, the performance of this dealer was highly satisfactory. However, six months back one of the partners decided to leave the partnership firm and had to be paid his share in cash causing financial problems for the firm. Mr. Patil believes that this is one of the reasons for the untimely payments to SWITCHEX for the sales. Moreover, the sales have also suffered. It is reported that the remaining two partners are also concentrating on their other business activities and consequently have less time for developing the business of SWITCHEX. Those partners have been assuring Mr. Patil that they will soon have another competent partner and, thus, will come out of their problems quickly. But no progress is reported in the matter till now.

In the meantime, another dealer from the same area has approached Mr. Patil for dealership. His is dealing with the electric panels till now and has good contacts with the switchgear buyers from Kolhapur region. But Mr. Patil feels that given the time, M/s. Kadam Brothers will recover and because of their experience and reputation as well as contacts, the firm will serve SWITCHEX satisfactorily. But he has no time as the Regional Sales manager is pressuring Mr. Patil to increase quotas of his dealers fast or get them replaced. "We want quick sales" is the motto of the Regional Sales Manager.

QUESTIONS

1. What alternatives should you suggest for Mr. Patil to solve dealership and sales problem?
2. What alternative should be opt? Why?
3. Examine SWITCHEX's policy of quick sales, in the context of its product range.

(Pune, M.B.A.)

Case Study-2

The Dilemma of A Sales Manager

RALLISON PHARMACEUTICALS LTD.

Rallison Pharmaceuticals Ltd. though Public Ltd. Co. is the one run by family of entrepreneurs with closely held shares. All along it had been concentrating on making bulk supplies to the Government. However, in 1990 the Company embarked on a scheme of scientific marketing with a slender field force. The sales force was created by recruiting from experienced persons from departments like distribution, packing etc., who were thought to have "selling expertise." One such person, Dr. Ganguly, produced good results and was promoted to the post of District Manager and was given the responsibility of two states.

In 1991, the company, utilising its vast manufacturing infrastructure and experience, launched an entirely different range of products. To promote this new range, separate fieldforce was created by recruiting new personnel. Meanwhile, the Sales Department underwent an upheaval and the old sales force had to quit.

Mr. A.P. Sharma, the new Chief Sales Manager, young but credited with considerable experience, studied the existing organisational structure and its personnel and exposed the fraudulent activities of the Regional Manager, Divisional Sales Manager and a couple of District Managers of the new product division and, as a result, made them quit. He felt that for the present sales operation, the posts of Regional Sales Manager and Divisional Sales Manager were superfluous and abolished them. He then filled the District Manager's vacancies with persons whom he carefully selected with the help of the Personnel Director.

Everything was running smoothly till Dr. Ganguly, the erstwhile Packing Supervisor made-representative, was made District Manager of the old product division, picked up some problem with one of his representatives, Dr. Taneja, and wanted him to be removed. However, Mr. A.P. Sharma felt that Dr. Taneja was an excellent "selling material" and transferred him to the new product division. Mr. Taneja worked with great enthusiasm in the new division and proved a great success.

Under the new Chief Sales Manager, both the old and new product divisions made rapid strides. Dr. Ganguly made an excellent contribution through his team. In 1993, when the Management planned an expansion of the old product fieldforce, Dr. Ganguly was promoted as the Divisional Manager, considering his contribution, contacts, seniority and sense of honesty and integrity with a view to motivate him for better results.

While looking for suitable candidates to be promoted as District Manager to work under Dr. Ganguly, the Sales Manager thought that Mr. Taneja and shown sufficient maturity and had a good track record to deserve a promotion. When Mr. Sharma proposed Mr. Taneja's name, Dr. Ganguly opposed it owing to his past enmity and prejudice against Mr. Taneja. Mr. Sharma felt that with his abilities and performance and his exposure to the old product division. Mr. Taneja was the ideal choice, but was doubtful as to whether to overlook Mr. Ganguly's opposition and promote Mr. Taneja or not.

Meanwhile, Dr. Ganguly proposed the name of another successful representative for the District Manager's post. In Mr. Sharma's opinion the person recommended by Dr. Ganguly, though successful, was timid and did not have the ability to become a Manager.

QUESTIONS

1. Should the Chief Sales Manager promote Mr. Taneja, notwithstanding the Divisional Manager's objection to such a move?
2. If Mr. Taneja is not elevated to the position of District Manager, what is the next best course of action for the Chief Sales Manager to take? *(MBA Pune)*

Case Study-3

Marketing Plan

CUSTOMER COMFORTS LTD.

'A glorious morning!' muttered Ms. Shakti Rohilla to herself as she arranged her agenda for the day. Ms. Rohilla was the newly appointed marketing manager of Customer Comforts Limited (CCL) — a Rs. 20 crore company in Bombay. First on her engagements for the day, she had a meeting with her Director (Marketing) early in the morning. This meeting was to evaluate the initial thoughts of Ms. Rohilla on how to plan marketing efforts for 'water-beds'—a major product developed recently by CCL.

Customer Comforts Limited (CCL) was set up about a quarter of century ago in New Delhi by Harjinder Singh to create and market a variety of inflatable products. The organisation manufactured rafts, boats, life-jackets and collapsible containers for bulk storage purpose. It had acquired both quality image and customer satisfaction. Over the years, the only change that Mr. Singh had allowed in company philosophy, was to innovate and add more vigorously to the consumer products in the inflatable category to meet new customer desires.

Water-bed was a major offer in the series by CCL in the middle of 1991 to the Indian markets. The product had already been accepted, to a large extent, abroad and it was hoped that Indian consumers too will accept it. It may be noted that water-beds are made of PVC with mattresses full of water. This water needs to be changed once in six months. In winter, if customers desired, the water could be heated to a required temperature.

Among the major benefits of water-beds over the conventional beds and mattresses whether made of jutes, cotton, or foam, was that a water-bed applied equal pressure on every point in the body. This ensured its users a healthy and comfortable night's sleep. Ms. Rohilla believed that this benefit will be its chief attraction and needed to be communicated.

Further, the PVC used in making water-beds was of high quality. They are sturdy enough as the in-house research and limited field experiments proved to withstand children romping on them. One could even stub a cigarette without springing a leak. Ms. Rohilla knew that this would be a major hurdle to cross as it would take some communication to convince customers. However, she felt confident that the benefit would reach customers.

Ms. Rohilla was to design a comprehensive market plan for the water-bed,. Before it, however, she consulted her Director (marketing) with her initial thoughts. The Director seemed to agree but asked her to marshal them in writing and discuss the same again that afternoon.

As she began, as if on cue, her study room clock chimed. "Oh, nine-thirty! time to get ready for the office," said Ms. Rohilla and spurted out of her study.

QUESTIONS

1. Critically examine the opportunity as seen by the CCL ?
2. Suggest a suitable plan for marketing water-beds. *(AIMA)*

CHAPTER 25

Sales Promotion

- *Introduction*
- *Definition of Sales Promotion*
- *Purpose of Sales Promotion*
- *Importance*
- *Objectives*
- *Reasons for Growth*
- *Advantages*
- *Effectiveness of Sales Promotion*
- *Limitations*
- *Kinds*
- *Consumer Sales Promotion*
- *Dealer Sales Promotion*
- *Sales Force Sales Promotion*
- *Promotion Planning*
- *Case Study-1*
- *Questions*

Introduction

The word promotion, originates from the Latin word 'Promovere.' The meaning is ''to move forward'' or to push forward or to advance an idea. The aim of production is sales. Sales and promotion are two different words and Sales Promotion is the combination of these two words. Sales promotion increases the sales. Sales promotion methods aim to capture the market and increase the sales volume. It is an important instrument in marketing to lubricate the marketing efforts. Now-a-days sales promotion is a necessary tool to boost sales. Sales promotion becomes a fashion and luxury. In the broader sense it is not an expenditure; it is an investment, as it pays rich returns. It aims in creating demand. It is right to say that sales promotion moves the product. A manufacturer must make the customers to know the product and he must influence them to buy that product.

Sales promotion is one among the three pillars of promotional mix. The other two pillars are personal selling and advertising. Sales promotion is the connecting link between personal selling and advertising. Sales promotion is an important and specialised function of marketing.

Promotion is the final element in the marketing mix. After the nature of the product is decided, its price fixed and the methods of distribution adopted, the producer has to take effective steps in meeting the consumers in the market. In consumer-oriented markets, the producer must know what is required by the consumers and to make the consumers know from where, when, how and at what price, the products would be available. The most widely used methods of promotion are personal selling and advertising. Sales promotion is designed to supplement and co-ordinate personal selling and advertisement efforts.

Definition

According to the American Marketing Association, sales promotion is ''those marketing activities other than personal selling, advertising, and publicity, that stimulate consumer purchasing and dealer effectiveness such as display shows, expositions, demonstrations and various non-recurrent selling efforts not in the ordinary routine''.

According to George W. Hopkins, ''Sales Promotion is an organised effort applied to the selling job to secure the greatest effectiveness for advertising and for dealer's help.''

According to John F. Luick and Willian L. Ziegler, "Sales promotion is an activity and/or material that acts as a direct inducement offering added value or incentive for the product, to resellers, sales persons or consumers.'' It can be said that ''sales promotion is any action or decision that will promote or help to promote sales. It may further be said that the efforts of the selling force itself are part of sales promotion.''

"Sales promotions may be defined as all the marketing and promotion activities, other than advertising, personal selling and publicity that motivate and encourage the consumer to purchase by means of such inducements as premiums, advertising specialities, stamps, refunds, rebates, exhibits, displays and demonstrations. It is employed as well, to motivate retailers, wholesalers; the manufacturer's sales forces to sell through the use of such incentive as awards or prizes (merchandise, cash and travel), direct payments and allowances, co-operative advertising and trade show. It offers a direct inducement to act by providing extra worth over and above what is built into the product as its normal price. These temporary inducements are offered usually at a time and place, the buying decision is made."

— *Stanley*

The major function of sales promotion is to serve as a connecting link or a bridge between advertising and personal selling which are the two wings of promotion. Through effective advertisement work, sales promotion helps salesmen to boost up selling. Producers can introduce new products by sales promotion. It reminds the consumers about the product through advertisement. Sales promotion can promote the product sales. It stimulates them to buy the product. All the buyers must be attracted, urged and even persuaded to buy the products.

Purpose of Sales Promotion

Customers are more selective in their buying choices and a good promotional programme is needed to reach them. The main purpose of sales promotion is to boost sales of a product by creating demand, that is, both consumer demand as well as trade demand. It improves the performance of middlemen and acts as a supplement to advertising and personal selling. It helps in achieving the following purposes:

(1) The basic purpose of promotion is to disseminate information to the potential customers.

(2) Sellers use incentive-type promotions to attract new customers, to reward loyal customers and to increase the repurchase rates of occasional users.

(3) To encourage the customers to try to a new product. An interesting example: the Brooke Bond Tea of India used to distribute free tea to every household during 1930's, in order to promote tea drinking habits among the people of Chennai.

(4) Sales promotions yield faster responses in sales than advertising.

(5) Sales promotion is considered as a speical selling effort to accelerate sales.

(6) Brand switchers are primarily looking for low price, good value and premiums. Sales promotions are likely to turn them into loyal brand users.

(7) It helps to defeat competitors' promotional activities.

Importance of Sales Promotion : In recent years, the importance of sales promotion has increased. The amount spent on sales promotion now equals the amount spent on advertising. The sales promotion increase is due to the changes in the marketing environment. The importance of sales promotion increase is due to the thinking of new ideas for creating a favourable condition of selling, promoting sales and future expansion of sales. It is a part of marketing strategy. It is essential for the survival of a manufacturer. For the birth of new product or new brand, sales promotion is very important. Advertising reaches the customers at their homes, or at the place of business or in their travels, whereas sales promotional devices inform, remind or stimulate the buyers at the point of purchase. Hence it is the only device which is available to the consumers at the point of purchase. A good sales promotional programme will remove the consumer's dissatisfaction with respect to retail selling. Sales promotion increases as a result of the growing use of self-service and other sales methods.

In India lakhs of rupees are now being spent on sales promotional activities. Now-a-days it becomes a necessity and it is not a luxury.

All the marketing devices, by which demand for a product is stimulated and restimulated are known as sales promotion.

Objectives of Sales Promotion

The major objectives of sales promotion are :

(1) To increase buying response at the customers' level
(2) To increase the sales effort of dealers and sales personnel
(3) To attract new customers
(4) To inform the public about the new product and its specialities, attraction and advantages
(5) To capture the major share of the market
(6) To create a favourable attitude towards the product
(7) To simplify the job of middlemen
(8) To meet the competition of other firms
(9) To effect off-season sales to boost the sales
(10) To stock more at the level of traders, through whom aggressive sales can be effected
(11) To stimulate the demand by popularising the products
(12) To establish and maintain communications with large market segments
(13) To keep the memory alive
(14) To create additional talking points to sales-persons
(15) To create brand image
(16) To remove customers' dissatisfaction
(17) To bridge the gap between advertising and personal selling
(18) To retrieving lost account
(19) To motivate sales force
(20) To encourage repeat sales
(21) To clear excessive inventories
(22) To block competitors' moves
(23) To speed up the sales of slow moving products
(24) To genrate short-term cash
(25) To deflect customers' attention from price
(26) To secure shelf-space in the selling places
(27) To counter-balance price competitions
(28) To build goodwill
(29) To improve manufacturer-dealer relationship
(30) To differentiate the compnay and its product from its competitors.

Reasons for the Rapid Growth of Sales Promotion

This is due to several factors which contribute to the rapid growth of sales promotion, particularly in consumer markets. They are internal and external factors.

I. Internal Factors

(a) Promotion is accepted by top management as an effective sales tool. Now-a-days top level managers realise and accept that sales promotion effects sales. It will increase the sales volume.

(b) Product managers are qualified to use sales promotion tools. Product managers realise the importance of sales promotion. Hence they practise sales promotion tools effectively.

(c) It is the duty of the product managers to increase the sales volume, and this attracts the sales promotion tools to achieve the aimed objective.

II. External Factors

(a) There is widespread use of branding. Promotional activities are essential as they are more practical than advertising.

(b) Competitors have become promotional-minded. There is cut-throat competition, and the market is flooded with numerous products. Hence, promotional activities are essential.

(c) During the period of inflation and recession, the consumers are more deal-oriented and the promotional techniques facilitate sales.

(d) The present stage of trade demands more deals from manufacturers.

In addition to Internal and External factors, the following further points are worthy to be noted:

(1) Intensifying competition in almost all consumer product categories has led to greater use of sales promotions because consumer respond favourably to the promotional incentives. (Intense competition).

(2) Products are becoming more and more standardised. However, the appearances of the products are similar. Consumers fail to understand it. So, companies depend heavily on sales promotion. (Proliferation)

(3) Consumers today are getting better education, are more selective and have become less loyal to brands than in the past. Thus, they purchase products based on price, value and convenience. Loyal consumers switch back and forth among a set of brands they perceive as almost equal. (Brand Loyalty)

(4) The Shelf-space available with resellers is limited. It is important note that when consumers enter a store, where products are displayed, the consumers make a many unplanned purchases on a look at it. (Growing power of resellers)

(5) Media advertising tends to be remote whereas sales promotion is more personal. Audience are bored with advertising clutter and avoid looking at. (Advertising is less effective)

Advantages of Sales Promotion

1. It stimulates in the consumers an attitude towards the product.
2. It creates a better incentive in the consumers to make a purchase. It is a demand creater.
3. It gives direct inducement to the consumers to take immediate action.
4. It is flexible. It can be used at any stage of a new product introduction.
5. Sales promotion leads to low unit-cost, due to large-scale production and large-scale selling.
6. It is an effective supporter of sales. It helps the salesman and makes his effort more productive.
7. The promotional tools are the most effective to be used in increasing the sales volume.

Sales promotion is effective when :

(a) A new brand is introduced.

(b) We have to communicate a major improvement or attraction in product.

(c) Enlarging the result of advertising.

(d) Increasing the number of retail stores in order to sell out products.

(e) Engaging or embarking upon aggressive sales campaign.

Limitations of Sales Promotion

(1) Sales promotions are only supplementary devices to supplement selling efforts of other promotion tools.

(2) Sales promotion activities are having temporary and short life. The benefits are also short-lived for three or four months. Then the demand will fall down.

(3) They are non-recurring in their use.

(4) Brand image is affected by too many sales promotion activities. Consumers are of the opinion that due to the lack of popularity and overstocking of products of a company, these sales promotional activities are conducted.

(5) There is a feeling in the minds of the customers that sales promotional activity tools are used to sell inadequate or second grade products.

(6) Discounts or rebates are allowed by boosting the prices of the goods, with a view to sell at a gain, which is not real.

(7) Immediate increase in demand is stimulated by this. Hence it is a short-lived tool.

(8) It is expensive and leads to a rise in the price of products.

Sales promotion is ineffective :

(a) when there is a declining market for an established brand.

(b) when there is no product improvement.

Kinds of Sales Promotion

Sales promotion can be divided into three kinds.

I. Consumer sales promotion

II. Dealer sales promotion

III. Sales force promotion

I. Consumer Sales Promotion

Activities aimed at reaching the consumer at his home or in his office may be called consumer sales promotion. It is aimed to inform or educate the consumers and to stimulate the consumers. Success in sales depends on consumers' co-operation. Consumer sales promotion increases the use of product by the consumers, attracts new customers and stands straight among the competitors, to introduce new products and to promote established products.

The following are the various sales promotion schemes used at the consumers' level.

(1) **Sampling :** Free samples are given to consumers to increase their interest in the product. They are also given to introduce a new product and expand the market. It increases the sales volume when the product is a new one to the customers. It is an effective device when the product is purchased often, e.g., soaps, detergents, tea or coffee etc. It is a method of demand creation. Sampling gives a chance to the consumers to compare the products with other substitutes. Samples are given to doctors by medical representatives. Specimen copies of books are given to professors. The idea behind this is that they recommend their products for use to patients or students.

The samples may be delivered door-to-door, sent by mail, picked up in a store, attached to another product etc. It is the most effective way to introduce a new product.

It is costly to produce a sample. It is the most expensive method. It is costly to distributors also. It is not justifiable for well-established product, a product with slow turnover, a product having less profit, perishable products etc.

(2) **Coupons :** Coupons are supplied along with a product. It is a certificate that reduces prices. Coupons can be mailed, enclosed in the packets or printed in the advertisements. The

purpose is to attract the customers and bring them to a particular shop to increase the sales of a particular brand.

The coupons are used (1) to introduce new products, (2) to increase the sale of an established product, (3) to sell new and larger size of a product, (4) to encourage repeated sales, and (5) to switch on consumer from one brand to another brand.

It is a short-run stimulus.

(3) **Demonstration :** It is the instructions to educate the consumers in the manner of using the product. It is a promotional tool to attract the attention of the consumers. When products are complex and of a technical nature, demonstration is necessary, e.g., computers, field machinery, electrical pumping set etc. Demonstration is done in front of consumers for mixy, wet grinder in retail shops etc.

Further examples:

Demonstration at retail shops: Sometimes, the demonstrations are organised at the retail stores by company salesmen for the benefit of retailers as well as consumers.

School Demonstrations: When the products happen to be a costly one and a hi-tech one, companies arrange demonstrations in schools or hotels. Here the consumers are invited to a particular place and demonstrations are arranged.

Door-to-door demonstrations: Consumer products companies quite often resort to house-to-house demonstrations. It is considered a highly specialised field of sales promotion. Eureka Forbes, the consumer appliances firm etc. popularised their products through door-to-door demonstrations.

Demonstrations to key people: Sometimes, demonstrations are organised for the benefit of key people and influential persons. It is a good selling techniques.

(4) **Contests :** These are conducted to attract new customers or to introduce new products. The consumers are asked to state in a few words why they prefer a particular product. To enter into the contest, the consumers must purchase a product and submit the evidence (a label or package or a card attached to the product) with the entry form for contest. To take part in the contest the consumers must be interested in the product. Consumers' skill and their ideas are tested and the prize is given to the best entry. It stimulates sales at the retail level. Entry forms correctly filled are submitted to the panel of judges. They will select the best and prizes will be given to the successful consumers.

Like contest, sweepstakes and games are also employed in sales promotions, and prizes are offered to the winners.

(5) **Money Refund Offers :** If the purchaser is not satisfied with the product, a part or all of the purchaser's money will be refunded. It is stated on the package. It will create new users and strengthen the brand loyalty. Sometimes, the money will be refunded if 10 top covers or 10 empty bottles or 10 packages are sent back to the manufacturers.

(6) **Premium Offer :** It is a temporary price reduction which increases the instinct of the buyers. Products are offered free or at a reduced cost as an inducement for purchasing. It is offered to consumers for consumer goods like soap, brush, paste, washing powder, glucose etc. For instance, when the customer buys two soaps, a soap box is given free along with the soaps. The soap box is a premium. In certain cases, the price is reduced. The reduced amount is a premium.

There are many types of premium offers :

(a) direct premium

(b) a reusable container

(c) free-in-mail premium

(d) a self-liquidating premium

(e) trading stamps

(a) **Direct Premium :** A with-pack premium accompanies the product inside (in pack) or outside (on-pack) the package. e.g., one plastic spoon in Taj tea or one steel spoon inside glucose D. or cadbury sweets inside the bournvita refill pack etc.

(b) **A Reusable Container :** It is a container which can be reused after the product is used. Point soap powder, sway soap powder etc. are in plastic buckets or plastic containers.

(c) **Free in Mail Premium :** Premium items are sent by the company by mail to consumers who are requested to send the proof of their purchase. For instance cigarette companies offer a packet of 10 cigarettes against 10 empty covers.

(d) **A Self-liquidating Premium :** It is an item sold below its normal retail price to consumers. The cost of the additional product is collected from the buyer at a concessional rate. For instance, a steel tumbler is given free of cost if you buy a packet of 200 gms. of sunrise instant coffee; or a soap powder manufacturer offers two kilograms of soap powder along with a plastic bucket at 50% off price. This method increases sales and brings benefits.

(e) **Trading Stamps :** It is given for purchasing the product in a particular shop. It is a premium given to the consumers by the seller in the form of stamps. These stamps are redeemable at the stamp redemption centres. To attract customers the retail shops use trading stamps.

(7) **Price off Offer :** It stimulates sales during a slump season. It gives a temporary discount to the consumers, *i.e.*, goods are offered at a rate less than the labelled rate. Fans are sold at a reduction rate in rainy season.

(8) **Consumer Sweepstakes :** Consumers submit their names for inclusion in a list of prize-winning contest. A ticket (like a lottery ticket) is given to the consumer of a specific brand. At the specified time, lots will be drawn. The prize-winner gets the prize. This system is followed by retail businessmen to promote sales.

(9) **Buy-back Allowance :** Allowance is given following a previous trade deal. That is, trade deal offers a certain amount of money for new purchases based on the purchased quantity. It prevents decline in post-trade deal. Buyers' motivation is increased because of their co-operation on the first trade deal. e.g., when cinthol and marvel soaps are concerned, the salesmen give one mug and two coupons free. If we purchase the two soaps by giving the coupons to the shop, the seller will reduce Rs. 2/- from the original price.

(10) **Free Trials :** It consists of inviting prospective purchasers to try the product without cost, in the hope that they will buy the product. Thus, buyers are encouraged by free trial to stimulate purchase interest.

II. Dealer Sales Promotion

The other name for dealer promotion is trade promotion. Manufacturers use a number of techniques to secure the co-operation of wholesalers, retailers or the middlemen. These activities, which increase the interest and enthusiasm of dealers and distributors, are called dealer or distributor sales promotion. It is the middlemen who are important persons for the fast movements of products. Hence this must be offered with some incentive. Following are the dealer sales promotion devices :

1. **Buying Allowance :** It is an offer of money off or temporary reduction to dealers for purchasing in stipulated period of time. It is a very effective method to introduce new products in the market. It encourages the dealers to buy a quantity that they will not buy in ordinary time. This buying allowance gives the dealers immediate profit, and price redemption. A wet grinder producer will give one grinder free if one purchases five wet grinders at a time.

2. **Merchandise Allowance :** An advertising allowance is given to the dealers for advertising the features of the manufacturer's product. A display allowance is given to them for arranging special displays of the product. After verifying the promotional work of the dealer, the manufacturers will give a certain amount of money for promotional activities. They hope that additional efforts

will be taken to increase the sales at retail level. Some manufacturers, as an encouragement, offer additional quantities of merchandise. This technique is known as merchandise deal e.g., Godrej company offers the dealers one extra soap cake, free of cost, when one purchases a dozen soap cakes.

3. **Price Deals :** Apart from the regular discount, special discounts are also allowed to the dealers for a specified quantity of purchase. This special discount is over and above the regular discount. For instance, a regular discount of Rs. 10 per case is allowed; and if the dealer purchases 100 cases at a time, he will be given a discount of Rs. 12 per case, *i.e.*, Rs. 200 extra for the purchase of 100 cases.

4. **Push Money or Premium :** Manufacturers may offer push money. It is a payment in cash or gifts given to dealers or to their sales force to push the manufacturer's product. To push his brand, the manufacturer will offer free speciality items that carry company's name, such as pens, pencils, calendars, match boxes, memo pads and yard sticks etc. This is a device for aggressive selling.

5. **Co-operative Advertising :** Dealers spend money in advertising manufacturer's product with the consent of the manufacturers. The dealer can claim an allowance by giving the proof of the advertisement.

This is an indirect advertising for the manufacturer. It will increase the sales of the manufacturer's product. But it is a burden on the manufacturer's budget.

6. **Dealer Sales Contests :** This is an indirect way of boosting the sales. This type of contest is conducted at the level of retailers and wholesalers. This is in the form of window display, store display, sales (volume) etc. Prize is awarded to the outstanding achievements. This method is aimed at stimulating and motivating distributors, dealers, sales-staff etc.

7. **Dealer's Listed Promotion :** Listing dealer is an advertisement. It gives a list of dealers or retailers who stock the product or who are engaged in its promotion. For example, the advertisement of Bombay Dyeing in newspapers carries the names of the stockists of their products. The consumer can buy the product from anyone of the listed dealers. This method induces the dealers to stock the products; and the consumers are encouraged to buy the products from the listed dealers.

8. **Dealer's Gift :** Manufacturers give attractive and useful articles to dealers against their order. The articles are transistor, radio, television set, clock, watch etc. Some manufacturers offer free holidays family tours to dealers who place more orders. Ralli Fan Co., arranges for free holidays tours to those who sell the maximum fans in a year.

9. **Point-of-purchase :** This plays the role of silent salesman. Point-of-purchase is also known as dealer-aids, dealer displays, dealer hopes etc. The competition among the retailers or traders has encouraged point-of-purchase advertising, which is a significant method for sales promotion. It means advertising at the point of purchase by the consumers. It is generally at the level of retailer's shop. For instance floor displays, stands, overhead signs, wall signs, posters etc., are examples of point-of-purchase materials. Again, it may be exterior or interior items. Exterior items like banners, displays are utilised by firms like service station. Interior items like floor display, end of counter displays, displays at walls, shelves, hanging from ceiling etc. are found in the store. Retailers adopt this method to draw the attention of customers and create an interest in the minds of the prospects. This method is suitable for consumer goods as well as industrial goods.

III. Sales Force Promotion

As dealer and consumer promotion, the sales force promotion also is a necessary one. The activities of sales force must be induced. In the channel of distribution the role of salesman is very important. The idea of sales force promotion is to make the salesman's effort more effective. The tools for sales force promotions are :

1. **Bonus to Sales Force :** The manufacturer sets a target of sales for a year. If the sales force sell the products above the targeted sales, bonus is offered to them. This is an encouragement incentive given to the sales people to sell more products–to cross the quota or targeted sales.

2. **Sales Force Contests :** To increase the interest and efforts of sales by sales force over a specified time, these contests are announced. The prizes are given to the salesman who secures the maximum sales in sales contests. Thus it stimulates the salesmen to sell more products.

3. **Salesmen Meetings and Conferences :** The idea behind these is to educate, inspire and reward salesmen. Encouragement is given to them during the discussion. New selling techniques are described to them and discussed in the conference.

TOOLS OF SALES PROMOTION

Consumer Promotion	Dealer Promotion	Sales Force Promotion
1. Sampling	1. Buying Allowance	1. Bonus
2. Coupons	2. Merchandise Allowance	2. Contests
3. Demonstrations	3. Price Deals	3. Meetings and Conferences
4. Contests	4. Push Money	
5. Money Refund Offer	5. Co-operative Advertising.	
6. Premium Offer	6. Sales Contests	
7. Price-off Offer	7. Dealers Listed Promotion	
8. Sweepstakes	8. Dealers Gift	
9. Buy-Back Allowances	9. Point of Purchase	
10. Free Trials		

Sales Promotion Planning Guidelines

Planning porocess starts with situation analysis. To start with, the promotion planners must first consider the corporate policy with regard to sales promotion, Joseph Mair has recorded one such policy statement. In the Handbook of Sales Promotion; the policy says:

(1) "Sales promotion is an integral part of the marketing mix".

(2) "Sales promotion should be used as an offensive weapon in the brand's marketing arsenal, not merely as a defensive reaction when a problem arises."

(3) "Sales promotion should extend and reinforces the brand's advertising and positioning, whenever possible."

(4) "Sales promotion should be developed as campaign, not as single, unrelated events."

(5) "Good sales promotions are built upon sound strategic planning."

The first step in promotion planning is situation analysis. This would include product or brand performance analysis, competitive situation including the promotion activities of major competitors, distribution situation and consumer behaviour with respect to sales promotions. Legal aspects concerning sales promotion are also considered. Based on marketing objectives and strategies, the promotion objectives would be developed. It is critically important to set unambiguous and measurable objectives and these should be developed in coordination with advertising and other promotion mix elements.

Sales promotion, thus, encourages quick movement of products along the channel distribution. It gives extra incentive to consumers, dealers and salesmen, and thereby producers push out maximum products. Ever-increasing competition, amongst the manufacturers, in the same line, creates further increasing of sales promotion in almost all the product fields. On the basis of competition, appropriate sales promotions have to be geared or undertaken in order to achieve progress of the firm.

All the manufacturers use various sales forces in order to maintain the current sales and, more particularly to increase the volume of sales for their products. All vigorous efforts to sell more products by widening the market result in aggressive selling. The aggressive sales can be gained by utilising the various sales promotions, described in this chapter. These promotions will facilitate the progress of the organisation as a whole.

QUESTIONS

1. Analyse the distinctive features of the various elements of the promotion mix. Illustrate with suitable examples. (*B.Com., Delhi*)
2. Examine the various discounts and allowances offered to traders or buyers to promote sales.
3. What is sales promotion? What is its importance in marketing industrial products ? (*B.Com., Madras*)
4. What measures would you suggest for sales promotion of a consumer product ? (*B.Com., Madurai*)
5. What are the factors governing basic promotional strategy ? (*B.Com., Madurai*)
6. Discuss the merits and demerits of various sales promotion methods. (*B.Com., Madurai*)
7. Distinguish between coupon and sampling. (*B.Com., Madurai*)
8. Discuss objective of sales promotion. (*B.Com., Madurai*)
9. Outline the different methods of providing discounts in the selling process. (*B.Com., Madurai*)
10. Distinguish between marketing and selling. (*B.Com., Bharathiyar*)

Case Study-1

Sales Promotion

TRIPLE PLUS PROTEIN BISCUITS

Indra Pharmaceuticals was established in 1986 to manufacture, distribute and market pharmaceutical drugs. It is purely an Indian company which had to face tough competition from multinational companies during the initial years. The company mainly survived on institutional buying (*i.e.* various government and charitable hospitals) and in the last decade with the help of effective strategies. It has set up a place for itself, amongst the leading pharmaceutical companies in the country.

In 1999, the Managing Director of the company stressed the need for diversification and addition of new products to its existing product range. Looking at the success of '**Threptin**' brand of high protein biscuits, he floated the idea of manufacturing and marketing the biscuits rich in protein, minerals and vitamins. His advisers suggested that since most of the people in the country were suffering from protein deficiency, the product, enriched with protein, would be desirable, and should be a big success, specially in view of its competing brand having a high price. The marketing research department of the company also gave green signal to the project after conducting a brief survey.

The company launched its biscuits with **"Triple Plus Protein**' brand name in 400 gm. packet consisting of 60 biscuits and priced at Rs. 75. *i.e.* Rs. 150 per kg. The product was heavily advertised in the newspapers, health magazines, radio and television. The target audience was middle class, who, it was believed, suffered most from protein deficiency and can afford triple plus protein biscuits. The ordinary biscuits were available in the market at the rate of Rs.30 to Rs.40 per kg. The thrust of triple plus biscuits in the promotion campaign was that these biscuits contain 3 times more protein and have additional mineral and vitamin value.

The company has 50 stockists covering the entire country and has the sales force of about 150 medical representatives for promoting its products, through doctors and registered medical practitioners. The medical representatives of the company had very good repport with government and charitable hospitals. To promote the triple plus brand of biscuits, its medical representatives gave discount coupons to the doctors for passing on to their patients for buying their biscuits. The buyer was entitled to a discount of Rs. 5 per packet of 400 gms. The scheme continued for about 6 months.

Despite heavy advertisement and canvassing by the medical representatives, the product was unable to attract customers. It was observed that launching of this product has not affected the market position of Threptin biscuits at all which was being sold at Rs. 90 for a pack of 275 gms. Rather, it was observed that the sale of Threptin biscuits had increased marginally, consequent to the advertisement campaign by Indra Pharmaceuticals. The company could achieve only 25 per cent of its sales target in the first year and sales remained almost static for the next year.

QUESTIONS

1. How do you account for the failure of the company to achieve the sales target ?
2. Critically evaluate the advertising and sales promotion strategy of the company.
3. Suggest a suitable promotion plan that can increase the sales of the company.
4. Do you think that change in the channels of distribution can improve the sales of this product? Give reasons for your answer. *(IGNOU, MBA)*

CHAPTER 26

Advertising

- *Introduction*
- *Evolution*
- *Definitions*
- *Basic Features*
- *What is Advertising? Advertising and Advertisement*
- *Advertising and Publicity*
- *Advertising and Salesmanship*
- *Advertising and Sales Promotion*
- *Advertising Objectives*
- *Additional Benefits*
- *Advertising Goals and Models*
- *Functions of Advertising*
- *Central Theme*
- *Importance of Advertising*
- *PLC and Advertising*
- *Advantages of Advertising to Manufacturers, Salesmen, Wholesalers, Retailers, Customers, and Community*
- *Objections Against Advertising*
- *Classification of Advertising Copy*
- *Types of Advertising Headlines*
- *Qualities of a Good Copy*
- *Elements of an Advertising Copy*
- *Scientific Advertising*
- *Why and When to Advertise?*
- *Causes of Failure of Advertising*
- *Determinants of Advertisability*
- *Kinds of Advertising*
- *Selection of Advertising Media*
- *Kinds of Media*
- *Is Advertising a Waste? Follow up System*

Introduction

Advertising is as old as trade and commerce. The ancient Babylonians and the Romans contributed significantly to the early growth of advertising. The nineteenth century saw the introduction of magazines which also grew into a big advertising medium. The modern day of advertisement agency has its origins during this period. Starting as agents for newspapers, the agency diversified into other services such as copy-writing, and played the role of consultants to advertisers. This marked the beginning of the modern-day, full service and agency. The early twentieth century was the golden age of advertising. The great depression of the 1930's saw a temporary setback in advertising growth. However, there were some positive developments during this period, such as the introduction of radio as an advertising medium and the application of research in advertising. The positive developments during 1950's were the emergence of television, the application of psychology and research in advertising, and invention of the concept of Unique Selling Proposition (USP) by Reeves.

The decade 1960-1970, ushered in a creative revolution in advertising. Outstanding personalities like David Ogilvy, Leo Burnett and Bernbach etc. emphasized the creative side of advertising and developed campaigns that stood out for their creative brilliance.

The decade 1970-1980 is referred to as the positioning era, as it saw the emergence of the concept of positioning, developed by Ries and Trout. This concept has wide application in advertising today. The present era is aptly named the era of accountability. There is greater need for truthful advertising, for measuring the effectiveness of advertising in general, and for socially responsible advertising

In India, advertising, as a potent means of sales-promotion, was accepted hardly three decades ago. This delay is obviously attributable to its late "industrialisation". But today, India too has emerged into an industrial country, giving boost to "advertisements" that appear regularly, in local and national newspapers, magazines, periodicals, TV etc. These

- *Keying the Advertisement*
- *Advertising Agency*
- *Advertising Budget*
- *Evaluation of Advertising*
- *Slogans*
- *Questions*

days, people use "Advertising" in various walks of life, Manufacturers use large-scale advertising for impressing people with the utility of their products. Businessmen advertise inviting individuals to invest money in their concerns. Employers advertise for application for various vacancies in thier companies for selecting the best of the applicants. The unemployed persons advertise their readiness to serve. In this manner, "advertising" has become indispensable, in modern life.

The present era is of mass production and mass distribution. Similar products are taken to the market. This involves stiff competition amongst the producers. Many firms adopt the vigorous means to maintain their existence in the market, as there are many substitutes in the market. This tendency is a struggle for the producers for their survival in the modern business world. All businessmen aim to make profit by increasing the sales at a remunerative price policy. When we manufacture good quality products or offer expert services, these must be known to the public. For this mass communication is needed as the population is great or the market area is wide. We can adopt sales promotion and advertising as tools to mobilise the marketing machinery. In the present business world, suitable publicity is done through advertising, which is adopted by commercial and industrial undertakings and almost all types of concerns. Therefore advertisement is a method of publicity.

Evolution

Advertisement has the prominent place among the techniques of mass education and persuasion on the public. It is not a modern origin. It has been used from immemorial period. In earlier periods, advertisement was displayed in the form of sign boards, writing on historical buildings or inscriptions on stones, stone-pillars, stone walls etc. The development of printing has greatly boosted the ideas of advertising through newspapers, magazines, hand-books etc. In earlier periods, it was used only in a limited manner. The evolution of printing technology and the changes of the marketing policies have been greatly utilised and many are benefited from advertising. Now, manufacturers, businessmen, employers, institutions, new shop owners, marketers etc. are benefited greatly by displaying advertisement. Increasing literacy, modern techniques of printing, stiff competition etc., add to the necessity of advertisement.

Definition

Littlefield defines it as ''Advertising is mass communication of information intended to persuade buyers as to maximise profits.''

Hall defines it as ''Salesmanship in writing, print or pictures or spreading information by means of the written and printed word and the pictures.''

Stanton says, ''Advertising consists of all the activities in presenting to a group a non-personal, oral or visual, openly sponsored message regarding a product, service or idea.''

American Marketing Association defines advertising as any paid form of non-personal presentation and promotion of ideas, goods, or services by an identified sponsor''.

From the above definitions, it is stated that advertising indicates that:

(a) Advertisement is a **message** to large groups.
(b) It is in the form of **non-personal communication.**
(c) It persuades the **general public** to purchase the goods or services, advertised.
(d) It is **paid for** by advertiser to publisher.
(e) Advertising messages are **identified** with the advertiser.

Basic Features:

After a careful scrutiny of the above definitions, the essential elements of advertising can be listed as follows:

1. **Matter of Record :** It is a matter of record furnishing information for the benefit of buyers. It guides or helps buyers to make satisfactory purchases. The contents of an advertisement are what the advertiser wants.

2. **Non-personal Communication :** It is a mass non-personal communication, reaching large groups of buyers. It is not delivered by actual person. It is not addressed to a person. Whatever the form of advertisement—spoken, written or visual, it is directed at a mass audience and not at the individual as in personal selling.

3. **Persuasion of Buyers :** Advertising complements or may substitute for personal selling. To persuade the buyers the advertiser makes his products buyer-satisfying. It is an art of influencing the human action to possess one's product.

4. **Paid Form of Publicity :** Advertising is a paid form and hence commercial in nature. Thus any sponsored communication designed to influence buyer's behaviour is advertising because advertiser pays for it.

5. **Identifiable with the Sponsor :** Advertising is identifiable with its sponsoring authority or advertiser. It discloses or identifies the source of opinions and ideas, it presents.

What is Advertising ?

Advertising is that activity by which visual or oral messages are addressed to the general public. Its purpose is to inform or influence them in order to increase the sales of the advertiser. It is done with a view to sell the goods or services, offered by the advertiser. It may also draw the readers or viewers to act favourably towards the idea or institutions featured. It is paid for by a seller (sponsor). The seller or the advertiser has to pay for the space (or time) through which the message (advertisement) appears. The aim is to persuade people to buy more. Advertising creates desire for new products. The success of advertising greatly depends upon effective advertising programme. An effective advertising naturally necessitates mass production, thereby reduces unit cost by lowering the price of goods in favour of consumers.

Advertising and Advertisement

The 'message' is known as advertisement. Advertisement is nothing more than a message. Advertising is a process. It is a programme or series of activities necessary to prepare the message and bring it to the intended persons or market. The reader knows who is behind the advertising as the sponsor is openly identified in the advertisement itself. Payment is made by the sponsor to the media, who carry the message.

Advertising and Publicity

Advertising is defined as any paid form of non-personal presentation and promotion of ideas, goods or services by an identified sponsor. ''Publicity'' has been defined by American Marketing Association as ''non-personal stimulation of demand for a product, service or business unit by planting commercially significant news about it in a published medium or obtaining favourable presentation of it on radio, television or stage that is not paid for by the sponsor.''

To be brief, both, advertising and publicity make a non-personal presentation to the masses. Tell the aspects of product like quality, price, usefulness, special features etc. The advertiser has to pay for advertisement. In case of publicity, it is not a necessity. For instance in election, the expenses of popularising a candidate may or may not be paid by the candidate. Advertising is a purposeful attempt sponsored by the party, whereas publicity may or may not be sponsored by the party. It means, in publicity, the person passing the message may not come to the stage: someone or a third person initiates the publicity; for instance good or bad remarks appearing in newspapers about anything–a film, a book, a policy, an adventure etc. Advertising is a method of publicity. In other words, publicity involves a number of methods including advertising.

Advertising and Salesmanship

There is no doubt that advertising and salesmanship are essential and play a vital role in marketing. These are designed to achieve the same ultimate goals. Advertising, a bulk method of selling, is to make effective sales at less expense. Distinctions between the two are:

The FIVE M's ADVERTISING

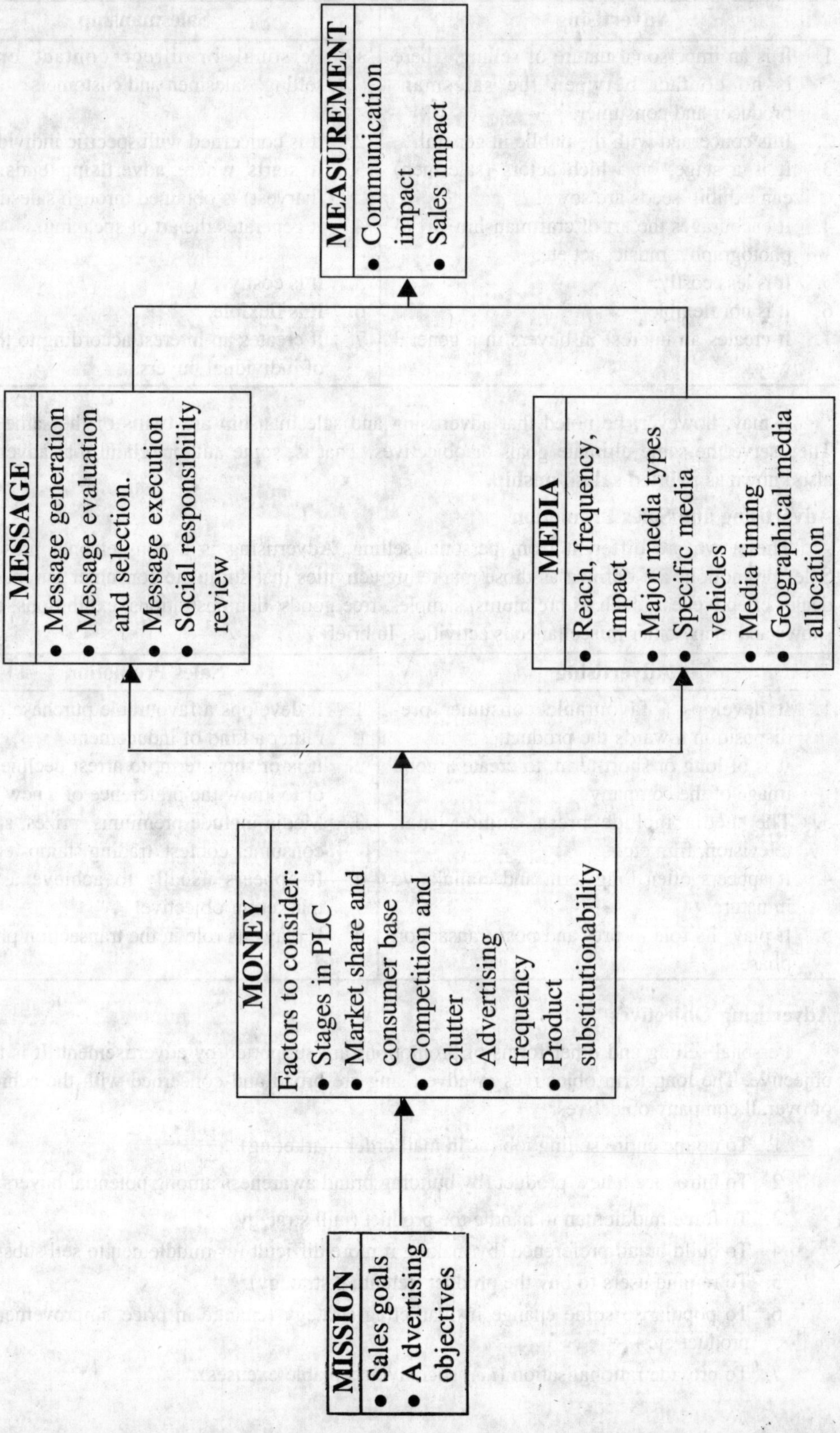

Advertising	Salesmanship
1. It is an impersonal nature of selling. There is no contact between the salesman, producer and consumer.	1. Personal or direct contact exists in selling–salesmen and customers.
2. It is concerned with the public in general.	2. It is concerned with specific individuals.
3. It is a stage, on which actors (salesmen) can exhibit–seeds are sown.	3. It starts where advertising ends.–Result (harvest) is obtained through salesmen.
4. It encourages the art of craftmanship–art of photography, music, act etc.	4. It generates the art of speaking.
5. It is less costly.	5. It is costly.
6. It is not flexible.	6. It is flexible.
7. It creates an interest in buyers in a general way.	7. It creates an interest according to the needs of individual buyers.

It may, however, be noted that advertising and salesmanship are **twins** of the same parents. They serve the same ultimate goals or objectives. That is, some authors claim that advertising is also known as **printed salesmanship.**

Advertising and Sales Promotion

These two are different from personal selling. Advertising is a non-personal presentation. Sales promotions are defined as those marketing activities that stimulate consumer purchasing and dealer effectiveness, such as premiums, samples, free goods, demonstrations, exhibitions, displays, shows and many other miscellaneous activities. In brief:

Advertising	Sales Promotion
1. It develops a favourable consumer pre-disposition towards the product.	1. It develops a favourable purchase decision, rather a kind of inducement.
2. It is of long or short term, to create a good image of the company.	2. It is of short term, to arrest decline in sales or to know the preference of a new product.
3. The media include press, audio-visual, television, film etc.	3. Media include premiums, prizes, sampling, consumer contest, trading stamps etc.
4. It appears often long term and cumulative in nature.	4. It appears usually to achieve a specific marketing objective.
5. It plays its role in pre- and post-transaction phase.	5. It plays its role in the transaction phase.

Advertising Objectives

Personal selling and other forms of promotions are supported by advertisement. It is the main objective. The long term objectives of advertising are broad and concerned with the achievement of overall company objectives.

1. To do the entire selling job (as in mail order marketing).
2. To introduce a new product (by building brand awareness among potential buyers).
3. To force middlemen to handle the product (pull strategy).
4. To build brand preference (by making it more difficult for middlemen to sell substitutes).
5. To remind users to buy the product (retentive strategy).
6. To popularise some change in marketing strategy (change in price, improvement in the product etc.).
7. To provide rationalisation (*i.e.,* socially acceptable excuses).

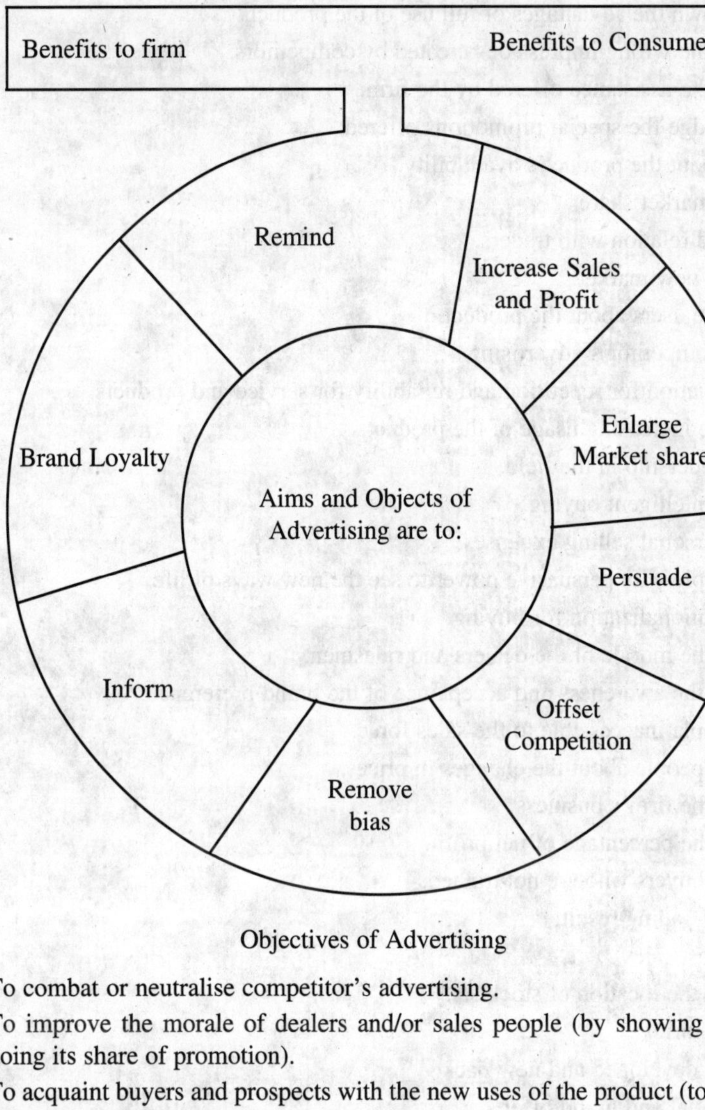

Objectives of Advertising

8. To combat or neutralise competitor's advertising.
9. To improve the morale of dealers and/or sales people (by showing that the company is doing its share of promotion).
10. To acquaint buyers and prospects with the new uses of the product (to extend the product's life cycle).

Additional Benefits

In sum, the primary objective of advertising is to increase sales. The following are the additional benefits, in brief:

(1) To encourage the potential customers to buy.

(2) To induce professionals to boost the sales.

(3) To open door for salesmen.

(4) To create an awareness or interest of the products in the minds of customers.

(5) To increase sales in off seasons.

(6) To build a good business image.

(7) To introduce new product and services.

(8) To maintain a brand loyalty.

(9) To introduce price deal.

(10) To make known the advantages of full use of the product.

(11) To wipe off the wrong impressions created by competitors.

(12) To describe the assistance offered by the firm.

(13) To acknowledge the special promotions offered.

(14) To inform about the product's availability.

(15) To increase market share.

(16) To keep good relation with traders.

(17) To enter into new market.

(18) To remind the users about the product.

(19) To combat competitor's advertising.

(20) To create situation for repetition and reliability for service and products.

(21) To spread the increasing usage of the product.

(22) To secure leadership in the field.

(23) To promote intelligent buying.

(24) To reduce personal selling expenses.

(25) To make people with persuasive power to see the new ways of life.

(26) To provide rationalization for buying.

(27) To improve the morale of the dealers and salesmen.

(28) To publicise the awareness and acceptance of the brand preference.

(29) To reach people inaccessible to the sales force.

(30) To convince people about the changes in prices.

(31) To stabilize the firm's business.

(32) To increase the percentage of net profit.

(33) To teach the buyers who are not trained.

(34) To announce trading result.

(35) To retrieve lost sales.

(36) To announce the location of stockists.

(37) To invite enquiries.

(38) To announce developed and new pack.

(39) To make special and grand offer.

(40) To attract investors.

ADVERTISING GOALS AND MODELS

Use of advertising requires some understanding as to how it functions through the use of suitable media. To understand this process of communication, various models have been turned to understand more about consumer responses to advertisement in terms of their involvement and feelings and on the other hand researches continue their interest in more quantitative approaches. The important models are as follows:

(1) AIDA MODEL

AIDA Model or theory is one of the early models of the subject. It was developed in the 1920s. The letters in the acronym **denote: Attention, Interest, Desire** and **Action.** The model suggests that any effective impersonal sales presentation should attract Attention, gain Interest, arouse a Desire and result in Action

(2) FIVE STAGE MODEL

An interesting model was put forward in the 1930 by rural sociologists studying the process of "innovation – adoption". This model suggested five stages in any adoption process: **Awareness, Interest, Evaluation, Trial and Adoption.**

(3) SIX STAGE MODEL

This model was put forward by Lavidge and Gary Steiner: **AKLPCP – Awareness, Knowledge**, **Liking**, **Preference**, **Conviction** and **Purchase – Model.** They give higher importance to the cognitive evaluations before the purchase. With an increase in competition and enhancement in discerning abilities of potential buyers and users, information is likely to play a greater role. The persuasive power of advertising in itself is a function of the information content. This models also take into account the prevailing degree of competition. The competition can arise between two brands or between substitute products in two dissimilar categories. The stage of liking (after the stage of awareness and knowledge) refers to the ability of advertising in creating and choice through its creativity and theme. Preference for the brand is the combined effect of product characteristics and their relevance in satisfying the need of target audience through creative advertising.

(4) DAGMAR MODEL

All the above models belong to a class that is commonly called the "hierarchy of effect" model.

In the 1950's came another model DAGMAR, belonging to the same broad category of hierarchy of effects model. Communication theories have proposed several models to explain the way of advertising works and each have some similarity. One model known as the DAGMAR Model (**Defining Advertising Goals** for **Measured Advertising Results**) describes the sequence of stages through which the prospective customer has to move: (a) unawareness, (b) awareness, (c) comprehension of the offer, (d) conviction and (e) action.

Through advertising, the retailer will make the potential customer aware of the store and its range of offers. As part of the advertising communication process, information has to be clearly transmitted so it can be decoded and comprehended properly. The process is then to make the offer credible so that the potential customer can show a favourable attitude to the store or product. The act of purchase may then follow.

Advertising Objectives

Five key words to summarise the advertising objectives (Corkindale and Kennedy)

1. **WHAT:** What role is advertising expected to fulfill in the total marketing effort?
2. **WHY:** Why is it believed that advertising can achieve this role? (What evidence is there and what assumptions are necessary?)
3. **WHO:** Who should be involved in setting objectives; who should be responsible for agreeing the objectives, coordinating their implementation and subsequent evaluation? Who are the intended audience?
4. **HOW:** How are the advertising objectives to be put into practice?
5. **WHEN:** When are various parts of the programme to be implemented? When can response be expected to each stage of the programme?

Functions of Advertising

The main objective of advertising is to stimulate or increase sales to all customers–present, former and future. Advertising increases the present sales and potential demand of the product. The above objectives are realised by the functions of advertising. Following are the functions of advertising:

I. Increasing the Number of Customers

(a) **By Increasing the Customers and Widening the Market :** Advertising through communication media informs consumers about the presence of a product in the market. This effective advertisement works in two ways. First it stimulates demand and then it strengthens the stimulated demand. The benefits and various uses of the products must be made known to the public of the area where the marketer wants to enter for marketing. To achieve the objectives, advertising is the only way. It serves to widen the market through increasing the buyers.

(b) **By Developing a Brand Loyalty :** All traders or manufacturers aim to attract the prospects in favour of their products and services. Development of loyalty to one's brand among the customers is important. For instance, if one is using a particular brand of soap, then advertising must aim at making him to use only this soap. Advertising and its impact make him a continuous and ever user and do not want him to leave it for another brand.

(c) **Offset the Competing Brands :** Many similar products are flowing towards the market and consumers are tempted to buy them through various promotional measures. Further, advertising facilitates the creation, direction and extension of demand for the particular products or service. A good advertising policy is always linked with the ultimate behaviours of customers. For instance, when one buys a bathing soap today, one may go in for a particular brand the next time. By focussing the qualities and merits of the product in a better way than other similar products, the competitors can be defeated by capturing their share of the market.

II. Increasing the Consumption Rate Among the Present Customers

(a) **Increasing Usage of the Products:** When a product is introduced in the market, it is meant for a specific use. But when the product is put into use consumers may come to know of its new uses. This is possible through research. Advertising will explain the multiple uses to the masses.

(b) **Reminding the Consumers :** The demand may be seasonal–cool drinks, woollen dresses, air-coolers etc. They are saleable during the season period; but during off season period, no sales may be possible. Again at the arrival of the season, customers may not remember the brand used by them, before making purchase. In these circumstances, advertising reminds the customers about the forgotten products.

(c) **Educating the Public :** Advertisement being a connecting link between the producer and the consumers, also plays its role by imparting knowledge. Consumers may not know the good or bad reactions of a certain product or services. For instance, when we purchase cloth, we are warned through advertisement, to go in for sanforized cloth. Sanforized cloth will not shrink. Those who do not know this, buy bad material and when stitched the dress becomes tight. Another example is baby milk food. The producer gives full instructions even on the package about the measurement of milk powder according to the age of babies. Take the example of new model scooter or car. The company appoints its own mechanics to see to the repairs and this will be published in newspapers. In case you approach any other mechanic to repair your new model vehicle, the inexperienced mechanic may spoil it. Other similar instances are shampoo, hair dye, soap, powder, hair oil, medicine etc. The understanding of the product, its uses, advantages etc., can be well-educated through advertising.

(d) **Shaping a Goodwill :** Almost every firm wants to establish a good name in the society. Like a human being, a firm doing good services to the society or offering products–different from others, better and cheaper than other products etc., earns a good name. Such a firm may ever be remembered by the consumers. The consumers may prefer a product, because of (1) low price (2) fashion (3) service after sales (4) multiple uses (5) quality merchandise (6) wider publicity. All these merits are known to the consumers through advertising, and sales are boosted automatically. Thus a firm can build a goodwill for its products.

Advertising plays a vital role in creating a background or **an interest** in the public; and the salesman easily convert the public into customers. It can tell a mass–thousands and thousands of people–about the product in the **shortest span of time** at the least cost. Publicity facilitates large-scale production, followed by mass consumption, creating **employment opportunities,** apart from profits.

"Advertising aims at:

(*a*) **benefiting** the Producer,

(*b*) **educating** the Consumer,

(*c*) **supplementing** the Salesman and

(*d*) **link** between Producer and the Consumer.

Central Theme in Advertising

Theme is the subject matter of advertisement. A theme represents a particular view-point or a central idea with which the message is conveyed to the public. An advertisement copy should bridge the gap between the advertiser and the readers, if it is to be effective. To achieve this, the advertisement has to provide the audience the information that is of interest to them. The two features of "message" are "message structure" and "message appeal." Message structure contains details (selling points) of the products and consumers' needs and benefits. A two-sided argument is effective in winning over an audience. The "message appeal" is the feature which brings about attitude change on the part of audience. The message appeals can be grouped broadly into two categories; (i) **the product-oriented appeals :** They may emphasise the physical features or the functions of the product or may attempt a comparison of the product with the other brands available in the market. (ii) **the consumer-oriented appeals :** They, on the other hand, are directed at the audience's attitude, faiths and beliefs. It may emphasise the attitudinal and behavioural patterns of the audience, the life styles of the audience or their social image. In actual practice, messages quite often combine the product appeal and consumer appeal.

The theme has an arresting quality, *i.e.*, it is capable of capturing attention of the people. In selecting a theme, all necessary information about consumers and about the product to be advertised must be collected with proper details. In collecting the details about consumers, information about the attitude and aspiration of genuine prospect for the product should be particularly known. Information about the product should include, characteristics of the product, benefits expected to the consumers and over the rival's products. Themes may change as the market conditions change. The theme or appeal points out the most important reason or driving force to the purchase of a certain product or service. It is an appeal based on human emotion, feelings, sentiments, needs, desire etc. We have the following common appeals with which advertising message can be effectively communicated, in brief:

1. **The Theme of Beauty :** The sales appeal for cosmetic, toilet products are usually based upon the theme of beauty:

Egs : "For charming appearance, use KUMARI TALC powder. Its pure, fine talc gives you that soft, smooth, silky feeling."

2. **The Theme of Health :** Food products and drugs are advertised through reliance upon the theme of health.

Egs : "Health brings happiness.
The key health is held by BABY PRODUCTS."

3. **The Theme of Pride :** The sales message in the case of jewelleries, TV sets, cars etc. laid upon the theme of pride.

Egs : "KUMARI Jewellery adorns fashionable ladies."

4. **The Theme of Comfort :** Products which aid in giving comfort to the people at work and at home are advertised through the theme of comfort.

Egs : "Stop Bad breath while you fight tooth decay all day.
What to do ? BABY TOOTH-PASTE
CALCIGUARD Great Refreshing Flavour."

5. **The Theme of Economy :** This is a common appeal used in many cases for saving money.

Egs : "Easy Care Fabrics !
BABY FABRICS that need no ironing."

6. **The Theme of Fear :** The theme of fear is utilised by insurance companies, banks etc. The advertiser tries to evoke feelings of fear or anxiety in the minds of public saying that the failure to use the advertised product might result in great loss or damages in terms of money, health or prestige etc.

Egs : "If it is GODREJ, it is safe."

7. **The Theme of Emulation :** The desire for imitation is strongly created human nature, by giving illustrations and factual information as to what some distinguished persons do.

Egs : "The successful men all over the globe use BABY FABRICS."

8. **The Theme of Distinction :** The desire for individual recognition, distinct social status and superior community standing is inherent in human nature.

Egs : Be a VIP by possessing a BABY pen.

9. **The Theme of Affection :** By directing appeal towards parental love, the copy of advertising becomes effective in securing action on the part of buyers.

Egs : "Glaxo Builds Bonny Babies."

10. **The Theme of Patriotism :** The appeal for products of national origin is sometimes based upon national sentiments.

Egs : "HMT watches are better than foreign made."

In modern times, advertising is used by men in various walks of life. Littlefield and Kirkpatrick observe that :

(1) **Advertising is not a game,** for here when advertising is done properly and profitably, both buyer and seller benefit.

(2) **Advertising is not a toy**, for advertising funds come from sales volume and, therefore, efforts are made to increase sales.

(3) **Advertising is not a racket**, only few advertisements are designed to deceive, majority are based on honesty.

(4) **Advertising is not an exact science,** for the sales are affected by number of factors such as competitors' decisions, manufacturers' promotional activities, change in price, personnel or policies etc. and these factors cannot be controlled as a physical scientist may control the experiments.

Importance of Advertising

The standard of living of the public is raised by introducing modern products and the latest techniques through advertising.

Mass production followed by large-scale consumption facilitates to earn more profits. Large-scale production decreases the unit cost. The selling price is also reduced, but not to the extent of decreased cost of production. It means, the price of the product is decreased, thereby consumers are satisfied and dividend rate is increased, thereby shareholders are satisfied. All these happen because of advertising. Items like, pens, radios, scooters, watches, refrigerators, television sets, cameras, footwares and many other modern amenities are examples.

Advertising reaches the masses, whereas salesmen find it difficult. Advertising covers a vast area. In the field of competition, advertising is a good helper to the producer to boost his products.

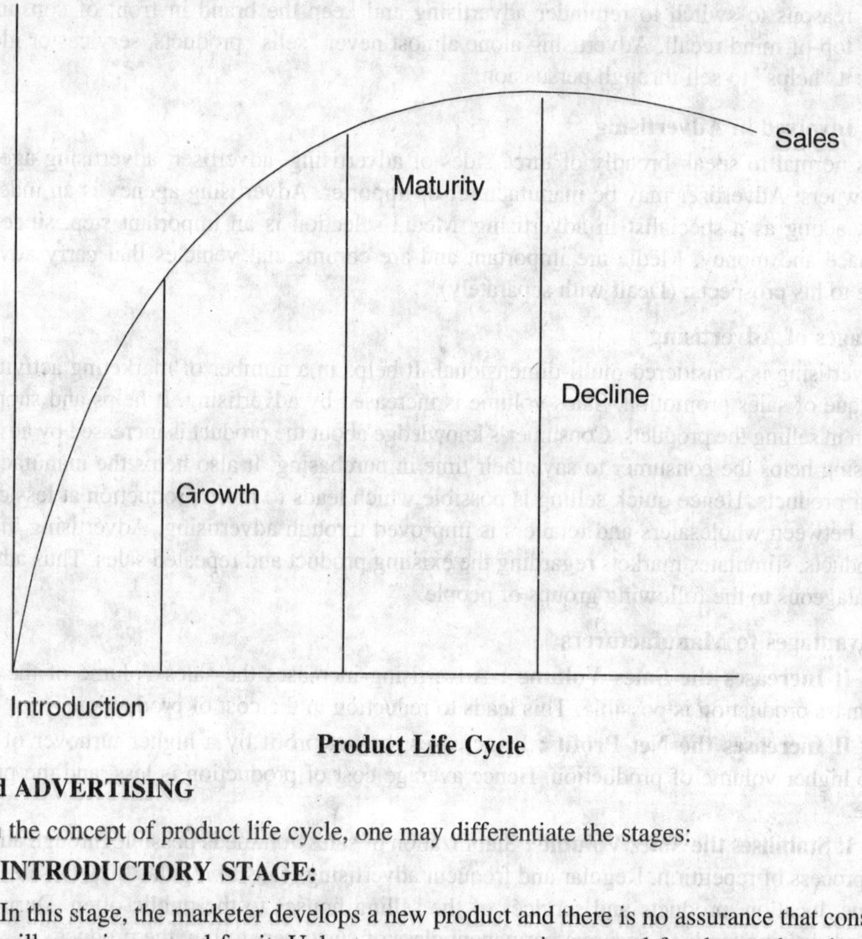

Product Life Cycle

PLC and ADVERTISING

Based on the concept of product life cycle, one may differentiate the stages:

(*a*) **INTRODUCTORY STAGE:**

In this stage, the marketer develops a new product and there is no assurance that consumers will perceive a need for it. Unless consumers perceive a need for the product, it will not sell. The job of advertising is to introduce the idea that the product is better able to meet the consumer needs than the existing ones. It must affectively communication that the new product has overcome the limitations of earlier alternatives that consumers tolerated for long, the role of advertising message in this stage is to furnish product knowledge, change existing habits, develop new usage, cultivate new standards of living, and implant a new way to look at existing approaches of problem-solution.

(*b*) **COMPETITIVE STAGE:**

The consumers have accepted the product and the competition has moved into the market-place sooner rather than later. The consumer faces the question, "Which brand should I buy? "Generally, in the early stages of competition, the combined total effect of competitors creates significant growth for the product category. The key objective of advertising is to clearly and convincingly differentiate the company's brand and effectively communicate its position.

(*c*) **REMINDER STAGE:**

When products reach maturity in their life cycle and are widely accepted, they are in their reminder stage. Markets may not feel much need for competitive advertising, as consumers already know all about the product. Some consumers like it and some others don't like it, or may be neutral. However, if marketers do not advertise, consumers are likely to forget about it and switch to other alternatives being advertised regularly. This is sufficient reasons to switch to reminder advertising and keep the brand in front of consumers for top-of-mind recall. Advertising alone almost never "sells" products, services or ideas. But it "helps" to sell through persuasion.

Groups Involved in Advertising

It is normal to speak broadly of three sides of advertising–advertiser, advertising agency and media owners. Advertiser may be manufacturer or importer. Advertising agency is an independent concern, acting as a specialist in advertising. Media selection is an important step, since it costs time, space and money. Media are important and are commercial vehicles that carry advertiser's message to his prospects. (Dealt with separately).

Advantages of Advertising

Advertising is considered multi-dimensional. It helps in a number of marketing activities. It is a technique of sales promotion. Sales volume is increased by advertising. It helps and supports the salesman in selling the products. Consumer's knowledge about the product is increased by advertising. Advertising helps the consumer to save their time in purchasing. It also helps the manufacturers to sell their products. Hence quick selling is possible which leads to more production at less cost. The relation between wholesalers and retailers is improved through advertising. Advertising introduces new products, stimulates markets regarding the existing product and repeated sales. Thus advertising is advantageous to the following groups of people.

I. Advantages to Manufacturers

(1) **It Increases the Sales Volume :** Advertising increases the sales volume of the product. Hence mass production is possible. This leads to reduction in the cost of production.

(2) **It Increases the Net Profit :** It increases the net profit by a higher turnover of sales. It leads to higher volume of production. Hence average cost of production is less, and the profit will increase.

(3) **It Stabilises the Sales Volume :** Stabilization of sales volume is possible through advertising by the process of repetition. Regular and frequent advertising leads to regular flow of sales. It gives the name, location, products and services of the selling houses to the public often. During slump period, advertising tends to ensure a permanent class of customers to buy the product.

(4) **It Controls Product Price :** Control of wholesale and retail price is possible by means of advertisement. The needy retailers are overcharged by some greedy wholesalers. The retailers charge higher prices for the products. Hence the consumers do not want to buy such products. This will lead to reduction in sales. Hence manufacturers print on the cover or announce the retail price of the product.

(5) **It Helps in Opening New Market :** Advertising is helpful in opening or creating new markets. It helps to get leadership in the market. It helps the manufacturers to take decision whether to expand the market share or not. It also helps them to sell new products or improved variety of products.

(6) **It Maintains the Existing Market :** Maintenance of existing market is essential for the success of a concern. Hence manufacturers, who look ahead, always have an eye on the future business. As such, by advertising he is very tactful to hold up the present market and to expand the market.

(7) **It Creates Reputation :** Advertising increases the reputation of the manufacturers in the public. It builds the image of the product and goodwill of the manufacturers. It protects the manufacturers from aggressive selling method adopted by his competitors. It creates an image in the minds of the customer about his brand.

(8) **It Secures More Dealers :** Advertising secures more dealers to buy the products. Due to the goodwill earned from the public, dealers are interested in buying such a product.

(9) **It is Less Expensive :** Advertising is considered to be less expensive. With a smaller amount of money, advertising reaches many people, and more people will buy the product.

(10) **Wide Information :** Wider information of product is possible through advertisement. Any change in quality or price can be made known by the manufacturers to the customers as and when it is necessary in a quick manner.

Manufacturers can change the habits and prejudices of customers by tactful advertising. Thus, it helps in establishing and controlling the buying habits of the customers.

II. Advantages to Salesman

(1) **Creates A Background :** Salesmen's mastery and skill satisfy the customers. A well-trained, active tactful salesman's job makes easy distribution work. The advertisement, which is the background, will help the salesmen very much. Customers know about the product through advertisement. When salesman contact them with the product, customers buy the product without any hesitation.

(2) **Curtails the Burden of the Salesman's Job :** If the advertising is done by the manufacturer, the work of salesman is reduced. Otherwise he has to advertise about the product and then try to sell the product. Salesman's function is supported and supplemented by advertisement. Selling and advertising are 'cup and saucer' or 'key and lock' words. Salesmen's work is made easier and more encouraging by advertisement.

(3) **Least Effort :** Advertised product can be sold very easily. Salesman's time is saved and he can contact more customers in a shorter period. He can meet many customers with the least effort.

(4) **Consumer's Need Can Be Studied :** A salesman's confidence is increased through advertising by educating and stimulating the consumers. Customer's demand and needs are studied by him correctly. The manufacturers are informed of this. They will supply the products according to the demand of the customers and thus equalise the demand and supply of their products.

(5) **Creates Enthusiasm :** Advertising reduces salesman's job. He can do his job in a better way to sell the products, crossing the fixed quota. Hence it creates enthusiasm and confidence in him.

III. Advantages to Wholesalers and Retailers

(1) **Creates Easy Sales :** Advertisement informs consumers about the quality of the product. Hence they know about the product. Sale of that product is easy for the wholesalers and retailers.

(2) **Increases the Turnover :** Advertising helps quick sale of the product which in turn increases the rate of turnover of the product. Thus, there is no question of old stocks. It reduces the expenses on overhead charges.

(3) **Attracts More Customers :** Advertising gives detailed information about the product and the availability of the product in a particular shop. As such, it attracts more customers in that particular shop.

(4) **Increases the Prestige of the Store :** Customers know about the store through advertising. The goodwill or reputation earned by the manufacturer is also shared by the selling shops. Thus the prestige of the firm increases.

(5) **Publicity :** In advertisement, product publicity and wholesale or retail shop publicity are done simultaneously. Thus, the retailers are also known to the public and thereby increase their sales too.

(6) **Economic Selling :** Advertising ensures more economic selling.

IV. Advantages to the Customers

(1) **Easy Purchasing :** Advertising helps customers in easy purchasing of the products. Advertisement gives useful information about the reasonableness of the price and the quality of the product. There are many tablets for headache, like anacin, aspro, coldarine etc. A good advertising can help in buying the best one.

(2) **Connecting Link :** Advertising is the connecting link between the manufacturer and the customers. It eliminates the middlemen. There is no profit for the middlemen. Hence the price is low.

(3) **Fair :** It helps the customers to get the product at fair price.

(4) **Saves Time :** It helps customers by giving information about the availability of the product, *i.e.*, where and when. The customers can select the best product in a particular shop. Thus it reduces their shopping time.

(5) **Best Quality Product :** Advertisement, generally stands for a quality product. Manufacturers advertise their product only for selling. If the product is not good, customers will switch on to other products (brand). Manufacturers maintain their quality to retain the market. As such, it is advantageous to customers. Benefits of standardisation are assured to the customers by advertising.

(6) **Educates the Customer :** The aim of the advertising is to educate the customers about the introduction of a new product mentioning its different uses. It gives information to the customers about the availability of goods and services in the market. The customers come to know about these things and purchase the products according to their standard. Thus the standard of living of the customers increases. The comparative type of advertisement of different products and substitutes will enable the public to understand more about a product or services.

(7) **Mail Order Business :** Advertising helps the people to get the products directly from the producers through mail order business. There are places, where the products are unavailable–villages, rural areas. Advertising helps them to get the products through post. Thus it improves the social welfare.

V. Advantages to Community

(1) **Increases Employment Opportunities :** Advertising generates employment opportunities directly and indirectly. Direct employment opportunities in advertising are artists, painters, singers, musicians, writers, photographers, pressmen, managing agencies etc. It creates mass sales, followed by mass production which in turn opens the door for more employment indirectly.

(2) **Uplifts the Standard of Living :** Advertising is an effective tool which raises the standard of living of the people of advanced countries. The standard of living is measured by the amount of national income and its distribution and the consumption pattern. Advertising gives stimulus to the consumers to buy new variety of products. It leads to large-scale production of more varieties of products followed by mass consumption. Thus advertising creates demand for standardised products.

(3) **Educative Value :** Advertising educates the members of the community in the various uses of products. As such, people know the varieties of products and their availability in the market and uses and benefits. Thus it educates the people. People become intelligent buyers. They become economic buyers. They understand the merits and demerits of products they come across.

(4) **Helps Press :** Advertising gives more income to the press. We cannot buy newspapers at a cheaper rate without advertisement. Commercial advertisement and broadcasting are undertaken by radios, television, newspapers etc. These lead to the cheaper availability of newspapers.

We can say that advertising is a boon to the producer and consumer. It is very important for modern trade and commerce. It stabilizes the sales volume and also the national income. It encourages large-scale production and increasing the profit. It reduces unemployment.

Objections Against Advertising

There are a number of advantages of advertising; yet there are some drawbacks too. Several criticisms and objections are put forth against advertising. Kenneth A. Longman, in his book 'Advertising' has mentioned the following charges against advertising:

1. Advertising sells people things they neither need nor want.
2. People are not really influenced by advertising.
3. Advertising generates senseless proliferation of variety in goods and services.
4. Advertising results in higher prices.
5. Advertising is false and misleading.
6. Most advertising is irrelevant.
7. Most advertising exhibits bad taste or sponsors it.
8. Advertising is too intrusive.
9. Advertising regulates discussions of public issues through its control of the news media.
10. Its life is short.
11. It tends to create monopoly.
12. In many cases, the public are cheated.

Apart from those mentioned above, economic, social and ethical objections are levelled against advertising. They are:

I. Economic Objection

(1) **Leads to Higher Price :** Large-scale production is possible taking into account advertising, and the price will be very low. If advertising fails to sell the product, then the price will be increased. Experience shows that advertising increases the price since manufacturers spend a lot of money on advertising, which increases the cost of production. But generally advertising increases sales and mass production resulting in less cost of production and reduction of unit cost.

(2) **It Forces People to Buy Things :** People are forced to buy things by the attraction of the advertisement. People do not need things like cars, refrigerators etc. but advertising forces them to buy this product. Thus it stimulates people to go in for things which they cannot afford. But it multiplies the needs.

(3) **People are Not Influenced By Advertising :** Some criticise that people are not influenced by advertising.

(4) **Creates Waste :** Advertising is regarded as waste. When there is a change in style or fashion, old things or half-used articles are not used any further. New products are purchased. The manufacturer must be very careful about this change. When there is a change in price, model, quality etc. it will incur another big amount for the advertisements. It is responsible for quick and premature changes in fashion and style. For instance, a particular product can easily be used for a year. But advertising shortens the life of the product through the publicity of the latest arrivals. Thus creeps in immaturity of the product growth. This is what happens in advanced countries, like the U.S.A. In America they change every year their cars and wives. Thus waste of resources multiplies.

(5) **It Exaggerates the Facts :** Advertising exaggerates the real fact to the consumers e.g., "the best medicine for headache," "the finest pain reliever" etc. These lead the consumer to buy that product even though it is of low quality or may be ineffective. Use of superlative degree in product description is also viewed by the readers in a negative way.

(6) **It is Fraud And Misleading :** Advertising is an instrument of cheating in many situations. A good advertiser can sell anything. Producers advertise their products not with a view to serve the public, but with a view to dispose of their products, which are really not needed to the customers. They aim at earning profits by pushing out the dead stocks. For this, by concealing the actual facts, the advertiser makes publicity with "make to believe" statements by using false statistics, tempered statements, false claims, exaggerated ideas, false comparison, misrepresented opinions of great people, false supported reports etc., without a base. For instance, film stars' opinions with photos and signature, generally appear in many newspapers. Big political leaders' statements, with signatures are ample now-a-days. Generally we may come across statements like the following. A film star says, "My **secret in beauty lies** in X brand soap". Some big star says, "I am dying for X brand cigarettes." "Do you know how we can enjoy and relax with the X brand drinks." "Our products are wonders of the world" etc. All these statements have no background but the public are cheated and this boosts the sale of dead and ineffective products.

(7) **Leads to Monopoly :** Advertising is done by large firms. It prevents the entry of small firms and new firms in the market. People buy a particular brand. By taking advantages of this producers raise the price. By using the advertising knife, they cut the necks of small or new firms. These lead to monopoly.

II. Social Objection

The Press : The major income for the press comes from advertisement. It is true that the cost of the newspapers is reduced. The advertising matters are presented in such a way that advertisers are favoured, but the public are not, so sometimes the public are affected adversely.

III. Ethical Objection

Cigarettes, brandy etc., are harmful to health. Advertising makes people to buy these. It affects their health. The way in which they are advertised is bad. The statements, poses of pictures etc., in many cases are offensive; they are vulgar and immoral. In many cases, advertising which excites emotions, nude poses of sex, vulgar statement etc., affect the morale of the younger generation and damage the ethical aims of a society.

A brief look at advertising. The key points to remember are as follows:

1. Be clear about what you are trying to convey.
2. Know why you want to convey such a message.
3. Know to whom the message is addressed.
4. Speak in the customer's language.
5. Choose the most appropriate medium.
6. Decide the best time to make contact.
7. Measure results.

Classification of Advertisement Copy

Advertising copy must arrest, inform, impress and impel the reader. As said earlier, a well defined advertising copy must perform the following functions:

(a) Attract Attention
(b) Command Interest
(c) Create Desire
(d) Inspire Conviction
(e) Provoke Action

An advertising copy may be classified as under:

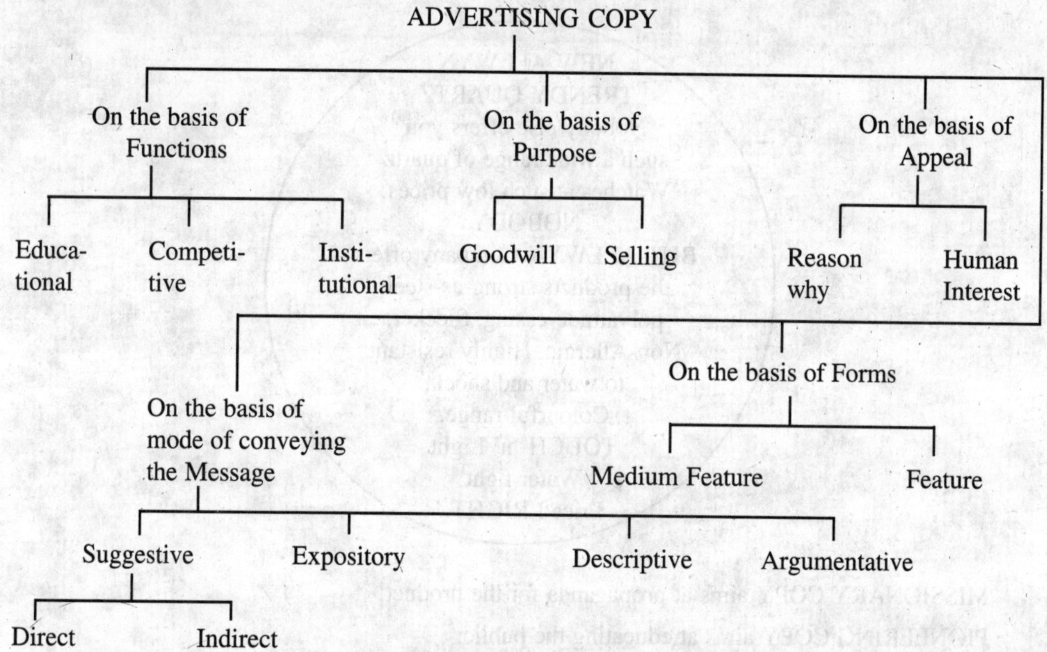

Educational Copy : It aims at educating the public, regarding the use of a product. Such an advertisement copy depicts the specialities of the product, in contrast to the existing ones. People keep certain habits which cannot be easily changed. Demand can be created when such habits are changed. This type of copy introduces new habits and attracts people towards the product.

Example : A small family is a HAPPY FAMILY.

HAVE A RICH LIFE.

Enjoy the pleasure in your life time.

Grow the small family with PROSPERITY.

Seek advice from your nearest FAMILY PLANNING CENTRE.

They are well trained to ADVISE YOU.

Why not make a VISIT, for your.

Family's sake, safe, pleasure, richness, unburdened life etc.

Competitive Copy : It aims at putting forth the special features of a product. It promotes to differ one brand from competitors' brands. It meets the challenge of the competitors.

Example : Kelvinator : LOOK

KELVINATOR is the best REFRIGERATOR you can buy.

All the other refrigerators put together cannot match its features and advantages.

Many of these are absolutely new in India.

Institutional Copy : It sells not the products of the institution but the name of the institution. Also known as PRESTIGE or CORPORATE advertising, this is the type of advertisement used to present the company's image. When a pharmaceutical firm takes space it describes its research skills, its contribution to society etc. The copy aims to develop and maintain a good-will for the product that the product comes from a reputed house.

Example :

NEW ALLWYN
TRENDY QUARTZ
Nobody else offers you
such a wide range of quartz
Watches at such low prices.
NOBODY
BUT ALLWYN Company offers
the products strong-as-steel,
polyamide casing, Sleeker.
Non-Allergic. Highly resistant
to water and shock.
Colourful range.
TOUCH 'n' Light
Water tight
Priced RIGHT.

MISSIONARY COPY aims at propaganda for the product.

PIONEERING COPY aims at educating the public.

GOODWILL COPY is one which does not try to sell a product but aims to sell the public some idea on the firm in general, on the quality of its product, its utility, etc.

SELLING COPY is used by the mail-order house to effect a sale by mail, or by the manufacturer who sells through retailers, to persuade the buyer to call for his brand at the retail store. It is used by the retailer to make an immediate sales of the goods, which he may have to stock.

REASON WHY COPY itself is clear as to its meaning. It explains the reasons to readers–why the advertised product is to be purchased. It aims at answering the questions raised about a product as to why, how and when the product is to be purchased.

Example :

BUILDERS OF
OFFICE MACHINES AND EQUIPMENTS
We possess all types of Labour Saving Systems
THROUGH MECHANISATION
OBJECT : Labour Saving, Time Saving, Accuracy and Minimisation of Fraud
If you are the MANAGER of your firm/office, Look the merits :
* Better Quality of Work * Lower Operating Cost * Improved Efficiency
* Facilitates Control * Greater Accuracy * Relieves Monotony
* Facilitates Standardisation
Available from Ready Stock
Available at all leading Shops

HUMAN INTEREST COPY makes its appeal to the emotions and the senses, rather than to the intellect and judgement. It may be of many forms:–Fear Copy, Humorous Copy, Story Copy etc. The examples and statements of these copies are funny and readers smile or laugh. It affects the heart rather than the mind.

Example : ''Life in perfect balance, offered by LIC''
''Retired life is made happier with BABY BANK''.

SUGGESTIVE COPY directly or indirectly conveys the message, which leads to sales.

Example :

Is interest losing on your money ?
Come, do your bank with KUMARI BANK,
Who pays good INTEREST apart from
Decent Dealings.
Remember KUMARI Bank is the only bank
you can rely on for Security of your money and
Regular Returns

EXPOSITORY COPY is not to conceal but to expose the facts as they are. Clear and concise ideas are given. It explains the construction, uses, merits, operation and superiority of advertised articles.

Example :

MAGNA RE-WRITES THE CHAPTER ON BALL PEN REFILLS
SPECIALLY MADE FOR PEOPLE WHO
LIKE TO WRITE BETTER.
Now, discover the International art of fine writing.
It is so simple:
Replace the refill in your pen
ASK FOR MAGNA REFILL
THAT IS IMPORTANT.
Then take a clear sheet of paper.
Touch pen to paper. And experience the sheer pleasure of writing.
So, look for Magna at your nearest shop.
Discover a whole new way to write with MAGNA

DESCRIPTIVE COPY conveys the ideas in words or pictures so as to impress the readers' mind and thus act upon it.

Example : ''NEW SHIRT ? ''NO, Washed in DET.''
''She is a Rexona Girl''.

ARGUMENTATIVE COPY is a message supported by facts.

Examples :

Use VIM. Vim can change DIM into SUPER WHITE.

Skin becomes softer, smoother–really
Lovelier–Thanks to BABY-KUMARI Soap.

TYPES OF ADVERTISING

The following are the important types of advertising:

1. **Brand Advertising:** This type of advertisements are done to build brands and develop unique brand identity for the firm. This is the most popular form of advertising in all possible media including TV, for examples, Pepsi, Coke etc.
2. **National Advertising:** These advertisements are uniform across the nation and are released through national media covering the nation.
3. **Local Advertising:** These advertisements are carried out in local and vernacular media to promote the product in a local region.
4. **Retail Advertising:** These advertisements are brought to promote retail outlets and dealer points.
5. **Political Advertising:** These are done for political parties, politicians and individual candidates during elections.
6. **Social Advertising:** These advertisements are brought out for a social cause like against AIDS, child-labour, women trafficking
7. **Directory Advertising:** These are the advertisements done in directories and yellow pages and followed by people while collecting a telephone number or a home address.
8. **Business-to-Business Advertising:** These kinds of advertisements are carried out targeting business and organizational markets, these messages are directed towards retailers, wholesalers and distributors.
9. **Institutional Advertising:** Institutions like colleges, universities, missionary of charities and large corporates bring out these advertisements. The purpose of such advertising is to create a positive goodwill, which will ultimately contributes towards achieving to overall marketing and brand building goal of the organization.
10. **In Film Advertising:** These are new forms of advertising in which brands are placed inside the film and actors are shown using these products during the movie for increasing the usage among the audience.
11. **Electronic Advertising:** These forms of advertising use electronic media like, TV, radio, video, audio-cassettes, etc.
12. **Interactive Advertising:** These are typical internet based advertisements, which are delivered to individ**ual consumers who have access to the World Wide Web**

THE HEADLINE

The first function of a headline is to attract the reader's attention to the advertisement. It is used to arrest attention and gain the buyer's interest. A headline is defined as a word or a phrase that is prominent and catchy, when compared to the other elements of the advertisement copy. It may be prosaic, poetic etc. depending on the type of product and atmosphere that has to be created. The following are the important models of headline:

(1) **News headline:** This type of headline gives some type of news – price reduction, product improvements, premium offer, a modification of an already existing product, the addition of a new ingredient in an old product, etc.

Egs: "Nescafe, the coffee that tastes so good."

"Glaxo builds bony babies."

(2) **Declarative headline:** This type of headline makes a bold positive statement, which is obvious in itself. The message is clear and direct.

Egs: "Buy Parker for success."

"Bring home the leader, VIDEOCON."

(3) **Affirmative headline:** Though the message is not assertive, it makes a statement.

Egs: "Growing children need COMPLAN".

(4) **Command headline:** The commanding headline urges the reader to some action. It creates an atmosphere of urgency in the text.

Egs: "Use VIM. VIM can change DIM into SUPER WHITE.

(5) **Interrogative headline:** This headline asks a question to the reader. Sometimes, the answer is contained in the headline itself.

Eggs: "Do you want a clear eye sight?"

Then, use "AMLA HAIR OIL".

(6) **Identification headline:** This type of headline is very useful for product identification either in terms brand name or the manufacturer.

(7) **Emotional headline:** These headline exploit human emotions. It is a deliberate and planned attempt at creating the right mood as the body copy also pour out emotions.

(8) **Bargain headline:** The bargain headlines are commanding, declarative and that an expensive product is a bargain, with some discounts or free offers.

(9) **Humerous headline:** Humour is a suspect element in advertising. Though it is extremely effective, it requires DEFT handling else it will fall flat.

(10) **Negative headline:** This headline is used indirectly to attack the competition and redirect the consumer to the advertisers.

The copy of the advertisement is defined as "all the written or spoken material in it, including the headline, coupons and advertiser's name and address, as well as the main body of the message." An advertisement copy is the written or spoken message in an advertisement including words, sentences, figures aimed to convey a desired message to the public. In short, the written matter and message used by the advertiser to convey his desired idea is known as advertisement copy.

The message is the heart of advertising. The words and pictures in the copy must win the hearts of readers. The main purpose of the advertisement copy is to influence the buyers and by that stimulate the sales volume. Advertisement copy is the written matter, or reading matter, the words, sentences, paragraphs, sub-heads, headlines, figures which the advertiser wants to convey to the public. A well-planned and drafted copy should:

(1) Attract primary and initial attention of the buyers.

(2) Hold the attention of buyers in an interesting way.

(3) Awake and stimulate the interest of the buyers.

(4) Create an impression in buyers to have memory value.

(5) Convince, persuade or induce the readers.

(6) Suggest and lead to specific response.

The aim of advertisement is to make the public to look, to like, to learn and to buy. The A.I.D.A. formula; Attention, Interest, Desire and Action is very important here.

Qualities of a Good Advertisement Copy

An effective advertisement copy must have certain qualities which make it the best one. They are:

1. **It Must Be Simple :** It must be simple and easy to understand. A copy writer must use short, simple, understandable words and sentences. The words or sentences used must be remembered by intelligent persons and non-intelligent persons. It must make people to see it, *i.e.*, it should arrest their attention.

2. **It Must Be Informative :** The copy must give the information which the reader wants to know about the products, in order to buy. Hence it must give the real fact. The information must be natural and straightforward. It must make people read it, *i.e.*, people should be informed.

3. **It Must Be Concise and Complete :** The copy must be complete and brief. If it is incomplete, it fails. Brevity is essential (condensation). Completeness should never be sacrificed for brevity. It must make people to understand it.

4. **It Must Be Enthusiastic :** Salesman's talk in the written form is the copy. The copy must tell the reader what the product or merchandise will do for him.

5. **It Must Be Honest :** It must be honest and truthful towards the public. If the copy is untrue, then the confidence and the value of publicity go down. The public should not be cheated. The public, who are the final users of the products, are the witness of the product quality. If inferior products are sold through false advertising, they have a short life. If the firm is hiding the facts, not exposing the real position, the product tells its own weakness to the users. If the advertisement is not honest, then the products will disappear from market and the firm will be closed down within a short span of time.

6. **It Creates An Urge :** It must reveal unknown or unseen features of the products. The public should be informed about the product's use and merits by the advertiser. It must create a goodwill in the minds of the public. Its aim must be to trust the firm and its products. It should have an effective salesmanship in absentia.

A GOOD ADVERTISEMENT COPY

1. It must make people to see it.
2. It must make people to read it.
3. It must make people to understand it.
4. It must make people to believe it.
5. It must make people to buy the product.

Elements of an Advertisement Copy

Apart from the quality mentioned above, there are certain principles, which an advertisement should have. That is it must aim to arrest, inform, impress and urge the readers to act on the advertisement. The elements are known as values and they are:

1. **Attention Value :** People are busy. They find time rarely. Almost all the people, who are able to make a purchase, do not have enough time. Under such situations, the advertisement must be able to attract the attention of readers, at a glance. There must be some speciality in the advertisement. To make it more attractive, we may adopt the following devices:

(a) Pictures and drawings should have a direct bearing on the product.

(b) The headline must be good with a proper border.

(c) It must have a pleasing colourful presentation.

(d) It should not be congested *i.e.*, there must be enough inter-space.

(e) The slogans must be lively.

(f) The coupons must be part of the advertisement. By filling the coupons the needy customer must be able to get full information and thereby it becomes repeated advertisement to the seller.

2. **Suggestive Value :** The message advertised should have some suggestive and useful value to those who go through the advertisement. The words or pictures in the advertisement should have commanding power on the readers. Repetition has good effect. When one comes across the advertisement every time, he begins to consider the product.

3. **Conviction Value :** To be more effective, the statements in the advertisement must be genuine and accurate. Misrepresentation or exaggerative words must be avoided. Simple and plain facts have more effect on the readers to convince them than colourful or flattering wordings.

4. **Sentimental Value :** The sentimental feelings or the prejudiced attitude of the reader should not be affected by the advertiser; but rather, they must be respected. The likes and dislikes, habits and customs etc., of the readers may be highly considered. It must appear that the advertiser is doing it for the readers.

5. **Educative Value :** When products are manufactured for the first time, it is the duty of the producer, through advertisements, to draw the attention of the people and to tell them the use, merits, ingredients, special features etc., of the products. All people are alike, but their behaviour is different. When the advertisement is able to change their habits and mould the tendency to use the products, the market for the products increases. People must have a feeling to see the advertisement through bearing eyes. It gives new information, suggestion and knowledge to people and directs them to go for the product.

6. **Memorizing Value :** Advertisement must create a good impression on the reader's mind. Slogan, if it is good to read and charming to hear, has good memorizing value. Repeating the advertisement often, through attractive brand name and catchy wordy slogans, may have a memorizing value in the minds of the readers.

7. **Instinctive Value :** The advertiser must have a well-thought out plan to make a copy to be advertised. The matter or message must be arranged in such a way that the reader is able to understand and act on the message. The presentation is brief with questions tempting or compelling the people to act on. We can come across, an inducement, an aroused feeling, a temptation, an inclination etc., in such advertisements.

Scientific Advertising

Advertising is necessary in the modern business world. A business without advertisement cannot be thought of. Advertisement aims at creating and maintaining the demand of the company. So an advertising programme should be prepared very carefully in order to serve the purpose fully. Scientific method should also be used to make the advertisement quite effective and attractive to those for whom it is meant. The principles of advertising have been established through a good deal of research. Scientific advertising programme is drawn by considering all relevant factors connected with advertising. A scientific advertising involves a careful study of the following factors.

1. Advertisability of the product (to be discussed later in this chapter).
2. Market usually consists of groups of buyers for a product or service. A group of buyers consists of children, grown-ups, students, women or men. An advertisement can prove successful in the market when the characteristics of the product can satisfy the main requirements of the customers for whom it is meant. Make a decision of the advertising media and type of advertisement copy.
3. Product analysis is necessary as to its acceptance by the customers. Needs and desires of the consumers are to be studied.

4. Preparation of advertising budget by analysing the competition in the market, area to be covered, and defined objectives to the firm.
5. Media to be evaluated through its cost, effect and result. Expert opinions may be sought to understand the effectiveness of alternative media, length of message etc.
6. On the basis of investigation and research, the actual execution of advertising programme should be done. Preparation of advertising copy may be entrusted to experts who have skill and experience.
7. Evaluation of the result is necessary. Advertising programme is effective if sales are increased, desired change in the consumers' habit effected and prospective customers become buyers.

Why and When to Advertise ?

The simple answer to the question "Why do we advertise ?" is that either we have something to sell or some one has something we want to buy. In other words, we may wish to give something away, seek an exchange or invite donors. We make known our offer or need. Many people use advertising and enjoy the choices available to them. We may sell a house, raise funds, sell products, buy second-hand products, launch a new product, employ people, find a pen-friend etc. as the result of facts known to others through advertising. Thus advertising is the means by which we make known what we have to sell or what we want to buy, so that we can sell or buy to our best advantage.

Advertising will be used only when it can fetch good result. It must have economy and be more efficient as compared to other means of selling. For instance, when you take the case of a book-seller, he sends his salesman from college to college to sell his books and this is more effective than advertising. Advertising is used to make the salesmen acceptable to the people. Immediate results may not be there to justify the increased cost of advertising, but future sales can be boosted by the advertisement.

Causes of Failure of Advertising

Advertising is the easiest and most economical means of tapping the wide market. But all advertisings may not be successful. From the point of view of advertisers and consumers, advertising may fail because of the following factors, (in brief):

1. Lack of consistent advertising policy.
2. Lack of confidence caused by exaggerated claims.
3. Lack of co-ordination between advertising policy and distributive policy.
4. Unimpressive appeals in the copy.
5. Wrong layout of advertising copy.
6. Failure to follow up advertisements.
7. Non-sensible preparation of advertising copy, lack of thinking and time etc.
8. Lack of experimentation with different types of appeals.
9. Selecting wrong medium.
10. Failure to inform the salesmen and dealers about advertising.

Determinants of Advertisability

It is said that "advertising can sell anything." The advertiser views that readers make purchases by going through the tricky phrases or clever slogans. "It is selling in print or presenting a commodity in print to the people in such a way that they may be induced to buy it." All products need not be advertised. Some products still have good market without advertising while others have poor market with advertising. Advertising programme is aimed at demand creation, and the manufacturer should know or evaluate its advertising opportunities. The question arises as to what factors determine the advertising opportunity. The ability of a product to be advertised is its advertisability. The following factors are to be considered.

1. The Product Should Have Primary Demand

A major criterion for primary demand advertising is whether the generic product provides important advantages for the consumer, when compared to other products that are capable of satisfying the same wants. A product enjoys primary demand when it is desirable. Flattering illustrations or glorifying descriptions are not sufficient to make the people buy. The stronger and more basic the consumer-wants are satisfied with the new product, the greater the primary demand advertising opportunity will be, that is, advertising is beneficial only when market demand is on the increase.

2. Advertising Must Be Continuous

There is advertisability expansion, if continuous advertising is adopted. Rare appearance of advertisement is insufficient to draw the attention of new or old customers. There are many advertisers, who constantly bring the products or services to the attention of readers.

3. Greater Chances for Product Differentiation

There must be opportunity to differentiate the products. This is a governing factor of advertisability. Product differenciation is the step to create preferences in the mind of customers. That is possible through colour, name, shape, size, package, taste etc. of the product. Product differentiation makes the public believe that a product is superior to others. For instance, appliances, automobiles or cosmetics are easier to advertise than wheat or rice. The more a brand differs from the competing brands of the same product, the greater the opportunity.

4. Product Should Have Hidden Qualities

The advertiser can inform the customers about the hidden qualities of a product through advertising. If the consumer can evaluate the qualities of the product at the time of purchase, there is less opportunity for selective-demand advertising, than if the product has hidden qualities which, to be evaluated, need purchase and use. For example, a cake-mix can be advertised and promises are made as to its simple preparation and its taste. To verify the qualities, one has to purchase and use. Advertising provides a major means of promoting these hidden qualities.

5. Presence of Power of Emotional Buying Motives.

The buying motives are in the minds of consumers but not in the product. The buying motives are just like petrol, with which a car or scooter moves on the roads. By making appeals of gains, economy, pride, prestige etc. of the product, emotional buying motives can be increased.

6. Sufficient Funds

A firm must have sufficient funds to support an advertising programme successfully. Advertisability can be increased, by spending enough funds through latest development of advertising. The policy of advertising depends upon the nature of products and the cost of advertising depends upon the sale of the products.

7. Product Price

The price of the product is also another important factór. The price must be reasonable, compared to similar products in the market. It need not be lower than other products in the market, but, the advertiser should not persuade the consumer to pay a very high price.

Kinds of Advertising

The important classifications of advertising are: Product and institutional.

1. **Product Advertising :** It aims at selling a particular product. This is the common way. A particular product with its brand is promoted through advertising. For example, Horlicks, Hamam, Bournvita, Viva etc. This type is again divided into primary and selective.

(a) **Primary Advertising (pioneer) :** This is a type of advertising used at the stage of introducing a new product to the market with the aim to inform the public as to its birth and other details. For example, pressure cookers, bicycles, scooters etc.

(b) **Selective Advertising :** This type of advertising is used when the market is loaded with similar products. There will be stiff competition among the producers. This generally happens in the growing stage of a product's life cycle. Since competition is there, the advertisers aim to capture the market by influencing the demand for a specific product, probably supported by promotion activities. This type is also known as competitive advertising. For example, Prestige Pressure Cookers, HMT watches, Rallie cycle, Rajdoot bike etc.

2. **Institutional Advertising :** This type of advertisement is displayed to create a goodwill for the firm rather than to sell its products. Its aim is to make people, members of the advertiser's firm. It gives importance to the firm and wants to create a good impression about a particular manufacturer or a shopkeeper. For example, Parry and Co; Godrej, etc. This may further be divided into three :

(a) **In Patronage :** In it, consumers are informed about the firm, its product and policies.

(b) **Public Relations :** It tries to create a favourable image about the firm, during strike periods etc.

(c) **Public Service :** Here, the advertiser tries to create an image on public support, social services etc.

3. **Commercial Advertising :** Commercial advertising or business advertising is concerned with selling products or ideas to increase the sales volume. They may be:

Trade advertising	– relating to trade
Industrial advertising	– relating to Industrial goods
Professional advertising	– relating to professions (Doctor, Accountant etc.)
Farm advertising	– relating to farm products

4. **Non-Commercial Advertising :** Non-profit organisations adopt this type of advertisement; for instance, inviting donations, financial aid etc.

5. **Rational and Emotional Advertising :** If the advertising explains the speciality of a product, such as use the B. K. Soap, Kumari powder etc., it is a case of rational type. When publicity is made to effect a lady look like a cinema star, associated with a charming beauty, it is a case of emotional type.

6. **National and Local Advertising :** When advertising is sponsored by manufacturers or producers, it is a case of national (general) advertising. When the advertising is done by retailers, it is a case of local (retail) advertising.

Selection of Advertising Media

Advertising medium is a means through which advertisers communicate their idea to likely customers to influence them with a view to know and decide about the product or service advertised. Selection of a particular advertising medium poses a problems for the advertiser. It needs a prudent calculation. It eats away the funds. The absence of correct decision will waste the money without result. There are a number of media available and one finds it difficult to make a final decision. The advertising medium should satisfy the objectives of advertising viz., the following:

1. It has to reach maximum prospects.
2. It must gain the attention of readers.

3. It must have wide coverage at less cost.

The selection of medium is made with reference to not only the above objectives but also the following factors:

1. **Objective of the Advertisement**

Media choices are influenced both by the purpose of a specific advertisement and by the goal of an entire campaign. For instance, if the goal of the campaign is to generate appointment for salesmen, direct mail method is suitable. If it is to include public, within a day or two, News-paper/Radio/TV may be used.

2. **Media Circulation**

Every medium has general circulation. That medium is to be selected which will reach the type of market with minimum waste circulation. The character of the medium and its coverage are looked into. One person buys a copy but there is likely to be a secondary readership by others. A magazine is passed round the office, read by the family, or given to neighbours. Sometimes, two media are circulated among the same people. But mere adding the two circulations does not give the actual number of persons who go through it. It is possible that 15 to 20% people read both. Duplication, wherever possible, is to be avoided.

3. **The Class of People**

The medium is to be decided by the kind of customers–sex, age, cultural, social, educational standard etc., again divided into rural and urban groups or rich and poor. The main thing is to determine which of the groups are to be approached. Buying habits play a vital role. If the products are for young people, better select radio or newspaper. If the products are for grown-ups, then sales-letters will be followed.

4. **Business Unit**

Selection of media is affected by the size and the nature of the business unit. It may be a departmental store, drug unit, grocery unit etc. Larger firms make use of radio, TV or News-paper, whereas small firms make use of cinema slides, handbills, posters etc.

5. **Message to be Sent**

The medium should fit the message. For instance meat product, floor covering, women's apparel etc. are best presented in pictorial form. Commodities of common use, like clothes, tooth paste, soap, tooth brush, radio, etc. need mass communication. The advertising for a particular group, for example grown-ups or ladies only, may be confidentially dealt with.

6. **The Extent of Competition**

By observing the competitors' success or failure, one can get better and bitter experience, as a lesson and can go for a suitable medium. One may follow the same line or think to develop new media with greater success.

7. **Cost of Space**

Cost of the advertising media should be considered in relation to funds available, circulation of media etc. The larger the circulation, the higher are the rates charged. Preferred positions are charged at higher rates and so is the case with advertisements in colour. The advertiser should try to develop some relationship between the cost of the medium and the size of the audience it will reach.

GUIDANCE TO CONSUMERS

Against untrustworthy advertisement

1. **Refuse to buy shoddy merchandise.** If your purchase turns out to be unsatisfactory, complain to the manufacturer or retailer.
2. **Don't buy on impulse.** Shop around, compare price, styles and models of any major purchase.
3. **Entertainment is no substitute for information.** Read and listen to advertisements carefully to find out what they really say.
4. **Get it in writing.** Don't rely on verbal promises.
5. **Credit buying doesn't create money, it costs money.** Do not buy on the instalment plan, or with a credit card, unless you can afford it.
6. **Read labels carefully** to be sure you know what you're really getting, what it costs and how to use it.
7. **Make a list before you do your grocery shopping and stock to it.**

ADVERTISING MEDIA

Medium is a means through which the advertising message is conveyed to the consumers. The proper selection of the medium, by which the message is to be conveyed, must achieve the pre-determined goals. In brief, the following facts, which affect the media may be considered:

1. Should the advertisement reach and influence the largest portion of the people?
2. Should it be possible to influence the pre-determined group of buyers?
3. Should it give a wide coverage at less cost?

There are some important factors, which are also to be considered:

1. The characteristics of the product and its demand.
2. Fund available for advertising.
3. Nature of the market *i.e.*, different segments.
4. The nature and extent of competition prevailing.
5. Medium to be adopted.
6. Coverage of the medium.
7. The product's nature.
8. The position of the product in the market.
9. Size of the advertisement.
10. The probable cost of advertising.

KINDS OF MEDIA

The media to be adopted, along with merits and demerits are discussed in detail below.

I. **Indoor Advertising**

1. Press Media :
   (a) Newspaper (b) Magazine
2. Radio
3. Television
4. Film

II. **Outdoor Advertising**

1. Mural (posters)
2. Advertising board
3. Vehicular
4. Painted display

5. Travelling display
6. Electric display
7. Sky advertising
8. Sandwich-man
9. Handbills (leaflets)

III. **Direct Advertising**

1. Sales letters
2. Circular letters
3. Booklets and catalogues
4. Folders
5. Package inserts
6. Store publications

IV. **Promotional Advertising**

1. Window display
2. Interior display
3. Show-rooms
4. Exhibitions

I. Indoor Advertising

When advertising is made through newspapers, magazines, radio, T.V. programmes or cinema programme in Video etc., so that people can get the message at home, it is known as Indoor advertisement. People read or listen to the advertisement when they are indoor. People can be benefited by indoor advertising as they can read the newspapers or see television programme when they are having leisure time. Indoor advertising can be studied under the following headings.

1. **Press Media :** Advertisement in newspapers, magazines, journals etc., can be called as press advertising. It is the most popular and widely used means of advertising. It is the most economical media of advertisement. Growth of literacy and development of press also pave the way for these press media.

Following are the **characteristics** of press media.

1. Wide coverage is possible.
2. Varieties of advertising are possible.
3. It is more effective for all purposes.
4. Reaching of the advertisements can be judged easily.
5. Detailed and informative sales programme is possible.
6. Permanency and mobility of publication are possible.
7. It is economical.
8. It is quick in action.
9. It has a longer life (magazine, journal etc.).
10. Detailed address and telephone number can also be given.

A. Newspapers

There is no doubt that the newspapers are the best and popular medium for advertising. It reaches every nook and corner of the country. It is the most powerful selling force. In India, there are many languages. Newspapers are being published in 91 languages. According to statistics, ''Indian Express'' daily newspaper is published from 10 places and prints 5,67,801 copies, ''The Times of India'' is published from 3 places and prints 5,30,565 copies daily and ''Malayala Manorama'' prints 5,27,657 copies. There is one paper, ''Anand Baazar''(Bengali) which prints 4,02,491 copies in Calcutta alone. Apart from this, newspapers are published in different languages. Current news can be known and a large number of people go through them.

Different types of newspapers are existing. They are National Dailies, Regional Dailies, Evening Dailies, National Weeklies etc. When the literacy rate is increasing, this medium can easily be adopted for good result through advertising.

Merits of Newspaper :

1. Newspapers are having a large demand and wide coverage.
2. The cost of newspaper is less when compared to its use.

3. Wide publicity is possible.
4. It contains interesting matter for everybody. 'Business news' for men, 'Ladies page' for women, 'Fashion pages' for youngster, 'Comics and puzzles' for children etc. As such it assures readership.
5. Speedy preparation and publication of advertising is possible.
6. Newspapers are read daily and hence continuous publicity is possible.
7. It makes quick results. The public response is quick. Advertisement given by sellers reaches the public quickly and they act accordingly.
8. Regular and frequent advertisement is possible.
9. It is flexible *i.e.*, number of pages and shape of the advertisement can also be changed.
10. It is suitable for direct and indirect selling.
11. Lengthy matter for advertisement can be given.
12. In local newspapers, preference is given to the advertisement of local products.
13. Effectiveness of advertisement can be estimated.
14. Selection of market is possible.
15. It is news apart from timely.

Demerits

1. It is having the shortest life. ''Today's newspaper is tomorrow's waste paper.''
2. Frequent advertisement become ineffective.
3. Newspaper advertising is affected by the illiteracy of the public. It affects the utility of newspapers also; the effectiveness is questionable.
4. Chances for display and demonstration are much rare.
5. People read newspapers in a hurry. Hence they do not take notice of the advertisement. Hence advertisement becomes a waste.

B. Magazines and Journals

These are periodically published. They are published weekly, fortnightly or monthly. Magazines are read leisurely. Magazines are published according to the tastes or liking of the public. There are different types of magazines.

(a) **General Magazines :** General magazines are read in easy-chairs. There is generally a lengthy advertisement. The standard of reproduction is also in a better way. They give more interesting and a longer duration. e.g., Illustrated Weekly, Blitz etc.

(b) **Specialists Magazines :** They are technical journals and professional journals. Technicians read technical journals. Doctors, lawyers, accountants etc., read professional journals. There are special magazines for industry, banking, politics, religion, agriculture, insurance, transport, literature etc. Special magazines for women and children are also available.

(c) **Special Issues :** Dipawali Malar, Directory (Telephone Directory) are also published which contain a large number of advertisements along with articles, stories, special features etc. Some magazines enjoy national and international circulations.

Merits

1. It is having longer life than newspapers. Hence it is a great help to advertisement.
2. It is having greater reference value of advertisement.
3. Colour advertisement attracts the people very much.
4. It is published for selected people. As such, it is having a high degree of selectivity. Famina is meant for women. Medical journals for doctors etc.
5. Cost is also comparatively low.

6. Advertisement in standard magazines creates a national image for the product, e.g., Reader's Digest, Illustrated Weekly etc.
7. It satisfies the need of a particular class of people, say "Commerce" for business.
8. Magazines guarantee uniformity of coverage.

Demerits

1. It is less flexible.
2. Limited circulation. It reaches only a limited section of people.
3. It is costly. High quality paper, colours and preparation cost of magazines are high. As such, the cost of advertising is also high.
4. Introduction of a new product is ineffective, as it takes time to advertise the new products. Hence timely information of arrival of a product is not possible.
5. Advance planning is needed to advertise in the magazine. As such advance submission of advertisement is necessary.
6. It is not suitable for regional advertising. For example, Reader's Digest is unsuitable for regional advertising.

C. Radio

Radio is the quickest medium of advertising when compared to newspapers or magazines. Sound moves faster than other media. It is a popular medium of advertising for a commercial firm. Radio makes its appeal to the ear. Commercial radio broadcasting has become popular and is widely used in all countries. It is also popular in India and the radio has started playing an important role as one of the media of advertising. It plays its role well, especially in rural areas where newspapers cannot reach. The maximum number of radio sets are in Tamil Nadu, followed by Maharashtra, West Bengal, Gujarat. Further, transistorised radio brightens the scope of advertising.

Merits

1. Coverage and appeal are wide.
2. It is the best means for illiterate people.
3. Spoken words are more effective than written words.
4. It is flexible and timely.
5. It adds to the prestige of the advertiser.
6. Spot programmes can be arranged.

Demerits

1. It is quite costly.
2. Only limited time will be allowed.
3. In many cases, listeners may be irritated with the commercial advertisements.
4. The effectiveness of advertising cannot be measured.

D. Television

It is of recent origin. It is more popular in advanced countries especially in the U.S.A. In Delhi the first television centre was set up in 1962, followed by Bombay, Calcutta, Lucknow, Madras etc. Television advertising is the latest medium of mass communication and is widely used for advertisement. It is an audio-visual medium, because one can see and hear. The maximum number of television sets are in Maharashtra followed by Delhi.

Merits

1. It appeals to the eye and the ear.
2. People are impressed by pictorial presentation.
3. Interest is further boosted by introducing colour televisions.

4. It has the characteristics of a salesman.

Demerits

1. It is an expensive medium.
2. The impact of advertising cannot be measured.
3. It is suitable only for large firms.

E. Film

The effects of television medium and film medium are the same. Film advertising is also advantageously used by advertiser. Cinema is an audio-visual medium of communication and offers opportunities to advertisers for screening commercial films and slides. In India, there are about 7000 cinema houses and 3,500 touring cinemas (approximate). The maximum number of cinema houses is in Andhra Pradesh, followed by Tamil Nadu, Maharashtra, Uttar Pradesh and Kerala. The maximum number of touring cinemas is in Tamil Nadu, followed by Andhra Pradesh and Kerala. For almost all consumer goods manufacturers are advantageously using this medium.

Merits

1. It can create a good impact on the audience.
2. It covers all classes of people–poor, middle and rich.
3. Explanation and demonstration are possible.
4. It has a wide appeal.

Demerits

1. Producing a film is costly.
2. Effectiveness cannot be measured.
3. The co-operation of theatre owners is essential.
4. The audience becomes irritated, where more such advertising films are shown.
5. Only cine goers can be covered.

II. Outdoor Advertising

Outdoor advertising passes the message to those people who are moving audience. Generally, almost all the people go out on some purpose or other–office, walk, sight-seeing, journey, park visit etc. This outdoor advertising has the best effects of advertising. Before discussing the types of outdoor advertising, let us discuss the merits and demerits of this advertising.

Merits

1. This is the best for local advertising; it has the widest appeal.
2. It speaks to everyone.
3. It engages few seconds of people's time and need no effort.
4. It always attracts the viewers, because of its style and colourful appearance.
5. Its effect is permanent.
6. It indirectly beautifies the place. With outdoor advertising, crowded places like Bombay, Calcutta, Delhi, Madras etc., appear beautiful to look on, and at the same time the unpleasant sights are covered up.
7. It is flexible.
8. It is a low cost medium.

Demerits

1. It has less advantage, compared to other media.
2. It reduces its value because of brevity.
3. The effect of prospects cannot be measured.
4. It can be used only as a supplementary type of advertising.

Types of Outdoor Advertising

1. **Mural Advertising** (Posters) : At present this is a common form of advertising. The posters are made in attractive colours in brief and printed. The poster is a sheet of paper. The matter is depicted on it. Then the prepared posters are pasted on walls or boards. Film showers use this medium for advertising and the posters are pasted in such a manner that they are projected to the people at bus stand, railway station, marketplace, parks, libraries, and crowded areas. The cost is less. It is flexible. It has a short life, because in cities, posters pasted in the morning, may disappear in the evening by pasting new papers on them. In certain places like cities, the space has to be hired for pasting posters.

2. **Advertising Boards :** These are also posters, but have better status than ordinary posters. The boards are fixed at the areas where people frequently assemble. Such boards are fixed at decent and neat places. They appear more attractive than posters.

3. **Vehicular Advertising :** This moving advertisement finds place on vehicles–buses, trains etc. The vehicle passes through many places and many people happen to see it.

4. **Painted Display :** It is an artist's work. This display is large in size. It is visible from a distance. It finds place at crossings, compound walls or erected structures built of poles or pillars.

5. **Travelling Display :** These are the advertisements as posters, small in size, written beautifully and placed inside trains, buses, tramcars, vans etc. The travelling people, in these vehicles, repeatedly notice it and keep it in their memory.

6. **Electric Display :** Electric display is more attractive. It is popular now-a-days. The beauty and attractiveness depend upon the skill of electrical engineers. Another method is that of running bulbs strap and it looks like moving. Such arrangements are common in big cities. During night time or in dark background, it is more bright and alluring. It is costly.

7. **Sky Advertising :** Sky advertising and sky writing have become popular. Big balloons with message written on them or attached to them, are allowed to float in the air. Big kites containing advertisement may be floated in the open air. Sky writing is a kind of advertising played by the pilot, through aeroplane, either by forming smoke or by illumination. Karnataka State Lottery Agencies have adopted big balloons for the sake of publicity. The inscription or writing on the balloon will speak about the products. Almost all the circus companies use the high powered revolving search lights to attract the attention of the public. All these types of advertisements can be seen from a long distance.

8. **Sandwich-men :** Sandwich-men are hired by the advertisers. They move or walk down through busy roads and streets. They dress in a peculiar way with fancy clothes. They carry posters of the product of the advertisers. They utter slogans. They create certain type of musical sounds. This sort of advertisement has short life, but is effective. Cinema theatres usually adopt this method of publicity.

9. **Handbills (Leaflets) :** Handbills are common and too cheap. Handbills, which are in the form of leaflets are distributed among the people through hired men. Sometimes, music bands are also played along with distribution of leaflets. Only interested persons may go through the handbills. The handbill distributor distributes copies of the handbill to all, who pass nearby. An uninterested person receives it by one hand and throws it away by the other hand. This type of advertising is suitable for small business people.

III. Direct Advertising

The object of direct advertising is to create a direct contact with the customers. The advertiser can keep a close touch with the customers or the public, who are supposed to have interest in his product. He contacts them and keeps a close touch with them through mail advertising. It is a common method. It is also known as direct mail advertising.

Characteristics of Direct Advertising

1. Through direct advertising, more or less a personal contact can be maintained.
2. There is a written form of communication *i.e.*, letter.
3. Contacts are through post.

Merits of Direct Advertising

1. A personal relationship with the customers can be maintained.
2. Detailed information can be conveyed.
3. Effectiveness of this system can be measured.
4. This system is elastic; addition or deletion is possible.
5. Privacy can be maintained.
6. It is highly selective; *i.e.*, sending the letters to those, whom the advertiser selects.
7. It is cheaper.

Demerits

1. In drafting mail, specialised skill is needed.
2. It is difficult to maintain an up-to-date mailing list.
3. The success depends upon the reaching of the recipient.
4. In many cases, it fetches no attention of the receiver.

1. **Sales Letters :** Sales letters are persuasive in nature. Many firms think every letter that goes out from the firm is a sales letter, because every business letter aims at an opportunity to sell the firm's product or earn a goodwill for the firm. To a certain extent, the salesman is substituted by the sales letters because the purpose of salesman and sales letters is the same, *i.e.*, push up the sales. Drafting a sales letter is in the form of advertising, to create an interest in the mind of the reader. Sales letters are cheaper and convenient.

Purpose of Sales Letter

1. To confer faith in the product.
2. To get an enquiry letter from the reader.
3. To create an interest in the recipient's mind.
4. To create sales and goodwill.

2. **Circulars :** It carries communication to a number of addresses. The circular letter contains information about the products. It is generally cyclostyled or is in the printed form. It carries less attention than the sales letter. The merits and demerits are similar to sales letters.

3. **Booklets and Catalogues :** These contain more particulars of the product and the firm. Booklets are in the form of a small book. Catalogue contains more information than a booklet. Fundamentally both are similar. Catalogue will be more attractive and it contains illustration of products with details and price lists.

4. **Folders :** These are letters or cards containing details of the products. They contain illustration. Folders can be sent without an envelop. The folders can be folded conveniently, as they are made of thick paper. These are generally adopted by publishers, medical firms, industrialists etc. The folders must be attractive.

5. **Package Inserts :** This is a system through which leaflets about the products are inserted in the packets of products. The package insert may contain details of the same product or other products of the same firm. Thus, it is an advertisement.

6. **Store Publication :** This is also known as 'house organs'. Certain firms may publish periodicals or magazines which contain information about the development of the firm. These will be distributed to wholesalers, retailers etc., free of cost. This will also explain the product in detail.

IV. Promotional Advertising

The object of promotional advertising is to increase the sales. These are also known as 'display advertising'. By this, we mean that the products are systematically kept in a place so as to attract the attention and notice of the lookers. It demonstrates the products. The following are the important types :

1. **Window Display** (outside display) : Window display is the medium used to attract the public by creating an interest in them. The products dealt in by the firm are placed at the front of the firm, trying to create an arousing interest in the minds of them. A good arranged system of window display naturally increases the sales. It gives a memorising attitude to the public, even if one is not entering the shop at the sight of the display.

How should a window display be?

1. It must be in a suitable position.
2. The window should not be crowded with items.
3. Good light and pleasing colours are essential.
4. Articles in display must be changed often.
5. It must create attention, attraction, interest, desire and action.
6. The price tag should be attached to products.
7. It must always be kept clean and neat.

Merits

1. It has "at the point of purchase" effect.
2. It attracts the onlookers.
3. It is used as an indicator of status to the firm.

2. **Interior Display :** In large-scale organisations, they use this type of display. Glass-doored cupboards, sunglass show-cases are used for internal display. Window display is arranged outside, but interior display is inside the shop. The related articles are displayed within easy reach. It is easy for the buyers to get the products needed by them.

Merits

1. Purchasing is made easier.
2. It facilitates to sell allied products.
3. The whole shop becomes attractive.
4. It is flexible.

3. **Show-Room :** Consumers always insist on prior inspection of the products, which they aim to purchase. Therefore sellers must provide facility for their inspection. Buyers are not satisfied with mere publicity. They want to have a close look at the product. In a show-room, not only the needed products are kept, but different products also. And this creates an inward interest on other products, when one makes a purchase of the needed item. In the show-room, salesmen are there to explain about the prospects. It must be highly decorated and must have good lighting arrangement with good atmosphere. For instance, textile mills, and firms producing furniture, refrigerators, television sets, radio sets and other luxurious items must have generally show-rooms.

Merits

1. The show-room appears as a sales centre.
2. Consumers can study the product and its proper functions as well as precautions.

4. **Exhibition :** It is known to everyone. This is also known as trade shows. The idea behind the exhibition is to promote sales of the goods exhibited. All, big or small, manufacturers reserve stalls in the exhibition area to exhibit their products. Exhibitions are popular and it is the place

where competitors meet. They are held on local, national or international level.

Merits

1. Variety of products display can be witnessed.
2. It is always interesting to the public.
3. It is a ready-made market.

When selecting a medium for advertising, the following should be considered:

1. Objective of advertising.
2. The financial ability of the producer.
3. The nature and extent of competition.
4. The prospective buyers.
5. The class of buyers (caste, age, sex, etc.).
6. Whereabouts of his customers.
7. Nature of message.
8. Medium to be adopted.
9. The cost of medium.
10. Circulation of the medium.

Is Advertising a Waste ?

When the objectives of an advertisement are not realised, then the amount spent on advertising is a waste. If it is so, this amount can be utilised for some beneficial purposes–improving the quality or other services. One should consider all relevant factors before taking a decision on its usefulness or waste. The aim of advertisement is to promote sales of products or service. Advertisement awakens the public at large. The cost of advertisement is included in the price, *i.e.*, increased price.

Advertising is mobilising marketing wheels. A country like ours, is developing in all fields, and this is because of advertising of new and developed ideas. Social advertising is a widely adopted method. As far as the consumers are concerned, advertisement is a waste, when it conveys incomplete information or a false information. However cost is finally paid by consumers. At the same time, if the advertiser increases the sales because of advertising, it is not a waste. If the expenditure is unproductive, then it is a waste. Advertising is a wheel, on which marketing moves.

Advantages of Advertising :

1. The commercial world has become one.
2. Close touch between consumers and producer is facilitated.
3. It furnishes necessary information to the consumers
4. It helps in disposing of products.
5. It is a boon for new products.
6. A brand gets popularity.
7. It is a boon to retailers.
8. Industries can flourish.
9. Consumers know the comparative benefits.
10. It creates goodwill.

In spite of its cost, advertising is preferred by all, as the advertising opens the door of progress and prosperity. All the advantages may be considered in understanding the merits in favour of ''advertising is not a waste.''

Follow Up System in Advertising

The follow up system, as the very name suggests, is a type of advertising to approach the customer by means of correspondence. The advertiser receives enquiries from customers in response to the advertisement made. The enquiries are properly entered in a book and replies are sent. By sending a mere reply it does not come to an end. An enquirer may be followed regularly through correspondence till it yields a result. Letters may be sent one after another, at an interval of about two weeks, till the result is achieved or finally stopped. Upon sending reply, if nothing is heard from the enquirer again he is approached by writing letters. This ''follow up system'' is effective in concluding a sale.

Keying the Advertisement

Generally, there arises a problem in choosing ''how to advertise'' We see the Newspapers, T.V., Radio, etc. are full of advertisements. Everybody advertises in one or the other way. However, one has to select the best medium, which fulfils one's purpose. This is possible by ''Keying'' the advertising. ''Keying'' means to adopt such methods while advertising that the result may be easily assured. The following are the methods :

1. By giving different addresses to different media, and when enquiries are received, it can easily be found out through scrutiny which publication fetches more enquiries. The publication which facilitates more enquiries may be selected and the rest may be dropped.
2. Different papers may be selected for the advertisement of different departments.
3. A coupon may be left with the advertisement with a request to make enquiries along with coupons.
4. Request may be made with the customers to name the particular medium through which he gets information.

Advertising Agency

Almost all good organisations have a separate department for advertising activities and is known as advertising department. It is headed by an advertising manager. It is not possible for all the organisations to maintain a separate department. Moreover, the present era is a stage of stiff competition in the field of marketing. And this invites specialised hands to deal with the advertising campaign, which is becoming more complex. Thus, the advertising agency has come up. The advertising agency is a service organisation. It is a specialised unit in the field of advertising.

An advertising agency is a group of persons, who are experts on various phases of advertising and related marketing areas. Such agencies are slowly progressing in India, whereas such agencies in advertising are well-developed in the U.S.A. The function of advertising is to sell goods and services to their clients, who have messages to be conveyed to the public. They are specialists who give expert assistance to their clients. An advertising agency is an independent concern. It acts as an agent or consultant for the advertiser. In early periods, they sold spaces to an advertiser and arranged for the publication in the newspaper on behalf of the advertiser. Now there are various media existing and new style of advertising has come up. The role of advertising agency has been upgraded. Thus, the advertising agency performs the following useful services :

1. They develop attractive and cheaper ideas for advertising.
2. The specialised agency, who has all facilities, such as artists, painters, photographers, expert personnel etc., can offer the best advantageous services to the advertisers.
3. They possess a closer relation with media owners and this facilitates in obtaining space and timely presentation at a competitive rate.
4. The burden of advertiser is undertaken by them, so that they are freed and can attend to other jobs.
5. The expenditure met by the advertiser for advertising can be turned into productive expenditure with the help of agencies.

6. Generally advertiser find difficulty in the preparation of advertisement copy. Often they make wrong copy. But the agency prepares the copy quickly and correctly. This relieves the burden of advertiser.
7. The agency also does the work of special packing, designing, sales training, research, test marketing etc., for their clients.

Selection of an Advertising Agency

The advertiser has to consider certain factors while selecting an advertising agency. They are :

1. The agency to be selected should have experience and must be peculiar to the business of the advertiser.
2. The line of products usually accepted by the agency, is to be considered.
3. The available facilities and equipments with them are to be ascertained.
4. The financial soundness of the agency is to be checked.
5. Goodwill and market reputation are earned through advertising.
6. "Time is money," specially to business people. Bringing the advertisement in time is an important factor.
7. Basis of remuneration for the work is to be considered.

Advantages of services of advertising agency, in brief are:

1. Advertiser is freed.
2. Benefit of economy goes to the advertiser.
3. The work is quick and satisfactory.
4. Advertising looks more attractive.
5. Market research is available at cheap rate.
6. It promotes sales.
7. Advantageous utilisation of fund is possible.

Remuneration of Agency

The advertising agencies are specialised in publicity. As such, experts are employed. The agency works for the advertiser either on commission basis or on fees basis. Under commission basis, generally the agency receives 15% of the cost media. The commission is paid to the media owners by the advertiser. In case, any special work is done on behalf of the advertiser, then the advertiser has to compensate him. In other cases, the agency is paid by the media owner at 15% of the cost, which is collected from the advertiser. In certain cases, the advertising agency collects the amount from the client, deducts 15% and the balance is given to the media owner. Under fees basis, a lump sum is charged by the agency.

Advertising Budget

Having determined the advertising objectives, the next important managerial task is to determine the advertisement budget. The amount set aside exclusively for advertising is known as advertising budget or appropriation. The firm may be spending the amount in order to achieve the sales goals. The question raised in this respect is how much amount can a producer or manufacturer spend on advertising? The financial manager has to tackle this problem. But it is a difficult task to be solved. Generally every year, an estimate will be made to calculate the amount for advertisement. There are different factors to be considered before making out a budget for advertising. Mainly PLC stages have to be looked upon. Here, the emphasis is given to the basis or methods available for determining the advertising budget or appropriation. They are briefly discussed below :

1. **Affordable Method :** Under this approach, a company, to determine the advertising appropriation, is to find out what the company can afford. It can spend for advertising as much as

the funds permit. From the name itself it is clear that the affordable amount set apart for advertising, is known as affordable method. It means that the advertising expenses may vary from year to year. Under this method the weakness may be (1) The opportunities of advertising are overlooked (2) It is difficult to plan long-term marketing development.

2. **Percentage of Sales Methods :** Here the budget amount is decided for advertising as a percentage of sales, *i.e.*, relationship between advertising expenses and sales revenue. For instance, a company may allot Rs. 5,000 which is 2% of the preceding year's past or forecast or anticipated sales *i.e.*, Rs. 2,50,000.

Merits

1. The method is simple in calculation.
2. A clear relationship exists between sales and advertising expenses.
3. Advertisement wars can be avoided.

Demerits

1. Past figures may be incorrect for the future.
2. Declining sales reduce the advertising expenses and is not a dynamic method. But, when sales decrease, advertising must be increased.
3. This system takes advertising as the result of sales. But it should be the cause of sales.

3. **Competitive Comparison Method :** A company sets its budget solely depending upon the basis of competitor's expenditure. That is under this method, the advertising appropriation is decided on the basis of spending for advertising by the competitors. For this a company has to collect relevant data about competitors. They will do simply what others have done.

4. **Objective and Task Method :** This is also known as research-objective method. The amount is set aside on the basis of objectives to be achieved and tasks to be involved. Under this method, three questions are involved: (1) What does the company want to accomplish? (2) What is necessary in order to accomplish this? (3) What will it cost to do this?

Merits

1. Advertising objectives are achieved.
2. It is flexible.
3. A clear advertisement programme can be drawn.

Demerits

1. The cost of objectives may not be estimated exactly.
2. It is more rational.

5. **Return on Investment Method :** Here the advertising budget is considered as an investment, thereby expecting a certain return in terms of profit. A clear study is made by emphasising the relation between advertisement and sales. Sales are measured with advertising and without advertising. That is, the profit obtained by advertising is compared with the cost of advertising.

Evaluation of Advertising

By the execution of the advertising programme, the responsibility of the management does not come to an end. It has to evaluate the advertising programme and this refers to careful exercise to evaluate the advertising result and the objectives, so as to assess the effectiveness of the advertisement programme.

Need : 1. What has been done and what is planned for the future–for an intelligent decision. 2. To plan for future improved decisions. 3. To adopt a proper and effective communication mix and media mix.

The methods, generally, adopted to evaluate communication of advertising are:

1. **Enquiry Test :** The number of enquiries received against advertisement is a test to know the effectiveness of advertising. To give more encouragement, the following techniques can be adopted:

(a) **Couponing :** Advertisements may carry coupons. The readers are encouraged to fill the coupons with address and return them to the advertiser. And in return, a detailed information of the product, generally, in the form of a booklet will be sent to the interested persons. An advertisement with the higher number of enquiries is considered favourable.

(b) **Split Run Test :** The advertising copy is differentiated, in approach, appeal or layout and of course with different addresses of the advertiser. The readers are encouraged to send enquiries. The copy generating larger number of enquiries is considered more effective.

2. **Recognition Test :** A sample of readers is selected with a view to measure the effectiveness of an advertisement, read by them. For this, a survey is conducted by the interviewers. The readers have also read other advertisements, including the one tested. They are asked to identify them. Here, a copy, which is recognised by a large number of readers is considered more effective.

3. **Real Test :** It is based on memory. It attempts to measure the communication effectiveness through a survey. The survey is made on those who have seen the advertisement. And copies of the publicity may be circulated among them. Opinions of both these (survey and copy) are collected from the people. Through this, the medium, accepted by the larger group is adopted.

Slogans are short catchy phrases used in advertisement. They strike the attention of readers and hearers. They are pregnant with sales ideas. They carry clear meaning and felicitous phrases. They linger in the memory for a long time.

A few examples

"GLAXO Builds Bonny Babies."

"Neither Birds nor Winds are faster–ABT Parcel Service."

"Nescafe–the Coffee that tastes good."

"Young Complexions love Pears."

"**Dunlop** leads the way."

"If it is GODREJ, it is safe."

"Don't say Ink–Say QUINK."

"COLGATE stands for quality."

"The World's Most Wanted Pen–PARKER 51."

"FIRE-STONE the only gum dipped tyre."

"DUNLOP equips the wheels of the Nation."

"No Bad Breath when you use BINACA."

A few specimens of advertisement are given below:

HOTEL KANYA AT KANYAKUMARI (T. N.)

Hotel KANYA has :

* 200 single/double rooms with/without A/C.
* Swimming pool.
* Rooms with telephone facilities.
* Roof garden.
* Personal attention.

* 24 hours smiling service.
* Delicious meals.
* Shopping complex inside.
* Banking facilities.
* Post Office Counter.
* Tour arrangements.
* Comfortable Theatre.
* Booking facilities for air/ship travels.

WELCOME FOR A PLEASURABLE HOMELY STAY IN HOTEL KANYA

***

AH! MEDICO TOOTH PASTE

Smile in confidence.
Breathe fresh air.
Preserve clean teeth.
Laugh always at close
Protect teeth decay.

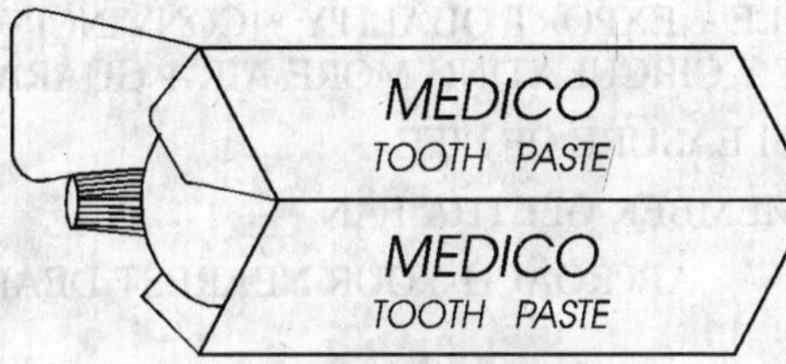

FRESH MORNING AND EVENING WITH MEDICO PASTE
WITH JOY FROM MEDICO PASTE

***

STOP LISTEN LOOK

HAVE YOU GOT BODY PAIN?

PAINKILLER

It acts in the following ways :

* Quick relief.
* Checks gas formation.
* Maintains correct pressure.
* Keeps digestive process.
* Stores energy to body.
* ONLY ONE PILL will push out your pain.

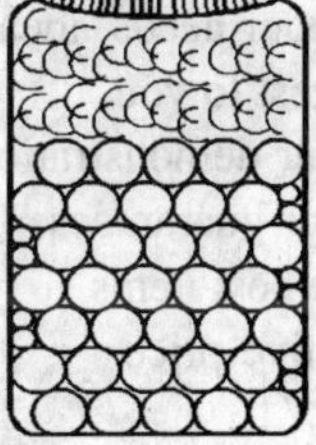

Swallow one pill along with cold water.
The pill acts in you.
How soon ?
WITHIN SEVEN MINUTES.
At the EIGHTH minute, you will forget PAIN
THANKS TO THE PAIN KILLER
Available in all medical shops, throughout India.

***

Geetha Fans

STOP ! HAVE FRESH AIR

AWARD WINNER FOR → STANDARD
→ QUALITY
→ DURABILITY

Here is the proof:

Manufactured in	1998	:	250 fans
	1999	:	2,560 fans
	2000	:	8,100 fans
	2001	:	35,000 fans
	2005	:	57,500 fans
	2008	:	2,50,000 fans

Because our FAN is:

CHEAPER + DURABLE + EXPORT QUALITY + CONVINCING + ATTRACTIVE
COMPACT + CIRCULATING MORE AIR + GUARANTEED

TO ENJOY PLEASURE OF LIFE

REMEMBER GEETHA FAN

APPROACH YOUR NEAREST DEALER

* * *

B. K. Shopping Complex

OCEAN OF :

MIXIES : FANS : RADIOS
CLOCKS : WATCHES : TAPES :
TAILORING MACHINES : TV :
DVD : FRIDGES : CLOTHES :
GAS STOVES : AIR COOLERS : AIR CONDITIONERS:
UTENSILS : WASHING MACHINES : PLASTIC GOODS :
CARS : JEEPS : SCOOTERS AND EVERYTHING

Drop in and see for yourself.
Tell us your needs–ideas–budget
We suggest to you.
Watch our demonstrations.
Check our guarantees.
Have the best items.
Competitive price.

REVEAL YOUR DREAM
WE MAKE IT COME TRUE.

REMEMBER, VISIT, FULFIL YOUR NEEDS FROM :
B. K. SHOPPING COMPLEX

* * *

BABYTRON

WHY PEOPLE PREFER BABYTRON TV

BECAUSE IT HAS :

* Anti-glare imported glass screen.
* Built-in shutter.
* Double speakers.
* DVD input.
* Attractive model.
* Hi-fi double speaker.
* Auto frequency tuning.
* Moulded plastic cabinet.
* Colour tracking.
* Channel indicator.
* Electronic built-in stabiliser.
* High gain and quality picture.
* Remote control facility.
* Sleek European style design.
* Built-in voltage regulator.
* Feather touch off-on control.

QUESTIONS

1. What is advertising? Discuss its objectives and point out the problems of advertising in India. (*B.A., Allahabad*)
2. Discuss briefly the use and objectives of advertising. What are its limitations ? (*B.A., Allahabad*)
3. ''Advertising brings long-term benefit, but sales promotion is for quicker result.'' (*B.Com., Sardar Patel*)
4. Define advertising. What role should advertising play in consumer vs. industrial marketing ? (*M.Com., Andhra*)
5. How is advertising effectiveness tested? (*B.Com., Chennai*)
6. What are the important features of an advertisement copy? (*B.Com., Madurai*)
7. ''Advertising sells products''. Do you agree with this statement? Give reasons for your answer and explain the functions performed by advertising. (*B.Com., Madurai*)
8. Discuss the essential features of a sound advertising policy. (*B.Com., Madurai*)
9. Explain the steps in preparing an advertisement copy. (*B.Com., Mysore*)
10. Mention the functions of an advertising agency. (*B.Com., Madurai*)
11. Examine the factors that are to be considered in the selection of media for advertising. (*B.Com., Madurai*)
12. The success of the advertisement campaign depends on proper selection of the media. Discuss. (*B.Com., Bharathiyar*)
13. What are the purposes of advertising as a sales tool and as a communication tool? How does it fulfil its purposes? (*B.Com., Mysore*)
14. Explain the various sales promotion methods undertaken at dealer's as well as consumer's levels. (*B.Com. Bangalore*)

15. Explain the advantage of advertising to the manufacturers, traders and consumers. (*B.Com., Bangalore*)
16. Discuss the importance of advertisement in modern business. (*B.Com., Madurai*)
17. Is it essential to use an advertising agency? (*B.Com., Mumbai*)
18. ''Money spent on advertisement is wasteful.'' Do you agree? Give reasons. (*B.Com., Madurai*)
19. Why do we advertise ? Discuss. (*B.Com., Mumbai*)
20. What qualities should be possessed by a good advertisement copy? (*B.Com., Bharatidasan*)
21. Explain fully the key factors influencing media planning. (*B.Com., Madurai*)
22. How can advertising manager evaluate the effectiveness of a firms' advertising? (*B.Com., Madurai*)
23. What do you understand by ''keying the Advertising''? (*B.Com., Chennai*)
24. What is advertising budget? (*B.Com., Madurai*)
25. Do you think that advertising is an investment? Discuss. (*B.Com., Madurai*)
26. What do you mean by scientific advertising ? (*B.Com., Banglore*)
27. Why advertisement fails ? Discuss.

CHAPTER 27

Personal Selling

- Introduction
- Objectives of Personal Selling
- Salesmanship
- Definition
- Modern Concept
- Science or Art
- Is Salesmanship a Profession
- Objectives
- Importance
- Duties of Salesman
- Qualities of Successful Salesman
- Sales Personality
- Knowledge of Products
- Knowledge of Customers
- Classification of Customers
- Types of Salesman
- Theories of Personal Selling
- AIDAS Theory
- "Right a set of Circumstances"
- "Buying Formula"
- "Behavioural Equation"
- Features of Personal Selling
- Process of Personal Selling
- Why Salesman Fail?
- Questions

INTRODUCTION

Rovert Louis Stevenson stated, ''Everyone lives by selling something.'' The people who do selling are called salesmen, sales representatives, sales persons, account executives, sales consultants, sales engineers, field representatives, agents, service representatives, marketing representatives etc. Personal selling and salesmanship are used without distinction. But there are some differences between the two. Personal selling is a broader concept. Philip Kotler is of the opinion that personal selling involves oral presentation in a conversation with one or more prospective purchasers for the purpose of making sales. Personal selling is a greatly distinctive form of promotion. Like advertising and sales promotion, personal selling is also a method of communication. It is a two-way form of communication. It involves individual and social behaviour. Each person is contacted by face to face conversation. Personal selling influences the buyers to buy a product. Personal selling reaches the goal of marketing effort *i.e.*, to increase profitable sales. The purpose of personal selling is to bring the right products into contact with the right customers, and to make certain that ownership transfers take place. Personal selling creates product awareness, stimulates interest, develops brand preferences, negotiates price etc.

The American Marketing Association defines the term salesmanship as "the Personal or impersonal process of assisting and/or persuading a prospective customer to buy a commodity or service and to act favourably upon an idea that has commercial significance to the seller."

Advertising, sales promotion and personal selling ensure the process of selling. Of the three personal selling is more important. It contacts the concerned persons in person and hence it is more effective.

Objectives of Personal Selling

Personal selling has two types of objectives–long-term and short-term. The long-term objectives, which are more or less permanent, are broader. These are also known as qualitative objectives. The objectives under this head are :

1. To do the entire job.
2. To serve the existing customers.

3. To search out and obtain new customers.
4. To secure and maintain customers' co-operation in stocking and promoting the product line.
5. To keep customers informed of changes in the product line.
6. To assist customers in selling the product line.
7. To provide technical advice and assistance to customers.
8. To handle the sales personnel of middlemen.
9. To provide advice and assistance to middlemen whenever needed.
10. To collect and report market information on interested matters to company management.

Apart from these qualitative objectives mentioned above, certain quantitative objectives are also assigned, known as short-term objectives, to personal selling, and they are :

1. To obtain a specified sales volume.
2. To obtain sales volume in ways that contribute to profit objectives, by selling proper mix of products.
3. To keep the personal selling expenses within specified limits.
4. To secure and retain a specified share of the market.

Salesmanship

''The personal selling'' and ''salesmanship'' are often used interchangeably, but there is an important difference. Personal selling is the broader concept. Salesmanship may or may not be an important part of personal selling and it is never all of it. Along with other key marketing elements, such as pricing, advertising, product development and research, marketing channels and physical distribution, the personal selling is a means through which marketing programmes are implemented. The broad purpose of marketing is to bring a firm's products into contact with markets and to effect profitable exchanges of products for money. The purpose of personal selling is to bring the right products into contact with the right customers, and make ownership transfer. Salesmanship is one of the skills used in personal selling, as defined by Stroh, ''it is a direct, face-to-face, seller-to-buyer influence which can communicate the facts necessary for marketing a buying decision; or it can utilize the psychology of persuation to encourage the formation of a buying decision''. Salesmanship is seller-initiated effort that provides prospective buyers with information and motivates or persuades them to make favourable buying decisions concerning the seller's products or service. The salesman of today has to react and interact in many different ways to many different people. Apart from the knowledge of the product, a salesperson has to be a psychologist with one prospect, a human computer with another, an adviser with another, and at the same time a friend with some buyers. Salespersons must adjust their personalities on every call. Salesmanship may be implemented not only through personal selling but through advertising. Thus, advertising has been described as ''salesmanship in print.''

Some definitions emphasise that salesmanship is the art of influencing or persuading people to do what sales representative wants them to do. For instance, contractors, teachers, ministers, authors, politicians, industrial engineers etc. practice the art of influencing others to do what they want them to do. Every man is a salesman in his own walks of life.

''He who works with his **hands** is a **labourer**.

''He who works with his **hands** and his **head** is a **craftman**.

''He who works with his **hands, head** and **heart** is an **artist.**

''He who works with his **hands**, his **head,** his **heart** and his **feet** is a **salesman**.''

Salesmanship is the ability to persuade people to want the things which they already need. Salesmanship is the ability to convert human needs into wants. The work of salesman is a service *i.e.*, helping the consumer. The salesman gives a solution to the customer's problems. Salesmanship is the ability to handle the people and to handle the products.

Definition

According to W.G. Carter, "Salesmanship is an attempt to induce people to buy goods."

According to the National Association of Marketing Teachers of America, "It is the ability to persuade people to buy goods or services at a profit to the seller and benefit to the buyer."

According to Knox, "Salesmanship is the power or ability to influence people to buy at a mutual profit, that which we have to sell, but which they may not have thought of buying until call their attention to it. Salesmanship is the ability to persuade people to want they already need."

According to Prof. Stephenson, "Salesmanship refers to conscious efforts on the part of the seller to induce a prospective buyer to purchase something that he had not really decided to buy, even if he had thought of it favourably. It consists of persuading people to buy what you have for sale in making them want it, in helping to make up their minds."

According to J.C. Jagasia, "It is an ability to remove ignorance, doubt, suspicion and emotional objection concerning the usefulness of a product."

According to Holtzclaw, "Salesmanship is the power to persuade plenty of people to pleasurably and permanently purchase your product at a profit."

According to Carfield Blake, "Salesmanship consists of winning the buyers' confidence for the sellers' house and goods, thereby winning regular and permanent customers."

According to Sefred Gross, "Salesmanship is the art of increasing satisfaction by persuading those people who should do so to buy specific goods or service."

Thus, salesmanship is the process of persuading a person to buy goods or services. It does not mean that salesmanship is applied only to personal selling; it can also be applied to advertising–printed salesmanship. Salesmanship in its broader meaning, includes all types of persuasion means, by a seller, viz., advertising, personal selling and other methods.

Modern Concept of Salesmanship

In olden days, a salesman takes an order. He shows the goods. He waits for an order. Then he receives the payment. He never attempts to guide, or help or persuade the consumers.

But the modern concept of salesmanship is entirely different from the old concept of salesmanship. Modern concept is creative in approach. He creates needs and converts them into wants. Customer satisfaction is the main problem of salesman. Mutual profit is essential both for the buyer and the seller. Salesman guides the customer to buy things which satisfy his want. Salesman motivates the feelings of the customers to act.

Is Salesmanship a Science or an Art ?

What is Science ? Science is a body of systematised knowledge. When calling anything as a science, it must be able to build up a body of laws or principles. The characteristics and behaviour of facts are analysed systematically and laws are formulated. Science is a system of facts and principles concerning a subject. Science is defined as an accepted knowledge that has been systematised and formulated with reference to the discovery or operation of general law. The principles or the set of generalisation, universally accepted, are called laws of that science. It is the knowledge of research, discovery and experience and the principles are universally accepted.

Salesmanship is a systematically arranged and specialised knowledge. It has its own rules and principles. Salesmanship is a science based on human psychology. A salesman has to study the psychology of the consumers. He must have knowledge about their behaviour. He must have knowledge about the different characteristics of goods which he has to sell. As such, he requires a systematic knowledge of those goods. As a science, salesmanship tries to follow certain basic principles, approach, demonstration and concluding a sale etc. All these have to be followed systematically. Thus we may say that salesmanship is a science.

What is an Art? On the other hand, art is making of the knowledge more efficient by applying skill. Art is skill. Art is a practical science. Art is a knack for doing something which is acquired by study, practice and special experience. If science is knowledge, then art is action. By science we know a thing; by art we do that thing. An art is skill in performance acquired by study, observation and experience.

Art is the practical side of skill. It is a knack for doing something which is acquired by study and practice. Science makes a man perfect and arts makes a man exact. Art is difficult to learn. It can be studied easily by the person who has the skill. A salesman must possess the skill and it can be acquired and developed. Every customer is an individual, but individuals are different. And a salesman has to diagnose the customer by efficient dealings, of course by using his skills. A salesman must have necessary knowledge and skill to face the various types of customers. Exact human behaviour is unpredictable, uncontrollable and un-understandable. Therefore, we can say that salesmanship is an art.

Salesmanship, 'the ship' signifies skill or art, that is sales-art or sales-skill. The salesman must thoroughly master the science and the technique of skill. Salesmanship is neither a science nor an art, but the combination of both. A salesman must have inborn talents and must possess real interest in his profession. The art requires patient practice and application of correct methods. Therefore, salesmanship is art-science based.

Is Salesmanship a Profession ?

A certain degree of skill or specialisation is required for a profession. Professional people such as lawyers, doctors, writers and actors get along with their clients. Some people say, "Salesman are born, but not made." Others feel, "Salesmen are mostly made than born." Still others assert, "Salesmen are born and made." There are certain qualities–emotional, physical development etc., that are born qualities. With pleasing personality and through convincing approach, prospects can be made attractive. But for a good salesman, personality alone is not enough. There are specialised institutions imparting training in salesmanship. A professional usually considers 'service' as its aim. He offers his service to his employer, whose profit is increased. Again the profession requires skill. The skill is present in the salesmanship. A professional man secures the best regards for the mastery of his subject. In the era of stiff competition, personality alone will not make a sale. Training makes one a good salesman. Thus, salesman is nothing but a skilful dealer with the public and he converts them into customers. The knowledge of four fundamentals–prospect, product, personality and organisation together with mastery over sales process makes salesmanship a profession.

The **basic requirements** for a true profession include the following :

1. An organized body of knowledge,
2. A relatively long and specialized preparation,
3. An organised plan or programme to train individuals who plan to enter the profession,
4. An established and accepted code of ethics,
5. A set of standards for admission and disqualification,
6. Recognition that service to others comes before self-interest.

An occupation to be called a profession should satisfy the above requirements.

Hello ! Professional Salespersons

1. You must aim at success.
2. You must get along with people.
3. You must exercise self-discipline.
4. You must develop selling skills.
5. You must have product knowledge.

The Professional Sales Representative's Creed :

1. I will place customer and company interests above self-interest.
2. I will be constantly alert to the concept that successful selling must bring mutual and continuous benefits to both the buyer and seller.
3. I will maintain an optimistic and positive attitude towards my business at all times.
4. I will maintain loyalty to my company, my associates and my customers.
5. I will do everything possible to support the free enterprise system based upon open competition and freedom of choice in the marketplace.
6. I will continue to develop new knowledges, skills and attitudes to keep pace with the changing technological and social environment.
7. I will make every effort possible to utilize efficiently my total capacities in rendering quality service to my customers and company.
8. I will never violate the trust and confidence of my customers or associates.
9. I will maintain honesty and integrity in all of my dealings with my customers, competitors, colleagues and company.
10. In all of my personal activities I will attempt to do what is right and just for all parties concerned.

–Pederson and Wright

Personal Selling–Objectives : (Qualitative)

1. To do the entire selling job (as when there are no other elements in the promotional mix).
2. To ''serve'' existing accounts (*i.e.,* to maintain contacts with present customers, takc orders etc.)
3. To search out and obtain new customers.
4. To secure and maintain customer's cooperation in stocking and promoting the product line.
5. To keep customers informed of changes in the product line and other aspects of marketing strategy.
6. To assist customers in selling the product line (as through ''missionary selling'').
7. To provide technical advice and assistance to customers (as with complicated products and where products are specially designed to fit buyers' specifications).
8. To assist with (or hand) the training of middlemen's sales personnel.
9. To provide advice and assistance to middlemen on various management problems.
10. To collect and report market information of interest and use to company management.

Objectives (Quantitative)

1. To obtain sales volume in ways that contribute to profit objectives.
2. To keep personal-selling expenses within certain limits.
3. To secure and retain a certain share of the market.
4. To obtain some number of new accounts of given types.
5. To secure a given percentage of certain accounts' business.

–Still and Cundiff

Importance of Salesmanship

In the present day, salesmanship plays an important part. Salesman is the connecting link between sellers and buyers at every step., *i.e.*, from the collection of raw materials to the finished products. Of all, customers are the most benefited by salesmen. Present era is of large-scale production, which is in anticipation of demand. The market expands along with competition. This makes distribution a difficult and a complex factor in the face of still competition. The expansion of the market, growing competition etc., invite a better salesmanship.

1. **Important to Producers :** Salesmanship is important to producers and manufacturers. For pushing products into the competitive market, salesmanship is necessary. To capture new markets also salesmanship is very important. Salesmen increase the sales volume. It brings larger profits to the manufacturers. Salesmen work as the ''eye and ear'' for the manufacturers. They improve their products according to the taste of the consumers. They improve their sales policies by keeping in mind the suggestions, impressions and complaints of the consumers. He is the creator of demand. Hence it leads to increased production and increased business activity. As such it increases employment opportunity as well as personal incomes.

2. **Important to Consumers :** Salesman educates and guides the consumers. He gives them more satisfaction. 'Consumers are right' in the marketing. As such, he gives more importance to them. Salesman helps the consumers in making the right decision and proper selection of the products which they want to buy.

Salesmanship increases the rate of turnover, and hence reduces unsold stock. As such it minimises the economic stagnation. Consumers can select the best products according to their requirements, taste and money.

Duties of a Salesman

1. The principal duty is to make sales of products or services.
2. He has to do the assigned duty (travelling).
3. He has to make collection of bills relating to sale.
4. He has to make report–Sales made, Calls made, Services rendered, customers lost, competition and any other matters, relating to firm.
5. All complainants must be satisfied peacefully.
6. He has to attend sales meetings.
7. A salesman with his experience must supply information in order to solve problems relating to product or the firm.
8. He must maintain a good relation with the customers.
9. He must assist the customers to make good selection.
10. He must develop a goodwill for the firm and the products.
11. He must have cooperative habits.
12. He takes periodic inventories of the stocks.

Characteristics or the Qualities of a Successful Salesman

Reid gives the following characteristics of a good salesman :

1. Establishing good relationship with a variety of people.
2. Learning quickly and adapting smoothly.
3. Planning ahead and efficiently managing his time and efforts.
4. Working hard to achieve his goals, dedicating himself to provide long-term service, rather than having a get-rich-quick attitude.
5. Communicating clearly both in speech and in writing.
6. Thinking analytically and learning to break problems down to their basic components.

7. Producing constantly both in quality and quantity rather than performing erratically.
8. Persisting steadily his goal and not giving up easily.
9. Possessing and living up to high moral characteristics that enable people to admire, respect and trust him.

"Personality is the personal distinction or dynamic force which is felt by everybody who comes within the radius." Personality is the sum total of the impressions made on people with whom one comes into contact. The impression is the result of many qualities that one possesses. There are a number of qualities which make a salesman successful. To become a successful salesman, he must master all the traits. A number of evidences as given by R.G. Walters, J.W Windate, Russel etc. divide the qualities of a successful salesman into the following major factors. They are (1) Personality of a salesman (2) Knowledge of the product and (3) Knowledge of the customers and their buying motives.

Sales Personality

I. Physical Qualities

The physical qualities are (1) A good appearance, (2) Sound health (3) A good posture and (4) Pleasing voice.

1. **Good Appearance :** The outward appearance makes some impression on the customers. A good-looking salesman in a neat dress with pleasing appearance will succeed in capturing the minds of the consumers. People may not like to deal with or make purchases from a salesman, who is dressed clumsily, spreading bad odour with unclean hands. Cleanliness is important for a better look. He must have well brushed his hair. He must have a cheerful smiling face, which is considered as a mirror of the mind. If he looks serious, then he must learn how to smile. A weeping face is not welcome.

QUALITIES OF A GOOD SALESMAN

I. Physical Qualities	**II. Mental Qualities**
1. Good appearance	1. Quick-actioned
2. Sound health	2. Imagination
3. A good posture	3. Self-confidence
4. Pleasing voice	4. Enthusiasm
	5. Creative talk
	6. Initiative
	7. Observation
III. Social Qualities	**IV. Character or Moral Qualities**
1. Good manners	1. Determination
2. Courtesy	2. Sincerity
3. Tactfulness	3. Integrity
4. Helpfulness	4. Loyalty
5. Politeness	5. Courage
6. Co-operation	6. Industry
7. Friendly	7. Self-management
8. Dependability	

2. **Sound Health :** Sound health and good physique are very essential for a business salesman. Travelling salesman needs good health as he has to travel to many places, eating different varieties of food, face different kinds of wheather conditions. Health is wealth. A salesman who lacks a

healthy body, is unable to give a good appearance and fails to carry out his duties. A sound mind occupies sound body.

3. **A Good Posture :** The way or the style of holding the body is another controllable factor. A salesman must have a good posture when he meets his prospects. A defective posture makes his appearance unwanted. He must display a good posture while standing or sitting and while walking his head must be kept erect.

4. **Pleasing Voice :** The voice is very important for a salesman. It must be attractive. The voice is the index of one's own feelings. It should not irritate the customers. The voice should not be like that of a horse or donkey; it should not be a closed nasal sound. The words uttered by him must be clear, pleasant and sweet.

II. Psychological Qualities or Mental Qualities

The mental qualities are :

1. **Quick Action :** A salesman must be alert and quick in action. He has to face many prospects of different temperament. He must have the mentality to face any situations and be ready to answer any questions. He should not be an absent-minded man. He must have quick thought of answering–what to say, how to tell, how to tackle the situation etc., without throwing away the customers.

2. **Imagination :** Imagination is a key to success in selling. If one possesses a rich imagination, it is of great help in solving problems. He must have a creative mind. For example, take the case of an insurance agent. He gives the picture of the retirement period of life. When the agent gives a view, through the eyes of the customers, the latter is impressed much *i.e.*, salesman has to imagine things from the point of view of the consumers. He becomes consumer-oriented and tackles the difficulties and problems of the consumers. He must put himself in the buyer's position.

3. **Self-Confidence :** A confident man never fails. He has the confidence in his work, capacity and power. Confidence makes him optimistic and enthusiastic. He can meet any situation in the product line. He engages or talks with a customer, makes him believe and the customer acts on his suggestions. Confidence makes him to meet any situation with courage. Experience and knowledge are the base for confidence.

4. **Enthusiasm :** It makes the work of a seller pleasant. Enthusiastic talk is always listened to by prospects. It gains interest and confidence of buyers and in turn more sales, thereby profit enhances, apart from satisfaction of the firm and buyers.

5. **Creative Talk :** A good businessman will never be defeated by his prospects. Generally a salesman never gives 'no' replies. He should try himself to satisfy a customer and at the same time push his stocks, which may be different from those asked for by a customer. For example, a customer asks the seller to show "wooden chairs." The shop possesses no wooden chairs, but has steel chairs. The resourceful salesman replies, "We have exhausted the stock and ordered for wooden chairs." "By the way, sir, we have steel chairs, which are more durable but at the same price. Shall I show you ?" The customer cannot take leave of the shop. The salesman's reply and suggestions must create an interest in the mind of the buyers.

6. **Initiative :** A salesman must be initiative. He must learn the tricks of his trade and must have knowledge of the product line. An active initiative is a self-starter. His job can be successfully carried out. He must have skill and be able to face and tackle situations intelligently. He can also win the confidence of the buyers.

7. **Observation :** A salesman should have a keen observation. He must have up-to-date knowledge of his products, and changes in style and fashions, attitude of competitors and government etc., to make him a clever salesman. With all these latest information he can easily suggest customers and help them in their purchases. When a customer enters into a shop, an experienced salesman can imagine the possibility of a sale by a look at his face, talk and dealings.

III. Social Qualities

1. **Good Manners :** A salesman must cultivate good manners. Good manners are charming, while bad manners are irritative. Annoyed replies or irritated actions will sweep away the diamonds. Certain nervous habits will do more harm apart from losing a presentable. People get annoyed or develop a dislike towards the careless replies and actions of an approaching salesman, such as , playing with rings, rubbing shoes, rubbing the hair and moustache, biting the nail, adjusting dresses, making sounds on the table with fingers or pencils, coughing continuously, opening and closing of match box or drawers or pen, standing on one leg, swinging the chair while sitting, clearing the nose , picking the teeth etc. All these bad manners should be avoided, good manners be cultivated.

2. **Courtesy :** Using polite and courteous words, a salesman can turn prospects into customers. Courtesy in dealing with customer, by using pleasing words like 'thank you', 'please', 'excuse me' etc will win the hearts of customers. It costs nothing to a salesman , but it is profit to him.

3. **Tactfulness :** When a delicate situation is faced, a tactful salesman deals with it in a proper way, in time and in an appropriate manner. He always tries to avoid unwarranted happenings. Through tactfulness, one can avoid obstacles, troubles, calamities etc.

4. **Helpfulness :** He must have a helping attitude whenever customers are in need of information. The salesman must expose the merits and demerits of the topic relating to the product.

5. **Politeness :** A salesman's decent behaviours, courtesy, attentive attitude etc., are the base for politeness.Customers feel satisfaction through the polite dealings of salesmen.When one enters into a shop and has dealing with a salesman, who shows politeness, will be preferred.

6. **Co-operation :** Co-operative attitude is essential for the success of a salesman. He must co-operate with the customers. In the firm itself, among the workers, there must be co-operation; otherwise aimed result cannot be attained. Progress of firms depends on the mutual co-operation of employees.

7. **Friendliness :** Customers vary in opinions, age, economic status, ideals, temperament etc. A salesman must be able to give a grand welcome to all those, who happen to visit the shop, with friendly conversation. His dealings must be that of a friend-adviser. He must enjoy the arrivals of customers and must associate with them easily.

8. **Dependability :** The statement revealed by a salesman should be correct. The customers may test the statement. Therefore giving false idea will spoil the dependability of the salesman. For example, a pen dealer says that a particular pen is leak-proof and when the pen is really so, the buyer will have a blind belief on him and thereby he earns a good name from the customers.

QUALITIES OF A SALESMAN

1. Knowledge of **self**
2. Knowledge of **product**
3. Knowledge of **firm**
4. Knowledge of **customers**
5. Knowledge about **competition**
6. Knowledge about **market**
7. Knowledge of selling **techniques**
8. PERSONAL ATTRIBUTES ARE:
   - Good Health
   - Cheerful Disposition
   - Decent Manners
   - Imagination

- Keen Observation
- Infinite Optimism
- Self-confidence
- Tact
- Cooperation
- Decisiveness
- Sociability
- Courtesy
- Kindness
- Courage
- Honesty

IV. Character or Moral Qualities

1. **Determination :** A salesman must have constant effort and patience in his profession to improve further. It is the will to succeed. He must stick to his profession. Practice makes the man perfect. Ceaseless practice, as a game, a player or a professional wrestler, makes salesman to come up to the top.

2. **Sincerity :** It is an added quality. He must be sincere towards his assigned duties. By sincerity, one can win friends, enroll new customers, retain old ones and win similar other favours. Dependability is increased through sincerity. He must make true statements with full information of products and assist the customer in taking a decision.

3. **Integrity :** It denotes honesty, trust and purity. The talks and behaviour of a salesman must be believed, trusted, honoured and agreed by others; thus customers are satisfied. A goodwill must be created for him and also the firm through honest dealings. This is more essential for the progress of the firm and for keeping a good relation with customers.

4. **Loyalty :** A salesman must have a full desire to work in co-operation with the firm by adopting the policies laid down by the firm. He must speak in favour of the firm. Otherwise the situation becomes worse. Co-workers are to be respected to develop a team spirit. The success or failure of sales depends upon the salesmen. The team spirit through co-operation brings success to the firm. They must be loyal towards the firm as well as the customers.

5. **Courage :** This is the quality that enables one to meet danger without giving way to fear. One must have enough bravery or boldness. In business, there arise various situations, such as, happening of tactless deals, unfulfilled promises, errors committed, carelessness shown etc. In all these situations , a salesman should not fear but must face them courageously and frankly.

6. **Industry :** Hard work brings home success. Everyone works to achieve an aimed target of business. Without pain or trouble, profit cannot be earned. People must possess an industrious attitude. One must be able to work hard even in unpleasant atmosphere. Industrious habits are intangible asset for a salesman.

7. **Self-Management :** We must have a plan to construct a building, with an aimed idea. A self-governed salesman can meet any number of customers. This is because he plans his work in advance and works according to the plan. Such a salesman find enough time and has a feeling of self-assurance.

It is difficult to find a salesman with all qualities. Some of the qualities mentioned above are in-born and others are developed through experience. He must recount his own qualities, recognise which is good and which is bad, and make up his mind to root out bad qualities and at the same time allow to grow good qualities. It is not possible to have all qualities. If any desired quality is absent in a salesman, the deficiency may be compensated by some other qualities. For instance, if a salesman lacks personality this can be compensated by giving more respect, politeness and help to the customers. So customers may overlook the personality in the merits of other qualities. To sum up the qualities of a successful salesman in a nutshell, his dealings with the customers must bring goodwill and not ill-will to the firm. Argumentative attitude drives away the customers. A salesman through the positive qualities in him, finds a top position in the business world.

Knowledge of Products

When one possesses only the sales personality but lacks the knowledge, it is like a banker without cash or hospital without medicine. It is fundamental that a salesman should possess thorough knowledge about the product, in which he deals. If so, along with his sales personality, one can shine. A thorough knowledge of the goods provides many advantages. Mainly an enquirer can be turned into a buyer. This is generally known as a selling point. When the selling points are used in sales talk, it is referred to as talking points. Let us know , first why one needs product knowledge. In brief, they are :

1. **Sales, a Pleasant Task :** A salesman should have up-to-date information relating to the products he deals with the customers. When one possesses thorough knowledge, he feels joy to explain to others. Complete and useful knowledge of goods is fundamental requisite of a salesman. These will increase the sales and render better service to buyers. Correct ideas, not guess work, create self-confidence, which generate potential buyers through satisfactory dealings. Knowledge makes the salesman's job a happy one.

2. **Technical Knowledge** : There are certain products, which needs complete information regarding their function. Generally customers ask questions to clarify doubts or some may have thirst for increasing their knowledge. In such cases, the salesman will be in trouble to face such prospects who feel that a particular salesman adopts deceitful attitude. To overcome all these, salesman should have complete information of the products, which he deals with.

3. **Product Knowledge Coupled with Personality :** Product knowledge is a background on which salesman's personality acts as a scooter-plug. Customers are highly interested to see how a salesman explains the products and how he offers a helping hand for a proper purchase. Sales personality, without the knowledge of product is like a dry water reservoir.

4. **Deep Self-confidence :** If a salesman lacks full knowledge of the products, it is a shame. The confidence grows when he can explain the products's capacities, performance, merits and limitations to the perspectives. His perfect knowledge of the product will naturally increase the confidence in himself. All types of queries can be satisfactorily met by such a salesman. If a single question is unanswered or wrongly answered, there arises a doubt in the mind of the consumers.

5. **Winning Customers from Competitors :** At present, the products are of various types and the market increases. Competition is the order of the day. The success in selling solely depends upon the ability of the salesman. The merits and demerits of the rival products must be understood by the buyers, possibly with facts and figures. All these aid to win the customers from the field of competitors.

6. **Selling Points :** A proper understanding of a product has many advantages or selling points. Customers are highly concerned with the selling points, such as, durability, attractiveness of product, its package , discount sales, selling terms, designs, price reduction, comfortableness, easy operation etc. All these favour a sale and are related to buying motives. A salesman must know all these to boost the sale at the counter.

How does a salesman get knowledge of the products ? He can get product knowledge from:

Personal experience	Meetings
Trade journals	Conferences
Discussion with co-workers	Visit to factories
Going through advertisements	Training schemes
Sales bulletin	Sales manuals
Professional magazines	Demonstrations
Training programmes	Audio-visual aids

Knowledge of Customers

The selling process and talk must be adjusted to suit the particular type of customers. Customers buy with different motives and each customer requires a different type of persuasion. Apart from giving expression to his sales knowledge, a salesman must diagnose a customer. He must be able to 'size up' a prospect as a doctor diagnoses his patient. The ability of a salesman is to size up a customer. Sizing up means a psychological observation of a prospect in understanding his character and buying policy and converting his desire into want in a suitable way. By experience, a salesman of average sense studies a customer as soon as he enters into shop. A salesman observes a prospect, his carriage , clothes, expression, conversation, action, tone of voice, while sizing up a customer.

There are different types of customers. Each customer has his own mind. Customers are not alike. Customers have different backgrounds, different habits etc. A salesman must be able to recognise these individual traits. There are no clear cut descriptions as to the type of customers. The following are some of the important traits.

Classification On the Basis of Behaviour

1. **Silent Prospect :** It is very difficult to understand a calm prospect. He may know better about the product. He may not waste time. Because of his silence, the salesman may find it difficult to understand the mind of the prospect.

The salesman must be patient in dealing such a calm man. He cannot guess the attitude of the prospect. The salesman must deal with him with dignity and respect. The prospect must be made to talk. Friendly, tactful and courtesy talk will unlock his closed mouth.

2. **Talkative Prospect :** Certain type of customers are very talkative, as opposed to the silent type. These people are not good listeners. They go on talking endlessly changing from one topic to another. Salesman is not allowed to talk.

Now the problem, to the salesman is how to tackle him. First, he may be allowed to talk for some time. It is easy to handle such people. Patient hearing and tactful dealings help a salesman to divert the mind of the prospect, around the product to be offered. As soon as the prospect is about to finish the topic, he talks to convert his attention towards goods by pleasant and sweet talk.

3. **Disbelieving Prospect :** Here the prospect deals with salesman with a suspicious feeling. He is critical and unfriendly. He thinks that salesman is cunning. He inspects the goods in an insulting way. He fears to admit the opinions and doubts the statement of the salesman. He believes the doubts and doubts the beliefs.

The best medicine for such category is to give reliable data, with recommendations, demonstration etc. As a proof of his understanding and to remove his suspicious feeling the salesman must give polite answers against many questions put forward by the prospect, to cross examine the salesman. The sincerity and honesty of the salesman must be understood by the prospect to vanish the disbelief in his mind.

4. **Nervous Prospect :** Some customers are of a nervous type and lack knowledge and self-confidence in taking a decision over a product. They may be timid, or shy in character. They generally talk less. They do not show any direct objections openly.

These type of customers are not of the disturbing type. Salesman must render services. Through tactful dealings, polite and calm conversation from the part of salesman confidence must be gained. The customer, because of his nature, should not be exploited, but helped in taking decision. Through friendly dealings and respect, satisfaction must be gained. Satisfaction is a seed for future harvest *i.e.*, sales.

5. **Impatient Prospect** (impulsive) **:** Certain types of customers are impulsive. They take quick decisions and are quick in temper. They hate delay. They want to be attended to immediately. They want quick settlement of dealings. They have no patience. Delay irritates them. They shout unnecessarily. A little delay will arouse their anger, as if injustice has been done. If salesmen fail to attend to them they may even leave the shop.

The best solution for this is immediate action on the part of salesmen. Getting the product immediately is the prime idea and the price is secondary. The customer is not bothered about the price. Avoid detailed discussion and avoid bargaining. Such prospects can be stisfied with quick response, and less talk with a smile.

6. **Friendly Prospect :** This type of customers is in joyful attitude having no pride or egoism. They show a close relationship to the salesman. They start with pleasant conversation in a friendly way. Their attitude even makes the stones to talk. There arises a pleasant atmosphere.

Such type of customer can be handled easily. Salesman must also have friendly dealings with a smiling face. Such type of people should not be cheated. They propagate good impression about the shop to others. Such people are not interested in prices.

7. **Hesitant Prospect :** Hesitant or undecided or deliberate type of customers have no firm mind. Such persons appear to be serious, but are undecided. They lack discretionary right in making a purchase decision. They need more and more information and each information is analysed carefully. The hesitation may be of price change, quality variation, lack of buying authority etc.

The salesman must explain in detail information of the product along with the merits, by comparing other similar products. The prospect must be convinced with ample proofs to establish the merits of the product. A satisfactory flow of information is aimed about the product to make them take a decision. Tell "you are making the best purchase."

8. **Rude Prospect :** Certain type of people are ill-natured and behave rudely. This may be due to financial position, cultural background, friend-circle, family background etc. They think that they are heroes of strong groups or kings crowned with high powers. When they enter into a shop, they keep on smoking cigarettes or chewing betel or are under the influence of liquor etc. They love full and uncontrolled freedom.

A new salesman is not fit to face such prospects. An experienced salesman may satisfy them by polished talks with pretended smile. The salesman should not gear his temper to the level of the prospect. By tactful dealings, hearing to his royal talks, offering respects, asking for his advice, he can lead him to make a purchase.

9. **Prospect without aim :** These are the types of prospects who prefer bargained purchases. They look at the market position and try to make purchases in auction sales or seasonal sales. Actually, such people do not want to make a purchase. But they aim to enjoy economic purchases.

In such cases, the salesman describes the product which are offered under "clearance sales," "seasonal sales," "seconds sale" etc. They must be informed of such occasions and products may be shown to them for inspection, along with merits of the products.

10. **Shopper Prospect :** Usually people visit shops and make enquiries of products as to their price, performance, etc. Then they may say that they will visit later. In certain cases the actual buyer may be accompanied by a friend as an adviser. Then enquiry takes place.

The salesman must welcome them. He can talk to the adviser and explain about the product, but without ignoring the actual buyer. The salesman may give a positive suggestion to one of the two persons, who seems to be the superior.

11. **Argumentative Prospects :** These are the types of prospects, which possess a disputative attitude. They always find fault with salesman and others. They create arguments and are clever in dealings. They try to test the salesman's knowledge and patience.

An inexperienced salesman, naturally loses his temper and is unable to effect sales. The salesman should not argue. He should not talk too much, but answer to the questions to avoid controversial talk. He must clarify all the merits of the products and win them to 'make believe'. Tell them the real facts and then leave them to take a decision.

Classification by Sex

Women : In earlier times, women possessed no right in any field. Only men made decisions. Women were treated as having no right, but were only puppets in the hands of men. But now the stage has changed. Along with men , women are also stepping out on equal footing. About more than 75% of purchases of a family is being made by women. Their position and status have come up, and are still coming up.

Women customers like shopping. They wander from shop to shop. They are keen in style, colour, beauty and economy in purchasing. They look and compare the products with other products. They always compare the quality and the price of similar products. They take time in inspecting the products and in making a decision whether to buy or not. They are conservative. They need more products for less money. They may go even for comparison, after the purchase is made. They try to find difference in products purchased comparing them with the products purchased by a neighbouring woman. They want a superior position everywhere, even in purchase too. They may be given a warm welcome on their arrival. They may be asked with a smile, as to what their requirements are. The salesman may reveal the details of the products, showing many proofs for evidence. He must allow them to inspect the product at its attractiveness, its operational position, beauty etc. He must tell them clearly the merits and savings of the purchases. They are also interested in the sales promotional tool and are satisfied when they are presented with free gifts, coupons, prize offers and small household items. The salesman must respect them. He must have patience, as they take more time in concluding a purchase.

Men : They are quick, and the majority are unaware of fashions. They look for durability. The salesman, by studying the nature, as said earlier, may be able to conclude a transaction.

Classification by Age

Children : They follow their parents for shopping. They aim for toys, picture books, eatables etc. Once the shop is located, and they like the salesman, they become regular customers and a friend of the salesman. They also bargain for the price. Make it a point, that salesman should never cheat such innocents. The salesman must have a sweet temperament and must talk nicely.

Young Prospect : They are not mentally matured. They need the latest and the most fashionable items. The salesman must co-operate with them by mingling with them, and suggest good products, but avoid too much talk. If they talk more, the young blood may tease the salesman by using taunting words.

Middle-aged Prospects : They are grown ups in age and experience; and each may be from different walks of life—workers, people of status, educationists, administrators etc. They are proud of themselves. Motivation of purchase must be known. Effective sales talk, exposing the pride of the product etc. may be disclosed, by respecting them at the most.

Elderly Prospects : Matured people are always cautious in money matters. Probably they are leading a retired life. The salesman must respect them, seek their advice and should help them in making a purchase. They should not be cheated. A clear explanation and comparison of different products are essential; and leave them to make their own decision.

Handicapped Prospect : Prospects may be blind, deaf, dumb, stammering, disfigured etc. They are to be treated as normal persons. Salesman must give all facilities to such people and adjust himself to deal with them. Their physical weakness should not be wounded. Salesman should show more sympathy and respect to such people apart from fulfilling their requirements.

Classification by Area

The customer can also be divided into two categories on the basis of area where they live—urban and rural.

Urban Prospect : The prospects from the cities or towns are by majority educated and well - mannered. They are always interested in the latest arrivals of products. Any new product—calculator, watch, scooter, car, television set etc. of the latest design and modernised items is preferred by those who live in cities.

Salesman must give them a grand reception. They are decent and pleasant to handle. Latest information, special merits, pride of possession, various uses etc., are to be intimated to them along with comparison of other products.

Rural Prospects : They are from villages. They are straight-forward. They are simple. They have rural but semi-urban character. They aim at bargaining. They do not trust the salesman and are suspicious of him. Most of them are illiterate. They may not prefer fashion and are rude in talk with unpolished words

The salesman must convince them with the products, he handles. Give them advice and talk to them about the comparative merits of different products along with the advantages of the goods. Stress the multiple use. They too are respected.

Type of Salesmen

1. **Manufacturer's Salesmen**

(a) **Missionary Salesmen :** They are also known as Creative Salesmen or Pioneer Salesmen. They are employed by manufacturers and do the work of missionary nature. They create demand for the products. They usually develop goodwill. They call on distributors-wholesalers, retailers, customers, in order to educate, train and induce them to promote the products. Manufacturers of medical supplies use this type of salesmen to promote their products.

(b) **Merchandising Salesmen :** They assist dealers by giving suggestions on display, store-layout, service facility etc. They arrange wide publicity and conduct demonstration for dealer salesmen, by even working along with them. They are largely involved in drugs, medicines, grocery etc. There is a wide scope for this category

(c) **Dealer-Servicing Salesman :** These salesmen call on retailers in their territory and visit them often. They bring samples of new products, take orders and make up window display.

(d) **Sale Promotion Salesmen :** They are also known as Retail Salesman. They are specialised in promotional work. They are representatives of medical firms or publishers. They may not take spot orders but they try to convince people like doctors about the new drug, research work, testing, result etc. They create demand by calling on customers.

(e) **Technical Salesmen :** They are trained technically. They provide technical assistance to company's customers on matter connected with the product, its quality, its design, its installation etc. Generally these types of salesmen deal with computers, equipments, machinery items, chemical products etc.

2. **Wholesaler's Salesmen :** Products reach the hands of customers through a number of channels, the main channel being wholesalers. They are the nerve-centres of distribution between manufacturers and retailers. These salesmen are mainly concerned with retailers through whom the products are to be marketed. Their main concerns are : (1) to guide the wholesalers in giving credit

transaction to retailers, (2) to collect bills from retailers and customers, (3) to collect information of the market trend, (4) to help retailers improve sales and (5) to take orders from retailers.

3. **Retail Salesmen :** They are of two types : (1) Indoor salesmen and (2) Outdoor Salesmen. Indoor salesmen work within the store—counter sales over the counter. They do not need training as they have to face only customers and not the prospects. They deal with regular buyers. They are order filling salesmen. They receive orders and execute them. They must have good manners and a helpful attitude. They must be able to guide the customers and help them to make quick decisions. They must also be knowledgeable and honest. Above all, they must maintain products in the shelves in an attractive manner

Outdoor salesmen may also be called travelling salesmen. Their main job is to make regular travels, visit customers, canvass orders etc. They must possess all the qualities of **ideal salesmen** (which we have already discussed).

4. **Speciality Salesmen** : They are to sell speciality products—expensive durable goods, furniture, books, house furnishings, washing machines, automobiles, refrigerators etc. People purchase these products only after a personal and careful selection, because they do not buy them frequently. Salesmen of this kind must be masters of the art of salesmanship. They are representatives of manufacturers, who produce special items

Theories of Personal Selling

There has been a lot of research by behavioural scientists and marketing scholars to examine whether selling is an art or science and various theories have been developed to explain the buyer-seller buying process. The process of influencing others to buy may be viewed from four different angles on the basis of different theories: thus there are four theories of selling viz:

1. AIDAS theory of personal selling
2. "Right Set of Circumstances" theory of selling
3. "Buying formula" theory of selling
4. "Behavioural Equation" theory

The first two of the four above-mentioned theories, are seller oriented and the third one is buyer oriented. The fourth one emphasizes the buyer's decision process but also takes the salesperson's influences process into account.

1. **AIDAS THEORY OF SELLING**

This theory, popularly known as AIDAS theory (attention, interest, desire, action and satisfaction), is based on experimental knowledge. This theory is very common. According to this theory potential buyer's mind passes through the following stages:

(1) **Attention Getting**

It is the crucial step in the AIDAS process. The objective is to put the prospect into the right state of mind to continue the sales talk. The salesperson has to convince the prospect for participating in the face-to-face interview. A good beginning of conversation may set the stage for a full sales presentation. The salesperson must apply his social and psychological skills to draw the attention of the prospect to his sales presentation.

(2) **Interest Creating**

The second step is to intensify the prospect's attention so that it involves into strong interest. To achieve this, the salesperson has to be enthusiastic about the product. Another method is to hand over the product to the prospect and let him handle it. BROCHURES and other visual aids serve the same purpose. Throughout the interest phase, the hope is to search out the selling appeal that is most likely to be effective.

(3) **Desire Stimulating**

After the attention getting and creating interest, the prospect must be kindled to develop a strong desire for the product. This is a ready-to-buy point. Objection from the prospect will have to be carefully handled at this stage. Time is saved and the chances of making a sales improved if objections are anticipated and answered before the prospect realises them.

(4) **Action Inducing**

If the presentation has been perfect, the prospect is ready to act, that is, to buy. Very often there may be some hesitation on the part of the prospect at this stage. The salesperson should very carefully handle this stage and try to close the deal effectively. Once the buyer has asked the seller to pack the product, then it is the responsibility of the seller to reassure the customer that the decision was correct:

(5) **Satisfaction**

The customer should be left with the impression that the salesperson merely helped in deciding. After the sale has been made, the salesperson should ensure that the customer is satisfied with the product. The salesperson should sense the prospect's mind and brief his talks.

2. "RIGHT SET OF CIRCUMSTANCES" THEORY OF SELLING

It is also called the "situation-response" theory. It has its psychological origin in experiments with animals. The major emphasis of the theory is that a particular circumstance prevailing in a given selling situation will cause the prospect to respond in a predictable way. The set of circumstances can be both internal and external to the prospect. This is essentially a seller-oriented theory and it stresses that the salesman must control the situation in such a way as to produce a sale ultimately.

3. "BUYING FORMULA" THEORY OF SELLING

The buyer's needs or problems receive major attention, and the salesperson's role is to help the buyer to find solutions. This theory purports to answer the question: What thinking process goes on in the prospects's mind that causes the decision to buy or not to buy? The name "buying formula" was given to this theory by Strong. The theory is based on the fact that there is a need or a problem for which a solution must be found which would lead to purchase decision, as shown below:

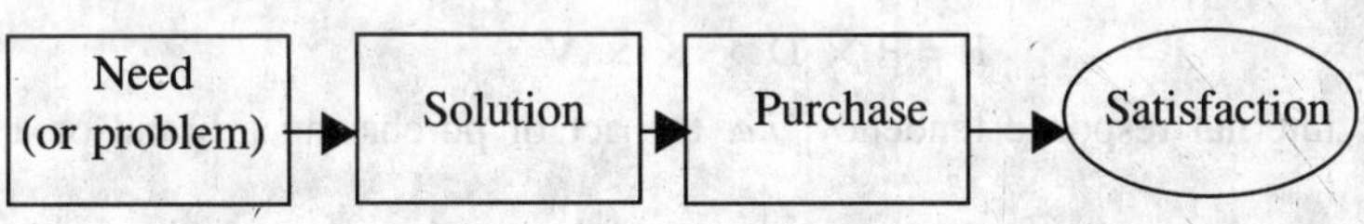

Whenever an individual feels a need, he is said to be conscious of a deficiency of satisfaction. The solution will always be a product or service or both and they may belong to a producer or seller. The buyer develops interest in buying a solution. In purchasing, the "solution" involves two parts: (1) Product or service or both (2) the brand name, manufacturer or the salesperson of the particular brand name:

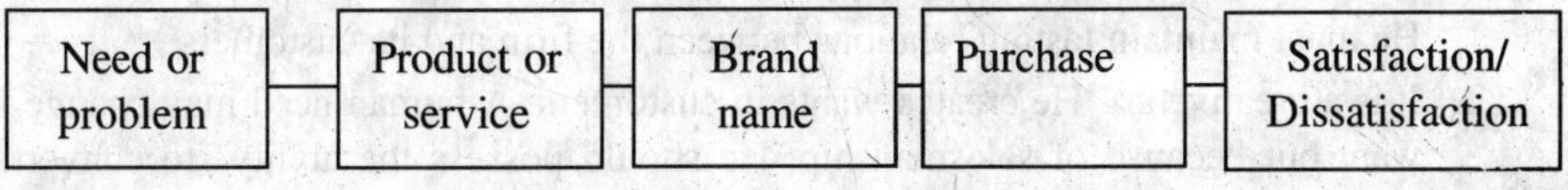

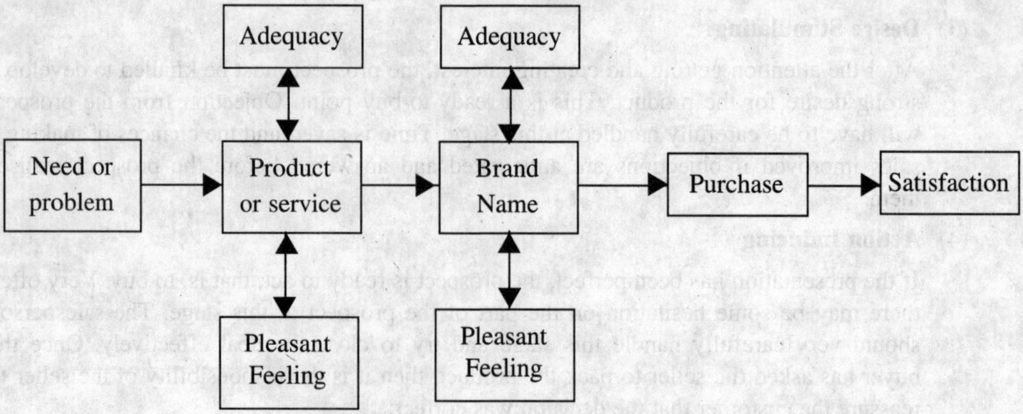

The product or service (Brand name) must be considered adequate to satisfy the need and the buyer must experience a pleasant feeling or anticipated satisfaction. This ensure the purchase.

4. BEHAVIOUR EQUATION THEORY OF SELLING

This theory is a sophisticated version of the "right set of circumstances" and this theory was proposed by Howard, using a stimulus response model and using large number of findings from behavioural research. This theory explains buying behaviour in terms of purchasing decision process, viewed as a phase of the learning process. Four essential elements of learning processes included in the stimulus response model are drive, cues, response and reinforcement, which are given below, in brief:

1. Drive is a strong internal stimuli that impel buyers' response. Innate drives stem from psychological needs and learned drives such as striving for status or social approval.
2. Cues are weak stimuli that determine when the buyer will respond. Triggering cues activate the decision process whereas new triggering cues influence the decision process.
3. Response is what the buyer does.
4. A reinforcement is any event that strengthens the buyers' tendency to make a particular response.

Howard believed that selling effort and buying action variables are multiplicative rather than additive. Therefore, Howard incorporated these four elements into a behavioural equation: that is:

$$B = P \times D \times K \times V$$

P = Response or internal response tendency, *i.e.* the act of purchasing a brand or a particular supplier.

D = Present drive or motivation level

K = "Incentive potential" that is, the value of product or brand or its perceived potential value to the buyer.

V = Intensity of all cues: triggering, product or informational

Features of Personal Selling

1. He must maintain lasting relations between the firm and its customers.
2. It is a creative art. He creates wants in customers. A human need may change into human want but because of salesmanship. He should possess the ability to convert needs into wants.

3. He must talk in the point of view of customers and engage their mind to his point of view. That is, the ability of the salesman must influence the customers' mind.
4. He must satisfy the consumers not only by selling products but also provides knowledge and assistance to satisfy the needs of consumers.
5. The new type of salesman has to play an important role in the total marketing process. Thus he must have the ability to learn and ability to communicate expert knowledge, in which he deals. Apart, typically, considerable weight has been put upon the importance of the art of persuation a necessary characteristic of good selling.

Personal selling carries importance, when:

1. The product is in the introductory stage;
2. The product's unit value is high;
3. The product requires demonstration;
4. The product must fit to the needs of buyers;
5. The company do not go for advertisement

Process of Personal Selling

The approach of selling method is different from salesman to salesman. Personal selling aims at oral presentation by talk or conversation between a salesman and a prospect. The salesman endeavours to convert the prospect into a buyer. Generally, the following are the processes involved in selling method and we discuss them in brief :

1. Prospecting
2. Pre-approaching
3. Approaching and Attention
4. Demonstration
5. Handling Objections
6. Closing
7. Follow up

1. **Prospecting :** A prospect means a probable buyer. Prospecting means searching for persons, to whom sales can be affected. Prospect is a person, who has wants to be satisfied and has ability and willingness to buy. Therefore this is a first step in identifying and locating of prospects, either from company's past records or customers or advertisements A list of such prospects is prepared, and this helps in planning the whole selling efforts so as to avoid waste calls.

2. **Pre-approaching :** It involves developing an understanding about the prospective buyers or qualified buyers as to their needs, problems, buying motives, preferences, personal character etc. This pre-approach is effective for making a ground for approach.

3. **Approaching and Attention :** This is a sales interview. This is a seed, with which sales tree grows up. This stage is important and vital. The first impression of the salesman may bring a long-run-benefit—repeated sales. This step is based on AIDAS formula. The salesman adopts all other selling points relating to the products.

4. **Demonstration :** The need-satisfying characteristics of the product are to be presented or demonstrated. The prospect may be made to understand the benefits of the product. He may also be informed of the special features, merits, benefits etc. of the products. The salesman can also show the survey reports, relevant data, free gifts, referring to specific problems in other products, telling examples etc. The prospects must be convinced and an interest in processing the product must be aroused. "You and not I" attitude must be followed.

Referral Approach: Here, the salesman, after seeking permission of a past or present customer, uses his name as a reference, in meeting another new prospect, thereby gaining easy entry. The main aim of all these approaches is to make an impression upon the "prospect. Advance planning of the "interview" is absolutely necessary for success in 'Personal selling". It saves time of both the buyer and the seller and helps in having an effective' sales presentation.'

5. **Handling Objections :** When one shows interest in buying the products, generally, every salesman faces objections from the prospective buyers. There is no wonder, when a buyer purchases products at a price, buyer asks questions and explanations. The salesman must face the buyer by giving satisfactory answers, sincerely and unhurriedly.

6. **Closing the Sales :** It aims at taking an order for the products from the prospective buyer. The salesman also asks questions as to the products—choice of colour, periodicity of delivery, quantity, terms etc. At the climax stage, the prospects place orders with the salesman.

7. **Follow Up :** Satisfaction of the buyer is important as a source of publicity. This stage is important, to have information from buyers regarding the product-use-problems, if any. The salesman keeps contact to know the problems, if any. After-sale service should be followed strictly *i.e.*, punctuality, personal attention etc.

Why People Object?

Negative Psychological Factors : Instinctively people are afraid of strangers. Reasons may be prejudice, bias or dislike of loud talkers etc.

An Un-welcome Salesman : Some people may simply dismiss the salesman, because they may not have the time for an interview, may not be interested in the product, may not be in the right mood, or may not have a happy past experience.

Paucity of Funds : When people say about insufficient funds , it is a valid objection.

Unwanted Product : Legitimate objections will arise when prospective buyers do not simply need the product.

Non-Recognition of Need : Some prospective buyers may say that the products to be sold, are of no use for them. It may be an un-recognised need.

Need for More Information : Some buyers offer objections in an attempt to get more information. There may be a conflict in buyer's mind. A struggle may be taking place between what emotion dictates and what reasons dictate.

Habit or Custom : Once a custom has been established by buyers, they are inclined to resist change. Many people resist anything new just because it is new and have no experience related to a new purchase.

Common Objections

Price : Some prospect say : "I cannot afford it". or "I was looking for a cheaper model" or "I always get a special discount".

Product : Some prospects say :

"The quality is too poor". "I do not like this design". "It is of wrong size".

Company : Some prospect say :

"Is not your firm a new one in the field?" "Your firm has to learn many things".

Miscellaneous

Additional objections :

"I buy always from friends." "I have no room for your product". "My brother is in the same line." "We are all stock up."

Some Buyers Object

At approach

At presentation

At the close

Preparation Required to Answer Objections

Develop a positive skill

Anticipate objections

Evaluate objections

Spot answer

Build skill

A trained and experienced SALESMAN

will LISTEN but will not INTERRUPT

will AGREE but will not COUNTER

will TURN objections into REASONS FOR BUYING.

Is Salesmanship Productive?

The activities of salesmen may or may not be productive. Pyle has five tests which may be used to determine, whether or not, selesmanship proves economically valuable.

1. Does the device tend to reduce the cost of marketing?
2. Does it reduce the cost of production, by an amount greater than an increase in cost of selling, so that the unit selling price is less than formerly?
3. Does it increase the utility of the product or service to the buyer to a greater extent than it increases the purchase price?
4. Does it produce more effective results, considering the cost, than some other form of selling?
5. Does it promote or encourage social well-being?

An affirmative answer to the above questions lend us to justify that salesmanship is productive; the comments are :

1. Salesman's job is to sell products and to find out the markets for the products. Moreover salesman is supposed to know the market where he can push the products. He does not dump products in the market where there is no demand. The meaning of the "salesman" itself is clear that he is a man, through whom products are to be marketed. It is implied that salesmanship naturally reduces the cost of marketing.
2. Sales increase through salesmanship , hence cost of production decreases. This is because only variable cost increases proportionately and fixed cost remains constant, against increase of production. Thus cost of production is reduced.
3. A salesman creates more uses with the products to the consumers by selling points and this increases the utility of the product.
4. The place given to the salesman is at the top, because he creates demand for the products by direct and personal contact. He, who deals with the customers, can know the drawbacks of the products. The drawbacks are rectified promptly, in order to increase prestige to the product. Thus the firm increases good result.
5. "Yesterday's luxuries" converted into "today's necessaries". This is due to salesman. Consumers can raise their standard of living.

On the contrary, the salesmanship is not productive when he fails to fulfill his objectives and when the product is not acceptable to consumers. However, the services of a salesman are needed in the field of marketing of today.

Why Salesman Fails ?

Primary Factors

1. Lack of planning ability , time utilization, poor work habit.
2. Lack of industriousness, drive.

3. Lack of resourcefulness, aggressiveness.
4. Lack of observation, an eye for sales possibilities, vision.
5. Lack of self-evaluation and self-development.
6. Lack of self-confidence, enthusiasm, too easily discouraged.
7. Lack of ambition or desire to succeed.
8. Ineffective calls could not develop interest getting sales presentations.
9. Inability to answer objectives, slow, uncreative thinker.
10. Inability to develop successful closing techniques.

Secondary Reasons

1. He could not work.
2. He was unstable.
3. He could not assimilate training.
4. He was immature.
5. He needed more money now.
6. He lacked good human relations.
7. He felt that the new job offered more security.
8. He did not like to sell.
9. He had outside interests.
10. He felt the need for the security of a salary.

Avoid the negative qualities:

1. Discourtesy
2. Harshness
3. Cowardice
4. Fear
5. Selfishness
6. Dishonesty
7. Disloyalty
8. Indiscretion
9. Gloominess
10. Ill-health

QUESTIONS

1. Define salesmanship. What are its features?
2. Describe the role and task of a salesman in closing of a sale. Illustrate with suitable examples. *(MBA., Delhi)*
3. What according to you are the qualities of a successful salesman? *(B.Com., Andhra)*
4. Comment on the qualities of a successful salesman. *(B.Com., Madurai)*
5. What are the essentials of effective selling? *(B.Com., Madurai)*
6. What are the advantages of personal selling? Are there any limitations? *(M.Com., Madurai)*
7. What do you mean by sizing up of customers? Comment on the different types of customers? *(M.Com., Andhra)*
8. Distinguish between personal selling and salesmanship. *(B.Com., Madurai)*
9. "Salesmen are born and not made." Discuss. *(B.Com., Madurai)*

Sales Organisation

CHAPTER 28

- *Introduction*
- *Need for a Sales Organisation*
- *Importance*
- *Functions*
- *Structure*
- *Sales Management*
- *Functions of Sales Management*
- *Field of Sales Management*
- *Sales Manager*
- *Qualities of Sales Manager*
- *His Knowledge and Attitude*
- *Duties and Responsibilities*
- *Type of Sales Manager*
- *Questions*

Introduction

Sales organisation consists of human beings or persons working together for the effective marketing of products manufactured by the firm or the products purchased for re-sale. Sales organisation co-ordinates the efforts of members of a group to bring about a desirable result. It provides an efficient, economic and flexible administrative set up to ensure timely movement of products from the warehouse to the ultimate consumer. Thus it provides satisfactory job to buyers and sellers.

A sales organisation has a number of departments. It has a planned and well co-ordinated structure. It performs the functions of planning, organising and controlling marketing and distribution of products. Sales organisation is a foundation for effective sales planning and sales policies. Systematic execution of plans and policies and programmes of a sales organisation control all the sales activities. As such it ensures maximum efficiency and profitability without losing consumer service and satisfaction.

According to Bolling, ''A good sales organisation is one wherein the functions or departments have each been carefully planned and co-ordinated towards the objective of putting the product in the hands of the consumers–the whole effort being efficiently supervised and managed, so that each function is carried out in the desired manner.''

Need for a Sales Organisation

''A sales organisation is like a power station sending out energy, which is devoted to the advertising and selling of particular lines; and there is a tremendous waste of energy between the power station and the points where it reaches the consumers. Therefore, there arises the necessity of organising the sales department.'' So long as the firm is a small one, there is no need for sales organisation, as the proprietor himself can sell all the output or in certain cases, he is assisted by one or two salesmen, under his direct control. But when the firm or the business itself expands, because of extension of markets, production in large-scale, competitive market etc., the need for a sales organisation is felt. The need arises because of the following factors :

1. Production in anticipation of demand, which must be sold.
2. To create demand for the products through efficient salesmen.
3. Execution of orders without delay.
4. Satisfactory action against complaints from customers.

5. Collection of credit sales.
6. Keeping enough stock by looking at the future demand.
7. Maximum contribution to profit.
8. To enforce proper supervision of sales-force.
9. To divide and fix authority among the subordinates.
10. To locate responsibility.

Importance of Sales Organisation

A sales organization is the mechanism through which a sales manager's philosophy is translated into action. The sales organization provides the vehicle for making decisions on planning, organization, selection and training of salesmen, their motivation, directing and controlling them. It also provides vehicle through which these decisions are implemented.

"A business organization is like a home. It has characteristic atmosphere. In some homes the head of the household and all its members are vitally concerned about religion, politics or some other interest – the occupations of the individual members being only of minor interest. In other homes where the personality of the head of the household dominates the activities and spirit of the members the opposite occurs. Like any group a business organization has its own culture, traditions, and to some extent its own language and climate." Hepner

"A sale organization is like a power-station sending out energy which is devoted to the advertising and selling of particular lines and there is a tremendous waste of energy between the power station and the points where it reaches the consumers. Therefore, there arises the necessity of organizing the sales department." Bolling.

''Sales are the life blood of business.'' Sales organisation is part and parcel of a business firm. All the departments are carefully planned in a good sales organisation.

The importance of the sales organisation, in brief, is :

1. Blood circulation of a human body keeps a man alive and in sound health. Similarly the sales strengthen the organisation. The more is the sales, the more is the profit.
2. Increasing sales means progress of the firm. If the sales fall down, it is fatal, because sales are the life blood of the business, as the blood is to a human body.
3. Consumers are the kings. Manufacturers produce goods for consumers. They must be satisfied in the market which is full of competitors with products for similar use. So suitable products are necessary, and for this an organisation is necessary.
4. To move the products from the factory to the consumers, the sales organisation is necessary–demand creation.
5. To handle the orders promptly *i.e.*, from the stages of enquiry to order at full satisfaction to consumers.
6. Collection of dues is also important. Several drops make an ocean; at the same time milking cows should not be neglected.
7. To keep good public relations by redressing the complaints if any, and to create a good image of the firm.

Functions of a Sales Organisation

Modern sales organisation is not only profit-oriented but also customer-oriented. The following are the important functions of a sales organisation:

1. Analysis of markets thoroughly, including product and market research.
2. Adoption of a selfishly sound but defensible sales policy.

3. Accurate market or sales forecasting and planning the sales campaign, based on relevant data.
4. Deciding about prices and terms of sales and pricing policies.
5. Packaging for the consumer wants a container which will satisfy his desire for attractive appearance, keeping qualities, utility, and correct price and many other factors.
6. Branding the product.
7. Deciding the channels of distribution.
8. Selection, training and control of salesmen and fixing their remuneration.
9. Allocation of Territory and quota-setting.
10. Sales programmers and sales promotion activities.
11. Arranging for advertising and publicity.
12. Order preparation and office recording.
13. Preparation of customer's record cards.
14. Scrutiny and recording of reports.
15. Study of statistical records and returns.
16. Maintenance of salesmen's records.

Structure of the Sales Organisation

The following factors are to be taken into consideration while designing the structure of a sales organization:

1. Nature of the market
2. Sales policies of the enterprise
3. Nature of the product
4. Number of products
5. Availability of financial resources
6. Level of distribution system
7. Size of the company
8. Price of the product
9. Ability of the professionals
10. Position of competitors' Products.

Sales Management

Sales management is concerned with mainly with the management of selling function. The sales function in a business is a basic function. The sales management represents one of the most important functional areas of business management, and all the principles of general management such as planning, organizing, directing, motivating, and controlling are applied to sales management too for securing better business performance, viz., reasonable profits through sales. Modern business performance, viz., reasonable profits through sales. Modern business is consumer centred.

The American Marketing Association has defined sales management as "the planning, direction, and control of personal selling activities of a business unit, including recruiting, selecting, training, equipping, assigning, rating, supervising, paying and motivating as these tasks apply to the personal sales force."

Functions of Sales Management

The general functions of sales management or marketing management are as follows:

1. Sales planning and policies
2. Pricing policies and price fixing

3. Advertising and promotions
4. Control of sales force
5. Marketing Research
6. Planning and control of sales
7. Management of distribution channels.
8. Branding, packing and labelling
9. After sale service
10. Integration and co-ordination of all functions.

The Field of Sales Management

The field of sales management includes the following tasks:

1. Setting sales force objectives
2. Human resource planning
3. Recruitment and selection of salesmen
4. Training of sales personel
5. Motivation
6. Compensation
7. Controlling the sales force
8. Organising and supporting the work of salesmen
9. Designing sales force objectives
10. Supervising and evaluating the sales force.

SALES MANAGER

The sales manager is the head of the sales organisation. He may also be known as sales executive, sales director or marketing manager. The sales manager is the key personnel in a sales organisation and is an important person. When he is in the meeting or inside the firm, he is more or less a representative of the consumers. But when he is in the market or when he is dealing with customers, he is a true representative of the firm and product. He plays dual role. He is responsible for directing all sales activities. A proper direction of the sales manager over the sales activities has a direct reflection on the progress of the firm. He steers the wheel of the sales organisation, as he is the driving force of the sales organisation. ''Under the old concept, the sales manager is primarily responsible for getting orders. This is the job of day-to-day selling, of hiring and training salesmen; order getting is his job, his life and responsibility. Under the new concept, the sales manager is still responsible for these activities but in addition, he has the responsibility of the transmitting to and imbuing the men on the selling front with the new company and management philosophy and thinking. The sales manager must become a planner, a strategy developer as well as an operator.''

Qualities of a Sales Manager

A sales manager must have requisite qualities of managerial and administrative capacity. To be a successful man in the field of sales, it is necessary that he should have the following qualities :

1. He must have adequate basic qualities, skill and experience.
2. He must possess pleasing manners.
3. He must be a good quick decision maker.
4. He must have all the qualities of a leader.
5. He must be able to set up, organise and operate the functions successfully.
6. He must have a spirit of co-operation. Co-operation is reciprocal–two-way traffic.
7. He must have ''your attitude'' and ''I'' attitude.

8. He must have an ability to teach others, which depends upon deep knowledge, mastery of language, clarity of expression etc.
9. He must be primarily a good trainer.
10. He must have the capacity to judge; he must be courageous, honest, reliable, dependable, ambitious, diligent etc.
11. He must be fair and firm while dealing with his subordinates.
12. He must have the power of inspiring and motivating sales-force

According to Pederson and Wright, a sales manager or sales executive must possess a wide range of abilities and the right mix of knowledge, skills and attitudes, if he is to be successful in administering the sales function within the company.

Knowledges

1. Knowledge of the external environment which may affect the operations of the company.
2. Knowledge of present practices and future trends with the firm.
3. Knowledge of the policies and the short and long term objectives of the company.
4. Knowledge of the other functions within the company, such as manufacturing, engineering, research and industrial relations.
5. Knowledge of the company's and competitor's product.
6. Knowledge of the new developments in non-selling functions–motivation research, data processing and inventory control etc. which have a future impact upon the operation of the sales organisation.
7. Knowledge of the strengths and weaknesses of personnel within the sales organisation.

Skills

1. Ability to work successfully with and through people.
2. Ability to communicate ideas.
3. Ability to inspire and motivate others.
4. Ability to size up and select new sales people.
5. Ability to evaluate the performance of present sales people and to train and develop them for future growth.
6. Ability to analyse and interpret facts.
7. Ability to weigh alternative actions and to make objective decisions.

Attitudes

1. **Open-mindedness :** The sales manager should be alert to new ideas and opportunities for new products or services.

2. **Natural Inclination to Look Ahead :** The sales manager, by the nature of the job, should be constantly planning and looking ahead.

3. **Flexibility :** Saleswork is not an exact science; therefore, its techniques, methods and practices will always be changing.

4. **Desire for Continuous Self Development :** The sales manger should strive to improve his knowledge and individual skills by strengthening areas of weaknesses.

5. **High Standards of Ethics.** The sales manager must lead the way in establishing high standards of ethical conduct.

Duties and Responsibilities of a Sales Manager

The important duties and responsibilities of sales manager are :

1. **Planning :** He has to formulate adequate plans *i.e.*, sales plans, sales policies and sales programmes and sales budget every year. He must plan for advertising.

2. **Execution of Plans and Programmes :** As he is responsible he must ensure the execution of the plans. He must go into every detail, organise on sound principles and execute them.

3. **Marketing Research :** The sales manager analyses the market thoroughly. He studies the market condition and method of distribution and organises, sales research of products. Marketing research gives solution to marketing problems. From the marketing research department, he can get up-to-date and reliable information, which will help him to take correct decision in marketing analysis.

4. **Control :** He controls sales. He controls selling operations and activities. He directs and fixes the sales target, territories, expense, transportation, quota etc., for each branch, selling agency or individual salesman, costing and budgeting.

5. **Physical Distribution :** He must be responsible for the physical distribution of products like order processing, packaging, transport and warehousing.

6. **Sales Policy :** He must formulate effective sales policy. He must ensure effective co-ordination of sales policy with production policy and the publicity department.

7. **Sales Budget :** He must prepare sales budget for the sales organisation. He controls selling cost analysis. Profit planning is possible with the help of sales budget and sales cost analysis.

8. **Distribution Channels :** There must be good relationship between the distributors and dealers. For that the sales manager has to select the appropriate channel of distribution.

9. **Sales Promotion and Advertising :** He must look after sales promotion and advertising campaigns to create consumer's demand. This will lead to secure more consumers' order for the goods.

10. **Management of Sales Force :** He is the leader of the organisation. His leadership has to be effective. He must guide, encourage and control the staff. For this he must possess ability, foresight and initiation. He is responsible for the recruitment, selection, training, promotion, supervision, motivation and control of the salesmen.

11. **Sales Office :** He is the chief executive of the sales office. He must assign duties to personnel so as to ensure efficiency of office and routine work–meetings, conferences, contests etc.

12. **Advising Top Management :** He has to advise the top management about the operation of his department. He has to account for closing branches, which have losses, and for opening branches after a deep and detailed study.

13. He must help in product planning and product design.

14. He has to study the markets. A comparative study of competitors' products will help him to draw a policy which will bring success or enable him to meet the competition effectively.

15. He has to set out policies by which continued patronage of customers is expected.

Types of Sales Manager

There are three types of sales managers based on their functions. They are :

1. Administrative Sales Manager.
2. Operating Sales Manager.
3. Administrative-cum-Operating Sales Manager.

1. **Administrative Sales Manager :** In a large company sales organisation has generally administrative sales manager. He has to develop the structure of the sales organisation. The sales organisation is divided into many sub-departments. An assistant sales manager or deputy sales manager is the head of each department. The sales manager is the administrative head of the sales organisation, and is commonly known as general sales manager. He must have effective control over all the sub-departments. He must direct and co-ordinate the activities of the sub-departments. Success or failure of sales organisation depends upon the ability of the general sales manager. He plans, directs and co-ordinates. As such the administrative sales manager is concerned more with

thinking. That is he formulates sales, sales programmes, sales planning, evaluation of performance, co-ordination of activities etc.

2. **Operating Sales Manager :** Operating manager works under the administrative sales manager. He works under the direction, guidance and supervision of the general sales manager. He is actual executor of the plans which are prepared by the general sales manager. The plans are implemented and worked out by the operating manager. He is responsible for the management and development of sales personnel. His job is to direct and control the selling efforts of sales personnel. Hence he is concerned with 'doing' or executing of the plan. He executes the sales plan with the help of branches or divisions; and he directs the manager and field supervisors. These managers are subordinate managers. They help the sales administrative manager in preparing plans and formulating the policies. The final decisions generally rest with the general sales manager.

3. **The Administrative-cum-Operating Sales Manager :** In a smaller organisation, this type of manager does all the functions with the help of salesmen and assistants in the sales office. He does the duties and responsibilities of administrative-cum-operating manager. In small firms involving a single product or limited products or restricted market, this type of combination *i.e.*, administrative-cum-operating manager is suitable. In short, operating sales manager is both an administrator and an operator. He combines 'thinking' and doing'.

QUESTIONS

1. Discuss the functions of a sales manager.
2. Discuss the importance of sales organisation.
3. What do you mean by sales organisation? Explain the part played by a sales organisation.
4. Bring out the importance of sales department. Discuss the role played by the sales manager in a sales department.
5. What is sales management? What are its functions? (*B. Com, Mumbai*)
6. What are the qualities of an effective sales manager ? (*B.Com. MS*)
7. Discuss the importance of sales manager. (*B. Com, Andhra*)

CHAPTER 29

Sales Force Management

- *Introduction*
- *Importance of Selection*
- *Sales Force Decision*
- *Sales Force Size*
- *Recruitment and Selection*
- *Selection Process*
- *Training*
- *Significance*
- *Objectives*
- *Advantages*
- *Training Programme*
- *Training Method*
- *Evaluation*
- *Questions*

Introduction

Personal selling effort is important in pushing the product manufactured. There are many ways, by which the goods can be pushed into the hands of consumers–personal selling, advertising, sales promotions, promotional tools etc. Of these, personal selling has many advantages in reaching the aimed goal. Personal selling is regarded as a key-man. It is an active striking power. Development, profitability and prosperity of a company greatly depend upon the salesmen's function. The word 'salesmen' applies to all persons who are engaged in the field of selling. Formerly the job of salesman was confined only to selling of products; but from the modern point of view, a salesman has to carry out the following duties :

1. He must acquire the knowledge of the basic needs to be satisfied through products or services.
2. Prospecting *i.e.*, searching for customers is one of his duties.
3. He provides information to the producer and consumers—co-ordination.
4. He must hold enough stocks to resell.
5. He must arrange for the display of products.
6. He has to maintain the purchase and sales account.
7. He must prepare sales slips.
8. He takes periodic stock inventories.
9. He assists customers in the selection of products.
10. He handles complaints.

In modern marketing, a new type of salesman has come up. He reflects the market trend by providing feedback to the producer about the customer's choice; and to the customers, about the product or changes made in the product, in accordance with their need, or the suitability of the product. Thus, it is the main job of the sales management to recruit effective and efficient personnel to serve the customers and the firm *i.e.*, he must be **prospect minded** and also **sales minded**. A successful salesman can satisfy both the customers and sales management. Moreover a salesman cannot be taken as 'born' but he is made.

It has been said, ''Salesman is born, but not made.'' It is true to a certain extent. There are some qualities which are inherent. A born salesman may not possess all the qualities, which are required and found in the salesman of today. There are doctors, engineers, actors, musicians etc.

who are qualified for their expert field work only after getting trained. In the same way born salesman can be improved through training. That is both recruits and born men, will improve further their performance through appropriate training. For instance, when we visit shops, we may come across sign boards, such as **'welcome', 'please visit again', 'thank you'** etc. Salesman may think he has done his duty by displaying the sign boards or telling the same words. These words become effective only when they are expressed in the appropriate time and tone. Otherwise the meaning will be different. When a buyer leaves the firm, if the salesman says '**welcome**', it is meaningless. The same is the case when a buyer enters into the firm, if the salesman says, **"Please come again"**, it is more foolish. Therefore, the sales management must choose proper person to attain the objectives–generating sales volume and developing salesman power. Thus, it is a task to select the sales force, which is the active striking power of the sales department, and this is a task before the sales management. As the sales management is defined, the planning, direction and control of the personal selling activities of a business unit, including recruiting, selecting, training equipping, assigning, routing, supervising, paying and motivating are tasks that apply to the personal sales-force. Thus, a carelessness in the process of selection will invite failure.

Importance of Right Selection

A sound recruitment policy and procedures are essential for a greater selling efficiency. A selected salesman must have all the qualities through which a firm can attain all fortunes—more turnover and more profit and the firm progress. Otherwise, the firm invites misfortune by unsound recruitment policy–selecting incompetent, uncared or disinterested sales army. A minor mistake, on the part of sales management, will doom the future of the firm entirely.

Therefore, the management of sales force is concerned with the following decisions :

1. Sales Force Decision
2. Sales Force Size
3. Recruitment and Selection
4. Training
5. Controlling
6. Compensation
7. Fixing Sales Territories
8. Evaluation

1. **Sales Force Decision :** Sales objectives have to be fixed by the sales manager in respect of total sales force and for each sales-man, in terms of volume, market share or profit for the firm. If the objectives are once decided, then the size of sales force has to be determined and this necessitates the following studies.

Job Analysis : Job analysis is a detailed study of a given job and reveals the job details, duties, abilities , responsibilities, working conditions, skill and knowledge needed to perform the job. This will help the sales manager to recruit the right man for the right job. This is further divided into :

Job Description : It is a brief statement describing the job and not worker. It includes :

1. Name of the job.
2. Nature of the job
3. Brief summary of the job
4. Duties to be performed
5. Relation to and with other jobs
6. Job responsibility
7. Working conditions for the jobs
8. Machines and tools to be handled

9. Criteria for each job
10. Evaluation standard aimed

Job Specification (Man Specification): The job description is followed by specification. The job or man specification indicates the exact requirements in performing a job. In brief they are :

(1) Educational qualification needed.
(2) Experience needed.
(3) Physical qualities expected.
(4) Skill needed to perform the job.
(5) Attitude needed for the job.
(6) Self-decision ability
(7) Responsibility to firm and customers.
(8) Emotional characters.

2. **Sales Force Size :** After having fixed the sales force decision, the sales force size has to be taken into account. More salesmen do not mean more sales. An existing firm possesses a sales force, and the question is whether to increase the number of salesmen. It is only the sales and profit objectives, both derived from sales forecast, that should establish the optimum size of the sales force.

3. **Recruitment and Selection :** Recruitment is a process of finding out candidates, who are encouraged to apply. Selection is process of choosing some out of many candidates. Therefore, we can say that selection is recruitment, but recruitment is not selection. Selection is a process of rejection of unfits. Recruitment precedes the selection process.

After deciding the number of salesmen and the objectives, the sales manager must select personnel. The usual sources of recruitment may be either internal or external.

Internal Sources : Many firms feel that the best policy to fill the vacancies of salesmen is from out of the existing employees of the same organisation. It may also be termed as promotion. This can well be adopted by analysing the ability and promising character of the staff and on the basis of seniority *i.e.*, length of services.

Merits

1. Much co-operation can be expected.
2. They are loyal
3. Since it is a promotion, sincere and honest performance can be expected.
4. They may not need training as there exists a familiarity.
5. They may not need high salary.

Demerits

1. There is limited scope for selection.
2. Favouritism plays its role.
3. New post may be unadjustable as the nature of work is changed.

Apart from the internal selection, ex-employees of the company can also be appointed if they are willing to accept a job. This policy is better and can profitably be adopted.

External Sources : We have the following sources :

(1) Employment Exchange
(2) Competitors' organisation
(3) Salesmen of non-competing firms
(4) Educational Institutions
(5) Recommended cases

(6) Advertisement

(7) Unsolicited applications etc.

(1) **Employment Exchange :** Private and public employment exchanges are the best source of personnel. They maintain proper registers with names and other full details of persons, such as job referred by those who seek jobs. The sales manager can call persons from exchange, by giving job specification to the officer concerned. In almost all cases the candidates may be untrained; and inexperienced hands requiring further training.

(2) **Competitors' Organisation :** The salesmen employed in other competing firms can be chosen. But this method is not morally accepted. He may be trained and may be developing his firm. Such a person can be drawn by temptation by giving more facilities and a higher salary. But it must be verified how far he is able to meet the sales objectives, considering his sincerity, loyalty, habits etc. Such a man, when he gets some additional benefits from some other firms, will follow the same tactics *i.e.*, leave the firm.

(3) **Salesmen of Non-competing Firms :** Salesmen can also be chosen from non-competing firms. Such persons may have experience in the line, if not touch with the particular product. They may need training to come up to the level of aimed sales objectives.

(4) **Educational Institutions :** Advanced countries like America, England etc., select students directly from specialised institutions, where theoretical and practical knowledge is gained by them. The institutional heads maintain complete records of students but as far as India is concerned, the chances are rare. It has been neglected with the feeling, 'just from egg' *i.e.* inexperienced.

(5) **Recommended cases :** The employees of the firm–managers, superintendents, section heads etc., may recommed candidates from their friend circles. They may have a moral responsibility when such persons are recruited. The employee who recommends personnel will be blamed, if the person is to be found unfit.

(6) **Advertisement :** This is a system generally accepted by firms in recruiting salesmen. Advertisements are displayed in newspapers, trade journals specifying the job and the required qualifications, experience and skill. There is the possibility of a wider scope of selection, as the news spreads over a wide geographical area.

Selection Process

Selection procedure is different from firm to firm. Each firm has got its own method in choosing men for employment. The requirement of quality in men depends on the job description. Similarly the selection method also depends upon the sales management. Generally, the following steps are followed:

(*a*) Application blank

(*b*) Screening

(*c*) Reference

(*d*) Personal interview

(*e*) Test

(*f*) Medical examination

(*g*) Final interview (appointment).

(a) **Application Blank :** Necessary information about the applicant is required to consider for appointment. Generally the candidates are asked to apply on company's application form, sent directly to applicants against a requisition or an application form, known as application blank given in the advertisement itself. This is with a view to gather only the necessary details of the applicants. It contains a number of questions, when filled in, gives a clear idea about the candidate. Generally, it may contain the name, sex, qualification, age, experience, health, social activities, references etc.

(b) **Screening :** All applications will not be considered. Screening is a process by which applications are to be screened out (rejected) from further consideration, on the basis of unsuitability. The remaining applications are formally considered by appointment, subject to further formalities. By rejecting the applications of unqualified applicants, much time and energy can be saved in further processing.

(c) **Reference :** Generally, it is a common practice to ask the applicant to mention the names of two references or referees, to whom the sales manager can make enquiries about the integrity, general character and ability of the applicant concerned. The qualities are checked with care and caution of the sales manager by contacting the referees. If the opinions are favourable, the applications pass to the next stage; and in case the referee gives unfavourable comment, the application is rejected at this stage.

Personal contact is necessary and it is better, because people are straightforward in tongue better than in pen. This is one-sided, but the effectiveness of such opinion is doubted, as there may be chances of telling only the good qualities of applicants. Moreover only the names of such favourable persons are mentioned in reference, with pre-intimation. To overcome this, personal interview is essential.

(d) **Personal Interview :** This is an important step in the process of selection. Only the screened applications are considered for selection and the firm sends out interview letters. Personal interview is a must. By this interview, the sales manager can understand the positive and negative qualities of the applicant, with reference to the job duties. A good interviewer must be unbiased, able to discover facts, a keen observer of the interviewee etc.

Interviews are also of two types : (a) Patterned and non-patterned. Under patterned interview, questions are designed and the same questions are asked to all, which is easy for comparison purposes. (b) In non-patterned interview no standardised questions are asked. The applicant is allowed to talk freely. A few direct questions are asked. By this type of interview, the applicant gets a chance of speaking about his attitude and interest freely. The interviewer must be able to make an easy evaluation of the interview.

(e) **Tests :** Test is an additional tool, with which the applicants are further tested to determine their suitability to the job. Generally following are the important types of psychological tests conducted:

(i) **Ability Test :** This test is devised to ascertain the capacity to grasp things, and is a measure to know how well a person performs a particular task with motivation. This can also be called as mental ability or intelligence test. Such tests determine the suitability of a candidate for a particular job.

(ii) **Habitual Characteristic Test :** A man may be intelligent but may hesitate to take a decision. This test is aimed to know one's aptitude and interest on normal, daily work, irrespective of the best behaviour occasionally.

(iii) **Achievement Test :** This test is designed to know as to what knowledge a man has gained from his education or training.

By all these psychological tests, the ability and suitability of a candidate can be verified. One can aim to evaluate the honesty, cheerfulness, leadership quality, assertiveness, co-operation, supervision capacity, emotional stability, determination, ability etc., of the personnel. The effectiveness and reliability of these tests are questionable, as the qualities cannot be measured exactly and the circumstances to be faced by salesmen are also different.

(f) **Medical Examination :** The important thing about any person, apart from all qualities and eligibility, is that he must be physically fit for the job. Diseases and physical deficiencies of the salesmen will affect the business. As such, selected applicants have to undergo medical examination.

(g) **Final Interview and Appointment :** The selected applicant is probably, called for a final interview and his suitability is measured from the different tests, physical reports etc. The job must be explained to him along with all relevant details, which are required in performing the duties efficiently.

If everything is in favour of the applicant, an agreement must be executed by him. Generally, the agreement contains duties and authorities, sales quota, sales territory allotted, salary and conditions of resigning. It is followed by an appointment order, which contains designation, jobs to be performed, salary and other financial benefits etc.

4. **Training :** Training is a continuation of selection. Having selected the salesmen, there are two options. They can be sent to the field directly with samples, order books etc., (born salesman) and/or they can be sent for training programme. Some people think that salesmanship is born in man, but there are only born salesmen, like born doctors, lawyer, engineers, teachers etc. However all these people need training to call them as qualified, and so also is the case with salesman. A man may have interest in the profession. The interest can be fully developed, through proper training. One attains perfection, self-development etc., through training.

Meaning

Training programmes are organised procedure or methods through which knowledge as well as skill, for a definite purpose, is acquired. By training, one can increase knowledge in a particular field. The salesmanship is not born but can be made effective through training.

1. Significance of Training

The present era of marketing world is full of stiff and cut-throat competition. The world is dynamic and not static. Customers are more benefit-oriented. Producers, to meet the ever-changing demand of consumers, produce new products, new devices, products with multiple uses, new working methods, etc. Thus, training or repeated training is essential to keep the salesman, with up-to-date knowledge, in respect of new or developed goods. Training gives scope for improvement.

2. Objectives of Training

The summarised objectives are given below:

1. To facilitate the salesman to acquire the technique and principles of salesmanship, process of sales, canvassing etc.
2. To bring down the labour turnover in the sales force.
3. To facilitate better sales performance.
4. To improve the relations with the customers.
5. To increase the efficiency of sales personnel.
6. To keep the salesman informed of the knowledge of products, market, competitors etc., to face all situations.
7. To lower the selling expense so as to increase the profits.
8. To maintain sound relation between employer and employee.
9. To develop better knowledge, and the ways and means to resist all situations.
10. To motivate the consumers more effectively.

Advantages of Training to Salesman

1. A trained salesman always wins customers by systematic approach.
2. Salesman acquires better understanding of the firm, as to its past history, policies and procedures and this helps the salesman for effective dealings.
3. A trained salesman takes less time in concluding a sale–early selling maturity.
4. A trained salesman brings increased volume of sales, in turn, more profit to the firm and himself.

5. A trained salesman is able to meet consumer's demand and help in solving problems.
6. Increased volume of sales facilitates reduction in cost of production *i.e.*, sales rise faster than expected. The cost per unit of order or per prospect can be minimised.
7. A better relation is created among the customers through reducing customer's complaint, increasing brand loyalty etc. Customer's satisfaction is gained.'
8. The ability of the salesman is increased by expert knowledge.
9. Controlling of salesman becomes easy.
10. Training facilitates better demonstrations, selling the products which have high profit margin, better methods of canvassing etc. Sales training helps to increase the sales volume. Supervision cost is reduced as trained salesman needs less supervision.

Training Programme

A firm should chalk out a programme for sales training. The training is based on the nature of the job and the products to be sold. A planned training programme should function with the following ideas or principles, often referred to as ACMEE.

A = Aim of the Training

C = Content of the Training

M = Method of the training

E = Execution of the Training-programme

E = Evaluation.

1. **Aim of Training :** The whole idea behind the training is to make a recruit a good salesman. It is true that some of the qualities of a good salesman may be inherent in him, but not all qualities. It is the training which makes him to have all qualities required of a salesman. It must aim to make him a guide to the buyer taking into account his needs, problems etc., and to make him a salesman of effective power by which an interest in the product may be aroused and a desire to purchase be created.

2. **Content of Training :** No hard and fast rules can be laid down as to the contents of training. The content of the training programme relates to the subject-matter of training. A training programme varies from firm to firm, because of the differences in products, markets, policies of the company, trainee's ability etc. In general terms, sales training is the teaching of salesmen and prospective salesmen how to do their jobs better. A good training programme facilitates the trainee-salesman to learn and understand the following contents :

(a) The knowledge of his job
(b) The products
(c) The company
(d) The markets and consumers
(e) The competitors
(f) The sales techniques
(g) The routine reports etc.

(a) **The Knowledge of His Job :** The job of a salesman is not complete, as soon as the transfer of goods takes place. But the salesman of today carries more weight than the salesman of mere order-taking. He must understand what the firm expected of him; what power he possesses; how to convince the buyers about the company's product and image. The company assigns responsibilities and powers, with which he works as a guide to buyers by projecting the merits of the products and on the other hand with profit to the firm. He is expected to do services, as a rope walker, to both the firm and the customers. He must have concrete plans as to his sales planning, meeting customers, sales talks, demonstration, presenting the goods, concluding sales, securing order, collecting dues, handling objections and complaints etc. Apart from these he must be a keen observer of market conditions–competition, consumers' likes and dislikes etc. He should co-operate with his senior fellows. Thus, he is trained with a purpose, the aim of his appointment being to know what the firm eagerly expects from him.

(b) **The Products :** A good understanding of the product is essential. The firm must give or ensure that the salesman has a thorough knowledge of the products, to be dealt with. In brief, they are :

1. Raw materials used in the product
2. Manufacturing methods in brief
3. Research and development undertaken
4. Improvement brought out
5. Its suitability to the consumers
6. Its trade mark, brand, characteristics
7. Its colour, weight, packaging, quality control etc.
8. Selling points of the products
9. Product merits and uses to consumers
10. Limitation of the product performance
11. Its price and discounts offered
12. Service after sales and guarantee period
13. Demonstration of its actual working
14. Availability of the products
15. Cost of operation and maintenance
16. Comparative study of similar products
17. Strength and weakness of competitors' products
18. The position of the product in the product line.

The above said knowledge of the products is essential for a salesman so as to shine himself as a creative salesman. When the salesman has a sound knowledge, he meets the public and converts them as buyers, in a better and more efficient way.

(c) **The Company :** A salesman should be well-informed about the following :

1. Brief history of the firm
2. Its marketing policies
3. Objectives and purposes of the firm
4. Economic and social objectives
5. Its position in the market field
6. Credit policies, sales policies, personnel policies
7. Capacity of the plant
8. Personnel of the firm-directors, stock-holders
9. Execution and handling of orders, sales accounting and collection methods
10. Salary, commission computation, travelling and daily allowances etc., and their payment procedures
11. Method of exercising control over the salesman
12. Allocation of quotas and territories
13. Marketing policies, pricing policies
14. Handling of complaints and their adjustment

All clear-cut knowledge about the company is essentially known to the salesman to enable him to work accordingly.

(d) **The Markets and Consumers :** Information about the market is an important and essential part of the training programme. The salesman must have a thorough knowledge of the size of market, demand for the products and the area under the competitor's side. Besides the knowledge of the market, salesman should know about the type of customers, buying motives, likes and dislikes of the products. Different types of customers need different types of approaches. People differ widely from person to person, sex to sex, age to age, place to place etc. Persons of different types require specialised way of persuasion. The salesman must adjust himself according to the nature of the customers. A blanket policy to all classes of people is not advisable. (See chapter 20. Buyer Behaviour, for more details).

(e) **The Competitors :** Salesman must be given a good knowledge or comparative study of the selling activities of rivals. Study relating to comparison with the rivals as to the merits and demerits of the product is important *i.e.*, strong as well as weak points. The salesman should know the rival firm's policies, method of approaching the customers, how they are paid, how customers treat him, how their product is, how they fulfil their duties, the area they like or dislike, their selling points etc.

(f) **The Sales Technique :** The Sales techniques are the essential part in sales training. After the training, the salesman has to be sent to the field, where he has to sell the company's product. He must be given exhaustive training in ''Sales Process'' (described earlier). The selling points must be correlated and sales talk be applied at the appropriate situation. A born salesman has to be instructed with the various selling techniques in detail. In short, training on the following items must be imparted :

(a) Selling process
(b) Method of gaining interview from consumers
(c) Method of approach to consumers
(d) Demonstration and presentation
(e) Method of handling objections of consumers
(f) Why salesman fails in the field etc.

(g) **Routine Reports :** Salesman should be trained to know the routine works and submit their reports to the firm.

(a) Amount of sales made
(b) List of new customers
(c) Credit outstanding of customers
(d) Collection of outstanding dues
(e) Competitor's position in the market
(f) Maintenance of accounts of expenses
(g) Demonstration and display of products
(h) Action taken on complaints, grievances etc.
(i) The attitude of market in respect of competitors
(j) Consumers' suggestion if any.

The reports may be sent to the firm, daily, weekly or monthly etc., as directed. The salesmen are eyes and ears of the selling firm. The salesman must be aware of the method of reporting and its importance.

Training Needs of Salesmen at Different Times

New Salesman Need

1. Facts about the company–history, policies etc.
2. Product details.
3. Company's system and procedures.
4. Fundamentals of selling their specific product.
5. Moral training.

Regular Salesmen Need

1. The above 5 items.
2. Changes in policies and procedures.
3. Facts about new products.
4. Future plans of the company.
5. Knowledge to supervise others.
6. Know-how to discharge responsibility.
7. Attitude or moral training.

Supervisors Need

1. Skill needed by others in discharging duties.
2. Ability to train others.
3. Ability to organise.
4. Ability to analyse and plan.
5. Ability to evaluate and follow up.

3. Training Methods

For imparting training to the salesmen, different methods are being used. Broadly, these methods may be divided into two:

1. **Group Training**

(a) **Lecture Method :** An expert or a lecturer speaks to trainee-salesmen about the various aspects of selling. It consists of oral talk in a classroom. This system is widely used. The trainees listen to the lectures. The instructor invites questions and answers from them. To make the lecture more interesting, visual aids, demonstration, suitable examples have been added. This system is more economical, and is the easiest and quickest in imparting theorctical training to a group of salesmen. But it is difficult to evaluate the effectiveness of lecture method. This method can be used more effectively in continuing sales training programme to provide new information or changes in the policies of the firm. This may include seminars, demonstrations etc., by expert salesmen.

(b) **Audio-Visual Method :** In order to supplement the lecturing (telling) method, training programmes include the use of visual aids, such as films, slides, posters etc., and are capable of making them more interesting.

(c) **Discussion Method :** This is a good method. Here an actual case or an imaginary case is given as a problem to be solved, to the different groups. The case or the problem may be typed or printed. Each group is asked to understand the problem and draw a conclusion. After this, the different conclusions or suggestions are analysed collectively, under the leadership of the instructor, in drawing generalisations from each case or problem. This type of training enables the salesmen in correcting their own views. It is suitable for a small group. It is slow and costly.

(d) **Conference Method :** Sales conferences and sales meetings are get together of concerned staff, either weekly, fortnightly or monthly. The thoughts of various persons are pooled in the conference. Meetings or conferences have motivating effects as the participants are given chances for creative thinking and to express their views. To make the conference more interesting, dramas, demonstrations etc., are included. Topics like, sales policies, facing competition, publicity ideas, dealings with complaints etc., are dealt with. And these will facilitate the participants in broadening their outlook and ideas. But this type of meetings or conferences is not suitable for new recruits.

(e) **Role Playing Method :** Role playing is a newly developed method. The sales trainees are made to act out roles in contrived problems. The trainer explains the situation of the problem and assigns the role of salesman and customers of different characters to the sales trainees. Each one has to act the assigned role. The trainer watches the role played by each and discusses their weakness and strong points. A few may be selected to act the play, while others may watch it. Thus, the salesmen have chance to see and understand the ideas in different situations. It is not suitable for new recruits.

(f) **Panel Method :** Members in the panel group may be permanent. The members, who are experts in the panel, discuss the problems, and solutions are passed to the sales-trainee groups, who may have further discussion. This system is ineffective.

(g) **Round Table Method :** It is similar to the discussion method. It consists of few members. The salesmen sit around a table along with a good discussion leader. They deal with the problems of actual cases. Every participant takes part freely in discussing the problems and solutions. Exchanges of new ideas take place advantageously.

(h) **Brain Storming Method :** Under this method, more or less, similar to round table conference, persons sit around the table. The leader tables the problems for discussion. The sales trainees have to understand the problems and find the solutions. The solutions are analysed by the leader or tested by the panel of experts. This method practically fetches no value.

4. Individual Training

(a) **On-the-job Training :** Under this method, a new salesman is placed under an experienced or senior salesman who trains him. First the coach explains the sales techniques under different situations. He also takes the trainee along with him on his rounds and gives him chances to observe the dealings with the customers. Doubts of the trainee are also clarified. Then the coach along with the trainee calls on customers; the sales trainee is allowed to deal with the customer and the coach observes the performance. If any weak point or short-coming is found in the sales trainee, they discuss how to overcome them. After some time, the sales trainee becomes a trained and independent salesman. This system is good for travelling salesman.

(b) **Sales Manual :** It is a compiled textbook. It contains details of the firm and products, job description, sales policies, opinions or reports required for reference purposes etc. Generally, it contains many problems with suggestive solutions. A copy of the book is given to a salesman to go through it and understand the ideas. It works as a ready-reckoner.

(c) **Initial or Break-in Training :** New recruits are given an orientation training so as to know about the company and its products. He may be allowed to work for some time in the firm itself to gain sufficient information about the products. After that he is sent to work in his field.

Apart from the above, salesman can also be sent to specialised educational institutions. The training cost is borne by the firm. There are many institutions in India which impart theoretical training along with practical work. Doors are open and firms can send their new recruits for training. Correspondence courses are also available for initial training. In certain cases, one can undergo training while one is fully employed. This is suitable for salesmen who are widely scattered. There are many firms which have permanent training departments like colleges.

It is important to note that even the trained or experienced salesmen need periodic training, called refresher training or follow up training. This is because of the changes in products, sales policies, changes in consumers and market, government policies, new developments, new ideas etc.

5. Evaluation of Training

Having trained the salesmen, the marketing manager must evaluate the usefulness or effectiveness of training, individually and collectively on the basis of the performance of the sales personnel. Money, effort and time have been spent on training. Therefore, it is natural to expect returns. Evaluation can be made on the basis of performance in terms of sales volume, sales profitability, order-size, expenses etc., between, before and after training periods.

Aims of Training

1. To prepare the salesman to discharge his job efficiently
2. To tell him what to do
3. To guide him how to demonstrate
4. To allow him to practise or to perform it
5. To check him in his performance

NB: (Controlling, Compensation, Fixing Sales Territories and Evaluation are dealt with separately)

QUESTIONS

1. What are the various kinds of tests commonly used in the selection of salesmen? What are the advantages of using tests ? Are there any dangers ? (*B.Com., Madurai*)
2. Enumerate the advantages of arranging training facilities for salesmen and state the types of training you would recommend for salesmen of a company manufacturing medicines. (*B.Com., Madurai*)
3. Outline a training programme for the sales force of your company. (*B.Com., Madurai*)
4. Explain the procedure involved in the recruitment and selection of salesmen. (*B.Com., Madurai*)
5. What is the necessity of training salesmen ? Explain different methods of training men. (*B.Com., Mysore*)
6. Discuss the various methods of training salesmen. Bring out the merits and demerits of each method. (*B.Com., Madurai*)
7. What are the external sources for the selection of salesmen and how are they applied ?

CHAPTER 30

Control of Sales Force

- *What is control ?*
- *Is Control Necessary?*
- *Pre-requisites of Control*
- *Elements Involved in Control*
- *Method of Control*
- *Bases of Control*
- *Reports and Records*
- *Sales territories and Sales Quotas*
- *Salesman's Authority*
- *Field Supervision*
- *Remuneration Plan*
- *Motivation of Salesman*
- *What is Motivation ?*
- *Need*
- *Types*
- *Techniques*
- *Methods*
- *Questions*

What Is Control?

The last but not the least significant phase is control of sales force operations. In any sphere of activity, supervision and control of salesmen is essential with a view to achieve the maximum success. The sales operations are to be materialised as per plans laid down, followed by scientific control of efforts and resources. A plan is necessary when you construct a building. In the same way, in business also a chalked out plan is a **sine-qua-non** and the plan to be under a successful control is essential.

What is control? It simply means a check, a means of controlling or testing. Control involves such functions as checking, verifying, standard selling, and directing or guiding. One may say, ''Control means watching results and translating them into positive action.'' Control is a process to establish the standard of performance measuring the work done. Through control salesman's performance can be appraised. All the organisations must have the operation of control, as a tool, for their progress and successful working. It is an act of checking or verifying the performance as per the plans. ''Control consists in verifying whether everything occurs in conformity with the plans adopted, the instructions issued and the principles established. Its objective is to point out weaknesses and errors in order to rectify them and prevent their recurrence. It operates on everything—things, people and actions.''

Is Control Necessary?

The manager exercises the control over the activities of salesmen through supervision. The planned sales operations are to be carried out systematically in order to get success over the aimed result. Salesmen are human beings; the need for supervision arises because of:

1. Salesmen may be working independently and may be at a longer distance from the sales manager. There may arise a problem of co-ordination, of salesmen's effort with the other sales efforts *i.e.*, publicity, sales promotions etc. To ensure co-ordination, control is a must.
2. The sales effected by each salesman should be known to the sales manager, who compares the actuals with the targets, to find negative variation, which should be rectified by corrective actions. There may be mistakes in the approach of a salesman, laziness in activities etc. These must be traced out and the salesman guided in order to channelise his efforts into desired path.

3. Efforts of the salesman have to be directed to maximise profits to firm in the light of progressive ideas and techniques to ensure the proper utilisation of men and materials.
4. "Of all the assets customers are the most valuable." To build a sound public relation, complaints of different types of customers are to be redressed. Thereby, it is possible to build a good image in the minds of the public. The salesman is guided by the sales manager, who tries to satisfy the customers through salesmen.

Prerequisites of Control

1. The sales manager should know what exactly he expects a salesman to do. (through fixing the sales quota).
2. Salesman should be given an idea of what he is expected to do. (through training).
3. Sales manager should know that the salesman is doing exactly what he is expected to do. (through reports).
4. Salesman should be made to know that the sales manager knows what he does. (through personal talk and reports)
5. Salesman should know that the sales manager appreciates what he does. (through reports).

Elements Involved in Control

The following steps are involved in the process of control:

1. **Analysis of Performance :** All controls involve the setting of a standard and the measurement of performance against their standard. The performances are analysed and compared with reference to the objectives, budgets and standards. This will reveal the variances between the performance and the standard.

2. **Analysis of Variance :** After finding out the variance, the first question is whether this variance is significant. If the variance is significant, the next question is usually, "What went wrong with the performance?" and possibly a better question will be "What is wrong with the standard?" Effective sales control should reveal poor execution of sales policies or indicate when sales policies need changing. Sales Control may not, however, disclose the reasons for poor execution. For instance, poor execution may be due to ignorance of sales policies, inability to perform the tasks, resentment, discontent etc. The significant variances are considered carefully to enable the authority to take corrective steps.

3. **Measures to Deal with Unfavourable Variance :** The function of control is to identify the weakness and errors in the sales efforts. Reasons and causes are found out and their remedial measures are formulated in order to correct the weakness and errors in a speedy manner. These enable the sales manager to guide the individual salesman when necessary. All these are done in order to improve the sales programme performance.

Methods of Control

Control is essential in order to secure optimum performance from salesmen. Sales managers effect controls, by common methods, through personal contacts, correspondence and report.

1. **Personal Contact :** Personal contacts are more effective than other methods. Sales manager himself or through branch managers or field supervisors, exercises controls over the salesmen. Salesmen can be assisted and inspired, and corrective steps can be taken.

2. **Correspondence :** This method is commonly accepted and is economical. Through correspondence, instructions are passed on to the salesmen and replies received from the salesmen. The salesmen are supervised or controlled through letters.

3. **Reports :** They are not in the form of letters. Printed report forms are used by the salesmen to make reports to the sales manager. In certain cases, the report may be oral.

Bases of Control

The control of salesman is based on : (1) Reports and Records (2) Sales Territories and Sales Quotas (3) Determination of salesman's authority (4) Field Supervision and (5) Remuneration Plans.

1. Reports and Records

Report : Every sales manager needs accurate and up-to-date information, on the basis of which he formulates policies for future business. Formulation of policies may not be practical in the absence of information. For the growing needs of the organisation, expanding the professions, widening activities of the business etc., it has become essential to look for the information. A report is a presentation of facts on the basis of activities. Salesmen's reports–daily, weekly, monthly, provide valuable information relating to the salesmen's activities for a sales organisation. Salesmen, who are the primary source of information, being the eyes and ears of the selling firms, are asked to send reports periodically. The report will reveal the following information:

1. Number of calls made on customers
2. Number of sales related to number of calls
3. Amount of sales made–volume and value
4. Details of sales made to regular customers
5. Details of sales made to new customers
6. Details of sales lost to old customers
7. Reasons for customers lost
8. Sales by product line
9. Outstanding accounts
   (a) Collections made
   (b) Bad debts due to bankruptcy
10. Credit worthiness of customers
11. Degree of competition existing
12. Number of complaints received
13. Number of complaints attended
14. Selling expenses total and per order
15. Impact of advertising and activities relating to sales promotion.

Report must be brief and in condensed form. It gives the needed information. Unnecessary or unwanted information is avoided, as many companies use standard forms for salesmen's report. Therefore, it is easy for the sales manager to understand the weak activities and suggest corrective measures to the concerned salesman.

Advantages of Reports

1. Salesman's report is a good guide and indicator for building future plan–a barometer.
2. Competitors' attitude can be known.
3. Sales manager does not waste time in formulating the policies for future, because of the brevity in reports.
4. Salesmen takes little time in writing the reports.
5. The report is a good form of control as it reveals the weakness and strong points of the salesmen.
6. The changes in demand and attitude of the consumers can be known.
7. It is a tool by which the activities of the salesmen can be sharpened.

8. Sales manager is able to divert his attention to the situation warranted on the basis of importance.
9. Salesman himself develops the habit of self-activity analysis.
10. The two-way communication assures employee morale.

QUALITIES OF A GOOD REPORT (or points to be remembered)

1. It should be brief and to the point.
2. It must be well-planned.
3. It must carry accurate data.
4. It must be clear and simple.
5. It should be specific
6. It should be realistic.
7. It should depict the correct picture
8. It should made in paragraphs.
9. It should avoid clichés.
10 Unwanted information should be avoided.

Records : Reports are the basis, on which the records of each salesman are prepared. They will reveal the following condensed idea relating to salesmen, based on actual performance:

1. Sales by product lines
2. Sales to regular customers
3. Sales to new accounts
4. Minimum, maximum and average size of orders
5. Account lost
6. Selling expenses for each order
7. Movements of products–slow or fast.

2. **Sales Territories and Sales Quotas**

Sales manager must try to know the sales field well in advance, before the production starts. He must know the area of demand for the products and for this he should know the habits and economic position of the customers; and the type of demand and quality of products usually in demand. In short, a detailed study of consumers is important. The sources of information are year books, census reports, publications, professional organisations etc.

Sales Territory

Almost all the firms, divide their markets, after the sales field is located into different territories. Sales territory is a particular grouping of customers and prospects assigned to a salesman. A sales territory is a geographical area which contains present and potential customers, who can be served effectively and economically by a single salesman. Its aim is to facilitate management's task in matching sales efforts with the sales opportunities. An efficient salesman can successfully discharge his duties and responsibilities if the territory allotted to him is of workable and suitable size. A good sales planning is based on sales territory, rather than taking the whole market area. That is, the market of a firm's product is divided into small segments or territories or areas, so that each territory can be allotted to each salesman. When allotting perfect sales territories, which have been planned carefully, the following objectives are aimed for the reasons thereof:

1. Sales effort can be fruited more effectively in the assigned territory.
2. It is possible to have increased market coverage, not losing the orders to competitors. He meets the competition wisely as it is pre-planned, because he knows the local condition.

3. It prevents the duplication or overlapping sales efforts.
4. Headquarters of each sales territory can be located in a place, where greater number of customers are located.
5. Work load for each salesman can equitably be distributed, in terms of sales volume.

Other aims :

6. A good territorial allocation brings higher sales volume at lower sales expenses.
7. It allows salesman to spend more time on calling customers rather than in journey, to serve the customers, to whom the products have to be sold. Customers can be served advantageously.
8. The activities of salesman can easily be controlled, more effectively, by the sales manager through comparisons of selling opportunities.
9. The interest and morale of each salesman can be improved in the respective territories.
10. A control of selling expenses is possible and at the same time it increases the sales volume.
11. It is a good basis to evaluate the salesman's performance.
12. Disparities in the work load can be known and be rectified easily.
13. A salesman can gain good knowledge over his territory, in respect of local problems and the existing competition.
14. The duties and responsibilities of each salesman can easily be defined, and thus salesman becomes more duty-conscious.
15. To bring co-ordination of personal selling and advertising efforts more beneficially, territorial assignment to each salesman is a must.

When allocation of sales territories takes place, the following factors may be looked into:

1. Equal earnings should be facilitated among all the salesmen.
2. Sales territory planning should aim in reducing the expenses *i.e.*, cost of travelling.
3. Work load must be justifiable to all; more or less equal work load.
4. It should be flexible, by giving room to the day to day changes.
5. A new salesman should not be given independent territory.

Apart from these, before the allocation of sales territories, the sales manager has to consider:

1. Density of potential customers
2. Distribution method
3. Degree of competition
4. Nature and type of product
5. Nature of demand–seasonal or regular
6. Administration facility
7. Equal work load
8. Frequency of contact with the customers
9. Knowledge of Government regulations
10. Facilities of transport available
11. Abilities of salesmen
12. Number of salesmen available
13. Facilities of communication means
14. Time needed to make a sale

15. Present volume of sales.

The territory allocation must aim at performing the activities in the most effective and economical way for mutual benefits of salesman and the firm. A salesman is expected to produce the best result from the area allotted, by concentrating his activities within the area.

Sales Quota

Apart from the allocation of sales territories, salesmen are further controlled by fixing sales quota. Almost all the companies use quota system of defining and evaluating the task expected of the salesmen. Sales quota, may be defined as the estimated volume of sales that a company expects to secure within a definite period of time. Quota is the amount of business, in terms of value or in terms of units of sales, which is fixed for every salesman. It may be fixed for a geographical area to be achieved within a definite period of time, a month or a year. Shorter the period, the better it is. It is a target or a standard of performance, that the salesman has to attain. The quota is fixed on the basis of sales forecast. For an effective control, smaller area and shorter period are preferred. A sales quota, to be effective, practical and successful, should satisfy the following:

1. Sales quota must be attainable and fair.
2. It must be scientifically calculated. It should not be too small or too big.
3. It must provide definite incentive to salesman.
4. It must be flexible.
5. It must be simple and must be fixed in consultation with the salesman.

Sales quota brings the following benefits :

1. The sales quota can be used as yardstick to assess the performance of the salesmen.
2. It is a measuring rod with which the sales operations are directed and controlled to more profitable channels.
3. It is possible and easier to locate strong markets and weak markets.
4. It is a device to adopt more effective compensation plans.
5. It fixes the responsibility on each salesman and so they work hard to attain the goal. The salesmen never allow the sales to fall below the quota.
6. It facilitates sales contests and is a base.

Weaknesses

1. In many cases the sales quota is fixed arbitrarily.
2. If situations are changed, the quota fixed may become ineffective.
3. If the quota is too small, the salesman will relax and if the quota fixed is too large or unattainable, the salesman loses initiative.
4. It is difficult to set an accurate quota.

Bases Necessary for Fixing Quota

1. Purchasing power of the prospects.
2. Past sales figures compared by analysis.
3. Demand trend for the products.
4. Position and degree of competition prevailing.

At the end of the quota period, it is a must to measure the effectiveness of quota by comparing the performance of salesman, in relation to the quota. To keep salesmen's effort on the right path, quotas can be used as a control mechanism. Departure of sales activities from the projected quota is a main problem to the sales management. If sales volume is not satisfactory, the fault may lie with quota plans. Quota, as a diagnostic aid, cautions the authority to take corrective steps and especially, when the sales volume takes a negative departure from the past sales.

In all fairness, quota should be aimed at equitable distribution. It should be equal for all salesmen. Should all the salesmen have the same quotas? The answer depends upon the territories, which are not the same in respect of competition, extent, customers etc. the ability of the salesman is also different. The 'better' salesman with 'better' territory exceeds the quota and 'poor' salesman with 'poor' territory fails to achieve even the quota. By considering all these, fairness of the quota decision takes place.

Types of Quotas

1. Sales volume, in value or units by product line, consumer type etc.
2. Salesmen activity, such as calls, new accounts, demonstrations, display arranged etc.
3. Expenses quota, either in value or percentage of sales obtained.
4. Gross Margin from sales obtained etc.

Quota can be used as a management tool, if it is set scientifically.

3. **Salesmen's Authority**

If the sales manager goes for doing all the works of a firm, it is very difficult to conduct the business. Moreover, he lacks time. Therefore, the job is divided and entrusted to the salesmen. When the authority is passed on to the salesmen, there is transfer of power to the salesmen *i.e.*, delegation of power. Delegation is the required authority to the salesmen to discharge their assigned job. When one is delegated the authority, it means permission is given to do the duties. When authority is conferred on salesmen, they know their responsibilities. Customers may not be willing to deal with a salesman having no authority. There are no hard and fast rules as to how much authority be given to a salesman. In modern time, the degree of authority is reduced. The authority and freedom of salesmen varies from firm to firm. To what extent the authority is given to a salesman depends upon the size and nature of the firm.

Since the salesmen are representing the firm and deal with customers, who have no direct contact with the firm, the salesmen's authority be well-defined. Generally, catalogue, price lists, advertisements etc., reveal the prices, guarantees, quality and other details of the products. And the salesmen are being relieved of these botherations. However, salesmen may be conferred with certain measure of authority in dealing with the matters, such as special concessions, discount rates, granting credit, settlement of claims, settlement of damages, defective, unsaleable items etc. But it is important that salesmen are watched in their acts which must be in accordance with the instructions by the sales manager and their activities are subject to the approval of the sales manager.

4. **Field Supervision**

Performance of a function or service by an individual is called duty; activities that an individual is required to perform are a duty on him. Authority is a right or power required to perform a job on the basis of duty assigned to one. An authorised person is empowered to do the assigned job. Responsibility must always be followed by corresponding authority or power. Authority and responsibility move in opposite directions. Authority always moves from the top downward, whereas responsibility moves upwards. Authority is derived from sales manager to whom the salesmen are responsible for proper performance of their activities. The individual responsibility and freedom of the sales personnel vary from firm to firm. A good degree of control is essential over the activities of the salesmen. Generally the sales manager or any senior sales personnel or field supervisors are appointed to check the activities of the salesmen so as to:

1. Know whether the salesman is doing his job in best way
2. Find out deficiencies if any
3. Make suggestions for further improvement
4. Check the procedure of orders taking

5. Evaluate the performance of salesman
6. Provide spot motivation to salesman
7. Secure maximum coverage of the market

Control aims at appraisal of salesman's performance. It must be done periodically and on continuing basis as to determine the compliance of policies and attainment of targeted quota in respect of job. Supervision and control are different. Supervision aims at direction for working and control includes supervision and evaluation of past performance.

Routing and Scheduling

Time must be used wisely while a salesman travels in his respective territorial area. Salesman will be encouraged to get maximum sales by reducing the wastage of time. Routing and scheduling is one of the techniques of controlling a salesman's day to day activities. A planned routing of the salesman will facilitate easy communication, maximum territorial coverage and thereby reduce the waste time. Management has a closer control. A clear tour plan is there and reveals route, location of customers, transport facilities, maps etc. The planned routes and schedules are to be followed by the salesman. The reports sent by the salesman can be compared with the planned routes and schedules and this reveals the deviations.

5. **Remuneration Plan**

Refer chapter 32

MOTIVATION OF SALESMAN

Salesmen are the backbone of a sales organisation. A good salesman make a poor selling house into a progressive one. And a bad salesman can make a sound selling house into a starving position. It is because the success or failure of a firm depends upon the ability and initiation of a salesman. It has been said, ''You can buy man's time, his physical presence, but not his will, loyalty and initiative.'' The selling firm can purchase the time of salesman or his physical presence for a job. His willingness to work or his loyalty cannot be purchased and these have to be earned. The will or willingness to work is an important matter as it is a motivation factor.

What is Motivation ?

Motivation means stimulus to achieve goals set out for salesmen by the management. Motivation is directly linked with the will–will to work it is the psychological encouragement or a process of hard work or work better feeling in the mind of the salesmen. To attain a good result through their activities, thcy have been trained. And compensation is paid for the services rendered by the sales personnel. Apart from this financial incentive, further encouragement in the motivation is needed–respect his personal ego, praise him, keep him in touch with the latest information, promotions, recognition of his merits etc., at the right place. These are non-financial incentives.

Need for Motivation

All the sales personnel like to have their efforts recognised. They like to feel that they are part and parcel of the firm. Some salesmen require no encouragement from the management and are able, ambitious and self-starters. Yet, most of the salesmen need encouragement and stimulation to work at their best. This is because of the following reasons:

1. **Nature of the Job :** Salesmen's job is to tell and to sell. He has a chain of incidents of happy and unhappy results from the customers. He has to face the customers of different attitudes–rude, shrewd, argumentative, impatient etc., as well as nice, friendly, good natured etc. He may successfully meet a few and end in orders, while a few may offer only arguments with no result. As such salesman will be in mental tension and will have no peace of mind. And his sales may be lost to competitors. This type of feelings will upset his mind, and he may lose his stamina, resulting in boredom apart from tiresomeness. Therefore, a strong stimulation keeps him to the desired level of performance.

2. **Human Nature :** A satisfied salesman will do better for the firm, but an unsatisfied salesman will do more harm than good. The financial incentive is not enough to keep him happy. Stimulation in the form of promotion, extra-financial benefit etc., are needed to keep him at the level of performance. His mind must be happy.

3. **Personal Problems :** A salesman passes most of his time away from his family. He is unable to attend to his family affairs. He may have sick or old persons at home or debts to be returned etc. His peace of mind greatly depends upon the condition of his family. His condition is correlated with condition of his family. Thus, he needs a good encouragement.

4. **The Loners :** By profession he is working in the assigned territory. He may feel lonely and monotonous. He must be kept in with the feeling of group identity.

Types of Motivation

When a manager wants to get more work done by his employees, he may either hold out a promise of a reward for them for doing the work. In a better or improved way, or he may constrain them, by instilling fear in them or by using force, to do the desired work. That is, he utilizes a positive or a negative motivation. Both these types are widely used by managements. A positive motivation involves the possibility of increased motive satisfaction, while negative motivation involves the possibility of decreased motive satisfaction. Thus, the following are the types of motivation:

(1) Positive Motivation and

(2) Negative Motivation

(1) Positive Motivation

Positive or incentive motivation is generally based on reward. People work for incentives in the form of the four 'P's of motivation: Praise, Prestige, Promotion and Pay cheques.

Positive motivation, in fact, includes (i) Praise and credit for work done; (ii) A sincere interest in subordinates as individuals; (iii) Competition; (iv) Participation; (v) Pride; (vi) Delegation of responsibility; (vii) Appreciation and (viii) Pay. Incentive motivation is the "pull" mechanism. It has its own benefits. The receipt of awards, due recognition, and praise for work well done definitely lead to good team spirit, co-operation and a feeling of happiness.

(2) Negative Motivation

Negative of fear motivation is based on force and fear. Fear causes persons to act in a certain way because they are afraid of the consequences if they don't work. If workers do not work, they are threatened with mechanism. Negative motivation has certain limitations; through its use only the minimum of efforts is put in to avoid punishment. Moreover, the imposition of punishment frequently result in frustration among those punished, leading to the development of maladaptive behaviour. Punishment also creates a hostile state of mind, and an unfavourable attitude to the job. Moreover, it may result in lower productivity because it tends to dissipate such human assets as loyalty, co-operation and *spirit de corps*.

Motivation Techniques

Generally, there are two types of motivation techniques. They are (i) Financial Motivation and (ii) non-financial motivation.

(*i*) Financial Motivation:

Financial motivation is connected directly or indirectly with money, wages and salary, bonuses, profit-sharing, leave with pay, medical reimbursement etc. are under this type of motivation.

(*ii*) **Non-Financial Motivation:**

Non-financial motivations are not connected with monetary rewards. In the word of Dubin, "non-financial incentives are the psychic rewards or the rewards of enhanced position, that can be secured in the work organization.

Some of the commonly used non-financial motivations are:

1. Appraisal, Praise and Prestige
2. Status and Pride
3. Competition
4. Delegation of Authority
5. Job Security
6. Job enrichment
7. Reinforcement, etc.

A few fringe benefits

- Medical leave with pay
- Free financial and legal advice
- Suggestion awards
- Pension, unemployment allowance etc.
- Holidays pay
- Lay-off compensation
- Parties and picnics
- Provident fund
- Disablement benefits
- Housing
- Transportation benefits
- Leave with pay
- Suggestion awards
- Maternity benefits
- Canteens
- Dependant's benefit
- Gratuity, etc.

Method of Motivation :

In addition to the remuneration, certain types of encouragement are needed. A few of them are:

1. **Sales Contests :** By sales contests, we mean a competition among the salesmen, by maximising their effort to boost up the sales, to earn the name of superior salesman. The aim of this contest is to increase the sales, to develop a team spirit, boosting the morale, encouraging to work hard, fast moving or slow moving items, to overcome the depression period etc. The successful salesman at the contests bags the prizes–cash, incentive, merit certificate or free travel etc.

2. **Conventions and Meetings :** This is a group motivation. All employees meet at a place. Everyone meets and contacts fellow workers. Exchange of ideas and opinions takes place. Salesmen have a close touch with the fellow workers and executives. Problems are solved and new policies are developed.

3. **Recognition and Honour :** Recognition and honour–title such as, "Superman for the year," medal or trophy, congratulatory greetings, appreciation letters etc., greatly encourage the salesman to do more hard work. These recognitions and honours satisfy a salesman greatly.

4. **Personal Meet :** The performance of the salesmen can be known from their reports. Further, to have more effect on the sales, salesmen may be facilitated to meet the sales manager in finding solutions to their typical problems. The sales manager gives satisfactory solutions to one's problems or discusses them to arrive at a satisfactory solution. This type of personal meet is a good encouragement.

5. **Promotions :** By considering abilities and experience, as a stimulation policy, the salesmen are promoted to a higher post on a higher salary. Thereby status increases, self-respect increases, remuneration increases; and naturally, it is the best motivation of salesmen. Further promotion is aimed at through further and more hard work.

6. **Personal Communication :** It is always good for the sales manager to write personal letters to the salesman, solving the problems of the salesman, who is performing his work. The two-way flow of ideas, facts, opinions, feelings is good in shaping a goodwill and developing a high morale apart from confidence and co-operation.

7. **Freedom :** In performing his job, he should not be controlled at a high degree. It is necessary that salesman be given a reasonable degree of freedom in doing his assigned job. The salesman should be permitted to do his job in his own pattern. Frequent calling for reports should be avoided. Such things create a good stimulus and generate a feeling that the salesman's job is important in the firm. When the sales manager gives more responsibility to the salesman, the better is the result.

8. **Timely Information :** Whenever any new product is introduced, a policy is changed, a new technique is adopted etc., the salesman must be informed, so that he can possess the latest news of his concern, which is a matter of pride for him. Some of the big firms, publish magazines, and bulletins which are meant for sales personnels and contain all the latest information. When the salesman is kept informed of all the changes–changes in product, policies, colours, prices, promotions, quality, guarantee, sales-after-services etc., he can act as a latest salesman.

QUESTIONS

1. Differentiate between advertisement and personal selling. Are they supplementary to each other ? Illustrate your answer with suitable examples. *(MBA., Allahabad)*
2. Why is formal evaluation of the performance of salesman necessary ? Discuss various ways in which such evaluation can be done. *(MBA., Allahabad)*
3. State the need for controlling salesmen. What are the various methods of controlling salesmen? *(B.Com., Karnataka)*
4. Discuss the different methods of controlling sales force performance. *(B.Com., Madurai)*
5. How are salesmen supervised and controlled ? *(B.Com., Chennai)*
6. Which selling methods - personal vs. advertising - would you recommend in the following and why ?
   (a) Watches
   (b) Motors (c) Pumps
7. What is sales quota? How is a salesman assigned a sales territory?
8. How is sales performance evaluated?

CHAPTER 31

Sales Forecast

- *Meaning*
- *Factors Influencing a Sales Forecasting*
- *Importance*
- *Methods*
- *Types*
- *Questions*

Future is uncertain. Man thinks about future. He may be a businessman, a broker, a manufacturer, a commission agent etc. All guess about the future in their respective field of interest. We try to know, through a clear imagination, what will be happening in the near future–after a weak, month or year. It can be called forecast or prediction. The process of forecasting is based on reliable data of past and present. Forecasting is not new, as it has been practised from time immemorial.

Forecasting is one of the important aspects of administration. The corner-stone of successful marketing planning is the measurement and forecasting to market demand. According to American Marketing Association, ''Sales forecast is an estimate of Sales, in monetary or physical units, for a specified future period under a proposed business plan or programme and under an assumed set of economic and other forces outside the unit for which the forecast is made.'' A sales forecast is an estimation of sales volume that a company can expect to attain within the plan period. A sales forecast is not just a sales predicting. It is the act of matching opportunities with the marketing efforts. Sales forecasting is the determination of a firm's share in the market under a specified future. Thus sales forecasting shows the probable volume of sales.

"Sales forecast is an estimate of sales during a specified future period, whose estimate is tied to a proposed marketing plan and which assumes a particular state of uncontrollable and competitive forces."

Candiff and Still

Factors Influencing a Sales Forecasting

A sales manager should consider all the factors affecting the sales, while predicting the firm's sales in the market. An accurate sales forecast can be made, if the following factors are considered carefully.

1. **General Economic Condition :** It is essential to consider all economic conditions relating to the firm and the consumers. The forecaster must see the general economic trend–inflation or deflation, which affect the business favourably or adversely. A thorough knowledge of the economic, political and the general trend of the business facilitates to build a forecast more accurately. Past behaviour of market, national income, disposable personal income, consuming habits of the customers etc., affect the estimation to a great extent.

2. **Consumers :** Products like, wearing apparel, luxurious goods, furniture, vehicles; the size of population by its composition–customers by age, sex, type, economic condition etc., have an important role. And trend of fashions, religious habits, social group influences etc., also carry weights.

3. **Industrial Behaviours :** Markets are full of similar products manufactured by different firms, which compete among themselves to increase the sales. As such, the pricing policy, design, advanced technological improvements, promotional activities etc., of similar industries must be carefully observed. A new firm may come up with products to the markets and naturally affect the market share of the existing firms. Unstable conditions–industrial unrest, government control through rules and regulations, improper availability of raw materials etc., directly affect the production, sales and profits.

4. **Changes Within Firm :** Future sales are greatly affected by the changes in pricing, advertising policy, quality of products etc. A careful study in relation to the changes on the sales volume may be studied carefully. Sales can be increased by price cut, enhancing advertising policies, increased sales promotions, concessions to customers etc.

5. **Period :** The required information must be collected on the basis of period–short run, medium run or long run forecasts (explained separately in this chapter).

Importance of Sales Forecasting

1. **Supply and demand** for the products can easily be adjusted, by overcoming temporary demand, in the light of the anticipated estimate; and regular supply is facilitated.

2. **A good inventory control** is advantageously benefited by avoiding the weakness of understocking and overstocking.

3. **Allocation** and reallocation of sales territories are facilitated.

4. It is a **forward planner** as all other requirements of raw materials, labour, plant lay out financial needs, warehousing, transport facility etc., depend in accordance with the sales volume expected in advance.

5. **Sales opportunities** are searched out on the basis of forecast, and thus discovery of selling success is made.

6. It is **a gear**, by which all other activities are controlled as a basis of forecasting.

7. **Advertisement programmes** are beneficially adjusted with full advantage to the firm.

8. It is an **indicator** to the department of finance as to how much and when finance is needed; and it helps to overcome difficult situations.

9. It is a **measuring rod** by which the efficiency of the sales personnel or the sales department, as a whole, can be measured.

10. Sales personnel and sales quotas are also regularised–increasing or decreasing–by knowing the sales volume, in advance.

11. It regularises productions through the vision of sales forecast and avoids overtime at high premium rates. It also reduces idle time in manufacturing.

12. As is the sales forecast, so is the progress of the firm. The master plan or budget of a firm is based on forecasts. "The act of forecasting is of great benefit to all who take part in the process, and is the best means of ensuring adaptability to changing circumstances. The collaboration of all concerned leads to a unified front, an understanding of the reasons for decisions, and a broadened outlook."

Methods of Sales Forecasting

Approaches to forecasting techniques and procedures vary from firm to firm. There are many methods. A firm may manufacture the products or distribute the products. Forecasting cannot be done on mere guessing, but on the basis of reliable statistical data collected for this purpose. A dealer or a manufacturer must anticipate the future need and provide necessities to fulfil the needs. The following are the various methods of sales forecasting:

1. Jury of Executive Opinion.
2. Sales Force Opinion.

3. Test Marketing Result.
4. Consumer's Buying Plan.
5. Market Factor Analysis.
6. Expert Opinion.
7. Econometric Model Building
8. Past Sales (Historical Method).
9. Statistical Methods

1. **Jury of Executive Opinion**

This method of sales forecasting is the oldest. One or more of the executives, who are experienced and have good knowledge of the market factors make out the expected sales. The executives are responsible while forecasting sales figures through estimates and experiences. All the factors–internal and external–are taken into account. This is a type of committee approach. This method is simple as experiences and judgement are pooled together in taking a sales forecast figure. If there are many executives, their estimates are averaged in drawing the sales forecast.

Merits

(a) This method is simple and quick.

(b) Detailed data are not needed.

(c) There is economy.

Demerits

(a) It is not based on factual data.

(b) It is difficult to draw a final decision.

(c) More or less, the method rests on guess-work, and may lead to wrong forecasts.

(d) It is difficult to break down the forecasts into products, markets, etc.

2. **Sales Force Opinion**

Under this method, salesmen, or intermediaries are required to make out an estimate sales in their respective territories for a given period. Salesmen are in close touch with the consumers and possess good knowledge about the future demand trend. Thus all the sales force estimates are processed, integrated, modified, and a sales volume estimate formed for the whole market, for the given period.

Merits

(a) Specialised knowledge is utilised.

(b) Salesmen are confident and responsible to meet the quota fixed.

(c) This method facilitates to break down in terms of products, territories, customers, salesmen etc.

Demerits

(a) Success depends upon the competency of salesmen.

(b) A broad outlook is absent.

(c) The estimation may be unattainable or may be too low for the forecasts as the salesmen may be optimistic or pessimistic.

3. **Test Marketing Result**

Under the market test method, products are introduced in a limited geographical area and the result is studied. Taking this result as a base, sales forecast is made. This test is conducted as a sample on pre-test basis in order to understand the market response.

Merits

(a) The system is reliable as forecast is based on actual result.

(b) Management can understand the defects and take steps to rectify.

(c) It is good for introducing new products, in a new territory etc.

Demerits

(a) All the markets are not homogeneous. But study is made on the basis of a part of a market.

(b) It is a time-consuming process.

(c) It is costly.

4. Consumers' Buying Plan

Consumers, as a source of information, are approached to know their likely purchases during the period under a given set of conditions. This method is suitable when there are few customers. This type of forecasting is generally adopted for industrial goods. It is suitable for industries, which produce costly goods to a limited number of buyers–wholesalers, retailers, potential consumers etc. A survey is conducted on face to face basis or survey method. It is because changes are constant while buyer behaviour and buying decisions change frequently.

Merits

(a) First hand information is possible.

(b) User's intention is known.

Demerits

(a) Customer's expectation cannot be measured exactly.

(b) It is difficult to identify actual buyers.

(c) It is good when users are few, but not practicable when consumers are many.

(d) Long run forecasting is not possible.

(e) The system is costly.

(f) Buyers may change their buying decisions.

5. Market Factor Analysis

A company's sales may depend on the behaviour of certain market factors. The principal factors which affect the sales may be determined. By studying the behaviours of the factors, forecasting should be made. Correlation is the statistical analysis which analyses the degree of extent to which two variables fluctuate with reference to each other. The word 'relationship' is of importance and indicates that there is some connection between the variables under observation. In the same way, regression analysis, is a statistical device, which helps us to estimate or predict the unknown values of one variable from the known values of another variable. For instance, you publish a text book on ''Banking'', affiliated to different universities. The permitted intake capacity of each and the medium through which the students are taught are known. Is it a compulsory or an optional subject ? By getting all these details and also by considering the sales activities of promotional work, you may be able to declare the probable copies to be printed. The key to the successful use of this method lies in the selection of the appropriate market factors. Minimising the number of market factors is also important. Thus the demand decision makers have to consider price, competitions, advertising, disposal income, buying habits, consumption habits, consumer price index, change in population etc.

Merits

(a) It is a sound method.

(b) Market factor is analysed in detail.

Demerits

(a) It is costly.
(b) It is time-consuming.
(c) It is a short run process.

6. **Expert Opinion**

Many types of consultancy agencies have entered into the field of sales. The consultancy agency has specialised experts in the respective field. This includes dealers, trade associations etc. They may conduct market researches and possess ready-made statistical data. Firms may make use of the opinions of such experts. These opinions may be carefully analysed by the company and a sound forecasting is made.

Merits

(a) Forecasting is quick and inexpensive.
(b) It will be more accurate.
(c) Specialised knowledge is utilised.

Demerits

(a) It may not be reliable.
(b) The success of forecasting depends upon the competency of experts.
(c) A broad outlook may be lacking.

7. **Econometric Model Building**

This is a mathematical approach of study and is an ideal way to forecast sales. This method is more useful for marketing durable goods. It is in the form of equations, which represent a set of relationships among different demand determining market factors. By analysing the market factors (independent variable) and sales (dependent variable), sales are forecast. This system does not entirely depend upon correlation analysis. It has great scope, but adoption of this method depends upon availability of complete information. The market factors which are more accurate, quick and less costly may be selected for a sound forecasting.

8. **Past Sales** (Historical method)

Personal judgement of sales forecasting can be beneficially supplemented by the use of statistical and quantitative methods. Past sales are a good basis and on this basis future sales can be formulated and forecast. According to Kirkpatrick, today's sales activity flows into tomorrow's sales activities; that is last year's sales extend into this year's sales. This approach is adding or deducting a set of percentage to the sales of previous year(s). For new industries and for new products, this method is not suitable.

(a) **Simple Sales Percentage :** Under this method, sales forecast is made by adding simply a flat percentage of sales so as to forecast sales as given below:

$$\text{Next year sales} = \text{Present year sales} + \frac{\text{This year sales}}{\text{Last year sales}}$$

or = Present year sales + 10 or 5% of present sale

(b) **Time Series Analysis :** A time series analysis is a statistical method of studying historical data. It involves the isolation of long time trend, cyclical changes, seasonal variations and irregular fluctuations. Past sales figures are taken as a base, analysed and adjusted to future trends. The past records and reports enable us to interpret the information and forecast future trends and trade cycle too.

Merits

(a) No guess-work creeps in.

(b) The method is simple and inexpensive.

(c) This is an objective method.

Demerits

(a) 'Market is dynamic' is not considered.

(b) No provision is made for upswings and downswings in sales activities.

9. Statistical Methods

Statistical methods are considered to be superior techniques of sales forecasting, because their reliability is higher than that of other techniques. They are:

(1) Trend Method

(2) Graphical Method

(3) Time- series method:

- (*a*) Freehand method
- (*b*) Semi-average method
- (*c*) Moving average method
- (*d*) Method of least square

(4) Correlation Method

(5) Regression method

NB: The above statistical methods can easily be studied with the help of statistics book.

Apart from the above, the following factors may also be considered:

1. Availability of raw materials
2. Plant capacity
3. Government policies
4. Buying habits of consumers
5. Fashion changes
6. Distribution system
7. Financial capacity
8. Market competition
9. National income movement
10. Sales promotions

Types of Sales Forecasting

The Economic Forecast : This type of forecast is important to understand the general economic trend through a careful study of Five Year Plans, Gross national products, National income, Government expenditure, Unemployment, Consumer spending habits etc. This is in order to have an accurate forecast. Big companies, in India, adopt this method.

The Industry Forecast : The future market demand is calculated through industrial forecast or market forecast. The expected sales forecasts of all the industries, in the same line of business are combined. Market demand may be affected by controllables–price, distribution, promotion, etc., and uncontrollables–demographic, economic, political, technological development, cultural activities etc. The executive must take into account all these conditions while forecasting.

The Company Forecast : The third step goes to the firm concerned to look into the market share, for which forecast is to be made. By considering both controllables and uncontrollables, based on chosen marketing plans within the firm, with that of other industries, steps are taken in formulating forecasts.

There are three classes of sales forecasts:

1. **Short-run Forecast :** It is also known as operating forecast, covering a maximum of one year or it may be half-yearly, quarterly, monthly and even weekly. This type of forecasting can be advantageously utilised for estimating stock requirements, providing working capital, establishing sales quotas, fast moving factors. It facilitates the management to improve and co-ordinate the policies and practice of marketing–production, inventory, purchasing, financing etc. Short-run forecast is preferred to all types and brings more benefits than other types.

2. **Medium-run Forecast :** This type of forecast may cover from more than one year to two or four years. This helps the management to estimate probable profit and control over budgets, expenditure, production etc. Factors–price trend, tax policies, institutional credit etc., are specially considered for a good forecast.

3. **Long-run Forecast :** This type of forecast may cover one year to five years, depending on the nature of the firm. Seasonal changes are not considered. The forecaster takes into account the population changes, competition changes, economic depression or boom, inventions etc. This type is good for adding new products and dropping old ones.

Limitations of Sales Forecast

In certain cases forecast may become inaccurate. The failure may be due to the following factors :

1. **Fashion :** Changes are throughout. Present style may change any time. It is difficult to say as to when a new fashion will be adopted by the consumers and how long it will be accepted by the buyers. If our product is similar to the fashion and is popular, we are able to have the best result; and if our products are not in accordance with the fashion, then sales will be affected.

2. **Lack of Sales History :** A sales history or past records are essential for a sound forecast plan. If the past data are not available, then forecast is made on guess-work, without a base. Mainly a new product has no sales history and forecast made on guess may be a failure.

3. **Psychological Factors :** Consumers' attitude may change at any time. The forecaster may not be able to predict exactly the behaviour of consumers. Certain market environments are quick in action. Even rumours can affect market variables. For instance, when we use a particular brand of soap, it may generate itching feeling on a few people and if the news spread among the public, sales will be seriously affected.

4. **Other Reasons :** It is possible that the growth may not remain uniform. It may decline or be stationary. The economic condition of a country may not be favourable to the business activities–policies of the government, imposition of controls etc. It may affect the sales.

The methods of forecasting discussed above have respective merits and demerits. No single method may be suitable. Therefore, a combination method is suitable and may give a good result. The forecaster must be cautious while drawing decisions on sales forecast. Periodical review and revision of sales forecast may be done, in the light of performance. A method which is quick, less costly and more accurate may be adopted.

QUESTIONS

1. What is the importance of sales forecasting? (*B.Com., Chennai*)
2. What are the types of forecasts? (*B.Com., Madurai*)
3. Explain the factors that influence sales forecast. (*B.Com., Madurai*)
4. What do you mean by sales forecasting? What are the methods used in sales forecasting?

CHAPTER 32

Remuneration to Salesmen

- *Introduction*
- *A Good Remunerative Plan*
- *Objectives*
- *Essentials*
- *Developing a Remunerative Plan*
- *Methods*
- *Incentives*
- *Fringe Benefits*
- *Questions*

Introduction

Every firm has to formulate a good compensation plan while recruiting salesmen. The salesmen's compensation plan or remuneration plan means the monetary payment by a firm to its salesmen, in consideration of the performance or service rendered by them. A good remunerative plan is a good tonic, with which employees put forth efforts in attaining the goals of the organisation and motivate more effectively. The salesmen play a significant role and are important, because they create income for the firm through sales. Moreover salesmen's role also decides the success or failure of the firm. Therefore, it is an important matter for the management to formulate a good and sound remunerative plan.

Reasons For A Good Remunerative Plan

1. A good remuneration plan, which makes suitable reward for the service, attracts the best sales personnel because they, through their efforts, bring revenues to the firm.
2. A salesman is happy when he is paid amply, which correlates his efforts and result. When he is satisfied with the payment, naturally he takes maximum interest in his duties.
3. Sales forces are not directly supervised. Labour turnover can be reduced. The selected salesmen serve for the whole life. All these bring economy and prosperity to the firm.
4. Handsomely paid salesmen create higher productivity to the firm, apart from a good relation between employer and employee.

Objectives of Remunerative Plan

1. It must facilitate the firm to attract and retain the sales force and make them efficient and loyal.
2. It should aim to motivate them so as to attain the sales volume of quota.
3. It should aim at a direct relation between salesmen's performance and firm's profitability.
4. It must eliminate the unwanted sales force.
5. It must have the capacity of controlling the sales force.
6. It should not be changed often.
7. It must provide extra benefit for sincere and hard working salesmen.

Essentials of a Good Remunerative Plan

1. It should be simple to understand.
2. It must be fair to salesmen and the firm.
3. It should be flexible enough to provide scope for adjustment of changes in business.
4. It should be reviewed periodically in order to keep it up-to-date.

5. It should provide adequate incentive to ensure living wages.
6. It should motivate the salesmen to boost performance.
7. It should ensure a minimum earning to a salesman.
8. Its monetary benefit should be in proportion to the objectives to be attained.
9. It should be easy and inexpensive to administer.
10. It should be competitive with the remunerative plan of rivals.
11. It must have provisions to reward a salesman whose performance is above average.
12. It should have provision for periodic increment or promotion from the lower to the higher grade.

Developing a Remunerative Plan

1. Development of a job description is the first job.
2. Then, through job evaluation, comparing other jobs, facilitates to have a remunerative plan.
3. A reasonable earning should be levelled.
4. Decide the total amount payable to a salesman.
5. The type of goods, slow moving items, small order, encouraging sales promotions etc., are to be considered.
6. Then decide the method of payment.
7. Test the plan, by applying it on salesmen and watch the reactions.

Methods of Compensation

Basically, the compensation is based on two factors–the time spent on the job and the amount of sales made. Based on these factors, the following methods are generally employed:

1. Straight Salary Method.
2. Straight Commission Method.
3. Combination of Salary and Commission Method.
4. Bonus.
5. Profit sharing

1. Straight Salary Method

It is the earliest of all remuneration plans and is the most common method. Under this system, salesmen are paid a predetermined amount, as a salary, generally at the end of every month. That is, a fixed amount of salary is payable to the salesman, regardless of his sales volume. The amount is fixed and does not vary. There is a fixed time-scale, with annual increments, for a continued service. Generally, the amount consists of basic salary, dearness allowance, and any other allowances. Other amounts to meet the business expenses will also be paid.

This plan is suitable at the following places:

1. Where a new market is to be explored,
2. Where several salesmen have to co-operate for a sale,
3. Where job needs missionary or educational effort,
4. Where new salesmen are employed,
5. Where the job needs pre-sale and post-sale service or the case of complex products,
6. Where the sales cannot be measured satisfactorily,
7. Where the salesman's job is just routine order-taking,
8. Where the salesman works at the sales counter,
9. Where the market, for the products, is seasonal.

Merits

1. The scheme is simple to understand.
2. It assures a definite guaranteed income to the salesman.

3. It exposes security and stability of income to salesman.
4. It helps to develop satisfied and loyal sales force.
5. It lowers labour turnover.
6. It is a good system when sales are uncertain.
7. When new salesmen are appointed, it is an effective scheme.
8. Consumers' needs and desire are better served.
9. The army of salesmen can be controlled easily.

Demerits

1. It makes no difference between the idle salesman and active salesman, as all get equal salary.
2. It does not stimulate the salesmen to work harder because salary is paid irrespective of sales volume.
3. Reward is unrelated to effort or effort is unrelated to reward, as under this system, there arises no relation between effort and reward.
4. It overcompensates the inefficient and undercompensates the efficient.
5. The selling cost is not related to the sales volume.

II. **Straight Commission Method**

This method is based on the result, and not on the basis of time. The productivity *i.e.*, volume of sales made by a salesman is a basis for remuneration. The commission is calculated usually as a percentage on total orders secured *i.e.*, total value of sales. The rate of commission may be flat or differential. Differential rates aim at lower commission up to a standard performance and a higher rate over and above the standard performance.

This plan is suitable in the following cases:

1. When high incentive is required to achieve sufficient sales,
2. When the financial position is not strong to meet the fixed cost of straight salary.
3. When the firm cannot control the activities of the salesmen.

Merits

1. There is a direct relationship between selling costs and sales revenues.
2. There is a clear distinction between efficient and inefficient salesmen.
3. Cost of administration is low.
4. It provides maximum monetary incentive to salesmen.
5. Salesmen are free birds.
6. The scheme works as a great incentive to efficient salesmen.
7. The plan is simple to understand and easy to operate.
8. It attracts salesmen of better ability and calibre.
9. An effective cost control system can be formulated, as there is a direct relation between selling cost and sales amount *i.e.*, both will move hand in hand.
10. Personnel management problem is the least.

Demerits

1. There is always uncertainty about the income and his position is insecure.
2. Fast moving goods are sold faster, but slow moving goods are sold still slower.
3. Salesman cannot be controlled as there arises a nominal relation, and he may quit the job at any time.
4. Salesman may use undesirable methods to boost sales.
5. The plan is unsuitable during depression or war periods.
6. Non-selling tasks are ignored and attention is focussed only on selling aspect.

III. Combination of Salary and Commission

The above two methods discussed, have merits and demerits. The combination of salary and commission plan takes the advantages of both the methods–Straight salary method and straight commission method. This plan is the popular method of remuneration. Almost all the salesmen are satisfied with a regular fixed salary, because people want economic security. In this method, a salesman gets a salary (fixed component) and a commission (variable component) on the basis of sales made. The system works in the following two patterns:

(A) Salary Plus Commission on Total Sales : Under this system, a salesman is paid a salary. (pre-determined) and also a commission on total sales made by him.

(B) Salary Plus Commission over Certain Quota : Under this method, a salesman is paid a pre-determined fixed amount as salary and a commission, which is calculated on the amount of sales over and above the sales quota. In case, the salesman cannot sell even the quota fixed, he is entitled only for the salary and there is a no question of commission.

Illustration :

A salesman who is appointed on a monthly salary of Rs. 1,000 plus a commission, is entitled at:

(a) 1.5% commission on all sales, (or)

(b) 4% commission over the sales of Rs. 25,000.

Total sales made by him was Rs. 40,000.

His total earning would be:

(a) Salary	Rs. 1,000	(b) Salary	Rs. 1,000
Commission 1.5%		Commission 4% :	
on Rs. 40,000	600	upto Rs. 25,000	nil
		above Rs. 25,000	
		i.e., 4% on 15,000	600
	1,600		1,600

Merits

1. There is a minimum guaranteed income.
2. Salesmen take more initiative to sell, as they know that more effort means more reward.
3. Efforts and rewards are well-balanced.
4. The plan is acceptable and is more suitable and appropriate to salesmen.
5. There is control over the salesman's activity.

Demerits

1. There is an increase in the office cost–administration cost.
2. More records have to be maintained.

INCENTIVE PLANS

IV. Bonus

Bonus is different from commission. The payment of commission is based on the value of the sales. Bonus is a financial incentive to the salesman. It is paid to the salesman in addition to the remuneration. The basis for the bonus is different from firm to firm. The basis may be:

(a) the profit earned in a particular territory,

(b) when the sales quota is exceeded,

(c) for any special services offered,

(d) for performing a certain promotional work,

(e) for creating a certain number of new customers,

(f) reducing the selling expenses.

The bonus amount is in addition to the normal remuneration.

The bonus plan must be drawn carefully such that:

1. The conditions laid down in the plan must be clear.
2. Misunderstanding or disputes should not arise.
3. Proper maintenance of relevant records is essential.

Merits

(a) It is an additional income to the salesman.
(b) Salesman becomes more loyal to the organisation.
(c) It reduces the turnover ratio in the organisation.
(d) A good understanding and co-operation are cultivated in the minds of the salesmen.
(e) The idea or aim of the firm can be germinated through the salesman.

V. Profit Sharing

This is a system by which a firm apportions a part of the divisible profit; and this part is shared by the salesmen in terms of their contribution to it. The bonus sharing plan is in addition to the regular remuneration. The profit or the loss depends upon the policies of the firm. The amount of divisible profit can be reduced by making reserves, increasing the rate of depreciation, undervaluation of stocks, secret reserve etc., to thin the profit to be exposed.

Fringe Benefits

This benefit is non-cash incentive, given to salesmen as a compensation, in addition to salary. This includes provision for meeting medical expenses, free medical facilities, free accommodation, provident fund schemes, pension benefit, getting company's product at cost price, children's education expenses etc.

Travelling Expenses

Salesmen, in finding the prospective customers, have to travel extensively. An amount may be spent by them to meet the customers, and this must be reimbursed. The trip must be unavoidable and essential for the business. The amount may be paid in the following manner.

(a) On receiving a detailed report of the actual expenses from the salesmen, after verification, the claimed amount may be paid immediately.

or (b) The amount incurred may be intimated to the company, and without demanding the detailed report, the full amount may be paid in good faith.

or (c) The company may fix an amount to be spent in sales territory, considering boarding and lodging etc. The fixed amount is paid.

or (d) The firm may fix a flat rate at which the amount is paid.

or (e) An amount may be fixed by the company for travelling purposes, generally monthly. The expenses reported by the salesman are paid, but not beyond the limit fixed.

QUESTIONS

1. How are salesmen motivated ?
2. Describe the types of selling situations where the payment of straight salary would be an appropriate method of compensating a salesman. *(M.Com., Delhi)*
3. Contrast the three basic methods for compensating salesmen.
4. Explain the characteristics of a good remuneration plan. Discuss the various methods of remunerating salesmen. *(B.Com., Madurai)*
5. Explain the essentials of a good remuneration plan. *(B.Com., Madurai)*

CHAPTER 33

Channels of Distribution–I

- *Introduction*
- *Definition*
- *Function*
- *Importance*
- *Types*
- *Different Channels*
- *Market Considerations*
- *Intensity of Distribution*
- *Channel Conflict*
- *Cause of Conflict*
- *Managing Conflict*
- *Logistic management*
- *JIT Techniques*
- *Benefits of JIT Technique*
- *Questions*

Introduction

The typical geographic separation of the manufacturer or producer from the ultimate consumer requires some means for bridging the gap. The movement of goods and services from the place of producer through middlemen to the ultimate consumers/users has been thought of as a channelised flow. At present most of the producers sell their products to the consumers through a host of marketing intermediaries performing a variety of functions–buy, take title to, resell, negotiate etc. Producers produce the products and finally make them ready for the market. The methods and routes to be adopted to bring the products to the market–to the ultimate consumers and industrial users, must be determined. This process involves establishing distribution strategies, including channel of distribution and providing for physical handling and distribution. Distribution system has two components : (1) channels of distribution and (2) physical distribution. By channel of distribution we mean the intermediaries or the process through which the products are transferred from the producers to the ultimate users. Physical distribution is concerned with the flow of goods to the ultimate consumers, including transportation, warehousing and inventory management. Marketing channels are the distribution networks. Products flow to the market through the distribution network. 'Marketing channel' or 'Channel of distribution' is a path traced in the direct or indirect transfer of ownership to a product, as it moves from a producer to ultimate consumers/industrial users.

The path between producers and users, that goods and services follow is called a marketing channel, trade channel or distribution channel. Today's customers have much more choice than their forefathers. Marketers have made this possible not only by offering choices but by distributing them at the consumption point at the right time. In fact, distribution has become increasingly important to marketers because of ever increasing competition and consumer concerns regarding prompt availability of products. Marketing efforts amount to nothing unless the products and services are made physically available at the hands of those who need them. In the 4 P's model of marketing mix, place element involves bridging the physical separation between buyers and producers.

Management of distribution is called third 'P' (place) in marketing. This involves processes to place the finished goods from a manufacturer to a customer for final consumption and usage. This encompasses flow of goods and ownership from manufacturer to the consumer. **We can say that whosoever is engaged between the producer and the consumer is a member of the distribution channel.**

Definition

According to American Marketing Association, "A channel of distribution, or marketing channel, is the structure of intra-company organisation units and extra-company agents and dealers, wholesale and retail through which a commodity, product or service is marketed."

According to Richard M. Clewelt, "A channel is the pipe line through which a product flows on its way to the consumer. The manufacturer puts his product into the pipe line or marketing channel and various marketing people move it along to the consumer at the other end of the channel."

According to Beckmen and others, "The course taken in the transfer of the title to a commodity constitutes its channel of distribution. It is the route taken by the title to a product in its passage from its first owner, the agricultural producer, or manufacturer, as the case may be, to the last owner, the ultimate consumer or the business user."

According to John A. Howard, "Marketing channels are the combination of agencies through which the seller, who is often though not necessarily the manufacturer, markets his products to the ultimate user."

Marketing channel may be defined as "a pathway composed of intermediaries, also called middlemen, who perform such functions as needed to ensure smooth flow of goods and services from the manufacturing ends to the consuming ends in order to achieve marketing of the produce of a company."

The distribution channel is the movement of goods and services between the point of production and the point of consumption through organisation, that performs a variety of marketing activities. The major participants in the distribution channel are : producers, intermediaries and consumers.

According to A. W. Shaw, "Distribution is the application of motion to materials as they move from the times, places, forms and conditions where they have no value, to the times, places, forms and conditions where they have value."

Function of Marketing Channel (Philips Kotler)

The functions of the members of marketing channel are:

1. **Research :** The gathering of information necessary for planning and facilitating exchange.
2. **Promotion :** The development and dissemination of persuasive communication about the offer.
3. **Contact :** The searching out and communicating with prospective buyers.
4. **Matching :** The shaping and filling of the offer to the buyer's requirements. This includes such activities as manufacturing, grading, assembling and packaging.
5. **Negotiating :** The attempts to reach final agreement on price and other terms of the offer, so that transfer of ownership or possession can be effected.
6. **Physical distribution :** The transporting and storing of the goods.
7. **Financing :** The acquisition and dispersal of funds to cover the costs of the channel work.
8. **Risk taking :** The assumption of risks in connection with carrying out the channel work.

GENERAL FUNCTIONS OF CHANNEL DISTRIBUTION

1. To distribute goods and services, with minimum losses.
2. To establish market for new products.
3. To offer after sale services to customers.
4. To facilitate maximum exposure of goods in the markets.

5. To establish brand loyalty.
6. To maintain competitive advantage to producuers.
7. To match goods and to the requirements of markets.
8. To persuade and influence the prospective buyers.,
9. To undertake all physical distribution functions.
10. To provide feed-back information.
11. To conduct market research.
12. To increase customer confidence.
13. To help in sorting processes.
14. To care all the flows involved in the distribution.
15. "**RIGHT** quantity of the **RIGHT** product/service to the **RIGHT** place in the **RIGHT** conditions at the **RIGHT** cost and at the **RIGHT** time with the **RIGHT** impression." (7 R's)

Importance of Channel of Distribution

A channel of distribution for a product is the route taken by the title to goods as they move from the producer to the ultimate consumer or industrial user. It brings maximum profit to all institutions concerned. The channel of distribution is very important to the producer and the consumer. The consumers are scattered in many places. The producer is situated in one place. There is a big gap between the producer and the consumer. The gap between the producer and the consumer is shrunk by the channel of distribution. Hence the channel of distribution is the connecting link between the producer and the consumer to sell the products.

The middleman in the channel of distribution (1) collects the outputs of various products, (2) subdivides the products according to the needs of the consumers and gathers this in the assortment wanted, and (3) disperses this assortment to consumers or industrial buyers. The middlemen are specialists in concentration, equalisation and dispersions. They create time, place, form and possession utilities. The channel of distribution helps in making products available at the right time in the right place and in the right quantity.

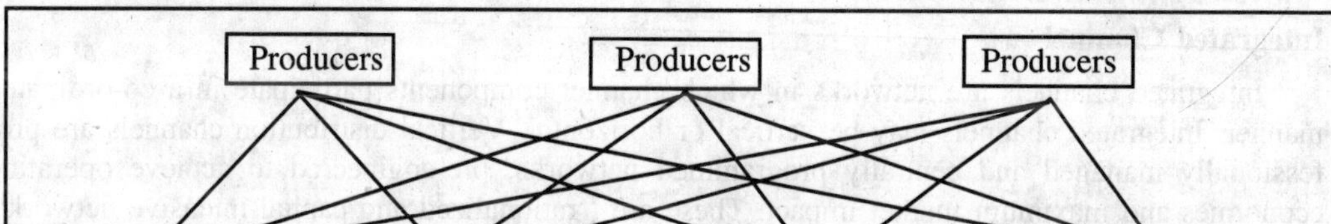

Direct Distribution

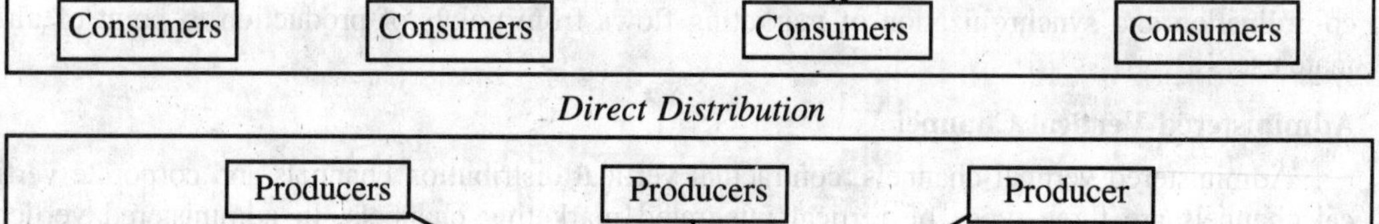

Indirect Distribution

Marketing and Distribution

Marketing is a comprehensive term which includes distribution also. Marketing is the process of discovering and translating consumer needs and wants into product and service specifications, creating demand for the products and services, and then in turn expanding this demand. Distribution is a function to distribute or sub-divide the producer's goods on a geographical basis to various specific markets.

Types of Channels of Distribution

Channels of distribution can be classified into Non-integrated and Integrated. The other name for Non-integrated channel is Individualistic or Conventional Market channel.

Distribution Channels

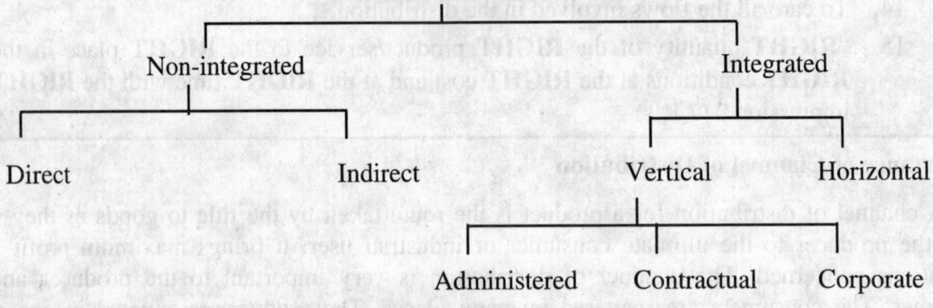

Non-integrated Channel (Conventional Marketing Channel)

In this channel each enterprise is a separately owned and operated concern. Manufacturers, wholesalers and retailers bargain with each other, negotiate over terms of sale and otherwise behave autonomously. In conventional marketing channels there are two types of channels and they are direct channel and indirect channel.

In the **direct or short channel,** the company sells the products to consumers directly. There are no intermediaries. In **indirect channel or long channel** the company uses intermediaries to channelise its products to the consumers. In the indirect channel, the company has more than one choice, depending upon the length of channel sequence.

Integrated Channel

Integrated channels are networks in which channel components participate in a co-ordinated manner. Integrated channels may be vertical or horizontal. Vertical distribution channels are professionally managed and centrally programmed networks, pre-engineered to achieve operating economies and maximum market impact. These are ''rationalized and capital-intensive networks, designed to achieve technological, managerial and promotional economies through the integration, co-ordination and synchronization of marketing flows from points of production to point of ultimate use.''

Administered Vertical Channel

Administered vertical channels, contractual vertical distribution channels and corporate vertical channels are three types of vertical integrated marketing channels. In administered vertical channels, one of a limited number of firms use developed programmes to achieve the co-ordination of marketing activities. A manufacturer controls the marketing of a particular line of merchandise.

Contractual Vertical Channel

Under contractual vertical distribution channel, independent firms are employed on a voluntary basis to develop a more efficient system on a contractual basis, so as to achieve systematic economies and increased market impact.

Corporate Vertical Channel

Under corporate vertical distribution channel, channel components are owned and operated by one organisation. The firms own both production and distribution facilities, e.g., Bata, Tata etc.

Horizontal Marketing System

Horizontal marketing system, also known as symbiotic marketing, occurs when two or more related or unrelated companies working at the same level come together to exploit marketing opportunities. By coming together they have the option to combine their capital, production capabilities, marketing strengths to gain substantial advantage by each company working alone This kind of joining forces is viewed as symbiotic relationship and can be between non-competitors as well as competitors. This arrangement can be on a temporary or permanent basis. For example: Auto manufacturers have joined hands with finance institutions to finance customers, TVs. Whirlpool and Onida joined hands to market washing machines etc.

Multichannel Marketing System

Multichannel system, also known as *hybrid channel*, involves different group of intermediaries. The system is also known as **dual distribution**, when a company uses two or more channels to distribute same products, use telemarketing to reach medium size customers, direct mail selling to small customers, retailers sell to personal consumers, and also uses online selling.

The companies can gain benefits because of adding more channels: (a) Increased market coverage, (b) Lower channel cost and (c) More customized selling.

The number of intermediary levels indicate the 'length' of a channel. The channel level is short if there is only one intermediary; and long if there are more levels. The following are the types of alternative channels:

1. Zero – level channel
2. One – level channel
3. Two – level channel
4. Three – level channel

1. Zero – level channel

A zero level channel consists of a producer and his customers/consumers. This is also called direct marketing. Here the producer or the manufacturer sells products directly to the consumers. For examples, (a) Door to Door sales, (b) Sale by mail order method, etc. Further, Bata shoes, Titan watches etc. are sold through the manufacturers' own show-room.

2. One-level channel

It consists of one selling intermediary in the distribution

3. Two – level channel

It consists of two selling intermediaries in the distribution.

4. Three- level channel

It consists of three selling intermediaries in the distribution. (see the chart given below)

The different channel choices are

A. Manufacturer-Consumer

This is the direct channel. Products are transferred directly to consumers by the manufacturers. It is the shortest and simplest channel.

Direct channel is conveniently adopted under the following circumstances.

1. Producer of perishable goods aims to avoid physical distribution, but tries to sell directly e.g., bakery products, ice cream, etc.
2. Manufacturers of fashion goods enter into direct sales for quick sales, before the fashion disappears.
3. When the plant is located near the customers, it is easier to sell the products.

DISTRIBUTION CHANNEL

(A) CONSOMER GOODS

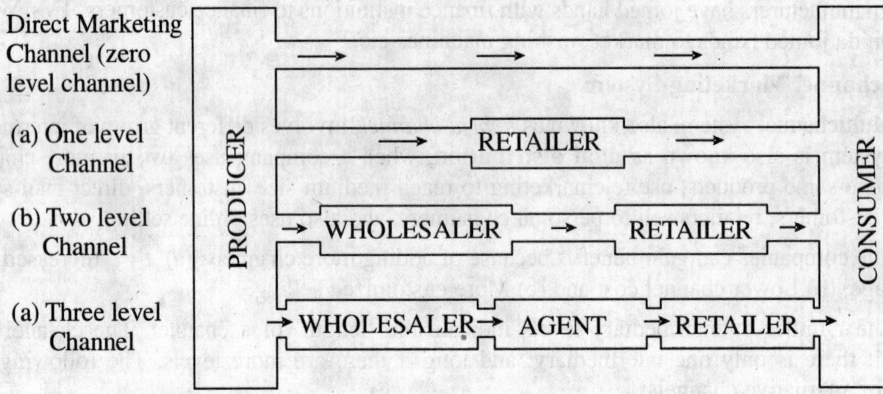

(B) INDUSTRIAL GOODS

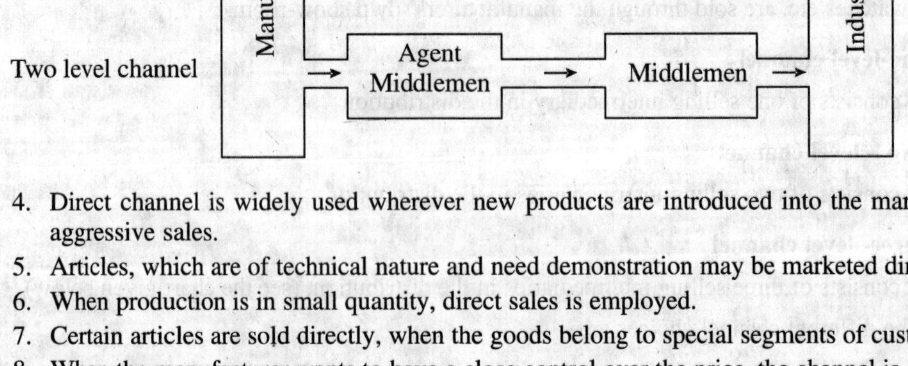

4. Direct channel is widely used wherever new products are introduced into the market for aggressive sales.
5. Articles, which are of technical nature and need demonstration may be marketed directly.
6. When production is in small quantity, direct sales is employed.
7. Certain articles are sold directly, when the goods belong to special segments of customers.
8. When the manufacturer wants to have a close control over the price, the channel is good.
9. The manufacturer is able to undertake various functions of marketing, by employing his own sales force or by retail shops. The system is good.
10. It aims to reach the specific target markets.

The drawbacks of this direct channel are :

1. It is uneconomical to have a direct contact with the customers, who are countless and scattered all over.
2. It is not possible for a direct contact with the multi-millions of potential customers for the products.
3. Manufacturers, generally, may not have talent of salesmanship.

The following are the methods used by producers, under direct channel.

(a) Opening sales counter at manufacturer plant.

(b) Door to door sales.

(c) Sales by mail order method.

(d) Sales by opening own shops.

(e) Sales through mechanical devices.

(a) **Sales Counter At Manufacturer's Plant :** Manufacturers of non-durable goods generally dispose off their products to customers who call on them; for example, bakery products, ice cream, cool drinks etc.

(b) **Door to Door Sales :** Salesmen employed by the manufacturers call at the door of customers. They move from door to door. This system works better when a new product is introduced into the market. Dealers may not have knowledge of the goods or they need a good margin of profit or they do not want to stock unknown products; for them this system is good. Selling under this system may be costly but when the market is known, it can be reduced. But, at the initial stage, when the market is unaware of the product, even at higher cost, this system is better; for example, ladies garments, utensils, coir products, household cleaning materials, rugs, housewares etc. To the customers it is easy to conclude a purchase, get personal service of the seller etc.

(c) **Sales by Mail Order Method :** It is a system by which products are sold to consumers. The post-office plays a significant role. This system is also known as shopping by post or mail order business or selling by post. It is an impersonal selling, branding, grading, standardising, packaging etc., facilitating the growth of this system. Customers are approached by sending catalogues, price lists, pamphlets etc., by post. Advertising adds further speed in the selling; for example, books, drugs, watches, toys, small appliances, clothes, seeds, jewellery etc.

The mail order system is suitable and profitable, when:

1. The goods are standardised and graded.
2. The goods are known to the customers.
3. The goods can be advertised precisely.
4. Wide publicity is made.
5. The price is low.
6. An improved system of post-office.
7. Merchandising is effective.
8. Goods are capable of being put into immediate use on buying.
9. Goods are not damaged in transit.
10. Goods are non-perishable.
11. Manufacturers have earned a good reputation.

Advantages of Mail Order System

1. Business can be housed in any place, by looking at the economy of rent.
2. Capital requirement is less.
3. The buyer gets home delivery.

4. The market is unlimited.
5. Bad debts can be avoided to a great extent.
6. Consumers get the products without shopping.

Disadvantages

1. Buyers cannot inspect or select the goods.
2. Demonstration is not possible.
3. After sales service is not extended.
4. No credit facilities are provided.
5. Generally high prices are charged.
6. Honesty of the seller is questionable.
7. Cheating is common.

According to Nystrom, the success of the mail order business has been to the following reasons:

1. The former isolation of farm life;
2. High literacy and wide circulation of periodicals;
3. Increased earning power and rising standard of the living of the people;
4. Inadequacy and unpreparedness of local retailers;
5. Lower prices;
6. Convenience of mail-order method;
7. Unconditional guarantee of satisfaction or money refunded;
8. A reputation for truthful advertising;
9. Improvement of post office system;
10. Rapid service in sending out orders;
11. Effective merchandising.

(d) **Sales By Opening Own Shops :** It is common that producers of perishable and non-perishable goods sell their products to customers, by opening their own retail shops. It is also common that manufacturers of clothes, footwear, certain electrical equipments etc., can push the goods quickly through retail shops and can offer satisfactory service to customers, thereby building goodwill. It also facilitates the producers to study the market trends, fashion preferred by buyers and style trend of people. This system offers a two way communication and the price is regulated.

(e) **Sales Through Mechanical Devices :** In advanced countries like Germany, the U.S.A., Japan etc., mechanical devices are employed to sell the goods directly to the customers. Commodities like coffee, soft drinks, newspapers, milk etc., are sold by mechanical devices. These devices eliminate sales personnel and economy in space with the help of automatic selling machines; sales are done on cash basis.

B. Manufacturer-Retailer-Consumer

In the channel there is an intermediary retailer. A manufacturer sells goods to consumers through these retailers. There is a gap between the manufacturer and the consumer.

If the buyers are large, this channel is preferable. For perishable articles which need speed in distribution, this channel is suitable. Large retailers are : departmental store, chain store, supermarket, big mail order house, co-operative store etc. Manufacturer acts as a wholesaler and performs the function of storage, insurance, financing and transport. Automobile appliances, clothings, shoes are sold directly to retailers. Bata India Ltd. use this channel. It sells its products through the large number of its retail shops. It is established in cities.

Under the channel, the wholesalers are by-passed and it is because of growth of many retailing institutions in and around the big cities. To by-pass the wholesalers the following are reasons:

1. Wholesalers lack interest in aggressive selling.
2. Wholesalers offer poor facility to store the products.
3. They demand higher amount of discounts on sales.
4. It shortens the journey time to the consumers.
5. Retailers prefer to have a direct dealing with the producers.
6. They may adopt hand to mouth buying.
7. Wholesalers, in many cases, start their own brands, competing with the manufacturer's brand.

Retailers offer the following services to customers:

1. They supply the goods in small quantities to consumers.
2. They stock variety of goods which facilitates proper selections.
3. They anticipate the consumer demand.
4. They guide the consumers in buying.
5. They offer credit facility to customers.
6. Replacement provision is offered.
7. They create time and place utility.
8. They undertake guarantee over the goods.
9. They act as specialists in selling.
10. They help the producers in display and demonstration.

Services to Producer and Wholesaler

1. They assist in the efficient distribution of goods.
2. They act as a market researcher.
3. Information of likes and dislikes of the customers is passed on to producers and thus changes in production are adjusted.
4. Sales promotion is strengthened only with the help of retailers.

Essential Requirements of Retailers

1. They must know the market position and the up-to-date trend in the selection. The unsold or unsaleable products and its stocks will be failure to retailing.
2. They must stock those goods which can be sold to customers.
3. They must compete in price and quality of goods to be sold.
4. They must be financially sound to keep an average stock so as to avoid overstocking or understocking.
5. They must have good facilities to display the goods.
6. The shops must be in places where customers are attracted.
7. They must show courtesy, friendliness, honesty etc., towards the customers in their dealings.
8. The Staff must be polite, courteous and attentive to customers.

Failure of Retailers

1. Lack of knowledge and experience in the work.
2. Limited finance.
3. Competition with others.
4. Fraud in dealings.
5. Lack of business care.

6. Keeping incorrect credit accounts.
7. Dishonesty in retailing.
8. Improper and careless credit system offered.
9. Unattended complaints by buyers.
10. Personal extravagance.

The chief requirements of the retailers given by Mr. Nystrom, summed up as follows :

1. Accessibility to consumers;
2. A satisfactory trading place;
3. Suitable stocks of merchandise, offering an opportunity for consumer choice;
4. Service offered and rendered to customers;
5. Personal relation of store employees towards customers, including not only promptness of attention but also courtesy, interest, friendliness and honesty;
6. Reasonable price;
7. Sales promotion, including all methods and devices for giving the public information about the goods and services offered;
8. Window display and counter display (which are the most effective forms of advertising);
9. The demand of customers should be aroused by means of suitable advertising so that they may be persuaded to pay a visit to the shop;
10. Trained salesmen, who are the backbone of the success of the retail house;
11. Staff employed should be polite, courteous and attentive to customers;
12. Clearance sales, which are usually organised at the end of a season, attract customers in large numbers.

C. Manufacturer-Wholesaler-Retailer-Consumer

Wholesaler and retailers are the two types of intermediary in this channel. A manufacturer channels his products to consumers through these intermediaries. The gap between the manufacturer and the consumer is widened due to these intermediaries.

D. Manufacturer-Agent Middlemen-Wholesaler-Retailer-Consumer

Agent Middlemen, wholesalers, retailers are the three types of intermediaries in this channel. The gap between the manufacturer and the consumer is very great. In this channel the manufacturer uses the services of the agent middleman (sales agent) for the dispersal of goods. The agent distributes the goods to the wholesaler who sells the goods to retailer and who in turn sells to the consumers.

The choice of distribution channel is affected by the following factors:

I. Market consideration.
II. Product consideration.
III. Company consideration.
IV. Middleman consideration.
V. Consumer consideration.

I. Market Consideration

(a) **The Nature of the Market** is one of the important factors in market consideration. Consideration is taken under this factor about the product which is meant for customer or the industrial buyer. Retailers will be employed if the product is for consumer market. Long channel of distribution will have to be employed if the product is meant for consumer market and industrial market.

(b) **The Number of Potential Customers :** There is the need for a number of middlemen service if the number of potential customers is large. If the number of potential customers is small, direct selling is suggestible.

(c) **Geographic Concentration of the Market :** Direct selling is effective if the customers are concentrated in a few places. If they are situated over the whole country, then a large number of middlemen will have to be employed. Companies' branches can sell their products in thickly populated area. In a thinly populated area, direct selling is costly and ineffective.

(d) **Order Size :** If the sales volume is large, direct selling is suitable. Industrial distributors sell industrial operating supplies.

(e) **Customer Buying Habit :** This affects the channel policies very much. When the buyers' habit and purchase pattern of consumers are frequent and small in size, we must adopt indirect channel. If consumers' purchase is impulsive, adopt indirect channel. If it is deliberate, adopt direct channel.

II. Product Consideration

(a) **Unit Sale Value of a Product :** When the unit value of a product is high, direct channel is effective. On the other hand, when the unit value is low, the direct channel is in-effective. If the product is of low value, larger and cheaper channels will be better. Short and costly channels may be used if the product is of high value; e.g., small equipments are sold through agents while industrial installation type products are sold directly.

(b) **Bulk and Weight :** To minimise the freight, heavy or bulky goods may be sent by train or truck.

(c) **Perishable Nature :** Perishable products such as milk, dairy products, bread, meat etc., are sent by shorter channel or direct channel, while long channel is used for non-perishable products. Delays causing product deterioration must be prevented by the channel chosen.

(d) **Technicality :** The technical nature of the product requires services. Hence sales and servicemen are needed to explain the use of the product to the customers. Pre-sale–and post-sale services can be provided. For products like computers, business machines etc., direct channel is more advantageous.

(e) **Nature of Product Line :** If the product line is narrow, longer channel must be adopted. If the product line is broader, shorter channel can be adopted.

(f) **Product Made to Order :** If the product is made for customers, the shortest channel may be used. Products can be distributed directly to the customers. If it is tailor-made, the customers select the products from samples, catalogues etc.

(g) **Seasonal :** Sales of the product are subject to seasonal variation, for example, woollen clothes etc. Hence to sell these seasonal products intermediaries are needed. Direct selling is ineffective.

(h) **Standardisation :** For standardised products and ISI marked products, indirect channel is more suitable.

(i) **Newness and Market Acceptance :** For new products with high degree of market acceptance, the indirect channel is necessary. Aggressive selling can be possible by these intermediaries.

(g) **Style Obsolescence :** Fashionable dresses must be sold considerably in a short time. This can be achieved by direct selling or to retailors who are specialists in selling fashionable goods.

(k) **Price Stability :** Direct channel is useful if the price of the company's product is stable.

III. Company Consideration

(a) **Financial Strength :** Financially sound companies are in a better position to select and design their distribution channel. As such, direct channel is adopted. On the other hand, financially weak companies have to select indirect channel, as they depend on the intermediaries.

(b) **Reputation :** It has been said that reputation travels faster than man. There are many companies, which have good reputation because of the product-preference by the customers. Many intermediaries are eager to have connection with such companies. There are queues for securing distributorship in standard firms like Tata, Bajaj scooters etc. In such a situation, it is better to adopt indirect channel.

(c) **Market Control :** When a firm wants to exercise control over the price, the way in which customers are served etc., direct channel is suggested.

IV. Middleman Consideration

The middleman, who is able to offer a good facility of storage may be considered. The channel which facilitates maximum sales must be preferred. The cost of each attractive channel may be estimated on the basis of unit sale. The best type of channel which gives a low unit cost of marketing may be considered.

V. Consumer Consideration

The characteristics of buyers as to their number, location, frequency of the purchase, quantities bought by them etc., influence the channel selection. If the customers are scattered geographically, a long channel can be adopted. Consumers may wish to have the product at a convenient place; for example daily consumption items like milk, paper, bread etc., consumers may like to have them at the door. The channel adopted must facilitate the commodities produced to be available to the consumers in time.

Intensity of Distribution (market coverage)

The producers decide the general channel of distribution, which is based on the number of middlemen to be engaged at each level. The nature of products, buying habits of buyers, competition etc., are considered; the number of intermediaries and the situations are not static. Three policy options are available:

1. **Intensive Distribution** (Mass distribution) : Manufacturers of convenience goods and common raw materials need intensive distribution; *i.e.*, the services of many types of middlemen. Thus, intensive distribution facilitates maximum sales for a product. These goods have place utility. For example, cigarettes, soft drinks, newspapers etc., have many consumers and a firm offers its products to as many markets as possible. Purchase unit and price per unit are very small. There are frequent purchases. Manufacturers take promotional activities and create brand loyalty in the minds of customers. Asian Paints have 6,000 dealers, apart from sales officers and Hindustan Lever has 3,00,000 dealers, apart from 4,000 redistribution stockists. Thus, they aim to reach every potential buyer.

2 **Exclusive Distribution** (Franchised distribution) : Exclusive distribution is preferred when the amount of product service expected by the final buyers is considerable. It is the opposite of intensive distribution. Only a limited number of dealers is granted the exclusive right to distribute the company's products in their respective cities. In the distribution of new automobiles, air condition equipments, expensive glassware, farm machinery etc., we can find the exclusive distribution. The manufacturer hopes aggressive selling through the exclusive distribution; he hopes that it will give more control over the price of intermediary policies, promotion credit and other services. It increases the product image and allows higher mark ups. Exclusive distribution creates a sole agency or sale distributorship in a given market area. Such an arrangement is arrived at with an agent middleman. It is known as sole selling or selling agency.

3. **Selection Distribution** (Limited distribution) : Selective distribution stands in between intensive and exclusive distribution. It is adopted by old companies and new companies.

Only the better middlemen chosen carefully are engaged here. The number of outlets at each level of distribution is limited in a given geographic area. The producer selects a few wholesalers and retailers, who are the best marketers. Nationally known branded products are marketed by adopting selective distribution. The system enables the manufacturer to concentrate his attention on a few intermediaries, who cover the entire market. The cost of selective distribution is usually lower than the cost of intensive distribution.

Channel Conflict

Channel conflict exists when one channel member perceives another channel member to be acting in a way that prevents the first member from achieving its distribution objectives. That is, when two or more organizations in a channel of distribution cannot reach an agreement on some issue, policy or operating practice etc. channel conflict is said to occur and hamper the functioning of the channel.

According to Stern and Heskett, "Channel conflict is a situation in which one channel member perceives another channel member (s) to be engaged in behaviour that presents or impedes it from achieving its goals. The amount of conflict is, to a large extent, a function of goal incompatibility, domain descensus, and differing perceptions of reality."

Types of Conflict

In any distribution channel arrangement, there can be three types of conflicts, viz:

1. Vertical channel conflict
2. Horizontal channel conflict
3. Multichannel conflict.

1. **Vertical Channel Conflict:** It occurs when conflict between members at different levels within the same distribution channel, for example, conflict between the producer and distributors, or between wholesalers and the retailers. This is between parties one level up or one-level below each other.
2. **Horizontal Channel Conflict:** Conflict at the same level between channel members is called horizontal level conflict. For examples, inter stockist conflict at the retail level among retailers on issues, like pricing, territory jumping etc.
3. **Multichannel Conflict:** This type of conflict exists when the producer has established two or more different channels to sell the product to the same target market. For example, a computer company may have its own retail showroom, authorized dealers, and also sells online. The conflict may arise if the company store or online prices are lower than what dealers charge for the same products.

Causes of Conflict

The channel conflict occurs largely because of financial and non-financial reasons. The best that can be done in certain cases is to minimize the seriousness of the conflict. Major causes of conflict include (*a*) Goal incompatibility, (*b*) Role ambiguity and (c) Differing perceptions.

(a) **Goal Incompatibility**

One major cause is goal incompatibility. That is, a major cause of conflict between manufacturer and wholesalers is the perceived goal incompatibility between them. For example while the manufacturer perceived his goals to keep the price low and go for rapid market penetration to capture a larger market share and earn profits in the long-run wholesalers perceive their goal to have more margin and profitability in the short-term. Such situations often create strained relations and both sides start accusing each other

(*b*) **Role Ambiguity:**

It refers to situations when the company sells its products to same customers directly, and the channel members also sell products to the same groups of customers. This may occur when a producer uses multichannel arrangement. For instance, if both the company sales force and dealers sales people sell products to institutions, an unnecessary conflict may arise because there is no clarity regarding such situations.

(*c*) **Differing perception:**

Different perceptions of the market and economic outlook may sometimes cause conflict between the producer and the dealers. The company may be optimistic about the economy and income growth in Indian middle class and want dealers to carry higher than usual inventories. Companies may also appoint more dealers and may come out with line extensions. The dealers, on the other hand, may be pessimistic and refuse to comply what company wants and may oppose appointing more dealers. All this may give rise to a conflict.

Managing The Channel Conflict

Though channel conflicts are a common occurrence, members of a distribution channel must work in tandem to avoid or resolve such conflicts in order to maximize profits for the entire channel chain. The following steps may be followed:

(*a*) **Communication**

One of the effective way to minimize channel conflict is to have regular communication between the manufacturers and the channel members. Regular personal contacts, formal meeting once/twice a year, acquaint them with future plan etc. can minimize the chances of conflicts.

(*b*) **Dealer Councils**

The chances of conflict can be minimized through formation of dealer councils. Such councils can resolve issues in horizontal level conflict and even vertical conflict. Councils are formed on regional or state basis and company remains focused on the laid down agenda, listens and accepts constructive suggestions. These councils can be effective means of managing conflicts.

(*c*) **Co-option**

This approach refers to include channel association leaders in the company's council or board of directors etc. to win the channel support. This can be quite an effective method to minimize conflicts if the channel concerns and opinion are listened to.

(*d*) **Arbitration and Mediation**

When conflict is chronic or acute, the parties may have to resort to diplomacy, mediation or arbitration, Diplomacy takes place when each side sends a person or group to meet with its counterpart to resolve the conflict. Mediation means resorting to a neutral third party who is skilled in conciliating the two parties' interests. Arbitration occurs when the two parties agree to present their arguments to one or more arbitrators and accept the arbitration decision.

Physical Distribution (Logistic Management)

Physical distribution is concerned with planning and control of distribution activities and it refers to the physical handling or products. It involves not only moving the product to fill customer order but also to meet customer needs.

According to Philip Kotler, "Physical distribution involves planning, implementing and controlling the physical flows of materials and final goods from point of origin to point of use to meet customer requirements at a profit."

In simple meaning, the process of physical distribution involves handling and movement of products from the point of production to the point of consumption or use.

According to Stern and Coughlan, "The term logistics management and supply chain management are widely used to describe the flow of goods and services and related information from the point of origin to the point of consumption."

Physical distribution and marketing logistics are the two sides of the same coin. The functions of logistics involves the following activities:

(*a*) Order processing

(*b*) Inventory management

(*c*) Material handling

(*d*) Warehousing

(*e*) Transportation

A brief explanation of each of the above is as follows:

(*a*) Order Processing:

Physical distribution begins when a customer places an order. That is, the starting point of a order processing system is the placement of an order by a customer. The order is recorded in sales journal book. The management must monitor two flows – the flow of goods and the flow of information. Efficient order processing contributes to customer satisfaction, reduces costs and time-cycle, and increase profits. After assembling the goods, as per specifications, the warehouse arranges delivery through an appropriate carrier. The customer is sent an invoice, inventory records are updated and the order is delivered.

(*b*) Inventory Management

A company's inventories are in the form of raw materials and finished products to fill customer's orders. The efficiency of logistics management depends on how it manages inventory because the company's investment is lying in the form of materials and products. Over-stocking of inventory will lead to increasing inventory carrying cost: and at the same time, running out of stock will result in loss of customers. So, it must maintain a balanced inventory which would be ready to meet a customer order immediately. The main objective of inventory management must be to maintain a balanced stock which would keep the inventory carrying costs at a minimum. The following are the connected topics:

(*i*) Ordering cost

(*ii*) Inventory carrying cost

(*iii*) E.O.Q.

(*i*) Ordering cost

The ordering cost is the cost of planning an order. That is, ordering cost is the total ordering expenses for the ordering or purchasing department. The ordering cost includes the following:

(i) The salaries and wages of the staff in the department.

(ii) Cost of stationery, postage etc.

(*iii*) Rent for the department.

(*iv*) Depreciation for furnitures.

(*v*) Cost of inspection, etc.

(*ii*) **Inventory Carrying Cost**

It is the cost of holding the materials in the store and includes:

- Cost of storage space
- Insurance
- Stationary etc., used by the store
- Loss of interest on investment
- Loss due to pilferage and deterioration
- Salaries of the staff etc.

(*iii*) **E.O.Q.**

Economic order quantity or reordering quantity or EOQ is not a stock level. It is a quantity to be ordered when the stock reaches the minimum level. Reorder quantity is such that when it is added to the minimum stock, it should not exceed the maximum stock level. It is the quantity of inventory which can be reasonably ordered at a time and purchased economically. It is also known as standard order quantity, optimum quantity or economic lot size. It means that the total cost is at minimum. The problem is, how much to buy at a time. In case, large quantities are to be purchased the cost of carrying the inventory is high. This includes interest on investment, losses, obsolescence, space costs etc. On the other hand, for frequent purchases, in small quantities, the cost is high because of ordering expenses. Therefore, the quantity to be ordered depends upon two factors – the acquisition cost and the cost of possessing materials. When order for material is placed, it must facilitate more trade discount, economy in transport etc. and at the same time it should not incur heavy charges on account of storage, insurance etc.

Formula (EOQ) = $\sqrt{\dfrac{2AB}{CS}}$

EOQ = Economic Order Quantity

A = Annual Consumption

B = Buying cost per order

C = Cost per unit

S = Storage and carrying cost

Illustration :

Calculate EOQ from the following:

Annual usage : 600 units

Cost of placing an order : Rs. 12

Price of material per unit : Rs 20

Cost of storage : 20% (*B. Com, MS, Madurai*)

Solution:

$$EOQ = \sqrt{\frac{2AB}{CS}}$$

A = Annual consumption = 600 units

B = Buying cost per order = Rs. 12.

C = Cost per unit = Rs. 20

S = Inventory carrying cost = 20%

$$\sqrt{\frac{2 \times 600 \times 12}{20 \times 20\%}} = \sqrt{\frac{2 \times 600 \times 12}{4}} = 60 \text{ units}$$

$$\text{(or)} \sqrt{\frac{2 \times 600 \times 12}{20 \times \frac{20}{100}}} = 60 \text{ units}$$

$$\text{(or)} \sqrt{\frac{2 \times 600 \times 12 \times 100}{20 \times 20}} = 60 \text{ units}$$

(*c*) Material Handling

Technique and procedures used for material handling can increase warehouse capacity, reduce the number of times a product is handled, improve customer service and their satisfaction. Various activities such as packaging, loading, movement, labelling systems must be coordinated to reduce costs and increase customer value and satisfaction. Correct internal packaging of materials is important to prevent any damage during handling and transporation. Companies use different methods of loading such as unit loading or containerization. Unit loading is grouping one or more boxes on a pallet and use forklifts, trucks or conveyer system. Container helps consolidate many items within the large inside space of one huge box, which is scaled at its originating point and opened after arriving at its destination.

(*d*) Warehousing

Warehousing provides a key link in the physical distribution chain and today's marketing managers closely scrutinize them. The location, size and capabilities of warehouses can profoundly affect a company's ability to satisfy its customers and deliver products. The purpose of a good warehouse is storage, bulk breaking, consolidation and utilization. There are various factors affecting the warehouse selection decision. This decision is influenced by the difficulty of moving goods directly from the assembly line to buyers or public warehouses. Factors like type of the product, cost of transportation, rent to be paid for warehouse, nature of market, labour supply condition, prevalent tax structure, geographical location and degree of competition have to be kept in mind while deciding on the location of a warehouse.

(*e*) Transportation

Transportation plays a key role in logistics management. The logistical system must be designed in such a way as to minimize the transportation cost. In our country, it has been roughly estimated that transport cost alone takes about 30% - 40% of product's price. In certain cases, the cost comes to 50% of product price. We may have to look two things – (a) Transportation cost must be at the minimum and (b) Speedy delivery to the customer. Look at the chart given on the next page:

RELATIVE RANKING OF VARIOUS TRANSPORT MODES

	Rank	*Cost*	*Speed*	*Damage in Transit*	*Dependability Points*	*Reliable Delivery*	*Points Served*
High	1.	Air	Air	Road	Pipe Line	Pipe Line	Road
	2.	Road	Rail	Rail	Road	Water	Rail
	3.	Rail	Road	Air	Rail	Road	Air
	4.	Pipe Line	Pipe Line	Water	Water	Air	Water
Low	5.	Water	Water	Pipe Line	Air	Rail	Pipe Line

SUITABILITY OF MODES OF TRANSPORT FOR DIFFERENT ITEMS

Mode of transport	**Items suitable**
1. Airways	Perishable items like flowers, eggs, vegetables, fruits, fish, costly instruments etc.
2. Vehicle (Road)	All consumer goods, books, clothes, fruits, paper goods, industrial goods etc.
3. Pipe Lines	Petroleum, gasoline, gas, lubricants, crude oil, etc.
4. Waterways	Fuel oil, petroleum, sand, stones, heavy goods, food-grains etc.
5. Railways	Iron and steel, timber, minerals, automobiles, canned food, agricultural crops etc.

Just-in-Time Technic (JIT)

The Japanese developed a time-based logistics management system known as just-in-time technique. It is based on the process of systematically controlling the supplies as well as production system of the organization. The concept of just-in time implies that raw materials are delivered in required quantities to the production plant as and when they are needed without any delay. Just-in-time process focuses on the reduction of elimination of inventory in the plant. Under this method it is assumed that whatever inventory is not used immediately is a waste. This concept also focuses on advanced production techniques like zero level inventory maintenance, manufacturing smaller batch lot sizes, rapid switch over, controlling the production with the help of preventive maintenance etc.

Benefits in JIT Technique

1. Increased inventory turnover
2. Eliminate waste
3. Increased quality
4. Inventory reduction
5. Increased manpower utilization
6. Increased equipment utilization
7. Stable production rate.

QUESTIONS

1. What do you understand by Channels of Distribution ? Explain the factors determining the choice of a suitable channel of distribution.
2. "One of the major assets of a firm is its Channel of Distribution." Discuss.

3. Define a channel of distribution. Discuss the factors governing the choice of a particular channel. *(B.Com., Madurai)*
4. Discuss various factors you would like to consider for selecting the channels of distribution for a consumer product which is sold all over India. *(MBA, Allahabad)*
5. Suggest the criteria for selection of applicants for the distributorship of colour TV. In what ways will the criteria be different for the distributorship for medicines. *(M.Com., Delhi)*
6. What channels are used for the marketing of agricultural consumer goods ? What are the methods of selling directly to consumers? *(B.Com., Karnataka)*
7. Write short note on distribution intensity.
8. Compare in details the advantages and disadvantages of direct and indirect distribution. *(B.Com., Bombay)*
9. Which channel of distribution would you consider most appropriate for a low priced mass consumer product such as soap to be sold all over India. Give reasons for your selection. *(B.Com., Punjab)*
10. Discuss various approaches to the selection of channels of distribution which may be taken by manufacturing concerns. *(B.Com., Allahabad)*

CHAPTER 34

Channels of Distribution – II

- *Middlemen in Distribution*
- *Agent Middlemen*
- *Functions*
- *Kinds*
- *Merchant Middlemen*
- *Functions*
- *Wholesalers*
- *Basic Characteristics*
- *Services to Manufacturers*
- *Services to Retailers*
- *Retailers*
- *Importance*
- *Functions*
- *Services*
- *Essential Requisites of Retailers*
- *Types*
- *Itinerant*
- *Fixed Shop*
- *Small Scale*
- *Large Scale*
- *Wheel of Retailing*
- *Elimination of Middlemen*
- *Arguments in Favour of and Against*
- *Questions*

Middlemen or business intermediaries act as the connecting link between the manufacturers and consumers. They are very important in marketing the products. Through them products flow into the market. The gap between the producers and the consumers is reduced by the middlemen. They specialise in carrying out the transfer of title between the producers and buyers.

In the channel of distribution, there is the producer and consumers; and in between them there are some middlemen–wholesalers and retailers. In our marketing point of view the middlemen and intermediaries are the same. The advertising agencies, warehouses, insurance companies, banks etc., facilitating functions in marketing, cannot be called middlemen. Middlemen perform the marketing functions more economically than the producers and more effectively at a given cost. Their specialisation and experience, offer to the producers, more than what producers can achieve on their own.

Definition

According to American Marketing Association, ''Middleman is one who specialises in performing operations on rendering services that are directly involved in the purchase and sale of goods in the process of their flow from producer to final buyer.''

Middleman is an intermediary between the producer and consumer or a seller and a buyer in a market.

Cundiff and Still say, ''All middlemen fall into two broad classifications–merchants and agents. A merchant middleman takes title to (buys) and resells merchandise. An agent middleman negotiates purchase or sales or both, but does not take title to the goods in which he deals.'' The merchant buys and sells. The agent specialises in negotiating on buying or selling transactions.

Classification of Middlemen

There are two types of middlemen in distribution : (1) Functional middlemen (Mercantile agent or Agent Middlemen) and (2) Merchant middlemen.

AGENT MIDDLEMEN

They are mostly engaged in wholesale dealing. They assist in negotiating sales or purchase or both on behalf of the seller or buyer. They do not take title to goods which they handle. The important types of agent middlemen are brokers, commission agents, manufacturer's agents, selling agents, resident buyers, auctioneers, and warehousers.

Characteristics of Agent Middlemen

1. They serve mainly the industrial users.
2. They get a certain percentage of commission on the volume of purchases or sales negotiated by them.
3. They act as a substitute for a manufacturer's sales force. Hence the manufacturer can sell products beyond the limit of the salesman.
4. They take more interest to work for the buyers.

Importance of Middlemen

Middlemen are very important in the modern ever-widening market, by making the distribution easy and smooth. Organised markets for many commodities are created by them. They create time, place, and possession utility. Middlemen concentrate their effort on marketing and distribution of goods. Hence manufacturers can concentrate their attention on production. The most efficient process of distribution can be performed by middlemen. In a wider market, the chain of distribution becomes longer. Hence the marketing machinery will be more elaborate.

Functions of Middlemen

Middlemen's functions are known as marketing functions. The marketing functions are : (1) the functions of exchange, (2) the functions of physical supply and the facilitating functions.

The functions of middlemen are :

1. The middlemen are the connecting link between the sellers and buyers. They help the sellers and buyers to enter into a contract of sale or purchase. This is the contractual function of the middlemen.
2. They direct the flow of goods from the manufacturer to the ultimate consumers.
3. Merchant middlemen perform the function of merchandising by making the goods fit for the market requirements.
4. They know the market condition, and hence they guide in pricing the products which is satisfactory to both the producers and consumers. The price will be profitable to both the parties.
5. Middleman is responsible for the flow of goods; *i.e.*, physical distribution of goods.
6. Middlemen look after advertisement and publicity.
7. Buyers' needs are fulfilled by middlemen.
8. They give advice to manufacturers on a small commission.
9. Large-scale production is possible with the help of middlemen. They collect huge orders; and large purchases of products lead to large-scale production.
10. Middlemen stabilise prices.

Wroe Alderson is of the opinion that the goal of marketing is the matching of segments of supply and demand.

Contractual	–	Finding out buyers and sellers.
Merchandising	–	Producing goods that will satisfy market needs.
Pricing	–	Process of attaching value to the product in monetary terms.
Propaganda	–	Sales promotion activities.
Physical distribution	–	Distribution activities.
Termination	–	Settlement of contract, *i.e.*, paying the value and receiving the goods.

Kinds of Agent Middlemen

1. **Broker :** A broker is an agent. He represents the buyer or the seller in negotiating purchases or sales without having physical control over the goods involved. His main service is to bring the buyer and seller together. He is the agent of the owner of goods, seeking a buyer other than the agent of a buyer who is seeking for supply.

He is acting as an intermediary. He has limited powers over price and terms of sales. He has no authority to bargain on behalf of its principal. The broker has no physical control over the goods. He sells the goods by description or samples. When the broker arranges the sales, the seller sells the goods directly to the buyer and the broker receives the commission from the principal. Thus the broker relays the buyer's demand to the seller and the seller's offer to the buyer. When the exchange takes place, he receives the commission.

Brokers are utilised by producers who sell their products at frequent intervals. It is cheap for producers to appoint sales force. Large manufacturers also appoint brokers. They act as the key middlemen in the distribution of the product. The broker's job is over when the transaction is over. They can be engaged when the producers need their services. Brokers are instrumental in opening new markets.

2. **Commission Agent :** Commission agent is an agent–individual, firms, or even companies. It negotiates the sales of goods belonging to the principal. It customarily exercises physical control over the sale of goods. It has the power on prices, and terms of sale under the condition that it must obey the instructions of the principals. Commission agent may arrange for delivery; he may extend necessary credit; he may grade and standardise the products etc. They collect credits. After deducting their fees, they remit the balance amount to the principal. Service merchants, wholesalers and the commission agents do the same activities except that they do not take title to.

The commission agent's services are mainly used for rapid sale of perishable commodities like, fruits, vegetables etc. It is very important in agricultural marketing.

3. **Manufacturer's Agent :** Manufacturer's agents are employed by the manufacturers to sell their products. The features of the manufacturers' agents are :

1. They have an extended contractual relationship with their principal.
2. They handle sales for each of their principals within an exclusive territory.
3. They represent manufacturers of non-competing, but related lines of goods.
4. They possess limited authority with regard to prices and terms of sales.

The agent receives a percentage of commission based on his sales. He uses his technique. He employs his sales representatives, who work for him. He has a large sales staff. Selling is his main function.

Manufacturers use such agents when :

1. They find the sales force to be uneconomical.
2. The firm is financially weak.
3. Experienced and knowledgeable representation is needed.
4. New product is introduced.
5. New market areas are to be opened.
6. The products are to be sold in the foreign markets.

Manufacturer's agents are important in the marketing of industrial goods. Furniture manufacturers also use them to sell their output. They offer advice to the manufacturers of industrial and consumer goods on matters of style, design, and pricing, because they are in close touch with the market.

4. **Selling Agents :** Selling agent is an independent middleman. He operates on a contractual basis. He negotiates all sales of a specified line of merchandise or the entire output of its principal.

He has authority over the price, terms and other conditions of sales. He is the sole selling agent for the line, he represents. He extends financial help to his principals or manufacturers.

Selling agents are in close contact with the buyers, and hence they guide the manufacturers on styling, design and pricing matters. They assist the manufacturers in sales promotion and advertising. Their services are used in the marketing of textiles, food products, coal, timber, metal products etc.

5. **Resident Buyers :** Resident buyer is an independent agent, and he specialises in buying for retailers. He receives compensation or a fee on commission basis. He operates in lines of trade, such as furniture, garments etc. He has his office in the market place. He helps the retailers to buy the product. The resident buyers are purely and simply an independent agent specialised in buying for principals who are retailers.

6. **Auctioneers :** They are generally appointed by business firms. The auctioneer receives the goods and invites bids for the goods. The highest bidder gets the goods and the auctioneer collects the amount from him. The auction may be ''**with reserve**'' or ''**without reserve**''. Under ''with reserve,'' the goods cannot be sold below the price fixed by the seller. Agricultural and livestock producers, used-car dealers, wool, cotton and tobacco merchants employ these auction companies. They sell goods to the highest bidder. They collect commission from the sellers for their services.

Other Agents

Packing and Forwarding Agents : Manufacturers find it difficult to collect, deliver and forward goods to the proper places. Hence they make use of the packing and forwarding agents. They are employed to collect, deliver and forward the goods to proper destination. Their remuneration is also less. They are expert and prompt in their dealings.

Warehousers : As their name suggests they receive goods from or on behalf of the principals for storing purpose. They receive remuneration for the storage. They will take care of the goods which are preserved by them.

Export and Import Agents : In leading port cities these agents operate. They arrange for the financing of purchases. They serve the principals in their needs of seeking foreign markets or overseas supply.

Purchasing Agents : They are independent middlemen. They specialise in locating the sources of supply for buyers of industrial goods.

Factors : Factors are persons. They are appointed to sell goods.

MERCHANT MIDDLEMEN

Contrary to agent middlemen, merchant middlemen buy and sell goods on their own account and risk. They take the title to goods. They resell the goods at a profit. They are divided into two categories–Wholesalers and Retailers.

Functions of Merchant Middlemen

1. They are the connecting link between producers and consumers and goods are supplied where they are in demand–distribution of goods.
2. They match the demand with production.
3. They perform the important function of advertisement, display etc.
4. They know the purchasing powers of customers and by informing the producers, fix reasonable price.
5. They offer too many communications between producers and customers.
6. They, in times of need, help the producers financially.
7. Their knowledge and experience can well profitably be used by producers and customers.
8. They are demand creators.

WHOLESALER

Wholesale dealing includes all activities involved in selling goods or services to those who buy for resale or business use. A wholesaler is a businessman who specialises in performing wholesale activities. The word 'Wholesaler' means to market goods in relatively large quantities. The term wholesaler applies only to merchant middlemen engaged in wholesale activities *i.e.*, they take title to the goods they handle.

Wholesalers are very important in the channel of distribution. According to American Marketing Association, ''Wholesalers buy and resell merchandise to retailers and other merchants and to industrial institutions, and commercial users, but do not sell in significant amounts to ultimate consumers.''

According to Cundiff and Still, ''Wholesalers buy and sell merchandise to the retailers and other merchants and not to the consumers.''

According to C.B. Giles, ''Wholesalers may be said to provide the economic utilities of time, place and possession which may lead to economy in distribution of adequate stock to be available at the right time in a convenient location.''

Stanton says, ''wholesaling and wholesaler includes the sale, and all activities directly incident to the sale of products or services to those who buy for the purpose of resale for business use.''

Basic Characteristics of the Wholesaler

1. Wholesaler occupies a very important position in the channel of distribution.
2. He provides information and advisory service to manufacturers and retailers.
3. He assembles the goods from many sources for the retailers to buy.
4. Normally the wholesalers sell large quantities.
5. He buys goods from the manufacturers and resells them to the retailers.
6. The wholesaler does not sell to the ultimate consumer.
7. Wholesaler is a merchant middleman. He is engaged in the wholesaling activities. He takes the title of the goods he handles.
8. He specialises in the product line.

Classification of Wholesalers

There are many classifications of wholesalers. Cundiff and Still classify wholesalers into merchant wholesalers, who are then first classified according to the range of merchandise they handle. They are :

1. General merchandise wholesalers
2. General line wholesalers
3. Speciality wholesalers

Second classification is according to the method of operation. They are :

1. Service wholesalers
2. Limited function wholesalers

For the convenience of studies, the wholesalers may be classified :

I. On the basis of area served.
II. On the basis of commodities they deal.
III. On the basis of method of operation.
IV. On the basis of the breadth of their line product.

I. On the Basis of Area Covered

(a) **Local Wholesalers :** They purchase the products from the producers and deliver them to the local retailers.

(b) **Provincial or State Wholesalers :** They purchase the products and sell them to retailers in a particular district or state.

(c) **National Wholesalers :** They purchase the products from the manufacturers located in a place. They distribute the goods to the retailers all over the country.

II. **On the Basis of Commodities They Deal**

1. The way by which certain goods are distributed.
2. The sources of supply.
3. Utilisation of the commodity by those who purchase it from the wholesaler establishment; for example, Fruit products, Agricultural products etc.

III. **On the Basis of Method of Operation**

(a) **Full Service Wholesalers :** Full service wholesalers, or full function wholesalers are merchant wholesalers who provide many services to their customers. They provide services of carrying stock. They are having sales force. They offer credit. They make delivery of goods and they give management assistance to their customers. There are three types of this wholesaler:

1. **Wholesale Merchants :** They sell to retailers and provide a full range of service to them. They buy and sell goods in their own name.

2. **Converters :** They operate as manufacturers and wholesalers. Their primary motive is that of selling; for example, they purchase material, perform certain operations, which the market approves of and the processed products are sold in the market. Such type of converters are rare in India.

3. **Industrial Distributors :** Industrial distributors are merchant wholesalers who sell to manufacturers. They provide several services to the manufacturers. They carry stock, offer credit and deliver the goods to manufacturers.

(b) **Limited Function Wholesalers** or limited service wholesalers : They offer fewer services to their suppliers and customers. There are many types of limited service wholesalers :

1. **Cash and Carry Wholesaler :** They have limited line of fast moving goods. Retailers who want to purchase go to the wholesalers, pass orders for the products, and receive the products against cash. They provide no credit and no facility for transportation e.g., fish stores.

2. **Truck Wholesalers or Truck Jobbers :** They perform selling and delivery functions. They also do the function of collection. They carry a limited line of semi-perishable merchandise, such as milk, bread, snacks etc. They sell them for cash. They sell them in supermarkets, hospitals, hotels, restaurants etc.

3. **Dropshipment Wholesalers :** They do not physically handle goods they deal. Dropshipper leaves the responsibility of storage and transportation activities to the producers. When the goods are ordered, producers will send them directly to the retailer but bill them in the name of these wholesalers, and finally recover from retailers. Generally transportation cost will be higher than the manufacturers' cost; for example, coal, timber, heavy equipment, sand, clay etc.

4. **Rack Jobber :** The market has a specialised line of products, such as toiletries and housewares. They serve in the area of perishable items. They sell on consignment basis. Retailers are supplied goods, but rack jobber retains the title to goods till the retailers sell them off. The main thing is that rack space is provided in the retail store for rack jobbers.

5. **Producers' Co-operatives :** Farmers are the members. They assemble farm produce to sell in local markets. At the end of the year the profits are distributed among the members. They improve their produce quality and promote a co-operative brand name.

6. **Mail Order Wholesalers :** This type of wholesalers sell goods by mail.

IV. **On the Basis of the Breadth of Their line Product**

Merchant wholesalers on this basis can be divided into three types. They are :

(a) **General Merchandise Wholesalers :** They carry a general assortment of products in two or more distinct and unrelated merchandise line. They may stock and sell dry goods, handwares, furniture, farm implements, electric equipments, sports goods, house-hold appliances etc. The importance of general merchandise wholesalers is decreasing due to the disappearance of retail general stores.

(b) **General Line Wholesalers :** They carry a broad assortment of goods within a single merchandise line. They also handle limited stock of goods which perish easily including vegetable, cereals, tea and coffee. They also carry the stock of razor blades, soaps and detergents, school supplies etc. General line wholesalers are more important than the general merchandise wholesalers and specialist wholesalers. Their total volume of sales is also greater. They are important distributors of consumer and industrial goods.

(c) **Speciality Wholesalers :** They carry only a part of a merchandise line. They specialise in canned foods. Coffee, tea, spices, dairy products, roasted and frozen foods or soft drinks. They give a strong promotional support to the restricted manufacturers brand. They create special displays handling in store products, demonstration and arranging for distribution of samples.

Services Rendered by Wholesalers

Services to manufacturers : There are many services rendered by the wholesalers to the manufacturers. They are :

1. **Acting As An Intermediary :** Wholesalers act as an intermediary between the manufacturer and the retailer. He is more close to the manufacturers.

2. **Selling Assistance :** He is the selling assistant of the manufacturer. They know the market condition well, as they are more in touch with them. Advertising and sales promotion activities are mostly undertaken by wholesalers. They know the customers' needs and act accordingly. They get order from them and sell the manufacturers' products.

3. **Storage And Transportation :** Manufacturers' cost of delivery and storage is reduced by wholesalers. They store goods in their godown. They deliver goods from the place of product to the place of demand. As such manufacturers do not invest more capital in storage and transportation.

4. **Price Stability :** Wholesalers hold stocks when the price is very low at the time of overproduction and sell the stocks when the price is high. They help in the price fluctuation.

5. **Financial Assistance :** Wholesalers offer financial help to manufacturers. Producers do not give credit facilities to retailers. But wholesalers give credit facility which will enable more sales of manufacturers' products.

6. **Help in Foreign Market :** They export goods. They have close touch with the foreign buyers and sellers. They help the manufacturers to sell their products in the foreign market also.

7. **Provide Market Information :** They provide market information regarding market condition, consumers' demand etc., to the manufacturers at the appropriate time.

8. **Adviser :** He is the adviser of the manufacturer regarding product features, packaging and advertising.

9. **Large Purchase :** Wholesaler purchases a large quantity from the manufacturer. The manufacturer can save time to sell the product, and he can utilize his full attention on production.

10. **Risk Bearing :** Manufacturer's risk is reduced by wholesaler. The wholesaler takes the title of the goods. Losses due to change in fashion, spoilage etc., are borne by the wholesaler.

11. **Maintaining Sales Force :** They recruit and train a number of salesmen to push the products. This is important for the manufacturer.

12. **Time Utilities :** They create both time and place utility through their warehousing operations.

Services to Retailer

1. **Large Stock of Varied Goods :** Wholesalers have a large stock of varieties of goods. Hence retailers are free from holding big stock of goods. The wholesalers' warehouses serve as reservoir for retailers. They can buy things as and when they need. Hence retailers do not lock up their small capital in a big stock.

2. **Facilitates Small Scale Purchasing :** Retailers have only limited capital resources. Hence they cannot buy large quantities from the manufacturer. Wholesalers buy large quantities and resell them to retailers in small quantity. Thus they help the retailers and remove their inconvenience and inabilities of large-scale purchasing.

3. **Prompt and Quick Delivery of Goods :** If the retailers purchase goods from the manufacturer, then there will be delay in delivery. On the other hand if the wholesaler has the stock of goods, he can deliver the goods to the retailers promptly.

4. **Financial Assistance :** Wholesalers grant credits to their permanent retailers. After selling the product, retailer settles the account with the wholesaler. He will repay the money once in a month or quarterly or as agreed upon. This financial help increases the effect of the working capital of the retailer.

5. **Advice to the Retailer :** Wholesalers offer advice to retailers. They give valuable service to the retailers. The retailer is not aware of the market condition of varied products whereas the wholesaler is specialised in one line of product. As such he knows the market condition. He advises the retailer about stocking, displaying, point of sale, promotion which adds to the value of products etc. Benefit of specialisation is reached by the retailer through wholesaler. Wholesaler can advise the retailer when to buy, how much to buy and at what time.

6. **Announcement of New Product :** The wholesaler informs the arrival of new goods to the retailers. The manufacturer advertises the new product. The wholesaler helps the retailer in efficient window display of the new products in his job.

7. Wholesalers undertake the risks involved in marketing functions.

8. Wholesalers help the retailers in maintaining a constant price for the goods.

Other Services of the Wholesaler

1. **Increase the Standard of Living :** It is the wholesaler who introduces fashion and new changes in the market. It increases the standard of living of the people.

2. Selection of goods is possible as he has a number of varieties of goods. Retailers and consumers can select the required goods from there.

3. **Low Cost :** Specialisation leads to decrease in cost and so the retailers and consumers can buy the goods at a low cost.

RETAILER

The word 'Retailer' is derived from a French word *retailer* which means 'to cut again.' Retail trade cuts off smaller portions from large lumps of goods. Retailer sells varieties of goods in small quantities to the final consumer. Retailing is an activity directly related to the sale of goods or services to the ultimate consumer for personal use. A retailer or a retail store is a business enterprise, which sells primarily to household consumers for non-business use. Retailers sell goods directly to consumers. Retailers' business is normally local in character. They sell goods in small quantity. They satisfy the unlimited wants of the consumers. As such, they deal in a variety of goods. A retailer is the last middleman in the machinery of distribution. A retailer is in between the wholesaler and ultimate consumer. He aims to satisfy the buyers, with the goods they buy and act as a good buying agent for his customers. He is the merchandising arm of the manufacturers, or the neck in the bottle of distribution.

Retailing covers all the activities involved in the sales of products to final consumers for personal, family or chain store, departmental store, supermarket or a service retailer etc. who link the producers and the final consumers. A producer who sell directly to ultimate consumers are performing retailing activity.

The retail sector is the second largest employer in India after agriculture. That is, retailing is high intensity competition industry and second largest globally. The reason for its popularity lies in its ability to provide easier access to a variety of products, freedom of choice, many services etc, to consumers. The largest retail store in the world is Wall-Mart of USA and the second largest is Carrefour of France. The Indian market is dotted by traditional market places called "Bajaar" comprising of numerous small and large shops, selling different or similar merchandise.

Retailing is becoming a significant marketing activity in all modern societies. The retail sector is changing at an over-increased rate. And this is leading to growth of retail marketing management and it is often stated that the only constant in retailing is change and more than ever before, we are witnessing the emergence of new forms of retailing, in part in response to demand from increasingly sophisticated consumers. For example, now ready-to-wear garments market has seriously affected what used to be strictly a made-to-order market for clothing. Almost all other retail businesses are undergoing changes with the passage of time. The increasing size of retailers and intensity of growing competition in the market in which they are operating has led retailers to search for new ways in which to grow their business. During the late 1980s and 1990s, the retailers moved away from their core areas into new service sectors like insurance, financial services and diagnostic clinics.

Retailing is not only important to consumers but more important to marketing companies as it helps in bringing the company's product closer to consumers. It helps consumers in making purchasing decision and subsequent buying easier. Effective retailing is a boon to increase sales of products. In other words, if retailing is not effective, everyone in the channel gets affected and some products are not sold well due to ineffective retailing. For example, Bata Shoe Company sells more shoes in rural and semi-urban areas because of their wide and well-knit retailing arrangement. Similarly, Leo toys are more popular and sell more because its retailing is more effective than its competitors. So retailing is an important activity of marketing plan for consumer products at all levels and for all segments of the market. Retailers are directly involved with the final consumers at the point of purchase and so their strategy is very vital for their success. There is a loss of business if a retailer losses a customer.

Definition : According to American Marketing Association, "Retailing consists of the activities involved in selling directly to the ultimate consumer for personal, non-business use. It embraces the direct-to-consumer sales activities of the producer, whether through his own stores by house to house canvassing or by mail order business."

A. Larson, Card, Mandell etc. are of the view that "if we think of production and consumption as the two poles of the distribution process, wholesaling would be nearer to the production pole and retailing would be nearer to the consumption pole."

According to W. Cundiff and R. Still, "A retailer is a merchant or occasionally an agent, whose main business is selling directly to the ultimate consumers."

Importance of Retailers : It is one of the important functions of marketing process. Cundiff and Still are of the opinion that, "If the buyer in a transaction is the ultimate consumer, the seller in the same transaction is engaged in retailing." The retailer is an intermediary in the marketing channel of distribution. He is both a marketer and a customer. He is a specialist in selling goods to the ultimate consumer. Retailers create place, time and possession utilities. He supplies the needed goods from the place of production to the place where it is demanded. He sells the goods at a reasonable price at the time when the customers want the goods. It is difficult, time-consuming, expensive and inconvenient for the producer to sell his goods directly to the consumer. Hence he takes risks through ownership. The retailers are having close contact with the producers and the ultimate consumer. The retailer has a twin role to play. He must satisfy the buyers with the goods they buy and earn the name as buying agent for his customers. He must please the producer for whom he handles the goods for sale. Retailers are subjected to ''selling in'' and ''selling out''. ''Selling in'' is concerned with the buying and stocking of the products. ''Selling out'' refers to the activities like consumer advertising, point of sale, display which are important to move the product from the retailer to the ultimate consumer.

Functions of Retailers

1. Provide personal services to all.
2. Provide two-way information.
3. Facilitate standardisation and grading.
4. Undertake physical movement and storage of goods.
5. Assemble goods from various sources.
6. Stock goods for ready supply to buyers.
7. Extend credit facility.
8. Create demand by window display etc.
9. Undertake sales promotion activities.
10. Assume risk.

"The Retailers perform various functions like providing assortments, sorting, breaking the bulk, rendering services, bearing risk, channel or communication, transport and advertising and holding inventory." They significantly contribute towards increasing the product value and satisfying the consumers.

Services of the Retailer

There is distinction between the producer and consumers in terms of distance, time and knowledge. This is the reason for the rising of the retailers' need. Retailers are helping in the physical flow of goods; storing them and providing a two-way communication between the producers and consumers. The following are the services of retailers.

1. **Assemble Goods :** The primary job of a retailer is to assemble different varieties of goods from various wholesalers. He assembles at convenient points a wide assortment of goods from various sources.

2. **Create Place Utility :** A retailer helps in the physical flow of the goods from the producer to the consumer. He aims at giving maximum local convenience to consumers. He transports goods from the point of production to the point of consumption. As such, the retailer satisfies the daily wants of the people by creating place utility. He undertakes door delivery and allows liberal exchange of facilities.

3. **Keep Varieties of Goods :** He provides the availability of many varieties of goods from many manufacturers. Retailers provide varieties of choice enabling the consumers to select the commodities easily.

4. **Provide Storage Facility :** The retailers store the required commodities for the consumer. Hence consumers need not purchase the commodity in a lot. The consumers can buy any article in any quantities at any time *i.e.* time utility.

5. **Create Demand :** A retailer attracts consumers' attention to new goods and their arrival by personal salesmanship. He brings new products and new varieties to the knowledge of consumers. He creates window display and demonstrative demand for new goods.

6. **Render Service to the Customers :** The retailer gives advice and guidance to the consumers regarding the purchase of goods. It is essential for him to establish permanent and continuous relationship with consumers. The customers are advised on the merit and suitability of the products. They help the consumers in the selection of goods. They improve the mode of living of the consumers.

7. **Provide Information :** They provide information about the nature, use, market trend of the product to the wholesalers and manufacturers. They have close contact with the consumers.

8. **Connecting Link :** The retailer is the connecting link between the wholesaler and the ultimate consumer. The wholesaler finds it difficult to sell the goods directly to the consumers. It is the retailer who helps both. He acts as an interpreter to the wholesaler and manufacturer regarding consumers' requirements and reactions.

9. **Extend Credit Facilities :** Customers' purchasing power is increased by extending credit facilities by retailers. Retailers' volume of sales is increased by credit facilities. Revolving credit plans, credit on open account etc., increase the purchasing powers of buyers.

10. **Marketing Function :** Marketing functions like sales and promotion, advertising, point of purchase display etc., are performed by retailers to create an interest to buy the products.

11. **Meet Day to Day Demand :** Daily demands of consumers for foodstuffs, vegetables, fruits, milk etc., are met by retailers at the right time.

Essential Requisites of Retailers

The success of the retailer depends upon various personal qualifications and qualities which are important for a businessman:

1. **Selection of Adequate Stock of Saleable Goods :** The selection of goods must be up-to-date and the stock must be adequate. The retailers are in close touch with the consumers. As such they will know the need of the consumers. Hence they must select the up-to-date goods which are preferred by the consumers. They must stock the goods in adequate quantities. Overstock or dead-stock will lead to dead capital which will ruin the business. He must know the financial position and must keep reasonable stock.

2. **Location :** Location of the shop must attract customers. The best location assures continuous prosperity; localisation will facilitate the selection of goods.

3. **Effective Buying :** The success of business depends on the effective buying in the right market at the right time and at the right price. A retailer is a buying agent on behalf of his customers. Expert and intelligent buying decision gives more profit in retail trade. Over-buying should be avoided, if buying is made on credit.

4. **Knowledge of Merchandise :** A retailer must have the knowledge of the merchandise which is more up-to-date and satisfies the new demand. He must be very careful in appointing salesmen and selecting assistants who deal with the customers.

5. **Service :** The retailer must follow the policy of "The customer is always right." "Customer is the king or queen." He must give importance to service and not to profit. The retailer must give personal service to the customers; *i.e.*, prompt and courteous service, quality assurance, service after sale, free home delivery, grant of credit etc. Customers want such types of service from retailers. They prefer to buy goods from a retailer than from a shop.

6. **Competitive Fixed Price :** The competitive price must be lower than the other retailers' prices. The qualities of goods offered for sale by the retailer must be good and pleasing. Price must be fixed. There should be no bargaining. A quick turnover is possible only at a lower margin of profit.

7. **Counter Display and Window Display of Goods :** The goods must be properly arranged, and effectively displayed in the shop. The term counter display refers to displays of any type of

goods within the retailer's shop, whether they are on the counter or on the floor or on a special stand. Window display costs little; but it is very effective. It appeals to the shopping public and secures good business. The three cardinal principles of new window display are : (a) to exhibit reasonable articles (b) to show them in as simple a manner as possible (c) to show them so that the eye can determine every detail put at the window. Window display brings prospects into the shop; counter display reminds why the customers entered into the shop and induce them to buy.

8. **Trained Salesman and Efficient Management :** They are the backbone of the retailers organisation. Customers' satisfaction is more important. Retailers' best advertiser is the satisfied customer. As such a retailer must employ a well trained salesman. He must be polite, attentive and good-natured; he must treat the consumers in the best manner.

Efficient retail operation can be obtained by better planning, organisation and control; higher efficiency can also be obtained by proper selection, remuneration and motivation of sales forces.

TYPES OF RETAILERS

Itinerant Retailers

(a) Hawkers and pedlars
(b) Cheap jacks
(c) Market traders
(d) Street traders

Fixed Shop Retailers

(a) Street stallholders
(b) Second-hand Goods Dealers
(c) Speciality goods shops
(d) General shops

Small-Scale Retailers

(a) Independent Stores
(b) Automatic vending
(c) Discount houses
(d) Syndicate stores

Large-Scale Retailers

(a) Departmental Stores
(b) Multiple Shops
(c) Mail Order Shops
(d) Hire Purchase and Instalment
(e) Cooperative Stores
(f) Super Markets
(g) Hyper Markets etc.

Itinerant Retailers

These retailers move from place to place for selling goods to the consumers. They have no fixed business premises. They sell the goods in small lots. They work with a very small capital investment. They do not stick on to a particular line of business. They deal in varied range of products. Mostly they are dealers in agricultural products. Hawkers and pedlars, cheap jacks, market traders and street traders come under this type.

(a) **Hawkers and Pedlars :** Hawkers carry their goods from place to place in hand cart and sell them to the consumers at their doors. Pedlars carry the goods on their heads. The goods may be pens, towels, toys, household articles, vessels etc. The price is lower than the market price but the quality is poor. They sell the goods in the streets of busy cities and in places of exhibition etc. They have no fixed place of business. They move from place to place with limited stocks.

(b) **Cheap Jacks :** They have an independent shop in a business locality. They sell household articles, ready-made garments etc. The shop is not a permanent one. The quality of goods will be inferior. If it is not profitable in that place, they will shift the shop to another place. They are more than a well-trained man and take all possible measures to sell out goods. The difference between hawkers and cheap jacks is that hawkers move from place to place, as they have no fixed place of trading *i.e.*, shop. On the other hand cheap jacks have a fixed place of business. If the business is unprofitable, they change the locality.

(c) **Market Traders :** Market traders open their shops on market days *i.e.*, on different places on fixed days. Market days are fixed on weekly or monthly basis. They carry on their business in the locality when the market is open. They open their shops in different places on different days when the market is open.

(d) **Street Traders :** These retailers carry on their business in busy streets or on the footpath of busy cities and towns. They choose bus stops, railway stations, government and commercial offices and school area. They handle only highly demanded light goods. At a time they deal mainly in a particular type of goods.

Fixed Shop Retailers

1. **Small Shops**

(a) **Street Stall Holders :** In a street where there is a heavy traffic, the street stall holders have their stalls. They are very careful in selecting the location for the stall. Once it is located in a place, then more or less it is the permanent place for the stall. Wholesalers and local suppliers supply things to these retailers. They have the articles like pens, banians, socks, handkerchiefs, cosmetics etc. The stalls are decorated inside. The goods are properly arranged in order to attract the attention of the customers. It covers only a limited area. As such they handle goods on a very small scale of different types.

(b) **Second-hand Goods Dealers :** These dealers sell and buy second-hand goods or articles like books, furniture, radio, cloth etc. Customers who cannot buy new goods at higher prices, purchase them from these retailers. They get these second-hand goods at private and public auctions. Their representatives also buy these articles from door to door. The price will be fixed at a low rate about 50% less than the usual price. Responsibility for the durability or the quality of goods is not guaranteed by the dealers. Even then, there is a good demand for the second-hand goods from the low class people as well as middle class people.

(c) **Speciality Shops :** A particular variety of goods is sold in these shops. The dealers specialise in only one line of goods; e.g., shops exclusively meant for toys, sports goods, ready-made dresses, radios, plastic goods, leather goods, watches, books etc. Customers have a wider choice while making selection of goods.

(d) **General Shops :** These shops supply goods which are required for day to day use. From these general shops consumers can get all their requirements such as, presentation articles, toffees, biscuits, plastic goods, footwears, umbrellas, tooth paste, soap, oil, thread, pen etc. The owner is very keen about satisfactory dealing with the buyers and gives a personal touch with good salesmanship. These are established in the central place in a locality. As such, consumers who reside in that locality can purchase their requirements at any time. They have regular customers. They supply the goods for the whole month even on credit, and payment is made once in a month as fixed by them.

Small-scale Retailers

1. **Independent Stores :** These are small and independently owned shops. The independent stores are relatively easy to set up. It has greater flexibility of operation and freedom of action. The owner can take decisions with regard to buying, selling, pricing, working hours, sales promotion etc. A friendly atmosphere may prevail in the stores. They get supplies from wholesalers. Such type of traders offer liberal credit facility, delivery service, catering of the individual buyer's needs.

2. **Automatic Vending :** Automatic vending is a form of retailing without the aid of a salesman. A variety of products, mostly convenience goods, are disposed of by means of a machine, when the buyer inserts coins. These are coin-operated machines. They automatically sell or push out when a buyer inserts the required coin. The machine offers round the clock sales services. Such types of machines are popular in advanced countries. Items like cigarettes, milk, ice cream, bread, eggs, postage stamps, newspapers, coffee etc., can be sold by automatic vending system. This is

also known as robot retailing. The products sold are generally of low price, uniform in size and shape and weight. The installation cost is high and for operations no salesman is required. But it may have mechanical failures; sales can be effected only up to stock-capacity and varieties are limited. These are the disadvantages of this system.

3. **A Discount House :** It is a retailing business unit. It deals with large selection of general merchandise. It competes on a low price basis and offers minimum of customer service. They deal in well-known brands of jewellery, sports goods, household items, consumer durables etc. They usually sell the items at less than the advertised price. They generally deal in national brands. They buy their merchandise stocks from wholesalers or from manufacturers. They with their attractive discount on price, attract buyers.

4. **Syndicate Stores :** These types of stores, in most of the cases, purchase unbranded merchandise and sell them as own brand along with branded products.

Large Shops

The large-scale retailers are :

(a) **Departmental Store :** Departmental store is a large retailing unit. It handles a wide variety of shopping and speciality goods. There are a number of departments under such a store. Each department deals in a particular line of products. All departments are under one roof. Each specialises in an individual merchandise from pin to plane or pen to car. It is organised into separate departments for purposes of promotion, service and control.

Definition. According to Clark and Clark, ''A departmental store is that type of retail institution which handles a variety of merchandise under one roof, with the merchandise grouped into well-defined departments which are centrally controlled, and which caters primarily to women shoppers.''

According to Cundiff and Still, ''A departmental store is a large retailing unit, handling a wide variety of shopping and speciality goods including women's ready to wear and accessories, mens' and boys' ware, piece goods, small wares and home furnishings, and organised into separate departments for the purpose of promotion, service and control.''

According to G. B. Giles, ''A departmental store is a collection of shops under one roof and ownership, each shop or department specialising in selling a special range of goods.''

Characteristics

1. **A Wide Merchandise Line :** It tries to function as a universal provider. It supplies all the retail needs of the consumer, from a pin to a plane. It does not supply perishable items.

2. **Departmental Organisation :** There is departmental organisation; merchandise are classified into several classes. Each department is specialised in one or more related lines. Each department has a manager. He has the freedom to control the department as he thinks fit. All the departments have centralised control on advertising, salesmen promotion, accounting, credit, employment etc.

3. **Large Size :** Departmental store is large in size. It is centrally located. It attracts a large number of customers.

4. The store is a horizontally integrated institution. Cundiff is of the opinion that it brings together under one roof a range of merchandise offering comparable to the combined offerings of many stores specialising in single or fewer merchandise lines.

Location : The department store must attract many customers. The location and premises of the department stores are the two important factors to attract the customers. The success of the store depends upon these factors. The location of the store must be in a central place, so that there would be a flow of customers.

''The customer is always right,'' is followed as a principle. Stores may create a house-image to customers by offering the services of trained salesmen, recreation facilities, music programme, movies etc., restaurant bar, reading rooms, rest rooms, telephone booth, beauty clinic, lectures, demonstrations, fashion shows, information centre etc. They allow credit, accept orders on telephone, offer home delivery, exchange of goods, refund to the unsatisfied buyers etc.

Organisation : Departmental stores are organised as a limited company or joint-stock company. It has a board of directors to frame general policies and to delegate powers to subordinates. The managing director or general manager is the executive head of the whole concern. Departmental managers or section managers, are subordinates to the general manager; they are responsible for their respective sections and their progress. Each department is independent, but is centrally controlled in the activities relating to advertising, sales promotion, accounting, employment etc.

Advantages

1. **Centralised Location :** The central locality of the departmental stores attracts a large number of people. It is located at the heart of the cities, where large numbers of people move about. People are attracted by the reputation that these stores will offer quality goods.

2. **Shopping Convenience :** There is the availability of a wider range of goods in one location. Customers can buy their requirements under one and the same roof. Customers can fulfill their wants as it offers a wide variety of goods at different price levels. As such, all their demands are met. Their time and labour are saved.

3. **Economies of Large-Scale Buying** : It is a large-scale organisation. It has all the advantages and economies of large-scale purchase. Goods are purchased in bulk quantities, which lead to the allowance of discount, concession rate etc. The freight charge is also less. Mostly purchase is made from manufacturers directly. Hence there is no middleman charge. Due to these, the price of the commodities is cheap.

4. **Services to Customer :** There are many services and facilities offered by the store to the customer. There is the service of expert buying of quality goods at the cheapest rate possible. This attracts a number of people. There are recreation facilities to the customers. There are facilities of free delivery of the goods to the customers. They allow hire purchase system in buying house-hold articles.

5. **Mutual Advertisement :** A customer, who visits the store to buy an article, can be easily persuaded to purchase many other articles from other departments in the same building. One department advertises for the other. Hence there is a large turnover in all the stores.

6. **Economy in Publicity :** It has adequate capital. Hence continuous advertisement is possible. One advertisement is enough to cover the whole concern and that too at cheaper rate and under expert advice. Window display, store-display etc., can be beautifully and attractively decorated to have a good effect. It attracts the customers by allowing periodical grand sales and sales at reduced price.

7. **Lower Cost :** There are many departments. The total cost is divided among the departments. Hence the cost is very low.

8. **Higher Efficiency :** Skilled and expert men can be employed in these stores. They have higher efficiency in dealing with the matters of the stores. Hence the departmental store operation will be on a higher level to the fullest satisfaction of the buyers.

Disadvantages

1. **High Cost of Doing the Business :** The departmental stores provide many services to customers. The management has to maintain a large number of staff apart from meeting heavy overhead expenses. All these will increase the cost of functioning. Thus the prices charged by the stores are higher and the ultimate buyers bear the burden of increased prices.

2. **Need for Higher Capital :** Higher capital is required for establishment and operation and also for buying the goods in bulk. They are located in the heart of the city where the rent will be high.

3. **Lack of Personal Touch :** The departmental store is big. It has a large number of employees. Many of them are paid low salary. The work entrusted to them may not be done wholeheartedly, and this affects the high rate of employee turnover. The majority of customers are not properly attended to. Of course, it may not be possible to give a personal contact to each customer. But a customer may not be willing to buy from a store, where he is not attended to by the salesman. We all, when enter into a shop, expect a personal attention from the seller/salesman. If we are enquired about our needs, surely we shall make a purchase, because of the salesmen's salesmanship. Otherwise, when not attended to, we leave the shop without even attempting to see the products.

4. **Risk of Loss :** The stores undertake large-scale purchases. It may happen that the fashion or taste of the buyers may change, which leads to dead stocks. Prices also change frequently, and those changes affect the stores adversely.

5. **Excessive Departmentalisation :** When there are many departments, the cost of clerical job will increase. It is also seen that employees of some stores are overburdened, while others remain idle.

6. **Absence of Local Convenience :** As it is situated in the central place, it is generally far away from the residential area. So it is not easily accessible. Goods which are required at once are always purchased from the nearest available shop.

Chain Store or Multiple Store

The chain store has its origin in America. It is known as multiple shops in Europe and other Western countries. A chain store is a network of a number of branches situated at different localities in the city or in different parts of the country. Thus a chain store system is a group of retail stores of essentially the same type, centrally owned and with some degree of centralised control of operation.

Definition : According to Clark and Clark, ''A chain store system consists of a number of retail stores, which sell similar products, are centrally owned and are operated under one management.''

According to Converse, ''A chain store system consists of four or more stores, which carry the same kind of merchandise, are centrally owned and managed and usually are supplied from one or more central warehouses.'' A chain store is one of the retail store system, e.g., Bata Shoes, Corona Shoes, Indian Oil, DCM, Bombay Dying, Tata Steel, Usha etc.

Characteristics of Chain Store

1. It is nearer to customers. The customers' approach is aimed at. As far as possible chain store goes near to the buyers as against departmental store, inviting the buyers to the shopping place.

Such type of stores can be found in residential areas.

2. **Large Scale Retailing :** It is basically a system of large-scale retailing. Such stores deal with articles for every day use; they are branded; they have quick turnover and are of standard quality. It eliminates the middleman.

3. **Limited Varieties of Merchandise :** Chain stores concentrate in a limited number of merchandise and products fall under the category of convenience goods, which are required by almost all people.

4. **Horizontally Integrated :** Multiple stores are operated horizontally. Addition of new stores increases the customers. Buying takes place in large lots. It leads to specialised merchandising, buying and promotional services and central administration spread over to more stores.

5. **Vertically Integrated :** They have large distribution centres. They buy from producers. They have their own warehousing. They have their own trucks or station wagons by which they distribute the things from their stores.

6. **Specialisation :** Chain stores deal with a limited number of merchandise. Hence there is the possibility of specialisation in the line, in which they are dealing.

7. **Standardisation and Uniformity :** There is the same style and uniform practice in all the shops of the chain stores and they are directed by the central office. As such, customers can easily recognise the shop.

8. **Centralised Buying and Decentralised Selling :** The central organisation in the chain store buys the products and supplies them to all the branches. Selling prices are stamped on the article, which are sent to the branches. The articles are sold at the market price. As such, centralised buying and decentralised selling take place. The managers of the individual stores have nothing to do with the purchases of products in which they deal. The products are supplied with the selling price stamped on them.

Classification of Chain Stores

According to location :

1. Local chain stores are operated either in the city or near the city.
2. Sectional chain stores are located at different places within the geographical unit.
3. National chain stores operate throughout the country.

The chain store may be utility operated, when operated by public utility companies. A chain store may be manufacturer controlled, when owned and operated by a manufacturer or a group of manufacturers. A chain store managed and merchandised by outside agencies, is known as leased department chain.

Advantages of Chain Stores

A. Advantages to Manufacturers

1. **Low Operational Expenses and Overheads:** There is a centralised way of specialised management service, joint advertisement, high rate of turnover, better stock-keeping, elimination of middleman, cash and carry operation etc. which led to the low operating expenses and overhead charges. Hence the prices of the products in the chain stores are low.

2. **Less Cost :** The cost of goods is less due to the purchase of large quantities or own manufacture on large scale.

3. **Low and Uniform Price :** Low operational expenses and low cost of goods lead to low price of commodities. There is uniformity in price in all the chain stores. Customers have the confidence in price and there is no bargaining.

4. **Standardised Methods of Operation :** Standardised methods of operation are followed in all the chain stores. Standardisation is applied on laying out the plan of building, window display, advertising, selection and training of personnel, selling policies, and shop services, stores system and procedures. More effective and economical operations are possible by standardised procedures.

5. **Less Investment :** The chain store handles only limited varieties of goods. The price is low. As such, there is quick turn-over. This reduces the investment on inventory. Cundiff is correct in saying that the chain store works on its inventory harder than many competitors.

6. **Flexibility in Operation :** It can open new shops or close down any branch shop which is running on loss. This is an advantage of decentralised selling. There is multiplication of selling points.

7. **Specialisation :** Chain stores are having the advantages of specialisation in a particular line of goods. Expert opinions can be sought and applied to all chains advantageously.

8. **No Extensive Premises :** Chain store can be opened in small area. It need not have extensive premises. Hence the rent is very low.

9. **No Bad Debts :** The goods are sold on a cash basis. Hence there is no bad debt. Clerical work is also reduced to that extent.

10. **Less Advertisement Cost :** There is common advertisement for all the branches. They have uniform external and internal display. Furniture and fixtures also have the same colour and design. e.g., Bata Shoe Co.

11. **Transfer of Goods :** Shortage of stock in one branch can be remedied by transfer of stock from other branches having surplus stock.

12. **Offset Loss :** The loss of one store is offset by the profit in another unit.

B. Advantages to Consumers

1. **Easy Accessibility :** Chain stores are opened in many places. They are within the reach of the customers. They offer convenience to buyers. In every important locality there will be a branch.

2. **Elimination of Middleman** : Chain stores buy directly and sell directly. There is no middleman. Middleman's profits and commission are saved, and thus buyers are protected. This benefit is passed on to the consumer by selling the commodities at cheaper price.

3. **Assured Quality :** There is the assurance of quality goods, as there is no middleman. Deterioration in quality can be eradicated by the control office.

4. **Assured Supply :** There is assured and regular supply of the goods to consumers whenever they need. The stock levels are always kept satisfactory.

5. **Direct Contact :** There is direct contact between the seller and the consumer.

Disadvantages (to Manufacturer)

1. As the number of stores increases, greater will be the task to provide effective supervision over the personnel working in each store. This is becausc of separation from central management.

2. Since standardisation of systems and procedures are admitted by the central management they cannot be altered by the store manager to suit local condition.

3. The changes in demand cannot change the production easily. So stocks may be stored without moving.

4. No service is extended to customers like credit sales, door delivery etc. This will reflect on the sales negatively.

5. A satisfactory remuneration method is absent in the store system, and this will lead to non-cooperation of the personnel, and hence gives chances to competitive prices.

Disadvantages (to customer)

1. No personal service is offered to the consumers. Only limited variety of products is available. Individual interest cannot be satisfied.

2. Credit facility is absent. They deal on COD system.

Disadvantages (to society)

1. The chain stores tend to adopt monopoly in dealings through price policy.

2. The chain stores cannot give satisfaction to individual demand or local needs.

3. Such shops may play fraud by supplying inferior items.

4. Local conditions have not been adjusted.

DISTINCTION

Departmental stores	Chain stores
1. Departmental stores are located in central places–busy locality.	1. Chain stores are located at different places.
2. It handles a wide variety of goods.	2. It handles only a limited variety of goods.
3. It pulls the customers to its shop by being located in heart of the city.	3. It approaches the customers by opening shop near to them.
4. The price in departmental stores is high.	4. The price is lower than that in the departmental store.
5. Customers can buy a variety of goods under one roof.	5. Consumers can purchase only special or limited goods.
6. It requires more capital to maintain different departments.	6. It require less capital.
7. Huge stock of goods leads to the block of capital.	7. Large stock can be adjusted by transferring to needy stores, and so blocking of capital does not arise.
8. It gives credit facilities to regular customers.	8. Its policy is cash and carry.
9. It is a combination of decentralised buying and centralised selling.	9. It is a combination of centralised buying and decentralised selling.
10. Profit or loss is calculated on the entire stock.	10. Loss, if any is adjusted by closing that store and opening a new branch.
11. Overhead charges are more.	11. Overhead charges are low.
12. They cater to the needs of local customs and customers.	12. They follow on a nationwide basis.

Mail Order Retailing (Scc previous chapter 'Marketing Channel')

Hire Purchase and Instalment

Hire Purchase : Hire purchase trading is a system by which the seller agrees to sell the articles to the buyer on condition that the payment of the article will be made to the seller in a fixed number of instalments, till the sale price is recovered. Hire, the name implies that the article is not sold, but title to the article vests with the seller till the last instalment is paid. If the buyer makes any default in remitting the instalments due, the article will be seized by the seller and the amount, paid so far, will be treated as mere hire charges.

Instalment : Hire purchase and instalment purchase are similar except for certain legal differences. Under instalment system, title to article as well as articles are received by the purchaser. On default of payment, the seller cannot seize the article but can approach the court of law.

Both the systems facilitate the sellers to find large markets. Buyers will be at ease to possess the products, even if they lack financial power. Today commodities like, scooter, fan, TV, radio, refrigerator, cycle, furniture, clock etc., are sold in plenty. The product, to be dealt under these systems should be (1) standardised products (2) durable products (3) high priced products etc.

Advantages

1. The standard of living has improved.
2. Buyers enjoy the possession of articles beyond their means.
3. Sellers can increase their sales.

Co-operative Retailing : The tough competitive nature and criticism levelled against wholesaling and retailing is given frequent changes, mainly in the field of retailing methods. The following are the important types of co-operatives.

(a) **Consumers' Co-operative**

Consumers' co-operative is a retail business, owned and operated by ultimate consumers to purchase and distribute goods and services chiefly to its members. Co-operative stores are financed by the members in the form of shares of small denomination. The profits from the trading are shared by the members. The principles laid down are, membership to all, limited interest on capital invested, sales at market rate and on cash only etc. The purpose is to supply articles at reasonable price, elimination of middlemen, correct measurement, stabilised prices etc.

Advantages

1. To supply quality goods.
2. To sell without adulteration.
3. To adopt correct measurement.
4. To eliminate middlemen.
5. To stabilise the price.
6. To effect regular supply.

Disadvantages

The progress of co-operatives has been effected seriously because of :

1. Lack of finance.
2. Untrained managerial personnel.
3. Poor salesmanship.
4. Defective methods of stock-keeping and accounts.
5. Introduction of credit sales.
6. Dishonesty of managing members.
7. Lack of interest.
8. Keeping stocks at high cost.
9. Lack of business knack.
10. Weak organisational structure.
11. Want of publicity.
12. Honorary service.
13. Lack of co-operation among members.
14. Lack of link with other co-operatives.
15. Uneconomic home delivery and services.

(b) **Retailers Owned Co-Operatives**

It is an enterprise, owned and controlled by retailers, who are associated for joint purchasing and warehousing of merchandise. The finance is obtained by issuing shares to members. The fund so collected is utilised for building warehouses, purchasing merchandise etc. Certain such co-operatives assist in advertising, store location and operation, policy making etc.

Supermarket : A supermarket is defined as, ''A large retailing business unit, selling mainly food and grocery items on the basis of the low marginal gain. It has a wide variety and varied assortments of goods. It lays emphasis on self-service.'' To be simple, a supermarket is a large retailing shop, where goods are kept in open rack or almirah; buyers have to select products, place them in a box or trolley, bring them to the gate, where one counter clerk prepares the bill for the goods selected; the buyer pays the bill and takes delivery of the products.

It is a large retailing store. It sells a wide variety of consumer goods and articles of household use, under one roof. It offers goods at low price and has a high turnover. It offers minimum services. It operates on cash and carry basis. It is a self-service store.

Features of a Supermarket

1. It operates on self-service style.
2. The price charged is low.
3. There is no credit sale.
4. It offers a wide variety of products.
5. Its margin of profit is thin.
6. They offer minimum customer service.
7. There is no sales pressure.
8. Packaging plays a very important part.

Advantages

1. Buyers can get products at a lower price.
2. There is no pressure for sales and consumers enjoy perfect freedom.
3. Low operating cost gives higher profits.
4. Different products can be selected at one place under one roof.
5. There is no danger of bad debts.

Disadvantages

1. Supermarkets are located at places where there is population concentration and the benefit goes to them.
2. Spacious premises are needed and expensive location leads to high cost.
3. It is not suitable to villages.
4. Personal contact is absent.
5. It needs much capital.
6. There is the possibility of mismanagement or theft.
7. It is inconvenient to sell heavy products or goods in pieces.
8. There is lack of good organisation.
9. Administrative expenses are very high.
10. There is a lack of retailing intelligence.

In India, the supermarkets are in childhood. People's ignorance and lack of education are the reasons. Supermarkets must have well-trained sales personnels; and the management people must be honest in dealings of purchases and must enforce strict control over the salesmen. Then supermarkets can shine.

Hypermarket : Hypermarket is a recent innovation. According to Stanton, "Superstore, also called as hypermarket or supermarket is the newest and possibly the toughest innovative competitor of the supermarket." It combines the features of a supermarket and a general merchandise store. It is a very large store. A large area is needed and as such it is situated at the edge of the city or outside the city. It deals in a variety of goods. The self-service method is followed. In France, it is known as hypermarket and in Germany it is known as giant store.

One Price Store : The very name 'One price' indicates that the prices are uniform. The prices are fixed in advance. The products which are in great demand by people are sold at one price. Such shops are generally found in crowded places. The margin of profit per article is very low, but the profit on the total sales will be high. As the price is the same for the products, the buyers are at ease to choose any article. It is also known as woolworth chain store. We can come across such stores in exhibitions and at certain busy places.

Franchising : Franchise means a privilege. Franchise selling means exclusive distribution policies. A franchise is a conditional right given to a retailer to market the franchise company's products or services under the banner of the franchiser. Franchise companies are those companies whose products require great retail promotion. But they have insufficient capital to set up or expand their own retail outlets. Thus manufacturers approach wholesale distributors, who in turn grant retailing franchise in their territories. As manufacturers improve their finances, they absorb the distributors and grant franchise direct to retailers. It explains that franchising was first in the hands of wholesalers, after the position was sound and favourable, the manufacturer contacted the retailers directly on franchise basis. A franchising operation is a legal contractual relationship between a franchiser (the company offering the franchise) and the franchisee (the individual who will own the business). Franchiser offers to maintain a continuing interest in the business of the franchise in such areas as the site selection, location, management training, financing, marketing, record-keeping and promotions. He also offers the use of a trade name, standardised operating procedure etc. Franchisee agrees to operate under conditions set forth by the franchiser. Franchisee makes capital investment and receives commission on the basis of sales. For example, Ford Co. licenses dealers to sell its car, the dealers being independent business people who agree to meet various conditions of sales and services.

Wheel of Retailing

"The wheel of retailing" is the name Professor Malcolm P. McNair has suggested for a major hypothesis concerning patterns of retail development. This hypothesis holds that the new types of retailers usually enter the market as low-status, low-margin, low-price operators. Gradually they acquire more elaborate establishments and facilities, with both increased investments and higher operating costs. Finally they mature as high-cost, high-price merchants, vulnerable to newer types who, in turn, go through the same pattern. Departmental store merchants, who originally appeared as vigorous competitors to the smaller retailers and who now become vulnerable to discount houses and supermarket competition, are often cited as prime examples of the wheel pattern.

Elimination of Middlemen

Wholesalers and retailers act as middlemen between producers and consumers. Apart from the services offered, the cost of their function is an addition to the final price. The final price is recovered from the ultimate consumers. At the same time, by eliminating the middlemen, it is possible for the consumers to get the products at a lower price, reduced to the extent of the additional amount charged by the middleman. Some people are of the opinion that wholesalers may be eliminated, leaving the retailers, as they cannot be eliminated from the distribution system.

Manufacturers and producers also try to have direct contact with the consumer-owned retail shop, M.O. houses, multiple shops, chain stores etc. It is generally felt that a good amount of the final price is eaten away by the middleman. Let us go through the case for and against the elimination of middleman.

Arguments in favour of middlemen

1. There are many functions–assembling, grading, warehousing, transporting, risk bearing etc. performed by the middlemen. They also take an active part in the distribution of finished goods.

2. The important functions of distribution and its risk burden are assumed by middlemen, and the producers have been freed. Thus production will further improve.

3. Because of the services of the middlemen, goods are brought to the places where they are needed.

4. Specialisation, which is the result of division of labour, is important in modern marketing, when there are specialised dealers. There is further scope of division of labour, which calls for specialisation in marketing.

5. You can eliminate the middlemen, but you cannot eliminate their functions. It means someone has to perform the functions. The marketing functions cannot be eliminated. Now the aim is to perform the functions at the lowest cost and higher efficiency. Here the middlemen perform the functions satisfactorily and economically.

6. They perform the functions of concentration, equalisation and dispersion. The goal of marketing is the matching of supply and demand.

7. There are certain types of products–perishable food items etc., and their distribution can only be necessarily done through the middlemen, who is fast and quick in dispersion.

Arguments against middlemen

1. The appearance of middleman in marketing functions costs about 35%-50% of the price paid by the ultimate consumer. The cost burden of middleman is charged on the consumers.

2. There are large numbers of middlemen between the consumers and producers. Some of these middlemen do not perform any marketing function. But these people create hindrance in the free flow of goods towards the market. Elimination may be useful in reducing the cost and speeding up the movements of goods.

3. All types of risks arising out of depression and recession, strikes, scarcity of raw materials are not shouldered by the middleman.

4. They enter into black marketing in time of scarcity and emergencies with a view to earn huge profits, by boosting the price.

5. They always push the products of manufacturers who give better terms. Better terms, generally mean inferior products. Middlemen aim at maximum profits and are not concerned about consumers or producers.

6. Communications have been developed extensively, and different modes of transporting systems are available regularly. Hence the middleman can be eliminated.

Arguments Against Wholesalers

1. Most of them are only order-takers for profit at the cost of consumers.
2. Relation between producer-consumers is hindered.
3. Encourage black marketing for higher profits.
4. They aim only at higher commission.
5. They do not offer any valuable services to anyone.

Conclusion

1. Elimination of middlemen does not mean elimination of the marketing functions.
2. There is no sense in eliminating the functions of specialists.
3. Middlemen are essential to deal with the distribution of perishable goods and some of the convenience goods.
4. It is not possible for the producer to distribute the goods to the ocean of customers.
5. Middlemen can do better than the producers, in the field of distribution.

To be more effective, the chain of middlemen should be shortened. Longer the chain, greater the cost of marketing. Appearance of chain stores, departmental stores, large retail outlets, mail order houses, supermarkets, consumer co-operative stores etc., facilitates the consumer to get products at low price. However, disservices and manipulations of the middleman continue to exist in the channel of distribution. Small producers are not able to contact consumers directly. Therefore the services of middlemen are essential in the chain of distribution.

QUESTIONS

1. Give an account of the different types of wholesalers. *(M. Com., Madurai)*
2. What do you understand by the term 'Retailing'? What are the various forms of retail organisation ? Which method is popular in India ? *(M.Com., Allahabad)*
3. What is the role of a small independent retailer in a distribution channel ?*(B.Com., Chennai)*
4. What are the services rendered by wholesalers ? *(B.Com., Mumbai)*
5. What are the services rendered by retailers ? *(B.Com., Andhra)*
6. It is said that the wholesaler is a parasite and therefore an unuseful link in the chain of middlemen from the producer to the customers. Do you agree with this point of view ? *(B.Com., Mumbai)*
7. Define retailer. Explain their functions and types.
8. What do you understand by large-scale retailing? Explain its main constituents.
9. "The middleman can be eliminated, but his functions cannot." Discuss. *(B.Com., Calcutta)*
10. What are the fundamental reasons behind the establishment of cooperative ? Explain. *(B.Com., Bangalore)*
11. Contrast supermarkets and discount houses with respect to basic characteristics operating philosophy and buying practices. *(B.Com., Delhi)*
12. Explain the wheel of retailing hypothesis.
13. Discuss house-to-house selling as a retailing method. *(B.Com., Mumbai)*
14. Explain what is meant by an Independent store. *(B.Com., Delhi)*
15. What is a chain store system ? Discuss. *(B.Com., Mumbai)*

CHAPTER 35

Marketing of Consumer Goods

- *Consumer Goods*
- *Industrial Goods*
- *Characteristics of Consumer Goods*
- *Classification of Consumer Goods*
- *Consumer Goods Marketing*
- *Shopping Goods Marketing*
- *Marketing Speciality Goods Marketing Method*
- *Comparative Study*
- *Channels of Distribution*
- *Questions*

Goods are those tangible things which are described by human beings and for which they are willing to pay a price. That is, goods may be defined as any commodity, product or services which are useful for people and have monetary value. Again goods may be tangible or intangible. Tangible goods should have the characteristics of tangibility; *i.e.*, the goods must be touched, seen, felt etc., for example, car, scooter, soap, fan, cloth etc. Intangible goods may be in the form of services, such as repairing, services of banks and insurances etc.

Goods are also known as commodities or products. They may mean any property or wares which are transferable. Goods have been classified in various ways; but for our purpose of study, we divide the goods into three categories on the basis of consumer needs : (1) manufactured goods, (2) agricultural goods and (3) natural raw materials.

Manufactured goods are those goods that are semi-finished or finished goods; used by producers and consumers. Manufactured goods are of two types–consumer goods and industrial goods. Consumer goods are those goods which are meant for direct consumption by ultimate consumers and households; for example, car, television, radio, cycle, shoe, furniture, toys etc. Industrial goods are those goods which are used in the process of manufacturing other goods and services. For example, raw materials, machines, computers, maintenance supplies etc., and the best example is semi-manufactured goods. Agricultural goods, in a narrow sense refer to the produces out of cultivation; for example, vegetables, grain, fruit etc., and in a broader sense, include produces out of the cultivation, dairy farming, poultry farming, egg, meat etc. Of these agricultural goods, say wheat, rice, pulses etc., are food products for human consumption, whereas oilseeds, tobacco, cotton etc., are raw materials for industry. That is, these agricultural products are classified into two categories–industrial goods and consumer goods. Natural raw materials are the gifts of nature; for example, mines, forests etc., and these are raw materials which need further operation before use.

Differences between Consumer Goods and Industrial Goods

Consumer Goods	Industrial Goods
1. Goods bought are meant for consumption.	1. Goods bought are meant for further processing.
2. There is a direct demand.	2. There is derived demand.
3. The demand is elastic.	3. The demand is inelastic.
4. Purchase is made in small lots.	4. Purchase is made in bulk.
5. To make purchases, ordinary knowledge is enough.	5. To make purchases, expert knowledge is needed.

Goods which are used for manufacturing other products or services are called industrial goods and the goods sold to consumers for direct consumption are consumer goods. But it is important to note that certain goods fall under both the categories–industrial and consumer goods. Therefore, the purpose for which goods are bought, decides their classification. For example, papers, typewriters, kerosene etc., are bought for the use of industrial consumptions and individual consumptions.

Characteristics of Consumer Goods

Manufactured consumer goods are sold to the consumers for consumption purposes. Further processing is not required before consumption. It is defined: "Manufactured consumer goods or products include all those which are destined for use by ultimate consumers or households in such a form that they can be used without commercial processing." Manufactured consumer goods are purchased by the consumers. People are the consumers and everywhere the consumers purchase the goods in small quantities, that too without any pre-intimation to the manufacturers. The following are the features of manufactured consumer goods:

1. **Customers Are Numerous :** Where there is a population, there exists market for these commodities. People of the whole world are buyers. Goods are manufactured to meet the day to day needs of the public. The buyers of consumer goods are scattered and the markets are widespread. Because of the numerous buyers, it is not possible for the manufacturers to deal directly with the buyers individually. Hence, the producers of manufactured goods employ the middlemen services–wholesalers and retailers, through whom the distribution of goods is done.

2. **Purchase In Small Lots :** Generally, the unit cost of consumer goods is low. People buy in small quantities; for instance, paste, tooth brush, soaps, hair-oil etc. Such goods are available easily that too in any quantity. This is because of : (1) The goods are available at convenient places. (2) Most of the consumers are financially poor. (3) The goods can be purchased at frequent intervals in any quantity. (4) Locking up of capital is avoided. (5) Deterioration of quality is avoided. The manufacturers of consumer goods generally adopt mass method of selling. They advertise their products in radio, newspapers, television etc. They also adopt distribution of free samples, display of the products in various retail shops etc.

3. **Mass Production :** Consumer goods are manufactured in large scale. There are a few customers for industrial goods. The demand for the consumer goods is greater and as such large-scale production is essential. Because of the non-durability nature of the goods, continuous supply is needed. Moreover markets are wide-spread and demand is regular.

4. **Primary Demand :** The world is progressing. At the same time, human beings are also raising their standard of life. A scooter, which was formerly a luxury item, has now become a comfort item. People have more income, more advertising and other promotional methods, which induce them to raise their standard, accepting luxuries as if they are necessaries.

5. **Buyers are Poorly Informed :** Consumers may buy varieties of goods, though generally not interested in studying their characteristics. Manufacturers also do not inform the buyer-consumers about the characteristics of the product. Consumers may not be experts in buying the goods. They depend on the advice of the seller. Advertising and other promotional tools influence the consumer's choice. Varieties of similar goods are available in the market. The persuasive communication and advertising of a product satisfy many consumers, often with unrecognised wants.

6. **Competition :** When similar consumer goods are marketed, there arises competition. Competition may be with regard to price, quality, substitute products etc. To overcome stiff competitions, manufacturers adopt various methods through branding, packaging, etc.

7. **Changes in Fashion :** We may generally come across occasions of 'clearance sales'. This is because of fashion change. New developments arrive and new fashion comes in as a threat to the existing fashion. Many products disappear before they reach the maturity stage. Thus manufacturers adopt method of introducing some changes in the existing products or they go for clearance sales

8. **Personal Considerations Guide Purchases :** Consumer goods must give satisfaction to the consumer. Conditions of sales–home delivery, repair facility, fitting, guarantee installation etc., have influence on the buying decisions. When a person purchases a durable product, he makes an enquiry as to the facilities, such as service after sales etc., available to him.

9. **Manufacturer Exercises Control Over the Price :** Manufacturer has complete control over the price of his products, through the controls of quality or quantity. The demand for the products depends upon economical conditions, size of population, fashion, taste etc., of the consumers. A producer can produce goods that the buyers need. Thus the manufacturer exercises a good degree of control on the prices of his products.

10. **Buying Motives :** Consumer goods are bought by consumers because of buying emotional motives. This emotional motive may be of pride imitation, prestige, comfort, social status, affection etc. For instance, we get a colour television with the remote control; and to a great extent our status is raised by possessing such a latest and costly product.

Classification of Consumer Goods

Consumer goods are meant for final consumption. On the basis of buying habits, manufactured consumer goods are classified into three classes (1) convenience goods (2) shopping goods and (3) speciality goods.

Convenience Goods

Goods that the customer usually purchases frequently, immediately, and with the minimum effort are known as convenience goods. Low unit cost, available at convenient places, at frequent intervals, with minimum effort, etc., are important characteristics of convenience goods. Convenience goods are daily necessaries for human being; for instance, cigarettes, newspapers, soap, bread, sugar, coffee, tea, toothpaste etc.

Features of Convenience Goods

1. Most of the convenience goods are perishable.
2. Consumers possess full knowledge of the goods.
3. Shops, dealing in the goods, are located at convenient places.
4. There is a regular and continuous demand for these goods.
5. The goods are purchased frequently in any quantity.
6. Amongst the competitors, there is a keen competition.
7. All goods are standardised and duly branded.
8. To get the goods, minimum effort is required.
9. Each such goods has close substitutions; for example, soap, paste etc.
10. Almost all the goods are daily necessaries of life.

Marketing

Since close substitute products are available to consumers, there arises a keen competition. Convenience goods are produced by numerous firms, in large scale and in many varieties. Each producer tries to sell the maximum of his products. The following factors are given consideration.

(1) **Display :** It is important to have a display of goods. Window display and counter display are essential to attract the consumers at the point of purchase.

(2) **Advertising :** A wide advertising is essential. A retailer may stock several brands and he is interested to make a sale but not of a particular brand. Hence, the manufacturer advertises his products, in newspapers, television, radio, popular magazine etc.

(3) **Wholesalers :** Consumers are countless. Direct selling is not practical. The product must be available in almost all retail shops. If the desired product is not available, consumers may go for substitute brands. The services of wholesalers are essential to facilitate the distribution of convenience goods to retailers, who stock such goods in enough quantity.

Shopping Goods

Shopping goods are consumers' products. Consumers make comparison in the selection of products as to quality, price, style, suitability, etc. in several stores. Examples are cloth, furniture, television, radio, jewellery, washing machines, fans etc. Consumers compare the relative suitability of alternative products before purchase.

Features of Shopping Goods :

1. Products are durable.
2. Purchase is not frequent.
3. The unit price is higher than that of convenience goods.
4. Comparison and evaluation are done by buyers.
5. It is always a pre-planned purchase.
6. Branding is not essential.
7. Buyers devote time and effort in the selection process.
8. Great care is given when purchase is made.
9. Generally producers supply goods directly to retailers.
10. Retail shops may not keep all rival products.

Marketing

Shops, dealing in shopping goods are located in central places. Manufacturers generally have a few outlays for the sales of goods. Shopkeepers keep the right goods to satisfy the customers. Generally, manufacturers supply goods directly to retailers, and this is more common. For instance, a shop dealing in electrical goods, may stock electrical goods, but not other goods. Consumers are at ease to compare the qualities of goods, prices, performance etc. For example, a television dealer may stock television of thc following brands : Dinora, Crown, Solidaire, BPL, Keltron etc. The consumers can compare the prices, performance etc., at the demonstration time. Further the name of the store is more important than the product's brand name or manufacturer.

Advertisements and displays are commonly done by the retailer. The location of the store, reputation of the dealer, salesmanship, price, design etc., are important to the consumers. In short, facility of comparison, creative salesmanship etc., are important for consumers while selecting thc best goods.

Speciality Goods

Speciality goods are those "goods with unique characteristics and/or brand identification for which a significant group of buyers are habitually willing to make a special purchasing effort." In the words of Copeland, speciality goods are "those which have some particular attraction for the consumer, other than price, that induce him to put in special effort to visit the store in which they are sold and to make a purchase without shopping;" for example, watches, radios, cars, shoes, cloth, television, tape-recorder etc. These are also known as luxurious goods.

Features of Speciality Goods :

1. Consumers insist on a particular brand.
2. Goods are high-priced ones.
3. The buyers are well-informed.
4. There is a limited demand.
5. Goods have their own unique attraction.
6. Consumers are prepared to spend considerable time and efforts for the wanted goods.

7. Customers make purchases without shopping around.
8. Substitute brands are not generally accepted by consumers.

Marketing Method

Speciality goods enjoy brand loyalty. There are a few outlets. Generally, manufacturers may run their own retail outlets for the sale of speciality goods. If the preferred brand is unavailable or out of stock, customers prefer to wait until they arrive in stores. Manufacturers and retailers advertise the products extensively. In the marketing of goods, repair service, installation etc., are very important. The retailer's reputation also plays an important role. For instance, a buyer purchases a scooter, 'Bajaj Chetak' and he has made the choice after comparing it with other similar scooters or may be because of certain unique features or the brand name or the confidence in the dealer.

Clear demarcation or distinction, which is found between the convenience goods and shopping goods, is difficult to find between shopping goods and speciality goods. Many products fall under both the categories. For instance, Mr. A wants to buy a scooter and he goes to different dealers studying the advantages and limitations of various models; then he comes to a decision. This is a case falling under shopping goods. But if the buyer has in mind a definite model, say Bajaj Chetak then he goes to the agencies, who are dealing in the particular Bajaj Chetak and purchases it; this is a case falling under speciality goods.

COMPARATIVE STUDY

Character	*Convenience Goods*	*Shopping Goods*	*Speciality Goods*
Unit price	Low	Medium-high	High
Selection time	Little	Considerable	Depends on nature of goods
Purchase frequency	Very often	Infrequent	Infrequent
Comparion of price and quality	No comparison is made	Comparison is made	No comparison is made
Importance to buyer	Unimportant	Usually very important	No generalisation
Purchase plan to buy	Very little	Considerable time is spent for purchase	Considerable, often long time is spent for purchase.
Purchase time taken for want-satisfaction	No time taken	Medium time taken	Long time taken
Time gap between decision and purchase	Generally no time is lapsed	Considerable time is lapsed	Considerable long time is lapsed
Availability	Nearest shop	Shopping around	Speciality shop
Examples	Soap, cigarettes, pastes, cold drink, bakery products. milk etc.	Furniture, refri-gerators, radios, sewing machines jewellery, shoes	Television, car, watches, goggles, bikes, photographic items
Marketing Methods			
Turnover	Quick	Medium	Low
No. of outlets	Many	A few	Very few

Character	*Convenience Goods*	*Shopping Goods*	*Speciality Goods*
Advertising done	Manufacturer	Retailer	Manufacturer and retailer
Window display	Very important	Important	Less important
Packaging	Very important	Relatively less important	Not much important
Length of channel	Long	Short	Very short
Brand name	Not important	Not necessary	Important along with store name
Sales promotion	Not needed	Required	Essential
Sales to buyers	Through whole-salers and retailers	Through retailer	Through retailer
Importance of retailers	Any store	Important	More Important

Channels of Distribution

A channel of distribution or trade channel for products is the route through which goods move from the manufacturers or producers to the ultimate consumers. "A channel of distribution consists of many specialised marketing institutions that relate to each other as sellers and buyers." In other words, a channel of distribution or trade channel for a product is the route taken by the title to the goods as it moves from the producers to the ultimate consumer or industrial user. The channel opens with the producers and ends by the ultimate consumers. In brief, the types of distribution or channel for consumer goods are :

1. Manufacturer to consumer.
2. Manufacturer to retailer to consumer.
3. Manufacturer to wholesaler to retailer to consumer.
4. Manufacturer, through an agent to wholesaler to retailer to consumer.
5. Manufacturer through an agent to middleman to retailer to consumer.

(A detailed description of these has been done in Channels of Distribution Chapter No. 33).

QUESTIONS

1. Explain briefly the common channels of distribution for the consumer goods.
2. Distinguish between convenience goods and shopping goods.
3. Define convenience goods. What are their characteristics, marketing consideration ?
4. Explain the special features of market for industrial goods. (*B.Com., Madurai*)
5. Is middleman necessary for marketing consumer goods ?

CHAPTER 36

Marketing of Industrial Goods

- *Introduction*
- *Buying Motives*
- *Characteristics of Industrial Goods*
- *Classification*
- *Marketing Consideration*
- *Questions*

Introduction

Industrial goods are those goods which are destined to be sold primarily for use in producing other goods or rendering services in contrast with goods destined to be sold primarily to the ultimate consumer. Stanton defines, "Industrial goods are those intended for use in making other products or for rendering a service in the operation of a business or industrial enterprise." Industrial goods are those goods, which have been brought by industrial users for the purpose of production. Industrial users–business, manufacturers, government, service organisation, institutions, other middlemen etc., buy products to use for the operations in making other products. Ultimate consumers buy products for their own personal or household uses. Goods bought to satisfy non-business want, can be called consumer goods. The industrial goods, are not final products; they are used for further production of goods to be consumed. Goods bought may be industrial or consumer goods, this depends upon the ultimate use. Industrial goods are sold in industrial markets and consumer goods, in consumer markets. Industrial goods are also known as producer's goods.

Buying Motives of Industrial Users

Industrial buyers are rational. The buying motives of industrial users can easily be determined when compared to consumers' buying motives. The following are the motives in brief, generally found in industrial buyers:

1. **Reduced Price :** There are many industries which produce similar products. Thus competition comes up in the market. Consumers prefer low price. Producers aim or wish to sell their products at the lower price, and at the same time keep the quality, quantity etc., as those of other rival products. This enables a manufacturer to increase his sales. When it is so, industrial goods are purchased at the lowest possible price. When a few items are purchased, negligible price change is not considered. But industrial users purchase goods in large quantity and therefore the buyers are rational; *i.e.*, price is a major consideration.

2. **Regular Supply :** Regular supply of goods is preferred for production. The source, from where the supply is expected, must be dependable. The supplier must be able to supply required quantity of right quality goods. If the production is regular, work will not be interrupted, and loss on account of losing business can be eliminated.

3. **Durability :** The goods purchased may be aimed to be durable final products. Consumers always prefer durable products, even at a higher price. For example, a screw driver, we purchase, is used to loose a screw, but if the tongue of the screw driver bends, we immediately take a decision not to purchase the screw driver of that particular brand. As such, only durable and quality products can be sold easily in the market. This fact is always remembered by the manufacturer.

4. **Greater Economy :** Industrial users prefer to purchase plants and machineries by which they can increase production at less cost. An efficient machine can yield more output at improved quality.

5. **Protection :** Purchases of goods are also desired to be protected against risk–theft, fire etc; fc example, purchasing of steel furniture instead of wooden furnitures. When industrial goods are purchased, their various uses are carefully considered.

Industrial buyers aim primarily to increase their profits; and thus their buying goal is to have quality items at cheaper rate and to increase saleability of goods having durability.

Characteristics of the Market for Industrial Goods

All those engaged in production need industrial goods. An industrial market consists of manufacturers, government service organisations, industrial distributors, middlemen etc. All these categories, who are engaged in business or process of operations in making other products, constitute the market for industrial goods. Industrial goods are differentiated from consumer goods on the basis of their ultimate use. The following are the features of industrial goods:

1. Geographically concentrated.
2. Limited buyers.
3. Derived demand.
4. Large-scale individual purchase.
5. Technical consideration.
6. Reciprocal buying.
7. Leasing instead of buying.
8. Buying decision.

1. **Geographically Concentrated :** The market for the industrial goods is generally concentrated in certain geographical area. This is because industries are located at a particular region. The demand for the goods comes from the area where industries are located. At the same time, the market for the consumer goods is spread over a wide area, as buyers are scattered over the whole country. For example, there is a good demand for automobile spare parts from Bangalore. Bombay etc., because automobile industries are concentrated there.

2. **Limited Buyers :** Compared to the number of buyers of consumer goods, there are only a few buyers of industrial goods. The number of buyers of consumer goods may run into millions of million, whereas the buyers of industrial goods may be only a few thousands. And the number of buyers of industrial goods is less than the number of buyers of consumer goods; roughly 10% of the total number of consumers are industrial users, because a few industries exist. Hence, there is a limited number of buyers of industrial goods.

3. **Derived Demand :** The demand for industrial goods depends upon the demand for consumer goods. Industrial goods are used in manufacturing consumer goods. The increase or decrease for industrial goods depends upon the increase or decrease for final products, *i.e.*, consumer goods. That is to say, when the demand for consumer goods increases, the demand for industrial goods also increases and vice versa.

4. **Large-scale Individual Purchase :** Individual orders may be few in numbers. At the same time, each sale will generally be of a high value in terms of money. That is large-scale purchase is there and, partly, the value of industrial goods is high, for example, lathe, computer, elevators, etc. The smallest purchase of these machines may run into several thousands of rupees. Here, the seller of industrial goods pays maximum attention to please his customer, because the buyer of industrial goods may order for a large quantity and the sales amount may run into lakhs. Thus, the seller or his agent must have salesmanship and direct sale is possible.

5. **Technical Consideration :** It is important to note that industrial goods are purchased for making other products. A buyer of industrial goods may have special requirements, and these are carefully considered before making the purchase. The manufacturer or his agent is a professional buyer, who possesses thorough knowledge of the industrial goods. For example, a manufacturer of transistor radio may purchase materials and parts, which will go into the final product of transistor radio. The

...ms to purchase good quality materials and parts, which facilitate to produce good ...os. If any change in the quality of material or parts occurs it will create trouble in the final ... Therefore, a buyer of industrial goods studies or carefully considers quality, durability, cost, ...ability, performance of the industrial goods.

6. **Reciprocal Buying :** Reciprocal buying is nowadays common amongst the industrial goods purchasers. The principle is simply based on 'I will buy from you on the condition that you buy from me.' For example, a paper manufacturer buys chemicals from a chemical firm, which buys considerable amount of paper from the paper manufacturer. Another example is, a truck manufacturer purchases tyres from a firm, which purchases trucks. The purpose of these types of dealings is that to some extent the demand for the products is assured on mutual understanding.

7. **Leasing Instead of Buying :** Heavy costly equipment of industrial goods are leased instead of purchasing. For example, parcel service agencies may not purchase trucks, but hire trucks; a building contractor may not purchase cement concrete mixer, but he may use a hired mixer; distribution agencies may use hired vehicle for distribution; a farmer may hire tractor to plough his land etc. Because of leasing system, the firm leasing out (lessor) and the firm using it on lease (lessee) are benefited. Lessor enjoys more income than the lessee in this sale promotion method.

Advantages To a Lessee : (1) He enjoys the use of the product, (2) He can return it after use, (3) The latest techniques are available, and (4) He enjoys the products whenever he wishes.

8. **Buying decision :** Comparing to consumer goods, the period of negotiations for a sale of industrial goods is generally longer. This is because (1) Many persons are involved in taking a purchase decision. (2) It needs advice of engineers, production manager incharge, cost accountant etc. (3) All formalities of the purchasing department calling for quotations, preparing comparative statement etc., have to be undergone. (4) Finance has to be arranged. Therefore the period of negotiation in buying industrial product is longer than the time taken for selling consumer goods.

Classification of Industrial Goods

Industrial goods may be classified, based on the broad uses of the product, but not on the basis of buying habits, into five categories.

I. Raw materials
II. Fabricating materials and parts
III. Installations
IV. Accessory equipment
V. Operating supplies

I. Raw Materials

Raw materials are those industrial goods which in part or in whole, become a portion of the physical product, but which have undergone no more processing than is required for convenience, in production or economy in storage, transportation or handling. These raw materials are of two types–farm products and natural products. Farm products *i.e.*, agricultural products which include wheat, cotton, vegetable, tobacco, fruits, groundnuts etc., and natural products which include fish, iron ore, petroleum etc. Here we deal only with natural products as agricultural products have been dealt with separately.

Features of Natural Raw Materials

The following are the important features of natural raw materials.

1. **Limited Supply :** The supply of natural raw materials is limited. Moreover, such materials cannot be reproduced. The supply is scarce, mainly in relation to demand. We search for new source or reproduction may be done; but these take a long time.

2. **Huge Capital :** Production of natural raw materials needs specialised activity and generally requires much capital investment. And apart from this, highly skilled personal services are needed. Further the producers of natural raw materials are few in number.

3. **Variation In Quality :** The producers can exercise control over the quantity or volume, but possess no control over the quality. The quality of the raw materials may differ from place to place.

4. **Bulkiness :** The materials are bulky in nature. But intrinsic value is low, when we compare size or shape. For example, the paper industries use 1,000 kilograms of bamboo, which may produce 500 kilograms of paper.

5. **Perishability :** Certain types of natural raw materials are perishable, while others are not perishable. For example, sea products are perishable.

6. **Production Can Be Controlled :** The output of the products can be controlled by producing the required quantity to meet the demand. That is, overproduction can be controlled. And this avoids the expenses of storage.

7. **Production Is Concentrated :** Compared to the farm products, the production of natural raw materials is relatively concentrated and not widely scattered.

Marketing Considerations

There arise some problems in marketing natural raw materials. Since the materials are bulky, having less intrinsic value, shorter channel of distribution is required.

The following problems are involved in marketing:

1. **Transportation Cost :** Bulkiness is a problem. Transportation cost of these bulky materials to a longer distance will cost more. At the same time the intrinsic value is less, lesser than the transportation cost. Thus the transportation cost is a deciding factor. That is, the transportation cost will decide whether the materials should be processed before they are carried to the factory, in order to reduce the transportation cost. In processing, the waste is removed and thus the materials are thinned, which reduces the transportation cost. For example, sugar mill industries are located near the place where sugarcane is cultivated. If the factory is too far off, the canes are to be transported to the factory and naturally, a greater amount will have to be spent on transporting.

2. **Needs For Standardisation :** The qualities of natural raw materials are widely different from place to place and time to time. At the same time, manufacturers for finished goods need a specific quality of raw materials. As is the quality of raw materials, so is the quality of the finished product. That is, the finished product is of high quality, when standard materials are used. The raw materials, which are extracted from nature, are of different qualities. When manufacturers are concerned with materials of specific quality for their finished goods, grading and standardisation are essential. As stated earlier, producers have no control on materials extracted from nature. Therefore, the producers of natural raw materials have to standardise and grade the raw materials. And such, materials fetch high price and possess a good demand; and have increased power of bargaining. Buyers of such raw materials, carefully inspect the materials, on the basis of their needs, before purchase.

3. **Adequate And Guaranteed Supply :** Manufacturers of finished goods generally invest huge amounts in fixed investment and employ many persons in the firm, and aim at mass production. For successfully meeting all these, regular supply of raw materials is to be assured by the supplier, who is particular about the uninterrupted supply of materials, which facilitate regular production of finished goods. These may be done with, either by entering into long contract with the supplier purchasing from open market at low price or by owning the source of supply.

II. Fabricating Materials and Parts

Fabricated materials and parts are industrial goods. These goods become part and parcel of the finished goods to be manufactured. They have undergone processing. **Fabricating materials**, which have been processed will go further processing in the course of manufacturing of finished products. The original entity cannot be recognised or identified in the final product; for example, **flour going** into bread, **yarn** going into cloth, **pig iron** going into steel etc. Fabricating parts are also industrial goods that have undergone complete manufacturing process, and generally do not require further processing. They become part of the finished product and can be recognised easily. This is because no change in

...ther processing is done on these parts. These fabricated parts, without any substantial ...n, are assembled or combined into the final product; for example, battery, spare parts, ...t, speaker etc. These items can be taken out from the finished products, in their original form.

Characteristics

1. **Adequate Supply :** A manufacturer of finished goods needs regular and adequate supply of fabricated materials and parts. These are required for the production of finished goods. Storage of these materials will affect the production of finished goods. For example, without tubes, cycles cannot be produced; without flour, bread cannot be prepared; without yarn, clothes cannot be made etc.

2. **Competitive Price :** There are many producers of fabricating materials and parts. This means there arises competition in selling. These materials must be priced at competitive price, so that the manufacturers are facilitated to produce their finished products at competitive price.

3. **Inspection :** Buyers of these goods, generally, possess good knowledge of these products. They are particular about the quality, suitability, price etc. They personally go to market in the process of selection and make thorough enquiry before taking a decision to buy.

4. **Uniformity :** Standard of quality and uniformity in size are of vital importance to the buyers. If one supplier is unable to supply standard materials and parts, buyers have many choices. As such, industrial users go in for the materials, which are of standard quality and uniform in size, quality, durability, price, shape etc.

Market Consideration

1. **Motives of Buyers :** Fabricating materials and parts are purchased in large quantities. Buyers need better quality. Brand has little to do with the buying motives. The price is also not, too much, considered. They look to the quality, performance and durability. The buyer's specification is important and accordingly the materials are to be supplied.

2. **Timely Supply :** The purchase is always based on timely supply and uniform supply. This is because the finished products are manufactured along with the fabricated materials or spares. If these are not supplied regularly and timely, an industrial user cannot produce finished products. Therefore the buyers need surety of supply on the basis of needs. Thus, the buyers prefer to buy these materials on a contract basis, six months to one year, so as to ensure regular and timely supply.

3. **Dealings :** Most of the fabricating materials and parts are sold directly to industrial users, with orders placed often a year or more in advance. Maximum dealings are direct; middlemen are used for small quantity. The firm, supplying the materials has its own salesmen and they call upon the users.

III. Installation

Installations are manufactured industrial products–the long-lived, expensive major equipment of an industrial user. Installation consists of building factories and offices; fixed equipments–power-looms, generators, elevators, boilers, cranes, locomotives, sawmills, lathes etc. Installations are major purchase. Generally they are brought directly from the producer. Its negotiation period is also long.

Characteristics

1. **Specification :** Specifications are always designed by the purchaser/user. Before making a decision to purchase, suggestions of experts in the line are sought. The installations are manufactured strictly according to the specification laid down by the user. Since it is highly costly and durable, much care is taken while designing installations.

2. **Obsolescence :** Fashion habit, behaviour of consumers in the market etc., may change often. The finished product must suit the market. Because of the development of science and technology, new inventions or economical methods. may come up. This may cause the machineries or installations to become obsolete.

3. **Durable and Costly :** Installations are costly and are meant for longer period; for example, installations of locomotives, or a sugar factory can be used for a long period.

4. **Testing :** Generally it is found that the working of installations cannot be judged exactly. Wh the installations are put into use, the workings or performance can be decided.

Marketing Considerations

1. **Pre and After Sale Service :** The buyers of the installations, which cost a huge amount, always expect sale service. In many cases, pre-sale and after-sale services are needed. Even a single sale is important to the seller. As such, the seller keeps a constant touch with the buyers and makes provision for repairing in order to earn goodwill.

2. **Sale Effort :** Generally no middlemen are involved and the channel is also direct from the producer to the user. The negotiation period is longer. A high degree of talent and sales effort are needed. A high calibre sales force is needed to market installations and generally sales engineers are employed. Personal selling is more effective than any other method. The purchases are also made when new plants are erected or when expansion or replacement of worn out machinery takes place.

3. **Leasing :** It is a problem to the management to have huge amounts locked up while starting new installations. As the price is high, buyers may go for getting them in lease instead of downright purchase; the leasing system is widely followed.

IV. Accessory Equipment

There are minor machines and/or machine tools; for example, welding equipment, speed reducers, typewriters, cash registers, trolleys, fans, conveyers, computers, etc. All these, commonly called accessory equipments, are industrial products. These are used as an aid in the production. They do not enter into final products. They do not have influence on the scale of production, as they do not perform any basic operation. But they facilitate and smoothen the manufacturing process. Their life is also shorter than installations, but more than operating supplies. They do not become part of the final products. These are standardised products and are not made to order whereas installations are made to order in almost all cases.

Characteristics

1. **Standardised Products :** Since they are equipments and tools used by different customers, most of the products are standardised in respect of quality, durability, size and price. They are produced in anticipation of demand. These items have standardised design.

2. **Obsolescence :** Accessory equipments do not become obsolete. These items are meant for certain purposes; for example, loose tools are required for fitting or loosening machines. Machines may become out of date; but it is not so with the accessory equipments.

3. **Durability :** The cost of these items is cheap. Its life is longer than that of operating supplies. These are subjected to wear and tear because of regular use.

4. **Brand Preference :** The buyers have brand preferences over the buying decision. Preferences of the workers and reputed manufacturers are important in marketing these products. For example, you may purchase a calculator of A company, some others purchase a calculator of B company. Each product has its own originality.

5. **Choice :** There is a difference in appearance or material input. It differs widely from firm to firm. Industrial users make enquiries from those who are already using them before taking a decision. They are purchased frequently.

Marketing Considerations

1. **Aggressive advertisement :** There are many producers of accessory equipments and tools in the market. They compete among themselves. To attract the industrial users, wide publicity is made, apart from sales promotional methods, for example, typewriters, fans, hand tools etc.

2. **Sales Policy :** Manufacturers of these products like to sell to industrial users through their own salesmen and through middlemen—direct selling and indirect selling. When the market is geographi-

the services of middlemen are adopted. Direct selling is adopted where the unit value ... demand is for several units.

. **Promptness of Supply :** In the absence of these items, the scale of operation is not affected. However, the flow of production is affected. As such, timely supply is preferred.

V. Operation Supplies

Items such as lubricants, oil, grease, petrol, stationery, distilled water etc., are operating supplies. These are similar to convenience goods, and are required in the firm's operation. They do not become part of the end-product. They are consumed in the operations. Their life is short. They are used up in the process of operations.

Characteristics

1. **Short Life :** The life of operating supplies is short. They are low priced. Such products are consumed in the office during the operation of a plant. They are used up or lose value immediately–oil, grease etc. used in the machine.

2. **Effort to Buy :** Almost all such supplies can be purchased with minimum effort. They are readily available in the market, apart from low unit value. They are purchased in small quantities frequently.

Marketing Consideration

1. **Price Competition :** The producers of these goods are numerous and hence competition arises specially on the basis of price. Generally the buyer's decision is based on price. This is because many manufacturers produce similar goods. When there are many sellers, price competition arises.

2. **Widespread Market :** Almost all the producers need the operating supplies. There is widespread market throughout the country. Sales of these items are in small quantities as they are available anywhere and at any time. They are similar to convenience goods.

3. **Effort to Sell :** Most of the supplies are indirect, as these resemble convenience goods. These industrial operating supplies necessitate broad distribution. The producers of these products, through extensive wholesaling middleman, sell them. Their unit value is less; they are bought in small quantities and they go to many users.

(Channels of the distribution of industrial goods are dealt separately in Ch. 33).

QUESTIONS

1. Bring out the special characteristic features of industrial products.
2. State the different classes of manufactured industrial goods. Explain the characteristics of a market for industrial goods. (*B.Com., Mysore*)

CHAPTER 37

Marketing of Securities

- *Functions*
- *Benefits*
- *Organisation*
- *Management*
- *Membership Rules*
- *Procedure for Dealings*
- *Kinds of Dealers*
- *Kinds of Speculators*
- *Listing Advantages*
- *Disadvantages*
- *Reasons for Price Fluctuations*
- *Questions*

We have industrial Securities, such as shares and debentures as well as Government Securities. For example, Joint stock companies established under the Companies Act, 1956, raise their capital, by way of dividing the capital into small parts, known as shares and these shares will be issued to the public. Securities *i.e.,* shares, debentures, bonds etc., are dealt with in a stock exchange. Thus stock exchange is a market for the purchase and sale of securities. The Securities Contracts (Regulation) Act, 1956 defines a stock exchange as 'an association, organisation or body of individuals, whether incorporated or not, established for the purpose of assisting, regulating and controlling business in buying, selling and dealing in securities.'' Thus, it is clear from the definition that a stock exchange is ''a forum, a mandi or a market for the purchase and sale of industrial and financial securities such as shares and debentures of public companies, government papers, municipal and port trust bonds and debentures.''

Organised markets are of two types–organised commodity markets and organised stock markets. These are popularly known as Commodity Exchanges and Stock Exchanges. A stock exchange deals in securities, but a commodity exchange deals in goods. Stock exchange is also known as stock market or security market.

Functions

The stock exchange deals in securities. It has also been described in many ways. For instance, it is known as a barometer of a nation's prosperity and adversity; a mart of the world, an open sesame treasure, Ali Baba's Treasure, a place to get rich quick, whereas for others it is just a place for gambling, a game of chance etc. As stated earlier, stock exchange is a market for the purchase and sale of securities, and is an organised market. It is a place for regular and continuous purchase and sale of all securities. The important functions of stock exchange are as follows :

1. It is a **convenient and permanent place** of market, where sellers and buyers meet to deal with securities.

2. It facilitates a **continuous market,** where joint-stock companies can sell their security in order to raise funds. It acts as a ready market to raise finance.

3. It facilitates the **investors to know the prices** of their securities from day to day. The expert opinions of business people are made available to common investors.

4. It provides **maximum liquidity,** marketability and price uniformity for securities. The investors are able to sell their securities at a moment's notice into cash, when necessary. Open and continuous market gives mobility to capital and diverts capital into sound investments.

maintenance of fair price reveals the real worth of securities. The real worth, which is on the basis of the earning capacity, may be different from the face value and market value. This helps the purchasers to know the real worth of securities, they possess.

6. The dealings of the exchange are always under **effective supervision and control;** and avoid unhealthy speculation and cheating. These activities ensure safety, security and equity on all dealings.

7. It offers a **useful service,** through the system of listing regulations. A listing means that a particular company's share, stock etc., are permitted to be bought or sold in a stock exchange. Listed securities command a good price over the unlisted ones.

8. It is sometimes called **economic barometer,** which indicates the state of health of the industry as well as economy of a country. The business cycle is reflected on the exchange.

9. It helps in **mobilisation of savings** for productive purposes by inducing, directing and allocating the flow of savings into the most productive channels.

10. It provides a **ready market** for government securities which are known as gilt-edged securities.

Benefits to the firm

1. Credit worthiness of a firm increases through listing privilege.
2. The market for the company's securities is widened.
3. The company enjoys a good response to public issue.
4. The firm enjoys higher bargaining power in the event of merger or amalgamation.
5. Collection of capital, by selling shares, becomes easy.

Benefit to Investors

1. The stock exchange report enables one to assess the value of investment.
2. Investor enjoys liquidity and negotiability of his investments in securities.
3. The listed securities serve as a good collateral with banks for easy finance.
4. Investor takes less risk by buying a listed security.
5. The daily quotation helps one constantly to review his investment portfolio.

Benefit to Community

1. Facilitates the mobilisation of untapped capital to a stream, which assures returns to people.
2. This return is an inducement to save more and more.
3. Growth of industry means growth of employment chances to people and growth of economy as a whole.
4. It helps government in raising funds through sale of government securities.

"The legitimate function of a stock exchange is to provide consistent with the large public interest, a forum and a service which are so organised, in the interests of both buyers and sellers, as to ensure the smooth and continual marketing of shares."

Organisation

The stock exchanges in India operate under the rules, bye-laws and regulations approved by the Central Government under the Securities Contracts (Regulation) Act 1956. Under this act eight stock exchanges were recognised in India: at Bombay, Calcutta, Madras, Ahmedabad, Delhi, Hyderabad, Indore and Bangalore and one more stock exchange at Cochin came into operation in 1979. Of these, Bombay stock exchange has been granted permanent recognition; and other stock exchanges have been granted permission which is renewed after every five years. Again Bombay stock exchange is the most important and is the oldest.

Any stock exchange which needs to be recognised, may make an application in the prescribe form to the Central Government along with copies of bye-laws and rules of the exchange and other information. If the Central Government is satisfied, after making an enquiry, recognition is granted to the stock exchange.

Organisation of Recognised Stock Exchanges

Sl. No.	*Name of Stock Exchange*	*Type of association*	*Recognition*	
			Date	*Period*
1.	Bombay	Voluntary non-profit making association of persons	31-8-57	Permanent
2.	Calcutta	Public Limited Company	10-10-57	5 years at a time
3.	Madras	Company Limited by guarantee	10-10-57	–do–
4.	Ahmedabad	Voluntary non-profit-making association of persons	16-9-57	–do–
5.	Delhi	Public Limited Company	9-12-57	–do–
6.	Hyderabad	Company Limited by guarantee	29-9-57	–do–
7.	Indore (M.P.)	Voluntary non-profit-making association of persons	24-12-58	–do–
8.	Bangalore	Incorporated as a Private Ltd. Company and converted into a Public Limited Company on 3 April, 1962	11-2-63	–do–
9.	Cochin		21-12-79	–do–

Management

A stock exchange is an incorporated institution, and works according to the provisions of the Securities Contracts (Regulation) Act, 1956. The management of the stock exchange in India is vested in a governing body. The governing body is known as 'Governing Board' at the Bombay Stock Exchange; 'Council of Management' at the Madras Stock exchange; 'Board of Directors' at the Delhi Stock exchange and 'Committee' at the Calcutta Stock exchange.

Governing body is composed of member representatives and government nominees. The representatives are elected once in a year and the government nominees hold office at the discretion of the government. The governing body has wide administrative powers. This body may have many sub-committees to manage the day to day affairs of the stock exchange.

Membership Rules

Only the members are permitted to transact business in a stock exchange. The business transacted in stock exchange is a highly technical one. Only individual can become members. If any individual wants to become a member, the prescribed application form has to be filled in. Before a person is admitted as a member, an enquiry is made about the character of applicant, his integrity, financial responsibility and competence, and he is to be supported by two existing members. When a person is elected as a member, he is required to pay an entrance fee, a membership fee and an annual subscription fee. Firms and companies are not eligible for the membership. The rules relating to admission of members are :

1. He must be 21 years of age or more.
2. He must be a citizen of India.

3. He must not have been convicted of any offence involving fraud or dishonesty.
4. His financial position must be sound.
5. He should not be an employee in any firm.
6. He must not have been expelled from any other stock exchange etc.

The entrance fee for admission ranges from Rs. 250 to Rs. 10,000; membership security deposit, from Rs. 5,000 to Rs. 20,000 and annual subscription from Rs. 15 to 300.

Procedure for Dealings

Outsiders cannot enter into the trading floor and cannot buy or sell securities. The transactions in securities on a stock exchange are done through the members or brokers of the exchange.

Choice of a Broker

Since a non-member (outsider) cannot deal directly in the stock exchange, one who wishes to buy or sell securities, has to approach a broker. If the broker is satisfied with the financial position of the client, he gives his consent to work on behalf of the client.

Placing the Order

The non-member client has to send details about the securities he wishes to buy or to sell to the broker by placing orders.

The various methods of placing the orders are:

(i) **Fixed Price Order :** Here the broker is permitted to secure higher price but not lower, in case of a sale and prices should be lower and not higher in case of purchase.

(ii) **Limited Price Order :** The client specifies the upper and lower limits of the prices.

(iii) **Bargain Price Order :** The client gives full liberty to the broker to exercise his discretion.

(iv) **Immediate or Cancel Order :** ''Buy or sell 100 shares at 150 immediate or Cancel.'' This means the order must be executed immediately at the best price and if this is not possible, the order stands automatically cancelled.

(v) **Open Order :** No specific time limit or prices are dictated when there is a complete understanding between the client and his broker.

Making the Contract

After getting the order, the broker meets other brokers, who are dealing with the particular security. Bargains are closed when a bid coincides with the offer. The bargain is noted by both parties in the diaries. These details of the transactions are entered on a slip of paper and put in a box for being announced in the official list.

Contract Note

The selling and buying brokers prepare contract notes and communicate to their clients after mutual confirmation. Particulars of sales or purchase are found in the contract note.

Settlement

The last stage is the settlement of the transactions. On the basis of the nature of the transactions in the stock exchange, there are ready delivery contracts and forward delivery contracts.

The ready delivery contracts are to be settled either on the same day or within a short period of time, not exceeding 7 days. The forward delivery contracts are to be settled on the due dates. All such contracts are subject to speculation. Only those securities which are included on the forward list of an exchange can be dealt under forward delivery contracts.

The fixed settlement days occur either at fortnightly or monthly intervals. The buyer has no intention of taking delivery or effecting payment. When the buyer wants to carry over his transaction to a future date, by mutual agreement between the parties, the settlement is called ''carry over'' or Budla. When the buyer wants to carry over his transaction, he has to pay some charges, for the facility granted to him. This is known as 'Budla Charge' or 'Contango'. If the seller pays 'Bu charges' to the buyer for postponement, then it is called 'backwardation''. Even on the ne settlement day, if the party has not honoured the contract and if there is no request for furthe postponement the default can be intimated to the stock exchange. When a member is publicly declared a defaulter, he is said to be 'hammered' and he ceases to be a member.

Kinds of Dealers

Only full members are allowed to do business on the 'floor' of the exchange. Other members, for reasons of convenience with a limited right, are also allowed to do business on behalf of members. They are:

1. **Remisiers :** He is a sub-broker and is not a member of the stock exchange. He is an agent of the members for securing business for his principal. He is a half commission man. He receives commission on the business secured by him, but it should not exceed 40% of the commission received on this business. Only Bombay Stock Exchange has remisiers. They are not allowed to transact business on the floor of the stock exchange.

2. **Authorised Clerks :** These people are known as member assistants and are authorised representatives of members. They can transact business only on behalf of their members. They are paid employees of a member to assist him in exchange transactions. They can enter the trading floor and buy or sell on behalf of their employer. 5 authorised clerks per member at Bombay, 8 authorised clerks per member at Calcutta and 3 authorised clerks at Madras are permitted.

3. **Unauthorised Clerks :** Such types of unauthorised clerks are, in addition to authorised clerks, permitted only in London stock exchange. They are also known as blue-button boys. They have no authority to deal, but convey messages.

4. **Taravaniwalas :** Members are divided into commission brokers and Taravaniwalas. Taravaniwalas have no dealings with non-members. They deal on their own account and resemble 'jobbers' on the London stock exchange and 'specialists' on the New York stock exchange. They often encroach upon the field of brokers and manipulate the prices of the securities against broker members. Their motive is to earn profit arising out of the difference in the purchase and sale of securities. Their business is in the nature of gambling.

Types of Speculators

Speculating refers to that class of business enterprise which is undertaken in the expectation of a rise or fall in prices. That is, Speculation consists in buying and selling commodities or securities or other property in the hope of a profit from anticipated changes of value. In stock exchange a large volume of transactions is subjected to speculation. Speculation is different from gambling. Gambling is nothing but betting on mere guess. Speculation is nothing but attempt at intelligent anticipation. A professional speculator tries to estimate the future trend of prices and enter into contract for the purchase or sale of securities in future in order to make profits out of fluctuations which he expects. A speculator attempts to make a profit out of a change in prices rather than by performing services. Thus, when a speculator expects the future price of shares to rise, he purchases those shares presently, so that he can earn profit by their sale in future. Similarly when he expects the price to fall in future, he enters into transaction of sale at present, so that he can earn profit by buying that security in future. The speculators in a stock-market are called by different names depending on the nature of speculative activity, as follows :

Bull : He is a person, who buys shares or stocks in the expectation of a rise in their prices. He intends to buy the shares of stocks and to sell them at a profit on a future date. Bull is a 'Speculator'' who is also known as ''Tejiwala''.

Bear : A bear speculator sells his shares in the expectation of a fall in the price. He makes sales of his shares and stocks with an intention of buying them at a reduced price in future. He is also known as 'Mandiwala'.

~ : A bear who is unable to meet his commitment is called a lame duck. Such a when a bear speculator cannot postpone the deal or the securities are not available ket.

ting

A stock exchange does not deal in the securities of all companies. Only those securities that are listed can be bought and sold at the stock exchange. All stock exchanges maintain an official list–Quotation list. Listing means permission to quote shares officially on the trading floor of the stock exchange. The listed shares appear on the official list of securities for the purpose of trading. That is, listing shares means the inclusion of the securities in the official list for trading purpose. It constitutes an integral part of the machinery of an organised stock exchange.

Procedure for Listing

The following are the listing requirements :

1. Memorandum and Articles approving of the listing of securities.
2. Copies of documents–memorandum, articles, prospectus, a brief history of the firm, consent of the controller of capital issues, agreement with underwriters etc.
3. Particulars regarding capital structure.
4. Particulars of dividends, specimen share certificate, letter of allotment etc.
5. An undertaking regarding the compliance with the provisions of Companies Act 1956 and Securities Contracts (Regulation) Act 1956.

Advantages

1. Status of the firm is raised.
2. The firm enjoys a privileged position.
3. A continuous market with informed buyers and sellers is ensured.
4. Shares have a high collateral value of borrowings.
5. Tax reliefs are available.
6. Collection of capital for expansion is made easy.
7. It creates a confidence among the investing public.
8. It safeguards the interests of the public.
9. It ensures the solvency of the company.
10. Investors can easily dispose of their shares.
11. The market for the shares becomes wider and receives widespread recognition.
12. Easy evaluation of real worth of securities is possible.

Disadvantages

1. The directors, by obtaining prior information, start speculation to their advantages.
2. Free transfer of securities helps a particular group of persons to enjoy control over the company.
3. The prices of securities fluctuate because of speculation.

Reasons for Price Fluctuations

Prices are always unpredictable and uncertain because of many causes. The prices of the securities dealt in stock exchange may go up or come down. The following are the principal factors for the fluctuations of prices.

1. **Supply and Demand :** If supply of a particular security is more than the demand, it fetches lower price and vice versa.

2. **Bank Rate :** The interest rate charged by the bankers has direct influence. If the intere rate is low, people borrow money and invest on securities. Thus price goes up. If the interest rate is high, there is less demand for shares.

3. **Speculative Attitude :** The activities of bulls and bears introduce price changes of the shares.

4. **Dividend Rate :** When the dividend rate is higher, the share price increases; and when the dividend rate is lower, the share price decreases.

5. **Government Policies :** Taxation policies, political factors, national economic policy, budget etc., lead to unexpected fluctuations.

6. **Artificial Scarcity :** In order to create a favourable condition in the market, underwriters purchase the shares of new companies. Thus, by creating an artificial scarcity, the price goes up.

7. **Trade Cycle :** During boom period, the prices go up and during depression period, the prices fall down.

8. **Behaviour of Financial Institutions :** Life Insurance Corporation, Industrial Finance Corporation, Industrial Credit and Investment Corporation of India etc., influence the prices of securities. When these institutions purchase securities at large scale, the price naturally goes up. Public may also demand the same securities.

9. **Company Productions :** If a firm has excess supply due to over-production, price reduction is possible. This creates a fall in the price of securities, as in the case of under consumption. If the firm restricts the production, the price goes up and profit increases; in turn security value also increases.

10. **Reputation :** A company's reputation depends on the efficiency of the Board of Directors. If a few able directors go on retirement, the prices of security fall down.

11. **Sympathetic Fluctuations :** Sometimes, securities of a firm may be listed with more than one stock exchange. Generally the price quoted by different exchanges may be uniform. But in case, any one stock exchange quotes a low or high price, it will have immediate effect on the other stock exchanges.

12. **Natural Causes :** Earthquakes, flood, fire etc., affect a country's economic position. Banks and insurance companies reduce their loan on properties. This will affect the price adversely. Failure of monsoon, rumour about war, strikes, lockouts etc., will also affect the prices.

13. **Balance of Trade :** If the balance of trade is unfavourable, the general price level of securities will come down.

The price fluctuations in stock exchange are brought about by many causes, and not by a single factor; economic, monetary, fiscal, political, foreign, psychological etc. A person, in order to be a successful operator in a stock exchange, must be aware of the various factors (discussed above) that influence the prices of securities.

QUESTIONS

1. Define stock exchange and explain its functions.
2. Explain the types of speculators.
3. What are the advantages of listing the securities ?
4. Explain the differences between stock exchange and a produce exchange.
5. Explain the causes for price fluctuations.

CHAPTER 38

Marketing of Agricultural Goods

- *Classification of Agricultural Goods*
- *Characteristics*
- *Problems in the Marketing*
- *Kinds of Markets*
- *Defects of Marketing*
- *Remedies*
- *Questions*

Agriculture plays a very important role in the economic development of a country. Agriculture is the backbone of an agricultural country, like India. India's prosperity depends upon the agricultural prosperity. Agriculture is fundamentally different from industry. The marketing of farm products generally tends to be a complex process. The types of agricultural commodities produced in our country are various and varied. Agriculture is the largest and the most important sector of the Indian economy. Agriculture contributes nearly 40%–45% of the national income and provide livelihood to about 70% of the population of the country. Agricultural marketing involves many operations and processes through which the food and raw-materials move from the farm to the final consumers. Agriculture provides goods for consumption and for exports and manufacturing sectors. The marketing system should be so designed as to give proper reward or return to the efforts of the tiller of the soil. But unfortunately, in India, the middlemen enjoy the cream at the cost of disability, illiteracy etc, of the poor Indian farmers. A small part of the price paid by buyers reaches the farmers while the big part is sucked by the middlemen. Farmers are handicapped mainly in securing a fair and reasonable price for their produce. The reasons are many—lack of regulated markets, ungraded produce, no Agmark, inadequate storage and warehousing facility etc. At present, the conditions have been greatly improved. Today, agriculture being modernised, leads to manifold productions. The role of marketing is fast changing.

Classification of Agricultural Goods

Agricultural goods are raw materials for industries and consumers. As such, we can classify agricultural goods into three. They are :

(a) Raw materials for industries, for example, cotton, jute, tobacco

(b) Raw materials for industrial goods

(c) Consumer and industrial goods.

Consumer goods are those which can be used by the consumers in their natural form without any change by manufacturing process. They are fruits, vegetables, egg, milk etc.

Raw materials for industries, for example, cotton, jute, tobacco etc., are raw materials. They are processed. The ultimate consumers use these products after they are passed through any manufacturing processes. The process is long in some cases like cotton into cloth, sugarcane into sugar etc.

Consumer and industrial goods are those used by both consumers and industries. When vegetables and fruits are sold to the consumers for consumption purpose, then they are called consumer goods. When they are sold to a canning factory for further processing, then they are called industrial goods. Sugarcane and coconuts are further examples.

Characteristics of Agricultural Goods

Agricultural goods are having some special characteristics which lead to varied problems marketing the agricultural produce. The characteristics of agricultural goods can be studied unde three heads :

1. Production characteristic
2. Product characteristic
3. Consumption characteristic

1. Production Characteristic of Agricultural Goods

(a) **Small-scale Production :** Farmers have small holdings of land. The produce in those lands is also very small, which is sufficient for their family needs. Marketing surplus is very small for them. More than 75% of the farm products, arriving at the markets, are cultivated or produced by small land holders, who cultivate individually. They do not have the knowledge of efficient marketing methods, such as grading, standardisation, storing, warehousing etc. To be more effective and economical, there must be large quantity of goods. As such they depend upon middlemen or co-operative societies to market their produce. Small-scale agricultural goods are not suitable for demand creation. Advertising is not possible due to the small-scale production. Branding is not possible due to different qualities of goods. Further, sub-division of divided holding, under the law of succession, into many fragmented holdings, increases the problems.

(b) **Scattered and Specialised Production** : Agricultural production depends upon some natural conditions. *i.e.*, suitability of soil and climatical conditions. If the fertility of the soil is rich and the climatic condition is favourable for the agricultural production, then the place is suitable for agricultural production, Farmers are scattered over wide area. They are away from the consuming centres. Some land is suitable for a particular crop. Different crops need different fertility of the soil and different climatic conditions. Generally industries are concentrated, while farming tends to diffuse into scattered areas. As such, some localities are specialised for some crops and others are specialised for other crops. Hence agricultural goods are scattered and specialised. Large quantities of agricultural products are essential for industries, where they are located and thickly populated areas arc essential for consumption.

(c) **Seasonal Production** : Agricultural production is seasonal in character. But there is demand for agricultural goods throughout the year, whereas the harvest is seasonal. For example, paddy or wheat production extends only for three or four months a year. But the demand for paddy or wheat is throughout the year *i.e.*, the demand is regular and continuous. For smoothening, there must be adequate transport facilities, storage facility, apart from finance.

2. Product Characteristics

(a) **Different Quality and Quantity :** In agriculture, man and nature are the two partners. Nature is the important partner. As such, the quality and quantity of agricultural products are beyond the control of the producers. Flood, drought, hailstorm, plant diseases, insects and pests, etc. affect the agrucultural production very much, even in advanced countries. As such, the quality and quantity also vary from year to year, region to region, village to village, climate to climate etc. Mainly the weather is not under the control of human beings and greatly affects the quality and quantity of produce. Grading and standardisation become difficult; even the farmer cannot guess the quality and quantity of his products, in advance.

(b) **Bulky Agricultural Goods :** When compared to their value, most of the agricultural goods are bulky, and the weight and volume are also great when looking at the value. As such, their transportation cost are high, storage of these goods is expensive, when compared to manufactured goods.

(c) **Perishability :** Many agricultural goods are perishable by nature. Perishable products, like fruits, vegetables, milk, dairy products, poultry products, meat etc, need special storage and transport perishable products, cold storage and refrigerators are needed. Paddy, wheat, , can be stored for long time by storing them properly and carefully.

..ion Characteristic

..nelastic Demand and Supply : Agricultural goods are necessary for every human being. ..ce, their demand is also inelastic. Price changes do not affect the demand. Demand for foodgrains is not affected by fall or rise in price. In the harvest season there is more supply of agricultural goods which creates glut in the market. This leads to fall in price. In short supply period, there is rise in the price. Price fluctuates due to imbalance in supply and demand. As such, there is the problem of price stabilisation, Government takes necessary steps to stabilies price in order to protect the countless small farmers from the clutches of adverse price change. Government procures marketed surplus and release as and when needed. Agricultural goods are consumed regularly and in small quantities.

Problems in the Marketing of Agricultural Goods

There are many problems in the marketing of agricultural goods. In short, they are :-

1. Concentration process is very important for agricultural goods. A long channel of distribution is needed and hence there is a large number of middlemen.

2. There is high demand for transportation and storage facilities in the harvest seasons, in order to protect the produce from deterioration in quality. So special transportation and storage facilities have to be provided.

3. To finance seasonal requirements more finance is necessary in a particular period. Financial need also varies from year to year depending upon the quantity of production.

4. Grading and standardisation is important for agricultural products. But it is very difficult to grade and standardise the products, as there are many agricultural goods, and one produce has many qualities.

5. Agricultural products do not create demand. Advertising is not possible due to the limited resources of agriculturists. As there are many qualities, branding is also not an easy job.

6. There is price fluctuation in agricultural products due to the imbalance in supply and demand.

7. Production of agricultural products is seasonal. The consumption is regular and the demand is regular throughout the year. Commodities must be stored and made available to the consumers.

Kinds of Markets

Agricultural produce marketing includes all the business activities involved in moving the produce from widely scattered producers to the ultimate consumers. In the process, the produce undergoes a change in time, place, form and ownership, which adds to their value. The chains of intermediaries through which the various produces pass between producers and consumers constitute their marketing channels. The production is little and scattered; therefore, middlemen are necessary for arranging for the concentration of the output of small producers and their dispersal to manufacturers and ultimate consumers. As regards the manufactured goods there are relatively few number of wholesalers, compared to the agricultural goods which involve a large number of wholesalers. Many wholesalers and middlemen are required for concentration. equalisation and distribution processes. There are, the following types of wholesale markets, found in practice :

1. Local Markets.
2. Central Markets.
3. Jobbing Markets.
4. Secondary Markets.

1. Local Markets

This type of market is also known as "Village markets" or "Primary markets", "Grow[n] markets." This local market functions daily or twice in a week; wholesale markets are located [in] market towns in the production area. They are the major points of concentration. This type o[f] market generally function along the roadside or centrally situated localities. In this market the produce of individual farmers is collected into economical lots; grading and packaging are done before moving them to central markets. The middlemen functioning in market are of many types and in brief they are :

(a) **Local Resident Buyers:** They have a fixed place of business in a market. They function on their own account or as an agent, in the capacity of retailers or processors.

(b) **Travelling Buyers :** These buyers move from place to place or farm to farm or even open a collection shop in a convenient place and collect produces during seasons and move them to other areas.

(c) **Co-operative Societies :** Co-operative Societies or co-operative marketing associations provide services to their members. Members can sell their products to the wholesalers through the societies. (for more details study co-operatives)

(d) **Auction Companies :** Through auction, marketing of agricultural products has been done. When the buyers and sellers assemble, produces are sold through open and free competition method.

2. Central Markets

In the local markets, the assembly of agricultural goods is made and from there they move in large central markets or terminal markets. Here, the wholesaler looks after the marketing processes—concentration, equalisation and dispersion. The central markets are situated in towns. The produces concentrated in these markets, are partly sold for local consumption and the rest transported to consuming centres. They are better equipped with modern facilities.

Features of Central Markets

(a) They enjoy adequate transport facilities.
(b) They have a large number of specialised middlemen.
(c) They have suitable locations near to the producing and consuming centres.
(d) They have adequate storage, warehouse facility, and facilities of communications, finance, advertisement etc.
(e) They ensure protection to buyers and sellers.

Functions

(a) Assembling of goods.
(b) Adjusting the demand and supply.
(c) Determining fair price.
(d) Collection and distribution of marketing information.
(e) Financing.
(f) Risk bearing.
(g) Facilitating future trading and hedging.
(h) Warehousing facilities.

A number of middlemen are operating in central markets as wholesale receivers and middlemen such as brokers, commission agents, commercial warehouses, commodity exchanges, banking, insurance companies etc.

3. Jobbing Markets

Job marketers mainly assemble the produces for retailers. The small wholesalers purchase produces from the central markets and sell them in small lots to retail stores. Jobbing markets is a secondary distribution market. The wholesale distributing agents are called jobbers. Jobbers are in wholesalers, who are bigger than local markets, but smaller than the central ... importance of jobbers is reduced by direct dealing between retailers and central ...

...dary Markets

The secondary markets are similar to jobbing markets. The difference is that under jobbing markets only agricultural consumer goods are dealt with, whereas in secondary markets agricultural raw materials are dealt with. Secondary markets are called sub-materials markets. These markets assemble raw materials from central markets and sell them to local mills and factories. Like jobbing markets, the importance of secondary markets is reduced because of direct dealing between mill-owners and central markets or growers.

Defects of Agricultural Marketing

We discuss below the main defects of Indian agricultural produce marketing. In unregulated markets, we can witness many weak points. In brief, they are:

1. **Lack of Organisation :** There is lack of organisation among producers. Producers are small and scattered. They have no collective organisation of their own to protect their interest. But buyers, most of whom are business buyers, operate on large scale and are well-organised. As such, buyers who are business-minded exploit the producers, who are illiterate and poor.

2. **Forced Sales :** National Planning Committee is of the opinion that the farmer in general sells his produce at unfavourable terms. The cultivator is forced to sell his produce as soon as the harvest is over. He sells his produce in the village itself. The reasons for the second sales in villages are :

(a) Cultivators' poverty and prior indebtedness.

(b) Need of finance to meet various obligations.

(c) Absence of road facilities.

(d) Lack of storage facilities.

(e) Defective means of communication.

(f) Interference of middlemen.

(g) Element of time which is an important factor, particularly with regard to perishable goods.

3. **Existence of Large Number of Middlemen** : There are a large number of intermediaries or middlemen between the producers and the consumers of their produce. These middlemen sell the produce to the consumers at a higher price and give lower returns to the producers. There are more than 10 intermediaries depending upon the nature of the crop, e.g., village merchant, itinerant merchant, dalal, agent middlemen, co-operative commission agent, wholesale merchant, semi-retailers, retailers etc. They do the function of assembling and distribution of produce. The long chain of middlemen takes a large amount of the producer's share from the consumers' rupee. On a rough guess about 50% of the price paid by the consumers goes to middlemen.

4. **Multiplicity of Market Charges** : The producers pay numerous and various marketing charges. They are more than 20% of the income of the produce. As such it reduces the producers' returns considerably. They pay market charges at different levels such as; commission to the dalal, weighmen charges, brokerage, charges of labourers who help in unloading the cart etc, apart from the deduction for impurities in the produce by the wholesalers.

5. **Malpractices of Markets** : Malpractices are common in unregulated markets.

(a) Malpractice in scale and weights. There are no standardised weights and measures. This is due to lack of regular inspection.

(b) Arbitrary deduction for religious and charitable purposes.

(c) Large quantity of produce is taken away as sample.

(d) Secret bargain between the seller's agent and the buyer's agent (under a cloth cover system).

(e) The broker is in more contact with the buyer than the seller. As such he is in favour of the buyer.

6. **Multiplicity of Weights and Measures :** There is lack of standard weights and measures. Weights made of sticks, stones, bits of old iron are commonly used in the villages and markets.

The multiplicity of weights and measures employed have many effects :

(a) It cheats the ignorant cultivator.

(b) It gives rise to complication between one markets and another market.

(c) It affects the accuracy of statistical calculations.

(d) It makes supervision very difficult.

(e) It gives opportunity to cheat the producers.

7. **Adulteration** : Adulteration is often resorted to by the middlemen which affects the health of the people. Due to adulteration the quality of the produce is reduced. In international markets, adulteration brings bad name to Indian agricultural produces. The middlemen and farmers make the adulteration. Even the good produces are subjected to customary inclusion of impurities. The adulterants, such as papaya seeds are mixed with pepper; red brick powder is mixed with chilly powder; sawdust with supari; vanaspathi with ghee, etc. Many stone crushers and grinders function to supply sizeable pebbles, clay balls etc. These are mixed with produces such as rice and other grains, to increase the weight. In India, adulteration is found from the temple to the hell. Almost all the daily necessaries of life are not free from adulteration. Tea dust is mixed with saw dust and medicines are also adulterated. Even poison is adulterated and if one wants to commit suicide, he fails because of adulteration.

8. **Inadequate Storage Facility** : Storage facility is far below the requirements in rural and urban areas. The loss due to inadequate storage has been estimated from 5% to 15% in weight and quality. The inadequate storage does not protect the produce from dampness, weevils and other vermins. Grains lose weights due to change of weather. Crops like jawar, pulses and maize are found to be infested by insects even before harvest. Losses due to rodents are also great. Rats eat one grain, but waste ten grains. Insects, beetles, moths etc. increase the loss. On a rough estimate, the loss is figured out at 10% of the total production, thus leading to a loss of Rs. 600 crores a year. The loss is caused because of improper and insufficient storage facility.

9. **Lack of Transport Facility** : In India, the means of transport are inadequate. Mukherjee is of the opinion that communication from the field to the village amd from the village to the mandi is often extremely poor and defective. There are bad roads which lead to loss during transportation and cause strain to the animals. The freight policy followed by railways in India is also not satisfactory. Railways do not have the facility for quick and safe transport of perishable products. This reduces the interest for intensive cultivation.

10. **Absence of Grading and Standardisation** : There is no standard grade for important commodities like rice and wheat in the whole country. There is low price for the ungraded mixed quality. The reputation of Indian agricultural producers in the foreign market is poor. Generally, producers cannot demand better price as the produces are not graded on the basis of quality. Apart from this, the accepted grades are not uniform throughout the country.

11. **Lack of Market Information** : Most of the farmers are illiterate and ignorant of the accurate prices ruling in the markets. They depend upon inaccurate information. Even if they are aware of the prices they are not comparable due to :

(a) Lack of grading and sandardisation acceptable to the whole country.

(b) Various agencies that supply inaccurate information.

(c) Variation in the price quotation given by local Governments and the Central Government.

(d) Lack of standardisation of weight and measures that leads to variation in weights and measures used in several markets.

Moreover, farmers have practically no contact with outside world. They depend on hearsay reports of village merchants who never reveal the correct price. The amount of village refraction differs widely from market to markets. As such, they sell their produces to local merchants, who suck the blood of the poor farmers, by offering low prices.

12. **Lack of Financial Facility** : Most of the financial needs of the farmers in India are met by village moneylenders, who in turn are financed by arhatiya and the indigenous bankers. There is also lack of financial facility against the security of goods, is not provided for. The rate of interest charged by the moneylenders is always high, 24%–40% and that too on compound interest basis. The money has to be paid along with interest at the time of harvest. The moneylenders come forward, purchase the produce by paying low prices, under the loan agreement, and again issue loans for further cultivation or for their family needs. The loan is advanced on the condition that the produce will be sold to them or through them. A cultivator is born in debt, lives in debt and finally dies in debt.

Distinction between manufactured goods marketing and agricultural goods marketing

Manufactured goods marketing	*Agricultural goods marketing*
1. Production is market oriented production *i.e.*, a manufacturer carefully attends to production and marketing.	1. Farmers produce the goods and middlemen have control on marketing
2. Manufacturers' reputation can indicate the product quality-branding.	2. Since no brand is there for these goods, manufacturers' reputation is nothing, but quality is the basis.
3. Marketing process is simple.	3. Marketing process is complicated.
4. Demand creation activities are important to stimulate sales.	4. Demand is regular and continuous; and needs no demand creation.
5. Middlemen cannot exploit manufacturers.	5. Middlemen can exploit farmers.
6. Manufacturers have full control over quality and quantity.	6. Producers have no countrol on quality and quantity.
7. Transportation and ware-housing costs are normal.	7. Transportation and warehousing costs are high.
8. Demand may be elastic and may not be continuous	8. Generally demand is inelastic, continuous and regular.
9. There is product differentiation and branding.	9. No product differentiation and branding.
10. Manufactured goods are not perishable.	10. Farm goods are perishable in nature.
11. Sales promotion and advertising are common.	11. Sales promotion and advertising are not common.

Remedies for Removal of Defects in Agricultural Marketing

It is very important to remove the defects in agricultural marketing. Our country is an agricultural country. An improved system of agricutural marketing will secure a larger portion of consumer's price to the cultivators.

The Royal Commission on Agriculture recommended the following measures for improving agricultural marketing :

(a) Improvement of transport facilities including rural communications.

(b) Lowering of railway freight rates and grant of other railway facilities.

(c) Establishment of Regulated Markets under State legislation.

(d) Standardisation of weights and measures.

(e) Adoption of measures to secure improved quality of produce by organisation among buyers and traders to guard against adulteration.

(f) Fixation of standards and grades of commodities.

(g) Promotion of co-operative sales.

(h) Holding of auction sales by Agricultural Departments to ensure increased price to the cultivators, who produce improved varieties.

(i) Carrying out of market surveys.

(j) Appointment of expert marketing officers on the staff of the Agricultural Department.

The defects of Agricultural Marketing can be removed by the following measures :

1. **Establishment of Regulated Market** : Many defects of agricultural marketing and malpractices of middlemen can be removed by the establishment of regulated markets. This can be studied in the following chapter.

2. **Use of Standard Weights and Measures** : Cultivators and purchasers are safeguarded against cheating by false or under weights by the use of standard weights and measures. The Planning Commission has recommended to adopt the metric system of weights and measures throughout the country. Metric system is simple, easy to learn and remember. It is easy to calculate and hence saves time. In April 1963, the use of metric capacity measures became compulsory throughout the country.

3. **Storage and Warehousing Facilities** : Increase in storage and warehousing facilities is necessary to remove the defects in agricultural marketing. "Warehousing is the protector of national wealth."

4. **Improvement in Transport Facilities** : For proper marketing of agricultural goods adequate and appropriate transport facilities are very important.

5. **Provision of Marketing Information** : The Central Marketing Committee made a marketing survey and reported, "There is at present, a surprising lack of co-ordination between different markets. Prices do not move in harmony even in markets which are not far from each other. We often find a market glutted with a product which is scarce in another, perhaps only a few miles off." The object of efficient market news is to achieve effective distribution and fair pricing of farm produce both for the producers and the consumers. The important media of market information are: private arrangements of traders, newspapers, Government Publications, regulated markets, radio and T.V. Co- operative societies also help in this respect.

6. **Development of Co-operative Marketing** : The defects of agricultural marketing are removed by the development of co-operative marketing. The Royal Commission on Agriculture is of the opinion that "group marketing must be more efficient than individuals, especially in conditions such as those which exist in India, where the individual producer is a small unit. "The farmer's income can be increased if he sells his produce for a better price. In this respect co- operative societies are very effective instruments in assisting the farmers.

QUESTIONS

1. What are the main defects of agricultural marketing in India and suggest measures for their improvements.
2. Mention a few characteristic features of agricultural products.
3. Distinguish between primary markets and terminal markets.
4. What are the problems of agricultural marketing in India ? (*B.Com., Chennai*)
5. Describe the major difficulties that have to be faced by Indian farmers in marketing their products.

CHAPTER 39

The Marketing of Services

- *Introduction*
- *Definition*
- *Reasons for Growth*
- *Characteristics of Services*
- *Intangibility*
- *Inseparability*
- *Heterogeneity*
- *Perishability*
- *Ownership*
- *Goods and Services Compared*
- *Marketing Mix in Service Marketing*
- *Product*
- *Price*
- *Promotion*
- *Place*
- *People*
- *Physical Evidence*
- *Process*
- *Service Quality*
- *Case Studies*
- *Questions*

Introduction

In today's global environment, the service sector occupies a key role in every economy. For instance, two-thirds of the economies in developed countries are service economies. In India, about half of the economy is now in the services sector and this sector continues to move very fast. Service marketing has increased important over the last decade with the advent of competition. A decade ago competition was relatively less important to firm in service business. However, competition has increased at an alarming rate in most service sectors. Today more than 60% of the most of the Western economies are in service sector. Service sector has been considered as post-industrial development. Thus, according to Daniel Bell, "If an industrial society is defined by the quantity of goods as marketing a standard of living, the post-industrial society is defined by the quality of life as measured by the services desirable and possible for every one."

Most of the marketing books are dominated with examples of business practices of manufacturing and product marketing companies. This is due to rapid application of marketing concepts to product marketing and domination of manufacturing and product marketing in business across the world. However, the service sector has come to stay as one of the key drivers of modern economic systems. While, consumer affluence is propelled by increase in income level, and generation of wealth across majority of industrialised nations, it has also contributed towards growth in services. The service economy contributed more than half of the Gross Domestic Product (GDP) in many developed nations. In developing countries, like India and China, services have emerged as a key sector fuelling growth and success for business houses. Many successful manufacturing companies, like Tata, Birla and Reliancé have entered in the service business.

Although we have seen recent growth in the service sector, the sector itself is not new. Even the so-called 'Industrial Revolution' can more accurately be described as a service revolution, for it could not have taken place without the development of crucial service sectors. For instance, without the development of railways, goods could not have been distributed from centralized factories to geographically dispersed consumers and many people would not have been able to get work. Service sectors emerged to meet the needs of manufacturing, including the needs of intermediaries who were essential for the distribution and transportation of manufacturers' goods to increasingly dispersed markets. Today, we continue to rely on services to exploit developments in the manufacturing sector.

A few examples (Service Sector)

Traditional Services

- Utilities – such as, electricity, water supply, etc.
- Transport Services – rail, road, air, water etc.
- Communication Services – Post and Telegraph, Telephone, Telecasting, Broadcasting, etc.
- Entertainment Services – Cinema, clubs, video games, Amusement parks, etc.
- Educational services
- Legal Services
- Accountancy Services
- Health, Family Welfare service
- Banking Services – Banks, Stock brokers etc.
- Distributive Trade – Wholesale, Retail, Dealers, Agents etc.

Modern Services

- Travel Agency
- Advertising
- Public Relations
- Market Research
- Courier Service
- Health Clubs

Latest and New Generation Services

- Business Services
- Recruitment Services
- Computer Training
- E-Commerce
- Internet
- Fax
- Computer Maintenance
- Management Consultancy
- Technical Consultancy
- Video Conferencing etc.

Definition

According to Kolter "A service is any act OR performance that one part can offer to another that is essentially intangible and does not result in the ownership of anything. Its production may or may not be tied to a physical product."

According to Berry and Parasuraman, "A service is an intangible product involving a dead, a performance or an effort that cannot be physically possessed."

According to Christian Gronroos, (a more comprehensive definition) "A service is an activity or series of activities of more or less intangible nature that normally, not necessarily, takes places in interactions between the customer and service employees and/or physical resources or goods and /or system of the service provider, which are provided as solutions to customer problems."

Service has a number of unique characteristics that make them so different from products. We discuss them in details, in this chapter.

Reasons for Growth:

Services as products are widely used today by ultimate consumers, businesses, and non-profit organizations and are usually provided through the application of human and/or mechanical efforts directed at people or objects. As economies grow, the demand for services keep on increasing in numerous areas such as in education, health, finance, travels and transportation, entertainment, advertising, fast food, maintenance and repairs, childcare and so on. The demand for services has become an indicator of the economic growth of a country. As economies shift from developing to the developed stage, services will show higher demand-shift for existing and newer services. The demand to services at the personal consumer level is related to increase in per capita income. When both husband and wife are employed, spare time available for domestic activities is limited, the earnings are more, therefore, they hire domestic service providers to make life easier. Considering the domestic scene, during the past 10 to 15 years, services have increasingly become more important in Indian economy and the competition in service industries is gaining momentum. Because of this reason, the role of services marketing is becoming more relevant in our fast developing economy.

Certain types of services have been grown at a high speed. For instance, Higher Education, Health-care, Financial Services etc. are the fastest growing sector, which are growing at a compound rate of 30–40%, annually, between 1995 and 2005. Money spending on hotels and restaurants, entertainments, etc. have grown at a compound rate of 20%. Services backed by technology, like vending machines, sandwich dispensing machines, computer-based records etc. have registered very good growth.

More and more women going to work had led to a greater demand for services like fast foods, creches, baby-sitting, domestic help etc. The advent and spread of complex products such as air-conditioners, cars, home computers, etc. have led to a greater demand for maintenance services. The growing pressure on time has resulted in greater demand for services like 'home-delivery'; people do want to waste their time visiting shops, standing in Qs and waiting for billing and packaging of products bought by them. They place the order over phone and the shop-keeper arranges home delivery. Demand for medical services have grown rapidly on account of increased health consciousness. There are strong indications that in India, services will grow even more rapidly in the coming years.

Characteristics of Services:

Services have a number of unique characteristics that make them so different from products, as said above. Some of the most commonly accepted characteristics are:

(A) Intangibility,
(B) Inseparability,
(C) Heterogeneity,
(D) Perishability
(E) Ownership

(A) Intangibility

Betore and after buying a physical product like, for instance, tooth paste, or soap or talcum powder, the costumer can see, feel, touch and smell and use it to check its effectiveness and quality. But, intangibility of services mean there are no such aspects and a service cannot be seen, touched, tasted or smelt. For instance, a lady going to a beauty-parlour for facial cannot know how would she look afterwards, unless the service is performed. The intangible characteristics of services which make them distinct from products are:

- A service cannot be touched or tasted;
- Precise standardisation is not possible;
- There is no ownership transfer;
- A service cannot be patented;
- There are no inventories of services;
- Production and consumption are inseparable;
- The customers ought to have faith in the person providing service;
- Services cannot be readily displayed or communicated.

The consumer experiences the reliability, expertise, attentiveness, and personal care of staff etc., only when a service has been bought and consumed. Physical products have certain benchmarks against which quality can be evaluated but any quality parameters can often be defined in the minds of consumers. Much depends on the expectations of customers.

Intangibility of services poses some problems for service marketers. A service marketer sells a promise to customers and customers are forced to place some degree of trust in the service provider to get the expected level of service performed. Marketers also face problem in communicating with customers about pure services because there is nothing tangible to put in ads or display in a store. Where tangible products are an important part of service offer, the problems may not be so challenging. The visible part gives customers some basis to assess quality. For instance, an auto service garage may have reassuring tangible cues to build customer confidence, but there is really nothing tangible to show in case of life insurance.

Pricing of services also poses problems. In case of tangible products there are raw material and labour cost to have some pricing base, in case of many services, determining the cost of producing and delivering the service is very difficult. For instance, to determine the price of producing and delivering a message or haircut is very difficult. Besides, marketers may face difficulty for justifying the prices of services to customers because customers cannot evaluate services before their actual consumption.

(B) Inseparability (Simultaneity)

In case of tangible products, their production and consumption are two separate activities and consumers are not a part of the production. Goods are generally produced in some central location at different times, stored and transported to those locations where there is existing or potential demand. In personal care services, the customer must be present during the entire production process, for instance, a patient has to be there while a surgeon is performing a surgery. The services of a machine can only be realised when the consumers interact with the machine, for instance, a bank ATM machine. Inseparability happens in both the cases when the service is provided by a human being or by a machine. Inseparability has a number of important marketing implications for services:

- Both, the production and consumption of services take place simultaneously.
- Service cannot be separated from the person providing it.
- Services, such as education, health-care, hairstyling etc. the service provider is the service in the eyes of consumer.

A plumber has to be physically present to provide the service. Similarly, the beautician has to be available to provide the service, that is beauty. That is, services cannot be separated from the service providers. Stay in a hotel room, or travel in a bus or train cannot be separated from the provider of such services. A carpenter or an electrician has to be physically present to provide the service. On the other hand, products can be manufactured in the factory today, stored for few days and sold when an order is received.

(C) Heterogenity (Variability)

Most manufactured goods can now be produced with high standards of consistency. But people-based services are usually suspectable to variability. In the case of services like airlines, legal advices, financial services etc, it is very difficult to keep the services consistent and standardised. The opportunity for pre-delivery inspection and rejection of products is possible in manufactured goods but it is impossible in case of services.

Individuals vary in their ability and performance. So, the quality of service depends upon the ability of individuals. The services are variable because of:

- Equipment-based services are less variable than human-based services.
- The inseparability of the service from the provider leads to some variability. Variability automatically enters in the picture depending on the person performing the service.
- The service delivery of the same employee can vary from customer to customer, day to day or even hour to hour in the same day.
- Variability is inherent in human-based services. Thus it is impossible to bring consistency in service.

The behaviour of persons varies from person to person because this is subject to emotion, stress and feelings of every individual. Persons show different behaviour in different situations. Every visit to the hair-dresser's shop gives you different experience because your behaviour and that of the hair-dresser is not the same in every visit. For example, the Tamil Nadu Hotels have good reputation as providers of high standard service. But the same group may have efficient or not so efficient employees in different locations, or on different days in the same premises and their services will vary. Since the human element is very much involved in providing and rendering services, variations are normal and standardization is very difficult to achieve. Even the same doctor who gave his complete attention during a patient's last visit may behave a little differently the next time.

(D) Perishability (Transience)

Manufactured goods can be stored for future consumption whereas services cannot be stored. It is possible for the manufacturer to store and manage inventory levels to suit different market situations and demand patterns. The services in contrast neither can be stored nor can be carried forward. If few seats are lying vacant in an aeroplane, they cannot be stored or carried forward for the next trip. Very few services face a constant pattern of demand through time. Most services show considerable demand fluctuations. If the services of a doctor or a lawyer are not used by needy customers, they cannot be stored up for future use. That is why hotels give discounts in off-season to bring in more customers or hire more staff when the peak season starts. The peculiar features are:

- A service has a high degree of perishability.
- Time element assumes unique importance.
- If a service is not used today, it is lost forever.
- Unutilised services are economic losses.
- Mass production is difficult.
- Services cannot be returned or resold.

A person unemployed, a ship loaded to only 60% of its capacity, i.e., 40% is empty, vacant rooms in Five Star hotels, a house unoccupied, credit facility not used, unsold seats in a cinema hall, etc. are illustrations representing perishable nature of service and business which are lost forever.

(E) Ownership

Service is intangible in nature. So, Physical possession of a service is not possible. Without physical possession, transfer of title is not possible. That is, in the case of a service, one may pay for its use but one never owns it. But when one buys any consumer or industrial products, one becomes legitimate owner. When a service is performed, now ownership is transferred from the seller to the buyer. The buyer is merely buying the right to a service process, such as the use of a car park or an Accountant's time. A service is purchased or hired for the benefit it provides to its user.

Goods and Services Compared:

Basis	Goods	Services
1. Entity	Tangible A Thing (Homogeneous)	Intangible An Activity/Process (Heterogeneous)
2. Storage	Possible	Not Possible
3. Title	Ownership is possible	No ownership
4. Pricing	Materials-based	Labour-based
5. Repairs	Possible	Not possible
6. Quality Control	Fixed	Variable Standard
7. Life	Longer	Stillborn
8. Channels	Longer Channels	Shorter Channels
9. Cost Allocation	Easier	Difficult
10. Replacement	Common	Rare
11. Quality	Standard	Varies with time and person

Marketing Mix in Service Marketing

A service marketer must develop strategies that satisfy needs and wants of customers. First of all the firm must determine the needs and wants of customers, it aims to satisfy and select a target market. We know services are intangible and cannot be defined in terms of their physical attributes. This poses difficulties for at least first time consumers to understand offerings and evaluate other service alternatives. The aim of marketing is to satisfy customer needs and a marketer strives to deliver a complete offer that may involves a combination of some tangible and intangible products.

The marketing mix concept has become widely accepted. The marketing mix is a specific combination of four strategies-product, price, place and promotion. They are designed to satisfy customers. The focus of marketing is to do such an excellent job of developing, pricing, promoting and distributing products to customers, that the products automatically sells itself.

For marketing of products, the four elements of marketing mix are product, price, promotion and place, popularly known as 4 Ps; which are used in a specific combination to arrive at the marketing strategy. In the case of services, there are three additional elements. These elements are people, physical evidence and process. Thus, marketing mix for services is comprised of 7 P's.

1. Product
2. Price

3. Promotion
4. Place
5. People
6. Physical evidence
7. Process

The first four marketing mix elements are the traditional 4 Ps that work well for tangible products. The additional three elements are important and require attention in service marketing. We shall now take up each of these, in brief:

1. Product (Service)

Physical products can be inspected and tried before buying, but in the case of services, inspection or trial are not possible. This is because products are tangible and services are intangible. This means the customers of services suffer higher perceived risk in their decision-making process. They do not know whether they have purchased the right service until they have used it and in some cases like medical service or car service, they cannot be sure whether they have received the right service long after they have consumed the service.

Planning the right marketing mix is a key skill for a service marketer. The effectiveness of planning the marketing mix depends as much on the ability to select the right target market as an devising a service offer, which will generate high level of customer satisfaction and corporate profit. The elements of marketing mix should be so planned that the customer has to believe that service offers added value to the customer's life. The most important issue in the service product is understanding what benefits and satisfaction the consumer is seeking from service. For instance, from the point of view of a restaurant's manager (a business-man), he simply provides food. But the customers coming to the restaurant may be seeking an outing, an atmosphere different from home, relaxation or entertainment. The marketing of services can be a success only if there is a match between the service product from the consumer's viewpoint and the supplier's viewpoint. To find this match, the service manager or marketer must have a good group of the following ideas:

(A) Service Benefits:

Service marketers must thoroughly understand the nature of the service. The service must satisfy consumer needs. The service marketer must be clear about the service benefits involved in the concerned case. Service benefit means the customer benefits resulting from the service. The services, which one offers in the market place, must have its origin in the benefits which the customers are seeking.

(B) Service Concept

It refers to the service benefits, which consumers seek from the service. Service marketers must be clear about the benefits, customers seek from the service. The whole service concept has to be based on the benefits, customers seek and which the marketer is willing to provide.

(C) Service Offer

Service offer means the bunch of benefits that is offered by the firm in the service. Again service offer is concerned with giving more specific and detailed shape to the basic concept notion. The service marketer has to decide what benefits should be put into the service package. For instance, if dance is selected as the service concept, the club might choose out of classical Indian dances or western dances. Type of dance, the quality and performance of dancers are the intangible aspects of the service offer. Physical infrastructure, for example, dancing hall, seating capacity, types of seats, air-conditioning, toilets etc. are the tangible aspects.

The decision has to stem from the customer service expectation, that is, what benefits do customers seek from the service? The share of the service offer stems from managerial decisions concerned with what service will be provided, when they will be provided, how they will be provided, where they will be provided, who will provide them, etc. The success of a service depends on how closely the service offer matches the service expectation.

(D) Service forms

Service elements are offered to the market-place in different forms. Service form is concerned with examining in detail the various options relating to each service element. In what form should the services be made available to the customers is another area of decision-making. Service form explains in what way or how the services are to be provided.

(E) Service Delivery system

This implies the mode of delivery of service. For instance, a cheque is used to withdraw money from the bank. Similarly, a club may use ticket, passes or membership cards for entry into the hall. The two main elements in a delivery system are the *people* and the *physical evidence*. For example, the competence and the public relations ability of a lawyer represents the people component while his office room, letter-head etc. are all elements of physical evidence

2. Price

In the case of products, the term 'price' is used for all kinds of goods, fruits, computers, etc. but in the case of services, different terms are used for different services.

Price Terminology for Selected Services

Service	Terminology
Education	Tuition
Legal Services	Fee
Transport Service	Fare
Insurance Service	Premium
Property use	Rent
Public Utilities	Tariff
Use of Money	Interest
Road Use	Toll
Hair-dressing	Charge
Municipal Services	Rate
Employee Services	Salary/wage

The perishability nature of service makes pricing of services difficult since fluctuation in demand cannot be met through inventory. Hence variation in price depending on time or season of demand or consumption becomes the natural strategy. Hotels offering the lower tariffs in off-season and telephone services providers offering lower tariffs for after peak hour calls are examples of how service markets can offset the perishable characteristics of service through a pricing strategy.

The higher the intangibility the more difficult it is to calculate cost and greater the tendency towards non-uniform services, such as fees of doctors, management consultants, lawyers etc. In such cases, the price may sometimes be settled through negotiation between the buyer and seller.

In services, such as dry cleaning, the tangible component is higher, and service provided is homogeneous. It is easier to calculate the cost on a unit basis and have a uniform pricing policy. In general, the more unique a service the greater the freedom to fix the price at any level.

The another characteristic to be kept in mind while determining prices is that in many services, the prices are subject to regulations, either by the Government or by trade associations. For example, bank charges, electricity charges, water rates, fares for rail and air transport etc. in India are controlled by the Government.

The various pricing tactics that may be used to sell services are:

(a) Differential or flexible pricing
(b) Discount Pricing
(c) Diversionary pricing
(d) Guarantee pricing
(e) High price maintenance pricing
(f) Loss leader pricing
(g) Offset pricing
(h) Discrete pricing
(f) Price lining

3. Promotion

Buying a service is a riskier proposition than buying a product. As a marketing manager you must design a promotion strategy, which helps the customer to overcome these constraints.

The guidelines, which can be kept in mind while promoting services, are as follows:

(*i*) Use simple and clear messages.
(*ii*) Stress on the benefits of the services.
(*iii*) Build on word of mouth communication by using testimony of actual users in advertisements.
(*iv*) Provide tangible clues to services by using well known personalities to help customers identify the service.
(*v*) Do not make exaggerated claims and promise only that which can be delivered.

The four methods used for promoting services, viz., Advertising, Personal Selling, Sales Promotion and Publicity, are the same as used in the promotion of products. They are explained below:

(*i*) **Advertising:**

Advertising is paid for publicity transmitted through a wide variety of media. It is non-personal and involves mass media communication of messages to a large number of people. Certain services such as entertainment (cinema, theatre etc.), passenger and freight transport (roadways, airlines etc.), hotel, tourism, travel, insurance etc. have been advertising heavily in newspapers, magazines, radio, TV etc. to promote greater usage and attract more customers. Professionals - doctors, dentists, lawyers, accountants etc. have a negative attitude towards advertising their services. These groups have traditionally relied on word of mouth for attracting new customers. But this situation is changing at present.

(*ii*) **Personal Selling:**

Services often require detailed explanations and continuing relationship or negotiations. Therefore, personal selling is the backbone of service marketing. Inseparability and heterogeneity create problems in personal selling. The following guidelines may be followed:

(*a*) The personal selling services should develop a personal relationship with the client.
(*b*) He must adopt a professional orientation so that he makes a strong impression of competency, honesty and sincerity on the customers.
(*c*) He should use indirect selling techniques as he is promoting an intangible.

(*d*) He has to build and maintain a favourable image by managing word of mouth publicity.

(*e*) He must customise the service offering by showing that he is selling a service package (service) not just a service.

(*iii*) **Sale Promotion:**

In service, sales promotion techniques are used to offset their perishability characteristic and to overcome the problem faced by customers in evaluating and judging the quality before making the purchase. Sales promotion techniques reduce the risk associated with the purchase. Sales promotion tools include:

- Money off coupons and spacial offers.
- Competitors' price promotion.
- Point of sale display
- Free gifts and other incentives.

(*iv*) **Publicity (Public relations)**

Publicity refers to communication about the services, which is not paid for by the organisation. Publicity is unpaid for exposure which is derived by getting coverage as a news of editorial item. The important point about publicity is that your choice of the newspapers, magazine or journal should be correct. The vehicle chosen must be credible and enjoy a reputation of being trustworthy. Wrong choice of media vehicle will result in adverse publicity.

4. Place (Distribution)

Distribution channels for services are more direct. There is no storage of services. Production and consumption are simultaneous and direct contact between customer and service provider is essential for most services. Growth for many service companies means opening new facilities in new locations, due to simultaneous production and consumption. The evaluation of locations is a critical skill for such services. The inseparability characteristic of services such as those of doctors, teachers, consultants, mechanics etc. poses a distribution constraint since they are able to serve only a limited, localised market. The other characteristic of services which affects the distribution strategy is the fixed location of services such as hospitals, restaurants, universities etc. which necessitates the customer to go to the service location.

Distribution element of service marketing mix is concerned with two main issues - accessibility and availability. Accessibility refers to the case and convenience with which a service can be purchased or used. Availability refers to the extent to which a service is obtainable or capable of being purchased or used. Both criteria must be met in order to achieve successful service marketing.

There are many services - hotels, airlines, LIC, etc. operate through middlemen (intermediaries).

The services for intermediaries

Service	Middlemen/Intermediaries
Hotels	Travel agents, tour operators
Airlines	Travel agents, hotels
Insurance	Agents
Shares	Stock brokers
Employment	Employment agencies
Financial services	Banks, financial institutions
Products	Wholesalers, stockists, retailers

5. People

People constitute an important dimension in the management of services in their role both as performers of service and as customers. People as performers of service are important because, a customer sees a company through its employees. The employees represent the first line of contact with the customer. They must, therefore, be well informed and provide the kind of service that wins customers approval. The firm must recognise that each employee is a salesman for the company's service.

In the first place, in services, quality depends on people. The service customer rarely distinguishes or separate the service from the person who performs it. Secondly, services are also highly people intensive unlike physical products, which are material intensive. Thirdly, while in case of physical products, a bad product can be taken back or replaced, a bad service cannot be taken back or replaced. Therefore, it has to be performed right the first time and every time.

People are the most vital element of the marketing mix. For many people-intensive businesses, employees are business for them. If quality people leave the organisation, the entity and quality of the service is affected, dampening company's overall image. Human resource management is so central to the activities of the organisation that it cannot be separated as a separate activity.

For instance, the waiter's behaviour can win or loose customers for a restaurant. The service personnel must be well informed and must provide satisfaction to customers. Careful selection and training, neat and consistent appearance of service personnel are necessary. In addition, rules and norms can be laid down to ensure consistent behaviour. Wherever possible automation and computerisation should be used to reduce the need for personal contact.

Customers are actively involved in services marketing. Complete satisfaction should be ensured because one customer influences others, leading to a chain reaction. The physical appearance of the company, the behaviour of service staff, the delivery of the service etc. all should be turned into a desirable and composite package.

6. Physical Evidence

Cleanliness in a doctor's clinic, the exterior appearance and interior decor of a restaurant, the comfort of the seating arrangement in a cinema hall, adequate facility for personal needs at the airport etc. all contribute towards the image of the service (organisation) as perceived by the customer. The common element in these is that they are all physical, tangible and controllable aspects of a service organisation. They constitute the physical evidence of the service. The physical evidence may be two types - *Peripheral evidence and Essential evidence.*

Peripheral evidence is actually possessed as a part of the purchase of service but by itself is of no value. An airline ticket, cheque book or receipt for a confirmed reservation in a hotel are examples of peripheral evidence. A cheque book is of value only if you have money in the bank; but without that it is of no significance. In a hotel you may find matchbox, pen, writing pad, flowers etc., which you may take away.

Whereas peripheral evidence is possessed and taken away by the customers, the essential evidence cannot be possessed by the customer; the building, design, interior layout and decor etc. of the organisations are constituents of the essential evidence.

7. Process

Process refers to the system by which the customer receives delivery of the services. For example, in a fast food restaurant the process consists of buying coupons at one counter and packing the food against coupons at another counter. In service, the process mainly involves adding value or utility for customers.

The three kinds of delivery processes that are applicable in the case of service products are *line operations, Job shop operations and intermittent operations.*

In line operations, the customer moves through a logically arranged operations in a sequence. Self-service stores and restaurants use this process. This type of delivery process is appropriated when the service is fairly standardised and the customer's requirements is of a routine nature.

In job-shop process, a combination of services using different sequences is provided. For example, different patients need different services, for examples, X-ray, medicines, surgery etc. in a hospital. In a service that is rarely repeated intermittent operations are useful. For example, each advertisement campaign requires a unique set of inputs in advertising agencies.

Service Quality

In service marketing, managing service quality is very important. Customers form service expectations from many services, such as past experiences, word of mouth, and advertising. Generally customers compare the *perceived service* with the *expected service*. If the perceived service falls below the expected service, customers are disappointed. If the *perceived service* meets or exceeds their expectations, customers will continue to use the same service provider. Most of the successful service providers add benefits to their offering that not only satisfy customers but surprise and delight them. Delighting customers involves exceeding expectations.

Leading service and consumer durable companies measure the gap between the customer's service expectations against the perceived services as a routine feedback process. Zaithaml, Parasuraman and Berry developed a model which suggest that customers become dissatisfied when their perceptions about service performance don't match their expectations and the five gaps that can lead to customer dissatisfaction. The gaps are:

Gap 1 : The service provider does not know what customers expect.

Gap 2 : The wrong service quality standards are set.

Gap 3 : Standards are not met (Service performance gap).

Gap 4 : What is delivered does not equal what was promissed.

Gap 5 : This gap occurs when the consumer misperceives the service quality.

The evidence of poor service quality, in everyday life, for examples, Trains are late; flights are delayed, telephone faults remain unattended; sales-people are rude; water taps go dry; etc. Based on this service quality, the researchers identified the following five determinants of service quality.

(1) **Reliability** : The ability to perform the promised service dependably and accurately.

(2) **Responsiveness** : The willingness to help customers and to provide prompt service.

(3) **Assurance** : The knowledge and courtesy of employees and their ability to convery trust and confidence.

(4) **Empathy** : The provision of caring, individualised attention to customers.

(5) **Tangibles** : The appearance of physical facilities, equipment, personnel and communication materials.

Questions

1. Why has the services sector grown rapidly in recent years? *(B.Com Kerala)*
2. Define services and distinguish between services and product. *(B.Com. MS)*
3. Explain the distinguishing characteristics of services. What problems these characteristics present to marketers? *(M.Com. Madras)*
4. "Services marketing requires an extended marketing Mix". Explain *(MA. MS)*

5. Discuss the elements of marketing mix for services. (*B.Com. Kerala*)
6. Explain the role of promotion in services marketing. (*B.Com. Delhi*)
7. What is meant by services? How services are important in the present century? (*MA. Agra*)
8. What are the important characteristics of services? How they are different from the products? (*BA, Andhra*)
9. What are services? How services can be defined? What are the characteristics of services? (*M.Com. Delhi*)
10. Explain in brief the various kinds of services. (*B.Com. Mumbai*)
11. Discuss the role of promotion in services marketing. (*B.Com. MS*)
12. How for advertising and sales promotion are important in the marketing of services? (*MA. Delhi*)
13. Discuss the special characteristics of service marketing. (*B.Com. Calicut*)
14. Explain the factors contributing to the growth of service sectors.
15. How do services differ from tangible products?
16. What are the major elements of service quality?
17. How do consumers judge service quality? What a service marketer should do to ensure service quality?

CHAPTER 40

Regulated Markets

- *Introduction*
- *Growth and Development of Regulated Market*
- *Organisation of Regulated Markets*
- *Constitution of Markets Committee*
- *Finance of Market Committee*
- *Functions of Market Committee*
- *Advantage of Regulated Markets*

40.1 INTRODUCTION

The producer is forced to sell his produce in the local or central market at any price due to his indebtedness. In these markets there are many malpractices, like short weights, unjust deductions, unreasonably high rates of commission, adulteration of produce etc. These and other market charges prevailing in these markets reduce the producer's income. It is disadvantageous both to the producer and the seller. In 1928 the Royal Commission on Agriculture observed that these could only be removed by the establishment of regulated markets. Regulated markets have been developed to improve the markets, to increase the need of fair competitive conditions and of strong bargaining powers of farmers. The main object is to regulate sale and purchase of the agricultural products and create conditions for a fair competition.

40.2 GROWTH AND DEVELOPMENT OF REGULATED MARKETS

The first attempt was the Cotton and Grains Markets Law enacted in Berar in 1897. It was passed, "to make available supplies of pure cotton at reasonable price to the textile mills at Manchester." This law provided a representative committee which controlled the markets and bazaars.

In 1917, the Indian Cotton Committee was set up. It recommended the regulation of cotton market on the lines of Berar markets.

The next Act was in 1927, *i.e.*, the Bombay Cotton Markets Act. The produces of the farmers were sold to the trader-lender in the village, of course at a price which was lower than the market rate. In other cases, the produces passed through many middlemen; but the major portion of the price paid by purchasers went to the cultivator. So the Government notified cotton markets and appointed committees to manage the markets.

In 1929-1930, the Bombay Provincial Banking Enquiry Committee was appointed to point out the defects in the working of the traditional markets. The Hyderabad Agricultural Markets Act was passed in 1930. In 1935 the Central Provinces Agricultural Produce Act was passed. The Berar Act was modified in 1932-35 by the Central Provinces Cotton Markets Act. The Bombay Agricultural Produce Market Act of 1939 replaced the Bombay Act.

In 1933, the Madras Commercial Crops Marketing Act was passed and it applied to cotton, groundnuts and tobacco, and in 1948 it was extended to other crops. Bombay, Madras, Hyderabad, Gwalior and Baroda also passed similar Act. The total number of regulated markets increased after the passing of these Acts in our country. In 1939 it was 122; in 1950-51 it was 283; in 1955-56 it was 450 ; in 1960-61 it was 700 and it was 1012 in 1965-66. At the end of the third five-year plan it was 1600. In 1974 there were 3016 regulated markets in the country.

Market regulation is enacted by the State Governments, assisted by Central Directorate of Marketing and Inspection. The Central Directorate gives financial assistance for developing regulated markets in the following areas :

(a) Command areas.

(b) Economically backward areas.

(c) Areas producing commercial crops like jute, cotton and tobacco. In 1973-74 Rs. 31.75 lakhs was granted.

Foodgrains are regulated in all the states except Andhra and Kerala. Only a few markets cover agricultural products like fruits and vegetables, livestocks and their products.

When legislation is applied to a particular cash market, it is called a regulated market. A regulated market works under standard rules and regulations. It has an organised character in all respects. A market committee is in charge of management and operations of a regulated markets.

P.R. Dubhashi in his book 'Agricultural Marketing — Theme of the Seventies' says, "The regulated market is not only a place where certain legal conditions are enforced, it is also a centre which provides a package of facilities to agricultural marketing and an economic centre where adequate demand is built up for the sale of agricultural commodities which can bring satisfactory return to the cultivator. It would be possible to develop the regulated markets not only for marketing agriculture commodities, but also for providing numerous facilities to meet the needs of agricultural through the supply of fertilisers, seeds, pesticides and agriculturists machinery." The Governments are taking concerted action to bring about all round development in the field of marketing .

In a planned economic development programme the marketing and exchange of goods are important in equalising the supply and demand. In exchange function, agricultural products pose great troubles and difficulties. The need for a regulated market is felt to ensure fairness in transactions, free competition and regulation of unfair malpractices.

Various legislations have failed to maintain uniform rules and procedures throughout India. There is absence of uniformity in the methods and procedures of the Act, and it varies from state to state and from region to region within the same state. There is variation in area and enforcement of law, definition of agricultural produce, the bye-laws of the constitution, composition of market committees, licence fees, market rates, trade practices, method of sale price quotation. For example, in Tamil Nadu the cess is payable by the buyers, while in Karnataka, Andhra and Maharashtra, the producers bear them. Thus the Act lacks uniformity.

Regulated market is a wholesale market, where dealing of buying and selling are regulated or controlled by the state government through a 'Markets Committee'. This committee consists of representatives of growers, traders, local bodies, marketing co-operative and the government. The Agricultural Produce Marketing Act governs the establishment and working of regulated markets in the prescribed area. The committee is responsible to ensure fair marketing practices.

40.3 ORGANISATION OF REGULATED MARKETS

The object of regulated markets is to safeguard the interest of the producers-sellers and raise the standard of the local markets. The first exchange of goods takes place in the local markets. In each regulated market, committees are established. These committees consist of representatives of the growers, traders, local bodies, sellers, sellers' co-operative shops and the state government nominees. In these committees majority of representatives are producers.

40.4 CONSTITUTION OF MARKETS COMMITTEE

The seminar on regulated markets organised by the Ministry of Food and Agriculture in January 1959 was of the view that :

1. The committee should not be too small or too wide. The strength of the committee must accommodate the various interests in proper proportion.
2. The number of committee members should be between 12 and 18 depending on the size of the market and other considerations.
3. 50% of the seats go to the growers, as their interest must be predominant in the committee.
4. For traders the seat shall be 25% at the maximum .
5. The remaining seats go to the co-operative marketing societies, the local bodies and government nominees. One seat is for warehousing corporations.

Indirect election is conducted to elect growers' representatives. It is conducted through the grower-members of the panchayats and other registered growers associations and agricultural co-operatives.

The market committee frames and administers the rules and laws. All business transactions are conducted within the market area under those rules and laws. The market committee fixes the charges, allowances and deduction that can be levied. It looks after the weights and measures. Licensed weighmen do all weighing.

In regulated markets, dealers fix the price and they submit their accounts periodically to the market committee. The dispute sub-committee looks after the disputes, if any, arising between the sellers and traders.

40.5 FINANCE OF MARKET COMMITTEE

The marketing committee gets its finance from the borrowed funds (government loans), government subsidies and grants and other sources including fines, market fees and licence fees etc. Property incomes are rent on godowns, stalls, canteens, interests on government securities etc., sale of grass grown on the yards, sale of manures, fees like registration fee, licence transfer fee, copying fees, certification fee, dispute fee, water and weighment charges etc.

The fund is used for :

1. Maintenance and improvement of the market and its building
2. Maintenance of standard weights and measures
3. Salary and pension of the staff
4. Payment of interest on loans
5. Collection of market information
6. Propaganda for agricultural improvement

40.6 FUNCTIONS OF MARKET COMMITTEE

1. Maintaining and management of market.
2. Enforcing the rules and bye-laws of the Act in the market area.
3. Granting licence on the purchase and sale of agricultural produce regulated by it.
4. Granting, renewing, suspending and cancelling a general or special finance for purchase and sale of regulated agricultural produce.
5. Providing all facilities in the market.
6. Fee is charged on the produce which is purchased and sold in the market and it is collected by agents.
7. It manages the income, incurs expenditure and invests the surplus funds.
8. It prepares the budget.

9. It maintains a register of licensed traders and general commission agents and records the fees collected.
10. It prescribes the market charges for different market functions.
11. It prevents adulteration of agricultural produce in the market area.
12. It promotes, grades and standardises the agricultural produce.
13. It collects and maintains the price list of regulated agricultural produce and supplies it to the government when required.
14. It appoints the secretary of the committee.
15. It directs and guides the persons who use the market.
16. It settles disputes, if any, in the course of transactions.
17. It acts as clearing house market information—collection and distribution of essential data on markets.
18. It facilitates smooth transfer of goods and orderly transactions.
19. It facilitates the producers to get best possible price for their produce.
20. It provides proper storage facility.
21. It prevents adulteration in the produces.

40.7 ADVANTAGES OF REGULATED MARKETS

1. **Reduction in Market Charges** (paid by the producer-seller) : The reduction is between 28% and 69% in various markets. There is reduction in charges of commission , weighing fee, hamali, brokerage, charity etc. The net saving of producer-seller is about 3% to 5% of the selling produce.

2. **Increase in the Number of Sellers** : More sellers bring their produce to these markets. As far as rice and wheat are concerned, the producers assembling markets are about 73% in the Punjab, 80% in Karanataka, 74% in Madhya Pradesh and 90% in Andhra.

3. **Changes in the Socialistic Behaviour** : There is a change in the socialistic behaviour of the influential, powerful and economically well off trading sections towards the illiterate, ignorant, indebted and economically backward cultivators. They divert their attention on fair trading, and responsibilities are vested with the licensed traders and commission agents of the market committee.

4. **Clearly Defined and Specified Market Charges** : There is reduction in excessive charges, and prohibition in unwarranted charges.

5. **Assurances of Fair Dealings** : There are regulated market charges, and market functions are controlled in order to reduce the marketing costs.

6. **Correct Weighing** : Periodical verifications and inspections of scales and weights assure correct weighing of their produce. Standard weights and measures are used in the regulated markets *i.e.*, the metric system.

7. **Settlement of Disputes** : A machinery is set up for the settlement of disputes between traders and sellers. It creates good relation between the sellers and buyers by arranging settlement of disputes regarding quality, weighing and deduction, preventing litigation etc.

8. **Market News Service :** Current market news are available to the sellers. Price conditions in various markets are exhibited on the notice board. Newspapers and radio also give the market price. The ruling price are announced through loud-speakers in many markets.

9. There is perfect competition. Agricultural produces are sold by open methods, benefiting the producers.

10. Grading and storing facilities are provided in many regulated markets. Agmark standards, grade specification are framed by an expert committee.

11. Market committees have provided various amenities in the market yards. They are :
    (a) shed for the sale of produce.
    (b) car parking places.
    (c) drinking water facilities for human being and cattle .
    (d) rest houses, canteens, for farmers.

12. Propaganda is made for agricultural improvements such as, use of good seed, fertilisers, pesticides etc. Regulated markets undertake improved methods of cultivation, use of machinery in farming etc.

13. The producer can receive prompt payment of price—a fair price from the buyer.

14. Producers are usually unorganised. They are few, scattered and ill-informed about the market condition. Regulated market helps the producers in these matters. Producers' interest is protected and they get a fair deal in marketing their produce.

15. There is the availability of reliable statistics regarding the arrivals, stocks, price etc.

16. Elimination of unwanted middlemen is possible only by regulated markets.

CHAPTER

41

Organised Markets

- *Demerits of Unorganised Market*
- *Organised Market*
- *Meaning*
- *Characteristics*
- *Commodity Exchang*
- *Commodity Exchange Vs. Stock Exchange*
- *Importance*
- *Function*
- *Services*
- *Organisation*
- *Membership*
- *Management*
- *Future Contract*
- *Types*
- *Kind*
- *Advantages*
- *Hedging*
- *Hedging Vs. Speculation*
- *Questions*

There are many markets in India. Most of the markets of our country are unorganised or unregulated. In an unorganised market justice cannot be expected. One can witness the following demerits in unorganised markets:

1. There is no justice to buyers and sellers.
2. Consumers have to pay exorbitant price for goods.
3. Dealings are not subject to any code of rules.
4. Most of the goods are ungraded and unbranded.
5. Producers may not get fair price for their produces.
6. The functionaries are not licensed.
7. There is no machinery for settlement of disputes.
8. Legal status is lacking.
9. Producers are easily cheated by middlemen.
10. Scales and weights are manipulated.
11. Brokers approached by the seller, work for the benefit of the buyer-merchant.
12. Produces are heavily adulterated.
13. Wide price fluctuations are found.
14. Artificial scarcity of goods is created.
15. Malpractices are found common.
16. Dealings between agent of seller and agent of buyer are unknown to the ignorant seller.
17. Sellers are forced to sell in unfavourable condition.
18. There is multiplicity of market charges.
19. Middlemen and buyers dominate the market.
20. Fraudulent and unscrupulous practices prevail in the market.

The buyer-merchants are highly business-minded. The middlemen employed also work for and on behalf of the buyer. The poor cultivators, who bring their produces to the markets, are made fools by the brokers. The appearance of brokers or agents changes the market mechanisms from bad to worse and complicated. In order to improve the marketing system of agricultural commodities, the above-mentioned defects should be removed. In marketing certain manufactured goods and industrial raw materials of agricultural origin, certain specialised institutions have come up with functionaries and techniques of their own. The functions of such institutions are different from other marketing institutions. These specialised institutions are known as organised markets.

Meaning

An organised market represents a public market mechanism or organisation consisting of buyers, sellers, producers, processors, dealers etc., dealing in one or more commodities or securities which constitute the articles of trade in the market. An organised market is a private voluntary association, consisting of dealers and professional traders of one or more commodities or securities. Members meet, conduct buying and selling operations on the trading floor on behalf of their clients. The workings of the organised market are governed by the bye-laws of the market.

Regulated market is an organised wholesale or central market regulated and controlled by the State Government through a marketing Committee; whereas the transactions in an organised market are governed by some standard procedure. The rules are framed by voluntary associations.

Characteristics of Organised Markets

1. It is a convenient central meeting place for buyers and sellers.
2. It facilitates establishing a close and continuous interaction between demand and supply.
3. Usually authority governs all business by the established rules and regulations.
4. The exchange authority is a self-disciplined, self-administered and self-regulated autonomous body. Now there is legislation to control these organised markets.
5. In organised markets there is free competition and perfect freedom between buyers and sellers.
6. Here sensitive price registering device is used.
7. Each forward market has a clearing house organisation. It clears all dealings and their settlement. It guarantees payment of dues. It takes and gives the commodity or securities during the settlement period.
8. Margin system is common in forward dealings.
9. Organised market provides market information.
10. It acts as a price barometer. Perfect market requirements are fulfilled by it.
11. Speculative trading is important, which is necessary in an organised market.

These organised markets are of two types viz., organised commodity markets and organised stock markets. These are popularly known as Commodity Exchanges and Stock Exchanges.

COMMODITY EXCHANGE

A commodity exchange is an organised market that functions under established rules and regulations, a market meant for the purchase and sale of commodities. It is an organised and permanent place, where persons meet for the purpose of doing business in a commodity, which may be a natural product of the soil, a mining product or manufactured articles. It is set up by an association of dealers under definite rules and bye-laws.

Converse, Huegy and Mitchell define Commodity Exchange as, ''An organisation of dealers in certain commodities which provides marketplace where the members meet at definite times and transact business under the rules laid down by the organisation.''

Pyle has defined, ''Commodity exchanges are specialised, organised markets which provide a place where their members buy and sell commodities or contract for future delivery under established rules and regulations.''

Thus, a commodity exchange is an organised and permanent place, where members transact in buying and selling of commodities, both spot or future transactions. The transactions are according to rules and regulations laid down by the exchange. Spot transaction implies immediate delivery of goods against payment, while future contract refers to the payment and delivery at a future date.

Commodity Exchange and Produce Exchange

There is a difference between the two terms. The produce exchange deals in only those commodities which are used as raw materials, as agricultural goods and certain minerals and lowest products. The commodity exchange, is a broader term, dealing in agricultural goods, minerals and manufactured goods. e.g., agricultural products like wheat, jute cotton, tea, oilseeds etc., mining products like gold, copper, iron ore etc., and manufactured products like textiles, oil, sugar, jute products etc. A commodity exchange may be regarded as a specialised wholesale market, dealing in a particular commodity or a group of commodities. There is a difference between a wholesale market and commodity exchange. The goods intended for sale are physically brought to the wholesale market, but dealings in commodity exchange are on the basis of grades. In the wholesale market, parties are present to settle the transactions whereas, in commodity exchange, contracts for sale or purchase are made through brokers. The protection against risk of price changes is provided through mechanism of future trading and hedging in commodity exchanges, but these provisions are entirely absent in wholesale market.

Importance

A commodity exchange does not buy or sell commodities. It facilitates the market activities of its members. It provides a ready and continuous market for the commodities. Because of the commodity exchange, commodities worth crores of rupees are shifted from the place of production to the place of consumption. It serves as a barometer, indicating the price changes. The hedging operations are carried on to get protection by the producers or traders from price fluctuations. Price changes affect every commodity. The trader can transfer the risk of price fluctuation to professional speculators. The cultivators and growers of crops find a ready and continuous market. The operators in a commodity exchange serve as professional risk bearers and insurers. The market values of commodities are determined by the forces of supply and demand.

Functions

1. Commodity exchange provides a convenient place, where members can meet and transact business in commodities, according to established rules and regulations. It facilitates in getting together of interested parties, settling their intents by safeguarding the interest of interested parties.

2. Marketing risks could be shifted or minimised through the commodity exchanges–hedging transactions.

3. It collects and disseminates market information–price, current consumption, supply, demand etc., of commodities collected by the exchange and made available to the public. These data are useful to the dealers to guess and conclude contracts of selling or buying, with confidence and certainty.

4. Arbitration committee of the commodity exchange brings about quick, cheaper and amicable settlement in case of disputes and avoids unwanted litigation. Disputes may arise in respect of price, quality, weighing, quantity etc., and are settled under the established rules and regulations of exchanges.

5. It establishes and maintains grades and standards. This facilitates trade on sound lines. Future contracts can be entered into and settled only by means of grades, which facilitate satisfactory price fixing of commodities.

6. The commodity exchange, situated in a central place, has facility in gathering information from other markets regarding price, supply and demand, and then the price is fixed.

Services

1. Commodity exchange provides a ready and continuous market for both the producers and consumers. Forecasting is one of the main functions of successful business management, facilitated by the commodity exchanges.

2. The commodities dealt in exchanges are standarised and graded. They are acceptable within the nation and outside the nation, and help the producers and traders to enjoy credit facilities, specially from banks.

3. Hedging transactions in exchanges help the producers and traders reduce or eliminate the risk shocking fluctuations arising from price changes.

4. The malpractices, we come across generally in the unorganised markets, have no place in commodity exchanges. Elimination of malpractices enables in crystallising market value.

5. Speculation is another way that helps to shift risks to the shoulders of others and at the same time earn profit.

Commodities Suitable for Dealings in a Commodity Exchange

All types of commodities cannot be dealt in a commodity exchange. Only commodities which fulfil the following conditions will be allowed to trade in a commodity exchange.

1. **Homogeneity :** A commodity is said to be homogeneous when the customers do not have changes of choice. Every unit is a perfect substitute for another. It means all units of any lot of the product must be identical in quality, size, colour, shape, price, appearance etc. For future trading, homogeneity is the backbone and is a pre-condition for effecting exchanges.

2. **Amenable to Grading :** Agricultural products are natural products. The commodities must be capable of being graded according to certain pre-determined standards. Unless they are graded, they cannot be dealt in the commodity exchange. Thus commodities should possess the characteristics of gradation.

3. **Durability :** The goods must be durable for a certain period–more than a year. Perishable commodities are not dealt with. However, cold storage system facilitates even the perishable items to be dealt in a commodity exchange.

4. **Price Fluctuations :** The commodity must also be one with ample fluctuations in price, *i.e.*, there should be frequent fluctuations in the prices of commodities. Thus speculators get interest to speculate in the commodities at the exchange.

5. **Wider Demand and Supply :** Certain commodities have local demand and supply, whereas some enjoy a national demand and supply while some enjoy international supply and demand. The demand for the products must also permit frequent dealings. Continuous dealings by large volume of trading are facilitated by commodities, which have market prestige. That is, for a continuous market, the commodities must have good demand.

6. **Free Flow of Goods :** The supplies and prices of commodities should not be controlled by government or private agency. There must be a free flow of goods to the market. The commodities have a free play on the position of supply and demand. Apart from large quantities the commodities must be natural and free-movement is unrestricted.

7. **Demand and Supply Must Be Uncertain :** Speculation depends on uncertainty factor and this is an inducement to speculators to make forward contract. Uncertainty of supply and demand is the life blood of speculators.

8. **Market Information :** There must be availability of getting information relating to products–supply, demand, price etc.

9. **Commodity Must Be Storable :** The commodities to be deat in the commodity exchange must be suitable to be stored. This factor enables the trader to sell the commodities at a future date as and when, there appears a price change.

10. **Seasonal Supply :** The commodity must be of such a type that it should not be possible to adjust its supply easily and quickly according to demand fluctuations. This element is esential for future transaction.

Organisation

Commodity exchanges in India are known as 'recognised association.' It is generally governed by the rules and regulations of the Forward Contracts (Regulation) Act, 1952 . All the commodity exchanges working in India are controlled by this Act. It is a practice throughout the world to organise commodity exchanges as the bodies of corporate managements. In India, commodity exchanges have been established mainly for transacting ''future dealings.'' However, we may find some commodity exchanges in India, transacting spot dealings. The commodity exchanges are registered as companies under the Indian Companies Act, 1956. They are of two types—profit sharing exchanges and non-profit sharing exchanges.

Membership

One can become a member of a produce exchange by purchasing its share and paying the prescribed fees of the association. The main requirement is that one must be a man of character and of good financial standing. The Committee examines the applicant and the sponsors. The sponsors are the members of the exchange and two members endorse the application for membership. If the Committee is satisfied with the applicant, he is elected. On his election, he is bound to abide by the rules and regulations of the commodity exchange. The members are classified into two classes—Trading Members and Non-Trading Members. Trading members are interested in 'future' trading on the exchange and non-trading members are not interested in the operation of future transactions on the exchange. Only members are allowed to transact business on the exchange. Members can do trading directly or through brokers, who are called floor operators. The brokers must be registered by the association and do trading only in the name of the members.

Management

The management of exchanges is controlled similar to that of the joint-stock exchanges. Most of the commodity exchanges are registered as companies under the Companies Act. The management of the association is generally classified into two sections—clearing section and administrative section.

The clearing section of the association is headed by a supervisor, specially meant for supervising the registration of future contracts, receipt of contract forms and 'slips' from brokers, receipts of deposit money and payment of profit to trading members. The administrative section looks after the functions relating to correspondence, filing, keeping the accounts, keeping the minutes of various meetings etc.

Generally, the power of management is invested in the Board of Directors, with a president, vice-president, secretary, treasurer and other officer-bearers elected. The composition of Board of Directors varies from exchange to exchange.

In order to assist the Board of Directors there are various committees to look after day to day affairs :

(a) **Floor Committee :** Business takes place in a hall called trading hall or floor. Brokers assemble at the fixed time. To enforce the rules of the exchange a floor committee is appointed.

(b) **Quotation Committee :** This committee settles disputes arising out of Quotation price.

(c) **Arbitration Committee :** This is a powerful committee. It settles the disputes among the members. The decision of this committee shall be binding on members and brokers.

(d) **Clearing House Committee :** This committee helps the smooth functioning of clearing works of innumerable transactions.

(f) **Bye-Law Committee :** This committee frames, alters and amends the rules and regulations of the exchange.

(g) **Finance Committee :** This committee looks after financial matters.

(h) **Commission Committee :** This committee settles the disputes relating to commission to brokers.

Transactions on Commodity Exchange

Commodity Exchange

- Cash Contract (Cash Market)
  - Spot Contract
  - Forward Contract
- Future Contract Exchange Market
  - Speculation
    - Waida
    - Option
    - Straddle
    - Badla
  - Hedging

Generally the function of commodity exchange consists of buying and selling of commodities on the basis of the rules of the exchange. There are two parties to the contracts—seller and buyer. In a commodity exchange, a broker, who is nominated by a seller or a buyer, completes the transactions on behalf of both the parties. On the fixed date, the transaction takes place.

The transactions that are traded on the commodity exchanges are of two types—Cash Contracts and Future Contracts. Cash Contracts involve payment of the price and delivery of the goods immediately or within a short period. This Cash Contract is also known as physical contract where actual delivery of goods is to take place in the transaction. Cash contracts are classified into two—spot contract and forward contract. In spot contracts, the payment and delivery of goods take place immediately, *i.e.*, on the spot. This is just like ordinary sale, where no problems arise. In forward contracts, there may be postponement of payment of price or of delivery of goods by a short period; sometimes both the payment of price as well as delivery of goods is postponed to a future date. But the prices are fixed on the date of the transaction. This type of contract, need not necessarily be dealt within exchange, this can well be fulfilled even outside.

FUTURE CONTRACTS

The word ''future contract'' implies that it is a contract to be fulfilled at a future date . In Cash Contracts payment for goods and delivery of goods take place immediately or after some fixed period. In a future contract, there is an agreement between the paties to buy and sell a particular commodity and take delivery of the goods on a future date. The transaction is based on rules of the commodity exchange. No actual commodity ever changes hands unless the contract falls due. Prof. Emery defines future contract as, ''A contract for the future delivery of some commodity without reference to specific lots made under the rules of some commercial body; in a set form by which the conditions, as the unit of amount, the quality, and the time of delivery are stereotyped and only the determination of the total amount and the price is left open to the contracting parties.''

G.W. Hoffman in his book 'Future Trading upon organised Commodity Markets' defines a future contract as, ''An agreement to buy or sell, in accordance with laws and rules of the exchanges, a definite quantity of a commodity at an agreed price at a future date being entered into for the purpose of speculating on or hedging against price changes and being usually closed out by another offsetting future trade.''

Characteristics of Future Contracts

On the basis of the definitions stated above, the following are essential characteristics of a future contact :

1. It is a contract for the sale of a pre-determined quantity, of a particular grade, at a fixed price at a future date.
2. The rules of the commodity exchange are strictly followed in the contract.
3. Such contracts are entered into only in the 'ring'or 'pit' of the commodity exchanges. The trading ring or pit refers to a specific place in the premises of the exchange.
4. A specified amount, as a percentage of contract price known as 'margin monyey' has to be deposited by the parties; it is a form of insurance and protects the seller and buyer, when contracts are not executed.
5. Only the members are allowed to enter into such dealings.
6. Settlement of the contracts takes place only during the months, adopted by the exchange.
7. If no time is mentioned in the contract, the seller can settle on any day during the trading exchange.
8. A basic contracts means the commodity to be delivered under it may be either of the contract grade or some other grade at the seller's option.
9. Future contracts are to be made only in multiples of trading units, such as 100 quintals or as stated in the rules of exchange.
10 Disputes, if any, are to be settled by arbitration machinery of the exchange.

Distinction between Forward Contract and Future Contract

Forward Contract	*Future Contract*
1. It is meant for actual sales and purchase of commodities. It means and aims at merchandising.	1. It is meant generally for speculation or hedging.
2. Contracts are made anywhere.	2. Contracts are made and entered into within the premises.
3. Margin money is not required.	3. Deposit of margin money is required by the parties.
4. Quality, quantity and the time of settlement are specified in the contract.	4. Dealings depend upon the rules of the exchange.
5. Parties to a contract need not be members. Seller can deal directly with the buyer	5. Parties to a futures contract must be members.
6. There is no specified unit of trading	6. Exchange prescribes the unit of trading.
7. Delivery of the goods must be made on the date stipulated in the contract.	7. Delivery of goods to be effected on any day of the trading month.

Types of Transactions in a Future Market

The transactions are of two types—speculative transactions and hedging transactions.

Speculation

Speculation consists in buying and selling of commodities in the hope of a profit from anticipated changes of value. A speculator welcomes risks in the hope of making a profit in accordance with his expectations of future price. To speculate means to look at from a distance. Speculation is not a game of chance. "It is the struggle of the well-equipped intelligence against the rough power of chance." That is, speculation is the intelligence forecast of price changes. In speculation also, there is an uncertainty about the future. But the activity involves right thinking and intelligent work.

Experts, based on sound judgement of forces of supply and demand, can calculate (speculate) the future trend of markets. Then it becomes a scientific and genuine work. At the same time unscrupulous men, who enter into speculation, invite evils to society. Speculation is a science as well as an art. It needs up-to-date information, rational interpretation and analysis, expertise and foresight. It signifies future happenings or events. Estimating the fall or rise in the price of commodities in future by taking advantage of market situation for profits, is known as speculation. A person, who practises speculation in trade or business of any kind is known as speculator.

Kinds of Speculators

1. Bulls : A bull is a speculator expecting a rise in the price of goods. He believes that the prevailing present price is the lowest and it will advance in future. Therefore he buys goods with a view to sell them at a good price and thus makes a gain. The person who does this speculative work is called Bull or Tejiwala. He is also called a 'long buyer,' long means the buying side of a future market. He forecasts rising prices. He is an optimist of future price trend. He points out that market demand is greater than market supply.

2. Bears : A bear speculator expects a fall in price. He expects that the current price of the commodity is high and the price will go down in the future. He sells commodity in the hope of buying back cheaply. He is a pessimist. He is a short seller. Short means the selling side of a future market. He forecasts declining tendencies; that is, demand is less and supply is more. He is also known as Mandiwala.

Kinds of Speculative Dealings

1. Waida or Forward Deals : The bulls and bears anticipate fall or rise in prices in the future. Hence they sell or buy at current price and sell or buy at higher or lower prices in future. And these deals involve unlimited gain or loss depending upon price differences. In these deals, the risk is at the greatest.

2. Option : An option contract is a privilege or a right to buy or a right to sell a certain commodity at an agreed price on an agreed date. The option may not be exercised. The option is a right—a right to buy or sell. The special right acquired to buy or sell a certain commodity at a certain price on a certain date is called option dealing. For example, A enters into a future contracts to sell cotton @ Rs. 1,000 to B who deposits "premium" or "option money" of Rs.100. On the specified date the price goes up to Rs.1,300. If A executes the contract, he is to lose Rs. 300 but if A exercises the option *i.e.,* not to carry out the contract, he is to gain Rs. 200 by losing the option money of Rs. 100. When the contract falls through, the option money cannot be claimed back, but has to be foregone in favour of other party who is ready to execute the contract. Option dealings are of 3 types.

(a) **Call Option :** It is a right to buy or not to buy within a certain period a certain commodity at a certain price. In a call option, the granter of option gives the right to the buyer of the option to buy during option period. The buyer of the option is required to pay the consideration money called 'premium' or option money. If he wishes to exercise his right to buy, he can do so as per terms already agreed upon. But if the price is unfavourable—declining price tendency—to him, he will not exercise his right, and lose only his option money. When price remains stationary or fall, no right of option will be exercised. The call option offers a limited loss or an unlimited gain.

(b) **Put Option :** This is opposite to call option. Put option is a right to sell or not to sell some commodities at a future date at the option of the option holder. It is an agreement giving the buyer of 'put option' the right to deliver to the other party a certain quantity of commodity at a fixed price. If price decline by exercising the right to sell, the seller makes profit. Otherwise, if prices rise, he does not exercise his options and loses his option money. The put option also offers a limited loss or an unlimited gain.

(c) **Double Option :** It is a combination of put and call option. Its working is based on the same line as that of put or call option. One can enjoy the double right by paying double premium. It gives the holder of the contract the right either to buy or sell at his choice. Such contracts are largely entered into when wide price fluctuations are expected.

In case of price rises, he may decline himself as a purchaser, by exercising the call option. At the same time if the price falls, he may declare himself as buyer, by exercising put option. He is secured on both sides, makes unlimited profit, irrespective of price rise or fall, that too on a nominal amount of premium.

3. **Straddle :** A straddling operation involves buying in a market where price is low and selling at a market, where the price is high. The same operation in stock exchange is known as 'arbitrage' and in commodity exchange, as 'spreading'. In cotton exchange it is known as 'straddling'. Straddling is used to equalise the difference in prices. It equalises the prices in the two markets—spot market and future market—or even in the same exchange. By this, the price differences can be eliminated.

4. **Badla (carry over) :** When prices of commodities do not move according to the expectation of the operators, the transaction is carried forward from one settlement period to the next. When the operator feels that the current price is unfavourable, the party carrying over the transaction by this type of postponement, must pay compensation—badla charge—to the other party as per the rules of the exchange.

Advantages of Speculation

The following are the summarised advantages from the speculation—through an intelligent forecast of future trend.

1. Speculation helps in equalising the demand and supply between periods of gluts and shortages, and protect against wide fluctuations in the markets.
2. Equalisation of prices is favoured by directing flow of goods from surplus market to deficit market.
3. It acts as a sponge, which absorbs the price rises or price falls, *i.e.*, price variations are reduced.
4. It creates national and international market for commodities; and cultivators have a ready market even in bad times.
5. In the absence of speculation, the sellers are to move in search of buyers, as the speculation offers liquidity to the commodities.
6. It broadens the activity of grading and standardisation and ensures the quality of commodities.
7. With the wide publicity of prices, the agriculturists and people interested in the disposal of commodities, can know in advance the speculated price. The market information is the best guide to farmers, sellers, buyers etc., to know the prices prevailing in the market.
8. It shifts the risks of price fluctuations from manufacturers or producers to the body of professional risk takers.

Abuses of Speculation

1. When this speculator becomes unscrupulous or selfish, the whole market gets spoiled.
2. The creation of false opinions, twisting of the price structure, spreading false news etc., are the most common form of manipulation adopted.
3. Innocent people enter into speculation through inexperienced speculators, and thereby speculators and people get ruined.
4. Bad intention, artificial scarcity, cornering etc., have bad effect on the society.
5. Fictitious dealings, pretended sales etc., conceal the real position of the market.

HEDGING

Hedging means the practice of entering simultaneously into two contracts of opposite, though corresponding nature, one in the spot or cash market and the other in the future market. That is, hedging involves the practice of entering simultaneously into two contracts of the same value in two different markets, namely cash market and future market, one setting off against the other. Protection against losses due to price fluctuations may be achieved through the use of future market. This type of practice is termed hedging. Hedging is a form of insurance to minimise loss due to price changes. Commodities, specially agricultural produces, may face wild price variation, sometimes contrary to our expectations. Either the buyer or the seller has to face the loss of price variations. ''The hedger had made two equal and opposite transactions, and if the price moves either way, he makes himself largely independent of speculative fluctuations.''

For example

Spot Market		Future Market	
April 1 Purchased 200 units		Sold 200 units	
Rs.1,000 units (Now)	2,00,000	Rs.1,200(June)	2,40,000
May 15 Sold 200 units		Purchased 200 units	
Rs.1,200	2,40,000	Rs.1,000 (June)	2,00,000
GAIN	40,000	LOSS	40,000

Benefits of Hedging

1. Risk at price change can be insured by hedging.
2. Agriculturists get proper price for their produces.
3. A hedged property is a good security for obtaining finance.
4. Hedgning assures normal profit.
5. It stabilises the prices and facilitates smooth supply of goods.
6. Because of reduced risk, a trader is able to supply at reduced price and thus consumers are benefited.
7. The risk of price fluctuations is met by risk-takers and speculators.

Evils

1. Harmonious relationship in the prices of cash market and future market must exist. That is the prices must move in the same direction. If the prices in both markets move in opposite directions, the hedger will be a loser.
2. The quantity involved in the contracts must be the same, but in practice it may vary.
3. Hedger cannot protect manufacturers if the cost of production increases due to increase in wages or other reasons.
4. When contracts are entered into two different grades in the market, the expected insurance cover cannot be attained.

Hedging Versus Speculation

Hedging	*Speculation*
1. Hedger is insured partly.	1. Speculator is an insurer.
2. He operates in two markets cash and future.	2. He operates only in future market.
3. Physical delivery of goods is essential.	3. Physical delivery is not aimed.

4. He intends to protect himself against adverse price change on buying or selling.	4. He intends capital gain.
5. He transfers the price risk to the speculator.	5. Speculator assumes the risk from hedger.
6. Hedger does not change his position frequently in the future markets.	6. He does change his position frequently.
7. He is free from price risks. to price	7. He voluntarily assumes risk of loss due change.

QUESTIONS

1. Explain the demerits of an unorganised market.
2. What is a regulated market?
3. What are the functions of produce exchange?
4. What are the qualities required for a product to be handled in organised markets?
5. Explain the characteristics of futures contracts.
6. Distinguish between forward contracts and future contracts.
7. What is meant by an option dealing? State the various kinds of option dealings.
8. Explain the advantages of speculation.
9. What do you understand by hedging?
10. Differentiate between hedging and speculation.

Co-Operative Marketing

CHAPTER 42

Co-operation

- *Co-operative Marketing*
- *Objective*
- *Need*
- *Features*
- *Structure*
- *Functions*
- *Advantages*
- *Working Methods–Questions*

The word 'Co-operation' stands for the idea of 'living together and working together to achieve common goals through united and joint efforts.'

Co-operation is an organisation or an association of persons who voluntarily associate together for the promotion of their common economic interest and is based on the principles of unity, economy, democracy, equality and liberty.

Prof. J.J. Worely observes, ''A social philosophy of co-operation, observes that, a co-operative society must rest on free universal association, democratically governed and conditioned by equality and personal liberty.

The International Labour Office defines co-operative organisation as, ''an association of persons, usually of limited means, who have voluntarily joined together to achieve a common economic end through the formation of a democratically controlled business organisation, making equitable contribution to the capital required, and accepting a fair share of risks and benefits of the undertaking.''

H. Calvert defines that, ''Co-operation is a form of organisation wherein persons voluntarily associate together as human beings on a basis of equality for the economic interests of themselves.''

Prof. Paul Lambert defines that, ''A co-operative society is an enterprise formed and directed by an association of users, applying within itself the rules of democracy and directly intended to serve both its members and the community as a whole.''

Co-operative Marketing

Co-operative marketing is co-operative association designed to perform one or more marketing functions, relating to the agricultural produce of its members. It is a form of business organisation. Its principle is co-operation. It sells the agricultural produce of its farmer members. It gives to the producers the full share of money given by the consumers. Co-operative marketing does the functions of buying and selling of agricultural produce. The selling functions of these co-operative marketing are: marketing of produce, acting as selling agent, supplying market information, standardisation, storage, assembling, processing etc.

Objectives of Co-operative Marketing

The main objective of the co-operative marketing is to enhance the income of the members to the maximum level. The other objectives are :

1. **To Increase the Bargaining Power :** The main object of the co-operative marketing is to increase the bargaining power of the farmers in the market, so that they can get more profit. The fundamental idea of marketing co-operative is to sell the members' produce directly in the best market at the best price.

2. **To Eliminate Malpractices :** There are various malpractices prevailing in the agricultural marketing. These malpractices are ''nothing less than theft'' (Royal Commission). Farmers are indebted to the moneylenders. In this respect co-operative marketing can help to reduce and eradicate the malpractices.

3. **Replacement of Middlemen :** There are a large number of middlemen in every stage of agricultural marketing *i.e.*, in collection, storage, financing etc. It aims at the replacement of middlemen. An efficiently organised co-operative marketing performs the middlemen's function more economically and efficiently.

4. **Integrated Marketing :** To get good price for agricultural produce, the co-operative marketing has to develop sale of graded and processed produce, to improve quality, to adopt better selling methods, to arrange for storage and transport to adopt scientific methods of cost reduction in transport, storage and handling of agricultural produce. The co-opeartive marketing societies make arrangements for loans from co-operative sources and act as an agent for the recovery of loans advanced by the co-operative credit societies.

5. **Theme :** Promoting orderly marketing and ensuring reasonable prices for the produce of the farmers is the theme.

To maximise the income of the members of the co-operative society, it makes efforts to obtain better price through developing regulated markets, adopting better selling methods, improving quality etc. At the same time, it adopts methods to lower the marketing costs by eliminating middlemen, improving marketing methods, reducing the cost of production on the farm, the cost of transport, storage, material handling, packaging etc.

Need for Co-operative

The majority of Indian producers are illiterates and are scattered all over the country, besides being unorganised. These tillers of the soil are awfully exploited by business people–middlemen, manufacturers etc. The middlemen, who are intelligent, are well-organised, and try to suck the blood of the cultivators.

It is also experienced that the cultivators sell their produces in the village itself. This is because of prior indebtedness to the village moneylender or merchant-middlemen. Even before the crops come up, the crop sales take place, because farmers are badly in need of finance. The moneylenders who grant loan against the crops, pay low price on the strength of agreement. The cultivator is bound to sell them–a forced sale.

There are various malpractices prevailing in the agricultural markets–arbitrary deduction, manipulation of weights and scales, multiple market charges, existence of many middlemen etc., and increased cost of marketing and reduced price.

Farmers dispose of their produces in the village itself, because of the absence of good connecting roads, lack of storage facility, compulsory intervention of middlemen at the market, selling becomes impossible without middlemen etc.

To protect the interest of the agricultural producer, to eliminate the army of middlemen, to ensure that agriculture occupies a pivotal position in the national economy and well-being of the entire population etc., the need for a co-operative marketing of agricultural produce is very essential. ''Marketing is the crux of the whole food and agriculture problems. It would be useless to increase the output of food, and it would be equally futile to set up optimum standards of nutrition, unless means could be found to move food from the producer to the consumer at a price which is remunerative to the producer and is within the consumer's ability to pay.''

Features of Agricultural Marketing–Co-operatives

1. **Open Membership :** Any farmer can become a member of the society, irrespective of caste, creed or religion. He can join or cancel his membership at any time. His produce is marketed or processed by the society.

2. **Democratic Management :** Voting power is limited, *i.e.*, one member one vote is the principle irrespective of the number of shares. As such, the members can enjoy democratic freedom.

3. **Limited Dividend on Share Capital :** The dividend on share capital is limited to a nominal fixed amount from 5 to 6.5%. Even if there is more profit, the dividend is fixed.

4. **Distribution Justice :** The surplus or the profit after meeting all the obligations, is distributed among the members, as compensation for the patronage extended by each member to the society. It is distributed according to the business done by a member in the society.

5. **Co-operative Education :** The basic principle of co-operation is ''each for all and all for each,'' self-help through mutual help. More money, time and effort are spent on educational and missionary effort to spread the gospel of co-operation.

6. **Self-Government :** The control of marketing co-operatives is kept in the hands of the members. The benefits of co-operation go to the members as patrons and not as owners. As the members are having the voting power, they have part in the management of the co-operative. As such, it provides a training ground for self-government.

7. **Service Motto :** It is a servicing centre to its members. It aims to provide maximum services to its members and not to earn maximum profits. It provides service facilties like storage, assembling, packaging, processing, grading, selling the produce to members at favourable price etc.

8. **Cash Trading :** It is always good to keep the transactions on cash basis, so as to avoid loss on account of bad debts.

9. **Control :** The main principle of co-operative society is voluntary organisation. Yet they are subject to considerable state control, under the co-operative laws a co-operative society must be registered under the Co-operative Society Act of 1912. By registration, a society becomes an incorporated association; it gets legal status and can function in its own name.

Structure of Marketing Co-operatives

There are two types in the structure of marketing societies. They are two tiered structure and three tiered structure. The two tiered structure consists of primary marketing societies organised at the market level or block level or taluk level and the apex marketing society is organised at the state level.

The three tiered structure consists of an intermediate organisation between the primary marketing societies and apex marketing societies. It is organised at district level. It is called a Central Marketing Society. The National Agricultural Co-operative Marketing Federation is framed at the national level to co-ordinate the functions of apex marketing societies.

Farmers who are organised on co-operative basis are responsible for the marketing of agricultural produce. There are two tiered and three tiered systems. The area of operation of a marketing society is fixed in view of local conditions. The structure of the organisation is as follows :

Two Tier System	*Three Tier System*
National Agricultural Co-operative Marketing Federation (NAFED) State Marketing Society Primary Marketing Society	National Agricultural Co-operative Marketing Federation (NAFED) State Marketing Society Central Marketing Society Primary Marketing Society

Membership : The membership of the marketing society is open to individual farmers, large-sized credit societies, service co-operative societies or other rural credit co-operative societies and multipurpose societies.

Source of Capital : Deposits from members, shares, loans from central financing agencies are the sources of the capital. It is up to 8 to 10 times the value of paid up shares capital. Government or the Reserve Bank of India grants loans or subsidy for the construction of godown. Capital is also got by issuing debentures. Money is borrowed from State Bank of India against securities of warehouse receipts.

The marketing societies need short-term, medium-term and long-term capital. Short-term capital is repayable within one year. It is needed for the following reasons :

1. To finance for production
2. To give advance against pledge (produce)
3. To meet contingent and establishment expenses
4. To purchase produce from farmers
5. To purchase under price support schemes
6. To purchase agricultural implements and inputs for supplying to farmers
7. To meet its running expenses on staff, rent of building godown etc

Medium-term capital is needed for purchasing motor-trucks, motor engines etc.

Long-term capital is needed for the following reasons :

1. To purchase machinery
2. To construct godowns, processing sheds and administrative building
3. To purchase furniture, equipment and transport vehicles
4. To invest in other co-operatives and financial institutions
5. To pay security to the government

In 1958, this Federation was set up in New Delhi. It covers the entire country. Its object is to co-ordinate and promote the marketing and trading activities of its members in agricultural and other commodities.

Its functions are to render technical guidance and advice to the State Marketing Societies. It co-ordinates the activities of these societies also. NAFED undertakes the business of internal trade in agriculture. The business increased from Rs. 11.41 lakhs in 1969–70 to Rs. 10 crores in 1974–75. Export, import and inter-state trade are also undertaken by this federation. It also fulfils the needs of its members by procuring and supplying different types of farm products from other states.

State Marketing Societies of Federation

They serve as an apex institution for all co-operative marketing societies in a state. Their membership consists of individuals and societies. Inter-state trade is conducted by these societies. They buy and sell and give credit and provide other facilities to the central union and primary societies. They purchase farm inputs and supply them to the farmers through co-operative agencies. Their functions differ from state to state. Their functions are distribution of chemical fertilizers, cement, iron, sugar, milk, rice, wheat, oil etc. In some states, they process the agricultural produce. They provide market information, render advice and technical guidance to other societies. They perform developmental activities like assisting in the construction of godowns, erection of processing units etc. They also function in food procurement operations of the state government and inter-state trade of foodgrains. These societies act as the lenders of last resort. They co-ordinate the activities of primary and central co-operatives. The business of these societies increased from Rs. 154.68 crores in 1965–66 to Rs. 282.55 crores in 1970–71 and to Rs. 962.12 crores in 1974–75.

Central Marketing Societies

These federations operate over a part of district or an entire district. They are engaged in the work of buying and selling and extending credit facilities and other helps to primary societies. These societies are the connecting link between the primary societies at the bottom and state co-operative marketing societies at the top. Their main function is to co-ordinate the functions of primary co-operative marketing societies in order to market their agricultural produce and distribute the agricultural inputs. They undertake the business of inter-district trade. They distribute consumer goods among consumers, through co-operative agencies.

Primary Marketing Societies

Primary marketing co-operative operates in small areas like a taluk or a block. Farmers who do agricultural work and produce agricultural produce, are the members of the societies. The object of these societies is to encourage self-help, thrift and co-operation among members. Their functions are :

1. Advance loans to members on the security of their produce
2. To purchase and sell agricultural commodities for the benefit of their members
3. Provide manures, fertilizers, equipments etc
4. Propagate and supply quality seeds
5. Provide short-term loans to their members
6. Act as an agent to their members and provide godown facilities to affiliated societies
7. Give advice and guidance to their members regarding the latest improvement in agriculture. Demonstration is carried out on the members' land with the help of the agricultural department
8. Process and grade the agricultural produce–for the benefit of their members, they have own machinery or hired machinery for these purposes

Functions of Marketing Co-operatives

1. **Purchase and Sale of Produce :** The marketing co-operatives purchase the produces from their member growers. They sell it in bulk quantities. As such, the marketing cost is reduced. This enables the members to get more reasonable price and also to sell to their best advantages.

2. **Commission Agent :** Farmers bring their produce to the headquarters of the society or bring it through the service co-operatives where they are members. These societies make arrangement for the sale. When the sale is over, payment is made to the farmers after deducting the commission which is a small amount. Thus the marketing societies are functioning as commission agent. It is financially a safe system, as there is no risk of cheating in price.

3. **Distribution of Agricultural Inputs :** In integrated co-operative marketing plans, the co-operatives supply the agricultural inputs such as fertilizers, improved (high yielding varieties) seeds, pesticides, agricultural implements etc. The supply of quality materials takes place at the right time at reasonable price. They give these inputs on credit basis. The credit is recovered when the produce is sold through the society.

4. **Supply of Agricultural implements :** They supply the needed agricultural implements like tractors, power sprayers etc., if needed by the cultivators.

5. **Providing Storage Facility :** For providing storage facility, the societies may have their own godown or hired godown. Loans are granted to producers against the produce kept in the godowns. When the price is high for the market produce, the societies sell them.

6. **Processing of Produce :** Some societies undertake processing of agricultural produce. They provide employment opportunities. They ensure high prices to the producers. The economic position of the society is strengthened.

7. **Provide Financial Assistance :** They give financial help to farmers. They make advances to the members on the pledge of produce and support them in the period between deposit of produce and sale. Members can get advances up to 75% of the market price of the deposited produce.

8. **Protect Members From Several Malpractices :** They protect the members from unauthorised deduction, incorrect weighing etc.

9. **Elimination of Middlemen :** They act as a connecting link between the producer and the consumer.

10. **Reduce Waste :** They reduce waste and help to get fair prices for the produce.

11. **Teach Business Methods :** They teach the farmers the best business methods and supply up-to-date market information.

12. **Stabilize Price :** They adjust supply according to the market demand. As such, in the long run the price is stabilised. The farmers are saved from the evil effects of the seasonal fluctuations in the price level.

13. **Inter-state and Foreign Trade :** These societies participate in the export trade of the country which helps to get better price for the growers. Through export trade, the marketing co-operatives provide wide market to the agricultural produce. In 1974-75, the export trade amounted to Rs. 68 crores, and in 1975–76 it was Rs. 140 crores.

Advantages of Co-operative Marketing

The co-operative marketing is advantageous to the producers, consumers, and the society. The advantages of marketing society are given below :

1. **Improved Bargaining Power :** In the co-operative societies a number of producers become members. Hence they have collective bargaining position, which is stronger than individual bargaining. As such, the bargaining power of the society as a whole improves.

2. **Development of Orderly Marketing :** Demand and supply position is studied carefully and co-operative societies act accordingly. They plan to sell the members' produce in the best market at the most favourable price and at the proper time. Producers and consumers are safeguarded from the seasonal fluctuations.

3. **Greater Holding Power :** Co-operative societies have greater holding power of their products for a longer time after the harvest.

4. **Better Price :** The producers can get better price for their produce, if they sell their produce through the co-operative society.

5. **Lower Cost of Production :** The market charges of co-operative societies are less than those of the private traders. They have a bulk quantity and a large volume of business. Hence there is economy in assembling, grading, storing etc. As such, the marketing cost is less. This benefit goes to the consumers, and the prices for the commodities become cheap.

6. **Better Selling Methods :** Co-operative societies sell the products like fruits, vegetables etc. directly to the ultimate consumers. For that they resort to advertising and branding. Thus they increase the sales of these products.

7. **Elimination of Middlemen :** The functions of middlemen are taken away by the co-operative societies. By eliminating the middlemen, the co-operative societies do their duty efficiently and economically. This benefit goes to the consumers and producers.

8. **Elimination of Trade Abuses :** Trade abuses, malpractices and waste are considerably reduced by co-operative societies.

9. **Lower Cost of Production :** Co-operatives take steps to decrease the cost of production of their members. They supply farm inputs. They encourage the members to grow the best crop to increase their yield. They help the members in purchasing the best seed, fertilizers and machinery at cheaper price. Thus there is large production at cheaper rate.

10. **Credit Facility :** Co-operative societies give credit facilities to their members to buy agricultural inputs and other agricultural requirements. The interest rate is very low. They grant loans on the pledge of produce. Hence the members are saved from the clutches of moneylenders.

11. **Division of Surplus :** The profit of the co-operative society is divided among its members according to their contribution to the society, as the profit is the property of the members.

12. **Educative Value :** Co-operative societies give advice and guidance to its members. Their problems are solved by the co-operative societies. From these societies they know the economic truth. Farmers, who are ignorant of the importance of marketing, can understand that marketing is as important as production. The economic development of a country depends upon the marketing of agricultural produce. They give up-to-date information about marketing. They inform new methods of cultivation and new development in science and technology, which help to improve their economic conditions.

13. **Help the Government :** Co-operative societies help the government in implementing the programmes. It helps the government in price stabilization. The government's new programmes and policies are passed on to the farmers through these marketing societies.

Working Methods

The following are the principal methods adopted by co-operative marketing societies in respect of produces of farmers :

Society may adopt the method of outright purchase, as if it is a private dealer. Here the producers sell their produces at the agreed price. Later, produces are sold by the society on their own account. Cultivators can dispose the produces against cash and meet their financial needs. However, the society must have enough capital, godown facilities apart from qualified staff. The loss or gain on account of price fluctuations is met by the society. To reduce the risk, there is a Price Committee that fixes the price for the produces.

Society works as a commission agent in selling the produces of cultivators. The produces are sold under open bidding system. Immediately after the sale, by deducting a nominal amount as commission, farmers are paid. Thereby society needs limited amount of capital apart from safe system. The grading and standardisation are done. No blocking up of capital is there. Members get good price. Here produces are pooled together so that grading becomes easier. This is a drawback to the cultivators, who bring produces of superior quality.

Society works as a pledging centre. Members pool their produces to the society and store them in the godown. Farmers get loans against security of goods up to 75% of the current market price. The loans can fully be recovered against sales amount. The glut or shortage of grains is avoided through this system. At the same time the risk and marketing cost are spread over all the producers equitably.

Limitations of Co-operative Marketing

1. The employees–managers, secretaries and other staff are paid poor salaries and are less qualified. Hence marketing operations cannot be carried out successfully.

2. Due to lack of whole-hearted co-operation of members the progress of co-operative societies cannot be attained.

3. Electing unscrupulous persons by personal considerations to the managing committee, ignoring efficient and experienced persons will check the progress of co-operatives.

4. Private business firms are well-organised, and have a sound financial position followed by professional character. Co-operatives may not compete with these firms.

5. Lack of scientific management is another drawback.

6. To raise the capital amount is difficult, as the dividend offered is low. The legal limitations of dividend are not attractive.

7. Most of the societies lack godowns, facilities for grading, processing, transport etc. so satisfactory services cannot be provided.

8. In many cases, the prices offered are lower than the market rate.

9. Cultivators have no confidence in the staff of co-operatives, as the staff have less interest in the society's progress.

10. Illiteracy of farmers is not understanding the benefit of co-operatives is another drawback.

QUESTIONS

1. Give reasons for the regulation of agricultural markets. What are the important features of the regulated market?
2. Discuss the role of co-operative marketing in solving the problems of agricultural marketing in India.
3. Discuss briefly the defects of agricultural marketing in India and suggests measures for its improvement. (*M. Com. Andhra*)
4. What are the problems of agricultural marketing in India?
5. What are the reasons for Indian farmers getting low price for their products? How far have regulated markets and marketing co-operatives helped in improving the conditions of agricultural marketing in India?
6. Define co-operative marketing. What are its advantages and limitations?
7. Explain the features of agricultural co-operative societies.
8. Explain the function of marketing co-operatives.

CHAPTER 43

Marketing Control

- *Introduction*
- *Meaning of Control*
- *Concept of Control*
- *Nature of Control*
- *Relationship between Planning and Control*
- *Purpose of Control*
- *Significance of Control*
- *Limitation of Control*
- *Control Process*
- *Requisite of Control System*
- *Marketing Control*
- *Tools and Techniques of Marketing Control*
- *Questions*

43.1 INTRODUCTION

In any management practice, the functions of planning, staffing, directing and controlling are very crucial. Controlling is an important element of management and measuring and correcting of activities to assure that events conform to a marketing plan. It measures performance against goals and plans, shows where negative deviations exist and by putting in motion actions to correct deviations, helps assure accomplishment of plans. Marketing control is a crucial function of marketing management. Using suitable controls, any deviation in marketing programmes and plans could be detected and corrected to direct it towards the marketing objectives and goals. Marketing control provides the means of testing whether desired goals and results are actually being achieved or not. During planning of marketing programmes, the marketing objectives and targets are set and controls are used to check the implementation of marketing programmes and plans will lead to the set target and if not, then corrective action must be taken to ensure that at the end of the period, the actual performance of the marketing department and its activity is close to the desired results.

Marketing control is the most important task of the marketing department of a company. It is a control tool for ensuring that the marketing activities of company get directed towards its marketing objectives. According to Kotler, "Marketing control is the process of measuring and evaluating the results of marketing strategies and plans and taking corrective action to ensure that marketing objectives are attained."

Marketing control is a crucial part of the marketing job. It is the role for ensuring that the marketing programmes and activities of the firm are always directed towards its marketing objectives. Marketing control provides the means of testing whether the desired goals and results are being achieved or not. Inherent in the process is the assumption that the desired results are known beforehand. And knowing the desired results in advance, involves planning. In this sense, planning and control are closely interrelated.

Therefore, marketing control is defined, as the set of process that determines the deviation, if any, between the actual sales performance and the desired sales results and guides the marketing activity to the corrective action to achieve the desired marketing goals and objectives. The actual performance may deviate from the desired performance due to many reasons including organisational factors and environmental factors. The marketing organisation will have to develop suitable strategy in terms of marketing mix programmes to counter environmental factors and necessary steps to correct any organisational factors.

43.2 MEANING OF CONTROL

Controlling may be defined as the process of analysing actual operations and seeing that actual performance is guided towards expected performance. It involves comparing operating results with plans and taking corrective action when results deviate from plans. It is a mechanism by which someone or something is guided to follow the predetermined course. As a plan is put into operation, it becomes necessary to check results to find out whether the work is proceeding along the right lines. In case of any deviations, necessary corrective action is taken to ensure that in future the work proceeds in the desired manner.

According to Koontz and O'Donnel, "The managerial function of controlling is the measurement and correction of the performance of activities of subordinates in order to make sure that enterprise objectives and the plans devised to attain them are being accomplished."

43.3 CONCEPT OF CONTROL

The essence of the concept is in determining whether the activity is achieving the desired results. In other words, the managerial function of control consists in a comparison of the actual performance with the planned performance with the object of discovering whether all is going on well according to plans, and if not, why? Remedial action arising from a study of the deviations of the actual performance with the standard or planned performance will serve to correct the plans and make suitable changes in the process and structure of organisation, the staffing process and the process and techniques of direction. In this sense, the controlling function of management enables management to be self-corrective.

43.4 NATURE OF CONTROL

The main characteristics of the controlling function of management are given below:

1. Control can be exercised only with reference to and on the basis of plans.
2. The managerial functions cannot be completed effectively without performing the control function.
3. Control is in fact a follow-up action to the other functions of management.
4. It is an ongoing process. That is, as long as an organisation exists, some sort of control is required.
5. Control is forward-working because past cannot be controlled.
6. Control is a process of measurement, comparison and verification.
7. The essence of control is action.
8. Control is dynamic and not static.
9. Control aims at preventing unacceptable or incorrect performance.
10. Control is a check-up measure. It comes in the end so as to ensure the proper implementation of plans.

43.5 RELATIONSHIP BETWEEN PLANNING AND CONTROL

Planning is the basis of control. Control implies the existence of certain standards against which actual results may be evaluated. Planning provides such standards. Where there is no plan there is no basis for control. Planning sets the course and control makes operations adhere to that course. Planning initiates the process of management, control completes the process. Without plans, control is blind for when one does not know where to go, one cannot judge whether one is on the right truck or not.

"Hicks stated that "Planning is clearly a pre-requisite for controlling. It is utterly foolish to think that controlling could be accomplished without planning,. Without planning there is no pre-determined understanding of the desired performance." Control makes planning a meaningful exercise just as planning provides the guidelines for control. Planning is meaningless without control and control is aimless without planning. Planning and control are the inseparable, the twins of management. Unplanned actions cannot be controlled, for control involves keeping activities on course by correcting deviations from plans.

Planning is looking ahead and control is looking back. Planning is the determination of objectives, goals, strategies, policies, programmes of an organisation to give purpose and direction to the activities of the organisation over a specified period of time. It is anticipatory. It reduces confusion and uncertainty. Control, on the other hand, is the direction of the operations of an enterprise towards pre-determined standards and monitoring the process in this regard for the purpose of correction and feed back. The purpose of control is to see that the structure and the pace of events in a business are conforming to plans.

All controls imply existence of goals and plans. No manager can ascertain whether his subordinates are operating in the desired way unless he has a plan. Control will be much better if the plans are more clear, complete and well coordinated and cover a long period. Without planning, there may be no control. Planning and controlling are inseparable functions of management. Planning and control are inter-related and interdependent.

43.6 PURPOSE OF CONTROL (OBJECTIVES)

A sound control system is needed for the following purposes:

1. Control reveals deficiency in planning : thus, plans and policies can be improved.
2. Control helps managers to discharge their responsibilities.
3. Control consists in verifying whether everything occurs in conformity with the plan adopted, the instruction issued and the principles established.
4. A sound control system not only reveals deviations but suggests the corrective actions required to overcome the deficiencies.
5. Control keeps the subordinates under check and creates discipline among them.
6. Effective control ensures efficiency and effectiveness in the organisation.
7. A control system ensures the achievement of objectives.

43.7 SIGNIFICANCE OF CONTROL (BENEFITS)

A good control system offers the following benefits:

1. A good control system provides timely information to management which is very useful in taking corrective actions. Control reveals deficiency in planning so that suitable action can be taken to improve plans and policies.
2. Control facilitates delegation and decentralisation of authority. It helps to expand the span of supervision.
3. It forces the individuals to integrate their efforts and to work as a team for the achievement of standards.
4. It measures progress towards the goal and brings to light the adjustments, if any, required in day-to-day operations.
5. Control enables management to verify the quality of various plans. Control helps to review, revise and update the plans. Without an efficient control system even the best plans may not work out as expected.
6. Absence of control leads to a lowering of morale among employees because they cannot predict what will happen to them. They become the victims of the bias and repression of the superior.
7. According to Terry, "Controlling helps ensure that actions proceed according to plans, that proper direction is taken, and that the various factors are maintained in their correct

interrelationships, so that adequate coordination is attained. "Control provides unity of direction.

8. In the content of predetermined goals, control keeps all activities and efforts within their fixed boundaries and makes them to move towards common goals through co-ordinated directives.
9. An effective control system stimulates action by spotting the variations from the original plan highlighting them for the people who can get things right.
10. A person is likely to act according to plan, if he is aware that his performance will be evaluated against the planned targets. Therefore, he is more inclined to achieve the results according to the standards fixed for him.

43.8 LIMITATION OF CONTROL

A control has the following limitations:

1. A firm cannot control the external factors – technological changes, changes in fashions, Government policies, social changes etc.
2. In some cases, standards of performance cannot be defined in quantitative terms, for example, human behaviours.
3. Control is a time-consuming and expensive process.
4. Control may not be acceptable to employees.

43.9 THE CONTROL PROCESS

The process of control involves the following steps:

1. Fixation of Standard

The first step in control process is the setting up of control standards. Standards represent the criteria against which actual performance is measured. Standards serve as the benchmarks because they reflect the desired results or acceptable level of performance.

2. Measurement of Performance

After the fixation of standards, the actual performance of various individuals is measured. This involves setting up the methods of collecting accurate and up-to-date information on the progress of work. All measurements should be clear, comparable and reliable. Measurement of performance against standards should be on a future basis so that deviations are anticipated and necessary corrective actions are taken to prevent them.

3. Comparing Performance with Standards

This refers to the comparison of the actual performance with the standards. It should be remembered here that appraisal of actual performance becomes quite easy if the standards are properly determined and methods of measuring performance are clearly stated. It is also important to note that while making appraisal of performance, the manager should concentrate mainly on those matters where major deviations are noticed.

4. Analysis of Deviations

All deviations need not be brought to the notice to top management. A range of deviations should be established and only cases beyond this range should be reported. This is known as control by exception. When the deviation between standard and actual performance is beyond the prescribed limit, an analysis of deviations is made to identify the causes of deviations. Then the deviations and causes are reported to the managers who are authorised to take action.

5. Taking Corrective Action

Mere reporting of actual performance or its comparison with pre-determined standards is not sufficient. Unless timely action is taken to adjust operations to standards, control process is incomplete. Corrective action may involve setting of new goals, change in organisation structure, improvement in staffing and new techniques of direction.

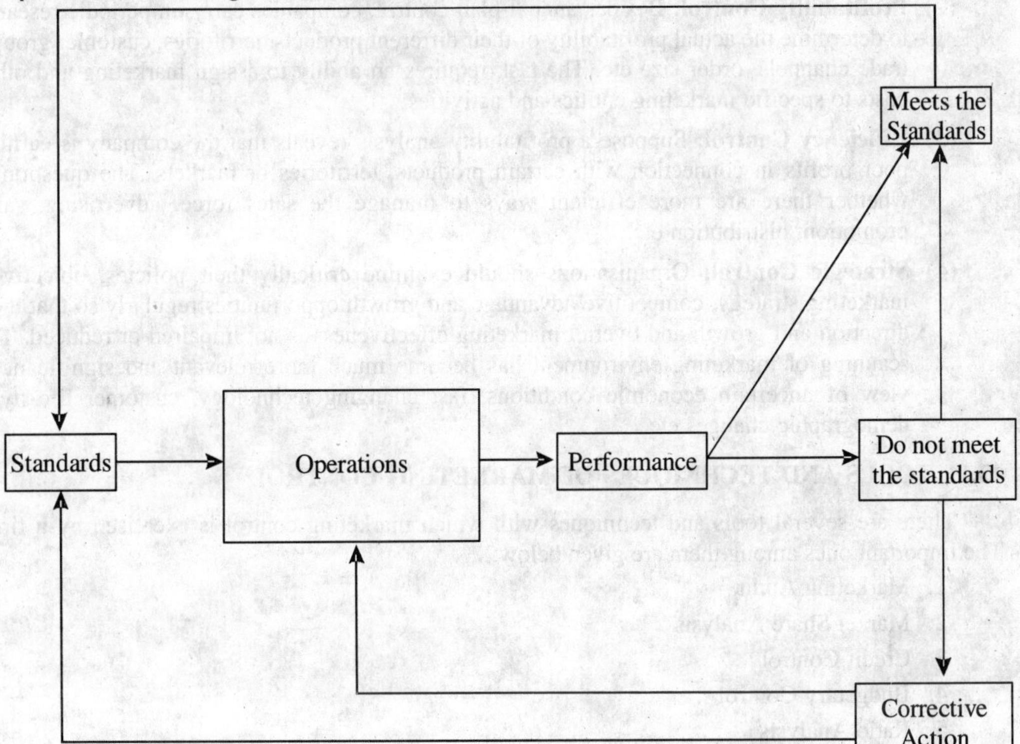

PRE REQUISITES OF A GOOD CONTROL SYSTEM
1. The objective and target must be clear.
2. The control system must be suitable
3. The system should be easy to understand and operate.
4. Selection of tools and techniques must be proper.
5. There must be speedy feedback system.
6. There must be prompt reporting system of variances.
7. It must justify the expenses involved.
8. There must be a good system of corrective actions.
9. It must fix individual responsibility for the poor performance.
10. Controls, which are essential, should be given priority.

43.10 MARKETING CONTROLS

There are several types of control available and the importance and purpose of these controls depend on the objectives for which these controls are to be used. All these controls have a common purpose, that is, monitoring the key results areas is marketing management. The key results are generally common for all marketing organisations. Some of the important marketing controls commonly used are:

(1) **Annual Plan Control:** This is the most basic of all controls used in marketing organisations. The main purpose of this control is to monitor and take corrective action to examine whether planned sales results are being achieved. The responsibility for this lies with the marketing departmental head and all others in the top management.

(2) **Profitability Control:** Besides annual-plan control, companies carry on periodic research to determine the actual profitability of their different products, territories, customer groups, trade channels, order size etc. The task requires an ability to assign marketing and other costs to specific marketing entities and activities.

(3) **Efficiency Control:** Suppose a profitability analysis reveals that the company is earning poor profits in connection with certain products, territories or markets. The question is whether there are more efficient ways to manage the sales force, advertising, sales promotion, distribution etc.

(4) **Strategic Control:** Organisations should examine critically their policies, objectives, marketing strategy, competitive advantage and growth opportunities regularly so that their direction and growth and overall marketing effectiveness is not impaired or reduced. The scanning of marketing environment has become much more relevant and significant in view of uncertain economic conditions, fast changing technology, customer life-style, demographic changes etc.

43.11 TOOLS AND TECHNIQUES OF MARKETING CONTROL

There are several tools and techniques with which marketing control is exercised by a firm. The important ones among them are given below:

1. Marketing Audit
2. Market Share Analysis
3. Credit Control
4. Budgetary Control
5. Ratio Analysis
6. Marketing Cost Control
7. Contribution Margin Analysis
8. SWOT Analysis
9. Variance Analysis
10. Market Information

1. Marketing Audit

A marketing audit is a comprehensive, systematic, independent, and periodic examination of a company's or business unit's marketing environment, objectives, strategies and activities with a view to determining problem areas and opportunities and recommending a plan of action to improve the company's marketing performance.

Marketing audit had four basic characteristics:

(*a*) Comprehensive

The marketing audit covers all the major marketing activities of a business, not just a few trouble spots. It would be called a functional audit if it covered only the sale force, pricing or some other marketing activity. Although functional audits are useful, they sometimes mislead management. Excessive sales force turnover, for example, could be a symptom not of poor sales force training or compensation but of weak company products and promotion. A comprehensive marketing audit usually is more effective in locating the real source of problems.

(*b*) **Systematic**

The marketing audit is an orderly examination of the organisation's macro and micro marketing environments, marketing objectives and strategies, marketing systems and specific activities. The audit initiates the most-needed improvements, which are then incorporated into a corrective action plan involving both short-run and long run steps to improve overall effectiveness.

(*c*) **Independent**

A marketing audit can be conducted in six ways: Self audit, Audit from across, Audit from above, Company audit office, Company task force audit, and outsider audit. Self audits, in which managers use a checklist to rate their own operations, lack objectivity and independence. Generally speaking, however, the best audits come from outside consultants who have the necessary objectivity, broad experience in a number of industries, some familarity with the industry being audited and the undivided time and attention to give to the audit.

(*d*) **Periodic**

Typically, marketing audits are initiated only after sales have turned down, sales force morale has fallen and other problems have occurred. Companies are thrown into a crises partly because they failed to review their marketing operations during good times. A periodic marketing audit can benefit companies in good health as well as those in trouble.

43.12 COMPONENTS OF MARKETING AUDIT

The marketing audit consists of examining six major components of the company's situation.

(*i*) **Marketing environment audit:** This audit calls for analysing the major macro-environment forces that might impact on the company and major trends in the key components of the company's task environment: markets, customers, competitors, distributors and dealers, suppliers and facilitators.

(*ii*) **Marketing strategy audit:** This audit calls for reviewing the company's marketing objectives and marketing strategy to appraise how well these are adapted to the current and forecasted marketing environment.

(*iii*) **Marketing organisation audit:** This audit calls for evaluating the marketing organisation's capability for developing and carrying out the necessary strategy for the forecasted environment.

(*iv*) **Marketing system audit:** This audit involves examining the adequacy of the company's systems for analysis, planning, and control in the marketing areas, as well as innovation.

(*v*) **Marketing productivity audit:** This audit calls for examining data on the profitability of different marketing entities and on the cost-effectiveness of different marketing expenditures.

(*vi*) **Marketing function audit:** These audits involve carrying out in-depth evaluations of major marketing-mix components, viz. products, price, distribution, sales force, advertising, promotion publicity.

2. Market Share Analysis

A company's sales revenue data would indicate its sales performance relative to the competitor and its growth relative to industry or market growth. This analysis shows how much the company is selling in the total market or total industry demand. The company should try to increase the market share gradually by improving sales performance, quality or delivery or after sales service. The decline in market share means company's sales are going down and the same is gained by the competitors.

Before a firm attempts a market share-based evaluation and control, it must have clarity on whether it is consciously seeking a definite share of the market or not. It is implied in any market share evaluation that the marketing performance will be assessed based on the market share. It is also implied that a definite minimum share is the real aim of the firm. Otherwise, the evaluation becomes mechanical exercise and loses its control potential. If the market share of a company is increasing, it is a sign of progress if it is decreasing, the company has to take necessary measures to arrest and possibly push back this trend.

3. Credit Control

Business firms are often forced to extend credit to increase sales. In certain other businesses, the entire sales take place on credit, cash sales being negligible. In certain other businesses, hire purchase and instalment payments are the normal practice. Even in those cases where sales to consumers are on a cash basis, credit is extended to the distribution channels. It is essential for any business firm to evolve a policy on credit and exercise proper control on it.

The firm must ensure that customers and channels do not explicit the credit policy of the firm. Credit transactions should not turn into bad debts. Credit transaction has two cost dimensions: (i) the interest on the money involved in the credit transaction and (ii) the risk of bad debts. Bad debts must be seen and understood as an important part of the cost of credit. They eat away the profits of the firm.

As in credit control, control on price cuts is also very essential. Enthusiastic marketing men often try to push up sales by reducing prices. Sometimes price wars among competitive firms become acute and salesman start selling below costs. Even when there are no price wars, there is usually a strong temptation the part of salesmen for striking special deals with customers, by offering price cuts, discounts and rebate of various kinds. Usually, firms institute clear procedures in this regard and sales personnel can operate only as per such procedures.

4. Budgetary Control

"The establishment of budgets relating to the responsibilities of executives to the requirements of a policy and the continuous comparison of actual results with budgeted results, either to secure by individual action the objective of that policy or to provide a basis for its revision."

Budgetary control has become an essential tool of management for controlling costs and maximising profits. The technique of budgetary control is, in fact, a must for every business enterprise. To control through the budgets, an organisation has to set up an effective Budgetary Control System.

Budgetary control essentially involves preparation of control statements at specified intervals of time, showing the budgeted figures, the achieved figures and the variance. Review and remedial steps are the other parts of budgetary control. In marketing, sales volume, sales expenses and profits are the main aspects to be controlled through the budgetary control device.

5. Ratio Analysis

Ratio Analysis is a powerful tool of marketing control. It helps in identifying correctly the financial strengths and weaknesses of a company. Different ratios can be calculated for different purposes. For instance, profitability ratios help to determine profitability of a company. Several ratios can be calculated from the accounting data contained in the financial statements. Some of the important ratios used in marketing control are given below:

(*i*) Return on Capital Employed Ratio
(*ii*) Return on Shareholders Equity Ratio
(*iii*) Gross Profit Ratio
(*iv*) Net Profit Ratio
(*v*) Expenses Ratio
(*vi*) Inventory Turnover Ratio
(*vii*) Debtors Turnover Ratio
(*viii*) Net Working Ratio
(*ix*) Operating Ratio

(*x*) Return on Investment Ratio

A few are explained below:

(i) **Return on Capital Employed:**

$$= \frac{\text{Operating Profit}}{\text{Capital Employed}} \times 100$$

It indicates the percentage of return on the capital employed in the business and it can be used to show the efficiency of the business as a whole. The term capital employed refers to long-term funds.

(*ii*) **Return on Shareholders Equity:**

$$= \frac{\text{Net Profit}}{\text{Shareholders Fund}} \times 100$$

This ratio establishes the profitability from shareholders point of view. Shareholders equity is also referred to as Net Worth. Here the net profit is after tax.

(*iii*) **Gross Profit Ratio:**

$$= \frac{\text{Gross Profit}}{\text{Net Sales}} \times 100$$

It indicates the earning capacity of the business. A ratio of 25% – 30% may be considered good.

Gross profit is the result of the relationship among price, cost and sales volume. A high ratio of gross profit is good and preferable.

(*iv*) **Net Profit Ratio**

$$= \frac{\text{Net Profit}}{\text{Net Sales}} \times 100$$

It indicates the overall profitability and hence it is useful to proprietors.

This measures the relationship between net profit and sales of a firm. The ratio of net profit (after interest and tax) to sales essentially expresses the cost/price effectiveness of the operation.

(*v*) **Expenses Ratio:**

$$= \frac{\text{Particular Expense}}{\text{Net Sales}} \times 100$$

The lower the ratio, the greater is the profitability. It is computed by dividing expenses by sales, then multiply by 100. The expenses ratio is very important for analysing the profitability of a firm. It should be compared over a period of time, as well as firms of similar type. A low ratio is favourable and high ratio is unfavourable.

(*vi*) **Inventory Turnover Ratio:**

$$= \frac{\text{Cost of Goods Sold}}{\text{Average Inventory}}$$

Cost of goods sold = Sales minus gross profit.

$$\text{Average inventory} = \frac{\text{Opening stock} + \text{Closing stock}}{2}$$

This ratio indicates how fast inventory is sold. A high ratio is good. A low ratio signify that the stock does not sell fast and stays on the shelf for a long time.

(*vii*) Debtors Turnover Ratio

$$= \frac{\text{Net Credit Sales}}{\text{Average Debtors}}$$

Net credit sales = Gross Credit Sales – Returns, if any

$$\text{Average Debtors} = \frac{\text{Debtors at beginning and at end}}{2}$$

This ratio measures how rapidly debts are collected. A high ratio is indicative of shorter time lag between credit sales and cash collection. A low ratio shows that debtors not being collected rapidly.

6. Marketing Cost Control

Marketing cost analysis is an important tool of marketing control in determining the profits and expenses and this has become a very crucial factor in view of escalating prices of sales administration, transportation and government levies. Due to escalating marketing costs, increased sales do not contribute to the improvement in profits.

The marketing cost control helps to identify unnecessary and avoidable costs and helps in reducing these areas of avoidable costs. It also helps in improving competitive position of the products of the firm. Cost reduction can help to improve competitive position as well as profits. It also helps identifying improfitable market segments, customers, distribution channel and also products and brands which do not contribute to the company's profits.

7. Contribution Margin Analysis

We often come across instances where a particular product or customer does not bring in any net profit to the firm, but still makes a useful contribution by carrying a part of the overheads. It is unwise to summarily drop such products or customers on the ground that they do not bring in any net profit. At the same time, they cannot be carried on blindly. The firm should know to what extent these products and customers absorb the firm's overheads. The control technique that comes to the rescue of the marketer in this respect is called contribution margin analysis. It is useful in both pricing and marketing control.

8. SWOT Analysis

All marketing executives today, trained in modern management techniques, are familiar with SWOT - *strengths*, *Weaknesses*, *Opportunities* and *Threats* – analysis. They use it at regular intervals, especially in corporate planning or marketing. Based on SWOT analysis, effective executives chart out a progress chart for the company and strive to keep it on a steady move.

The firm needs to conduct a strength, weakness, opportunity and threat analysis for the business unit. While strength and weakness analysis is analysis of internal strengths of the firm, opportunity and threat analysis is the analysis of external environment to identify the potential risks and returns opportunities in the business.

Faced with a constantly changing environment each business unit needs to develop a marketing information system to track trends and developments. Each trend or development can then be categorized as an opportunity or threat, and an assessment made of the feasibility and action needed if the organisation is either to capitalize upon the opportunity or minimise the impact of the threat. When you are planning strategically with any company. It is useful to complete an analysis that takes into account not only your own business, but your competitor's businesses and the current business environment as well. A SWOT is one such analysis.

9. Variance Analysis

Comparison of the standards with the actuals is required to understand the performance. The difference of the actual from the standard is known as variance. The variance may be favourable or unfavourable.

When the actual cost is more than the standard cost, the same is known as unfavourable variance. When the actual cost is less than the standard cost, it is known as favourable variance. When the variance has been calculated, it needs proper management attention. Variance should be analysed. Significant variance should be reported to the appropriate levels of management for corrective actions. Mere calculation of variance does not imply control. The analysis of variance helps to locate and to pin-point responsibilities.

8. Marketing Information

Timely and relevant marketing information facilitates the timely identification of variances between targets and achievements in respect of sales volume, market converage and market share. It also throws light on market standing, advertising and personal selling effectiveness, and chennel and physical distribution effectiveness.

While using marketing information for marketing control, it is essential that control information, planning information and general purposes statistics are properly distinguished from one another out of the various marketing outputs. Only then, marketing information can be used for control purposes.

Marketing information cannot in itself produce decisions: it merely provides data which must be interpreted by marketing managers. A timely supply of appropriate information provides feedback on an organisation's performance, allowing actual performance to be compared with target performance. On the basis of this information, control measures can be applied to put the organisation back on its original targets.

In the nature of things, any deviation between plan and actual can be identified only after the event has occurred. As such, the time lag between the occurrence and noticing of the deviation, and the time lag between noticing of the variance and taking corrective action becomes very crucial in the control process. If the interval is long, control becomes infructuous. Once planning is completed and implementation is underway, the feedback should start flowing fast. In other words, the crux of control is speedy feedback and speedy action that adjusts the operations to the pre-set norms. It is through feedback that control is achieved. Thus feedback and action have to viewed as two sides of the same coin, feedback is essential for timely understanding of what is happening against the targets. Action is essential for modifying the direction and level of performance so that it comes back in line with the pre-determined norms.

Questions

1. What is marketing control? Explain the various types of marketing control. *(B.Com. Madurai)*
2. "Coordination and control are the inseparable twins of management." Comment. *(M. Com. MS)*
3. Examine Important features of controlling. What are basic steps in the process of controlling? *(M. Com. Chennai)*
4. "Planning without control is an empty exercise: control is impossible without planning." Discuss *(B.Com. Kerala)*

5. What characteristics would you seek in a sound system of control? *(B.Com. Bhopal)*
6. Budgetary control is a tool of planning, co-ordination and control. Explain. *(B.Com. Mumbai)*
7. What are requirements of an effective control system?
8. Examine critically the various techniques of marketing control. *(B.Com. MS)*
9. Discuss the importance and role of marketing audit in modern business.
10. Explain the concept of marketing audit. *(B.Com. Ujjain)*
11. Explain the inter-relationship between planning and control.

CHAPTER 44

International Marketing

- *Introduction*
- *Deciding whether to go Abroad*
- *Main Activities*
- *Imporance of International Marketing*

44.1 INTRODUCTION

International marketing involves all the activities that form part of domestic marketing. An enterprise engaged in international marketing has to correctly identify, assess and interpret the needs of the overseas customers and carry out integrated marketing to satisfy those needs. That is, in international marketing as well as in domestic marketing, the basic functions are the same. Marketing principles are common and are universally applicable whether a marketer sells in Calcutta or America. In any market we need blending of four ingredients of marketing mix (product, price, place and promotion). International marketing refers to the marketing activities carried on by a marketer in more than one nation or country. It is marketing across national boundaries. It is the performance of business activities that direct the flow of goods and services to the consumers or users in more than one nation. When the business crosses the national borders of a given country, it becomes enormously more complex. A wide range of legal, political, cultural and sociological dimensions enter into picture.

The environmental and cultural dynamics of markets of different countries can be understood only by studying the respective people, their patterns of life , their social interactions, their sensibilities, their faiths and fancies. Kolde has eloquently described the environmental dynamics of the world in the following words: ''Multinational enterprises must function in a world of contrasts: old and new, primitive and modern, pious and agnostic, unutterably beautiful and sickeningly squalid, educated and ignorant, progesssive and stagnant, sophisticated and naive—all in constant agitation. To interpret this volatile diversity, to make sense of this apparent chaos, we must try to identify the underlying forces—prime movers—which produce the global dynamics.'

Modern commnication and transport systems have no doubt brought nations closer, but the cultural differences continue. A nation's history, its social and religious heritage, the value system of its people, the code of conduct handed down through generations—all these are components of a nation's culture. Moreover, culture is not a static entity. It undergoes a continuous evolution.

44.2 DECIDING WHETHER TO GO ABROAD

Not all companies need to venture into foreign markets to survive. Many companies are local businesses that need to market well only in the local marketplace. However, companies that operate in global industries, where their strategic positions in specific markets are affected strongly by their overall global positions, must think and act globally. Firms in a global industry must compete on a world wide basis if they are to succeed. Global competitors might attack the company's domestic market by offering better products or lower prices. The company might want to counter-attack these competitors in their home markets to tie up their resources. Before going abroad, the company must weigh several risks and answer many questions about its ability to operate globally.

1. Can the company learn to understand the preferences and behaviour of buyers in other countries?
2. Can it offer competitively attractive products?
3. Will it be able to adapt to other countries' business cultures and to deal effectively with foreign nationals?
4. What are the unique characteristics of each national market?
5. What products are to be marketed, at what price, through what channels, with what communications and in which markets?
6. What needs are to be satisfied by the products?
7. Do the company's managers have the necessary international experience?

Possible global markets should be ranked on several factors, including market size, markets growth, cost of doing business, competitive advantage and risk level. The marketer must decide which markets offer the greatest long-run return on investment.

International marketing involves the performance of marketing functions of buying, selling, transportation, storage, warehousing, financing, risk bearing, pricing, standardisation, advertising and sale promotion in foreign markets across the national borders.

44.3 MAIN ACTIVITIES

The following are the main activities involved in international marketing:

1. Market and Product Selection
2. Market Entry
3. Distribution Channels
4. Pricing for Global Markets
5. International Marketing Research
6. Marketing Communication
7. Procedure Complexities
8. Organisation for international marketing

1. Market and Product Selection

Proper market selection is an integral part of the strategies for international business. ''Market segmentation'' and ''Market targeting'' are concepts which are as useful in international marketing as they are in domestic marketing. Through careful market selection, the opportunities can be exploited and the risk involved in international business can be minimised. Product selection is as important as market selection. All aspects of the product such as the basic product constituents, the secondary features, brand names, packaging—package protection, package aesthetics, package size, lebelling and usage instructions—may need adaptation, depending on the situation, they have to be matched with the needs of the specific overseas markets. All products may not be amenable for globalised offers. In such cases, it is essential for the international marketer to ensure that the products are tailored to suit the different markets.

2. Market Entry

Export of products is the primary route to entry into global markets. Through joint venture, a firm literally gets close to foreign markets. In recent years, both exporting nations and importing nations have among themselves formed powerful cartels for various commodities.

Establishment of joint ventures and collaborations in foreign countries with some foreign firms for marketing the products and/or occasional manufacturing. A firm will have to determine the most appropriate method of entering into those international markets which offer good and feasible marketing opportunities.

3. Distribution Channels

The international marketer must take into account channels between nations and also channels within nations. Channels between nations include export through middlemen in one country or direct export to foreign customers who may be end-users or middlemen in foreign countries. Marketers should take interest with the entire channel of distribution from producer to the final buyer. The whole channel concept for each market is necessary for good international marketing.

4. Pricing for Global Markets

Generally, the principles and techniques of pricing are the same in domestic and international marketing. Firms which have a short-term interest in the foreign markets, may provide cost plus pricing strategy provided markets can be found at the price. However, firms with long-term interest in the foreign markets have to adopt a market oriented pricing policy. They have to take into account the conditions in each country and in each district market segment and formulate appropriate pricing policies for each market segment.

5. International Marketing Research

Marketing planning should rest on the foundation of marketing research. This is all the more true in the case of international marketing planning. Without reliable marketing information gathered through detailed marketing research, major decisions in international marketing cannot be taken. All the relevant information on the overseas target markets must be systematically collected, updated, analysed and stored. The markets must be classified by their size, customer requirements, channel patterns, distribution methods and other relevant characteristics. A good part of the data required for such studies can be collected from published and other readily available sources. To supplement this market surveys may be conducted.

6. International Marketing Communications

In domestic marketing, a marketer is appealing to people who are better known to him, using a known language, known symbols and familiar media. But in international marketing, we have to tackle unfamiliar people, a strange language, unfamiliar media and unfamiliar purchase motivations. Marketing communication has to be adapted to suit the foreign markets and the foreign audience. Advertising, trade promotion and high level personal selling are the major components of international marketing communications.

7. Procedural Complexities

A businessman is required to understand a variety of procedural complexities covering a number of areas like export-import licence, customs, foreign exchange, mode of payment, documentation, insurance regulations, quality regulations etc.

8. Organisation for International Marketing

Firms manage their international marketing activities in at least three different ways. Most firms first organise an *export department, then* create an International division and ultimately become a *multinational organisation*. A firm normally gets into international marketing by simply shipping out the goods. If its international sales expand, the company organises an export department consisting of a sales manager and a few assistants. Many companies get involved in several international markets and venture. A company may export to one country, licence to another, have a joint ownership venture in a third, and own a subsidiary in a fourth. Sooner or later it will create an international division or subsidiary to handle all its international activity.

Several firms have passed beyond the international division stage and become truly multinational organisations. They stop thinking of themselves as national marketers who venture abroad and start thinking of themselves as global marketers.

44.4 IMPORTANCE OF INTERNATIONAL MARKETING

(a) From the point of view of national economy:

(1) The developing countries need imports of capital equipments, raw materials of crucial nature and technical know-how for rapid industrialisation.

(2) An expanding export trade is a dynamic factor in a country's development process and the economic development of a country has a direct relation with exports.

(3) A high rate of economic growth, when contemplated by a country, is usually associated with a higher rate of export development.

(4) Sufficient export earnings are essential to cover import debt.

(5) Natural resources are valuable assets of a country and their economic exploitation necessitates import as foreign plants and machineries for the establishment of industrial units and calls for export marketing to earn valuable foreign exchange.

(6) The national income of a country can be increased to a considerable extent through organised export marketing.

(7) The standard of living of the people of a country is improved by imported items, quality products and use of improved technology.

(b) From the point of view of individual firm :

(1) A firm having an unutilised installed capacity after meeting the domestic market has to enter the international market for the economical utilisation of the capacity.

(2) A firm having a production system on a mass scale and facing severe fall in domestic demand has no alternative but to tap foreign markets for boosting up sales.

(3) A firm whose product life cycle is at the declining stage in the domestic market should have to find ways and means for survival and for this export trade has to be resorted to.

(4) A firm desirous to introduce new products likes to enter foreign markets with latest technology.

CHAPTER 45

Rural Marketing

- *Introduction*
- *Urban Markets*
- *Significance of Rural Markets*
- *Key Decision Areas*
- *Media Mix*
- *Questions*

45.1 INTRODUCTION

Rural areas in India is considered today as a huge storehouse of untapped marketing opportunities, by marketers. India is a very large country. Rural marketing is identifying and serving the needs of consumers living in villages. Three-fourths of India's population lives in rural areas. About 30% of our national income is generated by this sector. Some of these villages are located near cities and they enjoy facilities like electricity, water supply, communication infrastructure etc. Some other villages are located in remote areas and modern facilities have not yet reached them. The primary source of income for rural consumers is agriculture.

During the last four or five decades, India's progress on the industrial front and agricultural production has been significant and has resulted in substantial economic growth. The contribution of the Green Revolution and continued stress on socio-economic and technological development of the vast rural India have brought noticeable economic and social changes. India is a vast country with huge population and about three-fourths of the papulation lives in rural areas. The intelligent use of fertilisers, high yield agricultural crops and modern implements by farmers have brought about changes in the life-style and living condition of the large rural population.

A few years back, the rural market in India was an unknown area and many companies were not interested in entering the rural markets in India, as the demand pattern was fragile, seasonal, poor purchasing power of people, etc. Communication, transportation and infrastructure were the main blocks for growth of rural markets and penetration of urban products in rural markets. But these things of the past have been changed. Now everyone is looking at rural markets as the next growth driver in Indian market.

As a result of the Green Revolution in agriculture and White Revolution in dairy, and other developmental activities implemented through the Five Year Plans, the productivity, prosperity and disposable incomes of the rural population have improved. Thus, the standard of living and lifestyles of Indian rural people have also changed for better living, and this situation has generated demand for a variety of fast moving consumer products, consumer durables and services.

In the past, rural marketing was reckoned only as marketing of agricultural produce. Because of special interest taken by the Government, many regulated markets have been established in our country to facilitate proper marketing of farm produce. Adoption of scientific and commercial farming popularised the use of inputs like chemical fertilizers, pesticides, cattle and poultry feeds, high yielding varieties of seeds, and also tractors, tillers, other farm equipments etc: because of all these, the scope of rural marketing started widening. The penetration of television also gave an impetus to provide accessibility to marketers into rural India, for promoting consumer products.

The common myths of rural market lead us to believe that rural market is an area which is vast in size but amorphous in detail. And yet, the rural markets represent the largest potential market in the country. It encompasses over 70% of population. Its primary activities — agriculture, animal husbandry, fisheries, forests etc. — account for 50% of national income. Rural assets also amount to more than 50% of the country's tangible wealth.

Rural marketing is now a two-way marketing process. There is inflow of products into rural markets for production or consumption. There is also outflow of products to urban areas. The urban to rural flow consists of agricultural inputs, and fast moving consumer goods, such as soaps, detergents, cosmetics, textiles, and consumer durables like two-wholesalers, cars, television sets, electrical appliances etc. The rural to urban flow consists of agricultural produce like rice, wheat, sugar, tobacco, vegetables, etc. Products of cottage and village industries like handloom textiles, handicrafts etc. enter urban areas. There is also a movement of rural products within rural areas for consumption. Rural marketing, therefore, concerned with the flow of goods and services from urban to rural and vice versa and within the rural area itself.

Rural consumers live differently, their environmental conditions are different, and their source and pattern of income is different. Rural markets are different from urban markets in significant ways.

Now we examine the present conditions of urban markets:

1. The urban markets have almost reached a saturation stage that further tapping them with a normal profit margin has become difficult.
2. Increasing competition in urban markets make rural markets attractive new markets for marketing products.
3. Competition is becoming tough in urban markets, compelling many firms to incur heavy amounts in promotional expenditure.
4. The awareness level of urban consumers is high and hence product features have to be changed often. This leads to heavy investment, which will have a negative impact on profitability.

45.2 SIGNIFICANCE OF RURAL MARKETS

There are a large number of reasons for growing interest in rural markets. Due to various developmental programmes, today, the rural markets offer vast untapped potential to marketers. In order to facilitate full exploitation of the rural market potential, the marketers have to understand the factors involved in the rural marketing environment. The major reasons for growing rural markets are:

1. Growing Population

India's rural market is indeed a large one. It consists of more than 740 million Indians, forming 73% of the Indian Population in rural areas, according to census 2001. The rate of increase of rural population is higher than that of urban population. There are more than 5,70,000 villages in India of varying sizes based on the number of persons living in different habitations. The number of rural households is in excess of 120 million and accounts for over 70% of total household in India. The urban population of India lives in 3200 cities and towns, and just 9040 villages have population of 5,000 or more. The remaining villages have less than 5,000 people in each village. In urban areas the demand is limited to just 3,200 cities and towns and the rural market demand is highly scattered in our vast country.

2. Market Size

It is evident that the rural market of India is a geographically scattered market. Whereas the urban population of India is concentrated in 3,200 cities and towns, the rural population is scattered across 5,70,000 villages. And, of them, only 6,300 villages, or less than 1.1%, have a population of more than 5,000 each. More than 3 lakh villages, or more than 55% of the total number of villages, are in the category of 500 people or less and more 1.5 lakh villages or 25%, are in the category of

200 people or less. The inference is clear, unlike urban demand, which is highly concentrated rural demand is scattered over a large area.

The size of India's rural market is stated as 12.2% of the world population. This means 12.2% of the world's consumers live in rural India. In India, rural households form about 72% of the total household and this constitutes a huge market.

3. Current Consumption

The purchase and consumption of certain durables and non-durables by consumers in rural areas is more than that in urban areas. Some of the durables for which the demand in rural areas is more than that of urban areas are sewing machines, transistors, wrist watches, television sets, bicycles, batteries, table fans, coconut oil, tea, toilet soaps, washing powder, washing cakes etc.

4. Increasing Income

The growing opportunity in the rural market is no doubt the prime factor. The increased income or purchasing power of the rural consumer and the improved income distribution have enhanced rural demand for several products. Better access to many modern products/brands has added to this growth.

Different programmes undertaken by the government have helped to improve the economic situation of the rural areas.

5. Accessibility of Markets

The attractiveness and sustainability of a market depends upon its accessibility. The marketing programme can be implemented if the market has necessary communication, transport, storage and other necessary infrastructure facilities. The road network has considerably increased in last 30/40 years. Some states like Gujarat almost 95% of the villages and towns are connected by roads. Therefore, delivery and maintenance of stock of goods in interior rural areas is not a problem. At present, increasing number of companies and sending their stock directly to village markets in vans. These vans do delivery and promotion work and cover more than 5/6 villages, in a day.

6. Change in Rural Consumer Behaviour

Increased mobility between urban and rural areas because of improved transport and communication facilities, and also due to greater emphasis on literacy, etc. contributed greater awareness of products and services available to rural consumers. Product awareness with higher disposable income, have created demand for many products which were earlier thought to be urban products. The latest trends show increasing number of subscribers of mobile phones in rural and small markets in Maharashtra, Kerala and Tamil Nadu. In Andhra and Karnataka, about 40% of business of mobile service companies are in rural areas and smaller towns.

By and large, the rural consumers are marked by a conservative and tradition-bound lifestyle. But, what is striking today about this is not the basic conservative characteristic, but the fact that the lifestyle is undergoing a significant change. The lifetyle of a sizeable segment of rural consumers has already changed significantly in recent years, and that of a much larger segment is currently going through the process of change.

7. Competition in Urban Areas

The competition for market share, sale, profit etc. in the urban market is driving many companies to look beyond the urban market which has been their activity area for the least few decades. The costs have been increased and the profits are reduced. In such a situation, rural market is becoming more remunerative and profitable. The urban market is getting saturated and thus is unable to provide the much-needed market to many companies and in search of greener pastures, many of these companies are now targeting the rural market. The heat of competition in the urban market actually serves as the stronger driver behind the growing interest of corporates in the rural market. The fact that the rural market is still largely untapped and virgin market and the fact that the early entrants can tap it without having to face competition as in the case of the urban market, makes the rural market all the more attractive to them.

45.3 KEY DECISION AREAS IN RURAL MARKETING

Marketing in rural India requires hard work. While rural India does constitute an attractive and sizeable market, firms have to strive hard for securing a share of it. If rural markets have to be developed, each of the marketing elements — products, price, distribution and promotion, should be performed in a different manner. We shall examine the problems:

(1) Rural Market Segmentation

A marketer has certain important sources of data available and can consider several variables, to segment these markets. There are no hard and fast rules regarding what variables to choose. The following variables seem to be relevant to most of the rural areas in India and can be considered in determining the different market segments:

- Geographic location
- Population density
- Gender and age
- Occupation
- Income levels
- Socio-cultural considerations
- Language and literacy
- Lifestyle etc.

Other than the conventional methods of segmentation, we can also use few more variables as shown below:

- Land holding pattern (size of holding)
- Irrigation facilities
- Cropping pattern
- Education level
- Proximity to cities
- Occupation categories (labourer, farmer, employees etc.)

(2) Product Planning

Companies have to consider whether the existing successful products available in the urban areas can be marketed in the rural markets without any modification. It is advisable for companies first to determine what consumers in the rural markets need and want, and then select products from the available ones. Of course, much depends on the nature of the product under consideration. Product specifications like design, price and durability should be in accordance with the needs of the rural masses. There need not be too much sophistication, but the product must be simple in its function and, of-course, reasonably priced. The pacing should be simple, reflecting rural culture, Specifically, the following points must be kept when developing products for rural markets:

- Product must be simple in design-simple to understand, operate, maintain and repair.
- Functional aspects rather than sophisticated looks should be stressed.
- Price should be within the economic competence of rural consumers.
- Packaging should be simple, facilitate product use, should not add to cost and lead to economy in use of the product.
- The brand name should suit rural background.

The product strategy will focus on product market characteristics, product range, product positioning and packaging. The variation of rural market characteristics provide for opportunities to offer products to meet these needs of various segments of the rural market. The marketing firm must allocate its marketing effort based upon the relative ability to utilize opportunities in different product markets. Product market selection decision in rural markets require a careful assessment of relative capabilities on distribution and cost of the offering.

Economic and income realities of the market should certainly be considered while developing the product strategy for the rural market. In addition, socio-cultural realities should also be considered. When products are designed reflecting both these influences, the chance of success is greater.

Lower-priced product versions do help in many cases in the rural market, but no generalization can be made in this regard. Many companies try to reduce the prices of their products for the rural market by creating smaller size, or by decreasing the quality. The approach works sometimes and with some products, but not all times, with all products.

(3) Pricing Decision

The rural consumer in general, is price sensitive, or more appropriately, value conscious. Apparently, this has much to do with the income level of most of the consumers. The marketer will have to examine ways to make the product affordable to a large number of consumers in the rural markets. In case of a large number of non-durable consumer products, it is possible to design smaller pack sizes or unit sizes. In case of consumer durable and farm machinery, such as motorcycles, TV's, refrigerators, tractors, pumps, etc., the marketer may make arrangements with some banks for financing customers at low rates of interest or make arrangements with his dealers to offer products on instalments.

Pricing strategies are linked more to product positioning and packaging. Product packaging and presentation offer scope for keeping the prices low to suit the purchasing power of rural consumers but is wrong to presume that only cheap brands or low-priced products sell in rural markets. The decision of low income rural consumers is to buy something which has a value for its price, that is, utility value. Rural consumers are ready to buy higher-priced products particularly after harvesting time and festival season. The price and positioning decisions are therefore influenced not just by the income received but also on when it is received and how it is allocated among different needs of the rural consumers.

(4) Distribution Strategies

It is well known that transportation infrastructure in most parts of rural India is in poor shape. Though our country has the third largest system of railways in the world, many parts of rural India remain outside the rail network. Nearly 50% of the 5,70,000 villages in our country have no proper roads. While some improvements are taking place on account of the various road development programmes, many areas still have bad roads and most of the interiors have hardly any roads worth mentioning. As regards transport carriers, the most common ones are the delivery vans and the animal drawn carts. Because of the difficulty in accessibility, delivery of products and services continues to be difficult in rural areas. In warehousing too, there are special problems in the rural context. Business firms find it quite difficult to get suitable godowns in many parts of rural India.

In many areas, the number of available dealers is limited and finding a proper dealer may be difficult due to limited demand. Most dealers do not seem to have a reasonable turnover to make their operations attractive. Whatever extra a company spends in reaching these markets does not result in any kind of attractive incentive to the channel members and moreover, there is no assurance that all concerned will be benefitted.

For a large number of consumer goods, a typical village shop is unique. There are more than 3.6 million shops in the rural areas of the country. For any given product, the stocks are very limited because the shopkeeper has to maintain an inventory of a large number of products. The demand for many of these products vary considerably and it becomes difficult to establish any kind of pattern. Consequently, the inventories for many items are carried for a longer period of time. The supplies from various sources are off and on, generally involving longer lead-time, and sometimes the shopkeeper makes trips to down in a hurry to replenish the needed products. These factors block money and increase operational costs of the village retails. Any chance of earning more margins by increasing retail price at the shop level is self-defeating as consumers are otherwise quite sensitive to prices. Similarly, there is no way of increasing retail turnover. It is estimated that the average daily turnover of rural shop may be within the range of Rs. 400/500 to Rs. 600/700 and that too when the shopkeeper extends credit to its customers. This makes the picture of retailing in rural markets gloomy. But these retailers generally have their ups during festivals.

(5) Promotion

The masses in rural areas are highly traditional with high regard and compliance for deep-rooted customs. We have seen the rate of literacy among rural consumers is low and this drawback limits the use of printed words, Communicating the message to rural consumers has posed enormous problems due to diversity, distance and disintegrated rural markets.

The marketers have to make sure that their products are used by influential people of the village. If a particular brand of fertilizer is being used by the most educated and progressive farmer, all the farmers will start using the same brand of fertilizer. In buying products like fertilizers, seeds, pesticides, cements, farming equipment etc, rural consumers consult and emulate the most educated farmer of the village. It is important for the company to ensure that the educated farmers of the village use its brand.

Rural India has many fairs and festivals and marketers use these platforms for brand promotions. There is also use of mobile van publicity in rural areas where vans serve as a vehicle of product distribution and brand promotions. Salesman with vans move from village to village. Vans are fitted with projecting equipment or music system to catch the attention of people and announce for their assembly at some point in the village for entertainment. The salesman can then talk about his product and do spot selling. Wherever possible on the basis of these sales a local dealer may be motivated to keep stocks. Rural marketers use demonstrators for product display and promotion in village fairs and festivals.

Rural consumers are very fond of quoting statements of politicians, movie heroes, cricketers etc. Communicating with rural consumers effectively requires, a proper understanding of the rural consumers in different parts of the country. Some companies employ audio-visual vans, which are under the control of the firm. These vans provide marketers comprehensive means of promotion with added advantages. These vans screen films and carry ready stocks to deliver to the outlets and the vans are used for a variety of purposes, such as, demonstrations of products, selling products to retailers, collecting market information etc. Rural consumers are readers of newspapers. They scan every page of newspaper and are interested in local news.

(6) Communication and Personal Selling

Rural customers have poor literacy level, the scope for using print media – magazines, newspapers, periodicals etc. is not viable alternative. The situation is further compounded by the linguistic diversity. In the urban areas, marketing communication can be managed by and large with English and Hindi. Marketing communication in the rural area has to necessarily be in the local language. The constraints in media compound the difficulty.

45.4 POSSIBLE MEDIA MIX

1. **Formal Media**	2. **Non Formal**
TV	Audio Visual
Cinema	Publicity Vans
Radio	Puppet shows
Print Media	Demonstrations
Outdoor	Announcements
POPs, etc.	Music records etc.

TV : With the increase in coverage and increase in TV ownership in rural areas, TV is gradually becoming the prima medium for rural communication.

CINEMA : The cinema is a useful medium in the rural areas. Most large and medium villages have one or more cinema houses. On average, more than one-third of all rural people do see cinema, as a regular lifestyle.

RADIO : The radio is a well-established medium in rural areas. A big expansion in broadcasting facilities have taken place in the country over the years. The availability of radio sets has also expanded.

PRINT MEDIA : While the role of print media is certainly limited in the rural areas, it cannot be ruled out totally. Even the remote rural parts have a small group, which is literate. Moreover, while the group may be numerically small, its members usually happen to be the opinion leaders, influencing purchasing behaviour of a large segment of the rural consumers. Moreover, the younger generation in the rural areas is comparatively more literate.

OUTDOOR : The outdoors, which include hoardings, wall paintings, illumination and other displays works well for rural communication

POPs : Point of purchase or point of sale as promotion tools are quite useful in the rural markets.

AUDIO VISUAL : Audio-visual unit or the publicity van is very useful for rural communication. The van is comprehensive mobile promotion place at the exclusive command of the concerned firm. The publicity vans are quite popular with rural marketing firms.

Personal selling has special significance in the rural markets. It is important to note that the companies would do better to appoint sales people who hail from the concerned rural areas because they would be the one who are completely familiar and conversant with local conditions including language and culture. When such sales people are working in these areas, mingling and understanding rural consumers pose no problems. It is possible to develop beneficial relationships. Such sales persons need not resort to pressure selling techniques. They are more likely to be effective, if they adopt a position of a consultant. The sales people start by trying to understand in general terms the problems and needs that the company's products or services can solve, suggest more than one alternative, and explain the pros and cons of these alternatives.

Questions

1. Explain the importance of Indian rural market.
2. What are the key challenges of Indian rural market?
3. What problems companies face in the rural markets?
4. Explain four key challenges that a marketer faces while entering into Indian rural markets.
5. Distinguish between rural markets and urban markets.

CHAPTER 46

Marketing and Society

- *Introduction*
- *Social Responsibility*
- *How Marketing Influence Society*
- *Economic Aspects*
- *The Environment*
- *How Society Influence Marketing*
- *Social Criticism of Marketing*
- *Consumer Movement*
- *Questions*

46.1 INTRODUCTION

Marketing is no longer an activity confined to the exchange of goods and services in the conventional sense. With the passage of time, it has become highly versatile. The marketing concept is a philosophy of service and mutual gain. Not all marketers follow the marketing concept.

Business is marketing and marketing is business. A business firm is an economic institution of society and the businessmen and the marketers are members of society and their actions and performance are for the consumers, who are also members of society. Therefore, a business is something which has social implication. Society-oriented marketing rather than marketing-oriented society is a basic necessity. The marketing policies and objectives of business should be framed in a way that would contribute liberally to the social well-being. Marketing and society go hand in hand.

46.2 SOCIAL RESPONSIBILITY

Modern business is large and complex, catering to national and international markets. It exercises a definite and extensive influence on our economic and social life styles. As a social agency, marketing is responsible to deliver a standard of living and a standard of life-style consumers. Modern business must have society's approval in order to function successfully. In the present world, society is expecting much more from business than in the past. Society demands quality of life management. Integrated business plans and controls are expected to act as instrument of *social change* and these plans have to be implemented in order to promote social public welfare. Modern business must also demonstrate social awareness or sensitivity and social performance. Social responsibility means an intelligent and objective concern for the welfare of society that limits or prevents corporate behaviour from destructive activities - unfair trade practices. Such destructive activities may be immediately profitable to business but they cannot be tolerated by the society.

46.3 HOW MARKETING INFLUENCE SOCIETY ?

Economic Aspects

Marketing performs an economic role. Marketing serves as the mechanism through which production and purchasing power are converted into consumption, incurs substantial cost, which society pays. Marketing costs on an average amount to more than half of the total price paid by the final buyer. Marketing creates place utility. Time utility creation is also the function of marketing. These functions cannot be performed without incurring certain amount of cost. Thus total cost increases. But certain questions arise :

Does marketing cost too much ?

What is the benefit of marketing cost on total cost ?

Are there any offsetting benefits ?

What can be done to reduce marketing cost ?

Does Marketing Cost Too Much ?

The cost of marketing eats larger share in the prices that buyers pay—most experts say that out of each rupee the ultimate buyer spends, roughly half rupee goes for the cost of performing marketing activities.

To answer the question, we must compare the costs and benefits. Are the marketing activities performed here worth what they cost to the consumer ? Take for example, wheat produced in Punjab and is consumed in Kerala. Hence, the products need movement from one place to the other. This needs conveyance charges. Thus, the consumer has to pay for *place utility*. Again, wheat is grown at one time and is consumed at a later time. Thus *time utility* also enhances the price and consumer has to pay. Marketing activities add value to a product by changing the ownership, its time and place of consumption. Conversion of wheat into flour, also adds value to the product through adding *form utility*, but value is added here by manufacturing, not marketing.

46.7 THE ENVIRONMENT

Society is concerned with ecology and the need for preserving the environment from further human pollution. Business and industry are leading contributors to environmental pollution. Marketers are not responsible and not answerable. Packaging is pollutant feature of marketing. In order to differentiate the brands and buyer preferences, marketers use packaging, for butter, cream, cheese etc. Marketers also use disposable products. As paper napkins replaces cloth napkins, this require disposal. Disposable drinking cups, beverages are a few disposable products which add to environmental pollution due to marketing operations. Some people are of the opinion that the road side advertisement mars the road-side beauty.

46.5 HOW SOCIETY INFLUENCE MARKETING ?

Public opinion and political pressure are the results of pleasure and displeasure of the society. It has been aptly described by Cundiff that ''marketers have not often bothered to investigate society's reaction to their marketing practices. Society has often taken the initiative in communicating its displeasure through various forms of social pressure against offenders. The mildest form of social pressure is public opinion aimed at causing the offending marketers to change their ways. When public opinion does not accomplish the desired result, stronger action takes the form of political pressure, with an implied threat of ultimate legal action to force the offender to abide by society's wishes. And the strongest form of social pressure is restrictive legislation outlawing the unpopular product or marketing activities.''

46.6 SOCIAL CRITICISM OF MARKETING

Originally, the business firms based their marketing decisions largely on immediate profit calculations. Philip Kotler states that a firm should earn a satisfactory level of profit, no doubt, but it must also assume its social responsibility as a member of society. Further he states that a firm's profit must be harmonised with society's interest and well-being. Most of the companies did not grasp or embrace the social marketing concept until driven to it by circumstance. Consider the sale of cigarettes. Ordinarily, companies are free to sell cigarettes and smokers are free to buy them. Indian made cigarette packs are printed with statutory warning: ''Cigarette smoking is injurious to health.'' If it be so, then why should the companies manufacture cigarettes and harm the consumers' health. Smoking habits shorten the smokers' life. The people around the smoker may have to inhale the smoke and may suffer discomfort. Further, whisky, wine, brandy etc. are examples. Manufacturers continue to produce cigarettes to satisfy their own interest (*i.e.*, profit) and to meet the consumers want-satisfaction (*i.e.*, smoking),with utter disregard of society's interests.

Many types of criticism has been levelled at marketing. Social critics claim that certain marketing practices hurt individual consumers, society as a whole and other business firms. Let us examine how marketing affects the issue :

1. As a result of high cost in marketing, the consumers pay higher price. Modern marketing is accused of pushing up prices because of heavy advertising and sales promotion costs.
2. Marketers sometimes are accused of deceptive practices that lead consumers to believe that they will get more value than they actually do. Deceptive promotion include (a) over-stating the product feature, (b) misleading labelling, (c) describing size in misleading terms etc.
3. Sales people are accused of high pressure selling that persuades people to buy goods, they had no thought of buying. Many items are sold, not bought. Salesmen are trained in such a way that unwanted or unneeded items are imposed on buyers.
4. Another criticism is that products lack the quality they should have. There are unsafe products and unstated dangers in product-performance.
5. Urban buyers have to shop in smaller stores that carry inferior goods and charge higher prices. There are many marketers who advertise false value, sell old merchandise as new or charge too much for credit.
6. Critics have charged that the marketing system urges too much interest in material possessions.
7. Some firms have in fact used unfair competitive marketing practices with the intention of hurting or destroying other firms.
8. Marketers usually engage in unethical practices.
9. Marketers have introduced guarantee and warranty schemes against purchases. But customers are cheated.
10. Marketers unknowingly pollute the cultural environment.

46.7 CONSUMER MOVEMENT

Consumer Movement what is the consumer movement ? Consumerism is an organised movement of citizens and government agencies to improve the rights and power of buyers in relation to sellers. Traditional sellers' rights include :

* The right to introduce any product in any size and style, provided it is not hazardous to personal health or safety; if it is, to include proper warnings and controls.
* The right to charge any price for the product, provided no discrimination exists among similar kinds of buyers.
* The right to spend any amount to promote the product, provided it is not defined as unfair competition.
* The right to use any product message, provided it is not misleading or dishonest in content or execution.
* The right to use any buying incentive schemes, provided they are not unfair or misleading.

Traditional buyers' rights include :

* The right not to buy a product that is offered for sale.

* The right to expect the product to be safe.
* The right to expect the product to perform as claimed.

Comparing these rights, many believe that the balance of power lies on the sellers' side. True, the buyer can refuse to buy. But critics feel that the buyer has too little information, education, and protection to make wise decisions when facing sophisticated sellers. Consumer advocates call for the following additional consumer rights :

* The right to be well informed about important aspects of the product.
* The right to be protected against questionable products and marketing practices.
* The right to influence products and marketing practices in ways that will improve the quality of life.

Consumers have not only the right but also the responsibility to protect themselves instead of leaving this function to someone else. Consumers who believe that they got a bad deal have several remedies available, including writing to the company or to the media; contacting legal agencies and going to courts.

Questions

1. What do you understand by social responsibility of a marketer ?
2. Briefly describe the social criticism of marketing.
3. Does marketing cost too much ?

CHAPTER 47

E- Business

- *Introduction*
- *Telemarketing*
- *Automatic Vending*
- *E–Business*
- *E–Commerce*
- *Electronic Data Interchange*
- *E–Mail*
- *Internet*
- *E–Auctioning*
- *E–Marketing*
- *E–Banking*
- *E–Trading*
- *Questions*

47.1 INTRODUCTION

There have been dramatic changes in information technology over the past ten or fifteen years. Consumers and business-people no longer need to be near a computer to send and receive information. All they need is a cellular phone. While they are on the move, they can be in touch with their field personnel no matter where they are. Advances in information technology are revolutionalising the *modus operandi* of marketing and the business system. The business horizon is humming with buzzwords like internet, world wide web (www), cyberspace, information superhighways, etc., which are changing the way of contacting customers; order receiving and processing; and networking and intergrating business system. The revolutionary changes being ushered in by the internet are indeed exciting. The revolutionary changes in the information technology is sweeping across the global business. New information technology modes include electronic mail, corporate and public databases, application systems, fax, video and computer conferencing. These modes are considered to be some of the driving forces of internationalisation. These new information technology modes have a major impact on the coordination of head-quarter-subsidiary relations. In fact, most of the MNCs have developed these new modes of information technology. The internet is a world wide, self-governed network connecting thousands of smaller networks and millions of computers and people to mega sources of information. Quite simply, it is a technology no nation or enterprise can ignore. Technology experts are anticipating that the internet and the www would become the centre of commercial universe. Electronic markets will eliminate the need for the intermediaries and that direct contact between manufacturer and customer will bring down the cost of transaction and the cost of final product. The internet has the potential to evolve into an inter-connected electronic market place (cyberspace) bringing buyers and sellers together to facilitate commercial exchanges.

It is needless to say that the internet is a world-wide network of computer networks. Imagine a network of five computers in your office which are linked up together in a manner that you can exchange data, correspondence (mail) and even soft-ware, between these computers. Now imagine that you have a business associates or friends who also have several computers in their homes or offices organised pretty much like yours. Now imagine all these computers spread over different locations linked up in a manner so that they (meaning you) can communicate between each other. This is what Internet is all about. Except as mentioned earlier, this is a global network linking millions of computers and people cutting across all barriers and boundaries of countries, race, class or sex. The networking of computers that allow the managers, employees, customers, vendors, dealers, bankers, suppliers to deal with each other even across the globe. The networking of ATMs allow the customer to deposit money in Mumbai, to withdraw money in Delhi, to deposit cheques for clearance in Kanpur and to get his statement of accounts in Chennai.

47.1 TELEMARKETING

Telemarketing, sometimes called telephone selling, refers to a sales person initiating contact with a shop-keeper and closing a sale over the telephone. That is telemarketing involves the use of the telephone and call centres to attract prospects, sell to existing customers, and provide service by taking orders and answering questions. Many products that can be bought without being seen are sold over the telephone. Telemarketing helps companies to increase revenue, reduce selling cost and improve customers' satisfaction.

Today some companies have a sales force that goes to the customers, but not in person. These sales representatives, "going to the customers" by means of telephone, computer, etc. Thus, outside selling is becoming electronic, and the term telemarketing describes such communication systems. Telemarketing has become a major marketing tool. Telemarketing is increasingly used in business as well as consumer marketing. Telemarketers should have pleasant voices and project enthusiasm. Effective telemarketing depends on choosing the right telemarketers, training them well and providing performance incentives. Telemarketing is growing because: (*a*) many buyers prefer it over personal sales calls, and (*b*) many markets find that it increases selling efficiency. Sellers face increasingly high costs keeping sales people on the road; selling by telemarketing reduces that expense. Also routine selling by telemarketing allows the field sales force to devote more time to creative selling, major account selling and other more profitable selling activities.

47.3 AUTOMATIC VENDING

The sale of products through a machine with no personal contact between buyer and seller is called automatic vending. The appeal of automatic vending is convenient purchase. Products sold by automatic vending are usually well-known, presold brands with a high rate of turnover. Automatic vending is used for a variety of merchandise, including impulse goods like cigarettes, soft drinks, coffee, newspapers, magazines, etc. Vending machines can expand a firm's market by reaching customers where and when they cannot come to a store. Thus vending equipment is found almost everywhere, particularly in schools, factories, offices, large retail stores, gasoline stations, hotels, restaurants and many other places. They offer 24 hour selling, self-service and merchandise that is always fresh. Automatic vending has high operating costs because of the need to replenish inventories frequently. The machines also require maintenance and repairs.

47.4 E-BUSINESS

As computers became common business tools in the late 1950s firms were able to collect, store and manipulate larger amounts of data to aid marketing decision makers. Out of this capability developed the marketing information system—an ongoing, organised procedure to generate, analyze, disseminate, store, and retrieve information for use in making marketing decisions. Information is recognised as an important resource. A wide variety of information needs of a business are organised into what is called "Management Information System" (MIS). A management information system consists of inter connected subsystems. They provide the information necessary to stay competitive. The computer is an electronic tool that is used to collect, organise, analyse, interpret and communicate vast amounts of information with great speed.

E-business describes the use of electronic means and platforms to conduct company's business. The advent of the Internet has greatly increased the ability of companies to conduct their business faster, more accurately, over a wider range of time and space, at reduced cost and with the ability to customize and personalize customer offerings. Many companies have set up Web site to inform and promote their products and services. IBM defines e-business as "a secure, flexible and integrated approach to deliver differentiated business value by combining the systems and processes that run core business operations with the simplicity and reach made possible by Internet technology."

E-business can be (*a*) within the organisation, that is, Intranets facilitate employees communicating with one another and to facilitate downloading and uploading information to and from the company's computers. (*b*) Business to Business dealings, that is Extranet consists of two Intranets connected via the Internet, whereby two organisation are allowed to see confidential data of the other. (*c*) Business to Customer transactions, that is, selling the goods and services through Internet to the innumerable customers spread all over the world.

Electronic business is a super-set of business cases. E-commerce is one of the aspects of E-business. Some other important aspects of E-business, which are successfully carried through the Internet are e-auctioning, e-banking, e-mailing, e-learning, e-marketing, e-trading, etc.

47.7 E-COMMERCE

Prashant Jain defined Electronic Commerce (E-Commerce) as "the exchange of business information using electronic formats, including Electronic Mail, Electronic Bulletin Boards and Electronic Funds Transfer. E-Commerce technologies are designed to replace traditional paper-based work flow with faster, more efficient and reliable communications between computers." He further stated that "e-commerce" is the process of two or more parties making business transactions via computer and some type of network, *e.g.*, a direct connection or the Internet.

E-commerce (electronic commerce) is the buying and selling of goods and services via the communications capabilities of private and public computer networks including the Internet. Global business indeed is increasingly becoming e-business. This helps both the parties to efficiently coordinate their activities. Extranet also links dealers, retailers and distributors so that the company can have better controls on the delivery of finished goods. All consultants, ad agencies and market research agencies are linked with the company through the extranet making it possible for them to provide service of value to the company.

E-commerce is more specific than e-business; it means that in addition to providing information to visitors about the company, its history, policies, products and job opportunities, the company or site offers to transact or facilitate the selling of products and services online. E-marketing describes the company efforts to inform, communicate promote, and sell its products and services over the Internet. The 'e' term is also used in terms such as e-finance, e-learning and e-service. But as someone observed, the 'e' will eventually be dropped when most business practice is online.

47.6 ELECTRONIC DATA INTERCHANGE

The term electronic data interchange has many definitions. American National Standards Institute has defined it as: "Electronic Data Interchange (EDI) is the transmission, in a standard syntax, of unambiguous information of business or strategic significance between computers of independent organisations."

The principle of EDI is simple. It is a set of standards that define the way the paper forms should be rendered electronically. For example, EDI can be used to send an invoice or an order form from one company to another. The "sending computer" located at a customer's premises, used telecommunication technology to transfer order data instantly to the "receiving computer", located at the supplier's distribution centre. Software on each company's computer translates the item into standard codes, so it would not matter if one company calls a product a cog and the order calls the same thing a sprocket, EDI will make sure that the right part is ordered. After the order is received data are manipulated and formatted to match the order entry files, in the "order data base" of the supplier. The information is then transferred into the data base and appropriate error messages, and/or exception reports are generated. The "sending computer" stores the order and follows up on it. The "receiving computer" automatically transfers the data to the warehouse of the factory, the accounting and billing department and the shipping department. Electronic Data Interchange is the transfer of business documents, such as purchase orders and invoices, between computers as per a set of standards. EDI facilitates the transfer of business documents stored in structured format through mutually agreed messaging protocols – from one computer application to another.

47.7 E-MAIL

E-Mail is "the exchange of text message and computer files over a communications network such as a local area network or the Internet, usually between computers or terminals." It is also defined as "an electronic text message". Communication is the basis of all businesses. "The internet breaks into the traditional communication markets. Postal services and telecommunications companies are losing market share to the electronic communication, especially e-mail. E-mail combines the strengths of phone calls and letters. The internet enables combines the strengths of phone calls and letters. The internet enables instant communication in written form, either by e-mail or online chat.

47.8 INTERNET

Internet is "the world wide collection of networks and gateways that use the TCP/IP suite of protocols to communicate with one other. At the heart of the Internet is a backbone of high-speed data communication lines between major modes or host computers, consisting of thousands of commercial, Government, educational and other computer systems, that route data and messages. One or more Internet nodes can go off line without endangering the internet as a whole or causing communications on the Internet to stop.

47.9 E-AUCTIONING

Auctioning on the Internet has become popular nowadays. In traditional methods of auctioning all those who would like to participate in the auction either assemble at one place or bid over the phone. Some who are busy may find it difficult to spare time to participate in the auction. But nowadays all those who have Internet connection can participate in the auction by sitting in the home itself. The Internet enables everyone, irrespective of the country to which he belongs and where he is located, can visit the auction web site with a click and participate in the auction. In e-auctioning the people who want to participate in the auction visit the web site with a click, go through the details of the goods offered on the concerned web pages and place the price or price they would like to offer on the web page.

47.10 E-MARKETING

In traditional marketing the marketing team could not get immediate results on the customer reaction. They conducted market surveys, processed the data and prepared the reports. On the basis of those reports the management took decisions, formulated the policies, prepared the plans and implemented them. For all these they took lot of time. The Internet allows companies to react to individual customer demands immediately without any loss of time. It does not matter where the customer is located. This is called e-marketing.

47.11 E-BANKING

Electronic banking is one of the most successful online businesses. E-banking allows customers to access their accounts and execute orders through a simple-to-use web site. Electronic banking saves individuals and companies' time and money. Online banking allows the customers to self-service themselves. Customers can get money from an Automated Teller Machine (ATM) instead of walking upto the cash counter in the bank, can view their accounts, transfer funds and can pay bills.

47.12 E-TRADING

E-trading, where the basic requirements are a PC, a modem and the Internet connection, the investor can log on to an online trading portal, go through a comprehensive database of information, use the online analytical tools and pass on instructions to a friendly and reliable online broker. Online trading is the perfect combination of the medium of net catering to a real life concept. Online trading is the perfect solution to investor needs. It brings together under one site all the relevant factors to enable an informed investment, rather cheaply to the user.

QUESTIONS

1. What is meant by E-Business ?
2. What is E-Commerce ?
3. What is meant by EDI ?
4. Write short-notes:
   Automatic Vending
   E-Mail
   E-Marketing
   Telemarketing
5. What is meant by Internet ?

Total Quality Management

CHAPTER 48

48.1 INTRODUCTION

- *Introduction*
- *Quality*
- *Customer Satisfaction*
- *Customer Expectations*
- *Total Quality Management*
- *Quality Assurance*
- *Quality Circles—Guidelines*
- *Measuring Quality*
- *Benefits of TQM*
- *Investors in People*
- *Questions*

In recent years, many organisations have implemented **Total Quality Management** (TQM) programmes. TQM entails not specific procedures, policies and practices but a philosophy that commits the organisation to continuous quality improvement in all of its activities. One of the major values customers expect from vendors is high product and service quality. Most will no longer accept or tolerate average quality. If companies want to stay in the race, let alone be profitable, they have no choice but to adopt total quality management (TQM). Total Quality Management is an organisationwide approach to continuously improving the quality of all the organisation's processes, products and services.

For marketers, the best measure of quality is customer satisfaction. In a competitive environment, the ultimate indication of satisfaction is whether or not the customer returns to buy a second, third or fourth time. However, a firm can't afford to gamble that its marketing decisions are correct and then wait for repeat purchases to confirm or reject those judgements. Instead, managers realize that satisfaction is determined by how closely experience with a product meets or exceeds a customer's expectations. Therefore, marketers must do two things: (*a*) Ensure that all marketing activities, such as the price of a product, the claims made for it in advertising, and the places in which it is sold, contribute to creating reasonable expectations on the part of the customer. (*b*) Eliminate variations in customer's experiences in purchasing and consuming the product.

In business and management terms, there is an attempt to focus on a measurable concept of quality by concentrating on "fitness for purpose". A specification is supplied by the customer and the quality of the product is measured by how closely it conforms to this specification. It is based on the customer's perception of quality. In these terms quality can be defined as : "Continually meeting agreed customer needs" or "what it takes to satisfy the customer" or simply "FITNESS FOR PURPOSE".

In more general terms, quality is an elusive concept and the usual dictionary definition does not help to make it less so, that which makes a thing what it is, its attributes, its characteristics. The quality of a person may be measured by certain characteristics, such as honesty and courage.

One definition by the US Department of Defense is given below:

"Total Quality Management (TQM) is both a philosophy and a set of guiding principles that represent foundation of a continuously improving organisation. TQM is the application of quantitative methods and human resources to improve the materials and services supplied to an organisation, all the process within an organisation, and the degree to which needs of customers are met, now and in future. TQM integrates fundamental management techniques existing improvement efforts, and technical tools under a disciplined approach focused on continuous improvement."

48.2 QUALITY

Quality can be seen as an attribute of a product or service which ensures that it is attractive in the eyes of the customer. It is a relative property rather than an absolute one, in that a given product or service will be attractive to customers if it fulfils their expectations more fully than any other product or service under consideration. It means delivering the right product of service, which is fit for the purposes required by the customer, at the right price, and at the right time and place. A company that produces and delivers a beautiful-looking car to a customer will not be considered to produce quality goods if the car does not work well. Whatever the costs involved, the materials used, or the care taken in manufacture, the quality of the car will be considered poor if it is unreliable. A lawnmower that does not cut the lawn effectively is of no use to the customer whatever its price or however firmly the manufacturer describes it as a "quality" or "excellent" product.

There is no agreement on a definition of product quality, even though it is universally recognised as significant. One professional society defines 'product quality' as the set of features and characteristics of goods or service that determine its ability to satisfy needs. Despite what appears to be a straight forward definition, consumers frequently disagree on what constitutes quality in a product —whether it be a cut of a meat or a performance by a rock musician. Personal tastes are deeply involved, what you like, another person may dislike. It is important to recognize, therefore, that quality—like beauty—is to a large extent 'in the eyes of the beholder.'

Besides personal tastes, individual expectations also affect judgements of quality. That is, a consumer brings certain expectations to a purchase situations. Sometimes you have high expectations, as with a movie about which a read rave reviews. Other times you have modes expectations, as with a course for next semester that is referred to as "not too boring". Your evaluation of a product's quality depends on whether the actual experience with the goods or service exceeds, meets or falls short of your expectations.

48.3 CUSTOMER SATISFACTION

Whether the buyer is satisfied after purchase depends on the offer's performance in relation to the buyer's expectations. In general, satisfaction is a person's feelings of pleasure or disappointment resulting from comparing a product's perceived performance (or outcome) in relation to his expectations. If the performance falls short of expectations, the customer is dissatisfied. If the performance matches the expectations, the customer is satisfied. If the performance exceeds expectations, the customer is highly satisfied and delighted.

If it is accepted that high quality is a measure of excellence taken from the customer's point of view, then although producers may grade their goods in terms of quality, whether the producers' view of the grading is upheld will depend on customer perception. If customers like their strawberries to be large, firm, red and sweet, then fruit with those characteristics will be considered to be of the highest quality, and the producer of smaller, paler strawberries may not be able to convince customers of the high quality of their output, however, sweet they may taste.

The focus on the customer means that quality is conceptualised in terms of the customer's perceptions. The organisation's objective is to identify customer requirements so that both the customer's and the organisation's needs are met. It is also the intention to meet these requirements first time and thus avoid the cost of sorting out problems. The process involves: (*a*) Research; (*b*) Specification and Planning, (*c*) Delivery and (d) Review. The process focuses on the customer at key points and returns constantly to research into changing customer needs. When customer needs are identified, planning can take place into exactly what has to be delivered. The specifications and standards are determined so priorities can be established to ensure that the product or service delivered is what the customer needs and that it meets customer perceptions. Although costs and price play an important part in this, most customers will pay what is necessary in order to receive what in their view is good quality. This in turn will generate profits as customers demand this product or service above others.

48.4 CUSTOMER EXPECTATIONS

How do buyers form their expectations? From past buying experience, friends, marketers, and competitors' information and promises. If marketers raise expectations too high, the buyer is likely to be disappointed. However, if the company sets expectations too low, it would not attract enough buyers, although it will satisfy those who do buy. Some of today's most successful companies are raising expectations and delivering performances to match. These companies are aiming "total customer satisfaction". Ram cycles, for example, guarantee "total satisfaction" and will replace at its expense any dissatisfied customer's cycle within a period of three years after purchase.

A customer can be defined as anyone who receives a product or service. This approach has been extended by many companies beyond the satisfaction of the external consumer in order also to include the internal customer. One department in an organisation receives products or services from another department and passes these on to a third group. On an assembly line a commodity is passed along the line from one individual or team to another, each dependent on the other for the receipt of the commodity at the correct quality at the correct time, and aiming to pass it on with the correct added value and again on time.

The concept of the internal customer means that each process is viewed as a product so that evaluation takes place at once by the immediate customer or by the processor. This system will help to eliminate waste and reduce cost, while the overall objective will remain the satisfaction of the external customer. The product or service will be 'right first time' so that errors will be prevented through the need to satisfy the internal customer at each stage rather than through a final inspection.

48.5 TOTAL QUALITY MANAGEMENT

Quality is never absolute—It is always relative to certain other considerations. The first consideration is that the word 'quality' is meaningless unless the ultimate use of the product is also stipulated. The term 'good quality' means the article is good for the purpose for which it was intended. An article may be good for one purpose, but may be unsuitable for another. For example thin papers – type-papers—may be suitable for taking carbon copies, but they cannot be utilised as wrappers, for which thick papers are used.

"Quality control refers to the systematic control of those variables encountered in a manufacturing process which affect the excellence of the end product. Such variables result from the application of materials, men, machines and manufacturing conditions. Only when these variables are regulated to the extent that they do not detract unnecessarily from the excellence of the manufacturing process as reflected in the quality of the finished product can the control of quality be said to exist." Bethel etc.

As companies have made a conscious affort to 'focus on the customer', total quality management (TQM) and other methods have been introduced to implement this. It is possible to identify differences between total quality management (TQM) and titles such as strategic quality management (SQM). How important these are remains a matter of opinion. Total quality management is often described as 'value-based' approach to quality management; it may be seen either as a goal which an organisation aims to achieve, or the idea of a goal of total quality may be considered unattainable. On the other hand, strategic quality management can be described as both systematic and values based. It can be seen to suggest that the reason for improving quality is that it will have maximum strategic impact on the future of the organisation. Strategic quality management is designed as a practical and pragmatic framework in which the drive towards quality improvement can be sustained while not making claims on total quality. A counter-argument to this is to consider the word 'total' in the context of total quality management to mean that every part of an organisation is involved. The approach can be recognised, whatever its title, by its objectives. Total or strategic quality management can be defined as : "an intensive, long-term effort to transform all parts of the organisation in order to produce the best product and service possible to meet customer needs."

Product quality should be a primary consideration not only for manufacturers of goods but also for producers of services. It is virtually impossible for a services firm to achieve the same level of quality in all units of output. Quality varies because people, not just machines, are normally involved in producing services. In recent years, many organisations have implemented total quality management (TQM) programmes. TQM entails not just specific procedures, policies and practices, but a philosophy that commits the organisation to continuous quality improvement in all of its activities.

Total quality management is predicated on a commitment to customer interests, needs, requirements and expectations, and on the commitment of everyone to the constant improvement of the quality of everything that the organisation does and provide for its customers. Total quality management means an organisation culture to satisfy totally the customer needs and desires through an integrated system of tools, techniques and training. This involves reorganising management system, reengineering process of production and distribution radical changes in the organisation structure and processes. Such continuous improvements will give us high quality products/services. Effective management recognises productivity and quality as two sides of the same coin to increase profits and build customer patronage. An organisation that adopts TQM must implement changes in all areas of management. It must review its strategies, plans, policies, procedures and practices as per changing needs and desires of the market. The total quality is a way of life and not a magic formula. The management has to concentrate on achieving excellence in all areas of business and in all areas of management covering leadership, production process, distribution process, people management, resources management with continuous technological improvements, zero defects, ecology, social responsibility, etc.

48.6 QUALITY ASSURANCE

The quality assurance governs the ultimate fate of the enterprise in the market. No firm can really build up sustained bright product image merely through promotion. Only, through continuous managing for best quality—performance quality and market perceived quality—the firm can maintain bright product or brand image in the customer mind in a competitive market. Japan and Germany have emerged as business leaders today only through quality assurance and total quality management. If product features click with customer needs and expectations, even normal promotion is enough in a competitive market. Product becomes Unique Selling Point. Quality improvement is never ending. It is a relative value compared with the competition as perceived through the customer's eyes. It is an elusive concept because customer perception is itself difficult to predict.

Quality control often occurs at the end of the manufacturing process as a check to see if the commodity works. If it does not it is rejected and either scrapped or reworked. The problem with this approach is that there is heavy dependance on inspectors. This is expensive and obviously it is much better to identify the error at an earlier stage. Statistical process control (SPC) is a method of monitoring the conformity of a product to agreed specifications. By sampling units of the products, deviations from these specifications can be identified and adjustments made during the production process. Modern control techniques are based on the idea of an 'error-free' or 'zero-defect' approach or doing it 'right first time'. This concept arises because of the costs involved in correcting errors and the fact that the costs are usually greater the later they are identified. Under the TQM approach the team is made responsible for quality control, for reducing wastage and for ensuring that adjustments are made as soon as they are identified. Total Quality Management and Value-oriented Management are complementary and they must integrate in the management system to accomplish effective and efficient management. Indian Wisdom aims at maximum productivity and excellent quality and the same time enrichment of minds of all employees.

Quality assurance provides a framework for quality control and quality improvement. Quality assurance supports teams of employees with systems, resources and discretion appropriate to their unique contribution to the organisation, to keep them in tune with progress of quality management and improvements.

48.7 QUALITY CIRCLES

Quality circle is a small group of employees in the same works area or doing similar type of work who voluntarily meet regularly for about an hour every week to identify, analyse and resolve work related problems not only to improve quality, productivity and total performance of the organisation but also to enrich the quality of work-life of employees.

Guidelines for Effective Problem Resolution

1. Admit mistakes and don't be defensive.
2. It is better if the organisation takes quick action.
3. Employees should avoid jumping to conclusion with their own interpretation.
4. Don't argue with the customers.
5. Deal customer's feeling tactically.
6. Clarify the steps needed to solve the problem.
7. Keep customers informed of the progress made on the complaint
8. Consider remedial measures for inconveniences caused.
9. Give customers the benefit of the doubt.
10. Try to regain customer goodwill.

Dr. Deming opines that MNCs adopted quality circles without understanding what they are doing? He suggests 12 points for their successful functioning in the MNCs. They are:

1. Achieve consultancy of purpose
2. Learn a new philosophy
3. Do not depend on mass inspections
4. Reduce the number of vendors
5. Recognise two sources of faults: viz. management and production systems and production workers.
6. Improve on the job training
7. Drive out fear
8. Improve communication
9. Consider work standards carefully
10. Teach statistical methods
11. Encourage new skills
12. Use statistical knowledge

A quality circle is : "A group who meet voluntarily and regularly to identify and solve their own work related problems and implement their solutions with management approval." Small groups of employees, usually from the same work-place and under the same supervisor, volunteer to meet to identify problems and find solutions. They look at the problems that occur in their work area and that affect their own job. The group itself applies the solutions if it has the authority; otherwise management is presented with recommendations and decides on implementation. Team work and team spirit play a very important role in establishing quality management and quality environment. The total quality mission will fulfil the needs and desires of our customers, both internal and external. The mission can be achieved only through teamwork i.e. doing together. Only togetherness or unity of our afforts will create and sustain an environment, where all the self-activated towards the total satisfaction of customer needs and expectations, each one contributing his own special talents and abilities to the process. Through mutual trust, mutual respect, personal pride and above all through genuine team work, we will try utmost for excellence or perfection. This involves constant improvements in offering our services, products and processes. Team work does not happen by command at a moment's notice. It requires collaboration and spirit of co-operation. It needs action plan directed towards its accomplishment. Management's commitment, support and encouragement will be absolutely necessary.

48.8 MEASURING QUALITY

A simple indication such as profit growth, market shares or the return on capital invested can be used to judge how well a quality management system has worked, and these certainly should be among the measures used. A manager needs to be both a problem solver and planner and to be able to communicate the importance of medium and long term objectives to employees at all level so as to support the attainment of objectives and targets and measure performance against these. In Thriving on Chaos Tom Peters identifies 12 attributes of a quality system, which in themselves represent a check-list against which an organisation's management can assess the stage it has reached in the development of such a system.

1. Management is obsessed with quality;
2. The company has a guiding system or ideology;
3. Quality is measured;
4. Quality is rewarded;
5. Everyone is trained in techniques for assessing quality;
6. There is a shift of managerial philosophy from adversaria to co-operative;
7. It is recognised that there is no such thing as an insignificant improvement;
8. There is constant stimulation to improve quality;
9. There is a structure within the company dedicated to quality improvement.
10. Everybody is involved in quality management, including suppliers, distributors, customers;
11. It is understood that costs decline as quality increases;
12. It is recognised that quality is relative and improvement is never ending.

Benefits of TQM

1. A satisfied customer will likely to recommend the product to other buyers.
2. Manufacturing cost is reduced by reducing wastes.
3. TQM increases employee productivity and equipment productivity.
4. TQM reduces mistakes, thus savings are increased.
5. Increased pride of workmanship among individual workers.
6. Better justification for budgets because of efficient operations.
7. TQM ensures better profitability for the organisation.
8. Improved sustainability caused by extended time between equipment failures.
9. Streamlined maintenance and production processess.

48.9 INVESTORS IN PEOPLE

For many organisations people represent their largest cost, often 70 or 80 percent of the total. In the U.K., an initiative which recognises this fact and has the goal of attaining quality in organisations is "Investors in People". This rests on the premise that companies which have developed, or are developing, an awareness of quality acknowledge that people are the real key to achieving improvements. In a "quality" culture, people take ownership of their work and responsibility for the quality of their work.

"Investors in People" arose from the U.K. Government White Paper Employment for the 1990s which launched a partnership between business and Government. The National Training Task Force was established and the Training and Enterprise Councils and Local Enterprise Councils (in Scotland) were launched. A major priority of this initiative was to raise employer, commitment to training, hence the "Investors in People". The approach was to listen to businesses' ideas and needs, and look at the people factors which make one organisation more successful than another.

In all these practices, people are understood to be the key to achieving total quality and there is an emphasis on teams and seeing colleagues as internal customers, while being genuinely motivated to develop existing skills, develop new ones, accept the devolution of responsibility, make the best use of current or new resources, and if required, acquiring new managerial skills. Organisations need to recognise people as a valuable business resource, which can be used to create, protect or waste assets; that there are investment costs as well as benefits in this process; that the benefits will be greater than the costs; and that organisations will only benefit fully fron investing in people if they start with clearly defined objectives and actions. It is recognised that the foundation TQM is the human response and human efforts which can give extra-ordinary results with available material resources and achieve total quality. Japan is the pioneer in TQM.

The "Investors in People" programme aims to help organisations to improve performance through a planned approach that is,

(*a*) Makes a public commitment from the top to develop all employees to achieve its business objectives;

(*b*) Regularly reviews the training and development needs of all employees;

(*c*) Takes action to train and develop individuals on recruitment and throughout their employment;

(*d*) Evaluates the investment in training and developing to assess achievement and improve future effectiveness.

QUESTIONS

1. Define Total Quality.
2. What is meant by strategic management?
3. What is TQM?
4. How important is participative management for a total quality programme?
5. What part can management play in quality circles?
6. Explain "Investors in People". Summarise the benefit of it.

CHAPTER 49

Recent Trend in Marketing

- *Relationship Marketing*
- *Word-of-mouth Marketing*
- *Test Marketing*
  Case Study-1
  Case Study-2
  Case Study-3
  Case Study-4
  Case Study-5
  Case Study-6

Relationship Marketing

Companies in developed countries and many business in developing countries aim to satisfy customer needs and build lasting relationships. The issue focuses on reliability and trust between customer and organisation. As a result of this customer focus, a whole new subject, *customer relationship management* is now studied in marketing courses. According to Sheth and Sisodia, the term *relationship marketing* refers to long-term and mutually beneficial arrangements wherein both buyer and seller focus on value enhancement through the creation of more satisfying exchanges. This approach attempts to transcend the simple purchase exchange process with customers to make more meaningful and richer contracts by providing a more holistic, personalised purchase, and use or consumption experience to create stronger ties.

Pathmarajah (1993) defines relationship marketing as "the process whereby the seller and the buyer join in strong personal, professional and mutually profitable relationship over a time".

5 E's relationship marketing:

He characterised relationship as having the following properties:

- Effective
- Efficient
- Enjoyable
- Enthusiastic
- Ethical

Companies which are genuinely committed 'to the 5 E's are far less common than one may except, but those who are, aim to:

- Offer the most value, personally and professionally:
- Become a unique source in helping the buyer to build something better, egs, better peace of mind;
- Become a partner with the buyer in his objectives, and
- Establish a long-term trusting relationship with the buyer.

Relationship marketing is based on the principle that current customers are the key to long-term business success. According to Reichheld, the importance of customer retention can be judged by observing some of the following benefits it provides:

- Acquiring new customers can be five times more expensive than the costs involved in satisfying and retaining existing customers.

- The average company loses 10% of its customers each year.
- A decrease of 5% in the customer defection rate can increase profits by 25% to 85%, depending on the industry.
- The customer profit rate tends to increase over the life of retained customer.

Sheth and Parvatiyar are also of the opinion that it is to a company's advantage to develop long-term relationships with current customers because it is easier and costs less to make an additional sale to an existing customer than to make a new sale to a new customer.

Neighbourhood vegetable seller frequently reassure their frequent customers that if they are not satisfied with vegitables, they can return it, even after some use and get the full replacement.

Customer relationships are very basic to business and the growing importance of relationship marketing is a profound transformation in the way business think about customers. Many experts on marketing, like Philip Kotler. Theodore Levitt etc. predict that relationship marketing will become ever more important in the future. However, it is still in its infancy, although it has established itself as an underlying paradigm in modern industrial marketing and services marketing. Many marketers still stick stubbornly to the marketing mix. However, Philip Kotler, in a recent article concludes. "Companies must move from a short-term transaction-oriented goal to a long-term relationship-building goal". Webster, an another prominent American authority on marketing, comes to a similar conclusion in a recent analysis that "there has been a shift from a transaction to a relationship focus."

In these days of globalisation and privatisation, there is an innocent belief that competition will do everything. There is no known example of a market that has worked without any regulation. Also, there is no market without collaboration among suppliers, customers and others. "Collaboration through relationships, networks and interactions is the core of the contribution of relationship marketing." Therefore, relationship marketing is based on the existence of three forces viz. competition, cooperation and regulations and these lead to achieving a marketing equilibrium.

Relationship marketing has the aim of building mutually satisfying long-term relationships with key parties – customer, suppliers, distributors, and other marketing partners – in order to earn and retain their business. Relationship marketing builds strong economic, technical and social ties among the parties.

Relationship marketing involves cultivating the right kind of relationships with the right constituent groups. Marketing must not only do customer relationship management but also partner relationship management as well. Four key constituents for marketing are, customers, employees, marketing partners (channels, suppliers, dealers, etc.) and members of the financial community (shareholders, investors, analysts).

Relationship marketing is grounded in the idea of establishing a learning relationship with each customer, starting with the most valuable ones. The company gets smarter with each interaction with the customer and becomes more valuable to him. The customer tells the company of some need and the company customizes its product to meet it. Every interaction and modification improves the company's ability to fit the product to this particular customer.

Word-of-Mouth Marketing

Word of mouth marketing is strategy that encourages individuals to pass on the marketing message to others. It creates an exponential increase in the message's exposure and influence. The messages multiply rapidly and reach many in a short span of time. The advantages of this type of marketing are:

- Word of mouth accelerates the process of customer decision-making.
- It offers an authenticity to it because the source is normally independent of the company.
- The sources are convincing because the promotion method that is of the consumers, by the consumers for the consumers.

- The promotion is absolutely free of cost.
- It can take on a life of its own.
- There is long-term image of brand as well as company.
- It has the ability to override communication messages sent by the company.
- Among all promotional measures, it carried the greatest impact.
- It is a powerful means of communication among customers.

A few steps to create a word-of-mouth campaign are:

1. Offer special incentives and discounts for friends, who tell their friends. (Tell-a-friend programme).
2. Try to get the product into the hands of key influencers.
3. Run special sales
4. Network and brainstorm for ideas.
5. Programmes where useful gifts are given to customers, who give the gifts to their friends.
6. Arrange salesperson programmes and contests often
7. Employees are good tools for this type of marketing.
8. Create a club with membership benefits.
9. Arrange trade-shows, seminars, meetings etc. to popularise the product
10. Create "fun events" to bring users together and invite non-users.

Test Marketing

The term 'test marketing' is also sometimes called 'field testing'. The word 'test' means examination or trial. Test marketing means testing the product in the market before the product is commercialised on a large scale. This is done with a view to understand the market and the marketing considerations like nature of competition, nature of demand, the consumers' needs etc.

In test marketing, the following considerations are essential:

(1) Identification of the different uses of the product.

(2) Classification of the market from geographical angle with reference to the major uses or applications of the product.

(3) Selection of one or two such cross-sectional markets as samples that represent the features and conditions of the whole market where the product is contemplated to be sold.

(4) Classification of customers such as rural Vs. urban, white collar people Vs. working class, age-wise analysis etc. for the cross-sectional market areas.

(5) Identification and grouping of the customers into consumer market, industrial market, reseller market, Government market etc. in order to distinguish the marketing characteristics.

(6) Collection of pertinent information regarding the product and its features including the price from the different cross sections of the customers on whom the tests are made so that an in-depth analysis can be undertaken to understand their buying behaviour and interest.

The purpose of undertaking test marketing are:

1. To ascertain various uses of the product, the class or category of users, and the motives that prompt the buyers.
2. To gauge the nature of general competitive situations, latest trend in demand etc.
3. To elicit the following information necessary for the proper marketing decision:
   (*a*) Specific product advantages
   (*b*) Disadvantages of the product
   (*c*) New uses for applications of the product
   (*d*) Modification or improvement of the product, if any etc.

The basic objectives behind the test marketing are:

(1) To sharpen the knowledge of the territory for marketing:

(2) To decide marketing strategy with respect to price, promotions, distribution system etc.

In test marketing the following procedures are followed:

(1) The number of markets as test markets is determined at the outset, in doing so, the marketer should consider the factors, like representativeness of the area, cost of testing, regional differences, competitors' effort etc.

(2) While deciding the above for test purposes, it is examined whether such markets are having the characteristics like – existence of trade centres, industrial infrastructure, population mix etc.

(3) After the decision of test markets, the marketing manager carries out the test for a certain period. The duration of the test period depends on a variety of considerations. Of them, the important factors are:

- The existing position of competition;
- Probable expenditure;
- Average repurchase period, etc.

The competitive position influences the test duration in the sense that longer duration will give the competitors enough time to improve their products and introduce the same in the said markets. Too short a duration will not yield the desired results. Again, higher the test duration higher will be the cost of such tests. Further, the repurchase period is directly proportional to the test duration. If the repurchases by the customers are very frequent, then a shorter duration of the test may give the required data.

(4) During test marketing, marketing manager collects pertinent information for detailed analysis – customers' behaviour, habits, customs, etc. and distribution channels, competition etc.

(5) After the collection of required information, the marketing management decides about the marketing mix and marketing strategy. If the sales are excellent and promising, a decision to commercialise a product is taken up. If the sales are not so bright, the underlying reasons are investigated for improvement and a re-test is undertaken. If the indication of sales are poor, the management may drop the idea altogether.

Case Study-1

ALFA POWER NEEDS RESEARCH POWER

With the onset of summer, demand for the petrol/kerosene – operated domestic generators and battery – operated investors increases. The total market for portable generators and investors is estimated to be around Rs. 150 crores for North India which is badly affected because of the massive power cuts. There are two leading manufacturers of petrol/kerosene-operated portable generators. Both, along with a few other manufacturers, have 80 per cent of the market shares. The rest of the market is captured by large number of small-scale invertor manufacturers. The invertor uses one or two batteries and has a back-up time of 3-6 hours whereas the generator sets can operate uninterrupted for a longer period. The voltage obtained from the portable generator set is consistent whereas in the case of invertors, the voltage reduces drastically after the back-up time.

The batteries which are used in the invertors are automatically charged but have a life of 2/3 years. No other maintenance is required for the invertors, but in the case of portable generators, proper service is recommended after every 6 months. Some drawbacks which people have been observing in the use of portable generators are that they make lot of noise. Vibrations and emit lots of smoke also while in operation. Besides, the users will have to stock kerosene/petrol/diesel in the house for the operation of the set which has become a problem especially in small flats having working parents and small children. Recently in an incident it is alleged that because of the smoke emitted by the portable generator set, two kids of a family died.

M/s Alfa Power is a professionally managed concern. The chief executive of the concern, Sh. Kapoor, after completing electronic engineering has opted for self-employment instead of a wage employment.

He set up a unit for manufacturing electronic power generators in 1995 and within a period of one year other products such as CVT and Online UPS systems were added. All the products with state-of-art technology proved highly reliable and user-friendly. The foremost aim of the concern is to produce high quality products for total customer satisfaction.

The products of the concern were being used as OEMs for various concerns. Looking at the vast opportunities available for the invertor market. Sh. Kapoor decided to engage a marketing agency to carry out a market survey for its product which may be used for homes/shops/establishments as a substitute for the portable generator sets. The cost in the case of portable generator ranges from Rs. 15,000 to 30,000 (fuel extra). In case of invertors, the range is Rs. 7,000 to 19,000 (the cost of battery varies between Rs. 3,000 to 5,000 depending upon the brand).

QUESTIONS

(1) Draw suitable terms of reference highlighting aims and objective of the study for the market survey agency which Sh. Kapoor is proposing to hire.

(2) What are the salient features which Sh. Kapoor should look for in the selection of the marketing agency?

(3) What changes will Sh. Kapoor have to bring about in his marketing department?

(*AIMA, 1998*)

Case Study-2

DISPOSABLE CROCKERY — A NEW CONCEPT

Concept — Product Research

Packaging (I) Pvt. Ltd. was in the business of manufacturing packaging materials made of bio-degradable thermocol for the last six years. In the year 1994, it was thinking of diversifying into a technology-related product.

Product Concept

With nuclear families increasing in numbers, consisting of more number of working women, coupled with the difficulty in finding domestic help, entertaining at home has become a bane for every house wife, Food can be ordered from outside but cleaning up after the party is not easy. The available crockery range can extend from expensive. Chinaware to inexpensive disposable paper crockery. However, most housewives are reluctant to use their Chinaware for large gatherings in view of breakages and other problems like washing up.

That leaves them with the option of disposable crockery/cutlery especially for large parties, children's parties etc. The quality of disposable plates/glasses, etc. available in the market is not very good and, therefore, unsuitable for buffet meals, or are aesthetically unappealing. This leaves the average middle class housewife in a dilemma.

In this context, the product concept that Packaging (I) Pvt. Ltd. brought out was of disposable designer crockery made of thermocol. A pack size of 12 would include 12 dinner plates, 12 quarter plates, 12 bowls, 12 glasses, 3 serving bowls, 1 rice plate, 14 serving spoons and 12 spoons. The grocery would be made up of microwave-safe thermocol. Spoons would be made up of plastic. Three pack sizes, viz., 12 plates, 20 plates and 25 plates were envisaged.

Also, the company was wondering whether the pack should include designer disposable, matching high quality paper napkins, a matching table cloth (disposable) along with the napkins or simply the crockery. A preliminary exploratory survey had indicated that consumer is willing to spend Rs. 125-250 for the purpose of party crockery which is disposable. Three price intensions Rs. 125, Rs. 200 and Rs. 250 were to be considered.

QUESTION

Which technique of product research would you use to recommend for the pack combinations that the company must introduce? (*AIMA, Dec. 1997*)

Case Study-3

MARKETING TIME SHARE AT FUN AND FROLIC HOLIDAY RESORTS

The Background

The time-sharing concept (very popular in the Western countries) of enjoying life-long holidays year after year for only a reasonable one time investment in holidays for the future at today's low prices was entirely a novel one. The concept was based on the premise that since most people visited tourist spots annually, their requirements, as far as holiday resorts were concerned, could be met by periodical week-long slots being sold to others.

When the concept of time-sharing was introduced in India way back in 1985, it drew a lot of flak. This was due to several reasons:

- *First*, people were not very well aware of the concept although it was very popular abroad;
- *Secondly*, people did not want to be committed to going every year at a particular place for a fixed period of 99 years;
- *Thirdly*, the resorts being offered were very limited and locations unsuitable to the people. For example one company built just one resort and started selling time-share; and
- *Lastly*, resorts built in the North did not suit people staying in the South and *vice versa*, as this meant spending large amount of time and money in travelling.

Several companies, which had entered this business as it sounded very promising and exciting, had to close down their operations. The concept itself was left with a stigma attached to it.

The Revival

Fun and Frolic Holiday (I) Resorts was started in 1986 as a private limited company based in Southern India. It contacted customers door-to-door explaining to them about the time-share concept and extending additional facilities, gift your time share; rent out your time share, instalment payments, off-season discounts and most of all, honouring its commitments.

The company had to hire 50-60 bungalows in Ooty and Kodaikanal. The second resort at Ooty became functional in 1990. The year 1992 saw two more resorts at Ooty and Kodaikanal being added to the list. By the end of 1993, the company had six resorts functional. It had plans to come up with 25 resorts by the end of 1997. Today the company had an impressive 22,000 strong customer base with 45 per cent of market under its hold.

The Competition

The awareness and acceptance of the time-share concept has led to a number of companies enter the resort-share business, offering holidays at exotic places with competitive rates. The time-share concept has entered the growth phase of its life-cycle and it is imperative for Fun and Frolic to identify segments and new bases so that it can concentrate its efforts on them and maintain its lead. It may also have to review its various strategies to remain competitive in the market place.

QUESTIONS

(1) Outline the pricing strategy recommended for the company.

(2) What should be the overall marketing strategy of the company to retain its lead and remain competitive in the market place? *(AIMA, Dec. 1997)*

Case Study-4

HOTEL IN PUNE — "TO BE OR NOT TO BE"

Shri Ram Consultants have been appointed by a leading group in Hotel Industry to prepare a feasibility report for opening a five-star hotel in Pune. The group had been the most successful one in the Hotel Industry and had always kept its eyes open for new opportunities.

In view of the very fast industrial growth in the city of Pune, the city had attracted the attention of the group. Pune, apart from being a modern city, has the added advantage of pleasant weather and several places of tourist attraction in the neighbourhood. Moreover the closeness to Mumbai, city of international stature, made it very easily accessible to international tourists.

For Shri Ram Consultants, this was the first time that an assignment concerning hotel industry had been received. They, however, soon realised that the assignment was not as simple as it appeared to be in the first place. The feasibility of such a hotel would depend essentially on two factors. Businessmen visiting the city for work would constitute one segment of the market. While tourists would constitute the other. Further, the tourists could be Indians or foreigners. The success of such a hotel would also depend upon the relative attraction of other tourist centres in the vicinity.

Further, it was necessary to estimate seasonal fluctuations in demand for hotel accommodation so that attractive discounts could be offered during the off-season for business conferences, executive development programmes, etc.

The consultants realised that they would have to undertake a market research on a national scale to assess the tourist potential of the city. They would also have to survey the foreign tourists to estimate one of the most important segments of the market.

The Consultants wondered whether such a survey will have to extend over a period of one full year to completely take into account the seasonal variations in tourist traffic. They were also undecided about the manner in which the survey should be conducted. The company also feared that in the absence of an accurate definition of the problem, they may land up surveying the complete tourist market in India rather than studying feasibility of a hotel in Pune. They had heard that ITDC had appointed lady interviewers at several major airports for conducting such surveys and wondered if such a methodology could be of use to them.

The problem appeared much defined and they were concerned as the preliminary report explaining methodology of the research and the questionnaires to be used had to be submitted to the client along with the estimate of expenses within one month.

Questions

(1) How would you define the problem of assessing the feasibility of the Hotel so as to help design the survey?

(2) How would you plan a survey for actually collecting information on expected demand for hotel space? How would you estimate the cost of such survey? *(AIMA Dec. 1997)*

Case Study-5

ICPL'S FORAY INTO THE HOUSEHOLD MARKET

Indian Chemical and Pharmaceutical Ltd. (ICPL) is producing highly ethical products sold through doctors all over the country. The ICPL is planning to enter into the household insecticides market. They have the technical know-how to manufacture and the infrastructure to market the insecticides. Its sales force, of 250 sales representatives supported by 20 sales offices located in all major cities, contacted all the important doctors and chemists and made a direct distribution of company products to retail outlets.

The marketing research department was given the job to make a quick study and to provide suitable information so as to facilitate the company in taking a decision regarding entering the household insecticides market.

Questions

(1) Outline the information needs of the company for its new product planning and suggest the investigation process.

(2) Draw a suitable time frame, plan the manpower requirements and draw budget estimates for carrying out such a study

(3) Suggest a suitable format of the final report to be submitted to the Managing Director.

(*AIMA June 1996*)

Case Study-6

PLASTICS INDUSTRY VS. TNPCB — A CASE OF ENVIRONMENTAL POLLUTION

The plastics industry consists of more than 3000 units in Tamil Nadu and Pondicherry. It has provided direct and indirect employment opportunities for more than 4 lakh people. About 80 per cent of them are in the small scale sector, 17 per cent belong to the tiny sector and the rest are in the medium and large scale sectors. The industry contributes Rs 125 crore to the Tamil Nadu state exchequer.

Plastic products are part of our everyday life and we cannot simply imagine a day without plastic products. We use them in one way or an other in day to day life and it plays an important role in our disposable life-style -"use and throw away". The per capita consumption of plastics in India is about 2.4 kgs while the world per capita consumption is 18 kgs.

In January 2001, the Tamil Nadu Pollution Control Board (TNPCB), a state regulatory authority on environmental degradation, requested all the district collectors, municipalities, civic and local body authorities to ban the use of throw-away plastic products including carry bags, cups, plates etc. The TNPCB had already been cracking down on the plastic manufacturers producing plastic carry bags below 20 microns thickness as per the 'Recycled plastic Rules, 1999, Government of India (manufacture and usage). The rule bans the manufacturer and use of plastic bags of less than 20 micron thickness. But, other plastic products like cups, plates, sheets etc., do not come under the purview of the above said rule. Hence, the TNPCB requested all the municipalities, civic and local bodies to pass a resolution. Subsequently, in March 2001, TNPCB circulated a draft resolution to all the local bodies in Tamil Nadu to ban the manufacture, sale and use of one time use plastics and impose fines on the violators. As per the Board's direction, all the local bodies including Chennai Corporation voted for an anti-plastics campaign and almost every Metro Transport Corporation (Chennai) was displayed with 'scary' messages about plastics - 'emission of dioxins during the processing or burning of plastics will cause irreparable damage to human life'. The Board also insisted that the plastic units be classified in the green category to register with it.

The anti-plastics campaign of the TNPCB has pushed the entire plastic industry to the brink and it has created considerable confusion among the users as well as public mind. The plastic manufacture workforce is also quitting fast.

People in the plastic industry term the TNPCB's anti-plastic campaign as 'false and misleading'. The producers, under the banner of Tamil Nadu Plastic Manufacturers Association (TAPMA) have decided not to take things lying down and have geared up to fight back scientifically by creating awareness about the safe use of plastic products. In their campaign, the TAPMA decided that the objective should be to highlight the inevitability of using plastics in day-to-day living and its campaign was flagged off with a seminar on 'Environmental Plastics Recycling' in Chennai. Then, as part of the awareness campaign, the TAPMA and the New Delhi based Indian centre for Plastics in Environment (ICPE) have come out with a booklet containing points and counterpoints it was and presented as a memorandum to the minister for rural industries. The TAPMA explained to the minister that 'we are not against the guidelines, but only voicing concern at the TNPCB exercising extra authority and in the process, attempting to close down all the units in Tamil Nadu and Pondicherry.' Moreover, the Board is not only influencing all the local bodies to impose a ban on the plastic manufacturers and use of plastics items but also advising them to levy stringent fines on the users.

During TAPMA's interaction with the Board, they have expressed their willingness to cooperate in promoting general awareness about recyclability of commonly used plastic and initiate measures to reduce littering habits of people. They have also mooted the idea of having facilities for segregation and collection of waste at source to enable recycling. TAMPA claimed that the industry has already agreed to increase the minimum thickness and then make reuse and recycling viable. In any case, thick gauge bags are retained by consumers for multiple secondary use over an extended period of time. The campaign against plastics that they contain cancer inducing elements is a "malicious canard" as in reality they are made from polyethylene which is a polymer of pure carbon and hydrogen.

The TAPMA further suggested that the infrastructure and system support is a must for waste management as plastics industry does not litter, but people do. The TNPCB should seek information from the Central Institute of Plastics Engineering Technology (CIPET) located in Chennai itself, one of the premier institutes of plastics in South Asia.

The TAPMA argued that there is so much vehicle pollution which is hazardous to health and in some major cities it has reached an alarming level. so, can we ban all the vehicles? There are emission checking centres to monitor vehicle pollution and likewise, the TAPMA points that the industry and the regulatory authority could work together to find alternative ways to tackle this problem. It pleaded for an impartial support group to go into all the issues raised in the anti-plastics propaganda by TNPCB; and it appealed to the board to stop the campaign which is threatening the very existence of the plastic units. Further, TAMPA highlighted that the closure of units would result in thousands of people losing their employment and in turn create a socioeconomic crisis.

Questions for Discussions

1. Discuss TNPCB Vs Plastic industry as a consumer and public
2. Suggest ways for socially responsible 'Green' marketing taking into consideration the growing number of regulations against pollution by govt. agencies and consumer's demand for – harmless products.

APPENDIX

ONLINE ADVERSITING

Online advertising is a form of promotion that uses the Internet and the World Wide Web for the purpose of delivering messages to attract customers. Online advertising is also known as Internet Advertising.

The Internet emerged from a US Government project in 1970. The purpose was to develop some system of communication that would link researchers all over the world and allow them to access and exchange information. In 1989, World Wide Web (WWW) was developed. Web makes it possible for its users to share a complete range of communications including text, audio messages, graphics, etc. Any person or a company can create and register a WEBSITE that includes a homepage and other information, containing files, and anyone can access this website through a unique address and access the collection of available data contained in the web files. Today, web has become indispensable, for much of the communication that occurs between marketers and consumers in a large part of the world is through the Internet. Anyone with a computer and Internet connection can access websites sitting anywhere in the world, and buy or sell products and services.

The number of internet users is on a rapid rise world-wide. Internet is used by people of all ages and types. Internet has become a major medium for communication and entertainment this aspect of enteraiment is equally important when compared with the traditional entertainment and informative media such as television, radio, magazines, etc. The huge successes of Microsoft, Yahoo, Google, etc. have proved that online advertising is here to stay and flourish. Sensing enormous potential in online advertising, the marketing departments of most large companies have set up e-advertising groups. In practice, online promotional techniques such as search engines, banner advertising, direct e-mail and links or services from other websites to acquire new customers and provide services to existing customers that help to develop the customer relationship. However, for internet marketing to be successful there is a necessity of integration with traditional media such as print and television. Internet Marketing is the process of building and maintaining customer relationships through online activities to facilitate the exchange of ideas, products and services that satisfy the goals of both parties.

It is very commonly said that the new era is the Internet era. Everywhere everyone seems to be availing the facilities of online, that is, Internet.

ADVANTAGES OF ONLINE ADVERTISING

Online advertising is being increasingly used by advertisers. Some of the advantages of online advertising are as follows –

1. The online advertising gives the advertisement a wider coverage, and this wider coverage helps in making the advertisements reach more audiences.
2. The medium of online advertising offers unparalleled multimedia tools that can make advertisements very powerful and effective. The information may be presented with pictures, animation, sound, text, etc.
3. The benefits of targetted marketing and effectiveness tracking, conversion rates in online advertising are cheaper than in traditional advertising.

4. In online advertising, the advertiser is able to convey more details about the product to the audience, and that too at relatively low cost.
5. The biggest strength of online advertising is the direct response that it offers to both customers and advertisers.
6. Marketing on the web enables the marketers to adjust to fast changing conditions. They car know quickly what the market wants; and thus act accordingly.
7. The web also helps the marketer target the customers individually, because of the facility of direct, interactive and online communication with them.
8. A web marketer can attract customers located all over the world, compete for the global market, build global supply chains and operate with global strategies.
9. Like other direct marketing methods, web marketing helps to build relationship with customers. Being totally interactive and one-to-one marketing, web marketing is more effective when compared to other forms of direct marketing.
10. Channel costs, which are a significant part of marketing costs, are reduced considerably when a product is marketed through online advertising.

NOTES